ADVANCE PRAISE FOR WE SUFFERED MUCH

"Anyone that has spent a first day of winter on the Northern Plains can relate. Anyone that has spent the entire winter can certainly relate—and empathize with the highs and lows of the climate—and of the human spirit. Wilson has provided a masterful look at the work and dedicated project carried out by pioneer railroad surveyor C. W. Irish during his years on the Minnesota and Dakota prairies. Through a thoughtful and introspective view of Irish's own logs, journals, drawings, and personal correspondence, Cindy's weaving of this story makes for a unique look at a more-often-than-not overlooked time in the development of the Northern Plains. Facing illnesses, doubt, shortages of men and materials, and the ever-present challenges of geography and weather—Irish endeavored on in his quest to negotiate a path through the elements, and the inhabitants of the Dakota lands, in the lead up to the Great Dakota Boom of the 1880s. This marvelous work belongs in the collection of any student of Dakota history and of anyone who enjoy a riveting story of dedication and family interactions."

— RICK MILLS, CURATOR AND HISTORIAN,
SOUTH DAKOTA STATE RAILROAD MUSEUM, LTD.

"'Thar's gold in them (Black) Hills!' And the Chicago & North Western (C&NW) Railway was determined to benefit from the expected prosperity boom. But before their tracks could be extended from southwestern Minnesota to that far corner of what was then Dakota Territory, a route had to be surveyed. The C&NW assigned this daunting task to Charles Wood Irish, and author Cindy Wilson makes it immediately clear that her book is not about *surveying*, but *surveyors*. Over the next two years, 1879–81, Irish and his crew would suffer extreme heat, the historic winter of 1880–81, wildfires, floods, illness, separation from family and friends, horse thieves, gunfights, and the reluctance of the Lakota Sioux to have their reservation invaded by the 'iron horse.' Moreover, the C&NW was racing the rival Chicago, Milwaukee & St. Paul to be the first to reach the coveted Black Hills. Irish's crew did, indeed, suffer much while surveying the route, and the reader will find inspiration in Charles Wood Irish's fierce determination and endurance."

— JOHN BERG, DIRECTOR OF THE CHICAGO & NORTH WESTERN HISTORICAL SOCIETY AND RETIRED AMERICAN HISTORY TEACHER

"*We Suffered Much* is a monumental, never-before-told tale of a significant aspect of the closing of the American frontier: the building of railroads. This book is the gripping, adventurous account of Charles Wood Irish as he surveyed the most feasible routes for extending the Chicago & North Western Railroad through Dakota Territory. Author Cindy Wilson transforms Irish's 1879–1881 diaries and letters into a lively narrative. Her characterization of Irish creates the persona of a memorable Western trailblazer. Irish's accounts of weather, illness, and poor lodgings and nutrition typify his challenges in the unsettled Midwest. His brushes with the Lakota are poignant; they illustrate the clash between White progress and the resulting decimation of Native cultures. Irish's words read like a vibrant latter-day Lewis and Clark expedition narrative. *We Suffered Much* is a page-turner and an unexpected gift for those interested in railroad history and the development of the upper Midwest. This book celebrates an unsung hero whose sacrifices were necessary in linking the railroads from east to west. It is an entertaining and insightful read."

— William Anderson, historian, editor of *The Selected Letters of Laura Ingalls Wilder*, and author of many other titles

"Through the bitter cold and blazing heat of 1879–1881, Charles Wood Irish led a team of surveyors across south-central Dakota Territory on behalf of the Chicago & North Western Railway. As he confided to his diary over and over again, the men 'suffered much' from mosquitos, blizzards, subzero temperatures, disease, lack of water, and poor rations. Combining Irish's observations from his diaries, letters home, hand-drawn maps, and other notes, Cindy Wilson masterfully retraces the surveyors' journey, supplementing the story with her own field research. The result is a fascinating look at the strength of character it took to blaze the trail for the railroads across the Great Plains."

— Nancy Tystad Koupal, director of the Pioneer Girl Project

"Wilson takes the reader through the everyday life of Charles Wood Irish and his crew via her extensive research of letters, diaries, documents, historical publications, and Irish's hand-drawn maps. She also brings us along on her own investigative journey, weaving together her emotional insights and her connections to collection materials and the physical landscape. Wilson's work illuminates the critical need for support of the long-term preservation of our cultural heritage and speaks to the important role libraries and archives play in uncovering and understanding our past."

— Giselle Simón, director of Conservation and Collections Care, University of Iowa Libraries

"Cindy Wilson has produced another amazing book after her gem *The Beautiful Snow*. Railroads and weather are central to both books. While *The Beautiful Snow* told the story of how a railroad tried to remain in operation during an unusually brutal winter, her new book, *We Suffered Much*, describes the work of the survey crews who charted a route for a railroad in Dakota Territory between 1879 and 1881. While reading *We Suffered Much*, the word that kept coming to mind was *epic*. The conditions under which Charles Wood Irish and his crew often worked were so terrible that I often wondered how they were able to stay alive! This is a well-researched and well-written tale of incredible experiences, railroads, and fascinating nineteenth-century Midwest history. I highly recommend this unforgettable book!"

— Bob Sandeen, Nicollet County Historical Society, Minnesota

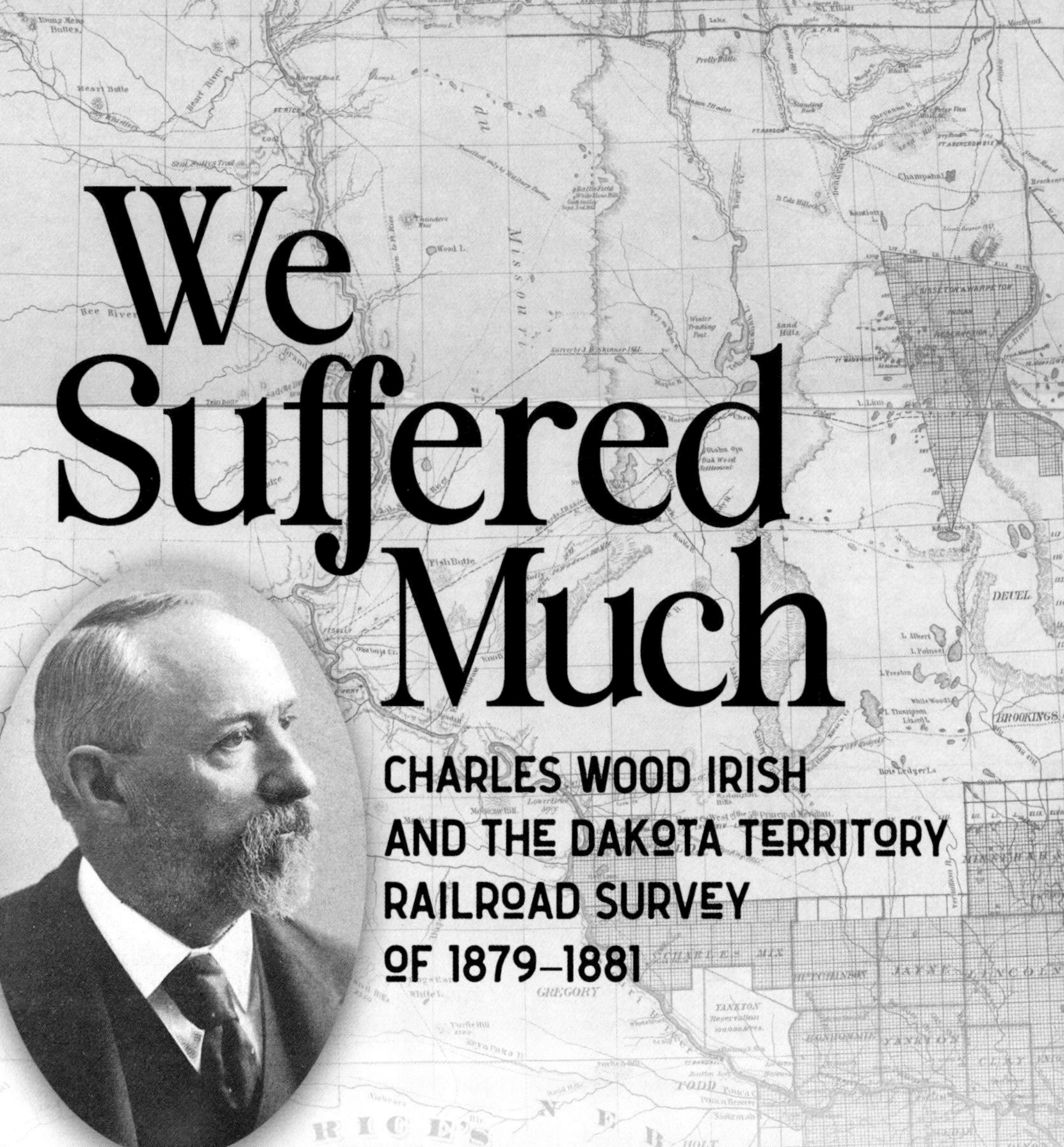

We Suffered Much

Charles Wood Irish and the Dakota Territory Railroad Survey of 1879–1881

Cindy Wilson

Softcover ISBN 13: 978-1-64343-567-1
Library of Congress Catalog Number: 2023924245
Printed in the United States of America
First Printing: 2024
28 27 26 25 24 5 4 3 2 1

Cover and interior design by jamesmonroedesign.com

939 Seventh Street West
Saint Paul, Minnesota 55102
(952) 829-8818
www.BeaversPondPress.com

To order or to contact the author, visit www.CindyWilson-author.com.

"Imagine yourself standing in a plain to which your eye can see no bounds. Not a tree, not a shrub, not a tall weed lifts its head above the barren grandeur of the desert; not a stone is to be seen on its hard beaten surface; no undulation, no abruptness, no break to relieve the monotony; nothing, save here and there a deep narrow track worn into the hard plain by the constant hoof of the buffaloe. Imagine then countless herds of buffaloes, showing their unwieldy, dark shapes in every direction, as far as the eye can reach, and approaching at times to within forty steps of you; or a herd of wild horses feeding in the distance, or hurrying away from the hateful smell of man, with their manes floating and a tramping like thunder. Imagine here and there a solitary antelope, or, perhaps, a whole herd, fleeing off in the distance like the scattering of white clouds. Imagine bands of white snow-like wolves prowling about, accompanied by the little collets* or prairie wolves, who are as rapacious and noisey as their larger brethren. Imagine, also, here and there a lonely tiger cat, crouched in some little hollow, or bounding off in triumph, bearing some luckless little prairie dog whom it has caught struggling about some distance from its hole. If to all this you will add a band of Indians, mounted on swift ponies with their long bows at their back, their knife and tomahawk in their belt, and perhaps a gun hanging at their side, and their shield, ornamented grandly with feathers and red cloth, and round as the full moon; if you imagine them hovering about in the prairie chasing a buffaloe or attacking an enemy, you have an image of the prairie."

— *Fort Randall Independent*, Dakota Territory,
December 20, 1865

---

* Possibly another treatment of coyotes.

An 1870 painting of Charles Wood Irish by Isaac Augustus Wetherby. AI-3

An 1870 painting of Susannah Abigail Yarborough Irish by Isaac Augustus Wetherby. AI-4

CONTENTS

Author's Note | xi

Preface: March 1881 | xxi

Introduction: The Panic of 1873—Period of Rest, Then a Boom | 1

SECTION ONE
SCOUTING TRIP: WHERE TO PLACE THE LINE 5

"Hard at Work on Dakota Trip": January 13–16, 1879 5
Initial Scouting Trip: January 17–February 23, 1879 7
Project Planning & Respite with Family: February 24–March 10, 1879 25
Final Preparations for the Surveying Work: March 11–20, 1879 28

SECTION TWO
THE SURVEY BEGINS! TRACY TO LAKE BENTON 33

Survey Work Begins West of Tracy: March 21–April 18, 1879 34
The Redwood Coteaus: March 29–April 9, 1879 37
On to Lake Benton: April 10–18, 1879 45

SECTION THREE
INTO DAKOTA TERRITORY AND BACK TO THE BEGINNING 55

On to Dakota Territory and the Big Sioux: April 19–24, 1879 56
Back to the Beginning for Three Trouble Spots: April 25–June 4, 1879 59
Back to Dakota Territory: June 5–14, 1879 73
The Lakes to the West: June 15–20, 1879 85

SECTION FOUR
MOSQUITOS, THE JAMES RIVER, AND THE WESSINGTON HILLS 91

Mosquito-Infested Sloughs and West to the James: June 21–26, 1879 92
Exploring to the North: June 27–July 5, 1879 94
Heading Back East and Battling Mosquitos: July 6–13, 1879 100
Even Farther East and Even More Mosquitos: July 14–24, 1879 105
Confronting the Wessington Hills: July 25–August 19, 1879 108

SECTION FIVE
ON TO THE MISSOURI, THEN BACK AND FORTH....119

On to the Missouri River from Wessington Hills: August 20–31, 1879....120
Exploring Medicine Creek: September 1–14, 1879....126
Back to the James: September 15–21, 1879....129
Scouting Volga to Watertown: September 22–October 4, 1879....131
A Furlough: October 5–19, 1879....135
A Return to Work East of the James: October 20–31, 1879....136
Another Furlough: November 1–14, 1879....141

SECTION SIX
SETTLING IN FOR THE WINTER....151

Yankton to Pierre via the Stage Road: November 15–24, 1879....152
Settling in for the Winter: November 25–December 2, 1879....156
Work along Medicine Creek: December 3, 1879–January 22, 1880....161

SECTION SEVEN
EXPLORING WEST OF THE MISSOURI RIVER....185

Exploring the Mouth of the Cheyenne: January 22–February 25, 1880....186
Over the Fort Pierre to Deadwood Trail: February 26–March 7, 1880....206

SECTION EIGHT
RIVER CROSSINGS AND LOTS OF UPS AND DOWNS....223

Exploring Another Route to the Missouri: March 8–27, 1880....224
A Furlough Home: March 28–April 15, 1880....232
A Riverboat Trip Up the Missouri River: April 16–27, 1880....235
Finishing Up between the James River and Medicine Creek: April 28–July 12, 1880....237

SECTION NINE
CRITICAL NEGOTIATIONS AND WORK WEST OF THE MISSOURI....257

Negotiation Duties: July 13–August 18, 1880....258
Crossing the Missouri and Up the Bad: August 19–September 25, 1880....272

SECTION TEN
THE FORKS OF THE CHEYENNE AND THE FIRST MONTHS OF THE HARD WINTER....295

Approaching the Cheyenne: September 26–October 12, 1880....296
The Start of the Hard Winter: October 13–28, 1880....303
Work Resumed: October 29–November 6, 1880....309
A Return to Pierre and Back to the Cheyenne: November 7–16, 1880....312
Back Down the Bad River to Fort Pierre: November 18–December 21, 1880....315

SECTION ELEVEN
WINTER CHANGES EVERYTHING. 327

Continued Work along the Bad River: December 22–31, 1880 328
New Year and Worse Weather: January 1–February 23, 1881 336
Work Comes to a Stop: February 24–March 26, 1881 344
Such Scolding, Swearing & Yelling: March 27–April/May 1881 350

Epilogue | 357

Acknowledgments | 367

Appendixes | 371

Appendix I: People | 371

Appendix II: Surveying before GPS | 377

Appendix III: Where Exactly Was Gap Creek Camp? | 380

Appendix IV: Township, Range & Section Delineations | 394

Appendix V: Steamboats Mentioned in the Diaries | 396

Appendix VI: Forts and Agencies | 398

Appendix VII: Biographies of the Irish Family | 404

Illustrations Credits | 415

Endnotes | 425

Index | 433

AUTHOR'S NOTE

Charles Wood Irish was an extraordinary man. He had endless curiosity and dabbled in many topics. He built his own observatory. He played a role in creating several railroads around the country. He was a father ahead of his time, raising daughters ahead of their time; in fact, he encouraged them to learn science, indulge their intellects, and not saddle themselves with marriage just for the sake of marriage.

His diaries and letters throughout the approximately two years of survey work on the new Dakota Central line on behalf of the Chicago & North Western Railway Company show wry humor, insights, frustrations, career aspirations, and a wide range of basic human emotions. It is a fascinating journey, and it has been a privilege to accompany him in his work nearly a century and a half after it took place.

Note: This is not a book about surveying. It is a book about a surveyor, his crew, and what they encountered in the course of their work.

Within the body of the book, unless otherwise noted via an endnote, anything in quotation marks came from a diary entry or letter. Letters are also offset and treated a bit differently from the main narrative. Outside of that, the text reflects a summary from his diary entries, descriptions from modern trips to the locations he mentions, and/or information pulled in to fill in details. If I'm musing on something, I let you know. If I'm describing a landscape, it will be as Irish would have seen it, or I let you know that I'm providing modern context. Because so much of the text is quoted or summarized from the diary or letters, they are not individually cited, but the endnote reference following this sentence will point you to them.[1]

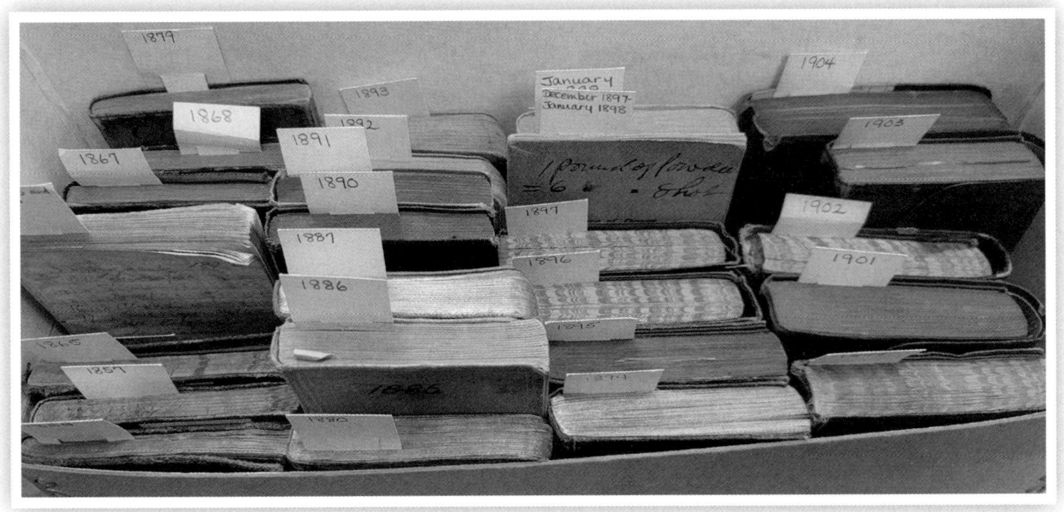

The marvelous box of diaries and notebooks. Such a tiny little gold mine! AI-5

Speaking of the diaries and letters, they are the core of this work and are essentially chronological. With a few exceptions, material will appear in the order he wrote it, including dates wherever possible. He would sometimes mention something in a diary entry, then delve more deeply into the same topic days later in a letter. I've worked to minimize duplication, but sometimes he presents certain things differently between the two, and it is interesting to see both. And while most of the story is from the perspective of Charles Wood Irish, you'll also read letters he received from his wife and daughters, which expand the overall perspective; these letters also help us get to know the three Irish women.

There are five basic types of content within this book: The main text comprises commentary on the diaries. Just as important are the family letters, which are tagged with and enclosed within a gridded box.

These items (the diaries and letters) are presented on the white paper, and you could simply read the main text and the letters and enjoy the story behind these two years, but there are three more types of content, presented on gray backgrounds; these "tangents" add flavor to the main narrative:

General tangents (tagged with) provide context or extra background for something mentioned in the main text.

News tangents (tagged with) bring in newspaper articles relevant to the work, appearing chronologically within the main text.

And research commentary tangents (tagged with) shed light on my own experiences during research and while hunting down the locations of survey team's campsites and other information; some of these, the shorter ones, appear in line with the main text, near relevant topics, and the longer ones appear at the end of their respective sections.

The preface blends my own writing with Irish's words, phrases, and descriptions from a letter to his daughters. To keep the preface visually clean, his words are not within quotation marks. Towards the end of the book, on page 350, is the letter to his daughters, in which you'll see which words were his.

As Mr. Irish frequently eschewed punctuation, capitalization, and even (sometimes) writing in complete sentences, I've cleaned up some of his spelling and punctuation to help with readability, but words within quotes attributed to him are his, and I've standardized most names to avoid confusion. The same is true for letters written by Mrs. Irish and their daughters, though to a lesser extent. Standard spelling and usage of certain words have changed since the time covered in this book. For the most part, those nonstandard spellings (such as *staid* instead of *stayed*) have been left intact, and [*sic*] is added only when it is an obvious mistake in the original document. Irish also often used shorthand when referring to the towns of Pierre and Fort Pierre, often calling either one Pierre. Using various contextual helpers, I've identified which he was referring to and have used the correct one in the text, even within his quotes. Finally, he almost consistently used "+" to represent *and*, and "+c" to represent *etcetera*. You'll see both frequently throughout the narrative.

Irish was dedicated to taking weather readings when possible and had equipment to do so. However, it is possible that his readings would not equate to readings using modern equipment. Some of his readings would indicate unusual or even record-breaking temperatures for time of year, etc. These may be accurate, or they may be the result of equipment variations. As an engineer, Irish tended to be careful about doing things "correctly," so one can assume he did his best to adhere to guidelines for ideal thermometer placement and standardized calibration, though those may not have matched modern specifications. According to Dr. Barb Mayes Boustead, a meteorologist with the National Weather Service, "the range of accuracy for any thermometer depends on the type of thermometer being used, which is true of thermometers from the 1800s through today."[2] The book includes the readings as he indicated them—temperatures in degrees Fahrenheit, barometer readings (atmospheric pressure) in millibars.

For the most part, very little is known about the individual crew members beyond their names (sometimes only their surnames), and in maybe only a quarter of the cases do we know what roles they served on the team.

Each chapter is segmented based on the work being done and illustrated with at least one map, created by me, that indicates the crew's locations, dates at certain camps, and any important landmarks. The included maps are general; I have highly detailed maps, but to protect the privacy of landowners, more generalized versions are published here. The campsites are located exactly unless noted as "approximate."

Hot or cold, roaming the windy prairies—where there is so little protection and oh so much wind nearly all the time—was not a pleasant thing, and Irish's diary frequently noted that he was ill from the effects. "We suffered much" was not an uncommon refrain within the entries, though the suffering rarely slowed him down. If he could not get out to investigate the countryside in preparation for the official surveying work, he was in his tent (or room) working on letters and papers related to the future Dakota Central, as we shall see over the course of the twenty-seven-month endeavor.

This book is not about surveying itself, but it does include surveying terms. Many of these terms may make intuitive sense as you read, but just in case, before beginning the book, you may want to flip to appendix II (page 377) for a list of basic surveying terms and concepts. Similarly, flip to appendix IV (page 394) for help with notations used to identify pieces of land. Irish frequently used these identifiers, and they are included in the text and maps to help show where the men were working or camping. It is not necessary, however, to understand these things, and the maps provide sufficient location information.

Sense of Place

One of the decisions I made early on was to visit camp and survey locations during the same time of year as the surveyors. I wanted to see, feel, smell, and hear the locations under similar conditions. Obviously this would be fairly general, as I would not be able (or willing) to travel to a remote corner of West River, South Dakota, for instance, during a fierce blizzard, but I could visit there in winter temperatures to get a sense of the area under winter conditions. Same with other seasons and other locations. It took at least a year of observations, but I felt these visits were important to capture the aura, as best as could be obtained, nearly a century and a half later.

I purchased three handmade notebooks from a consignment store near my home. On each expedition, I wrote observations. Sometimes these trips were not far afield. If it was a frosty morning, I would jump in the car and just drive around, writing down descriptions of frost on grass, branches, or cattails. Or on mornings of especially dense fog, I would simply stand at my window (I live in southern Minnesota) and write notes about what I was seeing, or not seeing, capturing the "essence" of a dense fog, so that when Irish described a dense fog that was thwarting their work, I could describe the scene with credible-ish words, if necessary. If nothing else, it enhanced the research experience.

Sometimes these trips yielded literal descriptions (such as the name of a modern road intersection). Sometimes they pushed into poetic ramblings about something that caught my imagination in the moment. Sometimes as I returned to the notebooks, often months later, I couldn't remember what I'd been thinking about when, evidently, a muse had inspired me. Other times, it led to additional research and discoveries to color the narrative. It was all a part of this journey, and all of it was a joy!

Today, state and county roads, whether paved or gravel, make travel fast and easy. Most roads follow the township grid established by the early land surveyors. Some roads follow earlier Native trails. And some of those trails are marked along their routes by signs established by researchers. This made it possible to get close enough to have visual sight lines on most camp and work locations. I stood in the surveyors' shoes, so to speak, though usually from a proper distance.

The biggest differences between then and now are in population, roads, and vegetation. Where Irish and his crew saw prairie, some early crops, and scattered trees (the last mainly limited to creek and river bottoms), today much of the eastern portion of the region is a solid mixture of soybean and corn fields. Farmsteads lie nestled within thick windbreaks, rows of trees serving to protect the yard from the strong west-southwest winds of summer and the north-northwest winds of winter, creating cozy little nooks within the wide-open landscape. Rarely can the eye sweep the horizon without it being broken up by these windbreaks.

The farther west you go, approaching the James River, the more arid it becomes, and the transition to ranch land begins in fits and starts between wheat and sunflower fields. By the time you are west of the Missouri River, it is firmly cattle country, mostly grass and grazing land, but likely a small percentage native vegetation. There are few places where you can stand, spin in a circle, and not see crops and trees, farmsteads and cemeteries, ranches and fences.

On the eastern end, the vegetation likely closest to what Irish saw is the sloughs. Those that exist today were either never drained for farming, which was common at the time, or drained but slowly filled back in by the ground water. Others are long gone. There are parks and occasional private lands where natural, unplowed prairie still exists, but it is rare and precious.

Another thing to consider is that for much of the route between Tracy, Minnesota, and well into Dakota Territory (now North and South Dakota, though Irish's crew worked in what is now South Dakota), the crew was conducting their survey across land claimed somewhat recently (at the time) by White settlers. West of the Missouri River, the land belonged to the Lakota.

Over the decades since Irish surveyed the area, there have been changes in the birds, plants, and animals. Some species are gone, while others have arrived on the scene. This means many of the scents and sounds experienced by Irish and his crew were different from what is available today. However, the general landscape—those wide-open vistas—remains mostly the same, though with more trees.

Despite these changes, standing at or near any of the camping or work locations that Irish and his crew experienced, it requires little imagination to look about, narrow your vision, and imagine being there before the fences, tree lines, and crops altered the views. It is interesting to drive along the railroad tracks today and consider the amount of time that Irish and crew put into determining the route, as well as the route options not chosen. It is even more poignant to realize that despite the considerable effort and resources that were poured into the railroad expansions that took place in the final decades of the nineteenth century, the heyday of rail traffic itself lasted but decades.

(This book includes historic photos as well as more recent ones taken by me. Photo citations are listed in the illustrations credits, beginning on page 415.)

Financial Buying Power Conversions

Irish made note of expenditures, and they are included as written. As a simple comparison, $1 in 1881 had the buying power of $25.15—roughly twenty-five times as much—when referenced in late 2019, according to the US Bureau of Labor Statistics.[3] You may find that conversion useful as you read about the fees paid for a night's lodging, a ton of hay, or a horse. I used the late-2019 rate because of its relative stability, before the COVID-19 pandemic and associated economic fluctuations, and also to tie this work to my previous book, *The Beautiful Snow*, which also uses the 2019 conversion number.

Native Land Loss

The story we are about to embark on took place less than three years after the Battle of the Little Bighorn, and during years when the Great Plains tribes were staging their final attempts to hold onto their ancestral lands in the face of White expansion. Most of the forts that are a part of this narrative have histories specifically linked to the conflict between the two cultures. (Others began as fur-trade posts).

Within Dakota Territory, much of the land Irish and his team were marking for the railroad had been off-limits just years before, or remained so. Especially in the early months, the diaries and letters mention nervousness about encounters with Dakota peoples, though there were no negative interactions with Irish's crew. Over time that nervousness faded, and by the end of the story, the survey team would include Lakota members.

American history and folklore are full of stories of those who helped "remove the Indian menace then preventing westward expansion."[4] That expansionist angle is only one perspective, of course, but the one most taught. I like to suggest that people look at moments in history more like a pie. What we are taught is usually only a single slice from that pie, from a certain perspective. Knowing that slice does not mean the rest of the pie did not happen. The other slices tell the rest of the story. Learning about the rest of the pie is not rewriting history, but rather helping one to understand the fuller story of what happened. Individual slices don't hold up well on their own, but together they create the whole, more substantial pie—the whole story, with full perspective.

The westward rush had an uncomfortable and very dark side, one I merely brush upon here. The land these settlers were rushing onto, of course, had been the home of various Native peoples, and they were being displaced with callous disregard, greed, and prejudice. It is a topic that deserves its own honest, humbling, and healing attention, and it is beyond the scope of this work.

While this book focuses on the work of one surveying team, the reader is encouraged to learn more about the ramifications that railroads such as the Dakota Central had upon the culture and lives of the people who had lived on this land for centuries before the White man came to "claim the empty spaces." The comparison maps below show the reduction of Native lands between 1850 and 1889.

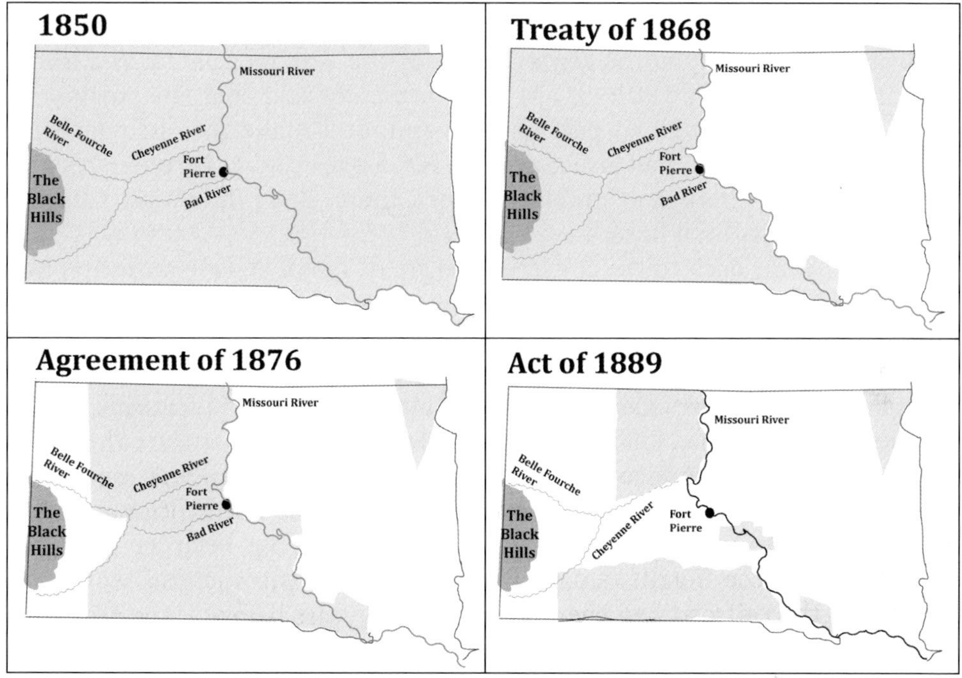

These maps show how recently the lands had belonged to the Dakota and Lakota peoples. Treaties ended in 1871. The next reductions of land happened via formal agreements and a legislative act. Most were executed less than honorably on the part of the US government. (Gray areas represent *approximate* boundaries of land that had not yet been ceded.) AI-6

Again, these maps are approximations only, formed with the input of dozens of other maps and the input of the archivists at the South Dakota State Historical Society. There is a wide range of opinions on what represented land ownership during these years, and it is not as simple to map as one would think. There are many papers and blog posts that detail this difficulty and the definitions that hinder mapping, and the reader is encouraged to dig deeper.

The letters and diary entries used language that today is considered antiquated. Similarly, locations such as the Great Sioux Reservation and legal documents of the era use similar terms to refer to the Lakota in the region. Throughout the book, quotes are as written, so words such as *Indian* and *Sioux* will appear.

In a letter dated January 30, 1880, Irish noted that he was among the "Sans Arcs, Blackfeet, Minneconjous [Miniconjou], and Ogallallas [Oglala]," each a division of western Sioux. When in Flandreau, he'd made note that he was among the Santee, a division of eastern Sioux. Those specific mentions were rare, and to avoid errors at that level, I refer to the eastern Native populations as Dakota and the western populations as Lakota, both of which are modern terms for the Sioux in those regions.

The Ingalls Story Within the Irish Story

When initially writing what became my first book, *The Beautiful Snow*, the text was going to include the construction of the Dakota Central as a lead-up to the Hard Winter of 1880–81. My editor wisely said that the story of the construction was enough to pull out, expand, and make into its own book. Prior to that decision, I had already transcribed over two years of Irish's diary entries, knowing there was a fabulous story there. But I didn't yet recognize that it deserved its own book.

When I came back to the construction story, I kept adding more and more (and more and more) of Irish's experiences into the narrative, until one day I realized that the construction story was very much secondary, maybe even tertiary, to Irish's story. The diaries and letters written by Irish during the surveying of the Dakota Central show an amazing set of adventures, humor, unbelievable conditions, and historic encounters. This book is the culmination of what bubbled up to nudge the construction story out of the way, once again.

Because all this research sprouted from my passion for the history behind the Ingalls family and because there are multiple overlaps between the activities of Irish and the Ingalls family within these two years, those overlaps are included here. As Charles Ingalls worked for the Dakota Central via a contractor, it is possible (maybe even likely) that Irish and Ingalls spoke with each other.

Introducing the People

This story covers nearly two and a half years of time, and as a result, many people play a role. Some people appear only once, while others appear consistently. For the most part, the reader is encouraged to remember the names of Irish's family members and the officers of the Chicago & North Western Railway Company (or just "Chicago & North Western"). For the rest, it is okay to just roll with the text and not be overly concerned about tracking who is who, as the reader should be able to intuit, through context, whether someone is a crew member, a local helper, etc.

The Irishes

- **Charles Wood Irish** is the star of the show, and the lead surveyor hired to identify a route, on behalf of the Chicago & North Western, from Tracy, in western Minnesota, to Deadwood, in the Black Hills of Dakota Territory.

- **Susannah Abigail**, or **Abbie**, is Charles's wife.
- **Ruth** and **Lizzie** are their daughters, both in their early twenties.

Officers of the Chicago & North Western

These men make frequent appearances in the book, so it will be helpful to remember their names and positions:

- **Marvin Hughitt** is the general manager and director of the Chicago & North Western.
- **John E. Blunt** is the chief engineer of the Dakota Central / Chicago & Dakota.
- **Albert Keep** is the president of the Chicago & North Western.
- **E. H. Johnson** is the chief engineer of the Chicago & North Western.

Irish's Surveying Crew

Many men participated in the job over the two years, some shifting out after a season, some staying on throughout. For the most part, if Irish named them in his diary, I also name them during the day's activities, as it felt impersonal to refer to any of them as "a crew member." However, don't feel that you need to remember their names and roles—just roll with the text. If you do want to track them, flip to appendix I (page 371) for a full list.

Local People Who Assisted Irish

From his initial visit to Currie, Minnesota, through the final months sequestered in Fort Pierre and Pierre, Dakota Territory, during the Hard Winter, there were area residents who helped with the surveying—by housing Irish, by escorting him on scouting trips, or even by braving fierce weather conditions to assist the men. They are mentioned within the text as appropriate.

Military Men

Once the men reached the Missouri River, Irish had frequent encounters with men at various forts, whether commanding officers or contracted store merchants. Some are prominent in the annals of the history of central Dakota Territory. They are mentioned within the text as appropriate, and appendix VI (page 398) expands a bit on their history.

Appendixes

Some of the topics covered lent themselves well to indulging in side research, but they could overwhelm the main text if included there. Instead, they are included as appendixes. As you read, if you want to know more about something, you can stop and flip back to the appropriate appendix (some of which I've already mentioned).

- **Appendix I: People** (page 371) is a list of crew members and their roles (if known), Indian police who were part of the crew for the final months of the work, and other Lakota that visited camp.
- **Appendix II: Surveying before GPS** (page 377) introduces some basic surveying definitions as Irish and his crew would have performed them, so that you'll have some understanding of what he means when he says they "ran a line" or "did levels" or calculated "curves."
- **Appendix III: Where Exactly Was Gap Creek Camp?** (page 380) outlines the journey taken to locate the campsite where some of the men spent the first storm of the Hard Winter of 1880–81 while living in canvas tents.
- **Appendix IV: Township, Range & Section Delineations** (page 394) explains the township-range-section method of identifying land.
- **Appendix V: Steamboats Mentioned in the Diaries** (page 396) provides a basic background for steamboating on the Missouri River in this era, as well as some basic information about each of the steamboats mentioned in the diaries or letters.
- **Appendix VI: Forts and Agencies** (page 398) expands a bit on the history of relevant forts to put context on their purposes (whether they served primarily as fur trade outposts, military fortifications, or Indian agencies, for instance).
- **Appendix VII: Biographies of the Irish Family** (page 404) is just what its title implies.

PREFACE: MARCH 1881

A collage of images from the March 1881 flood. AI-7, AI-8, AI-9

This section is a blend of my writing with words, phrases, and descriptions from Irish. It is presented without quotation marks in order to keep it visually clean. Towards the end of the book is a letter to his daughters, and in it you'll see which words were his. Within the body of the book, after this preface, his words will be set off conventionally.

Surveyor Charles Wood Irish stood at the second-floor window of the Chicago & North Western depot in the new town of Pierre, Dakota Territory. He and Mrs. Irish had been living there for many weeks, since the terrible winter cold and snows had driven his crew off the job west of the Missouri River.

An 1881 photo of the first depot in Pierre (right foreground). Irish was living on the second floor when the flood of 1881 hit. AI-10

The irony was that his work from the previous two years, almost to the day, had resulted in trains reaching Pierre in late November, just four months before. That should have meant an easy trip home to Iowa and away from the horrific winter in Dakota Territory. But the snows had started, the trains had stopped, and here they were in late March, trapped by ice that blocked the railroad tracks. Ice-blocked tracks didn't seem as disastrous compared to the ice-blocked river; a track wouldn't rise up to scour away its surroundings. A river, on the other hand . . . The scene below him was nothing short of calamity.

It looked for all the world like the roiling, churning waters of the Missouri River were trying to scrape away the new town of Pierre, along with its more established (but perhaps less civilized) sibling on the western shore, Fort Pierre.

The winter of 1880–81 had been historic not just for its lingering bitter cold but for the exceptional snowfall, which was melting, seeping its way into rivulets, then minor tributaries, then larger tributaries, and finally into the Missouri itself. Over the last few weeks, the waters of the Missouri had risen, reaching eight feet above the low water mark. But the ice on the river did not break up; it just rose with the water, as if trying to hold it down. Finally the cracks and fissures began, and the ice broke into chunks that began to float free, but not for long. They became jumbled, clogging together to create a dam seven miles south of the two towns.

The river began to lurk, to pool, to back up, to get fidgety, and—finally—to get downright agitated. It was a sudden menace to those upstream as the waters and energy built up behind the gorge, mile after mile after mile. Upstream, as those trickling waters drained en masse into the big river, seeping downstream upon that ice gorge, one last trickling drop changed the balance. Disaster exploded.

It was early morning. The residents of Fort Pierre were jolted awake by an unidentifiable, unimaginable sound. A low, terrifying, constant rumble of unknown source. Sharper crashes mixed in—whiplike, then gone—added to the confusion. Roaring splashes. Crunchings. Groanings. The earth itself trembled.

Dazed and groggy residents realized with a surge of adrenaline that the gorge had broken and the backed-up waters were on stampede. Freezing water and jagged slabs of ice slammed into the buildings closest to shore, scouring them away in the same easy manner, no matter whether they were made of canvas, wood, or stone.

Fort Pierre, on the western bank of the river, was taking the brunt of the assault. The inhabitants of Pierre, on the opposite side, stood watching from their own riverbank, some even laughing at what appeared to be little human ants scampering for the hills on the far side. Some of the human ants had just left their beds, sometimes without their clothes, and without the clearheadedness that the situation called for. They clawed their way, in a panic, to higher ground along the bluffs. Women, children, men, animals—all fleeing.

The people of Pierre were bemused, but not for long. The muddy, vexed water—as if it heard their laughter to the east and thought it a challenge—managed a four-foot surge, which reached into the lower grounds at Pierre, then began to rise. The witnesses there stood in horror for moments before they, too, began to run.

Perhaps from the top of those clay hills above Fort Pierre, the refugees on the west could now see human ants scampering towards the eastern bluffs too—at least those who ran for high ground. There was great confusion, and people ran in every direction. Regardless of which way they ran, the water continued its rampage south, with disastrous surges reaching inland east and west, filling the little valleys between the hills, turning the hills into smaller and smaller islands.

Irish was an engineer and a doer, and standing around helpless and afraid—or perhaps worse, running in confused circles—was not in his nature. He gathered the camp tents that had previously housed his surveying crew but now sat in storage. He gathered bedding. He gathered provisions. He took these items of comfort up to high ground above Pierre to house and protect the baffled refugees.

The sun began to sink behind the bluffs beyond Fort Pierre, but the water continued to rise, higher and higher, at one point rising ten inches in ten minutes. Meanwhile, it was claimed, some inhabitants had resorted to drinking—one method of drowning versus the other—followed by scolding, swearing, and yelling.

The shadows of twilight served as cover for the more dangerous types, and pistol shots could be heard. As darkness truly fell, the deepening shadows of approaching night conspired to fill the heart with terror.

Cakes of ice estimated at up to ten tons each came in singles, then groups, then entire herds. They crushed a small house as if it were a mere eggshell. When a hotel was hit, the sound was as if a bomb had gone off. A passenger railcar, standing on the tracks as peacefully as an unsuspecting cow grazing in a meadow, made a terrific noise when swept away by a particularly large berg of river ice.

Houses were turned over and broken up. It looked as if an earthquake, a tornado, or both had visited. Disaster. Irish heard people trapped in the second stories of buildings firing guns and ringing bells, desperately calling for help. He heard other sounds that simply defied description.

After what must have felt like an eternity, the rushing torrent began to slow. The slowing tide settled, then, at last, the terrible waters began to recede. Residents left their sanctuary on the bluffs to assess the situation. Pierre was bad, but not as bad as Fort Pierre.

The rougher sibling to the west was covered in ice eight to twenty feet deep. Less than a handful of buildings remained untouched. The great warehouses at the steamboat landing were crushed and gone, one of them apathetically relocated to the mouth of Bad River, to the south. The steam ferry had been abandoned atop ten feet of ice, two hundred yards inland. People were puzzling out just how they were going to get the ferry down off its new perch.

The surveyors' tents upon the bluffs above Pierre sheltered fewer and fewer residents as they made their way back down the hillside to inspect their now-battered holdings, the bits and pieces floating in an unpalatable soup of river water and debris.

Those same tents had once been the traveling homes and shelters and workplaces to an intrepid party of engineers who had spent the last two years creating the route for the Dakota Central railroad, a new entity of the mighty Chicago & North Western. The railroad was likely the thing that had lured many of the residents in the first place.

While neither the tents nor the engineers had needed to withstand a voracious flood during the surveying work, they'd experienced plenty else: A near 150-degree range of temperatures. Several multi-day blizzards. Winds that ripped the tents from their moorings. Virulent illnesses. Even a mutiny, accidental shootings, and one death. The job had been an adventure from beginning to end. Now Irish and his wife, trapped in Pierre and far from their peaceful Iowa home, were facing the angry waters of the Missouri River, swirling all around them.

How had it all come to this?

INTRODUCTION: THE PANIC OF 1873—PERIOD OF REST, THEN A BOOM

The Panic of 1873 put a halt to widespread railroad expansion. In hindsight, however, maybe it was more like a pause that allowed a great power to build up, to fortify, then to burst forth, not unlike 1881's ice dam. As the economy improved, a period of frantic railroad expansion ensued. In the coming decades, the frontier would close, sealing into myth and glory (and some amount of hidden shame) an entire era of American history. Much of that rapid spread across the landscape was made possible by the railroads. But that jumps ahead.

In the early 1870s, the Chicago & North Western had been expanding at an exuberant rate. One line, the Winona & St. Peter, had successfully reached the shores of beautiful Lake Kampeska, in eastern Dakota Territory, a long-sought goal. Towns sprang up along the rails, reversing the pattern of tracks veering this way or that to connect existing towns. Once the rails reached New Ulm, Minnesota, towns to the west were much rarer, allowing freedom to the surveyors to find the most efficient paths, knowing the towns would follow.

Steam locomotives needed to refill with water and fuel every so often, so towns were platted and watering stops set up. The towns platted were often upon land controlled by the railroad company via land grants, and they sold those town lots to merchants and businessmen who would then become the customers and vendors for the railroad. Towns were formally established, and farmers and merchants were enticed to purchase railroad land or homesteads as applicable along the lines, to form the social and economic fabrics of these new towns. It was a relatively new way of doing business, and it was successful. Western Minnesota experienced steady population increases by the early 1870s as various railroad lines moved westward and people followed the tracks.

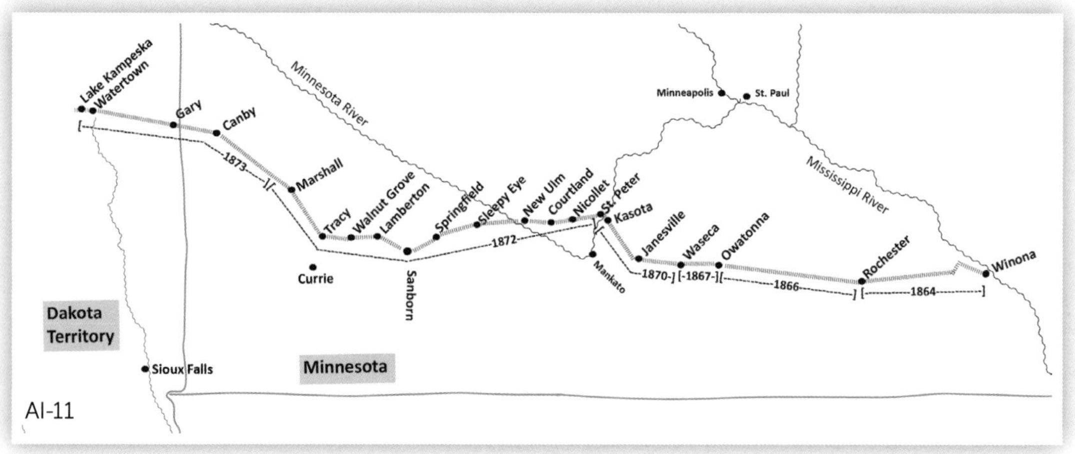

Then it all collapsed. In September 1873, officers of the Chicago & North Western, along with the leading businessmen of Chicago, Winona, and other cities and towns along the line, were celebrating the completion of the Winona & St. Peter Railroad (shown above) to its western terminus. While aboard a special excursion train headed to the end of the line at Lake Kampeska, Dakota Territory, near modern Watertown, the celebrants received news that bank Jay Cooke & Company had failed after years of overextension, much of it due to investment in various railroad endeavors.

The officers of the Chicago & North Western had been in the midst of calculating how to link that newly completed western end of the Winona & St. Peter with the transcontinental Northern Pacific, which was bound for the Pacific Ocean. The previous year, 1872, had seen jubilantly shared weekly newspaper articles—misty-eyed rhapsodies of the prosperity ahead—centering around that northern link between east and west. The officers had plans. Big plans. They saw dollar signs. Big dollar signs. Then, it all crashed to a halt, or at least to a crawl.

Despite the sudden lack of funds, the visionary minds remained at work. While the economy languished, deep what-if scenarios were raised, considered, argued, reevaluated, and considered again by the officers. By the late 1870s, the sleeping economy yawned awake and began to stretch. The officers of the Chicago & North Western took a closer look at the projects put on the drawing board during the quiet years. There were many options, each with its own costs and potential income, both short- and long-term.

The officers made their choices, and new opportunities shouldered aside the grand dreams of just a few years before. The biggest project to spike off from the Winona & St. Peter was no longer that connection to the Northern Pacific, with its coast-to-coast links. No. The officers now saw a greater opportunity heading to the Black Hills, where gold had been discovered. The sleepy little town of Tracy, Minnesota, was about to become the site of a great deal of frenetic activity. But for the moment, they had no idea what lay ahead, and the Chicago & North Western hoped to keep it that way.

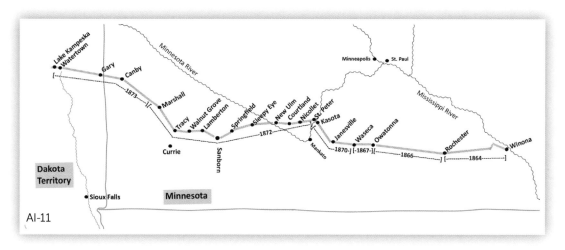

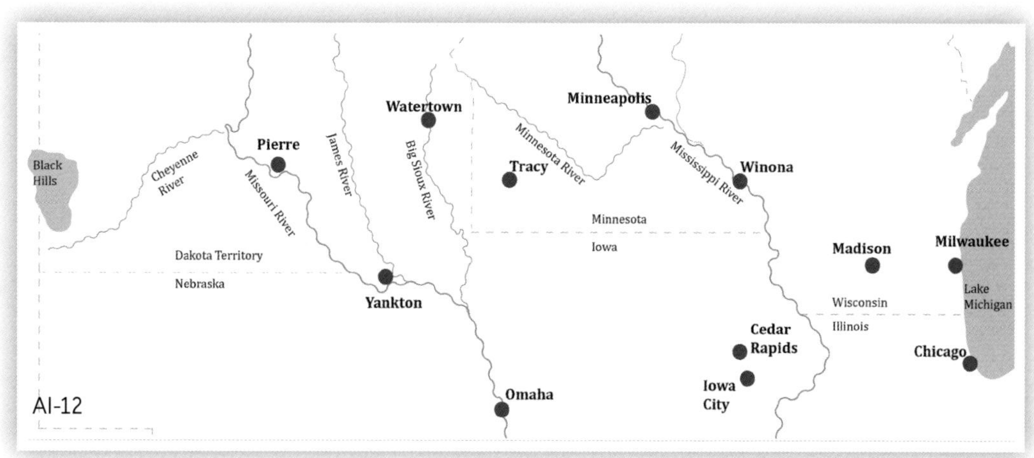
Black Hills
Cheyenne River
Pierre
Missouri River
James River
Watertown
Big Sioux River
Minneapolis
Minnesota River
Tracy
Mississippi River
Winona
Minnesota
Iowa
Dakota Territory
Nebraska
Yankton
Madison
Milwaukee
Lake Michigan
Wisconsin
Illinois
Cedar Rapids
Chicago
Iowa City
Omaha
AI-12

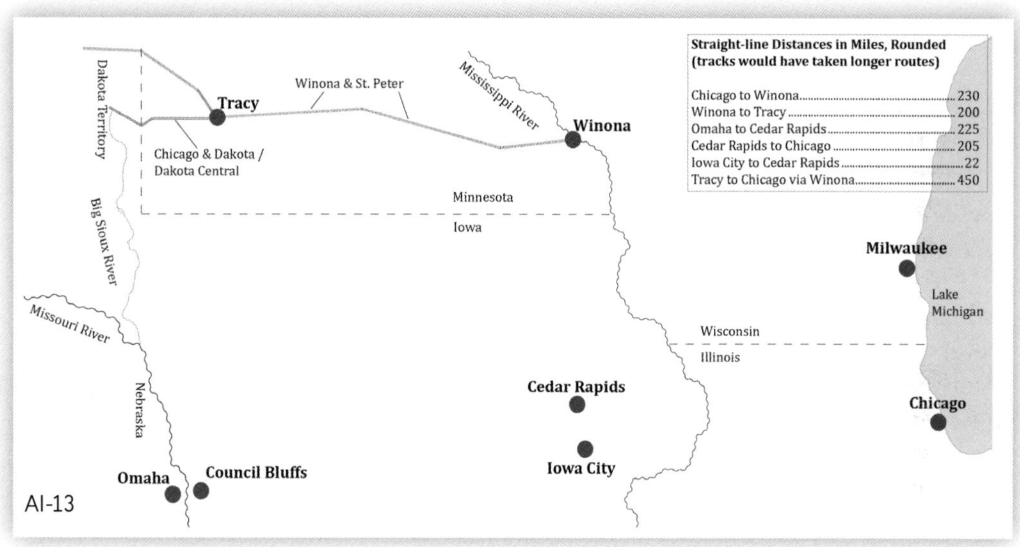
Straight-line Distances in Miles, Rounded (tracks would have taken longer routes)
Chicago to Winona 230
Winona to Tracy 200
Omaha to Cedar Rapids 225
Cedar Rapids to Chicago 205
Iowa City to Cedar Rapids 22
Tracy to Chicago via Winona 450
Dakota Territory
Tracy
Winona & St. Peter
Mississippi River
Winona
Chicago & Dakota / Dakota Central
Minnesota
Iowa
Big Sioux River
Milwaukee
Lake Michigan
Missouri River
Wisconsin
Illinois
Nebraska
Cedar Rapids
Chicago
Omaha
Council Bluffs
Iowa City
AI-13

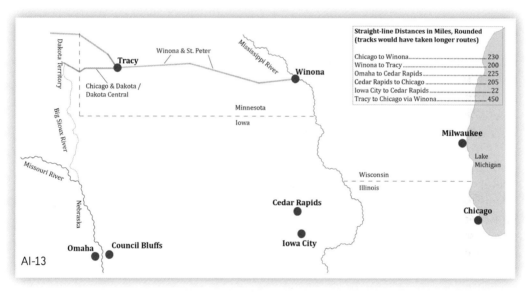

Section One

SCOUTING TRIP: WHERE TO PLACE THE LINE

JANUARY 13–MARCH 20, 1879

Surveyor Charles Wood Irish had been employed by the Chicago & North Western Railway Company to quietly scout out the land west of tiny Tracy, Minnesota, and on into Dakota Territory. Irish hired local guides to escort him, talked to many other people he encountered, and explored a wide swath of territory. He contended with cold, raging snowstorms and biting winds—and also escaped a hotel fire. Away from home, he missed his family, waiting anxiously for each letter. A hoped-for visit home was canceled when the officers requested that he investigate additional counties. The work was fruitful, however, and when Irish did go home, it was to prepare for his next endeavor: he would return to Dakota Territory to begin a surveying project, overseeing a large group of men.

"Hard at Work on Dakota Trip": January 13–16, 1879

In mid-January 1879, the nearly forty-five-year-old Charles Wood Irish was, uncharacteristically, at his home in Iowa City, Iowa. These were treasured moments, and he did not take for granted time spent in the company of his beloved wife, Abbie, and their two daughters, both in their early twenties. Nor did he take for granted the comfortable surroundings. A warm meal, a warm home, a comfortable bed.

Over a lifetime, he would accumulate significant professional and personal accomplishments. Right now, he was pulling together a plan for the Chicago & North Western. The officers had looked at their list of options, determining that a new line from Tracy, Minnesota, to the Missouri River and beyond was a top-tier opportunity. Gold lay in the Black Hills, and farms and ranches could sprout up along the tracks. It would be Irish's responsibility to plot an appropriate course.

His job was to begin that route, extending off the existing Winona & St. Peter Railroad in southwestern Minnesota, and get the rails into Dakota Territory, though it is unclear whether his initial task was to survey as far as the Big Sioux, the James, or all the way to the Missouri River. Whichever the target, it was a big task, but one Irish had done before. He would analyze an arc of territory, then determine a route based upon efficiency. How many cuts, how many fills, how many trestles or bridges, how straight or how many curves, what percentage of grade incline or decline—these were all factors that added to the calculations for not only construction but ongoing operations.

"Hard at work on Dakota trip"—these words comprised two-thirds of his diary entry for January 13, 1879, and commenced a two-year odyssey that resulted in the physical manifestation of the Dakota Central Railway.

LEGAL NAME OF THE RAILROAD LINE

For legal and operational purposes, the railroad was officially the Chicago & Dakota Railway while within Minnesota's borders, and the Dakota Central Railway once it crossed over into Dakota Territory. For our purposes, we will use the shorthand "Dakota Central" throughout.

The legal division between the segments also meant that Irish had to not only tally his expenses but separate them by legal unit. For example, in an undated notation in one of the expense journals he kept (right), Irish calculated $65.71 as belonging to the Chicago & Dakota and $34.29 to the Dakota Central.

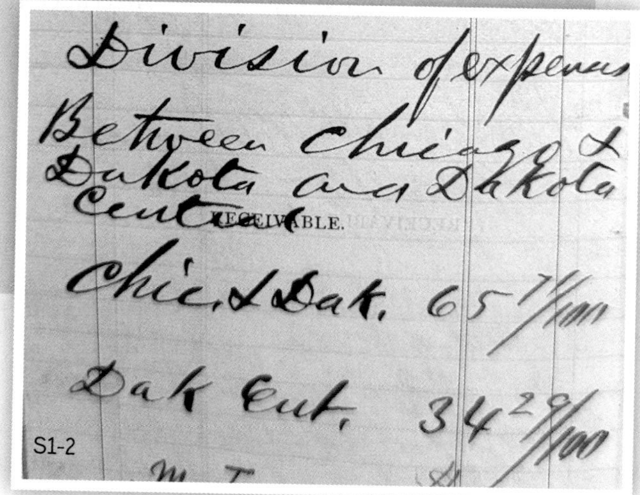

Division of expenses
Between Chicago &
Dakota and Dakota
Central
RECEIVABLE.
Chic. & Dak. 65 71/100
Dak Cent. 34 29/100

S1-2

Initial Scouting Trip: January 17–February 23, 1879

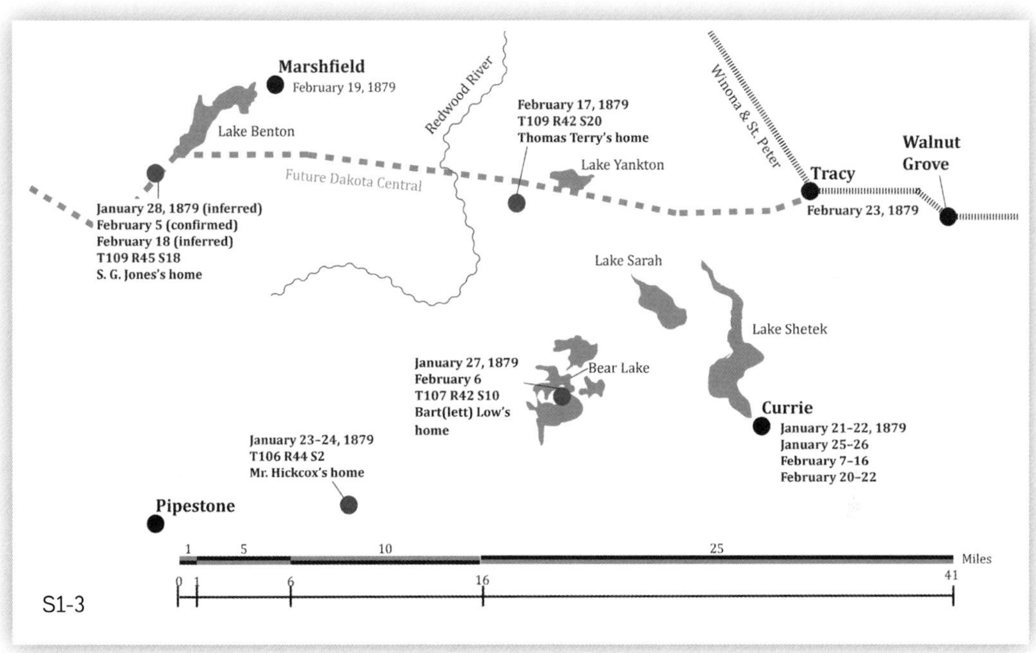

S1-3

By January 17, Irish was in Chicago, obtaining equipment, supplies, provisions, and—from the officers—"instructions." The next day, with $150 in his pocket, the gathered equipment in a box car, and instructions in his head, Irish boarded a Chicago & North Western train to head west. He arrived early on January 19 in a bitterly cold Winona, on the western bank of the Mississippi River, barely within Minnesota. There, he met up with John E. Blunt, a new resident of Winona and the chief engineer in charge of the Dakota Central. The two men had good rapport, and they attended a church service together the evening of Irish's arrival.

JOHN E. BLUNT, CHIEF ENGINEER OF THE CHICAGO & NORTH WESTERN RAILROAD

Born on Christmas Day 1828, John Ellsworth Blunt was a native of Tennessee. Educated in Massachusetts, he started his career doing survey work in Georgia, Alabama, and Tennessee. In 1862 he moved to Chicago, newly employed by the Galena & Chicago Union Railroad, which in 1864 became a part of the Chicago & North Western. Various promotions elevated him to chief engineer of the western divisions, which included the Winona & St. Peter and

S1-4

upcoming Dakota Central. He moved to Winona, Minnesota, in 1878 to oversee operations, and he was fifty years old when work began on the Dakota Central.[5] Blunt died in 1923 at age ninety-four; he was buried in Chicago's Rosehill Cemetery.[6] Perhaps imagine him speaking to Irish with a soft Tennessee accent colored with a bit of Massachusetts.

The proposed rail line that brought Blunt and Irish together in Winona was not yet even a rumor in the towns of western Minnesota, but these men in charge were taking the first concrete steps in its creation.

Irish and Blunt boarded the westbound Winona & St. Peter train at Winona on January 20, spent the night in Mankato, and completed the journey to Tracy by the following midafternoon. As they disembarked from the train, the day was warm enough for melting. Winter thaw often means mud, and their rented team of horses (he didn't say whether the team came with a wagon or whether this was a horseback endeavor) likely kicked up a bit of a mess as they traveled the approximately twelve miles south to Currie.

The road from Tracy to Currie was an easy trek—low, gentle hills flowing up, low, gentle hills flowing down. Sloughs spread out wider and wider, larger and larger. Ice flattened the surface of the wetlands and lakes, fissures etching across the open areas before disappearing among the reeds and cattails.

A ridge rose along the horizon to the southwest as the men approached the south end of Lake Shetek, where the road slipped down into the tiny town of Currie. The men then settled in as guests of a local man named Giles, no doubt an arrangement made well before the trip began.

Before leaving Tracy on January 21, Irish took a few moments to check in with his family, writing, "I am very well only quite tired out. I have only slept in a bed three times since I left home." It was warm, 46 degrees, and there was no snow to deal with. "It's a great plain of prairie like the Kansas plains but more settled up than Kansas or Nebraska." This trip required him to go "about half way" to the Missouri River, and he expected the explorations to take four weeks.

He told them to direct letters, for now, to "Tracy Lyon Co. Minn." Interestingly, he asked them to avoid putting "CE" (civil engineer) on the letters, only "just plain Esq." It seems they were not yet wanting to let any cats out of any bag as to his business in town.

On January 22, "a fine winter day," Irish roamed Currie looking for a team suitable for his upcoming scouting trip, evidently not considering the rented team from Tracy as an option. More immediately, he arranged for a horse and buggy for travel to Pipestone, which he found for the rate of $4.00, with an additional $5.60 for the animals' feed for the two-night trip. This outing would combine personal curiosity and professional duties.

A sample page showing expenses for the first month of scouting for the Dakota Central. S1-5

Irish left Currie the next morning, taking three hours to travel nine miles west. The high plateau allowed long views to the horizon, over hills and valleys. (Blunt may have also been along on this trip, as the diary uses *we*, though specifics as to who that constituted are lacking.) The day was cloudy, possibly featuring the low textured blue-grey clouds common in Minnesota during January, where one does not have to squint to see, making it an excellent day for evaluating the landscape.

West of Currie, the gently rolling hills are punctuated by wide sloughs that stretch outward from the low spots. The midwinter grasses would have brought a golden-copper color to the eye, a beautiful contrast to the slate grey of the clouds. There had not been much snow, and what little remained was huddled at the bases of the bunch grasses. While Irish was a keen observer who liked to share details with his family, he was likely putting his discerning eye instead to the wider terrain, looking for stretches that would—or would not—be suitable for a railroad bed.

West of Currie, showing the gentle undulation of the land and the mix of grassland and slough.

The midday meal—which Irish consistently called "dinner" and will be referred to thusly throughout this text—was eaten at the home of Bartlett, or Bart, Low (pronounced like the second syllable of *allow*), a resident of Lowville Township. Irish was likely eager to hear the man's experience with general weather, terrain, flooding, and the like, with an ear toward patterns and the availability of water (good for locomotives) or flooding (bad for railroad beds).

At the time, a collection of interconnected (or nearly so) lakes dominated the north-central portion of the township. They included Bear Lake, which Irish mentioned was his destination for the morning. Today, it takes squinting at a satellite map to see hints of these drained lakes; if you were unaware of their existence, it would not be easy to make out their ghostly outlines. A portion of those lakes live on in the guise of the Great Oasis State Wildlife Management Area, described as a "remnant woodland on the shores of a large drained lake basin."[7] In 1879, however, they were actual lakes, and likely surrounded by wetlands and sloughs. In other words, an expensive landscape for railroad track.

Having finished the meal at Bart Low's, the men headed southwest. The temperature was 28 degrees, which for late January was not uncomfortable. The wind, however, was blowing "a gale," reminding them it was winter on the northern plains. They traveled across a high plateau creased by the narrow, deep ravines of otherwise small creeks. Soon, the landscape began to feature more undulations—not bigger hills, but more in general—enough to create plenty of headaches for a railroad, each representing a cut-and-fill task (more on that later). As if knowing what was coming, the hills seemed to rise from the protective moat-like sloughs nestled at their bases.

By late afternoon, fighting that gale of a wind, they arrived at the home of a Mr. Hickcox, approximately eleven miles east of Pipestone. Looking north, Irish noted the land there was flatter, but more substantial hills were visible beyond. After spending the night under the hospitality of Hickcox (and likely inquiring about his local insights), they were up early. They took dinner in the fledgling town of Pipestone, then visited the famous quarry on its outskirts, a location sacred to many Native cultures for centuries. The red pipestone found at the site was carved into pipes that, through smoking, carried prayers to the Great Spirit. On his visit, Irish would have seen the sacred stone and learned of its power.[8] (Pipe making continues at the site today.)

After a second night at the Hickcox home, the men reversed their trek, having lunch at Bart Low's, near Bear Lake, and arriving back in Currie by 4 p.m. on January 25. Irish wrote, "The day was very chilly. This is a flat country + I fear a dry one." A dry country would make railroad operations difficult in an era of steam locomotives.

Perspective is a curious thing. It is interesting that Irish's eye saw flat country; the landscape in this region does not look flat, in most places, to this book's author. There are hills of varying degrees, from undulations to carved creek banks. But to the surveyor's trained eye, it was relatively flat for the purpose of finding a route for a railroad—and that was a good thing.

It is also interesting that he feared the region was dry. Irish was noted as a keen observer, and he knew that cycles of wet and dry years could have a big impact on the amount of water available to the locomotives. The presence of lakes and sloughs did not necessarily mean a wet climate, and his conversations with locals may have helped inform his concern.

Back in Currie, Irish spent January 25 and 26 writing letters, both to his family at home and to newspapers about a just-completed project in Arizona, as getting one's name in the newspapers was a way of boosting their résumé. (Over the previous three years, Irish had helped to route the Atchison, Topeka & Santa Fe Railway through Colorado, New Mexico, and Arizona.)

Writing to his family from Currie, Irish bemoaned his level of homesickness. Due to letters not having reached him, he teased that he would have "to go into the wilderness without a word from home." The mail may have been consistently delayed, but the weather was "very changeable." In particular, the wind had a habit of blowing from different directions over the course of a day or two—one day warm, the next cold. On top of all of that, he added, "The roads are dusty."

He was preparing to leave on a trip that would take him from Currie to Lake Benton in Minnesota, then into Dakota Territory—to Medary, up the Big Sioux River, and on to Oakwood. He would then retrace his steps to Medary before spending several days in Flandreau,[9] where he hoped to find letters from home waiting for him. He planned to be back in Currie by February 10.

It had been an unusual 48-degree day, strong winds drawing in warm air and transforming the frozen ground into a soggier substance. "It's quite muddy now," he noted in his diary as he made final preparations for his trip west.

The barometer was rising the morning of the twenty-seventh, possibly bringing with it a richly deep-blue sky, the dry January air holding no haze to filter what can be a painfully brilliant sun. Finally at 3 p.m., which would have been just an hour or two before sundown, he headed west for the scouting trip into Dakota Territory. At least one other man went with him, a W. H. Bell (or Bill—Irish's handwriting can be maddeningly sloppy at times). We do not know what became of Blunt after he traveled to Tracy with Irish on January 21, so he may also have been along. Or he may have taken his leave of Irish the week before. Perhaps Giles was along. At the very least, Giles provided the team and wagon that took the men west, as Irish's journal noted an expense of $20 for the use of Giles's team for eleven days.

After again spending the night at the home of Bart Low, the men scouted overland to Lake Benton. Irish was pleased with the terrain they crossed over, which, while gently undulating and covered in sloughs of all sizes, was deemed good and thus manageable. It was a promising start to the scout. The weather was likewise manageable, "thawing but chilly." Today, a good percentage of this area is completely covered by sloughs, and their edges alternate between dry and soppy, depending on the season.

Upon reaching Lake Benton at 7 p.m., however, Irish's optimism took a bit of a hit. There, he saw the formidably high north–south ridge, where the land takes a sudden rise as it stretches west. That ridge stood between him and Dakota Territory.

A modern photo showing the tree-covered ridge on the west side of Lake Benton. The notch to the left of center is where US Highway 14 crosses the ridge today. The incline is well beyond what a train could accomplish then or now. S1-7

Two nights were spent at Lake Benton, carefully scouting the area. The men then headed west on what Irish described as a chilly 36-degree day, analyzing the ground between Lake Benton and the town of Medary on the Big Sioux River in Dakota Territory. After climbing the 150 feet of elevation via that high ridge west of Lake Benton, Irish described the land as "flat" and "gradually [declining] to Medary." Medary, approximately seven miles south of what became Brookings, was firmly within the Prairie Coteau, a high plateau whose surface is today covered in small prairie pothole lakes. At the time, however, many or most of these were dry.

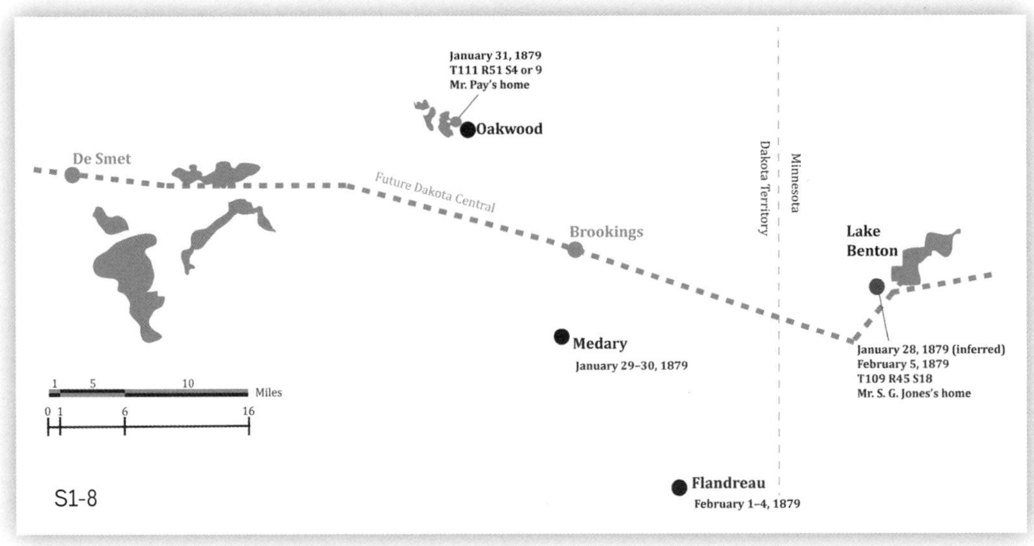

S1-8

THE PRAIRIE COTEAU

The Prairie Coteau (a.k.a. Coteau des Prairies, whose southeastern portion, in Minnesota, is called Buffalo Ridge) rises above the surrounding landscape, and its edges can provide sweeping views. Each railroad line that crossed it had to find a way up one side and down the other. The map image on the left does a good job of showing how the top of the coteau, or hilly upland, hosts many lakes (as well as countless marshes, sloughs, and potholes). But again, most of these wetlands were dry at the time Irish surveyed a route for the Dakota Central.

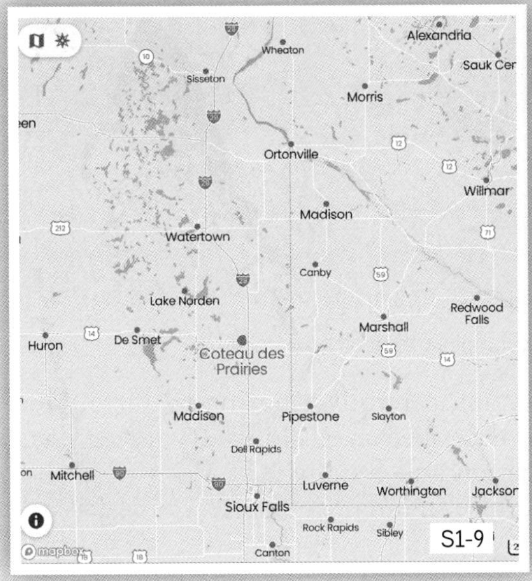

S1-9

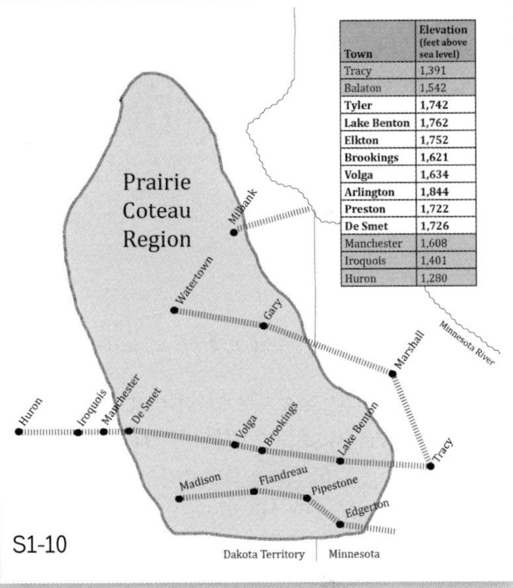

Town	Elevation (feet above sea level)
Tracy	1,391
Balaton	1,542
Tyler	**1,742**
Lake Benton	**1,762**
Elkton	**1,752**
Brookings	**1,621**
Volga	**1,634**
Arlington	**1,844**
Preston	**1,722**
De Smet	**1,726**
Manchester	1,608
Iroquois	1,401
Huron	1,280

S1-10

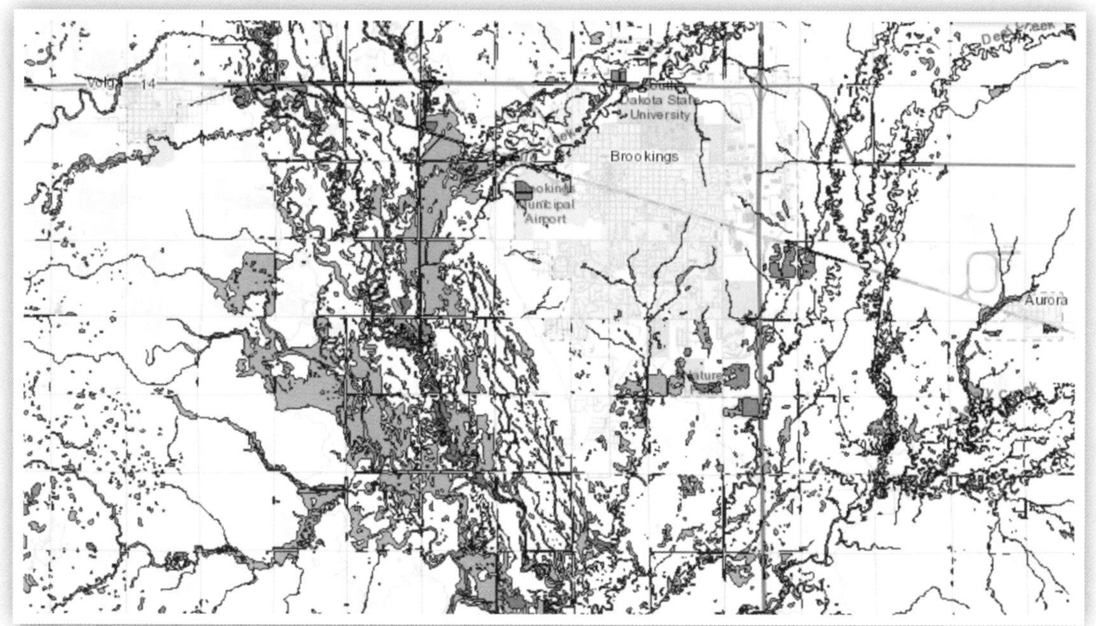

Modern map of wetlands and creeks around Brookings, in the core of the Prairie Coteau. S1-11

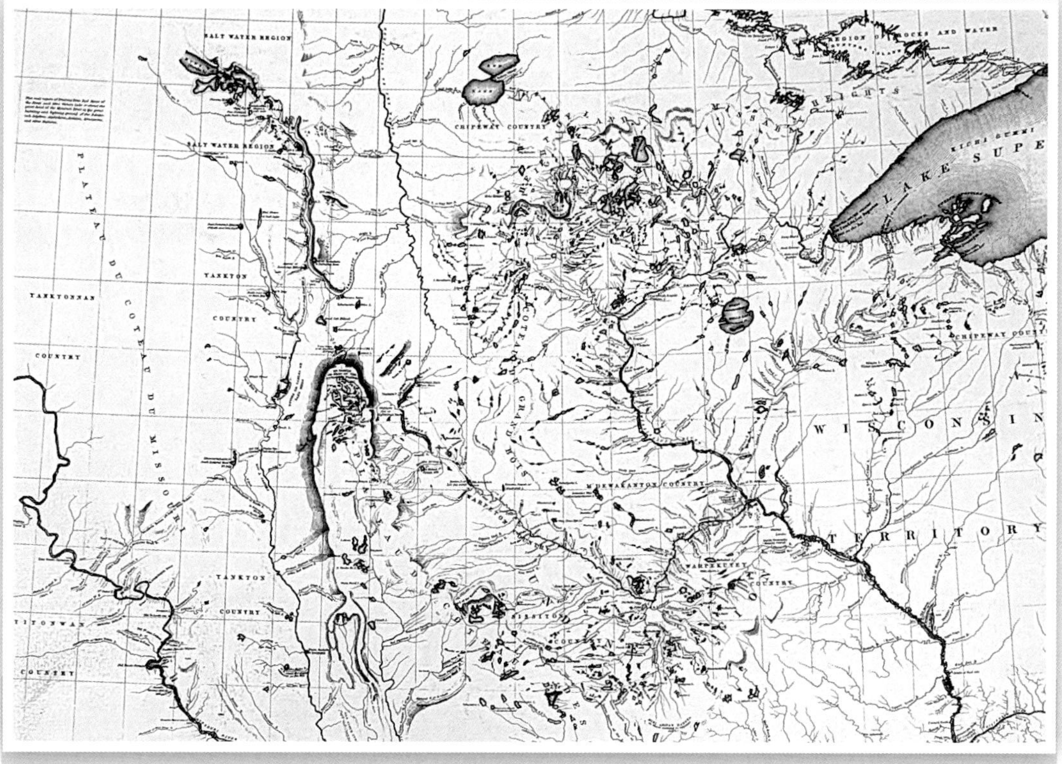

Joseph N. Nicollet's 1839 map of the Upper Missouri River Basin. S1-12

Irish spent January 30 exploring the ground around Medary, confirming his initial sense that the land between Lake Benton and the Big Sioux was perfectly suitable. There would be "no trouble in getting from west side of Lake Benton here nor in going west from here as there are no bluff[s] either side." The terrain appeared conducive to easy track laying, at least after the initial rise of the coteau.

On Friday, January 31, the men left Medary and headed north toward the little assembly of five houses called Oakwood. The day was raw; while the temperature hovered around freezing—not considered unusually cold for January—the northwest wind made it feel much colder, and Irish admitted that he "suffered much" as a result. At noon they arrived at the home of Byron E. Pay, whose home nestled on the eastern shore of Lake Oakwood. To the west of Lake Oakwood lay Lake Tetonkaha, with a handful of plowable acres separating them.

A view looking west toward where Oakwood stood, near the lakeshore. S1-13

BYRON E. PAY

Byron E. Pay was an early and leading citizen not just of the Oakwood area but of Dakota Territory in general, and his biography is fascinating. When four months shy of seventeen, he enlisted in the Union army and fought in the Civil War, participating in several encounters before being severely wounded at Chickamauga. He was discharged in 1864 due to "disability resulting from a gun shot wound in left shoulder." At nineteen, Pay obtained a job with the Northwestern Fur Company, taking wagons of goods from Mankato, Minnesota, to Fort Thompson, on the Missouri River in southeastern Dakota Territory. Over the next several years, he held various jobs in the Dakotas, either for the military or fur companies. He married, and his first home in the region was to the southeast of Medary, near the Big Sioux. In 1873, the couple moved to what became Oakwood Farm.

From 1872 to 1873, Pay served in the Dakota Territorial Legislature. In 1874 he became the area's postmaster, and from 1874 to 1885, he was a US marshal, a position he held while working with Irish. In 1878 he built a hotel, Oakwood House, which may be where Irish stayed when visiting. Pay also served as a land agent. In the mid-1870s, he was a frequent visitor to Marshall, Minnesota, where he sold butter from his dairy and brought beautiful specimens of potatoes and radishes to the editor of the *Prairie Schooner* newspaper as a proverbial (and literal) dangling carrot to lure farmers out to the fertile fields.

Considering the assistance Pay gave Irish in helping to site the Dakota Central and a branch between Volga and Watertown, perhaps it is ironic that the town of Oakwood was bypassed when that branch to connect the Dakota Central to the Winona & St. Peter was built, heading north from Volga but passing Oakwood several miles to the east. Eventually most of Oakwood's buildings, except Oakwood House, were moved east to the rails.

In 1897, President McKinley awarded Pay the Medal of Honor for his actions in a Civil War skirmish in Tennessee. Pay died in 1906 at age sixty-one, a well-respected man. He is buried in Arlington Cemetery in South Dakota.[10]

The terrain around Oakwood was a mix of flat and hilly, though the hills tended to be more numerous on the west side of the lakes, the flatter land more prevalent to the east. However, also to the east was a ridge that allowed one to look west over the top of the lake and assess the general landscape.

The area was "lush" and "fine indeed," except for one thing: "There is very little timber," wrote Irish, and what timber there was, was on the west end of the cluster of lakes. Thinking about the timber (fuel) needs of both locomotives and settlers, Irish made note of this resource—or the lack of it—multiple times throughout his upcoming diary entries.

Early on February 1, the men said their farewells to Pay and headed south, bracing against the "cold raw windy" day. They ate their early meal at Medary, then continued southeast to Flandreau, arriving in time for supper (late-in-the-day meal). Irish had let his family know he would be in Flandreau during the early days of February. A "great disappointment" awaited him, however: there was no mail from home.

In a letter fragment dated January 30, just before his arrival in Flandreau, he complained, "It seems harder to hear from you on this trip than when I was in Arizona so much further off." Distance wasn't really the problem, of course; it was infrastructure and population—or lack thereof.

The first night in Flandreau featured some frightening excitement. "We had quite a scare by a lamp breaking in a room near ours setting the house on fire," wrote Irish. The brief diary mention belies the danger of the situation, which he expanded on in a letter home.

THE FLANDREAU FIRE

In a letter home a few days after leaving Flandreau, Irish shared a longer account of the fire that had jolted him from sleep when he first arrived in Flandreau:

> The Hotel is a new building two stories high with very narrow hall and small rooms. I went to bed quite tired out, had just fallen asleep when there came a sudden Bang! a stifling smell and a cry of Fire!! fire! oh! how I jumped. I pulled on my pantaloons and rushed out into the hall to find it filled with smoke and flames. I ran back to my room intending to jump out of the window when I heard them call out all is right. I went back to find that a fellow had left a large lamp full of kerosene burning without a chimney, this made it so hot that it burst and threw the burning oil about the room + set it on fire. A brave fellow had the presence of mind to empty his water pitcher on his bed quilt and then throw the quilt over the flames. When by that time 3 or 4 buckets of water was brought in and dashed on the flames which checked them so that more quilts smothered them out. But it took an hour to entirely put out the fire, for the bed was burning and 4 buckets of water was all they could get, the wells being all dry, and they have to depend upon ice melting all over this country for water. I was so scared that I only got a few naps the rest of the night.

Flandreau's *Moody County Enterprise* also told its readers about the fire in its February 6, 1879, issue:

> A lamp exploded in B. D. Milam's room at the Sioux Valley House last Saturday night, which luckily resulted in [only] slight damage to property. It had been left a few hours previous partly turned down, and was shattered into a thousand fragments by the accident, while the oil was dashed over the wall and furniture and a calamity was only prevented by the prompt application of a smothering process. Moral—Don't leave your lamp burning while away from home.[11]

The next morning, Irish attended worship services at the local mission, where he "made the acquaintance of the missionary pastor." February 3 was a "stormy day and gloomy indeed," though his spirits immediately lifted upon receipt of a letter from home. Irish spent the next day writing letters of his own and preparing to return eastward. He had liked Flandreau, having found "many pleasant gentlemen" within its borders. He said nothing at all about the landscape, though.

To his daughter Lizzie, Irish shared his plans to stay a few more days in Flandreau, in case any letters were making their way to that town. He would have to move along soon, so he listed his next locations: Currie, Lake Benton, and Winona. The Winona stop would be on his way home, after he finished the scouting reports for the railroad. But that trip was not a certainty. "May not get the chance," he wrote, "for it looks as if they [the railroad company] are going to push ahead."

There was an overnight snowfall, and the temperature fell a few degrees below zero. Despite the souring weather, the men left town. It was miserable—over twenty miles of travel through a "very raw and cold" day. They stopped for the night, finding warmth and comfort in the home of S. G. Jones, a half mile or so southwest of the western tip of Lake Benton, along a wooded creek nestled at the base of the big ridge. Reflecting on his day, Irish lamented they had "suffered much from the cold."

February 6 dawned cold, but with the visual gift that "the air [was] full of frost . . . and all things were covered" with ice crystals. The men packed up, followed along the southern shore of Lake Benton, then dipped southeast to return to Bart Low's home, west of Currie. Wherever there was the rare timber, its dark, skeletal winter tree branches transformed as though dipped in sugar. Despite it being a beautiful ride—the sky likely a deep blue and the sun glittering off the airborne crystals and earthbound snow—it had also been a cold ride. On top of that, the glaring sun and reflecting crystals tired the eyes. Irish again told his diary, "We suffered much."

The next morning, February 7, they traveled approximately nine miles east to Currie. There, Irish received the gift of a letter from his daughter Ruth, which raised his spirits despite feeling "sick from the effects of cold." It had been a "very cold day," with the barometer rising—a condition that is often associated with plummeting winter temperatures. (As an aside, that was also the day Laura Ingalls turned twelve, her home less than fifteen miles to the northeast.)

Irish's traveling companion had only been mentioned by name on the day they left for the scouting trip, except when the diary mentioned that "we" did this or that. With the scouting trip concluded, so too went any mention of this mysterious traveling companion.

Irish spent the next several days writing letters and reports, recounting his explorations between Currie in Minnesota and Oakwood in Dakota Territory. He did take a few moments for himself at least, noting that the rise of the nearly full moon on February 8 featured beautiful moon dogs—an atmospheric optical phenomenon producing a halo and bright spots around the moon—reinforcing his observation that the weather was especially cold. They impressed him so much, in fact, that he made a sketch in his diary, despite the resulting art being a mere circle embraced by two arcs.

Among the letters Irish wrote from Currie on February 9 was a long one to his daughter Lizzie: "I got here last Friday in a sharp cold wind which as it came into my face + eyes caused me to cry a stream of tears 25 miles long. The tears ran down along my nose and wet the visor of my cap and my beard and there it froze into icicles and froze the tip of my nose but not more than skin deep." The weather was keeping him on his toes, he told her. "I dodged quite a severe storm while at Flandreau and another here yesterday and last night. I tell you it blew hard and went away below zero, but today it's warmer and thaws some at night."

He had anticipated heading home at this point, having explored the landscape from Currie to Pipestone to Medary. But a recent letter had changed his plans, he wrote: "I feel quite a disappointment for I was ready to start home when I got here and found a letter from Mr. Johnson [of the Chicago & North Western] ordering me to look over two more counties which will take me a week longer and I don't know what then." He described himself as "'sick, sore and sorry' [Irish's quotation marks] for I expected to be at home this week. Home! When will I be there. . . . You cannot imagine the destitution of most of the people in this plain of prairie. I will tell you more about it at another time."

He ended his letter by sharing, "[The company] are in earnest have ordered 200,000 ties to Tracy +c." This railroad was going to happen, but first he had to figure out *where* it was going to happen. Ten days later, the first rumors began to appear:

> **The Marshall Messenger says a rumor has been afloat there based on an order to leave a large number of ties at Tracy, that the C. & N. W. R. R. Co, intend to run a road next summer west from Tracy to head off the Southern Minnesota, and tap the country south of Lake Benton, thence to Ft. Piere.** S1-15

Irish had hoped to start this new scout on February 10, but the barometer was dropping, and he suspected that his departure would be delayed. Indeed, it became stormy and cold. He postponed the larger trip, but he did ride the twenty-four miles to Tracy and back (getting "chilled through" in the process) to get his letters and papers onto the train for delivery to, likely, Blunt in Winona, Hughitt and Johnson in Chicago, and his family in Iowa City. He then returned to Giles's home, where heavy snows and high wind on the eleventh further delayed his departure.

On February 11—his birthday—Irish remained stuck in Currie. To his wife he wrote,

> Here I am in this little place and the snow flying thick and you all so far away that I wonder when I shall see you again. I am today 45 years old! Think of it. Five more, Fifty!! Threescore and ten is not far off is it. I am very well, had some fever from the exposure of the last trip but that is all gone. My nose is quite sore but it is not badly [frost] bitten. I shall not leave here until fair weather comes. I hope I may get home now, so don't you fret about me, I have a barometer to go by + that saved me getting caught in this storm for had it not have been for it, I should have started yesterday out into the prairie.

His delay continued for several days while a storm blew "a stiff NW gale" and temperatures dropped to –18. He used the time to further review maps and notes he'd made from his scouting trip to the west, "wait[ing] for warmer weather" and greeting visitors who came to see him. Despite enjoying time spent socializing, the cold took its toll on him. "I am quite out of health," he complained, suffering a deep pain in his right side.

On February 14, Irish penned another letter home from Currie, regaling the readers there about his battles against the cold. By trusting the barometer readings, he had "escaped a very bad storm." He added,

> It has lasted 6 days, and all that time the temperature [was] from 6° to 20° below zero and the wind a severe gale all the time. My nose I froze the first day of the storm and chilled my chin we had to face the wind. . . . Oh! how it hurt. It's much better now. . . . With us [in Iowa,] you know we fear tornados. Here the great fear is of a winter blizzard as they call them, it's a high cold wind full of snow. . . . Well I feel happy that I got here for they have wood to burn and if it had not been for the barometer I have with me, I should have been out on the Dakota prairie in a sod shantie with only a hay fire to warm by.

(As a quick note, a barometer reads atmospheric pressure. In general, a higher reading indicates calmer weather, a lower reading indicates unstable weather.)

As an insight into how letters came and went, the family was directed to continue posting letters to Blunt, who would then see that Irish received them. At some point in the future, they'd be able to send letters "direct" to him, he assured them.

In an earlier letter, Irish noted the destitution of the people. He was seeing the region after several years of grasshopper scourge. The people who remained, perhaps, were the ones fighting hardest to hold onto their land and the work they'd already invested. Maybe Irish had more of an Easterner's point of view, writing,

> Well it's a pretty country, it's the people I find fault with. . . . You cannot imagine the poverty of nearly all the people here. They have but little to eat, not much pork even, very little bread either. . . . Then such clothes, rags + tatters, children are mostly bare footed + I have seen many little girls that had only a calico dress for clothing.

The letter from home must have included mention of clothes for Irish too, as he included,

> Wait about the clothes until I come home. I have slept on the prairie 3 nights but kept warm and comfortable. Those things of mine are admired everywhere I go and I have had to let the women cut patterns off of them three times now. They are just the thing. I am very well, but had a bad cold but got over it altogether. We have a continual raw cold wind blowing from all quarters which hurts my eyes very much.

He told Mrs. Irish, "The company is in real earnest, and I shall have work here for several months + when the weather is good I want you to come up here and live with me. I will rent a sod house." He hoped to be done with his work early enough to spend March home on a visit, assuming the storms didn't keep him from getting away.

A previous letter from the family had included the latest about the feud with the Goetz couple, neighbors of the Irishes. This one involved a dog, possibly just the latest in a string of troublesome dogs. "I don't believe that Goetz would be so bad a man if it was not for that old woman," Irish told his wife. He warned his family not to antagonize the neighbors, but to "give them to understand how you all feel about it, but don't get out of temper about it, that will do no good."

HAY STOVES

Another interesting piece of information Irish shared with his family was about hay stoves. During the upcoming Hard Winter of 1880–81, residents of the plains burned twisted hay for heat, being out of coal and wood. But Irish was not impressed by this option, writing in a February 14 letter, "You should see the hay stoves. My goodness you would go crazy if you had to use them. They fill up one end of the room with hay and it takes one all the time to put it in the stove, then the ashes fly out all over the room. The women have a streak of black ashes on each side of their eyes with a gutter or furrow down which the tears run in streams . . . They burn about 8 1/2 tons of hay (prairie grass) per year . . . The women look so funny with the white ashes sticking all over their hair like down from feathers."

February 15 dawned with the thermometer reading of –13, though by 2 p.m. it had risen to 25 degrees. As it had become "a very fine day," Irish went out to explore some of the locations associated with what is now more properly called the Dakota War of 1862 but at the time was widely treated as if an unprovoked massacre.

THE DAKOTA WAR OF 1862 AND SLAUGHTER SLOUGH

In late summer 1862, the local Dakota hit back against the US government by attacking White settlers, angry at the lack of promised food and annuity payments and at being treated as less than human. Some of the events took place very close to what became the town of Currie, including Lake Shetek, just to the north. It was at the lake that thirty-four frightened settlers gathered at the cabin of John and Julia Wright as news spread of killings.

The settlers began to run eastward, into a nearby slough. Gunfire was exchanged. The slough offered little protection, and those seeking a hiding place were either taken captive, left for dead, or killed. The captives were taken to various locations, ultimately traded into the care of a group of young Dakota men[12] who eventually delivered their captives safely to the US military. The tragic history of the Dakota War of 1862 is worth exploring, and the reader is encouraged to learn more and visit the locations of the conflict.

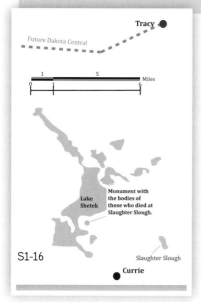

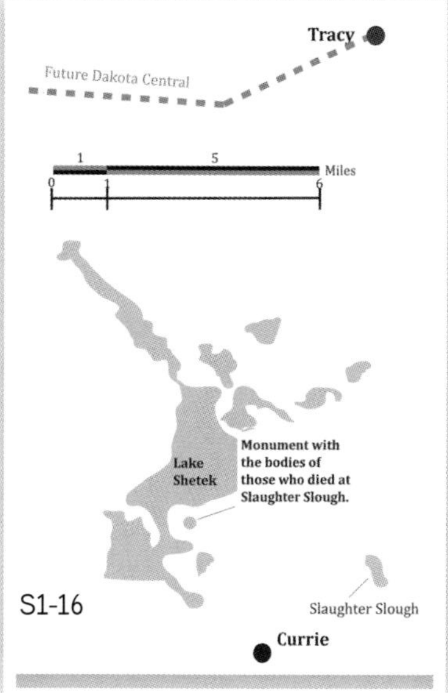

S1-16

Midafternoon shadows grew longer and longer, bathing the browns and coppers of the winter grasses in the rich light of the low-angle sun. In such circumstances, the warmth of the colors starkly contrasts with the cold bite in the air. As the sun entered its final hour above the horizon, the landscape became draped in dark, cool colors, until the setting sun dimmed altogether.

On a second day of touring sites near Currie, Irish ventured out with local businessman and town cofounder Neil Currie to visit the marsh named Slaughter Slough, where residents had fled when the local attack by the Dakota began. The site remains much as it was in 1862, and it is now a waterfowl production area, featuring individual monuments to the Dakota people, the White settlers, and the Fool Soldiers (young Dakota men who aided the White captives.) Irish and Currie also visited the site where fifteen of the victims were buried; a monument was placed there in 1925, and the area is now part of Lake Shetek State Park.

The view looking north from the center of Slaughter Slough, showing the undulating landscape. S1-17

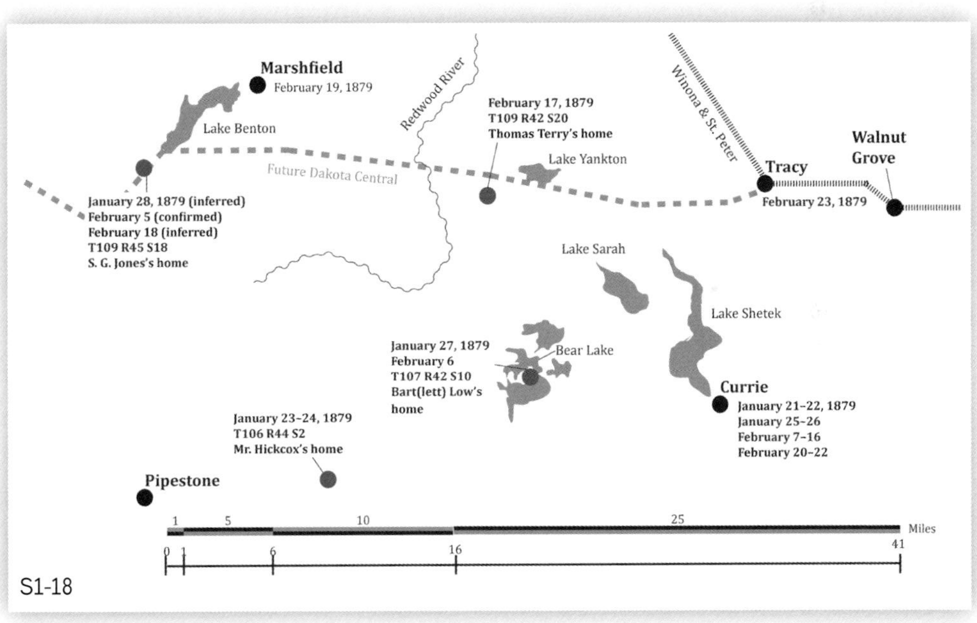

S1-18

After this brief hiatus, it was time to get back to work. The officers wanted Irish to evaluate two counties to the north (probably Lyon and Lincoln Counties). On February 17, Irish and Giles rode northwest to the home of Thomas Terry, southwest of Lake Yankton, near modern Balaton. On the way, the men swung eastward to take a look at Lake Sarah while enduring another "cold raw day," including a wind that switched from southeast to southwest. At Terry's home, Irish likely had many questions about the area, again soaking up information that would be relevant to the operations of a railroad.

The next morning, Irish and Giles left Terry's house in a light snow that was swirled by "a gale" from the southwest. It could not have been a pleasant trip, with snow whipping into their faces, getting into their eyes, and pricking any bare skin.

Their destination was Lake Benton, to the west, and they crossed gentle slopes that featured long views and big sloughs. Much of the land was a relatively flat, high plateau—much, but not all. The path also took them across the Redwood River, which ran through a carved landscape that Irish likely noted as being one of the main obstacles on the way to Dakota Territory (that and the high ridge west of Lake Benton). He'd have been right, as in the months to come, much time would be spent working and reworking both locations.

On February 19, in air that fought to reach 2 degrees above zero, they moved on to Marshfield, less than half a mile east of the frozen waters of Lake Benton. While Irish did not comment on the suitability of the terrain for building the rail bed, he did note that Marshfield was a "very poor, lonesome place . . . full of lakes + ponds and poor people." The barometer was rising, correlating to temperatures that would not be.

After an overnight in Marshfield, Irish and Giles awoke to a decision. The conditions outside were miserable: –18 with a strong wind from the southwest. The men decided to "face the storm," heading out into the frigid, turbulent air, intending to return to Currie.

They successfully reached Bart Low's at Bear Lake for dinner and, presumably, to warm up before heading out once again for the final nine miles to Currie. However miserable the travel, they successfully arrived in Currie at 7 p.m. "quite frozen through. No harm done however."

Several days of hard travel left Irish "quite sore" on February 21. He prepared a dispatch for Blunt, then had a local man courier it to Tracy, where it was either telegraphed to Winona or whisked away on the next train. The rest of the day—one that climbed to 48 degrees, described by Irish as feeling "like a summer day"—was spent writing letters and preparing to return home, as was the next day, five more long letters being the result.

Finally, on February 23, he bid farewell to Giles in Currie, rode north to Tracy, and checked into the Commercial Hotel to await the next train east. Irish closed this chapter of the project by noting, "The day was raw and chilly and brought on my rheumatic feeling in my right side." He was sore, but it had been productive work—so productive, in fact, that he'd return with an entire crew of surveyors, and together they would begin work selecting a route west of Tracy.

A REJECTED ROUTE

Let's step back a few years and do an extreme oversimplification of a significant situation. As the Winona & St. Peter (under the Chicago & North Western) was being routed about twelve miles to the north of Currie in 1872, Neil Currie was among a group who swayed officials to put in a freight drop to serve his and other villages to the south of the line. The planned route ran through what would become the town of Tracy, and trusting that a train station would be built there as agreed, Currie built a warehouse near the route. The tracks were built, Tracy was established, and the freight-drop arrangement worked well for several years, serving Currie and other settlements to the south. But there is a difference between having freight access and the clear advantage of being a railroad town.[13]

Speed ahead to 1879. It is possible that Neil Currie ("the John D. Rockefeller of the region"[14]) was again lobbying railroad officials, this time to head south from Tracy to Currie, *then* head west to Dakota Territory. Based on the first few weeks of Irish's scouting, this theory makes sense. However, the landscape west of Currie is more challenging—and thus more expensive to construct and operate a railroad upon—than that west of Tracy. The letter Irish received when he returned to Currie—the one that told him to explore two more counties to the north, ruining his plans to go home—explains why the rest of the work would cover a different landscape than where he scouted originally.

Project Planning & Respite with Family: February 24–March 10, 1879

At 10:30 a.m. the next morning, Irish was on the train. Tracy disappeared to the rear as the cars chugged eastward to Winona through rain, hail, and sleet—but no snow. There was no snow accumulation on the ground west of Tracy, though the ground was frozen. As the train passed through St. Peter and across the Minnesota River, however, there was enough snow for "good sleighing."

After a nearly fifteen-hour train trip, Irish arrived in Winona at 1:20 a.m., and despite the late (or early?) arrival, he met up with Blunt for breakfast. Irish and Blunt spent the day working on "a report and map of my explorations in Dakota," and both were aboard the 4:30 p.m. train for Chicago.

The men arrived in Chicago the morning of February 26, and for the next two days, Irish presented his findings to a collection of men who were anything but ordinary. In the room with Irish and Blunt were Marvin Hughitt, general manager and director of the Chicago & North Western, and Albert Keep, president of the same.

The eventual route of the Dakota Central was set in motion. At the conclusion of the intense meetings, Irish again boarded a 10 p.m. train, this time heading westward to Cedar Rapids, Iowa, then south to Iowa City. This was a route he would repeat frequently over the next two years. By the morning of the last day of February, he was home for the first time since January 16.

THE CHICAGO & NORTH WESTERN RAILROAD COMPANY

Albert Keep and Marvin Hughitt

To the average modern American, the names Keep and Hughitt may not be quite as recognizable as Carnegie or Rockefeller. But under the leadership of Keep and Hughitt, the Chicago & North Western had a crucial impact on much of the Midwest's economy and growth. Keep served as president from 1873 (around the time the Panic of 1873 began) until he retired in 1887. At that point, Hughitt succeeded him as president, having worked his way up from telegraph operator in 1851 through positions as trainmaster, superintendent, general manager, and second vice president and general manager. Hughitt retired in 1910, though he remained chair of the board until 1925. He died in 1928 at the age of ninety.

In a 1905 history of the Chicago & North Western, William H. Stennett wrote of the pair, "Under the management of these two men it will be found the road advanced from being not much more than 'a streak of rust' when they took hold of it until it has come to be the leading railroad of the West."[15]

A portrait of Hughitt closer to the age when this work was being undertaken. S1-19

A 1912 portrait of Marvin Hughitt in his early seventies. S1-20

The Chicago & North Western Offices

At the time, the officers worked in a building at the southeast corner of Kinzie Street and North Market (which today is North Orleans Street) in Chicago. This area was absolutely crawling with Chicago & North Western infrastructure, including tracks, warehouses, and the like.

The Kinzie & Market location, where the offices stood, was once the seat of a mighty empire. In June 2021, however, the lot hosted a mere few dozen yards of abandoned tracks and trees that appeared feral, held back by a sagging and locked fence. Across the street to the west, where the huge Chicago & North Western train station once imposed itself upon travelers arriving in or departing from Chicago, is a small parking lot of crumbling concrete, where weeds are doing their best to speed up the decay. The hustle and bustle of modern Chicago loudly rushes past without giving another thought to this inconvenient, empty block that hinders easy traffic flow. But when standing on that plot of land yourself, you can almost feel the ghosts of forgotten history. Go. Stand there. You may feel it too.

Modern view of where the Chicago & North Western offices stood, the remaining lengths of tracks a mere whisper of the frenetic pace that once characterized the area. S1-21

At the time of our story, the depot on Kinzie Street at the Chicago River was no longer able to handle the increased rail traffic. So construction of a large new depot began in 1880, a block to the east of the offices, and the facility was completed and opened the following year. With modern Victorian-inspired architecture, the new Wells Street Depot was visually up to the task of representing the mighty Chicago & North Western empire—only to be razed a mere thirty years later. Today, the Merchandise Mart building majestically holds down that same patch of dirt.

Chicago Itself

A recent book did a beautiful job of describing Chicago as a concept:

> No other city so fully embodied the seismic forces behind the nation's transformation from an overwhelmingly rural to an increasingly urban society: immigration and westward migration, industrialization and the mastery of steam power, and the conquest of space and time by the telegraph and the railroad. Situated between the vast productive power and consumer appetite of the eastern United States and the prodigious bounty of the farms, ranches, ranges, timberlands, coal fields, and mineral deposits of the continent's vast interior, Chicago was an irresistible attraction for investment capital and people of entrepreneurial spirit.[16]

Clearly, Chicago's role in the westward expansion of rails was critical.

After a single day of resting and catching up with his family, Irish attended church services on Sunday, March 2, then visited his wife's sister, Louisa Huffman. "She is very sick," he noted with concern. Despite this deeply unsettling time for his family, on Tuesday he was already "at work getting ready to go to Minnesota."

The spring weather in eastern Iowa was fluctuating, and an overnight thunderstorm starting on March 4 degenerated into a "cold raw blustery day" on the fifth, rebounded with a "fine warm day" on the sixth, and burst forth into a "hot" 76-degree day on the seventh. Of the eighth, Irish wrote, "The frost is almost out of the ground," and the temperatures pleasantly wavered in the seventies until March 10. The spring-like setting was a nice respite, however temporary.

On that day, less than two weeks after his long-awaited return home, Irish boarded another train. He was headed for Chicago, though feeling "quite sick from the heat." Spring had begun to awaken around him over the last few days, with the river ice melting and, he happily noted, the frogs starting their spring chorus.

Final Preparations for the Surveying Work: March 11–20, 1879

Irish spent time on March 11 at the offices of the Chicago & North Western, again meeting with President Keep and Chief Engineer Johnson. That complete, he began gathering the "camp equipage" as well as the various supplies needed to survey what would become the Dakota Central.

"I am very busy buying the outfit for the Dakota survey, " wrote Irish in his diary on March 13. By the end of the next day, he could say with relief, "Almost all my purchases [are] made."

On March 14, Irish wrote home from Chicago. He was worried about the health of his family as winter transitioned to spring:

> Now look out for colds and bad tempers, for this miserable cold spell will stop up the pores of the skin and also shut up the liver and then comes all these troubles. I want you all to take quinine as the warm weather approaches so as to avoid such debilitation as ensues and Ruth must be sure to resume her iron tonic.

He then brought them up to date about his activities in Chicago:

> I am quite well, indeed the cold weather has been very good for me and this morning I have my winter vest on. In fact I am well prepared for cold weather but not for hot weather. I have bought the horses, harness, and about all the other things and shall start this evening or tomorrow for Winona. . . . Well I got 14 buffalo robes, 20 pairs of blankets in addition to what the men may have, and you know that I have some good bedding. This storm began here at 11 last night, first a warm rain, then snow, and this AM the streets are all ice and a heavy NW gale with the temperature 18 above zero. . . . The Chicago river smokes as if about to boil.

More details were provided the next day, March 15: "Got all the wagons, harness + tents. Made out the provision bill and got all things ready." As he prepared to return to Minnesota, the weather began a decline, and he finished his last full day in Chicago in "cold raw wintry" conditions. On Sunday, March 16, another frigid day, he strolled around Chicago before finally boarding the 9 p.m. train for Winona.

On March 16, he wrote a letter to his daughter Ruth, teasing that as he was still in Chicago, she'd likely no longer trust him when he said he was, this time, actually heading out to Minnesota: "You all will think that I cannot tell the truth about my start west by this time. Well the fact is that they were slow shipping the stock and outfit so that I had to stay here to see to it. I am very well and start tonight at 9 o'clock for Winona."

He also shared about a near miss in Chicago:

> I have sent you some papers that had things in which I supposed you might read with interest. Today I send a [*Chicago*] *Times* which

contains an account of a man who nearly killed himself by blowing out the gas in his room. He was 17 hours under its effects and was as bleak as a mortified body could be and of the same color. The doctor thinks now he will recover. He has been 3 days unconscious but to day recognized his wife who came here to care for him. His room was the 3rd from mine, and I smelled the gas that morning.

After telling her of this scare, he admonished, "Dress warm, take camphor for sore throats, and you be sure to take some iron and quinine now."

In a letter home from Winona, he shared that on his way to the train station, he'd had yet another near miss, this time while riding on a horse-drawn bus, writing, "[We] ran into a hack, and it nearly demolished the buss. It was full as it could be. There is a bump on my head as big as [an] . . . egg." And in a nod to his oceangoing ancestors, who were ship captains and navigators, he added, "In about 3 days I go to Tracy to set up camp and then we will be out on the prairie ocean sailing."

Twelve hours after pulling out of Chicago, the train rolled up at the Winona depot, where Irish was greeted by Blunt and "some of the men who make up my party." It was less springlike in Minnesota, and the ground was still "frozen hard." After greeting his new crew members and welcoming them as a team, he "set at work to get things together."

The preparations hit a bit of a hiccup when Irish became ill. "Overworked, I suppose," he wrote hopefully. The items gathered while in Chicago arrived by train the second day, and he could rest easy. But his health degenerated throughout the day, and he began to dose himself with quinine to combat a fever. Despite his malady, he was able to get their goods loaded into a boxcar, buy a horse, and prepare for the trip to Tracy. All the while, he continued fighting an "intermittent fever."

Irish rarely passed up an opportunity to scold his family about overlooking their health. Ruth had described a pain she was experiencing, and her exasperated father wrote back, "That pain which you describe was malarial rheumatism or rather neuralgia, and had you have taken 3 good doses of quinine morning noon and night, it would have disappeared at once."

He himself also had some pains, but his were related to work. Within the office building of the Chicago & North Western, the offices of the engineers/surveyors (the terms were often used interchangeably) were on the sixth floor. He estimated that while in Chicago, he had climbed those six floors of steps, up and down, anywhere from "six to ten or more" times each and every day. "Think of it: climbing 300 to 600 feet on stairs each day for a week. It gave me a severe pain across my back, and by the time I got here, fever set in, and yesterday I was quite sick. I began the taking of quinine at once, and now it's broken up but I feel very weak."

Attention then turned to daughter Lizzie, who, he teased, would have to hand off a bug collection that she had become enamored with. Thinking it had been delivered for her father, she excitedly opened and explored the collection. Alas, he told her the fascinating insects were intended for her uncle Thomas.

While he did not reassure Lizzie that he would send her any bugs, he did promise his wife "a lot of fine feathers, fine ones at that." The women had asked for feathers for a feather bed, and Irish took this task to heart; letters in the future would keep the women updated of progress. All things were ready for the trip to Tracy, except for one horse that was not yet accounted for.

On Thursday, March 20, 1879, the train carrying Irish's crew and their gear, as well as other freight and passengers, pulled out of Winona, Minnesota, headed west. One imagines the various men in the party had questions for Irish, or at least images in their heads about the landscape they were bound for. We have names, but not ages. For some of them, we know the specific jobs they were hired to do, but not their level of experience. Were they young men excited to be going out to what they imagined as the mythic West? Or were they seasoned men who knew they were in for months of conditions that would run the gamut—temperatures ranging from –20 degrees or colder to nearly 110 degrees, beautiful skies, torrential downpours, and life-threatening blizzards?

Likely, it was some combination of the two. In the March 14 letter to his wife, from Chicago, he'd written that once in Winona, he'd "call together the men and boys" before heading into Dakota Territory. "Won't this be a fine introduction to camp life for gentlemen," he wrote, "and I have several of them in my party." Perhaps this was Irish's wry way of sarcastically predicting that some of these men—or boys—were in for a shock.

This initial party for the spring operation of 1879 was made of thirteen men, at least in theory. Some of the thirteen positions were not yet assigned a name. There would be a mutiny in the months to come, and three of the five men involved were on this initial crew. Meanwhile, however, a nice camaraderie would form.

Section Two

THE SURVEY BEGINS! TRACY TO LAKE BENTON

MARCH 21—APRIL 18, 1879

By the time the survey team gathered to head to Tracy, the project was no longer a secret in the region. After an inauspicious start due to illness and weather, the men began their work. As would become the norm, multiple line options were identified, analyzed, reworked, rejected, and accepted. Maps were drawn, reports written, officers kept in the loop. The men fought swirling snow, severe thunderstorms, and even a wildfire. They also began to fight homesickness and loneliness. Crossing the Redwood River proved particularly aggravating, but the men were coalescing into a team, and they observed their first holiday together as Easter came and went. The work was going well, and soon they would be crossing over into Dakota Territory.

Survey Work Begins West of Tracy: March 21–April 18, 1879

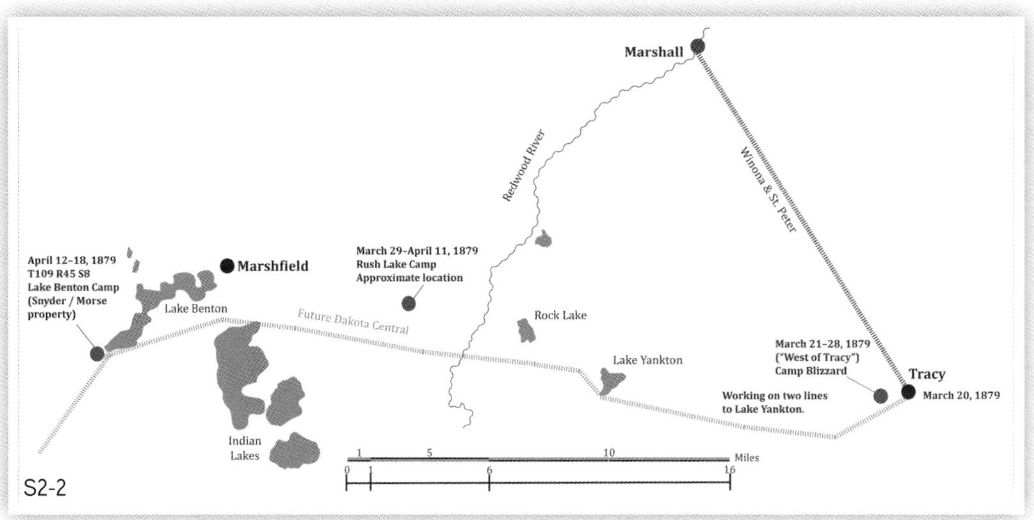

S2-2

And so it began! The survey team disembarked the train at Tracy, checked into the Commercial Hotel for an overnight (before thereafter sleeping in tents), and prepared for a monumental journey that would mix hard work and plain old adventure. Irish was concerned about his health, fearing he had developed "lung fever" (pneumonia).

Overnight, the men's horses arrived, but Irish's health took another downturn. He confided to his diary, "I am too sickly to go out but think I am getting better." A letter from his friend Neil Currie, which awaited his arrival, provided some level of comfort. Now that he was settled into a more consistent location, Irish let his family know they could now address letters directly to him at "Tracy Lyon Co Minn," rather than sending them via Blunt.

A snow set in and continued throughout their first full day in Tracy, leaving the men to restlessly mill about when they should have been out doing their first readings. "The worst and deepest snow of the season," Irish observed, remembering there had been no snow on the ground during his scouting trip a month prior. It was ironic and frustrating, but fortunately the snow was not long-lasting.

Saturday, March 22, was a momentous day, though the conditions weren't worthy of celebration. The day was stormy (though it "thawed some" in the afternoon), Irish remained sick ("sick enough to be in bed but [I] have to keep up"), and one of the horses had distemper. Despite all of this, Irish and the men ran three miles of measurements along the A Line. The physical work had begun, and the first potential stretch of the Dakota Central had been surveyed.

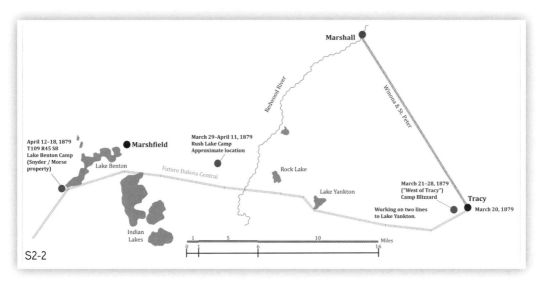

THE BIG CUT WEST OF TRACY

If the day's measurements were taken along the route that was ultimately graded, those three miles put them near the approach to a long hill that became known to readers of Laura Ingalls Wilder's novel *The Long Winter* as "the big cut west of Tracy," which begins about four miles west of town. Wilder set that cut as the location of the railroad blockades that kept the trains from reaching settlements to the west during the Hard Winter (1880–81). In reality, the problematic cut that inspired Wilder's story was about fifty miles to the east, on the west side of Sleepy Eye. Regardless, this cut west of Tracy has been immortalized.

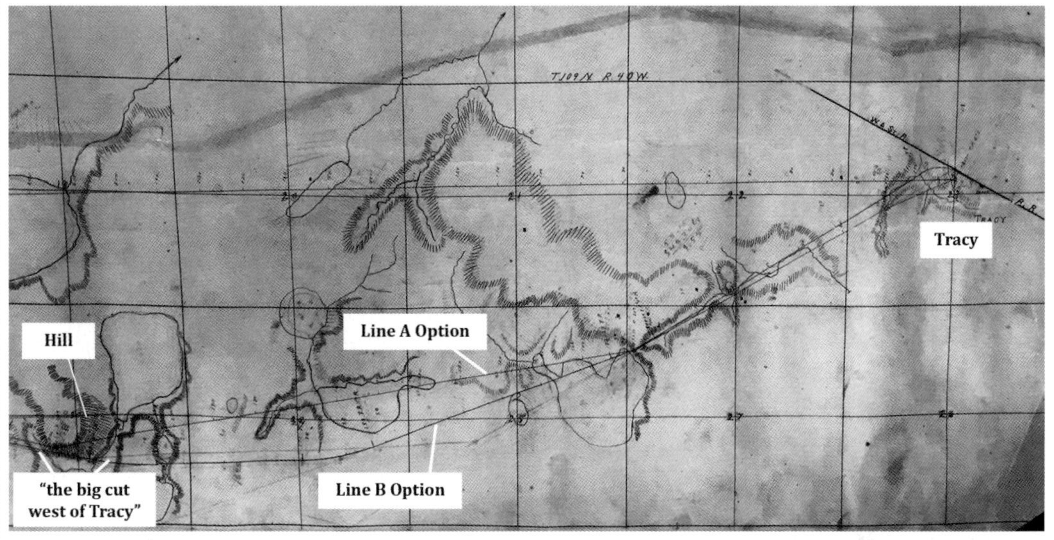

The multiple line options surveyed as they headed southwest from Tracy. The tight hash lines indicate the base of a hill, and the irregular closed shapes are bodies of water or marsh. The area in the lower-left corner of the map was immortalized as "the big cut west of Tracy" by Laura Ingalls Wilder. Both line options involved the hill (the dark area). Line A would have cut through the interior of the hill, and Line B skirted the southern edge of the hill. Line B was constructed. S2-3

Irish's first letter home from their camp near Tracy let his family know that he had arrived "sick as I could be." Not only that, but it had snowed, and the ground was covered in four to six inches of the nuisance.

He caught them up on the trip from Winona. Of the night of departure, he wrote, "Had to sit up until midnight waiting for the train; one of the men was with me. We went to sleep in the bar room in chairs and both took most awful colds, and we both had to go to bed when we got here." The sick crewman was out working on the line, but Irish was "lazing off," suffering from "spasmodic croup."

One crew member, a man whom Irish casually refers to as Old Joe, was obviously known to the family. "Old Joe is here the happiest man you ever saw." He gave just a general glimpse at the others. "I have a good set of men and they are gathered from all quarters. . . . I have 7 horses[;] one to ride good saddle +c. If the winter will only come to an end[,] we can have lots of fun."

The newspapers of the era provide a great deal of information about the progress of the railroad, but they cannot always be trusted as completely accurate. The March 27, 1879, edition of the *Brookings County Press* claimed the crew was near Lake Benton on March 22, a date on which they were actually about thirty miles to the east, running the first three miles of line west of Tracy. This kind of error may have been intentional, however, meant to excite readers about the coming of the rails and prosperity to towns along the tracks, as the article ended with, "We may expect them through this country soon."[17] A week later, the same paper republished a piece from the *Marshfield Tribune* noting that the surveyors were "making preparations for their survey," then adding again, "We may look for them in Brookings County ere long."[18]

The surveyor's camp had been set up since their arrival in Tracy, their large canvas tents providing not only shelter but space for meals, equipment, mapmaking, and conversation. On Sunday, March 23, a "blizzard came from the west and nearly tore our tents down," though the men were able to keep their lodgings upright. Intervening in a battle between a strong wind and large stretches of canvas, straining to hold back the gales, spent the men's remaining energy.

A large canvas tent of the type Irish and his crew used. This 1898 photo was taken at a Chicago & North Western camp near Pierre. S2-4

The next day was an improvement, though it remained cold with a strong southwest wind. While the men set about taking readings along the A Line, Irish went farther west "over the line [on] horseback and came back sore in every joint."

He may not have liked what he saw on the scout, as March 25 was again spent on horseback, investigating a new route west. While he scrutinized the alternate path in a "wind which blew a perfect gale," the workers were sent beyond the stretch of land Irish wanted to reconsider, to work on a route approaching Lake Yankton.

The alternate route that Irish identified that Tuesday was measured on Wednesday and designated the B Line. He and D. C. Dunlap, who worked the transit (a piece of equipment, similar to a small spotting scope, used to measure angles), got six and a half miles run. "It was a most beautiful day," Irish enthused in his dairy, and nearly 70 degrees. Work on the B Line continued the next day, and Irish rode as far west as Lake Yankton before returning to camp. Work was progressing well, but the weather was volatile, as is normal for a Midwestern spring. This time it was a thunderstorm with a strong wind that whipped at their tents, just four days after the blizzard that had tried to upend camp.

The night before the camp move from Tracy, Irish wrote a letter home to his wife. The last three days had warmed, and the frost was coming out of the ground, though "many of the lakes [were] still frozen over." He was happy in the work, with twenty-five miles recorded along the A and B Lines. With the move away from Tracy, he advised her that from this point forward (until the next big move), mail should be addressed to him at "Marshall Lyon Co Minn." rather than Tracy. Now that the work no longer needed to be kept secret, he added, "Be sure to put C+NW Eng. Corps at the bottom of the envelopes," likely to ensure they received proper attention and routing.

The Redwood Coteaus: March 29–April 9, 1879

At 4 a.m. on the morning of March 29, camp was packed up, and the men began the trek to Rush Lake, "on the west side of Lyon County." (See the end of this section for research commentary about the Rush Lake camp.) Along the way, Irish carefully evaluated the terrain between Lake Yankton and the Redwood River, including the hills through which the river flows, commonly called the Redwood Coteaus. The wind "blew with terrible violence" all day, and "a dog came near making my horse break my neck."

Sunday, March 30, was no day of rest for the men, who spent it doing camp chores. Some were sent out to hunt, but they returned to camp empty-handed after having "burnt a great deal of powder." The next day, the winds irritatingly whipped around from multiple directions, making the work cold and unpleasant. Despite this, much was accomplished, with six and a half miles of line run. Unfortunately, the men ran out of stakes to mark their route, delaying a portion of the work.

From the camp at Rush Lake, Irish wrote home to daughter Lizzie on March 30. He'd received her prior letter "just before moving camp," which they'd done the previous day, "in a most fearful gale of a wind." Otherwise, he reported the weather as "indeed splendid" and the farm fields as growing well.

He'd also witnessed one of nature's more violent yet beautiful scenes, writing, "I had a chance to see a prairie fire yesterday morning before the wind which blew so hard that I thought it would blow me off the horse. The fire travelled faster than I ever saw a railroad train run. It was at once a fearful and beautiful sight."

Irish's daughters were not conventional Victorian women, and Irish told Lizzie he was working to collect insects to replace the collection she'd become enamored with. "It's a most fascinating study," he wrote, adding that it "leads into every avenue of human knowledge of things terrestrial." Speaking of all things terrestrial, he was creating a collection of samples, in addition to the feathers: "I have made a beginning in the feathers. Shall bring home everything I can get in this country from feathers to rocks."

Irish's health was good, he reassured his daughter, but five crew members were still fighting off a cold that he himself had since recovered from. He reminded her that letters should now be sent via Marshall, further asking that she send "papers and all the news you can[,] for it's lonesome out here."

He brought some of Old Joe's personality into the letter, telling her that the man "calls the rabbits 'Jake Rappits.'" (Joe's accent will be written phonetically in future letters.)

April 1 began with a freezingly cold night, and the men abandoned their work after two miles, tired of fighting the "sharp and high" gale of a wind. The next day was no better, "a terrible day like winter." The men stuck to camp, doing "office work." One man, G. W. Thorn, who was assigned the responsibility of bringing provisions, had not yet made an appearance, and Irish wondered to his diary what had happened to him.

The bad weather continued, and by morning of the third, even the lake had frozen over again. It was another day stuck in camp doing "office work." Irish sent Joe DeBarr to Marshfield to collect needed supplies, as Thorn was still missing. Irish was debating sending out a rescue mission when the missing man finally appeared in camp, his delay unexplained.

While stuck in camp doing "office work," Irish wrote, "We are in camp in a nice little grove under a lot of hills and as snug and comfortable as we could wish for. . . . We are 8 miles southeast of Marshfield."

Old Joe must have had affection for Mrs. Irish, for he took it upon himself to tend to the feather collection. "Old Joe is perfectly happy," Irish wrote home. "The boys shot an owl and [Joe] asked me if Misses Irish would like to have the feters [*sic*—mimicking Joe's accent]. I told him yes, then he went and picked [the owl], so you see he thinks of you."

Irish shared his concern for the then-missing crewman. "I feel anxious for Thorn[,] the teamster who has been gone 4 days[.] I fear that something bad has happened to him. Shall look him up tomorrow if he don't come in tonight."

Irish admitted he had spent too much time in the recent hot-and-sunny weather: "I've sunburned badly. My nose is now peeling off and is quite sore." The days were hot, but the nights were cold. "Last night the temperature went 5° below zero and the lake froze over with good solid ice. It has been below 32° for 48 hours and the wind blowing a perfect gale. I hope this is the last bad day. I will not go out to work in such weather." With the benefit of hindsight, Irish's proclamation here could be attributed to naivete early in the job—he and his crew would be out in much, much worse weather.

With provisions and men accounted for and the wind having died down overnight, the crew set about serious work on April 4. The terrain they were working—the valleys and gullies around the Redwood River—was nothing short of difficult. Still, nearly eight miles of readings were accomplished by the time they returned to camp for the night, "all tired out." The day had been warmer, reaching 36 degrees, which, with the strengthening April sun and no wind, felt perfectly comfortable as they did their work.

Presumedly after re-scouting the area and recalculating some numbers, Irish and the men went back out on April 5, working on a second line option. They were able to survey a run stretching seven and a quarter miles, and Irish was pleased with the day's work. He also noted that while the lakes, wetlands, and ground were still "frozen hard," the migratory waterfowl were returning—a welcome sign of spring after having left similar signs behind in Iowa weeks before.

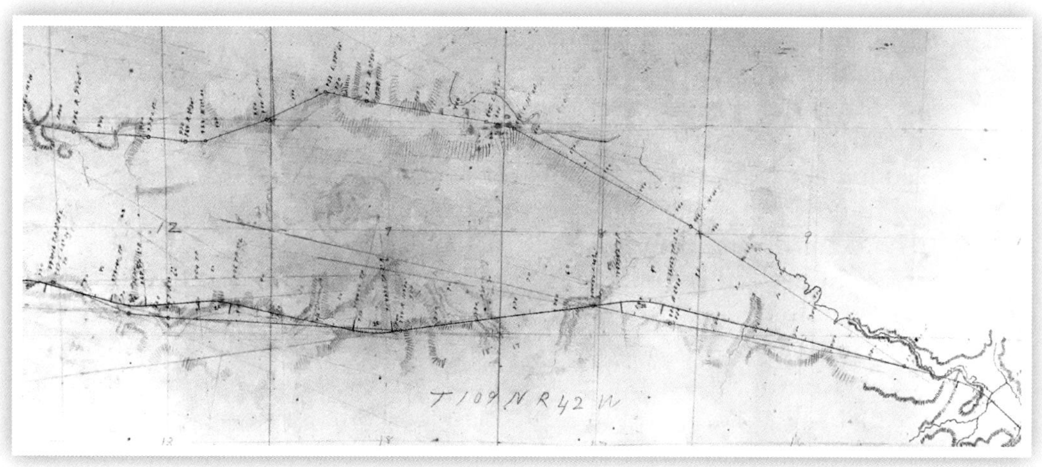

Irish's map with two possible routes away from Lake Yankton. S2-5

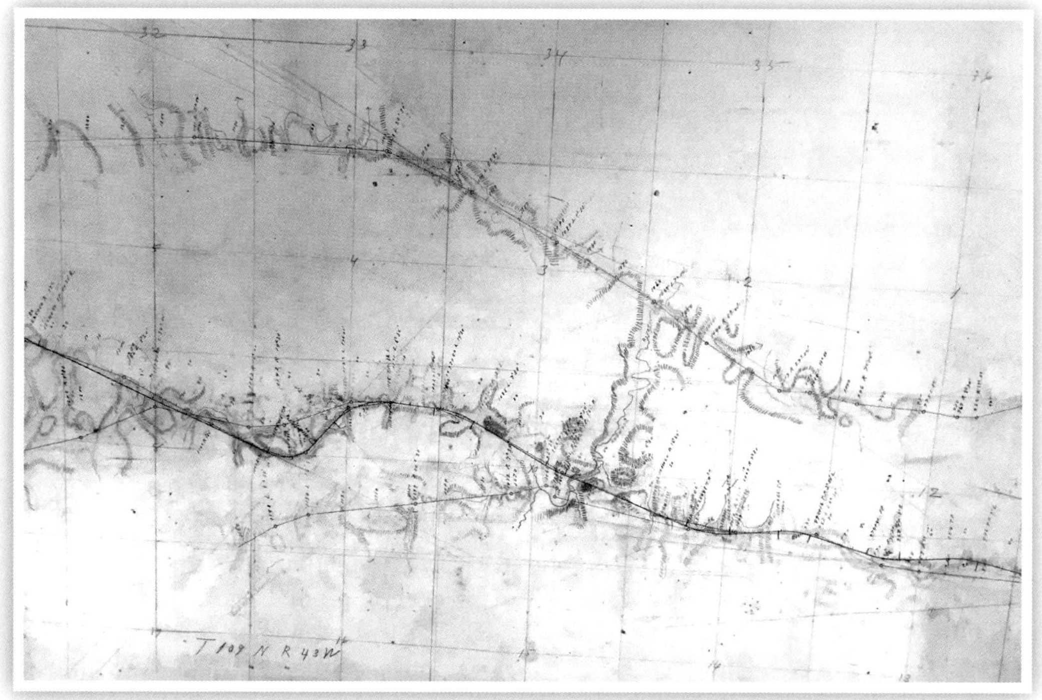

Irish's map with two possible routes through the Redwood Coteaus. S2-6

With multiple line options along the core route, Irish spent March 6 in camp creating maps, profiles, reports, and letters, wanting to get them sent eastward the next day and into the hands of the Chicago & North Western officers. The rest of the crew worked on various "camp chores," probably relieved they weren't out working in the high winds that buffeted the camp.

On the seventh, Irish sent the bulk of workers southwest to the Indian Lakes, with instructions to continue west to Lake Benton. Irish himself backtracked east, investigating an additional line option across the Redwood River, which he was still mulling over.

The location Irish sent the men, the Indian Lakes, had been drained by the time an 1898 map was published, on which they and several surrounding lakes were relabeled as "meadow land," though still drawn as lakes. The lakes had likely become their drier relative, a slough.

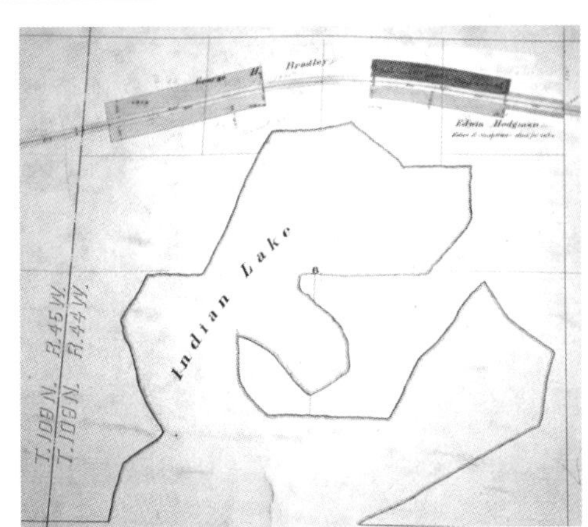

The linen roll map of the Dakota Central route, showing the northernmost lobe of one of the Indian Lakes, which itself was sometimes called Indian Lake (singular). S2-7

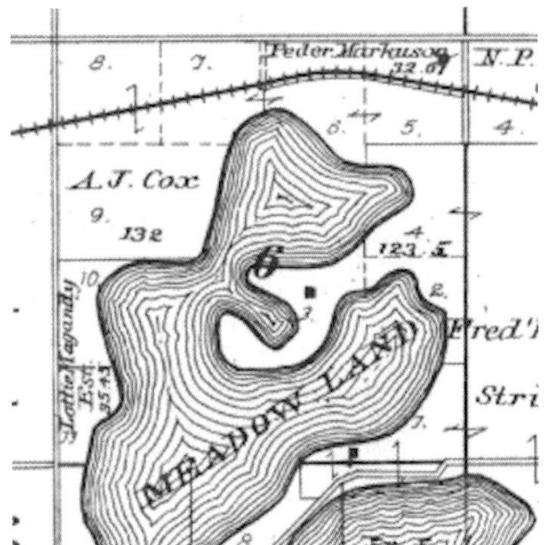

An 1898 map showing part of the Indian Lakes area as meadowland. S2-8

After his scout "reconsidering the Redwood crossing," Irish approached camp and saw smoke rising and fire blazing in the surrounding grasses. "A scoundrel," he indignantly declared, had set the fire. He "got back just in time to save it," with the help of several camp members.

A long letter home to his wife from the Rush Lake camp filled in details about the fire that seemed almost casually mentioned in the diary. It had, in fact, been "a great scare."

After a day's work, he was riding back along a ridge about four miles away. He wrote, "I saw a great fire burning about the camp. I started the horse into a full run thinking that the boys (Dunlap and Cole the cook) whom I had left in charge of the camp had let it get on fire." When as close as a quarter mile, he saw that the tents were still standing. Closing the final distance, he yelled out for Dunlap, who exited his tent "not knowing the great danger, for the fire was within 300 feet of the tents."

Irish drew a diagram of the setting to help the women envision the scene. The campsite was located at the triangles (tents) between the two timbered hills on the east side of the lake. The points designated B, C, and D show the "fire guard of several furrows all around the timber." Irish added, "Outside of this guard the prairie all burned off last fall and I did not fear fire in the timber unless we were careless ourselves."

The anger he'd expressed in his diary entry carried over to this letter to his wife, in which he bristled, "Well some scoundrel set the grass on fire at point C, 3/4 of a mile from camp and the wind happened to blow towards C, or else we would have lost all our stuff." Fortunately, in addition to Dunlap and Cole in camp, "strangers" from Lake Benton (G. Bryan, John Snyder, and A. W. Morse) were visiting camp and helped put out the blaze. Irish wrote,

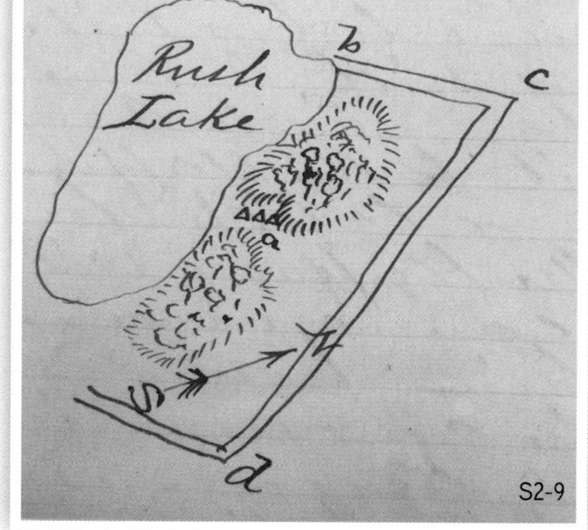

S2-9

> So there were six of us, and at it we went. O! Such a fight as we had, the three strangers worked as hard as if they owned the camp. Some brought water from the Lake to wet a ring about the camp while the rest of us with brush in hand swept the fire back. It took an hour and a half to subdue the fire fiend when we were all completely exhausted. Cole the cook carried water all the time on the run, and when we stopped he was speechless. We all fell on the camp beds and lay there the rest of the afternoon glad to be quiet.

It had been a harrowing fight. Bryan and Snyder had "cut their hands badly breaking the tall reeds that grew on the bank of the Lake." And Morse, a storekeeper from Lake Benton, "blistered his eyelids and cheeks." Irish himself blistered his eyelids, nose, lips, and cheeks, as did Dunlap—"I tell you it was a hot fight."

It was a lesson learned too. As noted, area residents protected the timber stand by plowing the fire break, and the grass outside the furrows had burned the previous fall. He'd felt the location was safe, but he amended that evaluation, writing, "After this I shall burn off a place upon which to put the camp before we set up the tents." He had his suspicions as to the fire's origin, but no real evidence.

After relaying the chilling story of the fire, he moved on to the feather collection: "You should see old Joe save the fetters [Irish's underline] for you[;] he sits down and picks off every good feather and all the down which he says is worth 180 a pound. But I fear that you have given me a great task to gather 80 lbs!! goodness what a pile of ducks it will take."

The birds that sacrificed their feathers to Mrs. Irish's feather bed were also supplying food, which led to a description of how the men stayed warm in camp:

> The boys have shot a nice lot of ducks which we will have in a pot pie tomorrow. You ask about the beds. We have splendid beds + you should see me with the blue pillow and the red night cap. Dunlap and I sleep together [called double bunking]. We have two water proof blankets, 1 buffalo robe, and 4 wool blankets under us on a bed of hay. Then 4 wool blankets and a buffalo robe over us and use my quilt for a bolster. Then I have another robe and my gray over coat, which I lay between me and the wall of the tent, so you see we cannot help but be warm. Then we have such a good tent! It is of cloth that weighs 12 ounces to the square yard. It's as thick as buckskin, and [I] have a large sheet iron stove to heat up with. We are comfortable you see. Then we have good provisions. As to the horses, we keep them in straw stables, but 4 of them are now sick. You should see my saddle + bridle. They cost $25 . . . When I go out, I put my gun before me and feel like a soldier.

The wind "blew so hard" on April 8 "that we could not work with the instruments." Without instruments, accurate measurements and readings for the survey were not possible. Instead, Irish rode along the line toward the Indian Lakes, after arranging for a wagonload of "camp stuff" to be taken to their next camp location, at the western end of Lake Benton. "This is the worst wind storm we have had so far," he observed to close out the diary for the day.

He'd finished the diary entry, but the weather was not yet done for the day. Before midnight, a thunderstorm swept in from the northeast. The rain continued throughout the next day, again preventing the men from working. "The camp is comfortable indeed," Irish happily recorded. In addition, some of the men "shot some ducks." Camp was comfortable and its inhabitants well fed with a hearty meal.

Possibly feeling he was falling behind schedule, Irish headed out on April 10 despite the continuing bad weather. The crossing of the Redwood River continued to worry him, and he scouted additional options to get the railroad tracks from one side of the river to the other. It wasn't an easy day's work. "It blows so hard that it is about all one can do to stick to the saddle," wrote Irish.

The Redwood River, not far from today's Black Rush Lake. S2-10

The terrain in this stretch of the Redwood is much steeper and more closed in than what is found just a few miles south, closer to the eventual crossing site (below). S2-11

The bridge that eventually spanned the problematic waterway. S2-12

IMPATIENTLY WAITING

While the surveyors were fighting the wind, the residents of Brookings County had worked themselves into their own dervish. The April 10 issue of the local paper implored the surveyors to "please hurry up a little" because the farmers wanted to know whether their land was near the new line and, humorously, whether "their farms are to be spoiled with depot buildings or not."[19]

On to Lake Benton: April 10–18, 1879

April 10 continued the "blustery and stormy" weather of the previous day, but Irish got the men back to work, running a line to the Indian Lakes. On the twelfth, they moved camp in a "very hard" wind from the southeast. Camp was reassembled on the lands of Snyder and Morse (two of the "strangers" who had fought the fire back at Rush Lake), at the western end of Lake Benton.

April 13 featured another "high wind," this time from the northeast, against which Irish and three others—one of them Snyder, who was quite familiar with the area—rode twenty miles, exploring options for getting over or around those high bluffs separating the Lake Benton area and the final few miles to Dakota Territory. The men returned to camp "quite tired out."

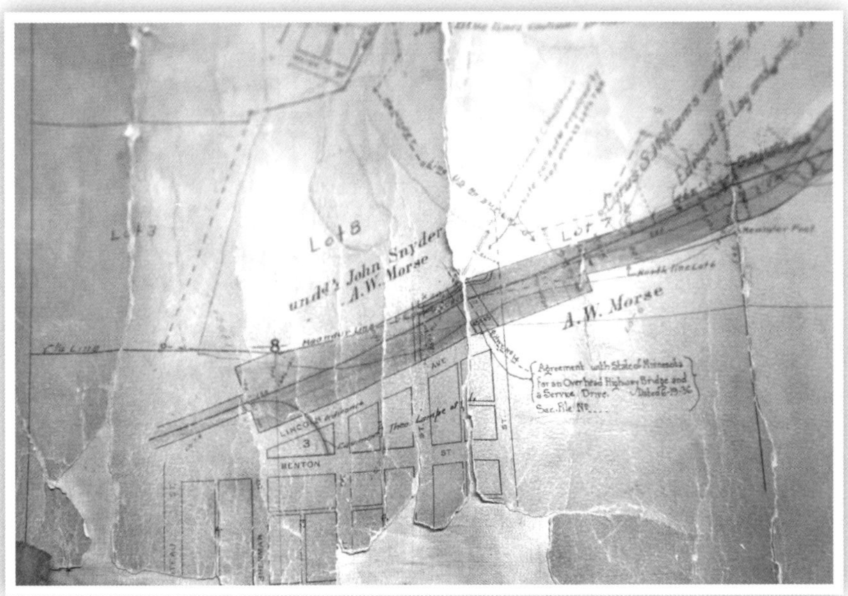

This map segment shows the location where Irish and the surveyors set up their camp on the west end of Lake Benton, on land owned by John Snyder and A. W. Morse (Lot 8). (This is also likely the camp location used by the graders and tracklayers that came through in the summer of 1879, and where Charles Ingalls ran the store for the contractor Wells & Company.) S2-13

Irish's diaries rarely mentioned holidays, but letters home did. To his daughter Lizzie he wrote, "This is Easter Sunday and we have celebrated it by eating two eggs apiece for breakfast[;] shall continue to celebrate at dinner and supper. Old Joe . . . has gone out to shoot a 'jeckess rappits.'"

And those jack rabbits were clever, Irish told her: "When you surprise one on the burnt prairie they will draw themselves up into a bunch and try to imitate a white stone and so will let you walk right up to them. When up [upon them,] they will jump and go leaping away like a kangaroo. They can out run the fastest dog or horse. We have a black dog named Nero. . . . Well our Nero tried a race after a jack rabbit the other day and was so soon left far behind that he suddenly gave up the chase and came frisking back to us as much as to say 'I only tried it for fun' [Irish's underline]."

The feather brigade was still in operation, and a "tuft" from a duck was tucked into the letter. "Mr. Thompson the leveler said that he'd bet you would have it on your hat within two hours after you get it," wrote Irish. "I thought so too. Well I think they are beautiful enough for any hat." In an undated letter segment that fits here as well as anywhere else, he added, "The feather stock grows slowly but surely. We have now duck, owl, prairie hen, goose, hawk and other feathers too numerous to mention."

The feathers were not the only samples collected on the prairies. Irish wrote, "I shall send you some flower roots to set out in our wild flower bed. They are beauties, and the first of vegetation to sprout and flower here." The enclosed roots/bulbs could have been for pasqueflowers, commonly the first prairie flower to bloom. This would be just the first mention of plants sent home for the gardens.

Irish closed the letter by giving us a glimpse into postal operations in 1879. A crew member was sent to town in the days prior to mail some letters. However, "the fool of a teamster did not pay letter postage," and Irish feared the letters lost. Irish asked the family to report to him the minute any of the sent items arrived—if they arrived—so he could rest easy. "I hope on Tuesday to get letters from you all as the team will come from Marshall then," wrote Irish. "That will now be our P.O. until the end of the survey [in this area]. I was there Thursday last and got letters for everyone in camp except myself + I felt lonesome when I got back." One can feel his disappointment in being left out of the communal camp joy of mail from home.

With the quick scouting trip done past the high ridge west of Lake Benton and on into Dakota Territory, attention refocused on the work still needing completion to the east. On April 14, the crew picked up the line where they'd left it and ran measurements along seven and a half miles, reaching the eastern shore of Lake Benton.

The next few days were spent surveying possible routes away from Lake Benton. On April 15, the men ran a line through large hills to the southwest, an area with a Dakota name that translates to "Hole in the Mountain." A meandering creek still nestles within the wide valley, creating a path through the hills. Wide river valleys play an important role for railroad surveyors, providing pre-carved gentle slopes through otherwise rougher terrain. It was the perfect exit point away from Lake Benton. To be thorough, they came back and did a second line north out of the valley, for a total of nearly seven miles of readings. With two options to consider, they returned to camp.

There waiting for them were Chief Engineer Blunt, Superintendent Sanborn, and a Mr. Bidwell, no doubt anxious to hear about progress and concerns. Conversations and tours likely took place, and on the sixteenth Irish wrote, "We got a good line out of the Hole in the Mountain."

A modern photo of the tracks running through the Hole in the Mountain terrain southwest of Lake Benton. The surveyors followed the flatter valley floor up and out of the ridges. This was just one of several lines the men experimented with to get up and over. S2-14

He did not indicate which of the line options identified on the fifteenth had been selected as "the one," but on the seventeenth, the men "began a new line for Big Sioux," starting from the selected route away from Lake Benton. It was a good day's work, with eleven miles of route being struck across the prairie. Irish again observed that the land was not ideal for farming, writing, "Drouth is making the farmers cursing. The grain cannot grow well, it's so dry."

With the surveyors moving westward, the April 17 issue of the *Brookings County Press* provided an update for their readers. The surveyors were on the western edge of Minnesota now (something they'd also reported in March but that was now accurate in mid-April), and the next step would be Brookings County. The railroad company planned to get one hundred miles of road built during the season, a distance that would "put the road beyond the Big Sioux" and, most importantly, "give this part of the domain a market for the coming crop."[20]

Those crops were, of course, of upmost importance to the railroad company. And those farmers who may have worried that their hard-won cleared fields would be torn up for railroad infrastructure now had a positive to think about instead. In the same issue, the editors noted that they'd finally met Irish, describing him as "a gentleman in every sense of the word, and . . . a man so well fitted for the position."[21]

The evening of April 18, the last night at the Lake Benton camp for now, Irish wrote home to his wife. He scolded her about not keeping on top of her health (she was caring for her ailing sister, Louisa Huffman, who was suffering a terrible, lingering illness that Irish knew would result in her death). He reminded her that when he'd first arrived in Minnesota, he'd been ill with a bad cold. "I was so weak that I could hardly walk about," he wrote, "and felt so depressed that I was worthless. Well I went to a drug store, wrote out a prescription for an iron tonic, and on taking it three days, I felt like a new man." He wanted her, too, to be taking her iron tonic to keep up her strength. (Prior to the Pure Food and Drug Act of 1906, there were few, if any, limits on access, quality, or control of pharmaceuticals. This note by Irish tells us he was somehow authorized to write medical prescriptions, but that does not necessarily mean he'd received extensive training.)

Illness was a fairly constant companion in camp, and the same was true now. "The men who were sick are all better or well except two," wrote Irish, "and I fear one of them will go into consumption, for he coughs all night long each night, and keeps us all awake so much. He is such a good man and has such great courage that I cannot send him off, but he won't take anything except some patent stuff. If he is no better when I come back, I shall send him home." The compassionate Irish also felt "a pity" for the men who worked so hard all day but were "kept awake through the night by the coughing of the sick ones," day after day. "Well so it goes," continued Irish, "and I really have a harder lot, for I must plan the work and must see that it is executed." Irish's dilemma between concern for one crew member versus the good of the whole crew is apparent, and this would have been a difficult choice to make.

"We crossed the line into Dakota Terr. yesterday," wrote Irish, "and shall move camp to the Big Sioux river tomorrow." The trip into Dakota Territory would be relatively short-term, and he anticipated being back in Tracy in a week or so to finalize the route. Therefore, while this letter was mailed from Lake Benton, he reminded her that letters should be now addressed to him at Tracy. He was disappointed too, writing, "[The] work, I fear, will prevent me from that home trip in May that I have looked forward to with so many hopes. I need not tell you. I am so tired each night when I get to camp that I cannot eat supper, and today staid to rest myself. The weather here is so trying."

He also shared a rare glimpse into camp relationships, such as, "Joe and Dunlap stick to me like brothers. They are my props." (Remember this statement, for there is an interesting development coming up.)

Camp was comfortable, but Irish was homesick: "Oh Dear, how I wish you were all here on the bank of this beautiful lake and in this bright sunshine. How you would enjoy it." Indeed, Lake Benton is a beautiful stretch of water. He also noted they were much farther north than Iowa City: "The day is much longer here than where you are, so the nights are shorter and we don't get the accustomed sleep to rest us." (A check of modern sunset times shows a twenty-three-minute difference, with Lake Benton being the later sunset).

An undated letter fragment was also likely written as they prepared to move camp away from Lake Benton. "We hate to move from this camp ground," mourned Irish, "as it's a perfect paradise, and [there are] such good people here. They remind me of our old neighborhood in Iowa." He continued, "We have now to deal with naked prairie, so you must not be alarmed if you hear that our houses have blown down, for if they do, it can't hurt us, as the frame roof and sides are cotton. Yet what a time we would have if they should blow away. It would scare half of the party into fits [another reference to the inexperience of a portion of the crew]. You can rest assured that we shall not camp on grass any more. One fire fight is enough for me in one year." Unfortunately, the episode at Rush Lake would not be their last firefight. This fragment may also have been written as they moved away from Rush Lake, though the reference to "good people" seems more suited to Lake Benton, where there was a small community.

On April 18, an additional eight and a half miles were run, placing the end of the line, he estimated, within ten miles of the Big Sioux River. Big leaps in distance had been made over the previous week, and it was time to move camp to the Big Sioux, a major milestone that would shift them into Dakota Territory.

THE QUEST TO LOCATE THE RUSH LAKE CAMP

A mystery sprang up while trying to locate the Rush Lake camp, and it consumed my curiosity for a considerable amount of time. I consulted with staff overseeing archives from county-level museums to university-level map collections—old plat maps, township and county atlases, even early highway maps were searched. The original maps drawn by Irish were referenced. The linen roll maps in the archives of the Chicago & North Western Historical Society were unfurled, their fragile, dried-out surfaces crumbling and cracking and leaving flakes and dust behind on the table. I cringed while ever-so-carefully searching them for a solution, but no lake named Rush was found.

Irish drew a diagram of the lake—the wooded hillocks to the east, the campsite between the hillocks, and the plowed firebreak furrows he'd assumed would protect them. Other drawings by Irish matched closely enough to modern satellite images that trusting his Rush Lake drawing—for general shape, at least—felt appropriate, though twentieth-century wetland-draining efforts make it difficult to match a modern water body to the lake drawn by Irish.

The survey crew spent a considerable amount of time encamped at Rush Lake. It was a cozy camp, and Irish liked it, describing the pleasant birdsong, nice evenings, and delicious meals of fresh fish. Other camps received little more written attention than a name, yet he fairly rhapsodized about the Rush Lake location. Plus, an exciting wildfire took place there. I felt it important to find at least a general location for this campsite.

Within the diaries and letters, Irish provided general clues: eight miles southeast of Marshfield; twenty-four miles west of Tracy; six or seven miles west of the Redwood River, which more or less runs north to south; being "on the west side of Lyon county." Seemed like it should be fairly easy to locate the lake. But . . .

Modern lake names do not always match historic lake names. Historic lakes may not even exist anymore. There is no modern Rush Lake "on the west side of Lyon county." There a Black Rush Lake, but it does not match any of his directional clues. There is a Rush Lake in northern Murray County, but again it matches none of his directional clues. As Irish was an expert surveyor, we can also presume he knew Lyon County from Murray. There is a Rock Lake about twelve miles southeast of Marshfield. Black Rush Lake is about fourteen or fifteen miles to the northeast. Rock Lake does not entirely match Irish's drawing, but again, much can change in 140-some years.

Old county plat maps from 1868 and 1872 showed lakes and marshes without names—but no shapes matched Irish's drawings. And the description "nice little grove under a lot of hills" could fit scores of locations. Modern satellite views often show the faint outlines of long-drained lakes if you know where to look (even railroad grades pulled up nearly a century ago, plowed and cultivated for generations, show their outlines). But none of the shadowy lines lined up to reveal the lake either.

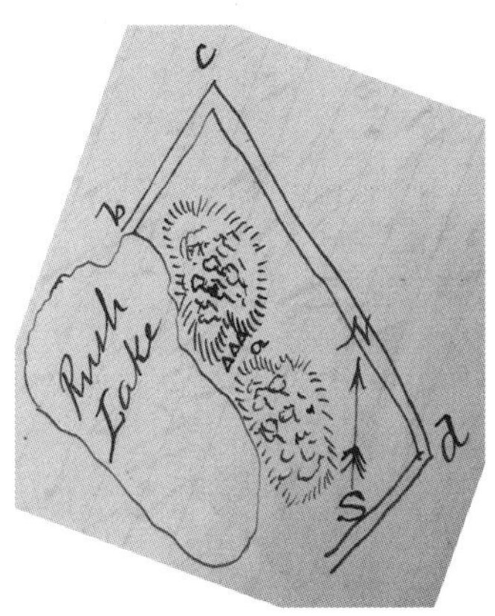

Irish's drawing of the Rush Lake campsite (the triangles between the hills), surrounded by the plowed firebreak. S2-15

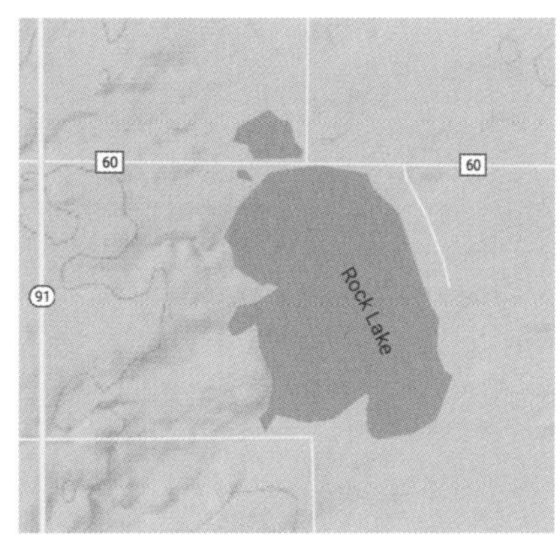

The shape of Rock Lake. S2-16

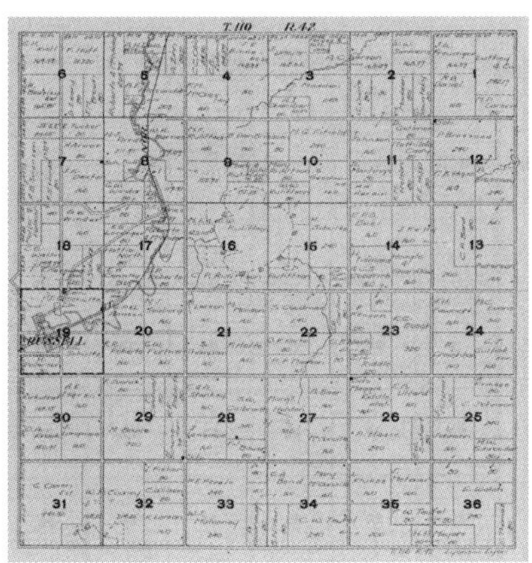

A 1918 plat map of the township southeast of Marshfield. S2-17

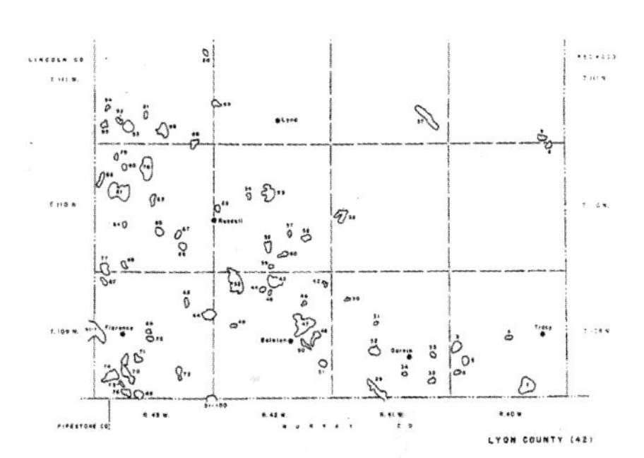

Lake shapes in western Lyon County. S2-18

The usually very-accurate Irish presented us with a dilemma here. But if you draw a line stretching eight miles southeast of Marshfield and another stretching twenty-four miles west of Tracy, then factor in the camp being "6 or 7 miles" west of the Redwood River, the resulting overlap allows us to draw a zone of possibility. However, the zone firmly excludes both Rock Lake and Black Rush Lake.

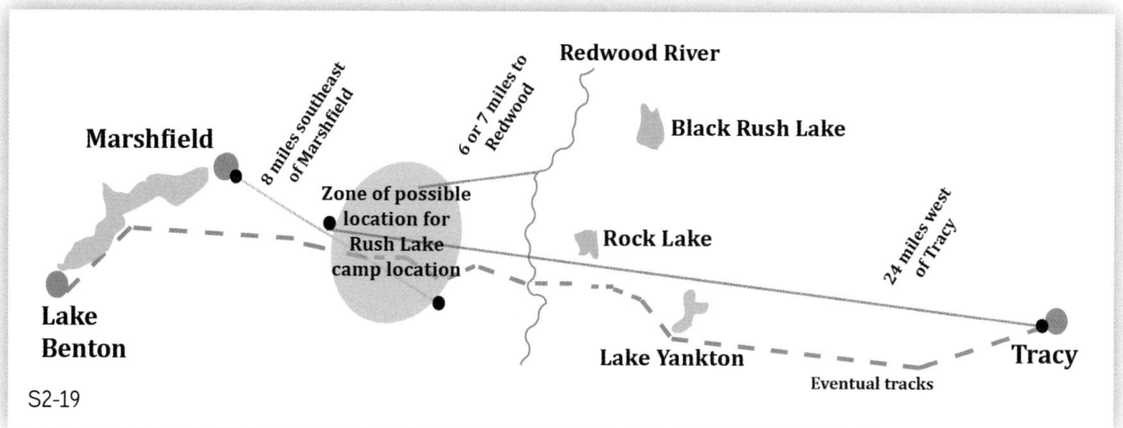

S2-19

Each bread crumb led to a new person with possible insights, who would lead to another, and so on . . . but each exciting lead seemed to pull deeper into the reeds and grasses, leading to nothing more than educated guesses.

Then I remembered an earlier trip to a satellite archive location for the Chicago & North Western Historical Society, where precious but moldering plat books were found by the dozens. On that visit, I had photographed the township pages that contained the built track of the Dakota Central. I had not, however, photographed the pages for the townships to the north of the built line. The moldering plat books themselves might reveal the location of Rush Lake . . .

A hopeful excitement erupted, and I emailed lead archivist Craig Pfannkuche, including a photo of the plat book in question and a list of townships and ranges for him to scour. Perhaps on one of the pages of that moldering book he would find a watery shape with a notch in the top, oriented north, west of the Redwood River, east of Marshfield, north of the built track.

A sample of the precious, moldering plat books held in the archives of the Chicago & North Western Historical Society. S2-20

Craig found the right plat book. He turned page after page. He located all the possible townships. But not one of them had any bodies of water shaped like Rush Lake, and none of the bodies of water that *were* mapped had labels. So promising, yet so disappointing!

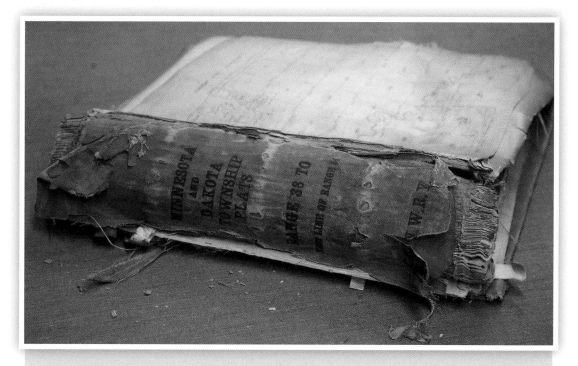

Section Three

INTO DAKOTA TERRITORY AND BACK TO THE BEGINNING

APRIL 19—JUNE 20, 1879

A major milestone was passed as the men advanced into Dakota Territory. Work soon called them back to Tracy, to conduct some minor adjustments and finalize the route for the grading and tracklaying contractors, who were assembling in Tracy to transform the surveyed route into a physical railroad. Activity was increasing for everyone as spring storms continued to lash the area. Another furlough was postponed as three trouble spots were reworked. Lack of information from home caused loneliness and anxiety, made worse when Irish learned that one of his daughters was ill. The weather was changing—cold some days, hot others, some days both. Once the work across the forty-some-mile Minnesota route was finalized, the crew returned to Dakota Territory. There they entertained a local journalist who provided a glimpse into the crew members' personalities. Later, the crew commemorated their goodwill by burying a time capsule with a treasure, which was unearthed just a few years later.

On to Dakota Territory and the Big Sioux: April 19–24, 1879

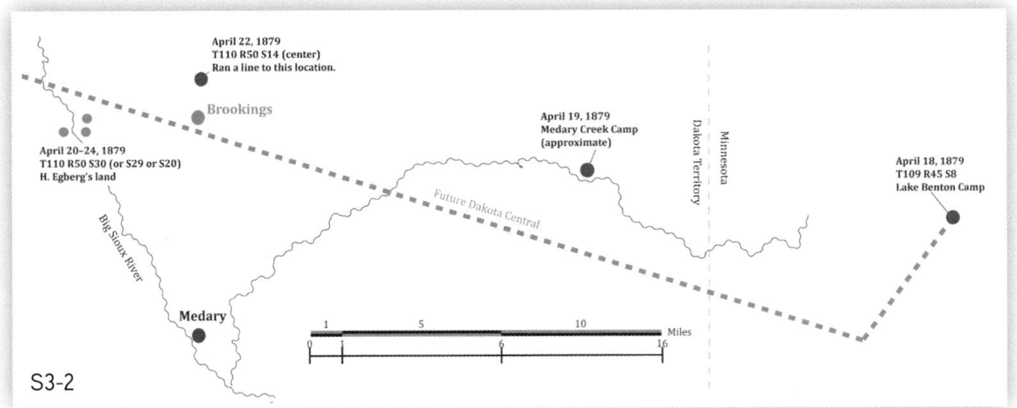

On April 19, camp at Lake Benton was pulled up and moved west, though some men and extra items were left behind in the care of landowner Morse. The main group continued west. The sky had looked as though a storm might brew up, so the decision was made to stop for the night somewhere along Medary Creek and put up a tent for shelter.

The storm didn't materialize, but the "wind came up with the sun" with such a force that Irish "could hardly sit upon [his] horse" while they made their way toward the Big Sioux. In fact, "it blew things out of the wagons." After retrieving the wind-flung items, the men forced their way against the gale, eventually putting up camp at the home of Halverson Egberg, on the bank of the Big Sioux River.

In a letter to Ruth from camp in the Sioux Valley, Irish noted the township-range-section coordinates of his camp at Egberg's, and as a mathematical exercise, told her to calculate the distance between them (with Irish in Dakota and Ruth in Iowa City) using the survey grid system.

The crew would head back to Tracy soon, and Irish reiterated that the work to be done would preclude his hoped-for trip home. He assured Ruth that their new camp was "safe from fire and in a pretty good shelter of small timber." He then mentioned that the southeast gale must have sucked all the air away from Iowa City. "I expect you all are now gasping for breath like fishes on a string," he wrote. "You cannot conceive how the wind blows here. I know that mother would be hunting a cellar half the time if she was here now."

As Ruth was about to embark on her teaching duties, Irish included some fatherly advice, writing, "Get some one in whom you have confidence to criticize you so that you can improve your self. Such help is called a prompter." In today's lingo, that's a mentor.

While the crew would soon return to Tracy to finish work there in preparation for the grading crews, a bit more work needed to be accomplished in Dakota Territory first.

On April 21, Irish scouted to the west, going as far as Lake Whitewood, which at the time was dry. In the meanwhile, his team was fighting the wind, trying to hold their equipment steady enough to do readings. After five miles, they gave up.

At 3 p.m. the next day, on the one-month anniversary of the survey, the line reached the Big Sioux River amidst the continued "severe gale." A notation in the diary for the day mentions, "We got west to the center of 14 south side T110-50 and went to camp," indicating that they were experimenting with running the line north of the location that became the town of Brookings (see previous map).

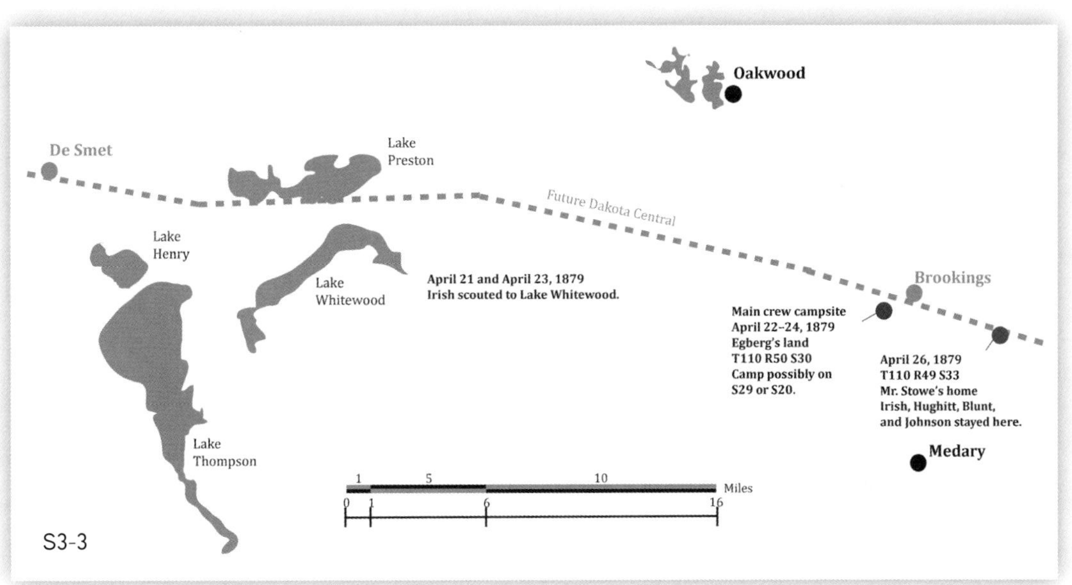

Conditions didn't improve on April 23, with Irish complaining, "Still the wind blows." Despite the difficulty of working with their equipment against a gale that could make their measurements less than accurate, the men ran a line west, "to within a short distance of Lake Whitewood." They spotted an antelope, but "could not get a shot." On April 24, Irish sent the men out to hunt while he worked on the profiles and maps from the recent work. They returned with . . . a solitary goose.

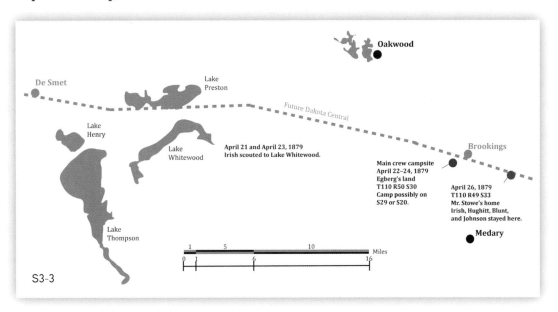

On the eve of the return to Tracy from camp along the Big Sioux River, Irish sat down to write to his wife. He was still hoping for a quick visit home. He'd suffered through a "violent headache" the last few days, a most draining circumstance. Most of the other men were again healthy "or nearly so. The warm weather put an end to the coughing."

Another entertaining camp story was included:

> We had a great excitement yesterday in the afternoon by scaring up some antelopes. One of the men took his gun and ran about two miles after them. They played with him nicely and would wait until he was almost near enough to get the shot, when away they would go to soon appear on the top of another hill, looking at him. I was afraid the fool would kill himself or get lost. Well he came back and we started on. When in a few minutes, here was the same antelopes looking at us from the top of a hill nearby. The fellow was so excited that he fired a shot at them, though they were 1000 yards away.

The antelope were not the only wildlife they'd be leaving behind. "I have got a goodly amount of feathers on hand," wrote Irish, "but as we are now away from ponds, [I] do not add much to the store. We will be in the lake region again soon, when we will begin to add to it. I may not have a chance to send them home until I come myself." Imagine—in addition to the heavy tents, stoves, and all the other "camp equipage," they were hauling around feathers. Lots and lots of feathers.

Over the last several weeks, it was a near daily occurrence to see local Dakota people, though the groups did not interact. Still, Irish was "in continual apprehension about them," unsure how to interpret their presence and watchful eyes. Nor did he provide any guidance as to whether his family should worry about his safety.

Back to the Beginning for Three Trouble Spots: April 25–June 4, 1879

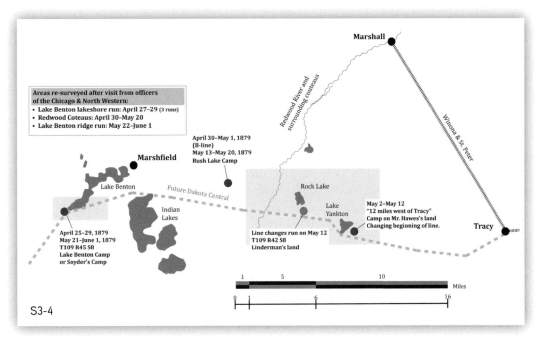

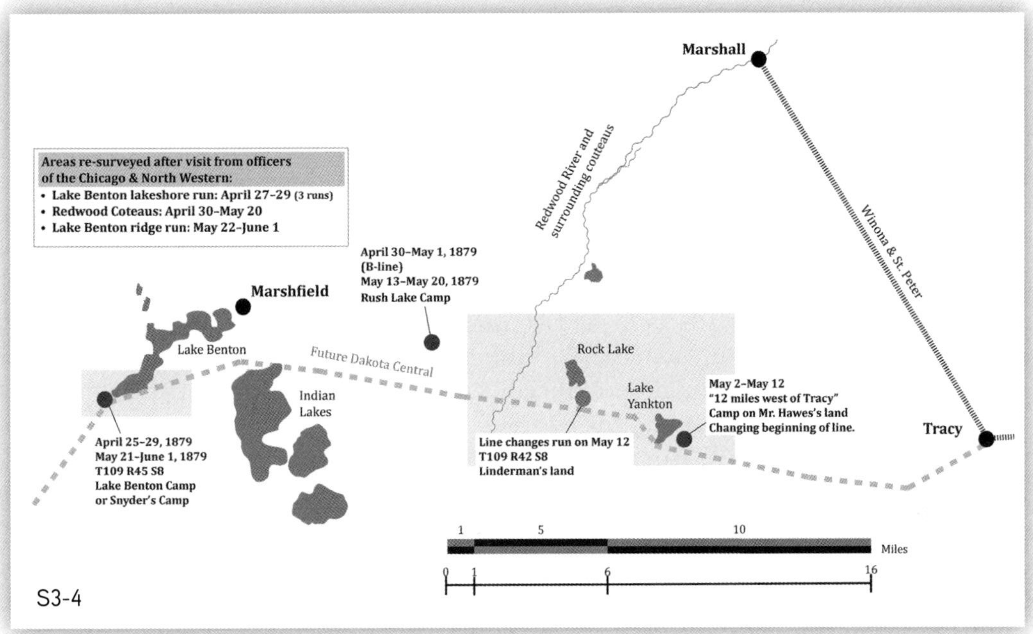

The plan for April 25 was to return to the campsite on the western shore of Lake Benton. Irish "sent the men and teams around by the road via Medary, and [he] went via the line." As he reached Medary Creek, he met up with Hughitt, Blunt, and Johnson, on their way west. Irish "turned about and took them to the Sioux River and back." The men stayed the night at the home of W. R. Stowe, southeast of modern Brookings.

The next morning, Irish and the railroad officers "rapidly" continued east, arriving at the Lake Benton camp by late morning. The "Chicago friends" enjoyed a midday meal with the men who were surveying the route, then continued traveling east. Irish was feeling a bit behind, noting that he'd accomplished "no line work." Regardless, the conversations with the officers likely yielded plenty of useful direction for the work, whether affirmations or concerns.

On April 26, following his rendezvous with the officers, Irish wrote home to Lizzie. Apparently, the officers had been pleased with his work, telling him it was "the best work of the kind . . . in years." In fact, they planned to keep him on and have him "build their line to the Black Hills," which would take two to three years. "So you see I am fixed for work now," he wrote. "If I am so busy this summer that I can't get home, I want you all to come up here to visit me." Based on that, it's possible the survey contract had been let for a specific distance, and that Irish had to prove himself before being entrusted with the entire route. He obviously passed muster. The short letter ended with a request of Lizzie: "Tell mother that we got the feathers of two geese into the sack today. I'll soon have enough for a bed."

On Monday, April 28, the men ran a new line along the south shore of Lake Benton. With this option, Irish was able to reduce the calculated "quantities," because the new line "reduce[d] curves and sharpness up to 10°." In this case, "quantities" referred to the materials needed to construct the track. All track required rails, spikes, ties, fasteners, and the like. But terrain that was already relatively flat allowed for the most inexpensive roadbed. Straight track was faster and easier to lay. If a trestle or bridge was needed, if a cut had to be made through a hill, or if land had to be filled in to bring a low spot up to grade, additional labor, expertise, and materials—"quantities"—would be required. And if those could be reduced, so too would the cost of that length of track as well as ongoing maintenance.

The next day, a third run along the shoreline was made, and Irish declared it "a perfect success." With this third, apparently successful line documented, the camp was again moved east, this time back to the Rush Lake site, which served as their base of operations while contending, yet again, with the pesky crossing of the Redwood River. Irish sent Thorn and a hired man to Marshall to bring back supplies. The rest of the men "got [the] maps ready to begin the change near here."

The men began their work on May 1, running five and a half miles of line. Similar to conditions in Dakota Territory, "the ground [was] very dry, and the farmers [said] that only about 1/3 the grain [had] come up."

On that day, the *Brookings County Press* alerted readers to "Indian troubles" along the James River. No details were provided, but the editor recommended that settlers living near the James move eastward to the Big Sioux valley as a safer option and an area of better land.[22] This may have been true (there was at least one report, months later, in early summer, of railroad surveyors being killed along a line just to the south), or it may have been that scourge of human nature called fearmongering. Or, since the lands near the Big Sioux were lauded, this may have been an opportunistic example of *boosterism*, in which, as in modern marketing, a town or region was enthusiastically written about, with negatives either glossed over or ignored, and often some things—such as weather—painted in glowing terms that outstretched reality.

On May 2, the "changes over the Redwood coteaus" were completed, and camp was moved "to Mr. Hawes 12 miles west of Tracy." As camp was being set up near Lake Yankton, Irish observed, "The bar[ometer] and the clouds look stormy." In fact, rain began to fall overnight and continued throughout most of the next day, May 3. Still, the men got out that day, running a three-mile alternative line to the one they'd originally identified. The clouds cleared, and they were rewarded at 7:30 p.m. with "a beautiful meteor in SW, 1st red then white."

Note: Meteor colors are influenced by the meteor's chemical composition as well as the speed by which it moves through the atmosphere. Nitrogen or oxygen will produce red, magnesium blue, calcium purple, sodium orange, and iron yellow hues. According to the American Meteorological Society, "the faster a meteor moves, the more intense the color may appear."[23]

In a letter to Ruth from camp on Mr. Hawe's land, Irish complained of having been "both very busy and part of the time sick." Well, perhaps sick wasn't it. He added, "I should say that I have been more tired than sick." The weather was stormy, but a lightning storm provided respite: "It seemed such a luxury to lie in bed until six o'clock and rest one's tired body."

By talking with local homeowners, he learned a construction technique he planned to deploy at home: "I want to take off the weather boarding and put building paper on under the weather boards. You have no idea how warm it makes a house. They have them here, and without being plastered, they are warmer than ours."

The sky may have cleared, but the conditions remained troublesome. "The wind came up from the NW very high," growing to a "40 mile gale so that [it was] hard work to save [the] camp with extra ropes and stakes." It is unclear whether the men did any line work, whether they stayed in camp and worked on paperwork and chores, or whether they simply rested. However the day went, Irish summed it up as "a most disagreeable day + an anxious one for me."

It had also become cold. The temperature dropped to 24 degrees by the morning reading on May 5, causing ice to form on standing water, including in camp buckets and area marshes. A strong wind from the northwest blew, and the day only managed to climb to 32 degrees. Regardless, out they went. Measurements were taken, changes made. "I am about down sick," Irish confessed. He didn't have the luxury of resting, however. Time was running out. Contractors were already organizing and planning to begin the physical work of turning that path of stakes into an actual railroad.

Despite feeling both rushed and ill, Irish spent time writing home from the camp twelve miles west of Tracy. On May 5, he penned:

> We had a very hard storm yesterday (Sunday) and we all had to work with all our might to keep our tents from blowing away. We had to put out our fires and stand in the worst storm that I ever experienced in a camp and pull ropes and drive pins all day long, and a part of the time it rained and hailed. So you see that our poor tired bodies got no rest on that day.

The camp would be on the move again, so he let the family know to send future correspondence to him via Marshall, Minnesota.

The next morning, May 6, was another cold one, and the surrounding location was full of complicating features. "We have several lakes to run over or around," wrote Irish. This area is still thick with prairie potholes, marshes, and sloughs with various degrees of liquidity, as well as many actual lakes. Plotting a straight route through it was no easy task, and additional costs of construction and ongoing maintenance had to be calculated.

May 7 was again "raw cold," though the work on the new line was going well. Blunt arrived to check on progress, staying in camp overnight. "I feel sick yet," wrote Irish, "it's by the cold weather that ails me." Blunt left camp on the eighth, and while the crew tried working despite a cold gale blowing, they gave up in the afternoon, knowing their measurements would be inaccurate in the wind. The weather had improved by May 9, but Irish did not indicate what work was accomplished. He did share that the afternoon featured a thunder shower, so we know the temperature warmed.

In a recent letter to Lizzie, Irish had mentioned the officers were so pleased with his work that he had been asked to survey the entire route to the Black Hills. In this May 10 letter to his wife, he shared yet another development: "Mr. Hughitt raised my wages to begin next month at $150. I take it as a high compliment." Irish was tickled—with inflation, $150 in 1879 equates to approximately $3,772.50 in 2019 value. The frequency of this wage (semi-monthly, monthly, etc.) is unknown, but it was nonetheless significant for the era.

The air was warmer, but again the weather failed to improve. Most of Saturday, May 10, was stormy, as was the eleventh, though there were "signs of a clear up," which turned to "threaten[ing] storms" on the twelfth. "Rain fell all day" on the thirteenth. In fact, some level of rain is mentioned within the diary entries until May 17, when actual rain turned to a "sprinkle."

Beneath those constantly rainy skies, the men tried to keep up the work. On May 10, the crew worked on the second line while Irish rode into Tracy seeking something that is frustratingly illegible in the diary. After failing to find what he sought, he returned to camp, getting soaked in the process.

May 11 was spent in camp, and despite the inclement weather, the temperature had risen a bit, and Irish declared that he felt much better as a result. Four miles of line were run on the twelfth, and when they stopped for the day, they were on the Lindermans' land, which allows us to determine, via online land records, that this line option was running through T109 R42 S8, a section that would soon see the graders preparing the roadbed. This became a built segment—and a successful approach to the Redwood River.

With the reworking done on the line west of Lake Yankton, the camp was moved west again to Rush Lake on the morning of Tuesday, May 13, despite an all-day rain. While the men worked to re-establish camp, Irish "went on horse back to Tracy," hoping to pick up funds that were to be delivered to him. The money was not there, so he spent the night in Tracy, and "sent the horse back to camp"—an entirely puzzling statement. It is not at all clear whether another person was traveling with Irish and escorted the horse back, or whether Irish's horse actually trotted himself obediently back to the Rush Lake camp from Tracy, a straight-line distance of about fifteen miles. Not likely. Nor, for that matter, does it tell us how Irish planned to return to camp himself once the money arrived. In any event, he took the train to Marshall the next day, where the expected funds were found. He returned to camp, somehow . . . Perhaps a crew member met him in Marshall with a horse.

One of Irish's main responsibilities was creating maps and reports of the terrain and surveyed route and getting them back to the officers in Winona and Chicago. The diaries make frequent mention of his working on maps, profiles, notes, and reports, sending those important items with one crew member or another to have them sent back to Chicago, or modifying said maps after the officers had time to digest the information. As we'll see, it was not at all uncommon for Irish to return to camp to find an officer (usually Blunt) waiting for him. Irish would hear what the officer(s) thought about the latest route proposals, and they would discuss pros, cons, and potential changes. Then, not uncommonly, the crew backtracked and reworked some portion of the route.

MAP PRODUCTION

When I was in the University of Iowa Libraries Special Collections and Archives department, working directly with the maps and profile drawings that Irish created during this project, Giselle Simón, director of conservation and collections care, casually mentioned that Irish was either hauling giant tables across the prairie or working with these large, unwieldy lengths of paper on irritatingly small tabletops. Some of the profile rolls are so long that they take ten minutes to roll up after looking at them. Some are so large that once unfolded they require two large modern conference tables pushed together. Irish crafted these documents from mobile campsites, on whatever surfaces were being carted along.

A few sample rolls of profile maps. These preprinted grid papers cover significant stretches of route, to scale. For instance, the roll on the left shows the elevation profile from Tracy to the Big Sioux River, approximately sixty-five miles. S3-5

On May 15, Irish sent Thorn to Marshall with reports, which could then be whisked away on the next train. During the day, the crew double-checked their work around Lake Yankton (at present-day Balaton) and felt good about the results. Irish was a bit concerned, however, when Thorn failed to return to camp that evening. One can imagine that in addition to being concerned for the welfare of his worker, there were the reports to worry about as well. Fortunately, daylight found the wayward Thorn approaching camp. He'd lost his way coming back from Marshall, having been forced to camp for the night at a location that, it turned out, had been relatively nearby. It should be noted that Thorn is the same man who arrived in camp late at the beginning of work, worrying Irish then too. This is a bit ironic since he was the camp courier.

The impact of the impending railroad line was being heartily discussed in Dakota Territory. At this point, the physical construction had not yet begun. The fact that a route was being surveyed was proof enough for settlers and potential settlers, and a correspondent to the *Brookings County Press* expressed happiness that the coming harvest could be shipped via the Tracy branch (the Dakota Central), saving them from having to haul their crop forty to fifty miles.[24]

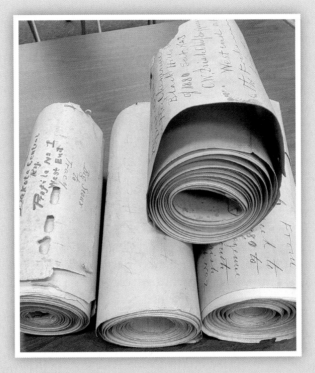

Just east of the Dakota Territory–Minnesota border, the happiness about the arriving railroad was a bit more hesitant. The people in the little town of Marshfield, Minnesota, on the northeast end of the waters of Lake Benton, noticed that the survey was routing the line along the south side of the lake, a location that would bypass Marshfield and therefore, in all likelihood, doom its existence. "We shall be glad to secure the road, wherever it may run; so send it along,"[25] the *Marshfield Tribune* article read. (Indeed, most of Marshfield's businesses would move to the center of rail traffic that was Lake Benton; today, the ghost streets of Marshfield lie beneath a farmstead and fields.)

The men ran a four-mile line that crossed the Redwood River, though it is unclear how many options for this crossing had been surveyed prior to this. One thing is certain, however: by May 16, preparations for building the physical roadbed were in high gear. Not only that, but the starting point of Tracy was less than fifteen miles to their east. The route had to be finalized, and quickly, or costs would begin to mount, with hordes of contractors potentially sitting idle. That would not go over well with the officers, whom Irish was determined to please.

The Redwood River had carved some of the more significant ravines in the area, and they presented a serious hindrance to the surveyors. On May 17, Irish recorded that the area was "the worst part of the line to go over." Each day, they steadily worked their way along the terrain, sometimes in the rain, often in some level of "gale," and even one "very hot" afternoon. The hard-working crew was rewarded one night when Perry Powers "got two nice strings of fish" for the cook to prepare. He obtained them in a most unusual way, however: he shot them. Or so said the diary.

Irish wrote home on May 18 from Rush Lake Camp, telling his family, "The team goes to Marshall in the morning, and I must let you know that I still live. I am well except a peculiar pain in the joint of my right thumb, which is so sore and has been for a long time that it hurts me much to write this letter." He was also still hoping for a trip home before "the busy trip west." He added, "I can't ask you to come so far to stay only a few days with me."

On Tuesday, May 20, work across the Redwood River was declared satisfactorily completed, and the men prepared to move back to Lake Benton. That was a big day. Not only had the Redwood Coteaus been dealt with, but the Dakota Central was officially incorporated. Two days later, the *Currie Pioneer* reported, "Contractors, subs and sub-subs without number have registered at the hotels [in Tracy] during the past few days. . . . Rails for the new road are fast coming in and tracklaying will begin in a few days. Quite a large number of tents are to be seen in and about town."[26] There was very little wiggle room in the surveyor's schedule, as the construction crews were massing at Tracy.

Irish wrote that a Mr. Perrine (also appearing in records as Perine), who was described in a regional newspaper as "the contractor's head man" and by "his very nature a bulldoser,"[27] arrived in camp at Rush Lake to chat with Irish. The graders, bridge builders, and tracklayers would soon begin work at Tracy, and Lake Benton would be the next major work camp west of Tracy. Perrine told Irish that Wells had the store contract. (The man who would be operating that store, on behalf of Wells, would be Charles Ingalls, the father of Laura Ingalls.)

The survey crew dismantled camp on May 21 and began the return trek west to Lake Benton. In their wake, they left the corrected survey line that would, in just a few weeks' time, be dug up, scraped, cut, filled, and mounded into the physical railbed.

As had become common of late, a rainstorm made their journey less than pleasant, and several of the men fell ill, including Irish. The party stopped shy of Lake Benton for the night, though that may have been planned. The next morning, with the "air . . . in a great state of commotion," they ran yet another line along the Lake Benton shoreline. The temperature reached 84 degrees while the men worked, and intermittent storms continued into the next day.

On May 22, the *Brookings County Press* shared that not only had the construction contract been finalized, but the contractor was looking for workers. This offered a double opportunity, with short-term wages as a construction worker and longer-term prosperity along the line after the trains began to roll. The editor, wearing his boosterism hat, reminded readers the railroad intended to connect Chicago with the Black Hills—both centers of wealth—and that everyone could get a piece of that pie by settling along the route.[28]

The work progressed regardless of the weather. Blunt appeared in camp on May 23, leaving after just a few hours. Irish was feeling better, though still "very weak." On Saturday, May 24, the men "broke ground in the Hole in the Mountain . . . at noon"—the area southwest of the lake where a creek's valley allowed for a gradual climb around the steeper bluffs to the north and west.

Once through the complex of hills and up onto the plain, the crew was gifted with one of the longest tangents of the entire eastern portion of the project, a straight run of approximately twenty-five miles, without need of any curves—a nice counter to the hair-pulling work on the Redwood River crossing. However, they couldn't move on just yet.

At Hole in the Mountain, the crew was setting slope stakes; the markings upon these stakes told the graders the necessary cut or fill work needed to get the railbed to the appropriate height all along the route. It was hot work, as the daytime temperature again hit 84 degrees, with a strong southeast wind. A rainstorm added a tinge of humidity into the mix as well.

The storm whipped up in the afternoon and continued overnight, with "rain and heavy thunder," causing less-than-restful sleep for the crew. Sunday, May 25, found contractor Wells himself in camp, checking out the location and getting his bearings. His grading, bridge-building, and track-laying crews would soon be progressing toward this location, and their temporary camps would move along with the work. Some would sleep in tents, others in railcars converted into bunkhouses. And every thirty or so miles, there would be a larger base camp, where the company store would be established. One of those locations would be at Lake Benton.

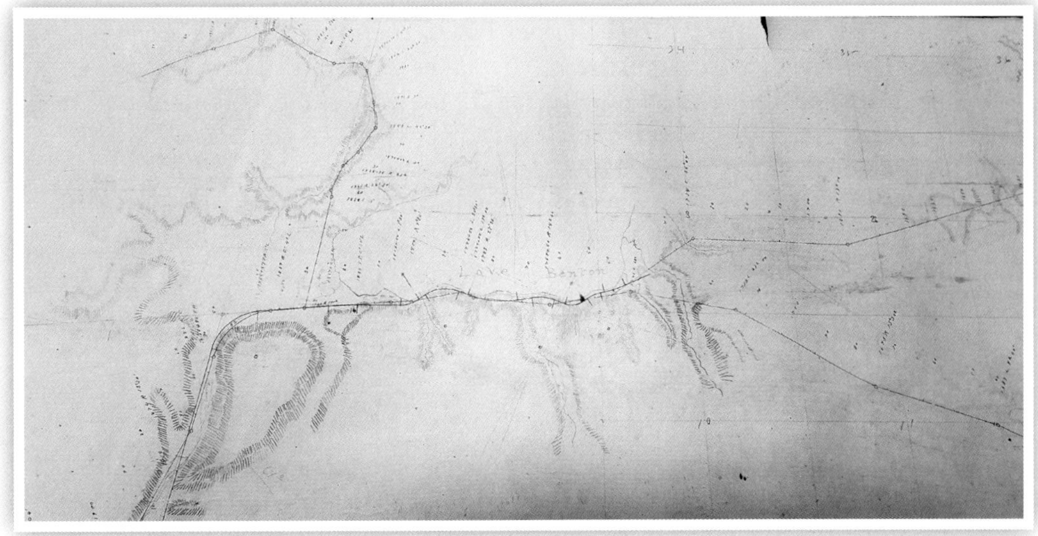

Irish's map detailing two possible routes to Lake Benton as well as two options away, one going to the south and one going north. The southern course was selected. The land on the western shore of Lake Benton (the body of water) is the camp location where Charles Ingalls worked. S3-6

While in camp at Lake Benton on May 25, Irish wrote to his wife, "I have not heard from any of you for a long time." The possible reason, he admitted, was that it had been so stormy that they'd not sent anyone to the post office for "a good while." In fact, it had "rained every day now for ten days past." Irish added, "Last night we had a most violent thunder storm all night long. The thunder was terrific and the rain a flood. The cook drowned out of his tent about midnight. He had to go out and ditch about it, a work he might have done in fair weather and daylight."

After giving instructions about which bills needed to be paid now and which could hold off, Irish turned his attention to items he needed sent to him:

> Get that saddle pocket made of good oil cloth lined with strong white muslin. And when you get the pants made, put my two botany books . . . into the pack and send it to Mr. Blunt at Winona Minn. with a letter saying that it's for me, and he will pack it and send it to me, so it will cost nothing . . . My old clothes have

taken a notion to fall to pieces all at once. For this reason I have to sit and patch them when I might be resting myself or writing to you.

Irish had sent home a map of his intended route with locations marked. His next focus, one that deviated from the main purposes of heading westward to the Missouri River, would be to examine a route across the Big Sioux, west to the James River, then north along the James, and finally back east to Watertown. "It makes me tired to think of those weary miles," wrote Irish. "I shall have 25 men with me." (The reason for those "weary miles" will become clear in the weeks to come as the work on a parallel survey is discussed.)

He ended the letter by reminding them all, "Take some quinine as the weather changes, also some good whiskey or else warm iron tonic." Speaking of consumables, "a piece of Dunlap's wedding cake" was sent back to Iowa City for the family to enjoy. "He brought it with him for me and for Mr. Blunt," wrote Irish. "Tell me what you think of it so I can tell him about it."

With the contractor on hand, the route away from Lake Benton needed finalization. On Monday, May 26, the men worked on estimates (how many cuts, how much fill, how many bridges, how many curves and at what angle, etc.) in camp during a morning rainstorm, then got out to "run the land lines at Lake Benton." The heat of the past week had suddenly given way, and Irish lamented, "It is very muddy and also cold."

The next day, they continued work on the lines along the southwestern tip of the lake, in section 8 on the 1916 map below, which shows the track as built, including how two curves were needed to navigate from the eastern run to the western escape from the valley. The circle shows the location of the Lake Benton camp, where the surveyors based their area work and the Wells camp set up for the first stage of construction, including the company store manned by Charles Ingalls.

On Wednesday, May 28, Irish declared the Lake Benton survey complete. At 11:30 p.m., he completed the map, and possibly none too soon, for Blunt arrived in camp the next day. The Lake Benton work must have included the line to the southwest that got through those pesky high ridges, and May 29 was spent working on the "long tangent," a twenty-eight-mile length of perfectly straight route leading to the bank of the Big Sioux River.

On May 30, Irish complained, "Cold, very cold. Winter clothes have to be put on." Despite the strong northwest wind adding to the chill, the surveyors continued their work on the long tangent. May 31 found Irish at the invisible line separating Minnesota from Dakota Territory. This was also the location where, legally, the railroad changed names from the Chicago & Dakota (in Minnesota) to the Dakota Central.

Back when a scoundrel had started a fire at the camp at Rush Lake, Irish noted three "strangers" in camp, though he had possibly made their acquaintance during his initial scouting trip. Irish wrote about one of them:

> Mr Snyder had the kindness to make a trip to Marshall for us and brought us the mail. He got here last night at 11 o'clock, and you should have seen the men arise from their slumbers. People who can get letters every day and live by a telegraph wire cannot know how it is to be out of reach of a P.O. Day after day passes, days become weeks, and no tidings from loved ones.

The joy of the men was palpable, and one can easily imagine the hoots and hollers of men leaping from their bedrolls to collect their connections to home.

Among the letters that arrived for Irish was one from his ill sister-in-law, Louisa Huffman, who Irish knew would soon pass. After reading the letters, he wrote to his wife, "Taking these letters together, I feel this morning quite mournful. How much sorrow there may be upon you today I know not but I greatly fear. Oh! How I wish I might be with you in this trying time." Abbie was Louisa's main caretaker in her illness, and Irish recognized that his wife "must be quite worn out with watching and daily toil." He added, "Louisa, poor soul, has suffered much, so much indeed that no doubt death, as it is inevitable, will be a relief."

The work was going well, and seventy miles of line was ready for the graders and tracklayers. Irish's crew was "scattered all over the line," doing their tasks, and it was expected that tracks would reach the Big Sioux by October. Here we also see Irish's quiet pride in his work. Hughitt mentioned that he wanted cars running to Deadwood by the next year, and he entrusted Irish to determine the route. "I always wished for such a chance but never expected to realize it," wrote Irish. He listed some of the "titled chap[s]" that had built the Northern Pacific Railway, garnering mentions in the newspapers, and compared himself to them, writing, "Here I am, a man who has hardly been mentioned in the papers of his own town, selected to do the next great work of the kind. Well I take it as a high compliment, I tell you, and I hope that we all shall hold out in strength and health until it's done." The goal to reach Deadwood by the end of 1880 was a significant project, and that accomplishment could bring significant career opportunities for Irish. He was organizing his aspirations and looking into the future, to Deadwood and beyond.

He reassured his family that he was not taking risks, nothing like those from the Arizona project. "We are on level prairie where we can see about us several miles," wrote Irish, making sure to include, "[We'll] have a large party of men so that at all times we will be on guard, and well guarded at that. Mr. Hughitt tells me to get anything I may want." Comparing this venture to the one in the southwest, he reminded them, "[In Arizona] we traveled in canyons all the time in which Indians could crawl up unperceived within gun shot of us." Letters in these first few months of the trip expressed some concern about being vulnerable to the local Native populations, but after plenty of exposure and no incidents, this concern disappeared from the narrative.

Crew member Dunlap's wife planned to come out from Chicago, to board in Marshall. The wife of A. B. Thompson was also set up in a shanty near the men. How many of the other men were married and had enticed their spouses to live nearby during the job is unknown, excepting what Irish shared in his letters, but he reminded his family in most letters that he would welcome and encourage their visit, if they chose to make the trip.

May 31 "felt as warm as summer," but June began quite differently, with temperatures ping-ponging up and down. The thermometer read a chilly 38 degrees at the morning check, and a "very severe gale" blew. The men "had to have a fire in all the tents" to keep warm enough. June 2 dawned even colder, at 36 degrees. The day itself, however, was again "warm as summer."

After having sent the men west to set up camp at the Big Sioux on June 2, Irish took a team and wagon over a dusty road to Marshall, staying overnight. At noon the next day, he retrieved Blunt from the depot, and they headed in the general direction of Lake Benton, likely inspecting the new run across the Redwood along the way.

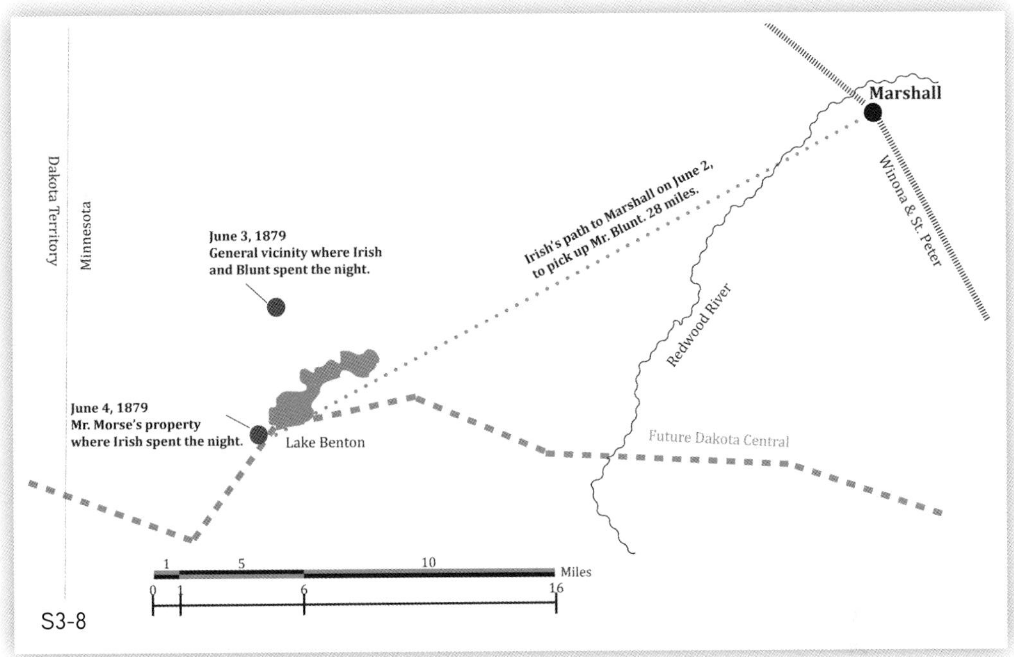

Irish and Blunt slept on the prairie that night, four miles to the north of Lake Benton. It is likely they were again looking over the landscape, to either confirm or reevaluate their choice of route up onto the coteau before the approaching construction workers committed to the route for them.

Either way, there was an overnight storm and a broken-down wagon, and June 4 was another cold day. In the mix, Irish became ill. Ill enough, in fact, that he sought the help of his friend Morse and his wife, who "did all they could" for Irish. This was likely A. W. Morse, who, along with John Snyder, owned several parcels of land around Lake Benton, including the location where the surveyors had been camping as well as that where the contractors were now setting up the "permanent" camp location for the work west of Tracy. The diary does not indicate whether or when Blunt may have departed. Irish mentioned sending Thorn "back after mail," so not all of the crew had been sent ahead to the Big Sioux. As the usual courier, Thorn may even have been with Irish on the trip to Marshall, but either way, he went unmentioned in the diary. Blunt may have returned to Marshall or Tracy, and thus the train, after seeing the new line at the Redwood River, or he may have been with Irish still. Again, the diary doesn't say.

While in Marshall on June 3, Irish received a note from Lizzie saying that Ruth was ill with "lung fever" (pneumonia). This deeply unsettled the man, who spent the next several weeks trying to pry information from his family while letters evidently either failed to reach him or arrived without updates about his daughter's health. Nonetheless, he immediately sent off a letter to Ruth, worried and scolding all at once. He feared she took on too much and failed to take her quinine and whiskey to ward off the ailments that were thought to come with spring weather.

It had turned cold in western Minnesota, and the men had to wear their winter clothing and keep the fires going. Irish himself nearly fell ill, but having taken his quinine and whiskey regularly (hint-hint, family!), he was now "quite well." The weather had also turned warmer, and it was now "warm as summer, very hot and uncomfortable."

Desperately wanting an update about Ruth's health, Irish sent a telegram to Lizzie before leaving Marshall on the June 3, imploring her to send a message back, to be picked up on the fourth. He had a man in camp ready to take the letter he was writing and get it to Marshall and return with Lizzie's dispatch (via telegraph).

To lighten the mood of his letter, he shared with her some of the "recommendations" that various crewmen had brought to him as part of their application to be a part of the team. One had been "shot through the hips" during the Civil War, even pulling down his trousers to show the scars. "I told him that was a good recommend[ation]," wrote Irish. A second man had "lost his health teaching school in Indiana." While that statement begs for more context and would likely yield some rather interesting backstories, none were given. Irish did share that the man "coughed to show . . . the need of camp life." A third man said that his best asset was that he was the companion of a "good watch dog."

Irish then jumped to a story about the camp's dog, Nero: Camp was on the move, and the dinner stop was underway, and Nero felt himself every bit a part of the crew as the humans. "Nero . . . slipped up behind the cook and stole our boiled hen," wrote Irish. The men were angry, but Irish "would not let them whip him for it." Nero did not go unpunished, however; for the next several weeks, any mention of boiled hen caused the poor dog to "drop on the ground and in the most abject manner crawl up to the accuser, testifying by his manner that he was the one who stole the hen."

Isolated as they were, the crew often employed humor to keep up morale. Nero wasn't the only one providing entertainment. A young man (Irish called him a "boy") named Pierre had been sent from Chicago to learn engineering. "He is the biggest fool I ever saw to be able to get an education," wrote Irish. It seems the more experienced men decided to take advantage of the youth's naivete. Leveraging rumors so prevalent "in the east"—the cause of much hand-wringing at the time—the men convinced Pierre that the "hills and hollows were full of Indians." His job was to carry the back flag for the line work, which meant he was often isolated from the others—the one that strayed from the herd, so to speak. The men added tiny nuggets of inuendo to heighten the boy's nerves.

"One day, he told me he must have arms to defend himself with," wrote Irish. "I told him to take all he wanted. Now there is not an Indian on the whole line, but he took a rifle, a shot gun, and all of our pistols and lugged them along for days . . . Strangers thought we made him carry the arms for the whole party." The letter ended without mentioning when the young man caught on or whether he was good-natured about the ruse. In camp life, being a good sport is often as important as having good job skills.

Irish included within the letter three wild roses, with the promise that he would soon send actual plants for the gardens. To finish the letter, a side note for his wife mentions that he convinced Hughitt to hire a second surveyor to take care of the test line from Watertown west to the James River, a significant relief to Irish, who was feeling overly stretched.

Back to Dakota Territory: June 5–14, 1879

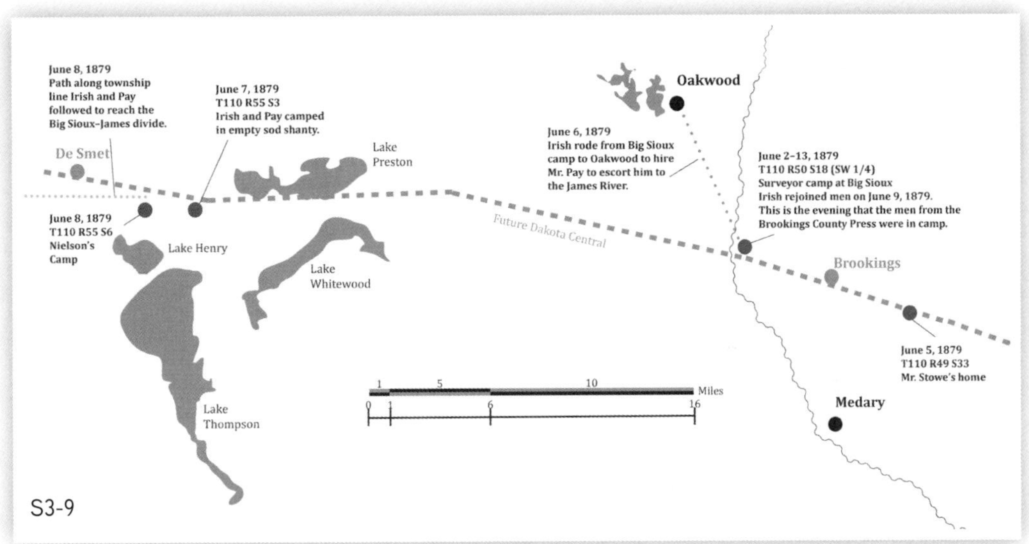

Thursday, June 5, was stormy and similarly cold, but Irish, along with Thorn, moved on to Dakota Territory. The men stopped again at the home of Stowe. Irish remained ill, but Stowe "treated [him] very kindly."

While Irish was recovering, the editors of the *Brookings County Press* were figuratively standing on their tip toes, looking over the eastern horizon, impatiently waiting for signs of flying dirt. They were so excited for "the hissing breath of the iron steed" that there was a flurry of squibs, one after another, that are almost the editorial version of a young child saying "Mom! Mom! Mom!" over and over. (Squibs are those short-and-sweet items in the newspapers that aren't quite paragraphs or articles.) The first handful of squibs in the June 5 issue read:

– The railroad will soon be here.

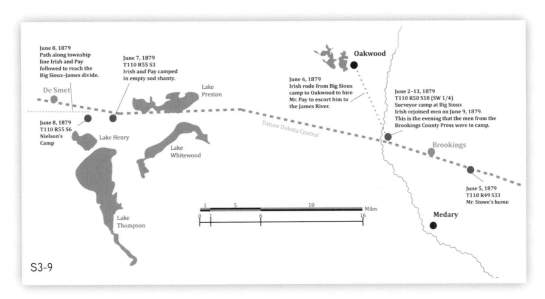

- The hissing breath of the iron steed will soon be heard in the land.
- Ship your grain next fall by the C. & N. W. R. R. from Brookings county.
- The right-of-way man for the C. & N. W. R. R. Co. was in town Friday night.
- Hundreds of men are throwing dirt on the C. & N. W. R. R. only 25 miles from Brookings county.[29]

Additional squibs more or less repeated the above using different words. It was clear that the progress of the railroad contractors would be the most important topic for some time to come—and the workers were barely over a week on the job back in Tracy.

Landholder Stowe, who had hosted Irish a time or two, visited the newly planted camp at Lake Benton to speak with the contractor in charge, who may have been Wells or Hiram Forbes, depending on timing. (Forbes's wife, Docia, a sister of Charles Ingalls, was responsible for the hiring of Ingalls to work for contractor Wells.)

Whoever Stowe spoke with to obtain the information, the same edition of the *Brookings County Press* repeated Stowe's news: "Work progressing rapidly all along the line from Tracy to the State line. Between three and four hundred teams with necessary men are now at work on this section. A gang of men are expected to commence laying ties to-day at Tracy, and track layers will soon take up the line of march."

Stowe himself was awarded a subcontract for a stretch of eight miles, beginning two miles east of Medary Creek. He expected to begin work within the week and was in immediate need of "thirty to forty teams and men."[30] In fact, less than two weeks later, he had broken ground.[31]

Lizzie had recently been appointed as notary public, and this greatly interested Irish, who, from his camp at Lake Benton, instructed her to fix up his old seal, claiming he'd been denied the job of notary public on account of being a Democrat, and he was "curious to know how [she'd] electioneered the matter." He wanted to see a sample of her seal, asking whether it had a symbol—vignette—similar to one he drew on the letter.

He again asked for an update on Ruth's health, reminding Lizzie, "Lung diseases are frequent here now [that] the weather has been so very changeable." With the arrival of

S3-10

summer, he promised to obtain from Hughitt a family pass so that the women could ride the rails to Tracy and come visit him at the camps to the west.

Irish was well enough to continue to the Big Sioux camp on Friday, June 6, arriving there at 9 a.m. He assigned Thorn and DeBarr to "fuel and wood" duty, though he doesn't say where he sent them, just that they were sent "back." While the two men on fuel duty headed east-ish (possibly into the heavily wooded area southwest of Marshall, which would then mean they were sent northeast-ish), Irish went northwest to Oakwood, the small village nestled near multiple lakes about eight miles to the northwest of present-day Volga, in Dakota Territory, which he had visited on his initial scouting trip.

In Oakwood, Irish hired B. E. Pay to escort him to the James River at a rate of $5 per day (equivalent to $125.75 in 2019 value). Irish and Pay traveled back to the Big Sioux camp, either that same day (the sixth), or early the next morning. Either way, the two men headed west from the Big Sioux Camp at noon on Saturday, June 7.

The region, he noted, was dry. It did not help that "the wind blew a violent gale" and that water was scarce. "Had battle with Norwegians for a bucket full of water," wrote Irish. "Got it and went on." Those few, terse words would be elaborated upon in a few days. The men scouted to a point a few miles west-southwest of the western shore of Lake Preston, where they found an unoccupied sod shanty that served as lodging for the night.

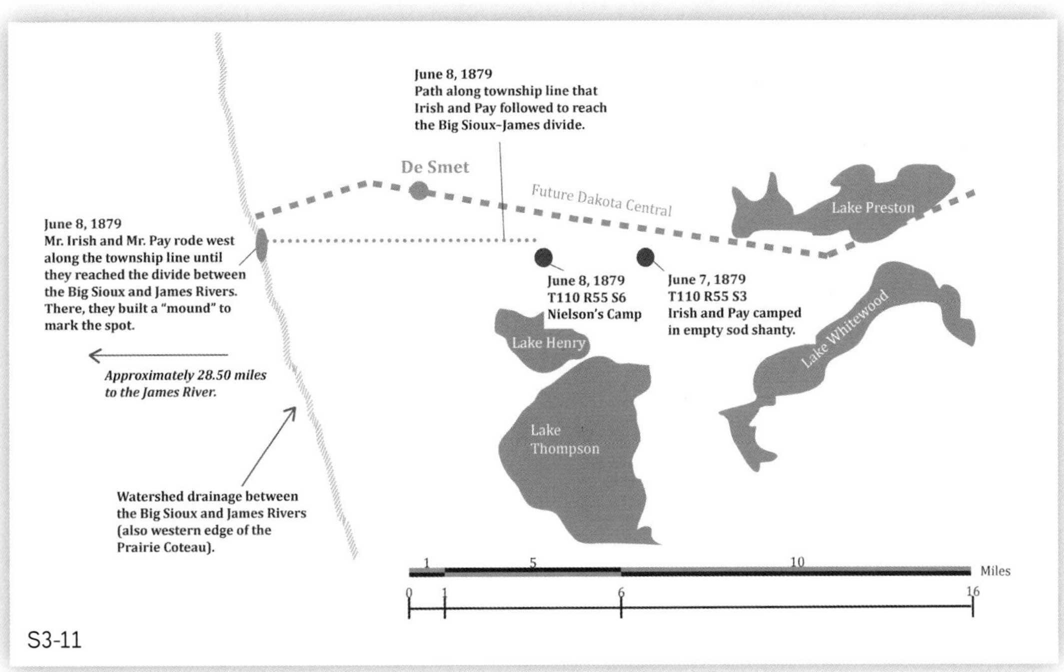

S3-11

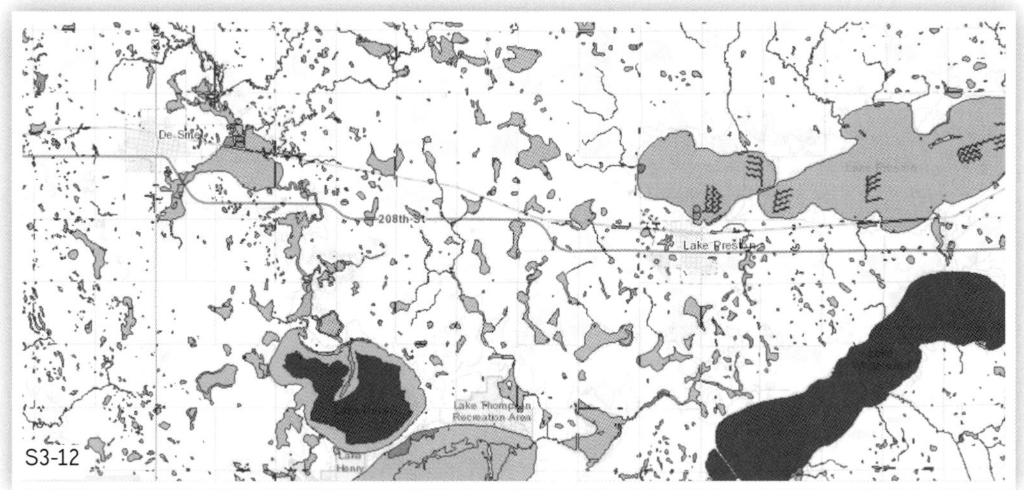

Modern map showing wetland locations between De Smet and Lake Preston. Most of these areas were dry in 1879, though rains produced plenty of breeding grounds for mosquitos.

Once camp was moved to the Big Sioux, Irish dashed off a quick letter, on Saturday, June 7, to tell his family that he would be unreachable until the next Wednesday (the eleventh) and that he hadn't had time to send a courier up to Canby to retrieve any waiting letters. He remained anxious to hear of Ruth's health, helplessly hoping she had improved and that her mother and sister were not wearing themselves out tending to her. As reflected over multiple letters, this lack of information was incredibly nerve-racking for the worried father.

After writing his own letter, a treasure trove was handed to him. The women sent a large bundle of materials to Irish, and in response, he sat down to write a second letter. "Never in my life was I more surprised," he wrote, referencing how much they'd crammed into the package. "That picture of the household including Mink [the family dog] made me see you all, and my joy would have been complete had I been able to know that Ruth was well or even better." Imagine how frustrated he must have felt, not hearing a definitive report on Ruth despite his begging, while otherwise newsy letters landed in his tent. One imagines him comparing the dates on letters received to their arrival dates, trying to piece the bits of information together.

Irish had sent courier Thorn back to Marshall to pick up the dispatch Irish had asked Lizzie to send. "I have been quite out of sorts for two days," wrote Irish. In fact, rather than being out on the line, he was being tended to by Mr. and Mrs. Morse, owners of the store in Lake Benton. His stomach was upset, which he blamed on weeks of eating salt meat. But his worry over not knowing Ruth's condition may have been as much or more a factor. He also mentioned that every time he became hungry, he also grew homesick, longing for good food.

A serious storm had hit the camp a few days before. In fact, he enclosed a newspaper clipping with "the doings of Sunday's storms" in the letter he'd written to Lizzie two days before, telling his daughter, "We were in bed and felt happy that we were on the Snyder's grounds here, the loveliest and safest camp ground that I ever saw."

Despite feeling safe and snug in their campground, Irish now told his wife, "Dunlap and I were so glad that we had not got our respective wives out here to be in that storm." He felt that the houses built by residents of the region were "flimsy" considering the weather, and "many a shell house went to pieces in" the wind. To Abbie he teased, "I know that if you had been here and could find no cellar to get into, I should have had to put you in a hollow tree or some other safe place. The loose stock started ahead of the wind and ran many miles before it."

After asking them to visit, he then, perhaps imprudently, regaled them with the volatility of the weather, writing, "The extremes of heat and cold follow each other so rapidly." It could be 85 one day, and 32 the next. He continued,

> You have to wear all of your winter clothes then suddenly toss them all aside . . . It's the worst place I ever saw for colds, and not only humans suffer from them but the brutes. I see so many horses sick with a regular quinsy, also the dogs. It lasts them about two weeks, and many horses have died from it this spring. Three of mine have had it, and [if] they don't get their strength, I shall have to leave them.

He reassured them that his inability to get home was not of his own making, but due to work. Perhaps realizing he was not doing a wonderful job enticing his family to visit, he changed the tone, writing, "On the other hand, I like the general appearance of the country, and it must be lovely when the weather is settled. These beautiful lakes with such charming groves by the side of them."

Irish was hoping for a brief lull in the work, but he was not optimistic: "I don't count much on that. . . . Mr. Hughitt the Gen. Manager wants to go with me across to the Mo. river. This all will take 4 weeks or 6 weeks at most, then I shall come home."

Writing from the innocence that comes without hindsight, he declared that he would not, "not for any pay," take on any more winter work. Remember that declaration—it will come up again. There was a possible trip to Deadwood, or possibly even Denver, on business. But "no more winter campaigns" were in his plans.

In the meanwhile, he hoped the women would take advantage of the family passes to either meet him at camp or, if they'd rather, meet him in Sioux City on his trip home, to prolong the visit.

Because the crew would be moving around for a while, his instructions for the foreseeable future were to address the next two letters to him at the Oakwood post office, the next to Canby, Minnesota, then back to Oakwood and so on until further notice. He added, "Should you desire to send me a telegraphic dispatch to come home or for other cause, send it to TJ Nichols Tracy Minn, and Mr. Nichols will send a man with it to me direct. I will write from the [Big] Sioux river tomorrow." It is no wonder that letters sometimes came late or failed to reach him. He must have wondered whether news of Ruth's health was wandering the countryside in the care of someone who couldn't find him.

FLIMSY BUILDINGS

Irish's ruminations on the flimsy, thrown-together buildings were valid. A month into the future, a correspondent from Oakwood would report that a "high gale" had grabbed hold of a twelve-by-eighteen-foot frame house without a floor, tossed it forty feet, and "crushed [it] into fragments." A man was in the house when the storm hit, and when found, he was initially presumed dead, though he was "only severely injured." Graphic descriptions of his injuries were included, and they did not paint a pretty picture. The lesson that the paper wanted to extend to its readers was that "frame houses, especially those without floors, should be firmly secured to the ground."[32]

On Sunday, June 8, Irish and Pay continued west, following the township line and buffeted by a strong, hot wind. "Our horses gave out for want of water," wrote Irish. "We turned around at 2pm having reached the James and Sioux divide." The two built a mound to mark the site, then returned east to settle again at Nielson's Camp; rain fell in the afternoon.

Nearly a century and a half of time and farming have obliterated the mound placed by Irish and Pay where the township line (the "road" visible in this image) met the divide. This photo looks east from the general vicinity of the divide between the Sioux and the James. S3-13

AN EARLY SETTLER'S ENCOUNTER WITH IRISH

In a reminiscence written years later, an early settler of De Smet wrote,

> Shortly after Crater and Ammundson took possession of their claims, R. R. Surveyor Irish with a companion passed through making a bird's eye selection of a route for the road, and soon his whole force, looking like a little army, was surveying westward and back again. The last survey varied but little from the first bend was adopted by the R. R. Company. During the autumn much grading was done and work there on was continued close up to Christmas. A cold snap about the holidays was the only severe weather of the winter of 1879–80.[33]

A check of land records show that George W. Crater held land in T110N 55W S6, which Irish identified as "Camp Nielson," where he and B. E. Pay—the mentioned companion—stayed the night of June 8, 1879.

The rain grew in intensity, lasting throughout the night and into the next morning, making quite the mess of things. "We had a wet time of it," wrote Irish on June 9. The men journeyed eastward in the rain, reaching the main camp along the Big Sioux at 5 p.m.

When the men returned to camp, they found not only that "a rain [had] flooded the camp in the night and the boys looked like drowned rats" (as he later shared in a letter home), but a representative of the *Brookings County Press* (and four of his friends, who may or may not have also been associated with the paper) had stopped by for a visit.

On June 12, the *Brookings County Press* would publish details of the visit made to what the reporter dubbed "Camp Irish," in honor of the "intelligent and entertaining leader" of the surveyors, who were currently camped in the southwest quarter of T110 R50 S18.

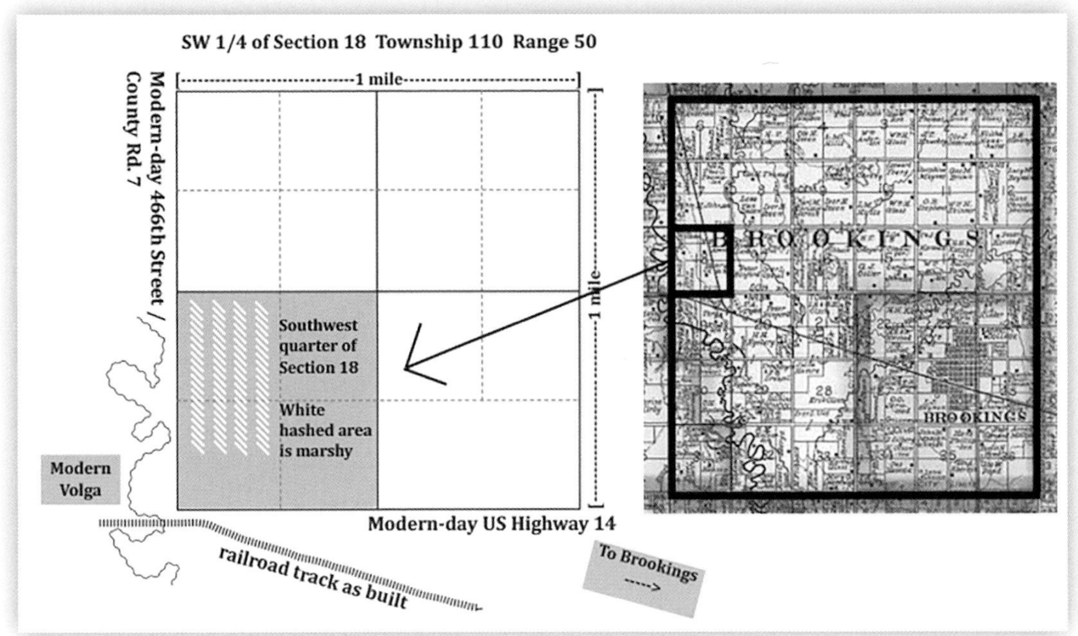

The location of Camp Irish based on an 1897 map of the township. S3-14

The visiting journalist and his friends had not been in camp long before Irish returned, surprising the crew, who had not expected him back so soon, as he had just departed a few days prior, intending to explore the land around the James River. The June 12 article relayed, "[Irish] had passed the center of Kingsbury county when he failed to find water, and the partched tongue and throat admonished him that a retreat would be the better part to act at that critical moment."

The men had been desperately thirsty, and Irish, said the reporter, "related one amusing incident of how he forced water from a well with his Winchester rifle. His team and himself nearly suffocated for [want of] water, he was even refused a bucket full." Not to be deprived of the necessary liquid, Irish told his listeners that "his rifle acted well its part in keeping three men at bay, while his traveling companion, Bryon E. Pay, proceeded to extract the contents of the well not only to the extent of one bucket, but all that was needed."

In the flowery prose of the time, the writer described the camp, the surveyors, and how they had dealt with a significant rainfall the night before:

> In a beautiful little grove near the banks of the silvery Sioux are pitched half a dozen tents. It is a cosy camp and occupied by a jolly company of men. . . . Mr. Irish, although tired with a long drive over the country, lost not a moment in at once proceeding to entertain the 'Visiting Statesmen,' of whom there were five.

A jovial meal followed, including buffalo meat (or so claimed the reporter, though buffalo were long gone from this area). He continued,

> Supper over we took a look about camp and discovered that the rain of the night previous had caused a slight commotion in camp and had lead [*sic*] the boys to inaugurate about their cloth houses one of the most scientific and complete system[s] of excavations known in the code of civil engineering. Nothing, however, saved them for this noble and great mechanical accomplishment but the craftiness of 'Shankland' [Shanklin] and his light canoe. Bravely did he 'rescue the perishing' on that terrible night and kept by his skill and bravery much life and property from jeopardy and destruction.

It is difficult to decipher from this vague insider retelling just what happened at the camp during that rainstorm, though we can surmise that crewmember W. N. Shanklin offered boat rides around the devised system of canals and trenches that drained the water away from the tents.

The article then provided some interesting information about what the surveyors, per Irish, were up to:

> The line is located to the Sioux River. It will cross at this point for beyond here the coteaus are narrowest and I propose to get through them in the quickest possible manner. I have been instructed to look up and survey a line to the Jim [James] river. I am not confined to any bounds or limits but shall run the line wherever I can find the best route. At the same time a line will be run from Watertown west to the Jim. After these two lines are surveyed, we shall compare notes and the best one selected as the main line for the extension. By best I mean best with reference to grades and curvatures. If the north line is built, this point will probably remain the terminus of this branch for the present. This is all I know about it.

Further, readers of the article were informed, "Mr. Irish knows nothing about the location of towns. Mr. Hughitt will be through here in a few days when that matter will be settled."

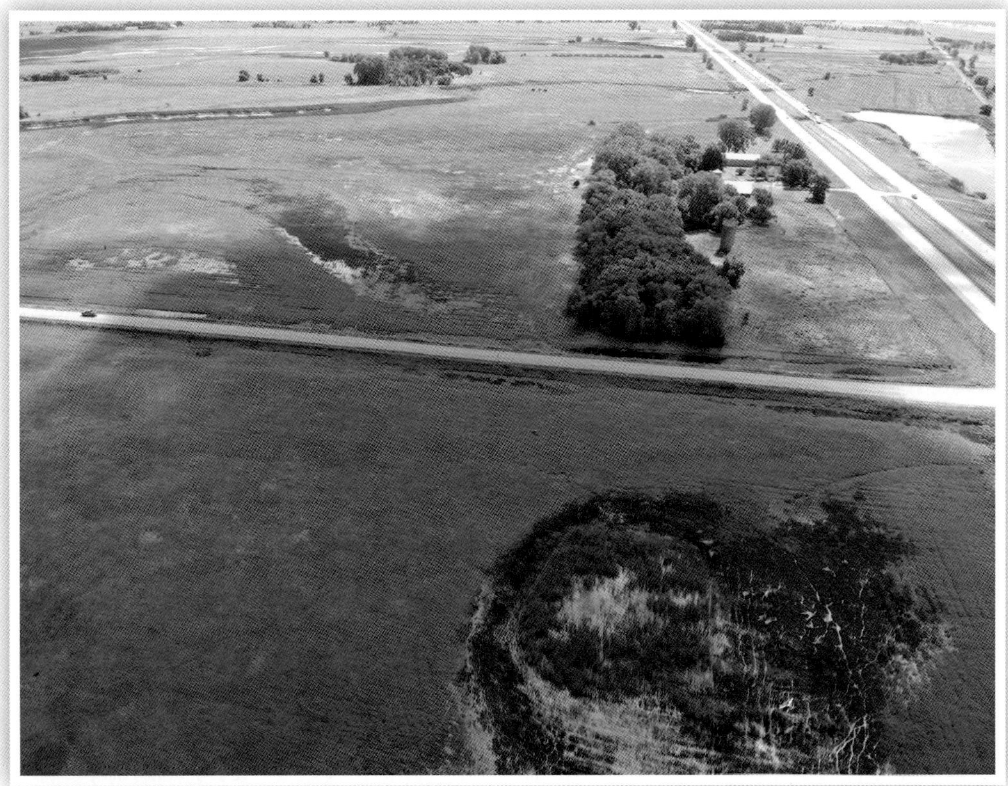

The area in the foreground is the approximate location of "Camp Irish," where the reporter from the *Brookings County Press* visited the surveyors before sharing tales with his readers. This image is from above the Big Sioux, looking east. The roadway along the right edge is US Highway 14. The photo was taken during the wet summer of 2018, and while it's difficult to determine by looking at the photo, what appears to be sandy ground is actually standing water. S3-15

After playing host to the lively reporter and friends, the crew got up early on Tuesday, June 10, and "began a line through the coteaus [west of the Big Sioux] and ran west to the 3 dry lakes." (Those dry lakes were likely what are now—filled with water—Lakes Preston and Whitewood, east of Arlington, and possibly the Twin Lakes, south of Arlington. Today the Twin Lakes and surrounding area are decidedly not dry. In recent years, sustained flooding required a two-and-a-half-mile rebuild of US Highway 81, with the grade being raised an average of two and a half feet.)

Writing to Lizzie from the camp on the Big Sioux, Irish mentioned, "It rained so hard Monday the 9th in [the] morning that the water ran into our camp a foot deep and drowned the men out of bed. They had to sit on the camp stools until daylight. We have not yet got things dry." It is surprising and a little disappointing that the reporter from the *Brookings County Press* did not include this humorous depiction.

It was wasted effort, however, as Irish decided that the route was not satisfactory. The next day, they ran through the "haystack slough" and dry marsh, but upon making some calculations, they discovered that option would require an unacceptably steep grade.

Finally, the tormented father received the letter that told him that Ruth was "so much better." Among the ailments she had suffered while Irish suffered from the lack of information were the mumps. "You must have patience and don't try to get out too soon," he beseeched in his June 11 return letter. He was also beginning to give up on the idea of a trip home, instead simply begging for more letters.

Line attempt number three was conducted on June 12, in the rain. This route proved successful, yielding a nearly flat grade, and they were able to mark out almost eight miles of this favorable path. The next day resulted in another five miles of line. Despite the productive work, it was "a most disagreeable day" due to heavy rains.

Camp Irish—On the Sioux.

News from any one in authority in the Chicago & Northwestern Company is always in demand. This week early we made a trip to the Big Sioux. On the south-west quarter of section 18, township 110, range 50, are the present headquarters of the surveying party, which in honor of their intelligent and entertaining leader we propose to call "Camp Irish." In a beautiful little grove near the banks of the silvery Sioux are pitched half a dozen tents. It is a cosy camp and occupied by a jolly company of men. Shortly after our arrival in camp, Mr. Irish rode in, to the surprise of all, as he had started but a few days before for the Jim river. He had passed the center of Kingsbury county when he failed to find water and the partched tongue and throat admonished him that a retreat would be the better part to act at that critical moment. He related one amusing incident of how he forced water from a well with his Winchester rifle. His team and himself nearly suffocated for water, he was even refused a bucket full. His rifle acted well its part in keeping three men at bay, while his traveling companion, Byron E. Pay, proceeded to extract the contents of the well not only to the extent of one bucket, but all that was needed.

Mr. Irish, although tired with a long drive over the country, lost not a moment in at once proceeding to entertain the "Visiting Statesmen," of whom there were five. And while he was thus offering us interesting and occasional amusing entertainment, his cook was exerting himself in another direction, preparing an entertainment that we all relished, and which was announced upon the bills as "supper!" The "Visiting Statesmen" were given a seat in a row and made a hearty meal

S3-16

ANTICIPATING A COMING HARVEST

On June 12, the *Brookings County Press* noted so much sod being turned over in the county that the next year's crop yield would be "immense."[34] This is an interesting piece considering that the referenced crop would be the one to help sustain the settlers affected by the railroad snow blockades during the Hard Winter of 1880–81. Trains would be unable to deliver needed food and fuel from mid-January until late April 1881, leaving thousands of people in new railroad towns throughout southwestern Minnesota and eastern Dakota Territory destitute as they endured blizzard after blizzard.

While looking forward to this upcoming crop, there was also some mourning for the current crop. The recent hail and wind had left affected crops "hardly worth gathering up," though, true to Dakota boosterism, some of the farmers "went to work and raked and scraped together what straw there was left on the fields." Even these leftovers in Dakota Territory, they claimed, comprised a harvest equal to those of farmers "in the most favored localities" in Minnesota and Iowa.[35]

For deeper details about the Hard Winter, see *The Beautiful Snow: The Ingalls Family, the Railroads, and the Hard Winter of 1880–81.*

The rain continued until the afternoon of June 14, tormenting the crew as they moved their entire camp west to the lakes, which are unidentified in the diary but were likely the "dry lakes" somewhere near the eastern edge of Lake Preston. It was relatively early in the day to settle into camp, compared to their usual working hours, but due to the "most discouraging storm," they decided to stop. One tent was set up, and everyone moved into it. "Rain! Rain!" was Irish's notation to describe the situation.

On June 14, the eve of a twenty-six-mile camp move away from Big Sioux Camp, Irish scrawled out another quick letter. The last two days had featured "very hard rains," but he was "feeling quite well" after hearing that Ruth was better. He included a newspaper clipping, calling it "an account of our camp which I wish Uncle John would print in full." It was likely the article from the *Brookings County Press*. (Irish's brother, John P. Irish, was in charge of Iowa City's *Iowa State Press*. Irish was finding various ways to get his name into print to help foster his résumé, and this was one of those channels.)

The Lakes to the West: June 15–20, 1879

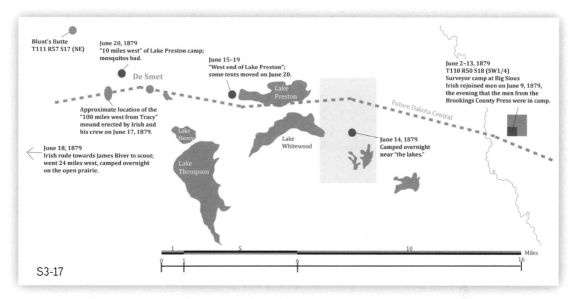

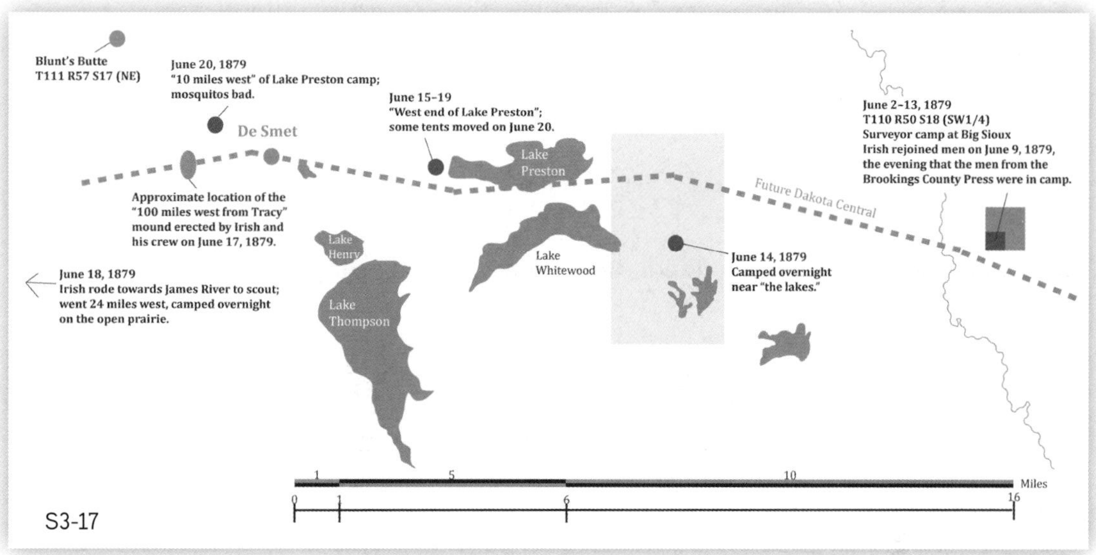

And still it rained, with the lovely addition of a "heavy gale" from the northwest. Nonetheless, the crew got up early on the fifteenth and continued westward into a "mist so thick that [they] could not see half a mile." It was most unpleasant travel, though the storm "cleared up some" around noon. Two hours later, the troupe reached their next camp, on the west end of Lake Preston.

After the new campsite was situated at Lake Preston, Irish penned a quick note to his wife:

> I send to the RR this day two sacks, one of which contains my heavy and worn clothes. The other feathers. The lot in the big sack, Joe picked off of the choice birds . . . I have stopped the boys [from] shooting birds as they are all nesting now. This lot contains about all the kinds that run these prairies.

The move west represented "one notch further towards the end." And, despite the "very heavy rains the past week," it remained difficult to find water. He was suffering from severe homesickness, writing, "Only duty to you and the girls keeps me here together with a desire to carry out what I have undertaken." It must have been difficult to send the packages rather than delivering them himself.

The crew was worn out from their difficult trek through the rain, but the work had to continue. On June 16, they successfully ran nine and a half miles. The next day, in a strong southeast wind, they ran an additional eight and a half miles, which tallied a total of 100 miles beyond Tracy. To commemorate the location, they built a "large mound." Using today's track as the base, that location is just east of the Silver Lake waterfowl production area, almost to De Smet. (In a straight line, one hundred miles beyond Tracy would be about four and a half miles west of De Smet.) They returned to camp feeling triumphant, ready to move camp again the next day, June 18, the men all healthy, excepting Dunlap.

MOUND BUILDING

When the land itself was being surveyed, especially before the prairies were encountered, it was common for locations—such as section corners—to be marked by blazing a tree (chopping a mark into the bark). Survey teams included axmen, who were responsible for clearing away brush and trees to make a clean line for the chainmen to do their work. On the treeless prairie, these axmen were called moundmen, as mounds would be built at important locations instead. There was also plenty of brush for them to remove with their axes, as Irish stated in his diaries.[36]

The camp move did not take long, reaching the new site by noon. Irish, J. S. Nettiburgh, and I. E. Segur went west on horseback to explore the region between camp and the James River. They rode twenty-four miles, in the process seeing several antelope and mistaking a herd of elk for a group of Dakota. The men camped on the prairie overnight, then returned to the main camp the morning of June 19 in a heavy rain that turned the camp into a muddy mess. When the rain stopped around 1 p.m., they were able to run three and a half miles of route before being chased back to camp again by more rain.

The June 19 edition of the *Brookings County Press* had multiple updates about the progress of railroad construction along the first miles of the survey. Most exciting perhaps was that there was a locomotive running on the tracks west of Tracy,[37] just weeks after graders had begun their work. This engine was supporting the track builders, but that didn't stop the editors from claiming that trains would be running to Lake Benton within the month and to the Big Sioux by mid-August. Their projections were off by several months on both counts, but they can be forgiven their excitement.

The *Press* also reprinted a piece from the *Marshfield Tribune*, meaning the information could have been a week or so old at time of printing, but it still provided some interesting details about what was going on at the beginning of the line. The editor had spoken with Hiram Forbes, who held the contract for ten miles to the east of Lake Benton, with "one hundred and forty teams and four hundred men."[38] Once that segment was complete, his next portion was the twenty miles to the west of the Big Sioux. This combined with Stowe's subcontract gives us a glimpse of how the railroad company broke up sections of the job, allowing some leapfrogging of the heavier work to take place.

Upon returning from the James through a hard rain, Irish was able to report on June 19 that all were well except Dunlap, who was suffering a fever. Irish likely planned to dose him with quinine, telling his family he would "cure him soon."

The camp was now well west of the Big Sioux, so he reassured his family not to be concerned if they received no letters from him over the next few weeks, as they were "out of reach of mails." He asked them to write plenty, though, and direct them to Watertown.

In a separate addition to the letter, he addressed his wife with comfort. She was caretaking at the "inevitable close of poor Louisa's life." He was concerned about the work and worry Abbie was going through in tending to Louisa, as well as the grief—he ached that he could not be there to support his wife. "You do not know how I dread opening [each] letter," he wrote, fearing that the next letter would hold the news of Louisa's passing. He commended her for comforting Louisa, writing, "That is all that you can do. Tell her that I think of her each day."

On the morning of Friday, June 20, part of the camp party moved westward as the surveyors ran another ten or eleven miles of route, at which point they decided to camp. Nearby was a "fine lonely butte," which they named Blunt's Butte, after their chief engineer. To commemorate the occasion, they created a time capsule of sorts, burying a bottle of whiskey along with the names of the men in the party and a copy of the *Chicago Times*. The bottle being full, it wasn't too many years before someone sought out its contents.

TIME CAPSULE UNCOVERED

Less than a decade after the time capsule was buried, the May 21, 1887, *Manchester Times* regaled its readers with the tale of a successful treasure hunt. It was C. H. Manchester himself—the town's namesake, one of two early settlers in the area[39]—who, having heard a rumor, was determined to find the bottle buried by the surveyors. Returning home from Spirit Lake, he "drove to the Butte and dug into the mound with the intention of possessing the spirits or disproving the statement." By then, the mound was "badly delapidated [*sic*]," and he dug a mere eighteen inches before striking pay dirt. He found the bottle oriented cork down, as any good whiskey connoisseur would have placed it. It and the paper listing the members of the party were "wrapped in a *Chicago Times*, dated May 27, 1879, and tied securely with a string."[40] The document read,

> This Butte is 110 miles from Tracy.
>
> This is a memorandum of an engineer's party at work surveying a line through Dakota for the Chicago and Northwestern railroad. We began work at Tracy, Minnesota on March 20th, 1879.—Have to

this date surveyed and located 70 miles of line from Tracy to the Big Sioux River and now we are on our way to the James River. We take the liberty to christen this beautiful mound, "Blunt's Butte," in honor of our Chief Engineer, J. E. Blunt, Esq. of the Winona & St. Peter Railroad Company.

The names of the party are as follows:

C. W. Irish, D. C. Dunlap, P. Powers, C. J. Hutchinson, A. J. Hughitt, C. J. Carse, L. Christianson, O. N. Hughitt, Joe Mudree [Mudra], E. S. Miller, H. M. Latio, G. Styers, W. N. Shanklin, G. W. Thorn, J. DeBarr, F. S. Meyers, I. E. Segur, W. C. Cole, I. D. Collins, I. M. Leighton, J. S. Nettiburgh.

We were visited by Mr. B. E. Pay from Oakwood, to-day, who brought with him letters from home. . . . This was done on the 20th day of June, 1879.

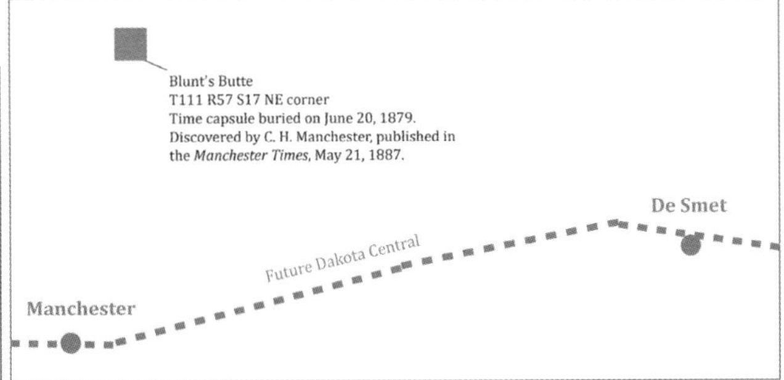

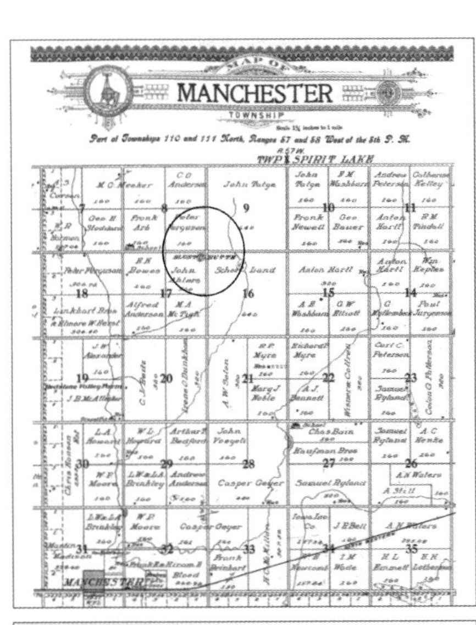

FRIDAY 20

Pulled up 1-2 & 3 tents left
4 tent and moved the
camp as we ran
10 miles west. The party
ran 11 miles. We camp
at a tank of water. as we
came on named a fine
lonely Butte after Mr Blunt
buried a glass bottle with
names of party & copy of Chicag

S3-18

The fun, companionable time commemorating Blunt's Butte disintegrated into a fight against one of mankind's greatest foes: mosquitos. After burying the mementos, Irish and Nettiburgh had continued west, then slept on the prairie with just blankets (no tents). The mosquitos "were dreadful," wrote Irish. "My horse acted so bad that I had to sit up with him all night."

The next morning, they moved "past an alkaline lake," making camp on the banks of the James River. The previous night's battle with mosquitos would be just the first of many.

Section Four

MOSQUITOS, THE JAMES RIVER, AND THE WESSINGTON HILLS

JUNE 21–AUGUST 19, 1879

The work to establish a route from the Big Sioux to the Missouri was well underway, and more was coming. The Chicago & North Western asked Irish and his crew to work on an additional survey—simultaneously—a request that had them moving back and forth. Much of the time was spent fleeing the torments of the early-summer mosquito bloom, in an area flush with sloughs, even if it was a "dry year." The extra work, mosquitos, weather, lack of easily found or potable water, heat, smoky skies, and news of a family death all made the time plod by for Irish. The company agreed to hire a second surveyor and crew for the second job, but Irish was assured by the officers that he and his crew had job security. The work was going well, and area towns were excitedly anticipating the coming of the rails.

Mosquito-Infested Sloughs and West to the James: June 21–26, 1879

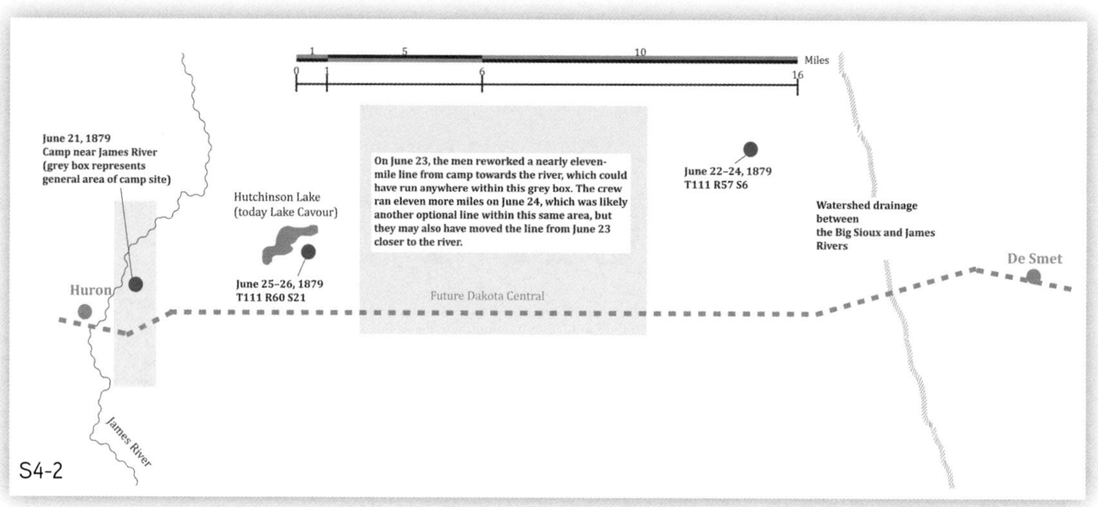

After another restless night fighting off the mosquitos, Irish and Nettiburgh headed back to the main camp, arriving six hours later, into the company of officers Hughitt and Blunt, who were waiting for them. "I am very tired," wrote Irish in his diary to finish the day. "They [Hughitt and Blunt] are about to leave for [the] east. Talked over the situation, got orders, and went to bed," read the entry in Irish's diary to finish the day. "We are to back up and run 70 feet N of [township] line to [the James] river." This set the line to its built location, south of where the men had been taking readings.

After a good night's sleep, most of the crew were up and at it the next morning, June 23, reworking a previous run. They "backed up 10 miles to [the] east side of the divide" (between the Big Sioux and James Rivers, the divide being just west of De Smet) and ran a different route of 10.75 miles. While the crew worked on the alternate route, Irish remained in camp, though his work was interrupted by "visitors looking up land," potential homesteaders investigating options.

From their camp "110 miles west from Tracy," on June 23, Irish happily reported he had escorted Hughitt and Blunt out to the James River and back and that the pair had returned east that morning. He further declared that in just three weeks, he would be allowed a furlough—the long-awaited trip home was on the horizon. He again begged his family to meet him in Sioux City, to prolong the visit.

There was more joyous news to share. The officers told him that he was now employed at this surveying task for all the next year. "They are sick of their other men," he wrote. "The man they sent to Watertown has been 3 weeks running 35 miles. While I have run 42 miles in the last three days!!" While Irish was running himself (and his team) ragged, he hoped that his family was not doing the same to themselves.

Keeping the women up on Dunlap's attempt to get his wife to board in Marshall and thus be near camp, Irish reported that her new plan was to come "with her sister [Irish's underline]," which evidently was not as pleasing to Dunlap. This segued into Irish's mention of the wild rose he'd included with the letter in the hope it would "retain its color and scent until it [arrived]."

A terrific storm hit at 4 a.m. on Tuesday, June 24, blowing down the two main camp tents, turning "their occupants out in the storm to hold them [the tents]." Irish's tent nearly blew down. After the storm dissipated, the crew was again out on the line, accomplishing another eleven miles of route measurements and readings.

On the twenty-fifth, camp was again moved, this time to Hutchinson Lake, north of modern-day Cavour (today, this fairly dry spot is called Lake Cavour). Disappointingly, and despite being "a fine body of water," the lake was so salty that the men became ill after drinking from it. Attempts to dig wells found water no more suitable. As a result, some of the men were sent about six miles west to the James River to retrieve water. Not only was Hutchinson Lake too salty to drink, but it smelled—horribly.

Exploring to the North: June 27–July 5, 1879

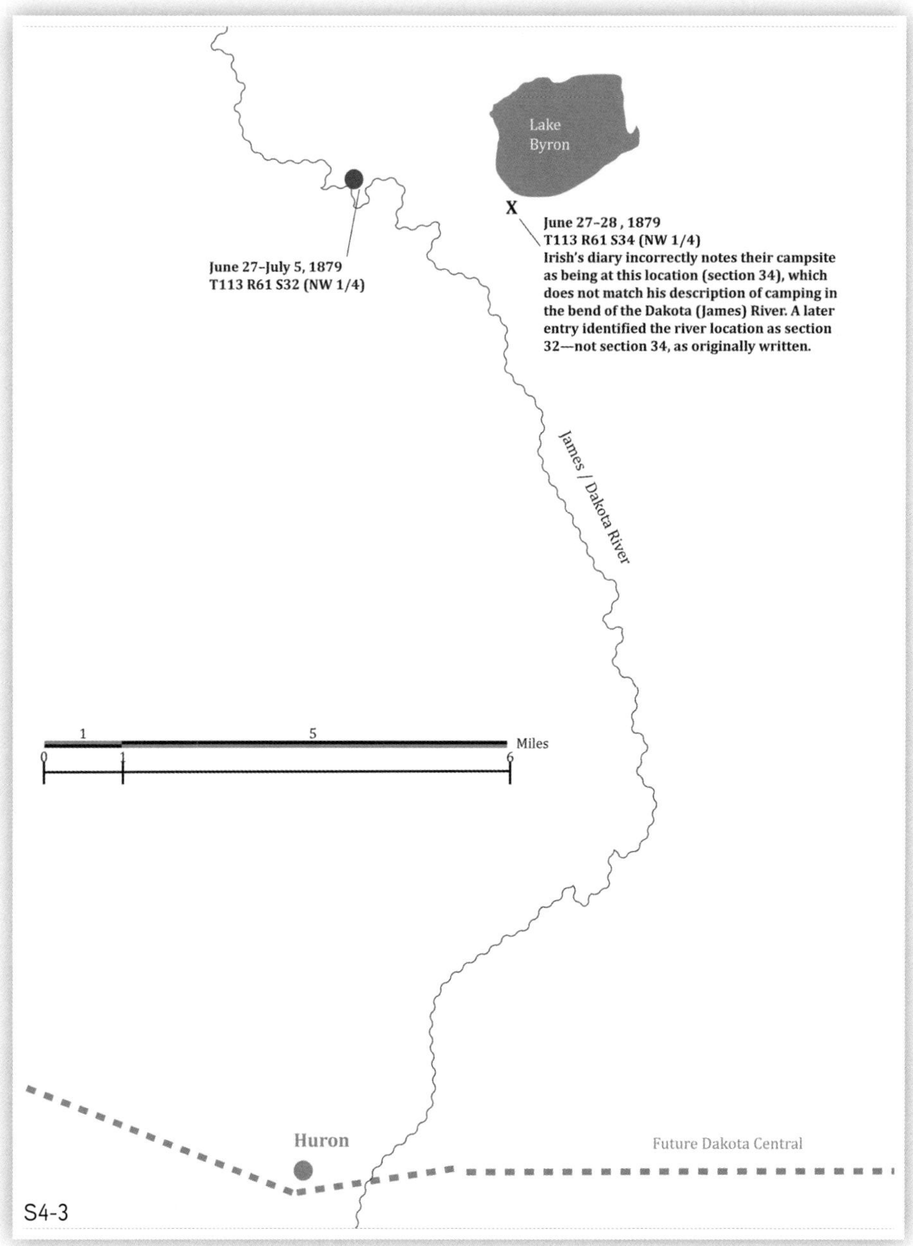

On June 27, after two days of heavy rain, the men pulled up camp, then set to their daily work on the way to a better campsite. The weather was good, and the men felt well and healthy. After running ten miles of line, they settled into the new camp, this one in a bend of the James (at the time also called the Dakota River), about thirteen miles north of the route that would eventually be finalized.

The new campsite was approximately where the barn structure is in the upper-left corner of this modern-day photo. S4-4

On the home front, Mrs. Irish reported that the beehive set up to nurture a stock of honey had not quite worked out as planned. The bees had simply up and gone. There would be no honey, and Irish was disappointed to hear it.

Hughitt and Blunt had again visited camp, and Hughitt observed that as Irish hadn't had time to write to the company concerning the passes for Abbie and the girls, Hughitt himself would take care of the matter. "I suppose he has done [it] by this time," wrote Irish on June 27. "It will pass you and the girls any where on the C&NW Ry if he wrote it as he said he would." Having free railway passes across the entire Chicago & North Western rail system was no small benefit, and that the head man himself was willing to arrange for it speaks volumes about his respect for Irish. With the passes, they could go anywhere, but Irish hoped they would choose to visit him.

He shared a little vignette from camp life on the James River:

> There are three men in the level party and two of them saw the antelope, and one shot at him 5 times, then Charley [Hutchinson] came and took the gun and killed him the first shot. The whole camp were rejoiced, as we had lived on salt meat so long. Charley is a hero now. Beg John [Irish's brother, editor of the Iowa City newspaper] to make a paragraph of it and send him [Charley] a paper.

The meal of antelope was the good side of camp life. The next paragraph was the other side:

> We have a real good time in camp except when it storms. Last Tuesday morning a severe gale of wind and a rain storm struck us.

> It blew down two of the tents. The one I am in came near going but we held it. The time was 2 o'clock in the morning. I looked out of my tent and saw the big one going off, Old Joe with two others [holding] the ropes, pulling back. They had only shirts on. The others had just raised up in bed and caught the curtain of the tent as it passed, and they slid along the ground in a sitting posture, the tent [acting] like a sail on a boat. They were badly scared but now have many a hearty laugh over it. So it goes in camp life. What scares you one day you laugh at the next.

He let the family know that he hoped to receive a passel of letters from home, though he'd soon be meeting up with the other surveyor to talk about the parallel surveys and a way to join the two lines together to reach the Missouri River.

The crew was up early the next morning, successfully surveying another 13.25 miles of route. It was a hot day, with temperatures around 90 degrees, but they were "in good spirits."

The next day, Sunday, June 29, they "did chores about camp," many of them "mending." June 30 was windy but still productive, resulting in another "18 miles 1700 feet with the chain and 15 miles 1300 feet with the level." Although he was "quite sick" that morning, Irish still found the energy to ride out to the dirt lodges with C. H. Meyers.

The night was spent in a shanty "1 mile east of the old dirt lodges where the medicine stone of the Yanktons and Brules is. . . ." Irish was a curious man and wanted to see the abandoned lodges of the local Native peoples for himself, having learned about them from his own readings and conversations. Heavy rains fell overnight, making the respite of the shanty even more welcome.

Note: Because the Dirt Lodges comprise a protected archaeological site, their location is not included on the map nor described in anything but general terms here. In centuries past, and where timber was available, these lodging structures were built using poles and sod, providing additional protection for the peoples of the Plains during the coldest months of the year.[41] *An internet search for the phrase "earth lodges of Spink County" will give you an idea of what they may have looked like.*

PARALLEL SURVEYS—AN EXPLANATION

To flesh out the issue of the parallel survey, let's step back a few paces. In 1857, the amended charter for the railroad line that eventually included both the Winona & St. Peter and Dakota Central was granted "full power and authority to extend its line of railroad from its terminus on the Big Sioux river to any point on the Missouri river, south of the forty-fifth parallel of north latitude,"[42] giving the Chicago & North Western a wide palette upon which to route their tracks.

Furthermore, since Brookings (via the Dakota Central) and Watertown (via the Winona & St. Peter) were both on the banks of the Big Sioux River, they were equal candidates for the eventual main line that pushed on to the Missouri.

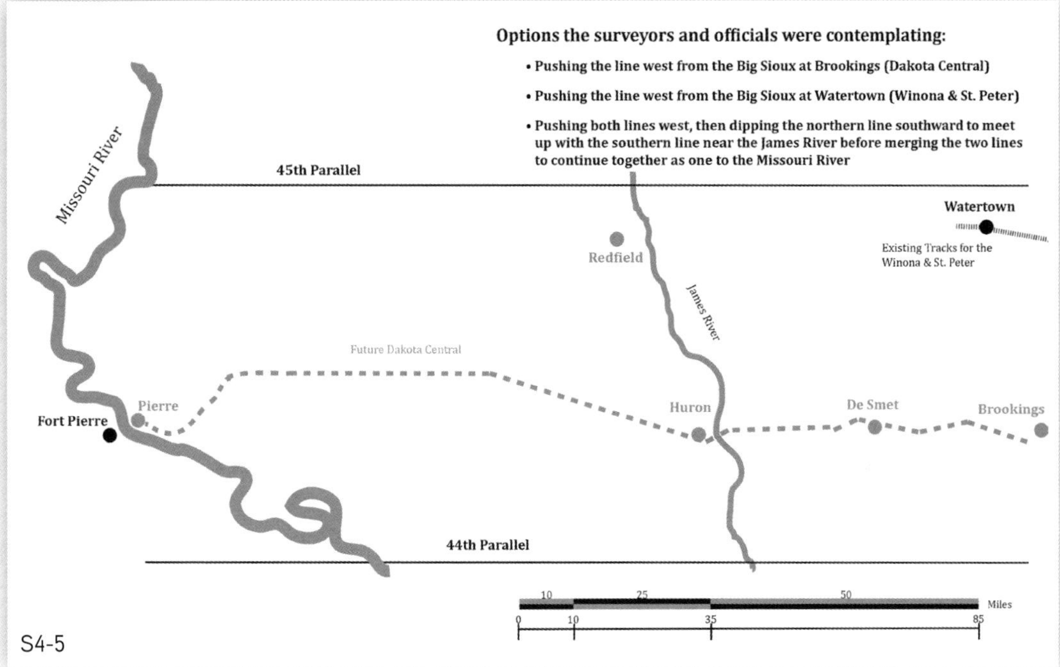

The indecision on whether Brookings or Watertown would remain the terminus for this round of track laying was a cause of great concern among the newspaper editors at both locations. If only one line was selected, the other town would languish, at least for the time being. The selected town would soon embark upon exuberant, excited, and enthusiastic growth, both in population and in prosperity. The "hurry up and wait" uncertainty must have been maddening for those champing at the bit to put down roots in the best location—the one served by the new railroad. But to make the decision about which route to invest in, the officers needed more information.

In a May 3 letter, Irish told Ruth of his orders (information that was not included in the May 3 summary in the last chapter, but the reader should know that he knew of this work by early May). "Shall begin the location and run west to the Big Sioux again," he wrote. "Then I shall go on to the James river, and begin at Lake Campeska [Kampeska] and run out to the James, joining lines and then run to the Mo. river at the mouth of the Big Cheyenne."

He reiterated those orders in a letter to his wife, written on May 25. After the trip for this side survey, he hoped to make it home. "It makes me tired to think of those weary miles," he wrote. "I shall have 25 men with me. If the good lord or some one else will help me, I shall run home before I go to the Mo.

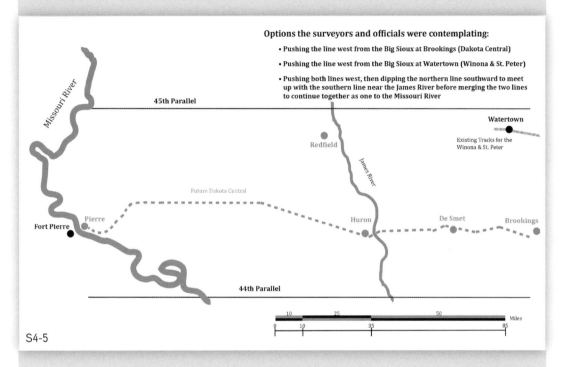

river." He had been subsequently and gratefully relieved of the northern portion of that duty by a second surveyor hired to handle that work, as shared by his letter home on June 4.

The June 18 *New Ulm Weekly Review* added more speculation into the soup by publishing that a "corps of engineers" (surveyors) under the employ of the Chicago & North Western were making a "preliminary survey from Watertown west [in preparation for] extending the road to Bismarck" in the northern portion of Dakota Territory. This was a reference to the long-planned-for route to connect the Winona & St. Peter with the Northern Pacific. That dream, still percolating for the officers, was interrupted by the economic shambles of the Panic of 1873.

Speculation about which single route the Chicago & North Western would invest in (west from Brookings via the Dakota Central or west from Watertown via the Winona & St. Peter) was at a high pitch at this point. The *Brookings County Press* published frequent—and hopeful—squibs and sentences which seemed to speculatively semi-confirm information heard via both rumor and legitimate conversation.

Further emphasizing the constant flux of information (and rumor), the August 27 *New Ulm Weekly Review* shared that the *Winona Republican* had "information from a pretty reliable source" that the line from Tracy would be pushed to the Missouri River near Fort Pierre, "just north of the Sioux reservation, and on a direct line to Deadwood."[43] Eventually, confirmation came that Brookings could celebrate its location along the chosen route.

At 3 p.m. the next afternoon, July 2, Irish and C. H. Meyers left the dirt-lodge area and returned to the main camp. However, the heavy rains had caused a creek to rise, and they "had much trouble to get across," not only due to the rushing water but because of increasing darkness. Once across the troublesome waters, they continued over the dark prairies in the rain, arriving in camp at 4 a.m., "all tired out."

Thursday, July 3, was spent resting in camp, dealing with heavy mud after all-night rainfall that continued into the day. Irish declared that they were "tired of rain now," but spirits were significantly lifted by the successful hunt of a "fine buck antelope," which meant a fine meal.

Rains had not only been heavy in the vicinity of the James and Big Sioux Rivers. The *Brookings County Press* let its readers know that "the Missouri is on a bender," having risen eighteen inches overnight.[44]

While the rest of the country was celebrating Independence Day, the survey team enjoyed the "fine hot day" by working on the maps and profiles for the routes they'd recently completed, then spent the afternoon entertaining themselves with a shooting match. "Did poor shooting all around," shared Irish, but it was a fun and relaxing day nonetheless.

A special treat also appeared in the form of the mail carrier, who arrived via horseback, "tired out and hungry." He brought news of "recent Indian troubles" and was "quite scared." Surveying parties for other railroads had, according to various newspaper articles, experienced different levels of encounters—from being told to turn around, to having their marking stakes pulled up, to being killed. This was not an insignificant bit of information.

Irish was an intelligent, steady man, not given to overreacting; he was not dismissive either. He likely tucked away the information and remained vigilant. Two days later, during an in-camp day, the crew "fixed up the rifles!" One can assume this was regular maintenance and cleaning tasks, so that the guns were in top condition.

On July 5, the team ran thirteen more miles of chain, to the vicinity of an alkaline lake. It was difficult work due to a "violent gale from the SE all day," and Irish was concerned that the camp would need to move again before the next rain.

FEARS FOR THE SURVEYORS

Weeks into the future, on July 31, 1879, the *Yankton Daily Press and Dakotaian* republished a July 24 piece from the *Brookings County Press* that read,

> It is reported that the Indians attacked and killed two of the Chicago, Milwaukee & St. Paul [the line running south of the Dakota Central by about twenty-five miles] surveying party, just after they crossed the Jim [James] river and that they refuse to allow any one to cross the country there. They pull up stakes and destroy all trace of the line as soon as surveyed.—Capt. Irish and his party have left for the Jim and will proceed to run a line from that river to the Missouri at once. Mr. Irish took twenty-five men along with him as guards. The Indians are reported quite numerous and hostile in that part of the country and preparing to prevent any party crossing the country there. Irish's men are all armed with Henry rifles."[45]

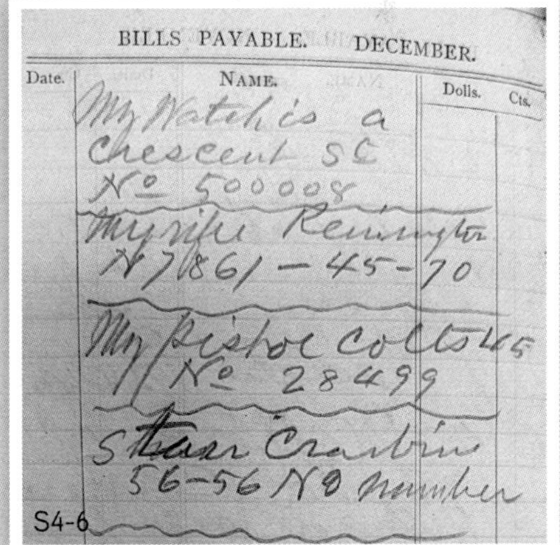
BILLS PAYABLE. DECEMBER.
Date. Name. Dolls. Cts.
My Watch is a Crescent SC No 500008
My rifle Remington N 7861 — 45-70
My pistol Colt 45 No 28499
Starr Carbine 56-56 No number

S4-6

S4-7

We of course cannot know all of the various weapons that the crew carried along with them throughout the two-year operation. However, early in his planning, Irish recorded in one of his ledgers some of the specific weapons he himself was taking. One rifle was a .45-70 Remington (serial number 7861-45-70), the other a .44 Winchester. His pistol was a .45 Colt (serial number 28499), and he also had a .56-56 Starr carbine.

Heading Back East and Battling Mosquitos: July 6–13, 1879

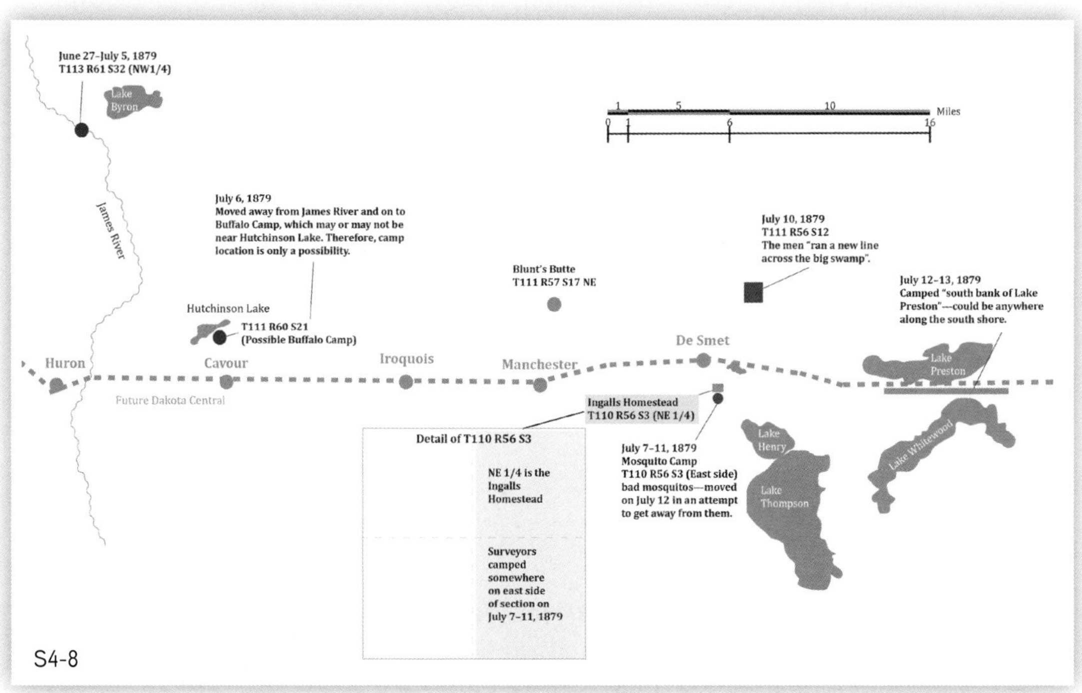

Camp moved east the next day. It was unpleasant work, as "the heat was intense" from 8 a.m. to 7 p.m., reaching at least 93 degrees. The new camp, possibly the same one they'd stayed at near Hutchinson Lake, was named Buffalo Camp.

Buffalo may have been a better problem to have. What they fought instead was an airborne plague of mosquitos in part brought on by the perfect breeding conditions of the frequent heavy rains. "Had the worst mosquito fight yet," wrote Irish. "Hardly an eye closed last night. The dew was also heavy." To top it off, Irish and Dunlap slept outdoors, which must have been nothing short of miserable.

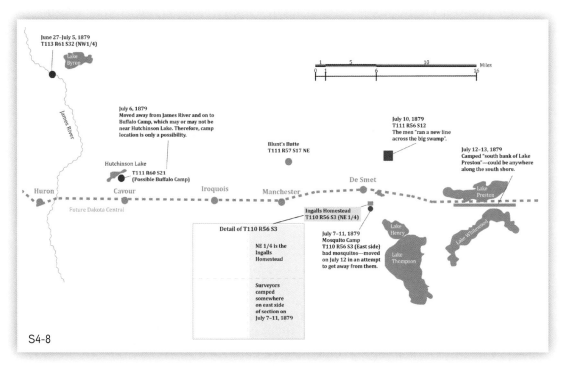

This modern map does a good job of showing the wetlands to the east of modern Huron, including around the lake where the men were camping. With rains, this entire area is a mosquito hatchery. S4-9

The next morning, July 7, the men continued eastward, passed Blunt's Butte, and camped after a pleasant day on the east side of Section 3, Township 110, Range 56. (This plot would, not too many months off, also catch the attention of Charles Ingalls, who would soon file to homestead the northeast quarter of Section 3.)

Irish sent the teams (wagons with horses) back to haul the remainder of camp to their new site, and they returned on the eighth. Once the entire party was reassembled, they were treated to a "beautiful meteor" which fell from east to southwest and was, visually, comparable in size to the planet Venus.

This new camp wasn't any more successful in terms of sleep than the last. "We had a hard night from mosquitoes," read his entry for July 9, relating the torture of the previous night. Not only that, but it was hot: 98 degrees at 10 a.m., 98 at 4 p.m.

Two of the crew members, Thorn and Meyers (he does not mention which Meyers, C. H. or F. S.), were sent to different locations to obtain supplies (Thorn to Goodwin and Meyers to Oakwood), while Irish himself continued east to Lake Preston. The two runners returned to camp at 11 p.m., where they encountered a strong windstorm that came in from the north and caused a significant and welcome drop in temperature. Work began a little late the next day (perhaps they allowed themselves a little extra rest in the wake of the heat and mosquitos?) when the men "ran a new line across the big swamp" about four and a quarter miles northeast of present-day De Smet (the southeastern lobe of the Muser Waterfowl Production Area).

Recent heavy rains were mentioned in a correspondence to the *Brookings County Press*, and the writer reported the Big Sioux had risen eight feet near

Flandreau.[46] That kind of rainfall and runoff would have left mosquito nurseries all over the prairie; their larvae hatch one to two days after being laid. The stage was set for more misery.

By July 10, the surveyors were recalculating options for getting across the Lake Preston area, ahead of the graders and tracklayers who had been at work on the eastern end of the line since late May. In fact, the tracklayers had caught up to the graders and were helping them shovel dirt in the eastern portion of Brookings County.[47] Irish was likely feeling an urgency to get this portion of the survey completed.

At noon on the tenth, Hughitt and Blunt appeared in camp with "a change of programme." They did not stay long, departing at 3 a.m. the following morning. As evidenced throughout the diaries, such early or late departures or arrivals were not uncommon, possibly due to train schedules farther east. It is not difficult to speculate, however, that the 3 a.m. departure had more to do with fleeing the mosquito-infested camp. Immediately after noting the early-hour departure, Irish added, "The mosquitoes were so thick that no one got rest in camp last night."

CONTRACTOR PROGRESS AND CHARLES P. INGALLS

The graders were making fast progress. While the surveyors were working between the Big Sioux and James Rivers, the graders were progressing from Lake Benton to the Big Sioux.

The July 10 *Brookings County Press* reported, "Mr. Forbes, who has been doing some heavy work at Lake Benton, has nearly completed his work and sent about fifty of his men further west. The dirt is flying fast. Trains are expected to be running to Hughitt [Lake Benton] by August 1st."[48] (As sometimes happened, exuberance overcame reality. Trains would not actually reach Lake Benton until mid-September, despite a steady work pace.)

It is not known whether C. P. Ingalls stayed on at the Lake Benton site or whether he was among the fifty or so who moved west when Forbes sent his employees onward. In each version of Wilder's autobiography, Charles stayed behind with Hiram Forbes at the Big Sioux Camp after others moved on, in order to settle accounts. He may have done the same at Lake Benton.

In either case, two weeks later, the July 24 *Brookings County Press* reported, "There is a scarcity of railroad work in this vicinity now, they having gone [back] to Benton to help Mr. Forbes out on his contract there which has to be done this week. They will then return to push the work here." It appears that after having sent many of his employees west in early July, Forbes called them back to help finish up duties in the Lake Benton area.

As Forbes's crew was working between Lake Benton in Minnesota and the Big Sioux in Dakota Territory, the "Walnut Station Items" portion of the July 24 *Redwood County Gazette* (in Minnesota) reported, "C. P. Ingalls, who is taking charge of a gang of men near Lake Benton, made a visit to town last night and reports work progressing rapidly and thinks in a short time trains will run to Lake Benton." The notation about Ingalls "taking charge of a gang of men" is intriguing. Had his role expanded beyond the storekeeper, bookkeeper, and timekeeper duties that he himself recorded? (Walnut Station, where the Ingalls family lived at the time, was the original name for the train stop that became the town of Walnut Grove. The two names were used interchangeably in these early years of the town.)

Despite having little or no sleep, the men "began [their] turn around Lake Preston." The day was hot, or as Irish described it, "perishingly" so, pressing in on the men at 98 degrees again for five hours straight at the height of the day.

The "change of programme" that Hughitt and Blunt had delivered days earlier concerned Lake Preston, to the east of the present camp. As Irish observed, it was a dry lake and had been "for many years." He says nothing else about the issue, though it would be something he would think of in the years to come.

DISASTER AVERTED

In that "change of programme" Hughitt and Blunt presented to Irish, the officers likely wanted a more direct route through dry Lake Preston. Irish advocated for a more cautious—but more expensive—detour. Irish prevailed, though the event and outcome evidently weighed on him.

The post-winter melt in March and April 1881 caused a relatively permanent alteration in the landscape of the Prairie Pothole Region of Dakota Territory. In 1884, three years after the Hard Winter, Irish wrote a letter to legendary explorer John C. Frémont, inquiring about lakes throughout east-central Dakota Territory. It read,

> When I constructed the Dakota Central Railway in 1879–80, all these lakes excepting Thompson, Poinsett, and Kampeska, were dry; and it took me a long time and no small research to ascertain when they last held water. They had been known to be dry for the twenty-five years preceding 1879, or at least persons who had lived there or in the vicinity for twenty-five years said that the lakes were dry when they came into the locality, and had, with numerous smaller ones, been dry ever since; and all who knew about them had a theory that they had dried up long since, and that they never would fill again; but I found an old Frenchman who had seen these lakes full of water in 1843–46, and I, in studying over the matter, found that you had seen and named them in 1836–38, and I would thank you very much if you will take the time and trouble to describe them to me as you saw them.
>
> I came very near locating the railroad line through Lake Preston, for the head men of the railroad company believed that it had dried up for all time; but on my presenting the testimony of certain

> reliable voyagers, they allowed me to go around it. It was well that they did, for the winter of 1880–81 gave a snow-fall such as had not been seen since the years 1843–44, and in the spring of 1881, all these lakes filled up, bank full, and have continued so ever since.[49]

It is obvious that the officers respected Irish's investigations and were persuaded by his arguments, and that likely saved them a great deal of money and trouble in the long run.

The marshy area near camp—what would become known as the Big Slough in the later Little House novels, near the eventual Ingalls homestead—was (and remains) a haven for mosquitos, which Irish said "swarmed by the millions above [their] tents." He added, "It pains me to hear the men and horses groan all night from such torment." So, possibly with great relief, they moved camp on July 12 to the south bank of Lake Preston, enduring another difficult creek crossing in the process.

The next day, July 13, was "a fine hot summer day," and the crew prepared to rework the survey as quickly as possible. Things were drying up; to find water to drink, they had to "dig 8 feet . . . where 4 feet" sufficed before.

Even Farther East and Even More Mosquitos: July 14–24, 1879

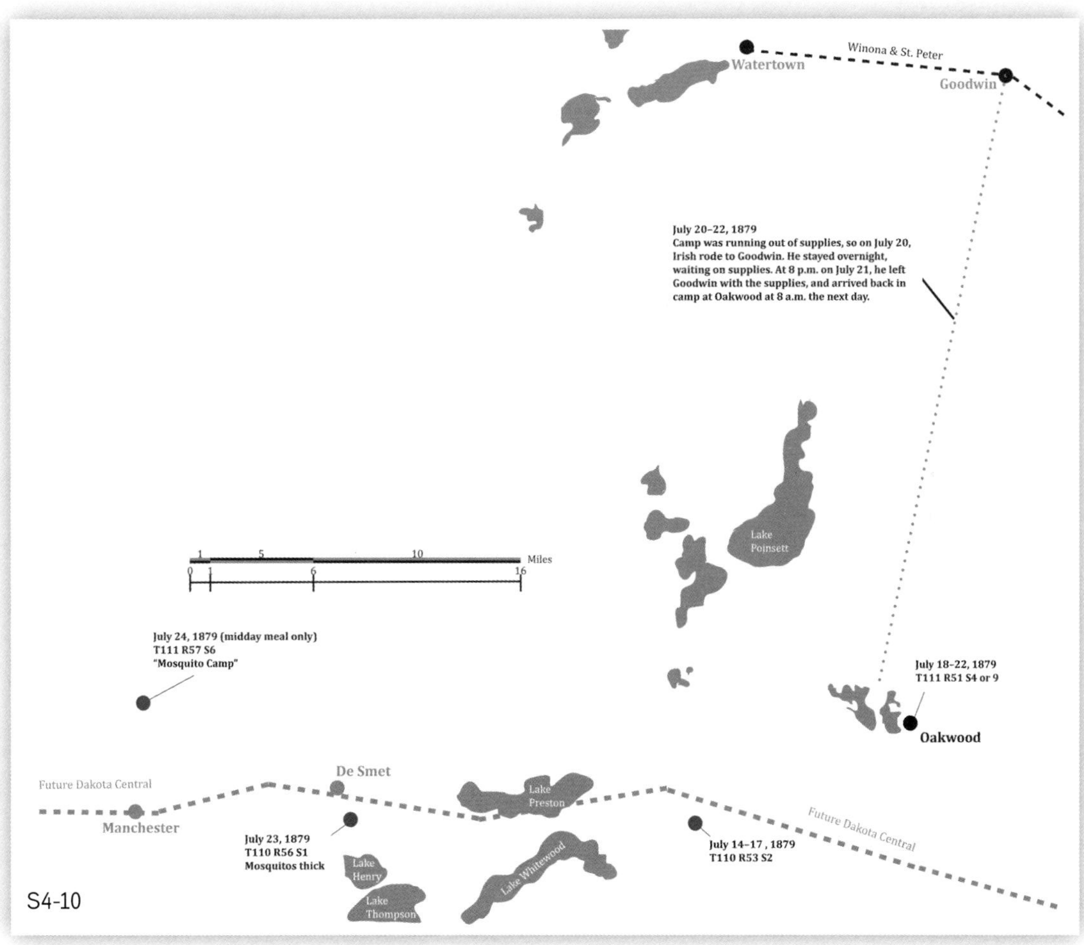

Disappointingly, the camp move did not provide escape from the pestilence. "Horror of horrors," wrote Irish. "What a night . . . mosquitos came by the million. Oh such mosquitos." Both horses and men were miserable and sleepless.

Beleaguered, they "got off with camp" the morning of July 15 and moved eight miles farther east, to clean up the survey near Lake Preston. The scourge continued, as Irish lamented, "Here we had more mosquito punishment." It wasn't all unpleasantness, as they saw another beautiful meteor, this one visually comparable in size to Mars.

That night, an organized defense was finally put up. "A relief of 15 men, 3 at a time, 2 hours each" were assigned to "smudge mosquitoes." This involved burning wet grasses at a smolder, producing a heavy smoke that deterred the wretched winged insects. With the new assault, the men "got some sleep." The coming day was hot, and maddeningly, there were "mosquitoes all day."

At 4 p.m. on Thursday, July 17, Irish declared the survey in the area complete. It should have been a time of satisfaction, but instead an emergency ensued: "Mr. Carse shot himself through the right leg with small pocket pistol. Wound not dangerous, but the shock to him was terrible. Pulse 15 per minute for 1 hour; did not recover for 4 hours."

Minding the status of Carse was not the only overnight task. The mosquito brigade did their shifts too, and in the morning, a Dr. Higgins from Fountain (about eight miles northeast of modern Brookings) arrived to tend to Carse. Afterward, the entire camp moved northeast to Oakwood.

ANTICIPATING THE TRAINS

Newspaper editors continued to excitedly anticipate the arrival of the trains, and rumors that they must have known were on the wild side were published. Sometimes they blamed other newspapers for the rumor, like a game of telephone, as when the *Brookings County Press* said they'd heard from the Watertown paper that trains would be running to Lake Benton by the third week of July.[50] Like many rumors, this was inaccurate. It was effective, however. People were coming and settling in advance of those promised trains. The same edition carried an observation from a correspondent who noted that the harvest would be a good one due to the number of settlers who had already claimed land. "Thousands of acres have been taken and partly broken up, and now waving the fine wheat, and more is left,"[51] said the correspondent.

Irish wrote up his final notes about this portion of the survey and sent them off with Thorn on July 19. The courier headed to Goodwin to get the notes onto a train headed east and to bring supplies back to camp.

Again, this milestone should have come with some celebration, but issues with the workers again deflected his attentions. "Collins got drunk, so [I] discharged him, discharged Cole and Shanklin," wrote Irish. "The boys took Cole and ducked [dunked] him in the lake for reason of his filthiness in camp."

As things settled down in camp, Thorn returned empty-handed; there had been no supplies to bring back. Irish was "much troubled by want of supplies," and despite the crew having already lost considerable time (presumably due to the rework at Lake Preston), Irish and Thorn took a team back to Goodwin, enduring a "very hot sultry" day, in hunt of the needed supplies. "I am tired out and sleepless," Irish penned on July 20.

Irish and Thorn remained in Goodwin the next day. "Mosquitos thick, nearly killed the horses," wrote Irish. "One of the poor things broke loose, and we had to scout in the dark for it." The two men decided to travel from Goodwin to Oakwood overnight, hoping for respite from the pests. They covered thirty straight-line miles overland in the dark. The diary for the next day lamented that the pesky bugs had been "terrible," Irish adding, "I tried to sleep on the sacks of corn in the wagon bed but failed."

The pair reached the main encampment in Oakwood at 8 a.m., twelve hours after leaving Goodwin. It took a few hours to pack up camp; the entire group headed west again at 10:30 a.m. They encountered mud five miles from Oakwood, and at least one of the wagons became stuck. They "lost but little time" after fighting to free the wagon, going on to camp two miles east of the land Charles Ingalls would eventually homestead. There, they "found the mosquitos very thick," and the evening became "very cold." It was entirely unpleasant, though there was some relief: the mosquito swarm was not as overwhelming as in recent nights.

They got up early on Thursday, July 24, then had their midday meal at what they called Mosquito Camp, north of modern Manchester, before continuing west to camp for the night at Hutchinson Lake. They had planned ahead, bringing plenty of good water, "so [they] did not drink the soda water" that the lake had to offer. There were, however, more mosquitos at night. Oh horror!

MR. BLUNT'S TRAVELS

Blunt, who had been out checking on his various survey parties, returned to Watertown "so sun burnt" from his travels west that the editor of the *Watertown News* had not immediately recognized him. "Mr. B. is a thoroughly competent man, and drives whatever he takes hold of with great energy," the article concluded.[52]

Confronting the Wessington Hills: July 25–August 19, 1879

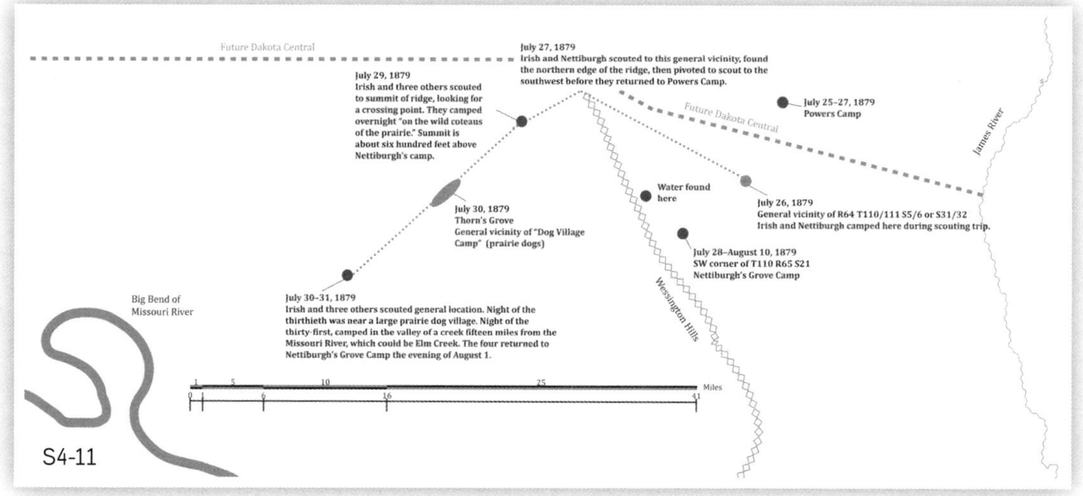

S4-11

At 10:30 a.m. on Friday, July 25, the crew momentously reached the banks of the James River and succeeded in crossing it—with all teams and gear—in an hour and forty minutes. Pausing only for a coffee lunch, they continued on to a campsite they named after team member Powers. It was a "bad state of affairs" there, however, as they were unable to find water nearby.

The next day, Irish and Nettiburgh began a multiday scout of the area to the west. For these trips, Irish's diary notes compass degrees, indicating what direction they rode (e.g., "S60W" meant 60 degrees from south toward west).

Sixteen miles to the southwest of Powers Camp, they found a "wide valley" with "timber and water." When they reached their turnaround spot, the pair and their horses took a half-hour rest. Among the scenes they took in while relaxing was a Lakota hunting party. Then they began their return trip, back toward camp but not to it. Instead, they went a bit to the northeast to scout a different section of ground.

For their evening camping location, they were "possibly" in the "vicinity" of sections 5, 6, 31, or 32 of township 110 or 111, range 64 (Irish's uncertainty). Those four sections meet at a center point, and that narrows their location down to an approximate spot within another approximate spot. Irish being a surveyor, we can probably trust his instincts and place this camp more or less as shown on the map, marked for the evening of July 26, as a pinpoint from which to base the next day's travel path.

Irish and Nettiburgh continued their scout the next morning, traveling three hours in one direction and two hours in another before heading back toward main camp. It was a "fine day," though some rain fell in the afternoon. As darkness increased, they spread their beds on the ground, only to notice the lights of the full camp not far away. They repacked their temporary bivouac and joined the main group at Powers Camp, arriving at 10 p.m.

After a restful night, camp was moved about eleven miles southwest of Powers Camp to the newly named Nettiburgh's Grove, to Camp Nettiburgh. A welcome Caldwell arrived with letters, pistols, and powder. He also brought news that just to the south was a camp of cattle rustlers, another thing for Irish to keep his senses attuned to. While the pistols and powder were welcome additions, the letters were treasured.

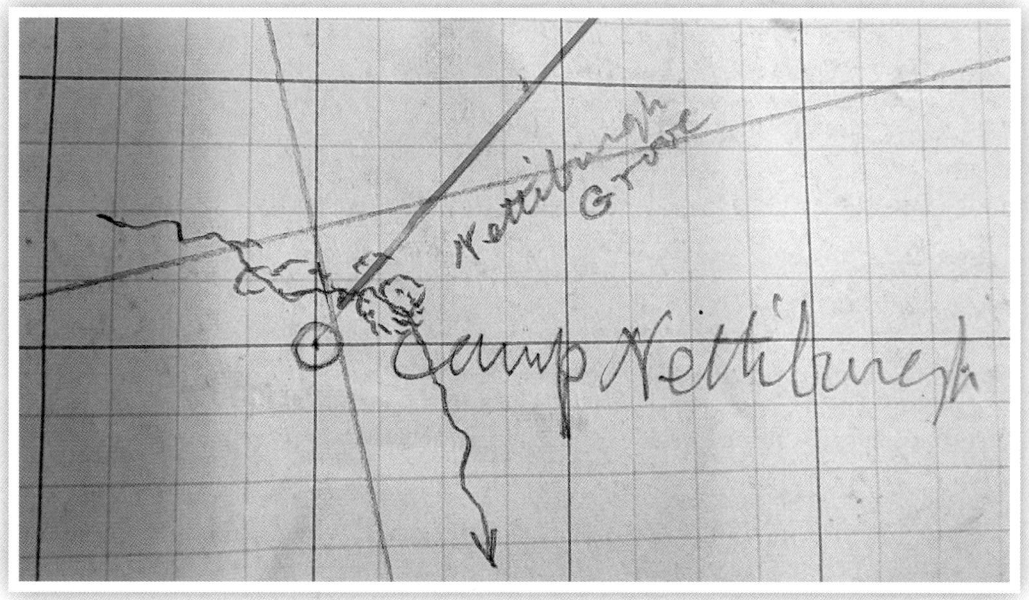

Irish's drawing of Camp Nettiburgh. A later Research Commentary tangent will delve deeper into why this is such a lovely little drawing. S4-12

On the morning of July 29, Irish, Thorn, Nettiburgh, and Cornell headed "up the valley" with forty-six gallons of water. The day was hot and dry, and the men had traveled for seven and a half hours by the time they reached the summit, where they "camped in the wild coteaus of the prairies" in the high point of the Wessington Hills. The landscape was drier, and there was no mention of mosquitos.

It was, however, cold. The men were up early, and despite having carried so much water with them, a team was sent in search of more, which was fortunately found a mere two and a half miles away.

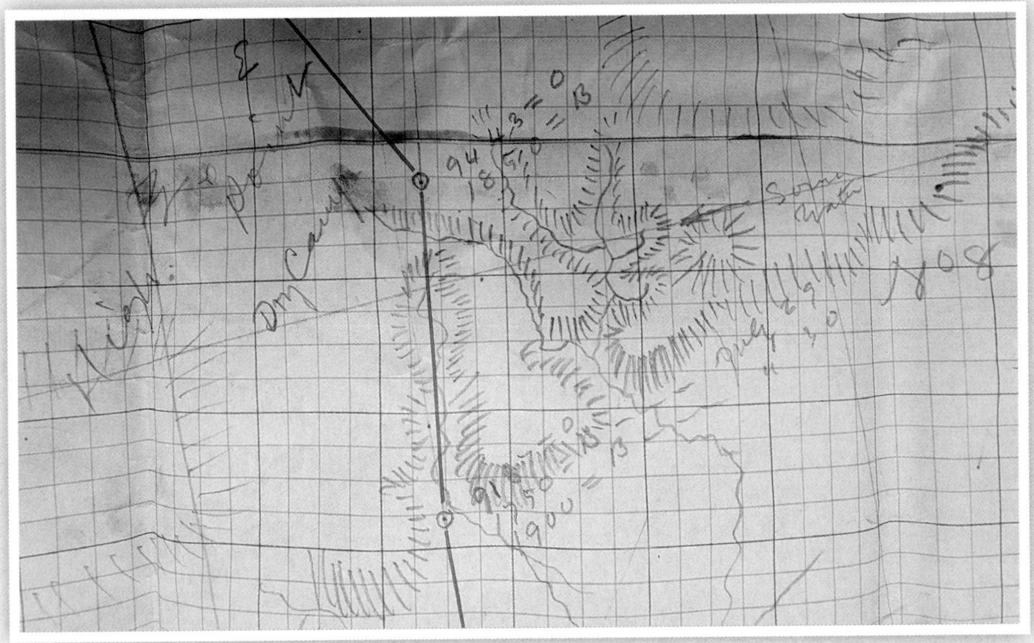

Irish's map of the Wessington Hills northern summit (see "High Point" notation in upper-left corner). The map is rotated so that the top edge points west. Their "Dry Camp" for the night is noted, as is the "nearby" water source they found (right side, "Some Water"). S4-13

Though the reason isn't mentioned, Irish had the crew change course to the southwest, following that line all day. The men were likely spread out on the scout, as they "discovered a village of prairie dogs 3 or 4 miles to S of [the] line." They also saw storm clouds forming. To prepare for the impending rain, they stopped, made "a dry camp," and hunkered down. "We are tired out and thirsty; so are the horses," penned Irish.

The diary does not indicate whether the clouds let loose any rainfall, but the next morning, July 31, Irish left Nettiburgh and Cornell to "dig for water" while he and Thorn continued on the scout. After crossing a Native trail, they "found water in large quantities."

Once the water had been found, "[they] brought up the team and camped for dinner." Then all went on ahead until they were about fifteen miles to the northeast of the Big Bend of the Missouri River. The day had been quite hot, as late July on the Dakota Territory plateau was prone to be. The need for fresh water was constant, especially with horses in tow.

August began with the scouting crew backtracking past the camp they'd named Thorn's Grove, near the prairie dog village. Again, it was "hot as blazes," at least after the misty rain subsided around noon. The environment was wearing on the men. Irish wrote, "We are all tired out, and the poor horses have only grass to eat. These plains are so barren, only grass and but little life." Despite that "little life" comment, there were plenty of prairie dogs, some of which became sustenance for the men.

After a full day of scouting along the return path, the men arrived back at the main camp at Nettiburgh's Grove. Over the next two days (the first being cooler, the second again hot and uncomfortable), additional lines were run "into the bluffs" as options to get through the hills.

A hastily written note to Ruth on August 3 from Nettiburgh's Grove let her know that Irish had been near the Big Bend of the Missouri. He was anxious to complete the final sixty miles of survey, "so as to get home and have some rest." The weather was fluctuating. "We have to put on thick clothes at night and in mornings, and in the middle of the day our thin ones," he shared.

Monday, August 4, brought Blunt to camp, this time in the company of A. G. Ryther, a forty-four-year-old Chicago & North Western officer who would continue to play some role for the duration of the project. Irish sent the rest of the party back to the James while he took Blunt (and presumably Ryther) "out to see the country west." The two officers left the next morning, and Irish turned east to rejoin his men, meeting them at 4 p.m., when he "set the men at work" despite the 98-degree temperature. Three and a half hours in, however, a "severe storm of wind and rain" hit camp. Fortunately, the worst result was that the men returned to camp wet. The storm did more damage at the supply camp, twelve miles west of Nettiburgh's Grove, where five inches of hail had fallen.

Note: The existence of this supply camp is another intriguing detail that had not been mentioned before, letting us know there were sometimes multiple camp locations for different purposes, not unlike the construction camps. With news traveling back and forth, there must have been regular runners keeping all informed of the various goings-on.

August 6 was hotter yet, with the thermometer hitting 100 degrees. The men began working an alternate line on the east side of the James, and once that was under way, Irish headed back across the James and to the southwest, returning to Camp Nettiburgh at 6 p.m., "tired out."

The next day's work along the James was carried out under conditions described as "hot as blixen," though the nights had become cold. Irish and Thorn left camp to "meet the boys," who he discovered had been "waiting since 9 1/2 AM." Soon enough, they were set to "work over the big gulch."

Temperatures dropped to 90 degrees on the eighth, which found the men working on the line that would get the tracks through the river valley. "Am so glad to get away from those bothering hills," wrote Irish.

Modern photo looking west toward the Wessington Hills. This photo shows how the hills dissipate on the north end, yet at this stage of the scouting, Irish and crew were investigating a route through the hills rather than around them. This is the view they would have seen as they left the James and headed west (minus the fence, of course). S4-14

The hills were not the only things vexing Irish and crew; the air was full of smoke from distant fires. Winds can carry smoke hundreds of miles away from the source, and the landscape can trap it and make the air heavy, irritating eyes and throats—not ideal conditions for the men working in the heat. The air remained smoky for several days, and on August 11, they could "not sight more than 1000 ft with transit and 350 with level" due to the smoky haze.

The relative respite of 90 degrees ended with three high-temperature days in a row, starting August 9—102, 101, and 96 degrees, respectively—the intense heat creating a similarly intense mirage. "Hot as blazes"; "Hot, hot, hot"; and "Hot again" were Irish's diary entries corresponding to each day. Three of the men—Leighton, Olson, and Joe Mudra—were "overpowered by the intense heat" and sent back to camp on the ninth. Irish declared, "Quite out of health and feel home sick."

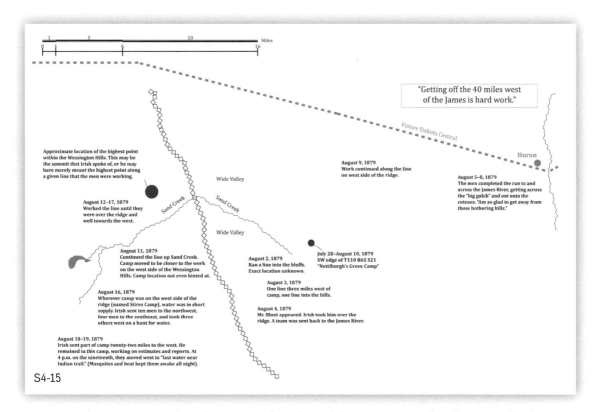

S4-15

As a way to give the men a break and keep up morale, the crew had a shooting match on August 10. It was also "a trial of the new guns." Irish finished his day writing letters and updating the account book, daily record-keeping being critical. Concern for the crew's safety was frequently on Irish's mind, and the shooting match helped keep the men from getting rusty, just in case.

Heading west just south of Sand Creek, east of the Wessington Hills, showing the gentle(ish) grade up the wide valley and through the hills. S4-16

Sand Creek after its descent out of the Wessington Hills. This was a foggy February day, but the conditions mimic the limited visibility encountered during the smoke-haze days the crew endured in early August. S4-17

Heat and homesickness were not the only maladies, unfortunately. On August 11, Irish wrote, "The camp diarrhea made its appearance among us." Four of the men were down sick and had to remain in camp. Irish kept the work going along the wide valley of Sand Creek as best he could with the others, but dejection was the tone of the day. "Smoky, very smoky," wrote Irish, "cannot see hills any more. I am still sick. Getting off the 40 miles west from the James is hard work."

While in camp along the northern end of the Wessington Hills, Irish received multiple letters from home with "the same sad tidings": the death of Louisa, his young sister-in-law. This news, though expected, was a terrible blow, and Irish spent much of the day mourning, reminiscing about Louisa, always "so kind hearted and lively," who always had a smile for the Irishes. In his August 12 return letter, he grieved, "There is no death to be deplored more than such a death at such an age as hers."

He wrote that after reading the news, he "left the party [crew] and all that afternoon shed tears," adding, "Everything looks so gloomy that I find myself thinking and feeling as I did when Mother died!" Unable to be home to comfort his family, he instead distracted himself by "working hard as to get done soon." It would not be easy, however. Three men were currently sick, with others recovering. So far, he himself was well. Saturday and Sunday had been so hot that "two of the men gave out and [they] all nearly melted."

On Monday, they would have put on their winter clothes for protection against the cold—had they had any along, which they did not.

"We were miserable as we could be," wrote Irish. Next in line of complaints was that the air had become so smoky that visibility was less than a mile. What a situation.

Note: There is a grave in Iowa City's Oakland Cemetery (Block B8, Lot 40, Space 1) marked as "Mrs. Hoffman." Records from Interment.net show a "Hoffman, Unknown Mrs., 32 years old, died August 3, 1879." This is most likely the gravesite of Louisa Hoffman, Abbie Irish's youngest sister, born in 1847. Louisa was her mother's youngest as well as the only child of her second marriage, after Abbie's father died in 1844.[53]

The next day, Irish sent Thorn, Nettiburgh, and Caldwell out to do some scouting work. The melancholy that draped camp was displaced when the men returned to camp with a stray pony. "It's wild as it can be," wrote Irish. "The boys are wild over the capture." The new addition to the crew was a welcome break from the work. The air quality remained poor, however. "Oh how smoky," he lamented, adding, "It's cold now, quite cold."

Despite the smoke, work went on. On August 14, the crew crossed the ridge and progressed "well in towards the west Hills." Not all work could take place, however. "The level party is behind, as Hutchinson is sick," wrote Irish. With a small crew, one man out could easily mean falling behind. In addition, two men had been sent out to scout for water, but they found none.

IN THE WAKE OF THE SURVEYORS

The August 14 *Brookings County Press* reprinted a piece from the *Winona Republican* reminding businessmen that the Tracy branch of the Winona & St. Peter was set to reach the gold town of Deadwood "with all possible celerity." The writer suggested that the businessmen should therefore push "their trade and enlarg[e] the scope of their operations" not only in Winona but along "the ever-widening field which is opened up to their enterprises."[54] The surveyors were working in a relatively unpopulated, quiet environment. But behind them, energy and activity was increasing significantly.

As Friday, August 15, dawned, the smoky haze had diminished somewhat, but not entirely. The crew "kept on west towards the big hill," though the smoke continued to obscure the view.

The lack of water was becoming a serious concern, and on August 16, Irish sent "10 men out to scout NW, 4 men SE, and [he] took 3 and went west to find water. . . ." He and his delegation "camped on a dry plain, no water." Joe Mudra, with the party that went southeast, "killed a mule deer," providing a hearty meal or two for the men. (This also lets us know there were at least seventeen men in the party at this time.)

The desperately sought water was found by digging near camp, though the entry does not indicate how deep they had to go. But perhaps Irish's news was superfluous, as "the NW party found plenty of water." The day had again been hot, with storms to the north during the night. "We all feel good over Joe's mule deer" was the contented final entry for the day.

The hot weather did not deter the crew in their work. Irish was determined to reach the Missouri River—and soon. In an August 17 reply from camp along Medicine Creek, he told his family to send a few letters to him at Fort Pierre, but not to write "more than you ought, as I may not get them." Also clear was that Fort Pierre was "on the frontier," and that led to all kinds of other uncertainties. "Continue to write to me via Watertown," he added.

With this letter, we also confirm the identity of Old Joe, who so faithfully collected feathers for Mrs. Irish. Irish wrote, "[He] shot a mule deer with that little gun of mine, and the fresh meat cured the men all up, so we named the creek after Joe"—Joe Mudra Creek, as it is labeled proudly and boldly on Irish's map of the area.

Providing a glimpse into Irish's personal ambitions, the letter included, "I shall have to survey a line to Bismarck yet, I think." The officers were asking him about other work he could do. The line to Bismarck (in what became *North* Dakota) would represent the connection with the Northern Pacific, one of the national-level projects of the time. Irish's connecting the Dakota Central—or any line, really—with the Northern Pacific would boost his résumé and bring with it some prestige. Irish was keeping his eye on this goal.

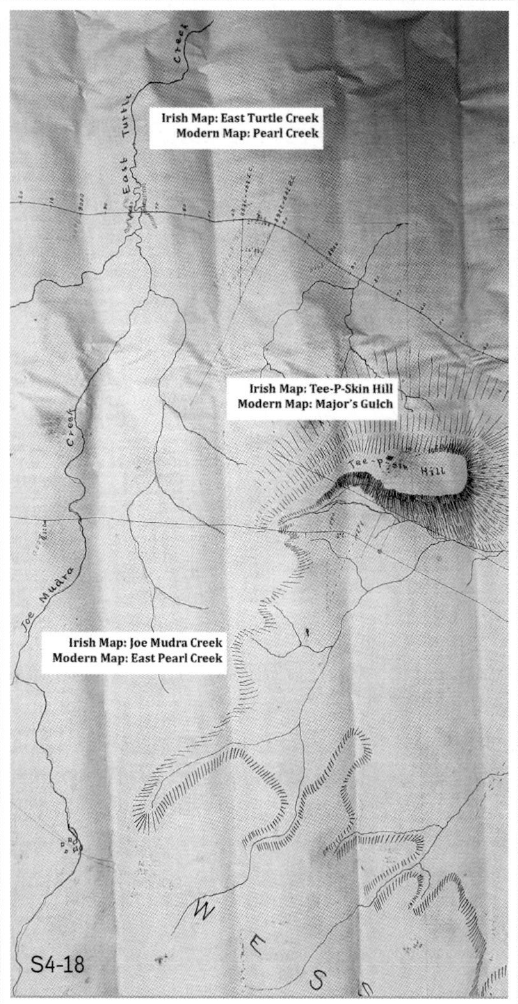

Irish Map: East Turtle Creek
Modern Map: Pearl Creek

Irish Map: Tee-P-Skin Hill
Modern Map: Major's Gulch

Irish Map: Joe Mudra Creek
Modern Map: East Pearl Creek

S4-18

Joe Mudra Creek, running through the center of the map, west of the Wessington Hills.

This letter has an excitement to it—he wanted to go home, but there was work to do. He knew that work could lead to bigger and better projects, so he was motivated to keep his nose to the grindstone, despite his deep homesickness. He still hoped to meet his family in Sioux City for the anticipated furlough, which he reminded them about in every letter. This letter was finished with, "We found a horse on the prairie the other day as wild as he could be. The boys caught it, but it nearly killed one of them." (He did not include this detail in the brief diary entry for the day.)

The night was windy and rainy, and as day awoke, the main camp was sent twenty-two miles "ahead." At this point in the route, that could have meant to the west, but it may have meant northwest, toward the northern edge of the Wessington Hills. Irish set to work on "estimates and maps" while the day blazed hot. The courier Caldwell came into camp, but he brought no letters from home. Irish was disappointed, but he again ended his daily report with, "We all feel better having fresh meat."

August 19 soared to 102 degrees—"a terrible hot day," wrote Irish, adding, "We worked on the maps and estimates and it nearly killed us in the shade of the camp." The heat wasn't the only irritation. Courier Caldwell was sent east again, as one of the sacks of flour was found to be contaminated with oil (though no indication as to the type of oil was provided). While Caldwell went east, the camp packed up and began to move west. They set out at 4 p.m. on August 19 and "came on as far as the last water near Indian trail."

They were working in unrelenting heat, and they needed water. Weather on the plains can fluctuate annoyingly, and the men were traveling back and forth across great distances, working to determine not only the route to the Missouri River but also another route farther to the east, both for the Chicago & North Western.

Section Five

ON TO THE MISSOURI, THEN BACK AND FORTH . . .

AUGUST 20—NOVEMBER 14, 1879

The Missouri River was finally reached, but the survey there was interrupted as the crew backtracked to again rework a stretch around Lake Preston, well to the east. The crew was also enlisted to conduct yet another side-project survey, this to find a route between Volga (just to the west of Brookings), to Watertown (twenty miles to the north), both along the Big Sioux. There were two treasured furloughs, but not everything was going well. A crew member died. There was extreme heat and storms, more illness, more prairie fires. While finally on furlough, Irish experienced the loss of a beloved pet. He also had to accept something he'd sworn would not happen: he was going to continue the survey throughout the winter.

On to the Missouri River from Wessington Hills: August 20–31, 1879

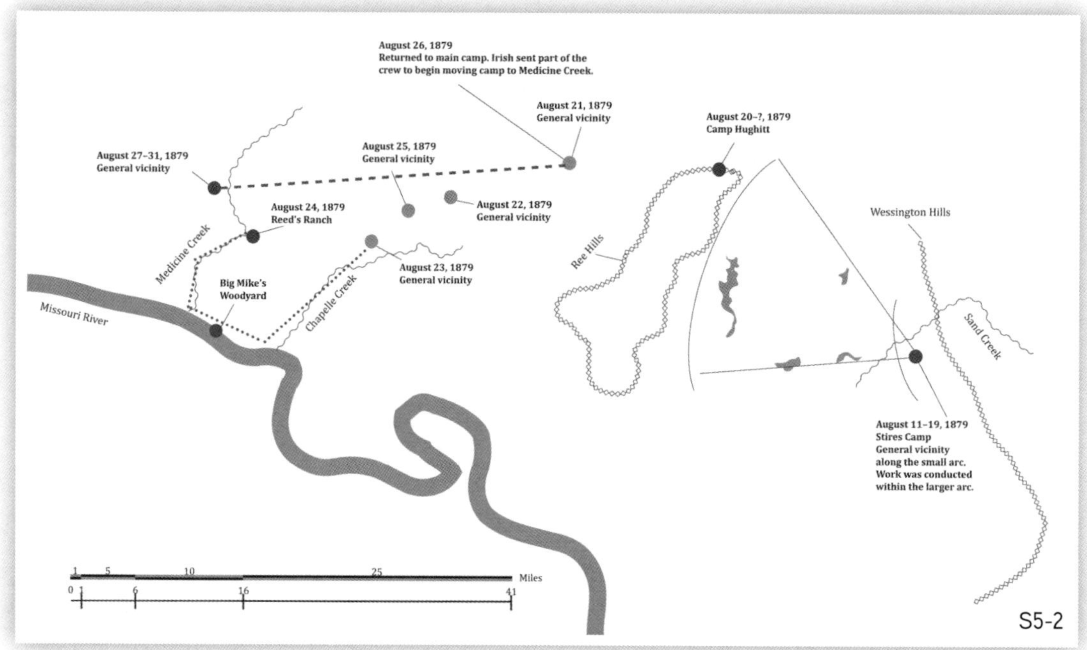

At 10 a.m. on August 20, the crew landed at their new site, which they named Camp Hughitt, "on top of the hills." It was "on top" both for being at the northern end of the run of hills and also above the plain below. It was another 96-degree day, but the men had the camp set up and orderly by nightfall, when rain threatened. An unfortunate correlation on the plains is that where there is water, no matter how desperately desired, there will, in all likelihood, also be the dreaded mosquito. The men had another restless night due to heat and the mosquito plague.

The location of Camp Hughitt, high above the valley, looking north. There is a water hole visible before the descent to the valley floor. S5-3

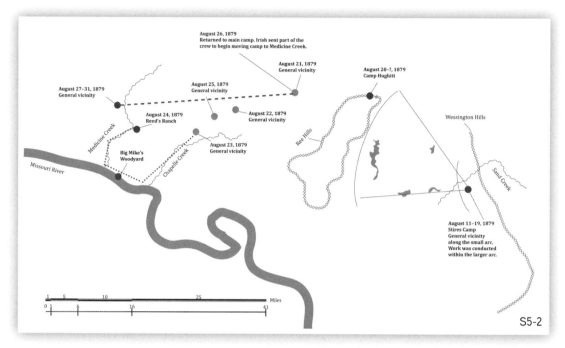

The threat of rain brought with it a serious cold front. High winds blew, and heavy rain fell. "But it did us much good," wrote Irish. "Cooled off the hot plains." Indeed! The temperature the next day topped out at 60 degrees, a 36-degree difference in twenty-four hours.

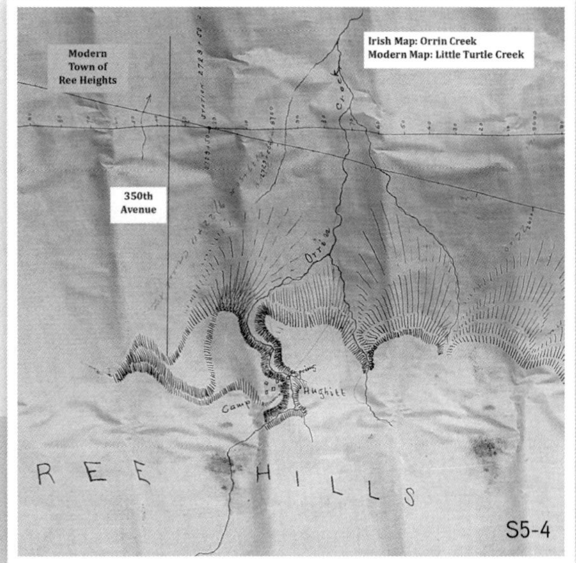

TOWN LOCATION UNCERTAINTIES

Before we return to the narrative, and while the surveyors were evaluating options between the James and the Missouri, the *Brookings County Press* was looking beyond the not-yet-arrived tracks to the next order of business: the location of the towns. (The *Brookings County Press* was published in the town of Fountain, which would find itself bypassed, and the *Press*'s staff and equipment would move to the new town of Brookings on the same day that the first locomotive pulled in, a few months into the future.)

There had been some confirmation of town locations along the route in Minnesota, but not yet in Dakota Territory. People were getting antsy, and it was perceived to be impacting business. "If the town matter was settled," wrote the *Press*'s editor, "parties intending to purchase grain would commence building their store-houses and elevators and contract for grain. Then when the road reached here, they would already have an accumulated business, and much of which is now moving away from them in other directions."[55]

The August 21 edition of the *Brookings County Press* also reported that grading in the Lake Benton area was nearly complete and that tracks had been laid to about twenty miles west of Tracy, with work progressing at about one and a half miles per day.

The lower temperature on August 21 made the day's work much more comfortable, and the men were able to run twelve and a half miles of chain. But as had become a pattern, the positive was balanced by the negative. One of the crewmen, Adams, became very ill. Irish diagnosed it as breakbone fever, a malady known today as dengue, though perhaps it was more likely malaria (or a related malady). Either way, Adams was shivering so severely that Irish worried the man's bones would break. The next day, Adams was much worse, and Irish attended him most of the day, writing, "Got his pulse down from 118 to 85 by the use of quinine and [indecipherable]"—Irish apparently added *something* to the quinine, but it is lost in his scribbles. (Not even the experts on frontier medicine that were shown the page recognized the scribble as a traditional medicinal ingredient.)

HANDWRITING, FRONTIER MEDICINE, AND QUININE

Sometimes Irish's handwriting appears clean and clear, simple to read. Other times it resembles a weak EKG reading. Oddly, it seems his handwriting was worst when he was feeling healthy; the more tired or sick he became, the more careful his writing. I suspect Irish was stressed by the work and Adams's illness, as the description of how he treated Adams is a mix of easy to read and entirely perplexing.

In researching "receipts" (recipes) that use quinine, comparing the various ingredients to the scribble pictured below (with a healthy dose of imagination thrown in, to boot), to see if a real word would emerge from the page, no helpful matches were found. The closest was "carbonate," which is, relatedly, an ingredient used in drug development.

It says, "... use of quinine and [indecipherable]." S5-5

Quinine was a commonly used medicinal on the frontier, especially when fevers and chills were involved. Originally derived from the bark of the cinchona tree, native to South America, the active ingredient had an unpleasant taste, and "tasteless" versions became popular at the turn of the century. Prior to that, syrups and elixirs were added to cover the flavor. An 1877 encyclopedia of medicinal recipes detailed one that included wild cherry bark, gentian root, orange peel, cinnamon, coriander seed, anise, caraway, cardamom, and licorice root, all infused into alcohol, all to cover the bitterness. The encyclopedia read, "This elixer is an excellent vehicle for quinine, the taste of which it completely destroys."[56] Still, none of those words look like the scribble. If you know what that word is, please contact the author!

Other than Adams's illness, Irish declared it a fine day. Once Irish felt that Adams was on the mend, he and Nettiburg rendezvoused with the rest of the party and slept on the prairie. "Had no blankets or coats, so we suffered very much with the cold," wrote Irish. They had followed a note from Dunlap that had unintentionally misled them, leading to some unnecessary wandering.

After a night exposed to the cold, Irish and Nettiburgh reconnected with the main party. The two men then joined up with Thorn and headed west to scout, exploring twenty-nine miles before stopping at dark along Medicine Creek. "All tired out" was a fitting end for the day.

More rains came through overnight, and the men were unable to stay dry, getting "wet through." The day, at least, was good for traveling.

After a heartbreaking situation earlier in the year (a letter in November will shed more light on that event), Ruth wrote of another adventure. She had gone to Davenport and visited with a doctor and his mother. The doctor, it turns out, was not much of a horseman, and during the buggy ride they took, the horse refused to do its duty and instead attempted to sit down. The doctor's mother "was having a nervous spasm" over the embarrassing scene. Ruth calmly "alighted from the vehicle and got the old lady into bed," then gave her a dose of camphor to calm her nerves.

Meanwhile, the doctor "succeeded in fastening the dashing steed [probably sarcastic] to a hitching post." He then came into the house to check on his mother, though Ruth's impression was that "he was more in need of a stimulant than she was." We won't spend more time on this, but that man was a Dr. Preston, and Ruth Irish would, in just a few years, become Ruth Irish Preston.

On August 24, they started early, stopped for breakfast at Chapelle Butte, then followed Chapelle Creek down to Jones's Ranch, then to Big Mike's Woodyard, which was on Fort George Island, at the Missouri River.

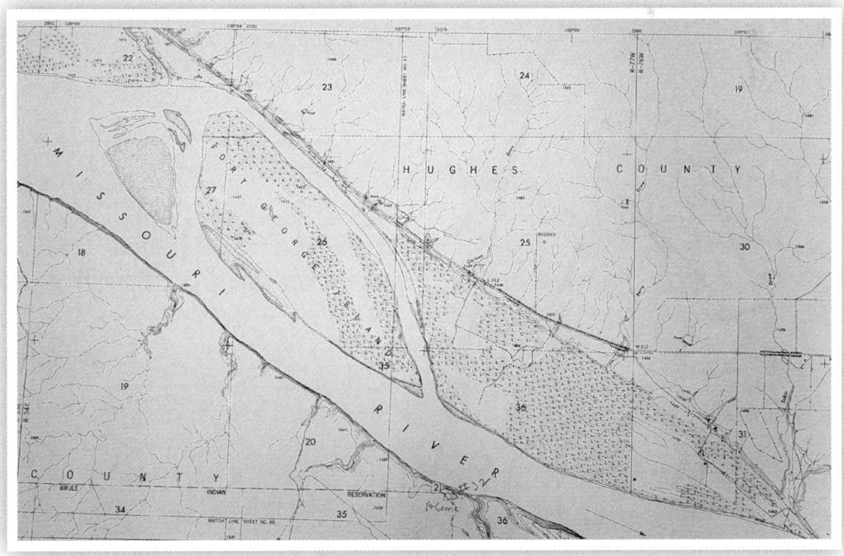

Map of Fort George Island, Missouri River. Irish and his crew would spend a portion of the upcoming winter on this island. S5-6

Reaching the Missouri was a big milestone, and it gave the men their first indication that finding a satisfactory route down the bluffs from the high plains was going to take significant scouting and experimentation.

After taking in the view of the big river, they headed north a short distance to the mouth of Medicine Creek, where they followed its valley back upstream to the ranch of J. Reed, where they spent the night. Reed's Ranch would become a significant location for their coming year.

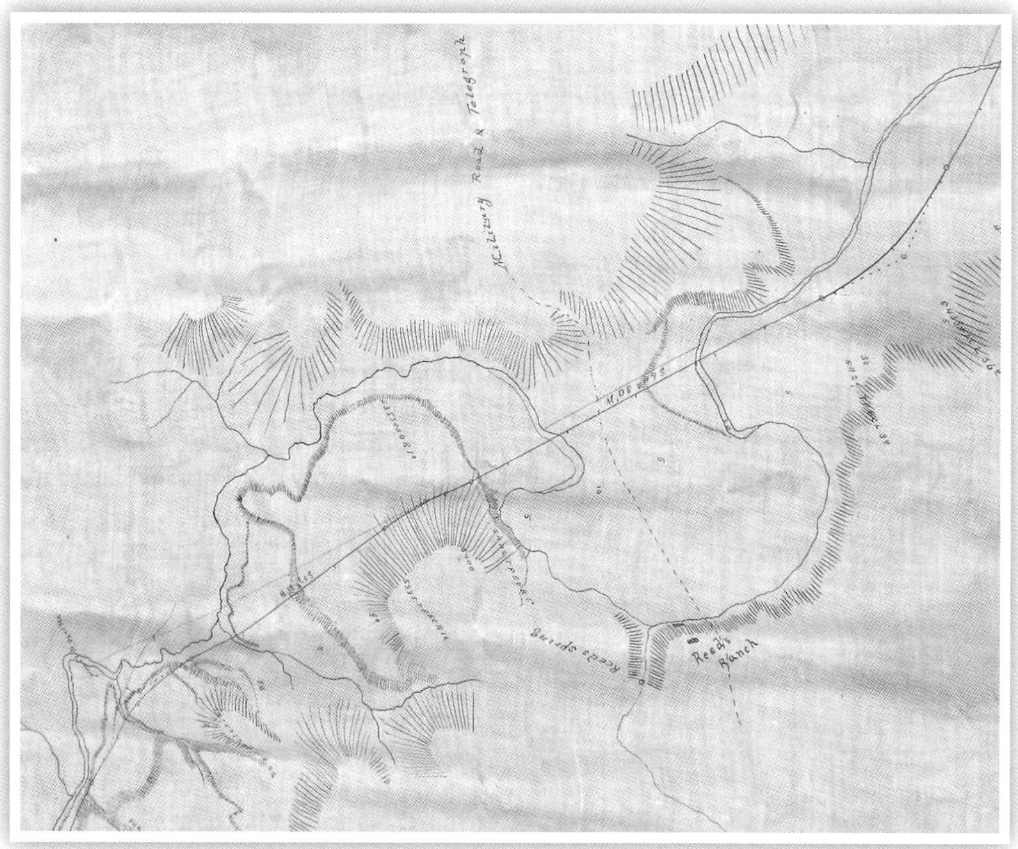

Irish's beautifully done linen map of the Medicine Creek valley, centered around Reed's Ranch, near modern Canning. The author had the privilege to walk the grounds with the current owner and see foundations that may have belonged to Reed's buildings (see the research commentary on page 181). S5-7

After another overnight storm, Irish and the others left Reed's and followed Medicine Creek four miles upstream, then connected with their previous trail to the camp location of two nights before. "A fine day," wrote Irish. "Have travelled in three days 81 miles. Am tired out."

The men may have camped without tents, as the heavy dew overnight caused their blankets to be "wet through as with a rain." Up and on the move, they rejoined the main camp by 11 a.m., and upon arrival, they learned the contaminated flour had been replaced with fresh, but "Dunlap [had] broken the transit and ran a crooked line." Surveying equipment could be finicky when functional, but it certainly created bad readings when broken.

Irish was worried about Adams, so he sent Caldwell to escort the desperately ill man to receive medical care, likely to one of the nearby military posts, though the diary does not indicate where.

Irish directed Thorn and Leighton to begin moving a portion of camp west to Medicine Creek. Irish and others stayed behind, and on August 27, they reworked four and a half miles to make the broken transit's errant line true. Reinforcing the cooling evenings, the morning had dawned with fog, the day was hot, and the afternoon saw the return of smoky skies.

Fog again greeted the men on August 28, and the day grew "excessively hot," with three men falling ill. Irish admitted that he was "almost so, but dare not say it." On this day, in a twist to the good-tempered-with-bad pattern they'd experienced, some bad was tempered with good: Irish killed a 150-pound buck, and "the men [were] so glad of it."

After a feast of good venison and "a good sleep," they all felt better, and though the heat was terrible, threatening to make them sick, they were able to do their work down the creek bed. Unfortunately, they discovered they didn't have the food they thought had been packed and brought along. Amid their frustration, Irish and Meyers went back to the main camp for provisions.

The heat, smoky skies, fitful sleep, and heavy work were taking a physical toll. "I am about sick again," Irish admitted on August 30. Still, work progressed, and the cooler day made for better conditions. The men ran their survey through a prairie dog town, killing two of the critters for food. They weren't the only successful hunters: "Saw a fight between 4 hawks over a dead one [prairie dog]."

On the final day of August, Irish and Dunlap explored "down the creek 8 or 9 miles, then onto the top of the great Medicine Butte." Irish added, "It's been a famous place for the Indians in bygone times. There is a figure of a rattlesnake made by placing stones in the ground."

(An online search for "Medicine Butte Rattlesnake Effigy" will yield modern information and videos on this site.)

Medicine Knoll, southwest of modern Blunt, South Dakota. S5-8

Exploring Medicine Creek: September 1–14, 1879

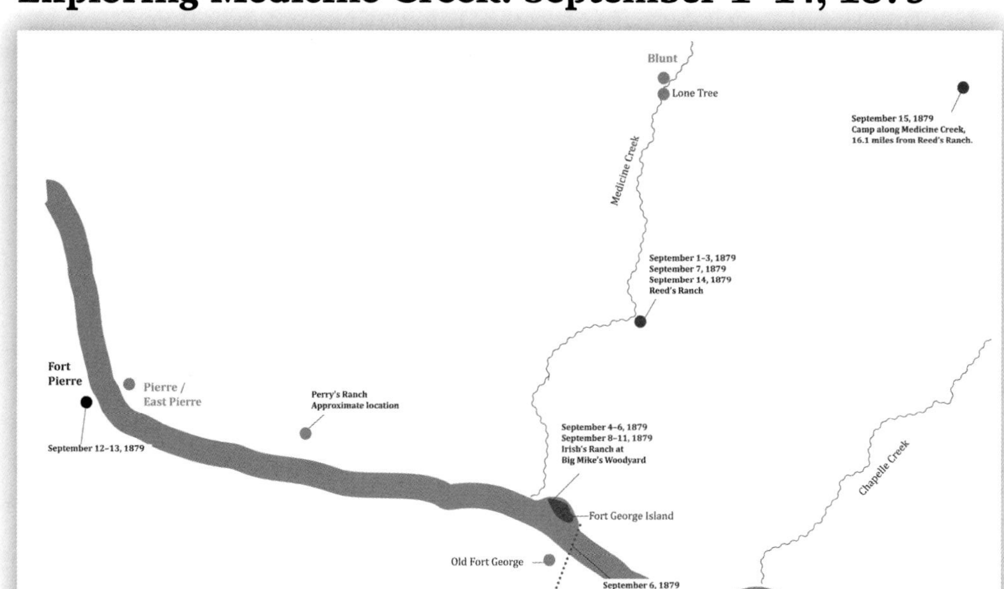

S5-9

September began with a "cold night and a hot day." Common of the era for that locale, the site of the day's work was designated as a tree, a rare-enough landmark to make it seem sufficient in the diary entry. In fact, the maps he drew denoted a stretch of route as beginning or ending at the sentinel tree. "We began our work at the lone cottonwood and ran down 9 miles," wrote Irish. "The creek is crooked but a favorable grade." Irish was "tired out" by the time they reached Reed's Ranch for the night.

The next day was productive—but possibly with a cost. "We ran 4 miles and a half and put in eight curves," wrote Irish. It had been "a good days work," but he felt sick, "very bad indeed."

He did not feel any better on September 3, "hardly able to go out with the men." He forced himself to duty, however, and they reached the mouth of Medicine Creek by the end of the day. There, he found a long-deserted village and artifacts.

A 2021 photo of the area near the mouth of Medicine Creek, the Missouri River visible at the left edge. S5-10

A pattern of cold nights (upper twenties) and hot days (upper eighties) did not make for pleasant conditions, but diary complaints remained minor.

The working camp (versus the supply camp) was moved to Big Mike's Woodyard (see tangent below), located on the north bank of the Missouri River, as a base for "examinations of the locality." A heavy hailstorm hit in late afternoon, which "scared the boys badly. No harm." Storms crossing the Missouri in central South Dakota can be legendary in their ferocity. It is no wonder the crew was frightened.

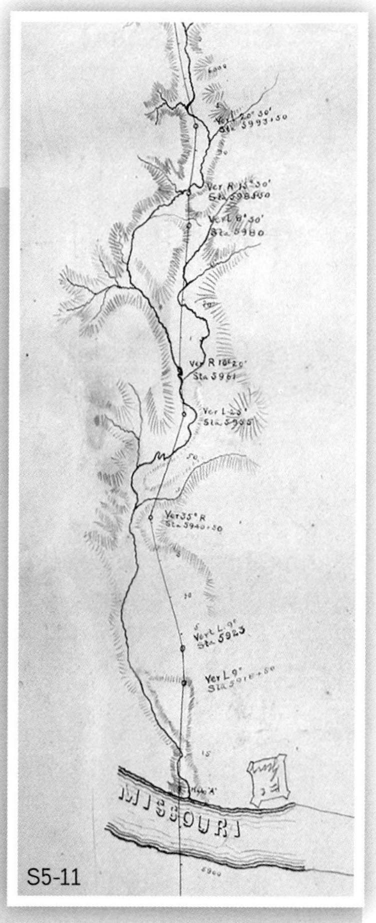

Irish's drawing of the lower portion of Medicine Creek as it empties into the Missouri River.

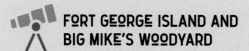

FORT GEORGE ISLAND AND BIG MIKE'S WOODYARD

Fort George Island, a large island barely off the bank of the river, was the site of Big Mike's Woodyard, one of many "wooding up" locations where private citizens cut down trees and chopped them into cord wood, which they sold to passing riverboats. (The island would disappear under the waters of the Missouri when the river was dammed, but there is a small area to pull over along the highway, on what would have been the north end of Fort George Island. From there, you can get a sense of the view the men had.) Irish will mention stopping at this island to take on fuel when he and Mrs. Irish steamboat from Yankton to Pierre in the future. However, many of these entrepreneurs were pilfering timber that belonged to the local Lakota, and this would become a problem a few months ahead.

On September 5, they "began work in dead earnest," as if the previous four months had not seen near nonstop activity. Irish wrote, "Set out triangulation points on N. bank and ran line down from Medicine Creek to woodyard. The river is very low." They'd seen no riverboats plying the waters since their arrival. The river wasn't the only thing that was low; the daily high temperature only reached 58 degrees, a big change from the weeks prior.

It climbed to a more comfortable 70 degrees on September 6, when they rented "a boat from an Indian and crossed over to the sunset side of the Missouri." The boat cost two dollars, and they hired an interpreter for an additional dollar. They crossed the river "600 feet below the site of old Ft. George" and "ran out 1 mile."

September 7 was another comfortable day, though it felt warm for work. Irish determined the high-water mark along the river to ensure (as best as humanly possible, at least) that the tracks would remain safe from flood waters. After accomplishing that task, he headed to the supply camp located at Reed's and attended to and wrote a prescription for Reed's sick child. A few days later, the diary noted that the baby was better.

More and more frequently now, the nights got cold once the sun went down. On September 8, Irish wrote, "Cold night +28, Hot day. We began run through the thick brush. We only got on a mile and a quarter the brush is so thick. I do not feel well. Have fever every afternoon. The men are well."

TOWN LOCATIONS ANNOUNCED TO THE EAST

Those in Dakota Territory who were anxious about the townsite locations being set finally got an answer. The September 11 *Brookings County Press* let it be known that a town would be placed generally in the center of Brookings County. The placement was a "judicious and generally satisfactory selection,"[57] even if it did mean that much of the town of Fountain, which housed the *Brookings County Press*, would soon be packing up to move (as would Medary, to the south). A squib within the same edition noted, "Friend Bandy [person] over at the Sioux gets a town too" (Bandy Town), announcing what would become Volga (though for a brief moment, it was also named Terra Coteau, a beautifully poetic name that sadly didn't stick.)[58]

While the newspapers had been clamoring for town locations, the mystery was not necessarily slowing down homesteaders. The same edition of the *Brookings County Press* that heralded the locations of the eventual Brookings and Volga also reported recent land-office business out of Sioux Falls. In August alone, sixty homesteads had been filed, accounting for just over nine thousand acres.[59] The region was not as empty as we now tend to believe it to have been.

The line through the thick brush that slowed the crew was finished on September 10, and they began a new option the next day, this one northward along the Missouri, reaching Perry's Ranch after seven miles. These last few days had brought pleasant weather and consistent work, but on the twelfth, Irish wrote, "The wind changed to NW last night and it's very cold today." Camp was moved north along the river, while the heavy northwest wind made it miserable. Sand along the riverbank was whipped around "like snow," and Irish wrote, "Quite sick, [could] hardly go on." Despite not wanting to keep going, the crew reached as far north as the site of modern Pierre, on the east bank.

The wind died overnight, but that merely helped the temperatures plummet. "I was so sick, I feared a permanent attack of fever," worried Irish, who remained sick throughout the next day and overnight, though he carried out his work, crossed the river to Fort Pierre, explored a few miles up the Bad River, and visited with friends.

By September 14, Irish felt better, having given himself three doses of quinine. So much better, in fact, that he recrossed the Missouri on the ferry and traveled the seventeen miles back to Reed's Ranch, midway up Medicine Creek. One suspects that Irish received news while in Fort Pierre: the crew was to return eastward once again.

Back to the James: September 15–21, 1879

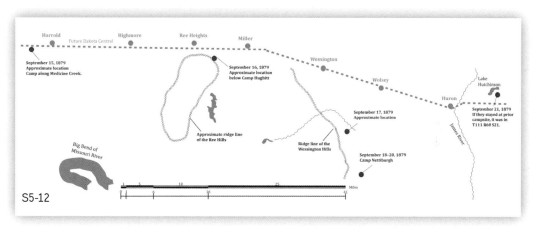

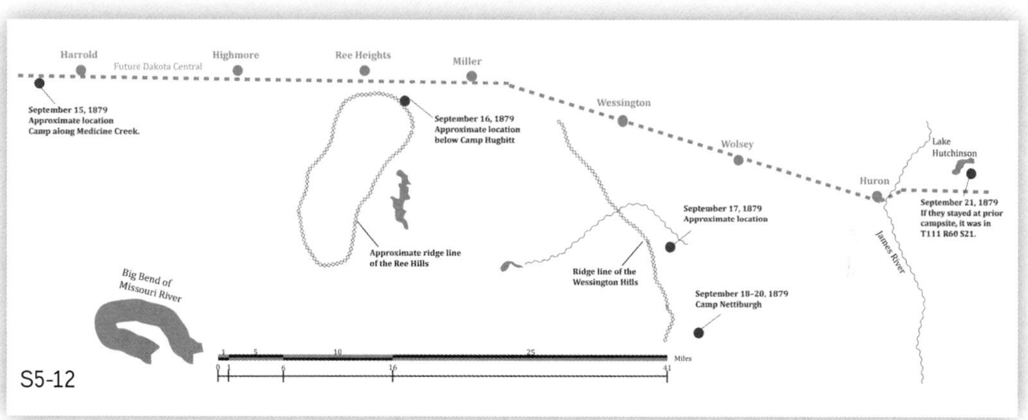

S5-12

On September 15, the men left Reed's Ranch and their work along Medicine Creek, and headed eastward, reaching a point sixteen miles to the northeast. Unfortunately, by the end of the day, Irish was "very sick" again.

After another "very cold night," his health improved, and the team continued east, camping for the night below the hill where Camp Hughitt was located, having traveled thirty-six miles that day. While they camped, Bancroft arrived with mail and the news that Adams, the sick crewman who had been taken out of camp on August 27 to receive medical help, had died. This must have been a somber moment for the rest of the crew and their leader. While they processed their colleague's death, a deer was brought in for dinner. The next day, another twenty-five miles were covered before camp was set up, and the work continued on.

SETTLERS SWARMING IN

In her novel *By the Shores of Silver Lake*, Laura Ingalls Wilder paints an image of a beautiful prairie devoid of humans, with the exception of the few railroad workers and her family. In reality, settlers looking for land were swarming over the area. Reminiscences of early settlers near De Smet also mention neighborly encounters with local Native peoples. The *Brookings County Press* of September 18 noted, "Land agents at Oakwood are busy locating land seekers in Kingsbury and Beadle counties."[60] Those are the two counties west of Brookings, extending twenty miles west of the James River.

Those already settled on the land were harvesting for the fall, and the yields were published. A farmer from Oakwood claimed to have threshed 653 bushels of oats that had been raised on 10 acres. Another yielded 24 bushels of wheat, 35 bushels of barley, and 52 bushels of oats from his land.[61] These reports show that the area around Brookings was, in fact, producing grain in the fall of 1879.

As the little site called both Terra Coteau and Bandy Town was swiftly renamed Volga, the September 18 *Brookings County Press* expected the new town at the center of Brookings County to be named Waterman, after the Chicago & North Western's officer Mr. Waterman.[62] That name did not stick either, and Brookings soon became the biggest town along the line west of Tracy.

A short move of just under five miles (making a total of one hundred miles from Pierre—99.9 according to Irish, but close enough) was made the morning of September 18, and the crew made camp again at 9 a.m. Provisions had run out, and temperatures dropped to the point that ice formed overnight. Over the next two days, Irish worked on notes about the surveyed route, and an antelope was shot and prepared for the crew's meal. Irish completed the notes from work along Medicine Creek and reported the levels finished. The next task was to create maps. The twentieth dawned under a "warmer, red sunrise," another antelope was shot to feed the men, and they prepared for another camp move.

On Sunday, September 21, the crew pulled up camp and started moving. At 4 p.m. they crossed the James River and found it to be "nearly dry." By 6:50 p.m.—"dark"—two men went missing. DeBarr was the hapless rider of a runaway horse, and Thorn again became lost while out hunting antelope (or as Irish recorded, "from zeal in hunting"), his sense of direction perhaps not being one his strongest attributes. With camp on the move, it was up to the lost men to find their way to the main corps, which both accomplished the next day.

Scouting Volga to Watertown: September 22–October 4, 1879

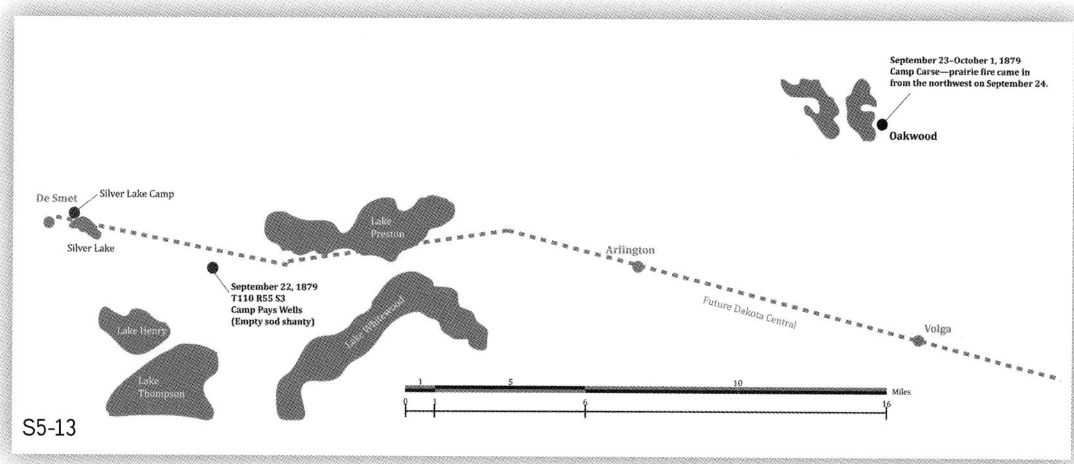

On September 22, as the crew moved farther east, they found that all water holes between Lake Hutchinson and Camp Pays Wells were dry—a concerning situation—but a cold rain settled in overnight. (Irish noted the name of this camp but did not explain its origin. The "Pays" portion likely referred to B. E. Pay, Irish's companion on this scout. The "Wells" portion may have referred to available water or, less likely, relate to the contractor Wells, but all of that is conjecture.) They moved an additional thirty miles east, arriving in Oakwood on the evening of September 23.

The rain provided drinking water for the men and horses, but the wetness led to shivering through the night, which was cold with a strong southwest wind. Also, while the rain sated the men and horses, it was not enough to protect the dry, parched grasses.

At about 1 p.m. on Wednesday, September 24, "a fierce fire" came rampaging toward them from the northwest. The men fought to save their camp and themselves all afternoon, succeeding after "a hard fight." The fire also burned into the edge of Oakwood, where "the citizens had a narrow escape."

PRAIRIE FIRE

This specific fire did not appear in the *Brookings County Press*, but in mid-November, a correspondent from Oakwood reflected on several of that autumn's fires. Much hay had been destroyed, and many expected the price would therefore go up.

In her autobiography, Laura Ingalls Wilder describes a wildfire that came into the Silver Lake railroad camp, sweeping in "out of the west after dark and [getting] into the tall grass in the Big Slough." Wilder continues,

> It looked for awhile as though the camp would be burned, but the men were all out with teams plowing furrows to turn the fire and setting back fires whipping them out on the side next camp while they were small and whipping out little fires with grain sacks. They headed it around the camp and it went roaring around on the other side of the lake and away to the east.[63]
>
> Wilder's autobiography is not reliably chronological, but this was a good spot to include her description of a fire like the one that threatened Oakwood.

Fighting a wildfire is an exhausting experience. Irish wrote, "We are cleaning up. All are tired out and I am sick. Day hot and the ashes and dust fly terribly." A "severe gale" blew all day, making the situation more difficult. Despite the blowing ash and dust, work continued. This time, Irish and crew were working on yet another side project for the Chicago & North Western. With B. E. Pay and two others, he scouted the land between Oakwood and Watertown, investigating the possibility of a rail route between, with the actual terminus at Volga—but Irish specifically noted Oakwood. This line would come to fruition.

The new route was graded in 1880, and the yet-unrailed grade was used by wagons and sleighs during the upcoming Hard Winter of 1880–81. Before that, the roadbed in Volga was used by Territorial Governor Ordway as the site of an inspirational speech full of the best boosterism of the day. That final grade did not, however, go through Oakwood. Instead, it passed several miles to the east. Most of Oakwood's buildings and population defected to the newly sprouted town of Bruce, with the exception of B. E. Pay's Oakwood House Hotel.

Irish arrived in Watertown on September 26 and stopped for a meal. Within popular culture of the time, the murders by the "Bloody Benders" of Kansas were famous. The Benders were a family who operated a roadside inn, killed their guests, then buried the bodies in the yard. They scattered and disappeared into thin air when authorities closed in on them. Irish took his meal at "Benders"—whether an establishment (he mentioned staying at the Central Hotel) or a private home is not known—but to his diary, he confessed that he'd teased the "old man about the Kansas murders." Honestly, one wonders whether that was wise, as the whereabouts of the murderers were not known (though one would think they'd have changed their names).

Irish did not sleep that night, feeling "quite used up." He also received a telegram telling him to wait for a letter from Blunt, expected to arrive on the afternoon train.

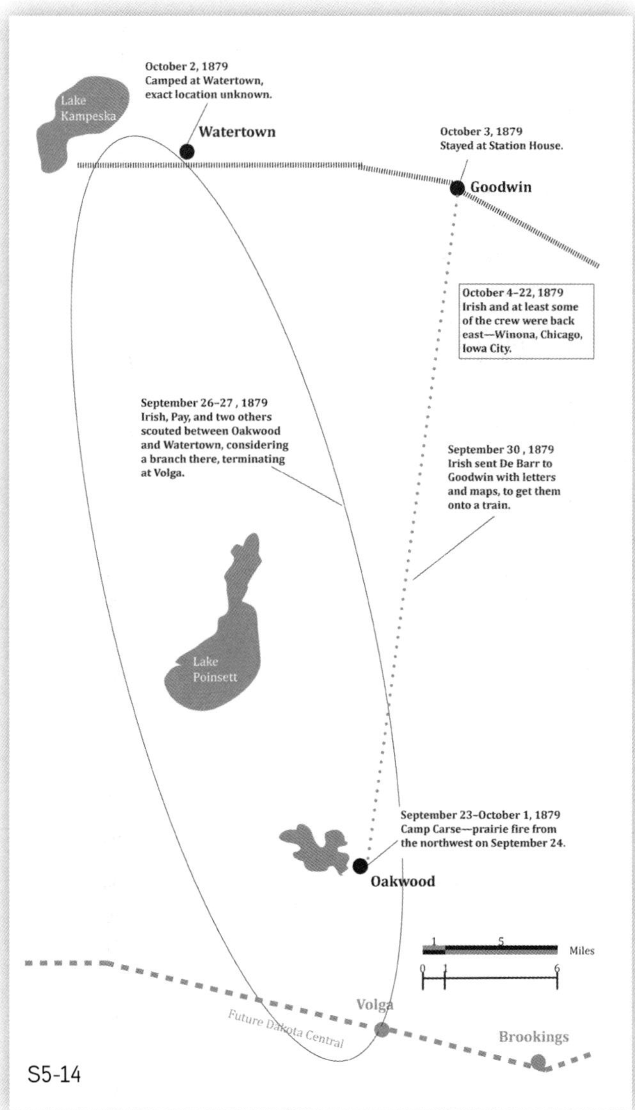

September 27 was a hot day that gave way to a rainy night, followed by a new day that brought rain in "torrents." As typical, rain did not stop the crew from performing their duties, and by late morning, the men had set off, reaching camp by evening. The day drained Irish, however, and he felt "quite sick" by nightfall.

The morning of the twenty-ninth, he still felt unwell but rode off to meet up with Blunt. After their midday meal, Irish gave Blunt "4 double blankets, 1 buffalo robe and 1 oil cloth, and a gun." Another downpour started at 3 p.m., and it continued for the next four hours.

Weather improved the next day, and with it Irish optimistically hoped "to soon get rid of this fever." The letters and maps prepared from the recent work were sent to Goodwin with DeBarr for transport, and two wagons were "packed up and loaded for Watertown."

October 1, which reached 91 degrees, was again spent taking down what they'd named Camp Carse and preparing for a major move, including pulling "down No. 1 tent for the last time." It was likely a difficult day, as the wind "blew a perfect gale all day," making tent takedown a pronounced battle between the men and the blowing sail-like canvas.

The wind preceded a storm that hit overnight, bringing heavy rain and shivering cold—46 degrees with a strong northwest wind. Lightning and thunder thrashed around the base camp, where the men may have been housed in the barest of shelters, as they intended to be on the move early next day.

They were mobile by 8 a.m., pausing to eat lunch near Lake Poinsett, one of the three lakes Irish mentioned in his letter to Frémont as not being dry that summer. After traveling throughout the cold, windy day, they reached Watertown at 9 p.m.

UPDATES ALONG THE ROUTE

The land that had seemed so remote when the surveyors came through just six months before was transforming at a startling rate.

The October 2 edition of the *Brookings County Press* was awash in news about goings-on in the wake of the surveyors. New towns had been platted along the route from Tracy to Huron at the James River. The first locomotive had rolled into the station at Lake Benton two weeks before. The bridge-builder camp had moved west to Medary Creek, and Hiram Forbes had moved his crew west of the James River. The tracklayers had been at work within Brookings County since September 30, which was the same day the telegraph stringers began work in Tracy, working their way westward.

The same edition allows a glimpse at how these new stations went operational ahead of the construction of the railyards. Boxcars were retrofitted to serve as temporary depots, allowing business to be transacted even before official structures were built.[64] In fact, an official letter from Chicago, written September 23 and published in the October 2 *Brookings County Press*, announced that Lake Benton would officially open for freight business on the new rail line on September 29,[65] four months after ground was broken in Tracy.

The towns sprouting up along the surveyed route were frantically at work putting up buildings ahead of winter. By early October, Volga—also called Bandy Town in this article—boasted a store building moved from a nearby community (perhaps Oakwood), a hotel under construction, a blacksmith shop, and many other buildings at various levels of completion. The railroad company also had, just to the north, a "large store building well filled with goods."[66] It was assumed that the railroad construction would continue through winter, and that this supply store would keep the men well stocked in their work. By the end of the first week of October, the tracklayers had made it to Medary Creek, closing in on Brookings, though building the needed bridges would be a slow process.[67]

It wasn't all rapid expansion, however. According to the *Brookings County Press*, the survey underway between Volga and Watertown was "abandoned by orders from headquarters,"[68] though no explanation was given. Interestingly, a November 13 article would report that a survey was again taking place between the two towns.[69] It may be that a second set of surveyors was put on this project so that Irish and his crew could focus on the main route west.

—A corps of engineers are now surveying and looking up a route for a railroad from Volga to W… This line will run through the town site of Oakwood, and that town is now happy. We hope they will be able to secure the road, but have little faith in its being built soon.

Brookings County Press, November 13, 1879. S5-15

The next day, October 3, remained cold, with a wind that "blew with violence all day." During the unpleasantness, the crew paid their various bills around Watertown, then Irish took a portion of the men east to Goodwin to pay off more invoices. The wind continued strong and blustery, which made travel on the fourth difficult too.

The wind wasn't the only problem impacting their travels. The men left Goodwin at 5 a.m., but not by train. The recent prairie fire had burned Bridge 589, between Goodwin and Gary, and until it could be repaired, trains could not run. They got around the still-smoldering structure by taking a wagon from Goodwin to Gary and catching the train there, finding themselves in the relatively cosmopolitan embrace of Winona by 5 p.m.

A Furlough: October 5–19, 1879

Conditions in Winona were a bit of an upgrade for the men. Irish and Joe Mudra spent the night of October 5 at Huff's House Hotel, then had dinner at Blunt's new home in the river town. While the day was hot and dry, at 95 degrees, there was no wind. Imagine, after months of wind—described using various adjectives, all of which translated, more or less, to "it is always very windy"—it must have been nearly delightfully disorienting to feel a calm air.

Winona's Huff's House Hotel, the "place to be." It was located at the southwest corner of Johnson and West Third Streets, three blocks south of the Mississippi River and the tracks of the Winona & St. Peter. It was set up to accommodate the needs of the business traveler. Irish, Blunt, and sometimes members of the surveying crew met and stayed there. S5-16

The rendezvous with the more established town may have been a bit too tempting for Joe Mudra, who, Irish wrote, "got drunk . . . and is still fuddled." Irish, himself an admitted occasional drinker, seemed bemused by his traveling partner, extending leniency since they were not officially on the job. The men left Winona at 1:30 a.m. on October 6 and arrived in Chicago by 4 p.m.

Irish did not mention Blunt traveling with them, but after having dined at the man's house in Winona on the fifth, Irish also met with Blunt in the general offices of the Chicago & North Western in Chicago on the seventh. The day was again hot ("awful hot," in fact), and Irish was "at work getting cooler clothes." Once in more comfortable attire, he went to work "on maps and estimates" and the "final papers" for the route of the Dakota Central to the Missouri River, a major step for the upstart railroad.

This trip to Chicago also began a well-earned respite for the lead surveyor. Mrs. Irish arrived in Chicago on the afternoon of October 9, and over the next two days, Mr. Irish happily escorted his "bonny wife" around the sights of the bustling city, including Lincoln Park, the Douglas Monument, and views of Lake Michigan. (Their visit also corresponded with the eighth anniversary of the Great Chicago Fire, which started on October 8, 1871, and burned for several days.)

After their time together in Chicago, the couple boarded a train late in the evening of October 12, arriving home the next evening. Irish spent the next several days enjoying the company of his family, then prepared to depart for Dakota Territory on the twentieth. He also found time to contract for a fourteen-by-nineteen-foot addition to the house, to be completed by November 10.

Sadly, he also dealt with the mournful loss of the family's "faithful watch dog and sure friend," Mink, who passed away overnight between October 17 and 18. The beloved pet was buried "under the Siberian apple tree," Irish writing, "Good bye Mink, good true old friend." Those final words in his October 19 entry still evoke his pain all these years later. A frost struck too, though it "did not kill the morning glories."

A Return to Work East of the James: October 20–31, 1879

The day after patting down the earth above their dear Mink, Mr. and Mrs. Irish again departed for Chicago, arriving at 7 a.m. Later that day, they boarded a train for Dakota Territory, arriving at Kasota, on the east bank of the Minnesota River, for breakfast on their third day of travel, which was also Mrs. Irish's birthday. Once on their way again, a telegram instructed Irish to continue to Tracy and wait there until Blunt could join him.

Irish did so, and he was joined in Tracy by not only Blunt but also Hughitt, Johnson, Burke, Keep, and two more of the key officers of the Chicago & North Western. This was a significant gathering of power; whatever the conversations were about, Irish did not intimate the details in his diary. The talks took place within the company's business car while the train returned to Kasota, where Irish found himself overnight before returning, again, to Tracy with Blunt. Back in Tracy, Irish was reunited with Mrs. Irish, who had waited there for his return, and the pair traveled on to Watertown together.

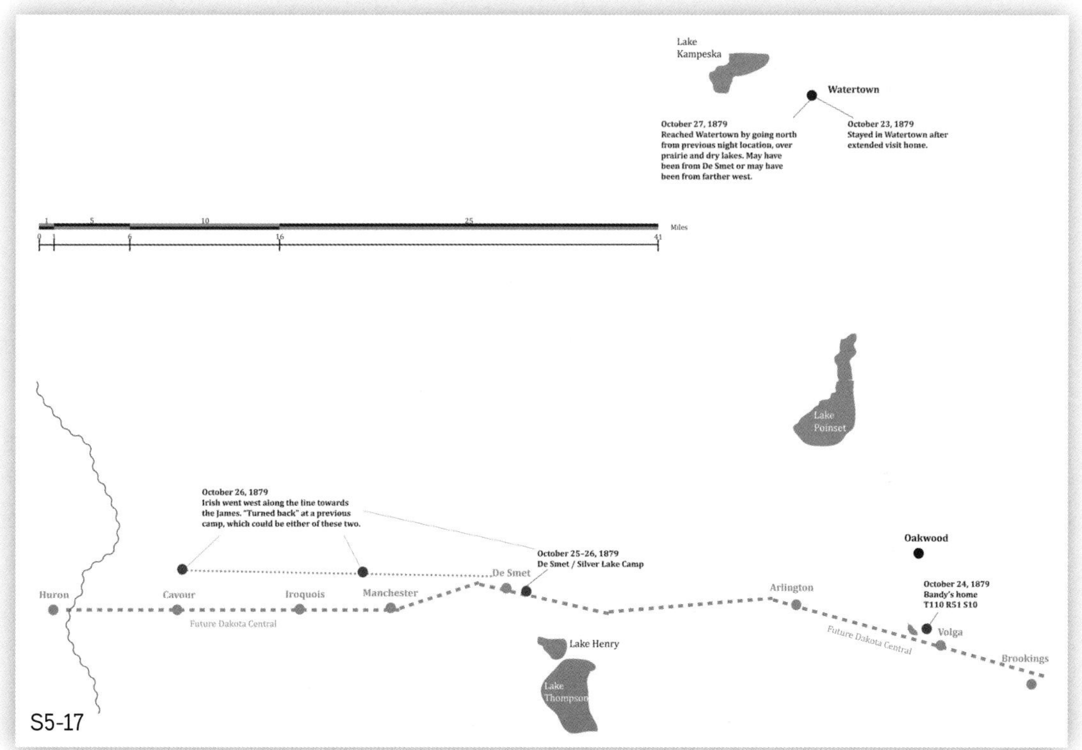

S5-17

RAPID PROGRESS

While Irish was home on brief furlough, the telegraph poles were set as far as the Big Sioux River, and they were functional to Aurora. (Communicating via telegraphy was often referred to as "lightning.")[70] The October 22 *Brookings County Press* announced that the first official building in the newly platted town of Brookings was a blacksmith shop, "which went up on the eighth," followed by a warehouse, a hardware store, and the post office.[71] Businesses were on the move too. The tracks were laid into Brookings the same hour the equipment of the *Brookings County Press* arrived ("six o'clock Saturday, October 18") during the newspaper's move from Fountain to the new, expected-to-boom town.[72]

Farther west, reports placed the graders within ten miles of the James, with "the heavy cuts nearly completed, and the entire grade [would] be ready for the iron by the first of December."[73] The first locomotive was reported to have crossed the border from Minnesota into Dakota Territory on October 2, and by the third week of the month, "the engine [was] almost near enough the Sioux River to drink of her placid waters."[74]

From Kasota, Irish regaled Ruth and Lizzie about the surprise meeting between himself and the officers of the Chicago & North Western, which had forced him to leave their mother behind in Tracy in the hospitable "care of a Mrs. Welsh at the Commercial Hotel."

The "special palace" car of the Chicago & North Western arrived from the west. The officers had been on a trip examining Irish's work. After greetings, the men started east. "[We] had a fine time and talked the RR situation over, and they authorized me to go on with the work," wrote Irish. "They also gave me two weeks more time to rest in, and visit at home so after I go up to Watertown today and go over the work, we will come home via Dubuque."

Talk of future trips home always seemed to be couched with "after this big amount of work is accomplished." But the officers trusted him, and as he sometimes mentioned, this was no small compliment.

The trip, he told his daughters, was proving beneficial for their mother. He then shared an amusing story: "We had a pious crowd on the sleeping car. Very pious. So we were afraid to drink our whiskey in public but lo! and behold! we found out that the pious ones had a bigger bottle than ours, and were going into the dressing room to drink, so we followed their example."

The parents would be home again soon, though for Mr. Irish it would be a short visit. He broke the news that he would "spend the winter at Fort George, on the Missouri." He wondered how his daughters would react to this news, especially after he had sworn up and down there would be no more winter campaigns. "Now be good girls, don't fly to pieces, nor run away," he teased.

On the morning of Friday, October 24, the Irishes departed Watertown and headed to Oakwood in less than comfortable conditions—"Very cold now, wind from SE it punishes us badly." The party pushed past Oakwood and spent the night at Bandy's home, to the northwest of modern Volga.

Following the line westward on October 25, the party fought a "hurricane" of wind but enjoyed more moderate temperatures, arriving for the night at an established railroad camp west of Lake Preston. Under the hospitality of W. D. Hodge, the party stayed at the "Engineers house" at De Smet, in the Silver Lake Camp. Readers of the Little House books will know that building as the Surveyor's House, which would shelter the Ingalls family for the coming winter.

S5-18

S5-19

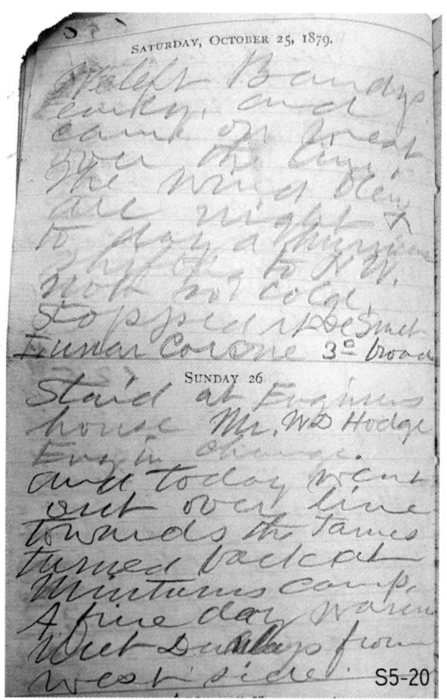
SATURDAY, OCTOBER 25, 1879.

SUNDAY 26

S5-20

A VISIT TO SILVER LAKE CAMP

For readers of the Little House series by Laura Ingalls Wilder, there is an interesting overlap between Irish and the Ingalls family. Irish and his wife were at Silver Lake Camp for two nights, so it would not be at all surprising if the gregarious Charles Ingalls spoke with Irish during this visit. Perhaps Mrs. Irish would have visited with the few other women in camp, which would have included Mrs. Ingalls (Caroline).

In Wilder's autobiography, she wrote about how others frequently ate with the Ingalls family. She then added, "The Co. men [the railroad company] when passing through came too and so Ma and I were very busy."[75] This makes it possible—maybe even likely—that Irish and Blunt were served their meals by Caroline and Laura.

Also, Wilder remembered that an "Irish baby" had been ill and that her mother, Caroline, had attended to the patient. Irish did not indicate any illnesses for himself or his wife, something he tended to elaborate on when not feeling well. So while it is unlikely that the "Irish baby" was actually an adult Mr. or Mrs. Irish, it is interesting to contemplate that Irish may have been a name, not a nationality.

The next day, the party left Silver Lake Camp and went west over the line, "towards the James," turning back east to spend a second night at the Engineers House. On October 27, they headed toward Watertown, but went north to explore the "rolling prairie with many dry lakes." The officers may have been seeking Irish's opinion on the conclusions reached by the second surveyor that had been hired to examine the route west from Watertown.

Whatever the purpose of the excursion to the north of De Smet and on toward Watertown, Irish left no hints within his diary. He did note, however, that it looked stormy, that the wind blew hard from the west and northwest, and that after some rain, it became "quite cold."

Travel across the prairies was long and tiresome. But so, too, could be train travel. The group reached Watertown the evening of the twenty-seventh, boarded the eastbound train the next morning, and were at Blunt's home in Winona by suppertime. Irish spent the next morning writing letters and preparing for the next step in the job, leaving "orders for stoves," as surveying work was to go on all winter.

Once the paperwork was complete, the couple boarded the afternoon train for Chicago, staying in a sleeping car for $1.50. After arriving in Chicago the next morning, they were soon aboard another train back westward to Cedar Rapids, then south to Iowa City, finally arriving home at 5 p.m. on October 31. What Irish's men were up to during his furloughs is a mystery. Perhaps they, too, had time off; it was never mentioned in any of the diary entries.

VOLGA WINTER TERMINUS OF WORK

The final October edition of the *Brookings County Press* let readers know that once the railyards (including the depots, stockyards, elevators, warehouses, etc.) were completed to the east, the Brookings railyard would be next, construction expected to begin by mid-November. Readers also learned that Volga would serve as the western terminus for winter operations.[76]

Over the last many weeks, the leaders of Brookings had been on a relentless campaign to have the new town named the county seat. By early November it was a fait accompli, and the editor seemed almost stunned by the ease of the election victory, writing with bemusement, "It wasn't such a hard job after all to move the county seat."[77] This claiming of the county seat for the newly formed town along the Dakota Central illustrates the importance of the coming railroad in the societal structures, how fully it impacted most aspects of public and private life at the time. While all this was going on along the freshly built tracks and while the surveyors were not that much farther west, they were seemingly in an entirely different world.

Another Furlough: November 1–14, 1879

Irish was only home for a few cold days (one of which was "cold as blazes"). He balanced time with his family and preparing a return to Dakota Territory, placing an order for a leveler (surveying equipment) from Wisconsin.

On November 3, Irish received a telegram from Hughitt, and on the fifth, he was again aboard a train headed to Chicago, amid an assault of howling winds and swirling dust.

There were issues with the proposed route, and Irish met with Hughitt in Chicago the next day, November 6. The survey crew were to return to Fort George Island and rework the survey approaching the east bank of the Missouri River, the first option being the route down Medicine Creek to its mouth, the second being farther north to allow for a crossing of the Missouri nearer to the mouth of the Cheyenne River (on the west bank). They were to also examine the head of Bad River, well west of the Missouri and within the Great Sioux Reservation.

OFFICIAL AGREEMENTS

On November 6, 1879 (while Irish was meeting with Hughitt in Chicago), the commissioner of Indian affairs received a telegraph indicating that a request by the Dakota Central, dated November 1, had been granted. This gave the railroad company permission to "construct its road down the valley of Medicine Creek crossing and [recross] said creek as the engineering necessities may require." Secretary of the Interior Carl Schurz requested that "Commissioner of Indian Affairs Hayt inform the Indian Agents at the affected Indian Agencies."[78]

Refer in reply to the following:

DEPARTMENT OF THE INTERIOR,

OFFICE OF INDIAN AFFAIRS,

WASHINGTON, Nov. 1, 1879.

To the Comr of Indian affairs
Washington D.C.

Sir:

The Dakota Central Railway Co. are engaged in the construction of a railroad connecting with the Winona & St Peter Railway at the east line of the Territory of Dakota, and comprising a part of the system of roads operated by the Chicago & North western Railway Co. For the purpose of obtaining a practicable crossing of the Missouri River, the company asks the right to construct its railroad down the valley of Medicine Creek crossing and recrossing said Creek as the engineering necessities may require. 2 To establish a ferry across the

Letter to the commissioner of Indian affairs requesting permission to construct a railroad down the valley of Medicine Creek. S5-21

Department of the Interior,
Washington November 6th 1879

The Commissioner
of Indian Affairs

Sir:

I return herewith the letter of Mr B. C. Cooke, solicitor of the Dakota Central Railroad Company, &c., asking that said Company be allowed to construct its road down the valley of Medicine Creek crossing and recrossing said Creek as the engineering necessities may require; also making certain other requests which you recommend may be reserved for future consideration.

In accordance with your recommendation authority is hereby granted to the said

(Railroad

Letter from Secretary of the Interior Carl Schurz to Commissioner of Indian Affairs Hayt granting permission for the Dakota Central to construct tracks along the surveyed route down Medicine Creek to the Missouri River. S5-22

After having vowed earlier in the year that he would do no more winter surveys, Irish was facing not only a winter survey but one covering a significant swath of land in a region already known for notorious winters. This had to have been a daunting thought as he left the offices of the Chicago & North Western in the hustling and bustling city of Chicago, which itself had two inches of snow on the ground. Irish may have made a mental note to check on the status of the stoves he ordered. They'd be needed.

He was also still anxiously looking for a replacement for the broken leveler, the one he ordered not yet having arrived. In fact, he spent the rest of the day creating a list of needed supplies, then headed back to Iowa City on the night train. The next few days were spent finalizing the return trip to Dakota Territory and enjoying his visit home. This time, however, he would be headed to Yankton—not the usual route through Minnesota.

CAMP LOCATIONS

As I tried to nail down campsite locations, identifying those in the general "west of the James and east of Medicine Creek before it descends down to the Missouri" vicinity was one of three long-term odysseys I became obsessed with. Part of that was due to my own impatience; when the maps that held the answers became off-limits—due first to COVID-19 restrictions, then to their physical fragility—I doggedly pushed ahead, trying to identify work locations based on vague clues from the diary entries, letters, area maps old and new, topography maps, protractors, rulers, and considerable contemplation. Then one glorious day, the mysteries were solved. But first there were, shall we say, some frustrations.

In March 2020, I was scheduled to dig deep into the Special Collections and Archives department at University of Iowa Libraries in Iowa City, Iowa. I'd done considerable research in 2017, but this was for deeper items to supplement the first round. The boxes and maps were reserved, plans coordinated with the archivists, hotel reservations made. Of course, that was all put on hold when the pandemic began and shutdowns were ordered.

The new plan was that staff would dig up what I needed, online video meetings would be held, and we would jointly work through the maps. The archivists were doing their best to keep up with research requests, not just from myself but many others. When my turn came, Rich Dana and I set up a teleconference appointment. While I waited for the virtual visit, I kept plugging away at the information I had on hand.

Like with Rush Lake, finding the locations of these particular campsites felt important for telling the story. But where Rush Lake was a single campsite, the region between the James and the northern end of Medicine Creek had multiple campsites. Of the creeks mentioned in the diaries or letters—or at least those between the James on the east and Medicine Creek much further to the west—only one can be matched to a modern map. One!

In stubbornly trying to reproduce their movements, I applied significant effort in deconstructing diary clues, a multi-powered magnifying glass in hand, squinting and scouring modern topographical maps of South Dakota and various historical maps from the second half of the nineteenth century. You might be surprised at how varied modern maps are. Most of them have the big rivers—Big Sioux, James, Missouri, Cheyenne, Bad. But the tributaries, sub-tributaries, or sub-sub tributaries? Not a chance. Or at least rarely. Oddly, tributaries to the Bad River west of the Missouri were easiest to tally between historic and modern maps (*that* odyssey will be touched on later). Even on modern maps (whether paper or online), creeks can be identified with different names, stream courses, and even (in some cases) actual locations, depending on the publisher.

Once the crew had moved west of where the official township-range-section grid was set, Irish could no longer identify locations by that designator. Thus he would often say, for example, that he'd traveled two hours "S30W," meaning 30 degrees west of south. If we knew where he'd started, we'd have a good idea of where he went. But that starting point was terribly elusive, and two hours could mean half a mile or several miles, depending on terrain or task.

Where Irish described a "valley with timber" after having ridden for some distance over so much time in such a direction, I analyzed maps for probability of timber considering an 1879 or 1880 topography: his timber was probably within a creek valley, but not necessarily, as wet spots such as sloughs could also nurture some scrub trees. The camp was possibly protected by a hill or hills, but not necessarily. Extra bonus points if the diary or letters also mentioned such features. But the odds that any feature he described could be easily correlated to a modern location were only so-so. Trees were cut down for housing and fuel, or simply died in the intervening almost century and a half. Creeks and wet spots in an arid land can appear and disappear almost at will depending on drought cycles (though clues to their existence usually remain), and of course, private ownership prevented full investigation of the landscape (though most owners were willing and even excited to show me around, offering any help they could provide; the people of this area are extraordinarily generous!).

In reality, there simply weren't enough solid clues within the diaries or letters to locate most of the campsites between the James River and Medicine Creek within more than a several-mile radius, or "zone of possibility." I was frustrated—I wanted to do better. I wanted to see the maps.

Finally, the long-awaited day of the video teleconference arrived, and Rich Dana had the documents on hand. A large table (or several pushed together) took up much of the room. There was plenty of space to lay out large documents or many smaller documents placed side by side. Beside the table were carts, and upon the carts were boxes—full of treasures.

I sat at my dining table, full of anticipation, an external monitor connected to my laptop, increasing my digital work space. Rich placed the first box on the table, removed the top, and pulled out a large accordion folder. He unhooked the clasp and removed a pile of documents, setting them on the table. I was excited, full of hope that answers would fly out of those boxes like magical moths.

As Rich carefully turned pages, I would tell him whether each item was relevant to my research. Because I'd already obtained most of the smaller documents related to the Dakota Central, these papers turned out to mostly be related to Irish's work before or after the Dakota Central. I had hoped some items had been misfiled in other boxes, but that turned out not to be the case. Finally the boxes were completed and set aside. The next items were the maps—the oh-so-important maps!

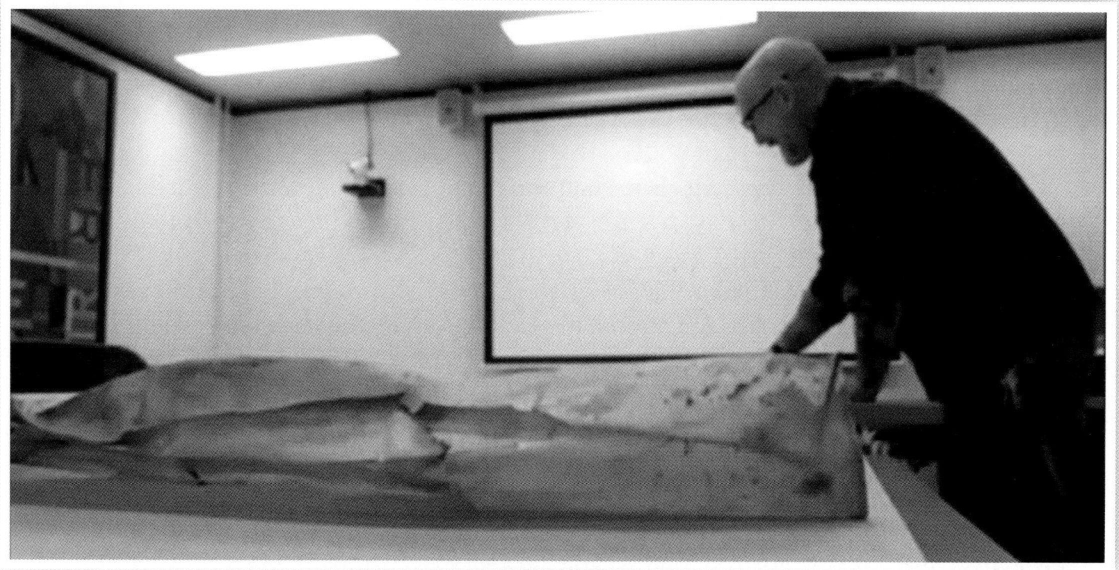

Rich Dana unfurling one of the frighteningly fragile maps. S5-23

Rich pulled out each map carefully, spreading it across the table, weights added to the corners. I turned my head this way and that as Rich moved the camera over each map, trying to orient my view to the layout of the maps. *Would the answers be on this map? The next?*

Some of the maps were dry parchment that crackled like stiff tissue paper while being unrolled. Some had nothing more than straight lines and calculations, with zero context as to what or where they were. These were set aside as unhelpful. My earlier enthusiastic hope started to shift toward cautious optimism.

One map, as he began to unroll it, objected to being disturbed from its long slumber. It crinkled so loudly that Rich and I both cringed. Despite Rich's gentleness, the map was cracking and crumbling in his fingers, bits of it falling to the table. It didn't seem to hold any important information, but it was an impactful moment. Was my quest important enough to risk these documents? Rich stopped unrolling that desperately fragile map and marked it as destined for the restoration department. The next few maps were similarly fragile, but they contained mostly unhelpful drawings.

Just as I was beginning to shift from cautious optimism to disappointment, a map wafted onto the table and seemed to shout to me. I yelped, "There it is! Nettiburgh's Grove!" then, "Look! There's Camp Hughitt!" These maps would help me locate several campsites, and from those, others. We'd hit pay dirt. Yet another map had the entire set of campsites up and down Medicine Creek—the route that took the tracks from the high plains down to the Missouri River. Any researcher who has found a cache of answers knows this excitement, this glory of discovery. I could finalize my own maps, and I knew the campsites were placed accurately, not based on conjectured guesses.

But wait . . . Let's back up a moment. It is important to mention that at the beginning of the teleconference, we'd agreed that recording the session would be sufficient, rather than photographing as we went, in order to get through more documents and maps in our limited appointment time. I'd then watch the resulting video after the fact, and from that be able to take screen shots and use those for my work. Makes perfect sense, right?

A few days later, an email arrived. The video had not been saved. Perhaps the two-hour appointment had been too long and the video too large. Whatever the reason, we'd have to do the appointment again. There was a long list of appointments in the queue, so it would be a while. The good news was that we now knew which boxes were relevant.

A few days later, another email arrived. Hooray—the video was found! I downloaded it and cleared my afternoon. I began to watch, ready to freeze the frame as each important location appeared on screen . . . then realized a catastrophic reality: the teleconference platform defaulted to recording whoever was speaking, not necessarily what the presenter wants to show. So each time an important document or map appeared on screen, I would say, "Yes, that one is important," and the screen would immediately switch away from the map to show the speaker—me. Thus, rather than seeing the precious map location that would tell me where Nettiburgh's Grove was in conjunction to the other camps, I instead saw my excited face, not the map. Not Nettiburgh's Grove. Not Camp Hughitt. Not the answers I sought. Just my face, over and over, except when maps and documents were being put back into the boxes and folders. Drat!

Not the view I wanted to see when reviewing the video that we thought would answer all my questions. Drat! S5-24

I sent Rich an email, sheepishly cowering over our folly, and the rescheduled dive into the map boxes was put back onto his schedule. It was several months before they could fit me in again. While waiting, I would sometimes go back to the clues, trying to sneak up on the diaries and maps as if, by some miracle, they would suddenly, magically, present to me the location of those mystery camps, surrounded by flashing neon lights and arrows. It never happened.

Then an email arrived saying that *all* the maps I sought had been deemed too fragile for research and sent to the restoration department, with no known date as to when they may be dealt with. After a few deep sighs, I returned to the video to try to obtain enough context from what was visible to make informed-enough guesses to suit my perfectionism, allowing me to place the campsites on the maps.

I even drove around the area, up and down the grid of roads, looking at locations within the "general vicinity" as mentioned by Irish, as if some waving patch of grass would suddenly provide a clue. Of course, there were no revelations, though several curious cows took a deep interest in my presence.

Finally, the research room reopened, having closed at the start of the COVID-19 pandemic, and I was able to go to Iowa City. People from different departments within Special Collections met and organized a game plan. After a couple of conversations, the marvelous Giselle Simón, director of conservation and collections care, set aside an entire morning to work directly with me so that I could see *each and every one* of those fragile maps (insert giddy, excited researcher noises here). Answers to two of the three most important mysteries eventually unfurled themselves across the table tops, and I was able to take photographs of the maps without any "technical difficulties" from the otherwise-helpful videoconference software. Along the way, I also learned about desiccated mold, live mold, animal glue and how it browns over time, and how to carefully unroll and reroll ridiculously long maps. Precious, lovely, wonderful maps!

One of the moldy maps, this one covering the James River to where Medicine Creek empties into the Missouri River. S5-25

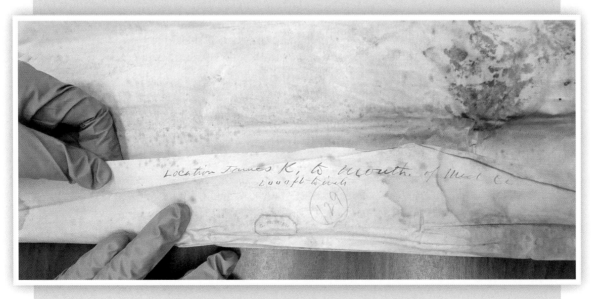

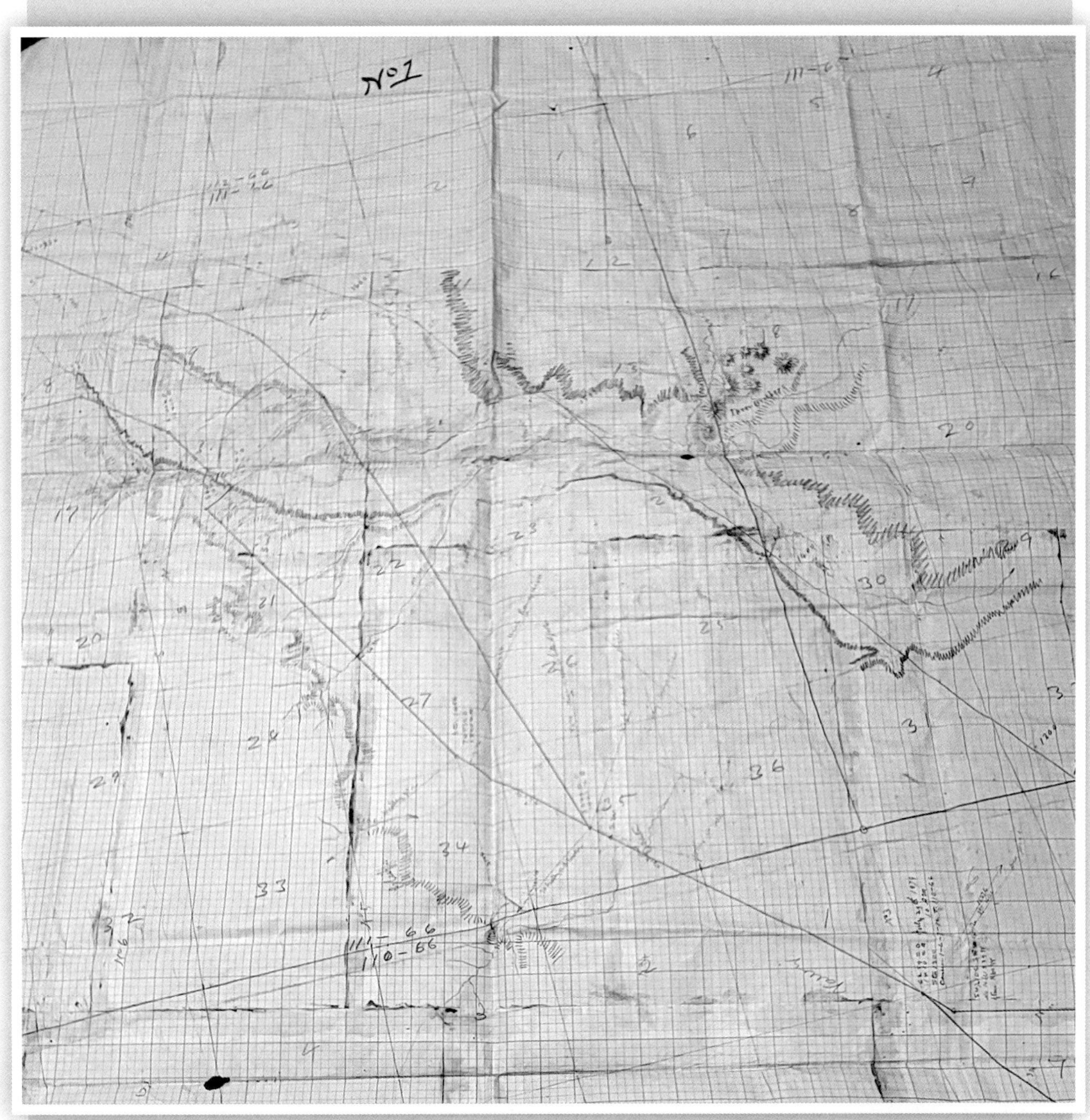

The full map of the Wessington Hills region, made up of individual pieces of graph paper glued together with animal glue, which has since browned along the edges. Each "seam" was beginning to separate, but we carefully unfolded the map, and it remained flat. S5-26

Section Six

SETTLING IN FOR THE WINTER

NOVEMBER 15, 1879—JANUARY 21, 1880

With winter approaching, the men rented a cozy log structure as a solid base camp during the difficult Dakota Territory winter. They spent considerable time and effort outfitting it to their needs, even setting out a mailbox so that hoped-for letters from home could be easily retrieved. Game was plentiful, comradery was good, and Christmas was observed as best they could. The survey work along Medicine Creek to bring the tracks from the high plain above down to the banks of the Missouri had to continue, however, and that involved going out in the field, sometimes for a week or more, away from their warm lodgings. Blizzards, wolves, and illness all came into play, including more than one race for shelter when a storm blew up out of nowhere. Worries for those at home crept in too, but progress continued day by day. Irish also came into the possession of a horse with a marvelous personality, which would serve as company and amusement in the months to come.

Yankton to Pierre via the Stage Road: November 15–24, 1879

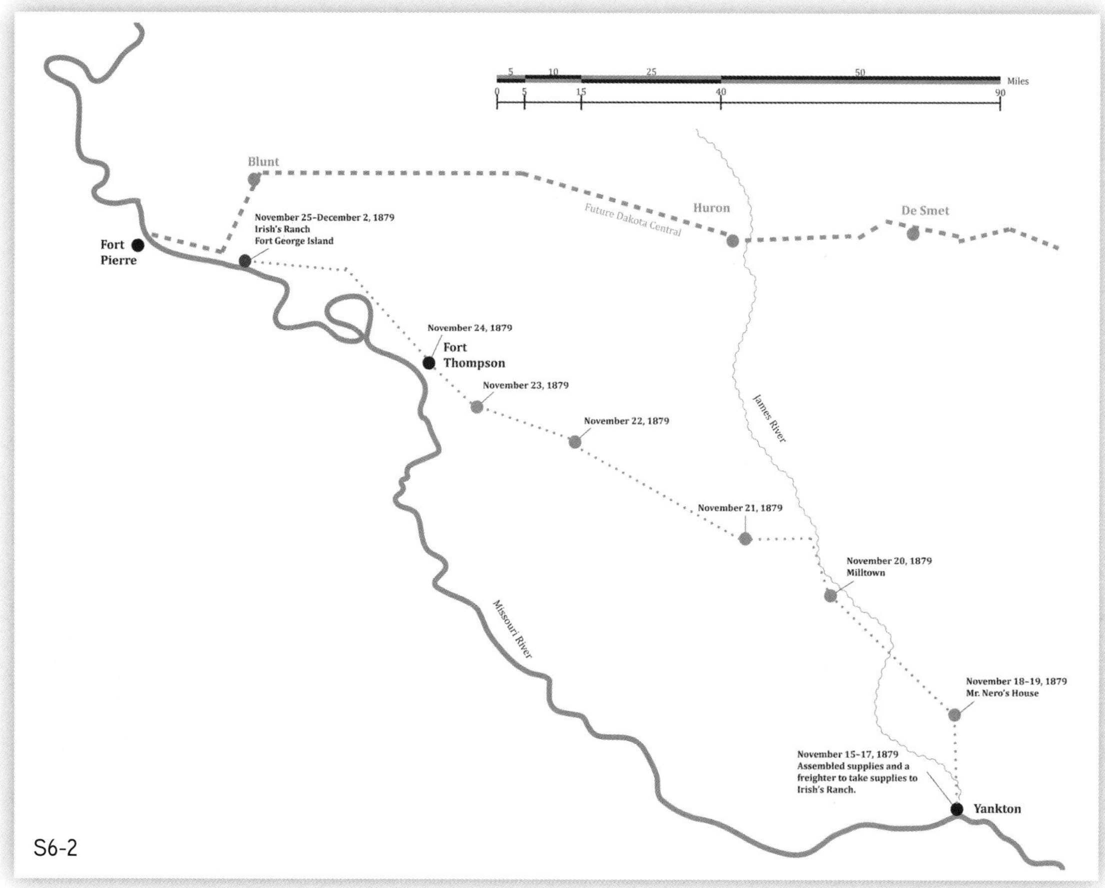

S6-2

On the morning of Friday, November 14, Irish was again on a train to Cedar Rapids. There, he boarded the 8 p.m. train west, across Iowa to Sioux City, then on to Yankton. Aboard the train, he had the opportunity to converse with P. A. Willson of Fort Thompson, though he didn't record any details about their discussion in writing. With his thoughts on crossing the Missouri River and beginning survey work beyond its not-yet-frozen waters, the conversation likely revolved around the residents and owners of that western property, the Lakota.

In a rather humorous note written during his trip back to Yankton from Cedar Rapids, Irish took a few moments to write,

> I tell you, Abbie, you must not risk me alone on the keers [Irish's underline—an accented pronunciation spelling of *cars*] anymore. Why, a lady took possession of me . . . and was

> determined to run off with me. She first thought I was John P. [Irish's brother] but when she found out her mistake, it made no difference. I tell you I was scared.

He then warned the women at home about a more serious matter: "They have an outbreak of dip[h]theria here and are badly scared about it." Cedar Rapids was not far from Iowa City, close enough that the disease's spreading was a very real fear. He provided plenty of recommendations for how and what to gargle with (iodine and carbolic acid) and the usual emphatic reminders about quinine and iron camphor.

Irish's diary frequently expressed anxiety about health (his own or that of others), the weather (too cold or too hot), and certainly mosquitos (horror of horrors!). Seldom, however, was the work itself a source of concern (a few "bothersome hills" being a rare exception). While in Yankton, however, he seemed restless, trying to round up supplies and get everything in order, worried about being fully prepared for the coming winter.

"I hurry them [the suppliers] up," wrote Irish, having seen stormy clouds to the south, "for I must get into camp before hard winter sets in." A hard freeze descended that night, making his impatience all the more timely. He contracted with a freighter at a rate of "$2.35 per hundred and $5 for the men," to be paid upon delivery to Fort George Island. (This meant that Irish would pay the freighter $2.35 for carrying one hundred pounds of cargo up to one hundred miles.) Arrangements were made just as a light snow was beginning.

STAGES.

DAKOTA DIVISION.

WYOMING STAGE CO.

From Yankton to Fort Sully,

And all intermediate points, including Bon Homme, Springfield, Yankton Agency, Fort Randall, Wheeler, Red Lake, Ft. Thompson, Ft. Pierre and Fort Sully.

Comfortable Coaches and Quick Time.

WM. KRAMER, Agent. S. P. GAMBLE, Superintendent.

YANKTON & PARKER

DAILY STAGE.

Mail and Express Line,

Tri-weekly to Sioux Falls.

The Shortest, Best and Cheapest Line to

SIOUX FALLS.

The route lies over the finest section of Southern Dakota, and passes through the counties of Yankton, Turner and Minnehaha, touching at Marindahl, Turkey Creek, Clay Creek, Swan Lake, Howard and Wall Lake.

YANKTON Office at American Express Office.

SIOUX FALLS Office at the Cataract House.

MOORE & SUMNER, Proprietors.

Dakota Central

STAGE LINE

Brinkerhoff & Jordan, Prop's.

The stages of this line run from Yankton to Utica, Lesterville, Odessa, Scotland, Maxwell, Olivet, Whiterburg, Milltown, Martella, Rockport, Rosedale and Firesteel in fifteen hours, leaving Yankton each morning at four o'clock. The return trip is made each day, leaving Firesteel at four o'clock a. m. and reaching Yankton at seven p. m.

Horses changed every ten miles.

Passengers and Express Goods Carried at Reasonable Rates.

Yankton office on Third Street, at Brinkerhoff's barn, just west of the Merchants hotel.

Mitchell office at J. O. WALRATH & CO'S. Livery stable.

Ads for just three of the stage lines serving southeastern Dakota Territory, giving interesting clues about how they were operated. S6-3

Irish arrived in Yankton "safe and well," taking up room 58 at the Jencks' Hotel. The weather was springlike, Irish writing, "The boatmen now wish that they had not pulled off their boats yet"; they were missing out on late-season business. With no boats plying the Missouri, Irish's "poor pilgrims" had to "hoof it up the road." He expected the stage trip to Fort George Island to take about two days.

He let Ruth know that since he'd left Reed's Ranch, the "whole property was burned by a prairie fire. . . ."—everything but the house, which was saved. Irish also observed that foot and wagon traffic to the Black Hills was significant, even at this time of year. He signed off with the not uncommon plea "Take quinine and iron +c , and keep well."

Before setting out from Yankton, Irish took the opportunity to drop another letter in the mail. He told Lizzie he expected to take "9 or 10 days to reach Ft. George with teams." That estimate is a far cry from the two-day estimate he had given when he first arrived, but a much more realistic one.

On Tuesday, November 18, at 3 p.m., Irish and his freighters left Yankton and began the trek northward toward Fort George Island, located off the east bank of the Missouri, about fifteen river miles downstream from modern Pierre and opposite the site that once held Fort George. After covering twenty miles during a pleasantly warm afternoon, the party retired for the night at 8:30 p.m. at a Mr. Nero's home, having traveled approximately 3.6 miles per hour on average.

—The Yankton *Press* of the 18th says: "A party of seven surveyors, under the leadership of C. W. Irish, left Yankton to-day for Pierre, by wagon, with instructions to run a survey for the extension of the Chicago & Northwestern road from Pierre to the Black Hills. The Northwestern will be the first road to tap the Dakota gold region."

Yankton Daily Press and Dakotaian, November 18, 1879, as reprinted in the December 11, 1879, *Brookings County Press.* S6-4

According to Irish's reading, the barometer sat at 28.925 on November 19, a drop from 29.5 the day before. The cold air mocked the clear, sun-filled sky, with a "severe gale" from the northwest "increasing [in] violence all day." While the wind rose throughout the day, the temperature dropped, eventually stabilizing at –12 degrees. The party had made the decision early in the day to remain at Nero's, as "one could barely stand against the wind." The lodging served well to keep the party warm, but the fare available—food, beverages, and other offerings—was "very bad."

It appears that Irish had appropriated a stash of letterhead from Jencks' Hotel, for he wrote home on it from Nero's Ranch, along the stage road. The first day's travel reached twenty miles to the north of Yankton, with "the first storm of our trip" lashing them not long after they set out.

"The wind blew from the NW with great violence, and it is now quite cold," wrote Irish. "I concluded to stay in this house; a Frenchman owns it. His name is Nero. We are all well, shall start on tomorrow if it stops blowing . . . I tell you it was a sight to see the wind carry the sand, dirt, and cinders of the prairie fires along. It looked awful black and lowering." Diphtheria was also a problem in the region, and he worried that the wind would blow *that* eastward too.

November 20 dawned at a frigid but manageable −6 degrees, so the group resumed their trek northward, passing a Mennonite settlement along the way. They also ate dinner at the stagecoach "Missouri Sta." of the Chicago, Milwaukee & St. Paul; passed the town of Olivet ("3 hotels and 6 houses"); and were denied lodging in Bellows ("They refused us to stay"). The party eventually arrived in Milltown at 10 p.m. after traveling thirty-two miles for their day's journey.

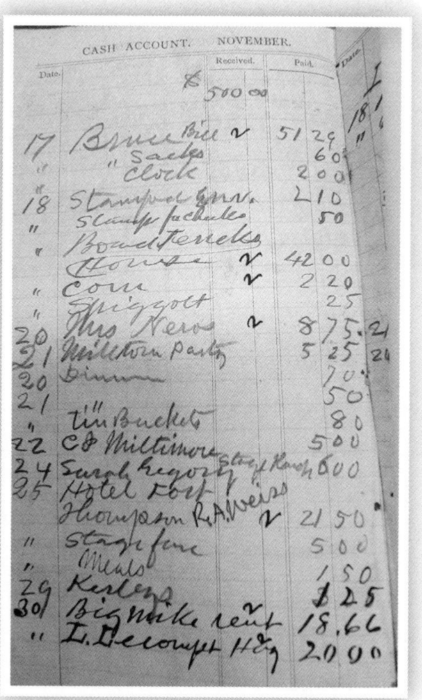

Expense ledger for the crew's time at Nero's, Milltown, and Fort Thompson, as well as rent to Big Mike and hay payment to Louison LeCompt. S6-5

November 21 and 22 were likewise spent huddled against the cold, yet the crew trotted along, twenty-five miles on the twenty-first and an astounding forty-two miles on the twenty-second, into a northwest wind that increased "to gales."

They spent the night of the twenty-second at Dewey's Camp, then deserted, "without fire or tents"—most likely an unpleasant night, as the morning was "very cold & frosty." After leaving camp at 7 a.m., they eventually crossed American Creek, then on to Crow Creek, where the night was passed at Sarah Gregory Stage Ranch, spending $6.00 for room and board.

The morning of November 24 was "cold, windy, clear," and the entourage made it to Fort Thompson, where they set up camp behind the hotel. There they found team member "Carse and his outfit" waiting, having arrived the day before (Carse had suffered the gunshot to his right leg in mid-July). Despite the presence of a hotel, the men slept in their tents overnight, though they took their meals at the establishment.

As Irish wrote Lizzie from Fort Thompson, the crew had traveled "over 90 miles of plains . . . no timber nor houses." Irish added, "We only got water twice on the way. As the tents went by the way of Watertown, we had to lie down on the prairie and sleep in a buffalo robe each and eat frozen victuals for two days." (*Victuals* means food provisions, a synonym being *vittles*).

This "hardship" was partially intentional, a hazing of sorts. Some of the men were new, and Irish wanted to toughen them up a bit. Dunlap and Irish "kept [their] mouths shut" while "the other fellows growled and grunted very much." Irish was evaluating their reaction to the situation, analyzing each man's character. He later wrote, "Lewis is the best one of the lot. He has such good sense."

Irish anticipated that one more day of travel would find them at Fort George Island—"Then comes the work of fixing up for the winter," he wrote.

Settling in for the Winter: November 25–December 2, 1879

At this point, Irish stayed behind at Fort Thompson, sending the teams and men ahead. He himself waited for the stagecoach, which he boarded at 4 p.m. after paying the $5.00 fee, and arrived at Big Mike's Woodyard on Fort George Island at 11 p.m., after a "cold and raw" day riding along "very dusty" roads. Arriving before the others, he was able to spend time making arrangements for their winter headquarters.

The next day, Wednesday, November 26, Irish tried to find a house and stable to rent on the island. Existing buildings were already occupied, so he negotiated a contract—$50 per three months—to rent Big Mike's own house and stable through February. Once that was accomplished, paying $18.66 to Big Mike up front, Irish "went in quest of hay" but was unsuccessful. At least the falling snow was "light," and therefore not much of a nuisance.

(This letter's heading indicates it was written from Fort George Island on November 6. However, Irish was in Chicago on the sixth and en route by the sixteenth. Taken in context, this letter was likely written on November 26.)

Ruth had written a letter that was intensely personal, addressing a heartbreak experienced earlier in the year. Because she requested in that letter that all correspondence about the matter be burned and no more be spoken of it, her privacy will be respected, and the details of her pain are not included here (though the letters do exist, seemingly never burned).

What is remarkable about Irish's response (below) to Ruth's letter is that in 1879, a Victorian-era father was giving his Victorian-era daughter this type of advice. Because it is such an exceptional offering within the confines of nineteenth-century society, much of it will be included here as he wrote it.

He began by admitting that he did not want to lose either of his daughters to marriage and face the changed relationships. "But then life is only a continual meeting and parting of friends and relatives," he wrote. "So it must come some time."

After encouraging her to leverage her intellect and engage in deep learning in the scientific fields, he turned to relationships. He told her how he had two relationships prior to her mother, but he had ended them because he knew the women were too wild or extravagant to suit him, and he did not want to spend his life in regret. He went on to write,

> And at last I met your mother. She was truly industrious, lively and not ashamed to wear coarse shoes. With her I made a match for life, and I have never seen the day when I had to regret my choice. Ill fortune brought sickness and great weakness to her, and this has saddened both our lives, but have we not done well so far, to bring up two girls as yourself and Lizzie of whom I get so many well meant conversations?
>
> Now I hold that a woman, a grown woman, should be deliberate in making a choice of a husband, for there are many more risks to run in taking a man for a life companion than the converse. The first requisite to my mind is intellectual capacity. I met in my travels so many couples where the woman naturally has a bright mind, though uncultured, while her husband is a dull fellow, though perhaps well educated, and yet her inferior, thus she has the greater burden to bear, for she has the cares of the family and to think how the living shall be made. Now, such a life must be full of bitterness for the poor woman, who though she can see the way, [she] cannot take it, the blockhead of a husband is in the way. Then I say the man should possess a clear intellect and thus be able to take the leap. Don't marry for the sake of marrying.

This advice demonstrates how Irish was an extraordinary figure of his time, and in this way well ahead of it.

The rest of the men and teams arrived, Big Mike moved on, and Irish and his men "went at work fitting up the quarters." There was much to do, and the "boys all work[ed] with a will." Wood was cut to build bunks for the sleeping quarters and to use as fuel, and water was hauled for all manner of uses. "It's a big job," Irish acknowledged.

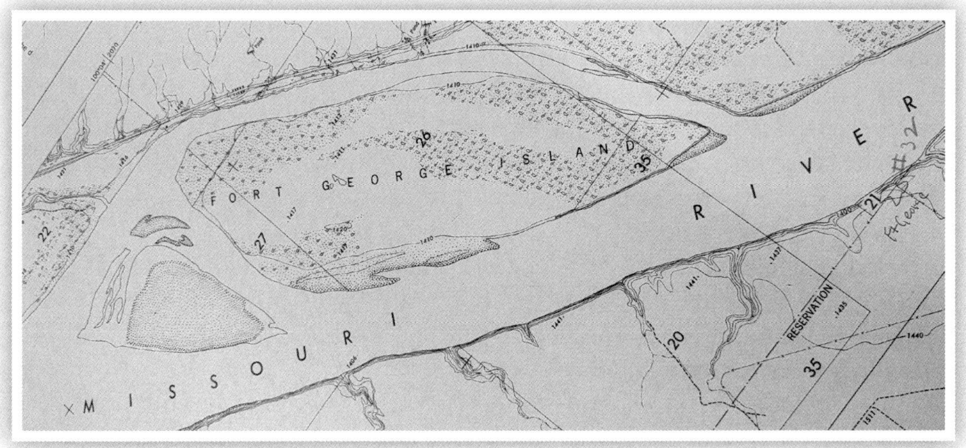

Map of Fort George Island, on the Missouri River. Irish and his crew spent a portion of the upcoming winter on this island. S6-6

By the second evening, seven bunks were completed, and Irish felt that one more day of hard work would complete the job. Still on the hunt for hay, he was able to purchase four tons from Louison LeCompt for a total of $20. The men remained "hard at work on the house and stable," and Irish was becoming homesick, "anxious to hear" from his family.

As the men worked to fix up their winter lodging on Fort George Island, Irish sat down to write home. There was no wind, but it was cold—"We expect it to get to 40 below." While the outside was less than hospitable, he was pleased with the rest, writing, "I have a splendid camp in a large log house with two stoves in it and in the thick timber, so [we] have plenty of wood." All were well except Dunlap, who continued to fight a cold. "I will have to doctor him soon," wrote Irish, and you can almost hear him insisting that the man take the quinine.

This is one instance where Irish's tendency toward shorthand causes confusion for researchers. The Missouri was "full of floating ice," and after recording in his diary that they could not cross the river to get to "Pierre" (again, Irish's frequent shorthand for Fort Pierre), he immediately added that he and Leighton had, in fact, gone to "Pierre" and back, having experienced "high wind and a sand storm on the river." Despite the contextual clues available, it is still unclear whether they crossed the river at this point (if so, presumably on a ferry that managed to dodge the floating ice chunks).

A clipping from the *Yankton Daily Press and Dakotaian*, December 11, 1879.

The surveyors, Mr. Irish and his out fit are at Fort George in camp. We have seen nothing of them yet. They will probably be up to the Christmas tree if they hear of it.

S6-7 **PIERRE.**

The crew spent the last day of November sprucing up the camp to their satisfaction, and the mail arrived from Fort Pierre at 10 p.m.—"All are happy now as it's the first news from home since we left."

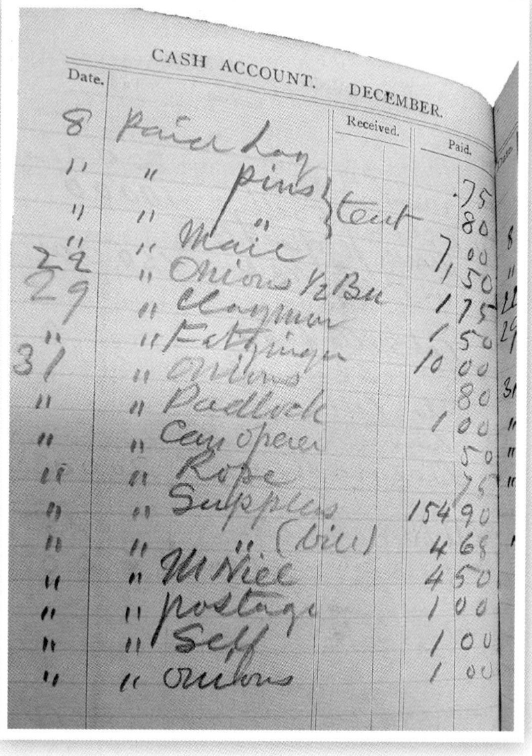

CASH ACCOUNT. DECEMBER.

Date.		Received.	Paid.
8	Paid Lay		
"	" pins } tent		.75
"	"		80
"	" Maie		7,00
22	" Onions ½ Bu		1,50
29	" Clayman		1,75
"	" Fetthinger		1,50
31	" Onions		10,00
"	" Padlock		80
"	" Can opener		1,00
"	" Rope		50
"			75
"	" Supplies		154,90
"	" " (bill)		4,68
"	" McNiel		4,50
"	" postage		1,00
"	" Self		1,00
"	" Onions		1,00

A sample page from the expense journal from December 1879, showing some of the items purchased in Fort Pierre, including onions, more onions, a can opener, rope, and more onions. (Onions are high in vitamin C, which helps ward off scurvy while enduring irregular nutrition.) S6-8

December began with the new camp in tidy order, the plot of land being dubbed "Irish's Ranch" for their winter stay. The crew had not only fresh news from home but a sturdy, warm, snug structure to protect them from the elements and animals, at least when they weren't out scoping route options. The upgrade over their previous canvas tents must have provided a bit of confidence about the winter—and something to look forward to when working away from base camp, making due with thin canvas walls.

Now that they had a stable location, regular weather observations commenced. It was a "fine day like summer," with temperatures in the low sixties, though ice was "8 inches thick on ponds." While the ponds were frozen solid, the ground was not, and Irish complained of the dusty roads. The pleasant weather ended abruptly, and December 2 was a "cold raw day."

After gently scolding the women for writing family notes on the letters others were sending to him by way of their household, he reminded them that had they taken better care of themselves, per his advice, they'd not have fallen ill as the weather changed, including, "Quinine is the best drug ever found for the use of the human family." Well, quinine and whiskey combined.

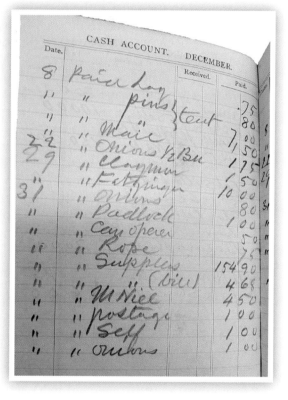

Now that he and the crew were well settled in their camp at Fort George Island, Irish caught the women up, sharing more details about the crew's frigid journey north from Yankton and the initiation process the new recruits had endured. After leaving Yankton, there had been little to eat, and the crew had endured ninety miles of barren prairie in the cold and wind. Some of that prairie had been burned over, the wind whipping ash across a blackened landscape. "We lay upon the ground two nights with only a buffalo robe apiece to keep us warm," wrote Irish. "I tell you the two infants [new recruits] howled. It was so cold that I found my head froze fast in the robe in the morning and [it was] such work to get loose. The boys were badly scared. We ate hard tack and raw bacon." This may not have been what the new recruits were expecting. "O! But Linkhart was homesick. Lewis got on very well."

Can you imagine waking up to find your head frozen to your bedding? He must have been worried about how the winter would go, despite presenting as a seasoned surveyor for the new recruits.

Now that camp was situated, the crew planned to leave the next day to make a work camp twenty-five miles to the north, along Medicine Creek. Irish expected it would take one or two weeks to run lines down the creek toward the Missouri, which had not yet frozen. They'd be away for a few weeks, but a nice little representation of home would remain at camp: "We now have a mailbox on a pole near the camp and the driver brings our news and leaves it for us there." This temporary camp was now a semi-permanent mail stop.

He ended the letter with two humorous personal items. One, the women must have told him that the neighbors' "yellow dog" was dead, and Irish wanted reassurance of its accuracy, writing, "How do you know he is dead? He has gone to hell for sure, he was so bad a dog." He also commented on a note that Mrs. Irish had included in an earlier letter, writing, "I had to laugh over Mother's note that 'in a weak moment I got some blue dishes.' 'In a weak moment' was Beacher's favorite sentence, and it sounded so funny coupled with blue dishes!"

Work along Medicine Creek: December 3, 1879–January 22, 1880

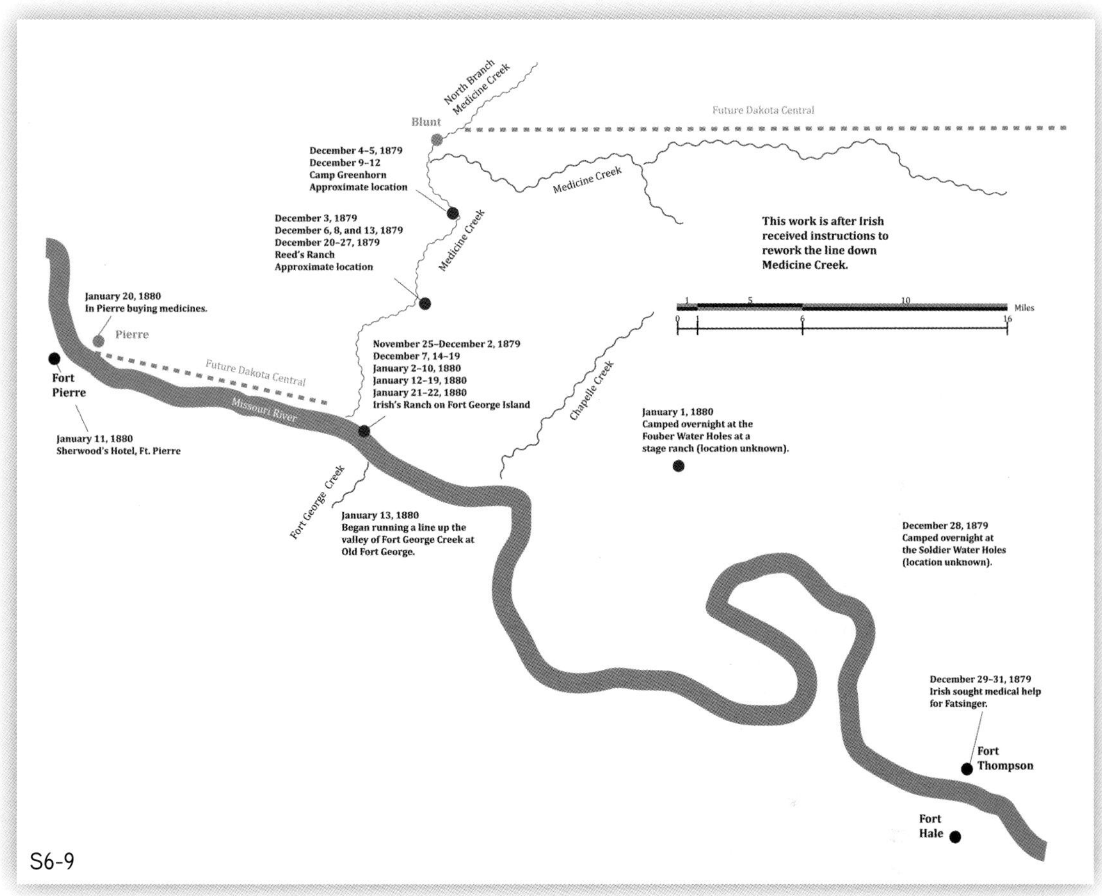

S6-9

The men left their settled headquarters "for camp 25 miles north" on December 3, stopping partway at Reed's Ranch for the night. The air was cold, but the ground, still unfrozen, allowed them to drive their tent stakes in "as well as in summer," Irish adding, "With a spade we dig easier than in summer time."

Their work resumed in full swing on the fourth, when the team "travelled up along Medicine Creek," setting up a new camp as sun began to set. The day had begun at 22 degrees with a southwest wind, and it rose to a grand 28 degrees, though the wind had swung around to blow from the northwest. This new campsite was named Camp Greenhorn, or Green Horn Camp (he used both)—"in honor of the green hands we have with us." The cold temperatures bothered Irish, and he was "not well."

As the men stirred the next morning, the air was a crisp 15 degrees, and a dense fog formed by 10:30 a.m. This complication did not seem to slow the men, who not only did a decent day's work on a line but harvested an antelope and jack rabbit, making the evening meal "a feast." It was a fitting reward for the new men, who Irish commented were doing "splendidly."

A photo of the terrain obscured by dense fog, taken in the Wessington Hills in 2022 by the author. While such a fog did not seem to slow the men in December 1879, when such conditions did occur, the men were forced to work in shorter segments so they could retain sight lines. S6-11

Saturday, December 6, found Irish prowling around the wider area. The day was cold, dawning at –14 degrees. Bundled against the chill in a wagon pulled by a team of horses, Irish left Camp Greenhorn at 9 a.m., traveled to the north branch of Medicine Creek, then followed it to examine twenty miles of its route.

During his trek, the wind changed around to come from the northwest, and "the cloud looked like a blizzard coming." Irish monitored the position of the looming dark-grey gloom that threatened as he headed cross-country to

Reed's Ranch at an urgent pace, arriving at 7 p.m., glad to be off the open prairie for the night. At 9 p.m. the thermometer read but 2 degrees.

The harsher weather that threatened the day before did not strike overnight, so early on the seventh, Irish departed Reed's to return to Irish's Ranch on Fort George Island, approximately seven miles downstream. The temperature was −8 degrees, but fortunately the wind was calm, and he arrived in time for his midday meal.

After eating, he wrote letters to his family. In his diary he admitted to being "very tired and sore." At 2:30 p.m., snow began to fall, ceasing at 9 p.m. after dropping a coat of two and a half inches (which, he determined, equated to about a quarter of an inch of rain.)

On December 7, the first letter Irish wrote from Fort George Island was to Ruth. His last letter had told the family he was headed twenty-five miles up Medicine Creek. In this new letter, he shared that the previous day he'd gotten the crew set up before going "alone over the country with a team [of horses], driving 40 miles . . . camping by [himself] on the creek. . . ." He returned to the work camp, the one dubbed Camp Greenhorn. "It's in a pretty place," he noted, including a "pretty good" drawing of it, adding, "The big hill to the right in the distance is the Big Medicine hill 15 miles off" (shown on the previous page).

Perhaps to reassure his family, he mentioned, "A herd of antelope ran up so close to us that I shot one from the wagon. This gave us fresh meat to eat. We also killed a jack rabbit. Dunlap shot it." Irish wanted his family to know the details, so he added that the rabbit "had on his winter dress of white fur, 2 inches long, white as snow." He continued, "I took the game to camp early in one of the wagons and a big wolf followed me 4 miles or more. I tried to get a shot but he was too wary. That night a gang of wolves came about the camp and stole the antelope skin." The letter did not express much concern about wolves skulking around the canvas tents, but the wolves weren't his only concern.

"What a time I have with the greenhorns," he lamented. "I do wonder if I ever was such a fool." Kindly, he does not elaborate. He wasn't hovering around, however, and trusted the new crew members to their tasks. He left them at their namesake camp and returned to Fort George Island to pick up provisions, which he would bring the next day after a cozy night in the cabin. Perhaps he even relished the errand, which provided an opportunity to return to the warmer, sturdier shelter of the lodge.

"I expect that if the weather is not too bad we shall be back here [Irish's Ranch on Fort George Island] in about ten days." He also expected that over that time, he'd come back to Irish's Ranch "from time to time" to check the mail. That part may have been said with a wink, as he added,

"I tell you we have a comfortable house and I wish we might have it all the time with us."

He was so pleased, in fact, that he drew diagrams of the layout (below), including sleeping assignments. Irish and McNiel, the cook, were the only two with private bunks, with the other men doubled up. The six bunks were each 7.5 feet long and 4.5 feet wide.

a: Lewis / Linkhart
b: Dunlap / Carse
c: Leighton / Vernon
e: DeBarr / Powers
f: Selby / Fatsinger
g: McNiel (cook)

S6-12

a: Irish's bunk, gun mounted overhead, big box off the ground, side table, and two water barrels

S6-13

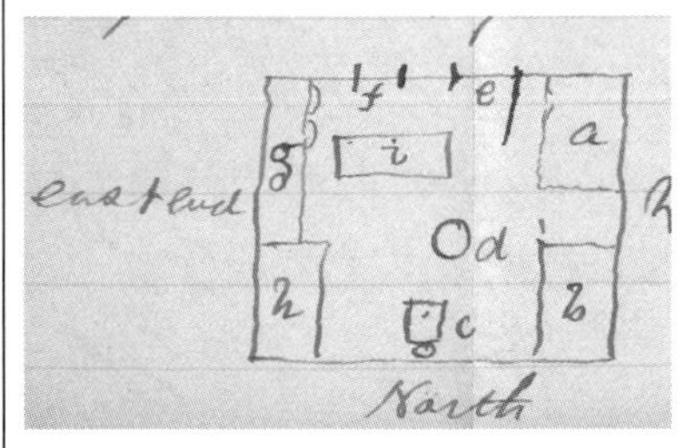

a/b: Men's bunks
c: Cookstove
d: Heating stove
e: Door
f: Window
g: Cupboard
h: Irish's bunk
i: Dining table

S6-14

Irish's special "big box," where he locked his private items such as correspondence and the like, was up on sticks to protect it from moisture. The solid walls of the lodge were the clear difference from camping in canvas tents, but he assured, "We have three pair of heavy blankets and two buffalo robes each, and some of the men have blankets of their own, so you see we are well fixed for cold weather." But at the time, most of the men were currently camped at the base of the hills along Medicine Creek; the blankets and robes would have to suffice for them.

Food was plentiful too. "Prairie chickens are thick in the woods about our cabin," he wrote. "The boys get 12 to 20 at a time. So, we have pot pies." Grazing cattle were numerous, as was wild game—"I shall try and kill some deer when we get back."

In a previous letter, he'd let the family know that a mailbox had been installed. While cozy in camp, he was inspired to make a drawing of the receptacle, adding, "We have two mail sacks with the inscription IRISH'S RANCH on them, and every other night at the witching hour of 12, the mail comes from PIERRE" [Irish's capitalizations]. Despite the midnight arrival, the deliveries were quickly sorted through, though not everyone received mail. "The ones who get no letters look so demure and chopfallen," wrote Irish. The disappointment of no news from home may have been harder on the men than the cold and the wolves.

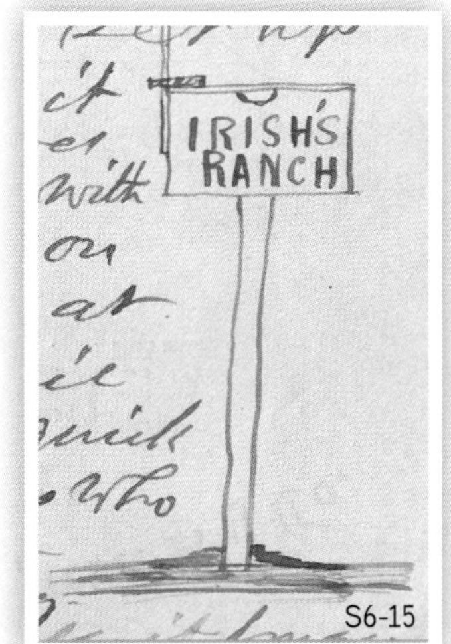

After closing his letter to Ruth, he began one to Lizzie. He asked her to collect and send to him the daily weather observations published in the local newspaper, the *Iowa City Press*. He wanted to be able to compare them to the weather readings he took on Fort George Island, to see if he could correlate weather on the Missouri with weather at home several days later. Irish's scientific mind was full of curiosity, adding, "We have a regular observatory here, [with a] thermometer, rain gauge, barometer, and wind vane."

His vow to avoid a winter campaign may have been lurking in his mind: "I do hate the plain now in winter. Not a living thing upon it except wolves and now and then a jack rabbit . . . If I had the 25 miles of Medicine Creek run and the men here, I should feel happy." He was seemingly not anxious to return to Camp Greenhorn, but he would. First he had to ask, again, how the family knew "the yellow dog" was dead, adding, "He had no soul as Mink had. He was a dog like the one Solomon spoke of." (This is a reference to the way dogs in the Bible, and specifically Solomon's proverbs, are framed as vile creatures, a metaphor for sinners).

At 5:00 a.m. on December 8, the weather reading showed a dangerously cold –24 degrees, and the day rose to all of 8 degrees. It's unknown what the main crew (still based at Camp Greenhorn) was doing, but they had likely been left with instructions to continue taking measurements along Medicine Creek.

Meanwhile, Irish loaded the wagons with provisions for their camp upstream, then went to the valley of Chapelle Creek to procure tent pins (presumedly made from tree or brush branches there)—the winds in the area are notorious, and the tents needed to be strongly secured to the ground. It was a long day, and he stopped again at Reed's for the night.

Another inch of snow fell overnight, and the next morning, the ninth, Irish "left Mr. Reed's in a snow storm." The wind was howling from the northwest, and when he "got to the top of a hill, the snow flew so thick [he] could not see 100 yards."

Conditions like this can be dangerously disorienting. Fortunately, he was able to descend the hill from Reed's and proceed into the creek's wide valley; by staying within its walls, he did not have to fear getting lost on the open plains. He made his way toward the camp where the rest of his men waited. The "wind blew hard all day," making for an especially miserable journey. Just as he was tiring of the trek, he found that, "much to [his] delight," the crew had moved the camp down into the valley, where it was more protected from the strong winds. The relocated camp was dubbed Camp Blizzard.

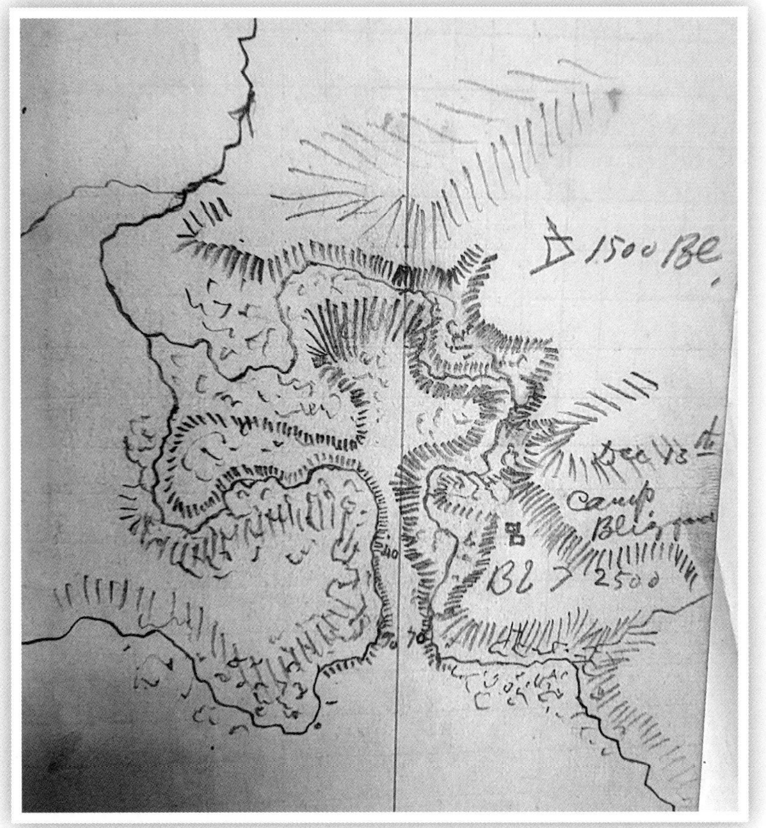

Irish's drawing of Camp Blizzard and its vicinity. S6-16

While the little camp was nestled within the creek valley and out of the worst of the wind, that did not mean they were in a cozy environment. Irish's full diary entry for Wednesday, December 10, 1879, reads, "Wind blew hard all night, zero at 5 AM, at 8 PM zero. The wind blew a gale of 25 miles an hour all day. For this reason the snow flew so thick that we could not travel at all. At 3 PM +3, I went out but could see nothing. This is a regular blizzard. Had to put the boys on short rations."

It appears the party had not expected an extended layover, and food had to be preserved until they could return to or replenish at base camp on Fort George Island. The next day, the eleventh, was clear, dawning at –28 degrees with low winds. Irish did not mention how much snow fell, but the ground was likely softened under a smooth, sparkling, brilliant blanket of white. A clear sky also meant a bright sun (though not a warm one). These ingredients would have combined to make a day that was painful for the eyes, though it would have been beautiful to look upon.

CONTRACTORS RETREATING FOR THE WINTER

While the men were huddled against the storm along Medicine Creek, a Volga correspondent to the *Brookings County Press* provided some interesting updates about what was going on to the east. The railroad section boss, McCormick, "had quite a respectable building raised and enclosed [the previous] Sunday," possibly providing a peer structure to De Smet's Surveyor's House. The contractor Wells & Company was "fast winding their season's business," and of the workers as they returned east for the winter, the correspondent expressed, "With regret we will follow the retreating shadows".[79]

They were there to do a job, and since they could see (however painfully), they could do their work. Five miles of "preliminary line along Medicine Creek" was accomplished, and they spotted five antelope and a wildcat. At 8 p.m. it was –29 degrees, and in an unusual act, Irish made a second evening weather reading at 9:30 p.m., showing the temperature had risen to –20 degrees, under a southwest wind. While there was hope of conditions improving, another notation hinted that things were, possibly, about to get worse: "Joe DeBarr is sick."

The crew was at work again the next morning, December 12, which greeted them with –20 degree air but a beautiful display of brilliant, fuzzy white arcs to the sides of the sun—sundogs, a sign of deeply cold air. Work commenced, but not as briskly as usual. Despite the men's best efforts to stay warm, their stiff hands shivered and their eyes watered—the cold was taking its toll. "The level party were slow," wrote Irish, probably with a sigh. "We are tired out."

Saturday, December 13, featured a cloudy sky, calm wind, and temperatures not far above zero, staying in the single digits. The work continued down Medicine Creek until 2:30 p.m., when a cloud from the northwest began to drop snow, paired with what Irish described as a "10 mile gale." Assessing the situation, Irish had felt it best that his party try to get to Reed's for the night, but they didn't leave soon enough—"In 30 minutes a blizzard was upon us."

After four hours of struggling against the swirling, confusing snow, seven of the men reached Reed's at 7 p.m., two hours after the sun had set. The remaining team—the level party led by Vernon the teamster—had been "so far behind that they had a hard time getting in." The men waited anxiously until the missing men finally straggled in. "All are safe," Irish wrote with relief after this brush with the fierceness of a Dakota Territory winter storm.

The strong northwest winds continued throughout the next day, though the snowfall itself decreased in intensity. The men moved from Reed's back to Irish's Ranch, arriving at 2 p.m. All the men were "tired out," and two more—Fatsinger and McNiel—were down sick.

Back in the comfort of the lodge at Irish's Ranch, Irish sat down to write home. He was happy with the thirty miles of work they had accomplished, despite two blizzards and temperatures as low as –29 degrees. It had only topped zero once, reaching a grand maximum of 10 degrees. "All the ears and noses which were too long for this climate got badly nipped," wrote Irish. "The party had four of its ears frozen. I came through all right. In truth I am the toughest man of the party, as far as human endurance is concerned." (Yes, he said that, despite his frequent whining about his physical condition.)

Perhaps he felt a little embarrassed by his claim, as the topic moved immediately to the family's house plants and their health: "I hope that you will not water that cactus which I brought you from here very much; in fact, keep it quite dry but not dusty." Mrs. Reed's mother had taken a similar cactus home the previous summer, and Irish shared that she'd called it "the finest flowering plant she ever saw," adding, "The blossoms are of a fine rose color."

While Irish wrote home from Fort George Island, Ruth was sitting in Iowa City, penning one of her own. It had been a snowy, stormy winter already, and it was barely mid-December. To distract from her irritation, she shared a funny story. A friend had made a new bodice for Ruth, one that required the wearer to be laced up in both the front and back. Lizzie and the bodice maker were dressing Ruth in the new bodice for the first time when it became quickly evident that "its size would not permit [it] to go further on or even to be removed." After a moment's pause, they realized they would have to remove it by way of scissors, cutting the bodice apart to liberate poor Ruth. "I laughed until I nearly gave up the Ghost," wrote Ruth. "I think I laughed more heartily than I should have done." How the poor seamstress felt was not included.

It wasn't all fun and games, however. Ruth and Mrs. Irish found it quite difficult to rouse Lizzie and Fannie (a hired woman) out of bed each morning. So, being inventive, Ruth marched off to the store and "purchased a small tin horn & a little whistle, which [she proposed] to use at the break of day, not to make the echoes of the early morn, but to wake the two girls." Ruth would blow one, and her mother the other. "Together I believe we will be able to awaken them," Ruth concluded.

After mentioning how she planned to wake the household, she noted that it was time for sleep. The family bird got a mention too: "George is hopping about quite lively, and sings a song most every night before we go to bed." The household wished their husband and father a merry Christmas, not knowing whether any later letters would reach him by the holiday.

With the men safely back at base camp, December 15 was spent gathering wood and water. Irish recorded that it hailed all afternoon, though it was likely sleet. On the other hand, he also noted, "It's so warm that we let the fire go out in our house." The thermometer read a mere 13 degrees.

While basking in the cozy room, Irish also observed there had been "no mail for a week," adding, "The drivers are afraid to strike out." Word from home went far to improve morale in such isolated camps, so this was a significant diary entry.

One hopes that the men rekindled the fire overnight, as the morning temperature on the sixteenth was –7 degrees, and it again snowed all day. Chores continued, and by the end of the day, Irish recorded, "We now have a good wood pile and plenty of grub. How we wish for the mail to come."

The night was stormy, but the next day, December 17, was partly cloudy and reasonably comfortable, at 7 degrees. He sent "3 squads of 3 each to hunt," despite having noted the previous day that the camp had "plenty of grub." The resulting haul included an antelope, a wildcat, and two prairie chickens. Irish himself spent the day working on maps and visiting a local Frenchman, Mr. Shampo, who was married to a Lakota woman.

That visit likely afforded Irish the opportunity to harvest knowledge from the couple, learning about flood and weather patterns and possibly asking about the personalities and moods of the Lakota and their leaders, knowing that the Chicago & North Western would need to negotiate access to travel across their lands.

On Thursday, December 18, Irish again sent out hunting parties while he worked on maps. The two teams returned with a combined haul of three more prairie chickens, and while that may have been welcome news for the men, an even more nourishing event took place—mail arrived from Pierre. Along with the mail came visitors: a Mr. Blake and others. While Irish managed to complete the maps, the rest of his work waited while he had the chance to entertain their visitors, fresh stories and conversation probably a happy respite for the crew.

December 19 found the men working to clear "a road for the stage," but it is not clear whether that meant they were lending their services (e.g., shoveling snow on the established road) to the stage company or whether they were creating a spur off the main road to their camp to allow the stage access to their camp location.

Whatever the purpose, the men did this work in conditions so frigid that a "fine halo" encircled the sun—again, a sign of deep, deep cold. While the road was being cleared, Irish ran an errand over to the valley of Chapelle Creek, downriver from winter headquarters. He was likely again harvesting timber. Whatever the purpose and however cold, the drive was likely beautiful. The "air [was] full of frost crystals this shape [see drawing] all about 1/20 inch in diameter." Irish was an observant man who appreciated the glittering created by the sunlight glinting off the ice crystals floating through the air or settling on some surface, be it grass tops sticking above the snow or the branches among the timber he was collecting. It was exactly

S6-17

the kind of scene he would recreate in words for his daughters through a letter home.

On December 20, the crew again moved up Medicine Creek to Reed's Ranch, setting up a semipermanent camp there to serve as another headquarters while they conducted survey work along the creek. The day was miserable: "It's very stormy, wind from NE a gale. We suffered much but got the camp up at sundown. –12."

It warmed up to 2 degrees by sunrise, and the men were at work by 7 a.m. Their efforts were successful, though the weather proved volatile. The winds began the day as a twenty-mile-per-hour gale (making for a windchill of –19 degrees, using modern calculations) from the northeast, then over the course of the afternoon, it changed to the southeast, then south, then southwest, then settled in at a solid forty-mile-per-hour northwest blow. The temperatures were similarly erratic, reading 16 degrees at noon, 6 degrees at 1 p.m., and zero at 4 p.m. Irish noted, "Snow flying heavy. We all got in safe."

That previous diary entry does a good job of describing the conditions under which the men lived and worked. At least they had been in the more permanent camp, with buildings to offer better protection from the elements. But this day, December 21 (and most others), they were out in canvas tents, some with stoves but some without. After a day working in the cold, wind, and snow, they "got in safe" to a camp made of canvas.

Monday, December 22, dawned clear and cold: –26 degrees. Despite this, the men "got out early" and were again at their work. The day was "very sharp," though the temperature did rise to –2 degrees at noon. The men "saw many wolves about" over the course of their day. Two more men joined them: a new man named BJ, and Perry Powers returned, having taken four days to get from Yankton to Irish's Ranch on Fort George Island, then another day to join them at Reed's Ranch on Medicine Creek. (See the end of this section for research commentary about Reed's Ranch.)

It snowed all night, and the 5 a.m. temperature reading offered a paltry –16 degrees. "The wind blew a 20 mile [per hour] gale all day and the snow flew thick," wrote Irish. The men did very little survey work compared to other days, but the effort was made, leaving an obligatory short distance of line measured before they retreated to the comfort of camp.

Irish's final sentence in his diary for the day was, "We think the mail carrier is lost." Given the transitory nature of this work crew, one might wonder how any of them expected the mail delivery person to know their whereabouts at any given time.

The sun peeked over the horizon on Christmas Eve but did little to warm the air. The 5 a.m. reading showed –38 degrees, spiked to –10 at noon, then dropped to –35 at 9 p.m. before plummeting to a staggering –46 overnight. It was the first fully clear day the men had experienced in two and a half weeks. Irish did not note what time the men began their work, but they "quit at sundown." While it is likely that most households across the country that day were having special dinners and reading stories from the Bible, Irish's crew spent Christmas Day at work. A thirty-five-mile-per-hour wind blowing snow over deep snow cover caused "hard walking" in the morning, but the afternoon was "fine." In fact, Irish optimistically declared, "It looks like better weather."

After work on Christmas Day, Irish sat down to write a letter home, including, "I have the pleasure to wish you a Merry Christmas. Have just got into quarters from a very cold trip up on Medicine Creek." Letters awaited them upon their return—as precious a gift as they could ask for.

The snow that covered the ground in Dakota Territory was not like the snow of Iowa. "It's dry and crisp and feels just like sand when it blows in your face or when you take it in your hands," wrote Irish. "Then again it's like sand when a wagon is driven through it. All this is because it's frozen so hard." After sharing how very cold it had recently been (well into the −30s), he told them, "Now remember too that we live in tents." Then perhaps fearing he would worry them, he added, "Our tents are more comfortable than any house here except our own." Whether true or meant merely to comfort his family, the words had the melancholy feel of a man who wanted to be home with his family for Christmas. Instead, he was on a frigid plain doing work that froze ears and noses.

On Friday, December 26, the temperature soared to 31 degrees by 2 p.m., and the men "took off [their] overcoats" while running over four miles of line in what feels like an exuberant show of energy. Powers delivered seven more prairie chickens to feed the men, adding to their well-being. The day ended with the notation, "I am quite tired out wading snow. Had a fine purple sunset."

The next day also delivered good weather conditions, enough to allow the team to run "into the bottoms at the mouth of Medicine Creek." This also allowed Irish to make "a topographical survey of the upper half of [Fort] George Island." The upbeat entries ended with the cautioning that the barometer was very low, reading 28.5 millibars.

Sure enough, snow began to fall overnight into the twenty-eighth, Irish writing, "Signs are that we shall have a hard storm." Not only that but one of the men, Fatsinger, had fallen ill enough that Irish felt the man needed medical attention. So despite concern over the weather, and perhaps thinking about the recent death of crewman Adams, Irish and Fatsinger headed out for Fort Hale, where a military doctor could tend to the man. By noon on the twenty-eighth, "a blizzard struck," and the trek to get medical help became dangerously difficult.

They reached a location called the "soldier water holes" (hereafter capitalized) at 5 p.m., during what Irish described as "a fearful storm of wind and snow" with visibility that dropped to fifty feet. They stopped there for the night, where men and animals could get water. Whether they slept on the ground, in the bed of the wagon, or in a structure at the watering holes, one hopes that they had something to protect themselves from the elements, especially since Fatsinger was so ill.

A recent photo of a watering hole, taken not far from the location of Fort Bennett. S6-18

This photo from a different location illustrates one example of "holes," locations that either provided consistent water, such as a spring, or held intermittent ponds, such as the one shown here. The vegetation around these transitory watering holes was different, marking their borders. In this image, the darker vegetation (in February, a deep burgundy), marks the outlines of what is, on occasion, an accumulation of water. Stage stations were often near these locations, to help ensure that the stage animals had plenty to drink. This one is near modern Ottumwa, South Dakota, along the Fort Pierre to Deadwood Trail. Irish would soon embark upon his own trip along the road. S6-19

The weather had cleared by the following morning, December 29, and an 8 a.m. departure brought them to Fort Thompson by 1 p.m. While Irish had originally noted Fort Hale as his destination, they remained at Fort Thompson, where there was medical treatment available for Fatsinger. Fort Thompson is a more logical destination, as it is on the east side of the Missouri, compared to Fort Hale on the west bank. Or perhaps Irish merely misspoke in the diary, meaning Fort Thompson all along. Regardless, this is also a good moment to stop and think about the level of responsibility Irish was shouldering, not only for the work of surveying a route for the railroad company and all that entailed, but also the care and lives of the men under his command.

While at Fort Thompson, Irish collected supplies and made two trips back to the Soldier Water Holes. The diary says that he "ran just two loads up to the holes 15 miles"—that "15 miles" could refer to the distance one way (presumed when creating the maps for this book), but it could just as easily refer to the round-trip distance or the total distance traveled over the two trips.

Overnight at Fort Thompson, Irish wrote a letter home that filled in some of the questions the diary left open. "Poor fellow," he wrote of Fatsinger, "he suffers from youthful indiscretions and will I think die before long." (A later diary entry would name one of those "youthful indiscretions" as syphilis.)

He turned from health dangers to what recent weather had left behind, telling the women, "The snow lies deep upon the unburned prairies and has blown off of the burned ground and filled up the hollows and gullies until it's very dangerous to travel." These conditions were not only dangerous but painful. "[The snow] flies about in the wind like fine sand and feels like it when it strikes and sticks to the face and hands, but it does not feel cold until it begins to melt. The snow is the only thing here which I dread."

Oddly, despite the cold, the ground was too dry to freeze—"fully as dry now as in any part of New Mexico." The soil was just deep dust, "over a foot deep in the roads." Irish added, "We dig it up with a spade as easy as we did in summer, and we drive the line stakes with an ax hatchet." The dirt may not have frozen, but the water holes had, and that made it hard to find water for the animals and crew, forcing them to get water from the river.

December had been cold and stormy. The northwest winds blew the snow to the southeast, making for unpleasant travel. Due to the thick dust in the roads, Irish had been unable to find anyone willing to haul provisions for the crew, so the men had to add "shopping trips" to their list of duties. And that was, in part, why Irish was gathering supplies at Fort Thompson and writing home.

"On Sunday morning the 28th I took two teams and started for this place," he penned. "It began to blow + snow at 9 AM and by noon we were wrapped up in a blizzard, the wind blowing at 30 miles an hour from NW." Frequently the cool head in a tense situation, Irish had to take the reins, later writing, "The men with me were scared and could not keep the road. I tell you it was bad."

They made it twenty-seven miles, reaching watering holes eighteen miles from Fort Thompson. After hunkering down for the night, they rose to a clear sky but cold morning on the twenty-ninth, and soon reached their destination.

Irish was there at Fort Thompson on a medical foray, tending to Fatsinger; thus it is unlikely that Mrs. Irish knew her husband would be there. Nonetheless, on his first evening at the fort, he was handed a letter from his wife. In it, she described symptoms she was experiencing.

After reading her letter, he was "taken sick by a very severe pain in [his] heart," which worsened to the point that he considered calling for help, but it eventually passed. "I think I brought it on by over exertion and eating a hearty supper," he surmised. Or perhaps the news of Mrs. Irish's illness caused an episode of anxiety.

His best news was that the survey to the mouth of Medicine Creek was complete. "We next go at work sounding the Mo. river," he wrote, "and I shall do some travelling in the nice spells of weather."

He again expressed sadness over his inability to get home for the holidays. The snow and storms simply wouldn't allow it, for while he could have arranged for a two-week break, it would have taken ten days alone by stage—due to the poor road conditions and overnight stops to prevent mishaps on the dark prairie—to get to Yankton. "Well we will have to bear what we cannot change."

The year ended with concern. On January 1—a "fine day," with temperatures around 30 degrees with low wind—Irish finished up his business at Fort Thompson, purchasing provisions before returning to Irish's Ranch; he did not provide any update on Fatsinger. He was uneasy, though. "The Indians are still turbulent," he wrote. "The inmates of Fort Thompson spent a sleepless night. The Indians threaten to kill them all." At least one of the men, "Gilmore the butcher," made out his will, just in case. This is a good reminder that this was still a time of discomfort among the peoples of the region, for many reasons.

As Irish was making the aforementioned preparations to return to camp, he received a visitor, later writing, "Mr. Felt the post trader came to get one of my guns. I let him have it and 40 rounds of ammunition." It is interesting that Irish felt safe enough to head back to camp, especially after handing over some of his own protection. Those at Fort Thompson (Irish just says "we")—minus Fatsinger, who was seemingly left behind—set out and reached the Soldier Water Holes at noon, then continued to Fouber Holes Stage Ranch, arriving at 6 p.m. The snow there was "quite deep in [the] track."

POST TRADERS

A settlement's post trader, or sutler, was usually a civilian. He would pay for the exclusive right to conduct business at the post—"ten cents a month, for each enlisted man and officer, to the post fund."[80] He operated the store from his own building, selling a wide range of items. The sutler's store was often a place of gathering as well.

Sometimes outside traders set up nearby to illegally compete with the authorized post sutler. On October 27, 1879, post sutler W. E. Caton of the Cheyenne River Agency (or just Cheyenne Agency) wrote the first of several letters outlining his situation to Commissioner of Indian Affairs Hayt, fearing he would suffer "loss and perhaps financial ruin." Another trader, J. C. Robb, had "succeeded in controlling the trade with the Indians," thus beating Caton out of transactions which legally belonged to him.[81]

The commissioner must have replied touting the nature of competition and free enterprise, as Caton replied on November 28 that he did not "fear honorable competition," nor would he object if the commissioner chose to replace him. What he objected to was that someone who had not paid the licensing fees and did not have to play by the rules which restricted Caton could "control the trade to which he has no right."[82]

While a post sutler paid for his privilege, the position clearly came with its own stressors, which Caton was dealing with during the same timeframe he became acquainted with Irish.

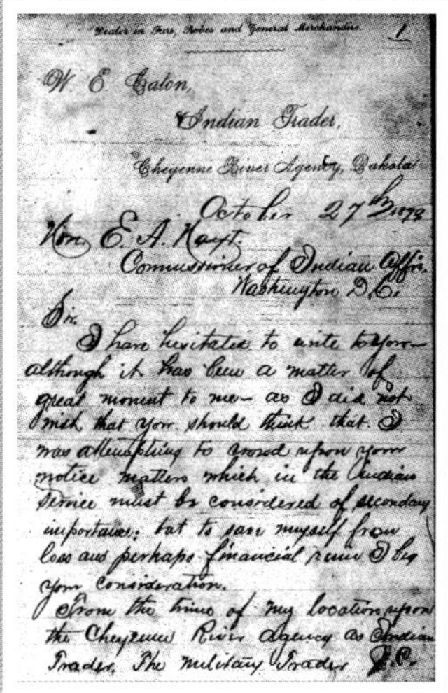
Dealer in Furs, Robes and General Merchandise. 1

W. E. Caton,
Indian Trader,
Cheyenne River Agency, Dakota
October 27th 1879
Hon. E. A. Hayt
Commissioner of Indian Affrs.
Washington D.C.
Sir
I have hesitated to write to you although it has been a matter of great moment to me as I did not wish that you should think that I was attempting to crowd upon your notice matters which in the Indian service must be considered of secondary importance; but to save myself from loss and perhaps financial ruin I beg your consideration.
From the time of my location upon the Cheyenne River Agency as Indian Trader, the military Trader J. C.

The first page of a letter from trader W. E. Caton to Commissioner of Indian Affairs Hayt, October 27, 1879. S6-20

It was also on January 1 that Irish obtained, for the promise of $40, to be paid later, a five-and-a-half-year-old Texas pony named Billy (he spelled it both Billy and Billey in the diary, but we'll stick with Billy). As time passed, this pony would show himself to be smart, patient, and gentle, with an entertaining personality. (For those familiar with the film *Dances with Wolves* and the main character's horse Cisco, that is how I imagine Billy.)

The January 2 overnight stay at the stage ranch near Fouber Water Holes, run by an "old Frenchman named Clermont," was a bit more eventful than the usual goings on at Irish's Ranch. A Mr. Millet, of Nebraska, had joined them as an overnight guest, and Irish had "a lively political discussion with him," though Irish did not record what the conversation was actually about. It likely paled in comparison, however, to conversations with other guests who arrived during the night. Irish wrote, "Regular Bull Whackers. Hard cases. Two of them engaged in a fight this morning. No harm done." Irish seemed anxious to get going, for they were trudging through the deep snow again by 6:15 a.m., fighting a strong wind from the northeast. After a "very hard day's march" they reached Irish's Ranch at 6 p.m. "tired out."

January 3 found Irish sick in bed with what he called "influenza," complaining, "It's severe on me." Things went downhill all day, and his entry ended with, "Still sick and sicker at 10 PM." The next day was also spent in bed, which was unfortunate, as the weather was warming, and considerable thawing was taking place. Team members Leighton and Vernon were sent back to the Soldier Water Holes to retrieve the supplies from Fort Thompson that Irish had stowed there; they returned to camp on January 6 with the goods, rather muddy for their efforts.

Meanwhile, "Sick sick sick" was his initial entry for January 5, noting he could hardly sit up. Things improved throughout the day, and he was able to spend time working on a map. It is possible, however, that he was still suffering issues due to his illness, as the diary for this day is repetitive, with the same few items written twice each with slightly different wording, as if he simply was not thinking straight.

It is hard to tell whether he was improving by the sixth or merely experiencing different symptoms. "I am better, got really at work on the map," he started, then complained, "I have such severe pains in my back and hips." To quell the pains, he was taking a concoction of "whiskey and quinine with muriatic acid," and he recorded the quantities for each. While convalescing, he sent the teams out to work on the route along the Missouri, upstream of where Medicine Creek emptied into the river.

The glimmer of improvement Irish's health had shown on the sixth faded. He remained "quite sick." He was also "unable to walk about," and was experimenting with his medicinal dosage. Instead of quinine, his new regimen required three daily doses of a mixture of whiskey and Jamaican ginger, as well as two daily doses of ten drops of muriatic acid.

Despite continued illness, he spent January 8 working on maps. "The ginger and whiskey [mixture] is a good diuretic + the acid is rapidly removing the excess of alkali from my system." The men were out working on the "line to the river," creating a five-degree curve in the route. This was an important step, determining where the descent down the Medicine Creek valley would stop and the curve to connect the line to parallel the Missouri River bank would begin.

WAXING NOSTALGIC AFTER A BRIEF BLOCKADE

After a brief blockade due to snow, trains began running again in eastern Dakota Territory. Material was being brought in and stockpiled at Volga in preparation for the resumption of grading, tracklaying, and bridge work in the spring. Despite the newness of the entire experience, the editor of the *Brookings County Press* wrote, "It seemed sort of old fashioned to see the old iron monsters roll through." Despite the nostalgic reaction to the chugging trains, the editor's focus was on the future. The tracks, they predicted, would reach the James by early June and the banks of the Missouri before the end of the season.[83] What a difference seven short months had made in the wake of the survey crew.

Finally, on January 9, Irish cautiously declared himself to be feeling better, thanks to the whiskey and ginger (the "quinine did no good"). While he kept working on the maps, the weather outside grew colder, and storm clouds began to drift in. The landscape that is ordinarily so grand and sweeping began to compress down, the clouds lowering, darkening the sky. Fortunately, it was more threatening than thrashing.

It was not much of a storm, with only about two and a half inches of snow and no mention of wind, though the temperature dropped to a reading that Irish interpreted as "quite cold." With the maps completed, Irish made plans to head to Pierre "to send off the papers . . . by express," which included letters, likely to the officers of the railroad and to his family back in Iowa. His health was improving, and his mood seemed to be upbeat as well.

On January 11, Irish and Leighton headed to Fort Pierre, staying at Sherwood's Grand Central Hotel (or just Sherwood's Hotel). He included some of his expenses in the diary, giving us a glimpse into costs: the bill at the hotel was $3.30, and he also had a $5.50 fee from the blacksmith.

Among the letters he wrote while at Irish's Ranch, mailed during this visit to Fort Pierre, was one to his daughter Ruth and a second to his wife.

He told Ruth that December had essentially been stormy "from the 7th to the 29th, unprecedented in the annals," the coldest since 1864. Further elaborating on the storms, he wrote:

> West of the Mo. river, the snow was very deep and many teams were blocked in between [Fort] Pierre and the Cheyenne river. One man was lost 6 days in the storm; he left his house unable to travel and kept on day and night and at last found settlements but with his feet and hands badly frozen. Another boy was out 4 days without food or fire, but saved his life. So it goes.

He also shared some glimpses into camp life, writing, "We all worked along in the storm and slept comfortable in our tents at night and on the worst days staid in the tents and played chess, checkers, and cards, told stories, and did all we could to pass away the very monotonous time."

He also let Ruth know about his recent cold, saying, "I have suffered from the worst one I have had for years; it has lasted me near 10 days and I am not well. Several of the others have it now . . . I have to doctor them however sick I may be."

To his wife, he shared similar news, though of his cold he added, "It came not from exposure but came in the warm, very warm east winds which immediately followed the past cold weather." This virus had some odd symptoms, which Irish described in detail:

> Every one [Irish's underline] that I know of in this region had the same trouble more or less in the same week . . . My lungs and throat are very sore, but the worst part of the visitation consists in the neuralgic pains which accompany it. I had it, and now have it in my right hip joint, it's so annoying to be sick and then unable to sleep or rest. Why, night after night passes without a practical rest for me. Last night I did not feel it until I got into bed. When up it starts, and I rolled over and over all night. Linkhart [the sickest of the men] has it in his face, so does Mc[Niel] the cook. The others in legs or back. Well so much for complaints."

He let his wife know that his Christmas meal had been "a frozen biscuit and a raw piece of pork," adding, "Walked 11 miles in the snow knee deep that PM, so you see I had a hollow day [Irish's underline] before I got supper. New Years day I ate two hard tacks for dinner and at night was taken very sick, which of course brought me to be very merry and thankful."

His wife and daughters had sent him a special package for Christmas, containing a cake. Irish was grateful, sharing, "I tell you I felt so [touched] that I went out in the woods and cried, I did. I could not help it. I really don't know what there was to cry about, but then cry I did, and at once felt better. The cake was in nice condition. I gave the boys each a small piece and they all pronounced it good indeed."

We also get a glimpse into how he was able to work in the cold: Johnson, the chief engineer of the line, had given him a nice pair of gloves. He also wore his buffalo coat whenever he went outside—"No wind can blow through it."

January 12 was very cold (–26 degrees), but thankfully there was no wind. Upon returning to Irish's Ranch, he found that Linkhart had improved, as had Irish, who declared himself "very much better." Linkhart had "been sick for some time with a catarrhal affection and quinsy." (Catarrh is inflammation causing congestion in the nose and throat, and quinsy is an infection of the throat and chest.)

Tuesday, January 13, was a fine day, and the men walked across the Missouri River ice and began work on a "preliminary line west of the river at Old Fort George." They worked their line to the top of the bluff, following Fort George Creek and an old trail.

The creek the men followed emptied into the Missouri River near the old fort site. There was "plenty of grass" at the location; this could be a note about the soil being sturdier and less prose to erosion, or it may have been a simple observation that there was plenty for the animals to eat. Back at camp, the team's cook, McNiel, was improving but not yet capable of providing meals.

January 14 was "very warm," and the remaining snow rapidly melted into the ground. The men worked the line from the "Cottonwood Forks" (likely a spot where a stream forked and there were cottonwood trees) to the summit of a butte that the men named Johnson's Butte, "in honor of Chief Engineer Johnson of the C&NW Ry," and "set a staff and flag" in the ground to commemorate the occasion. The butte, he observed, was "made up of gravel" and contained "numerous remains of vertebrates, some being land animals." Letters home indicate he may have pocketed some of these old bones to send to friends who would be interested in them.

Despite it being mid-January, Irish declared the day warm, and the next day, the fifteenth, followed suit. Water began to pool upon the Missouri River ice, and Irish was concerned about the speed of the thaw, that the ice would become weak and complicate their work. Despite that worry, the men began taking soundings—a process that required standing on the ice, making holes, and inserting long rods to measure the distance to the river's bottom. Reassuringly, the temperature of the water itself was a degree or two below freezing, making an ice breakup less likely.

While the work went well and the weather was pleasant, Lewis was "taken sick . . . with violent fever." He'd be the first to fall prey to whatever this particular affliction was.

The rest of the men continued taking river soundings on Friday, January 16. The weather remained warm, making for "muddy sloppy" roads, and there was "plenty of water on the ice." While the men worked on soundings, Irish focused on creating maps and profiles of the recent work. He also had time to wander around the grounds of their camp, describing the thick willow groves, poison ivy, and other types of vegetation in his diary.

By Saturday, January 17, two more party members had fallen sick—Leighton and Powers. It appeared they had the same fever that tormented Lewis. Irish finished the maps and profiles, then took observations to determine his exact location for use with the survey readings. The day must have been warm and windy, for he finished his entry with, "These winds are called the chinook winds, being supposed to blow from the Oregon coast."

Sunday the eighteenth was a rare though forced day of rest—most of the crew were sick. "I have the largest hospital now on hand that I ever have had," lamented Irish. "My medicines are nearly gone." Later that night he recorded, "The sick are no better." McNiel the cook (who had been recovering from an earlier illness), Joe DeBarr, Linkhart, Lewis, Powers, and Leighton were all now sick. And it wasn't just the men who needed tending: "Leighton's old mare tried to fight a bull last night [and] got fearfully gored. The gash in her thigh is 18 inches long and is deep up along the hip bone."

The night must have been terrible for the sick men, who Irish diagnosed as being in "the embrace of breakbone fever." Despite that being the same diagnosis that had killed Adams, Irish did not seem to be, at least in writing, entirely sympathetic: "Gracious, what a time I have, 7 whining sick men all groaning and making all the fuss they can." Irish was known as a compassionate man, so this brief diary entry may have been intended more as a reflection on his own overextension in caring for them, rather than a judgment on the men's uncomfortable situation.

It is also interesting to contemplate that illnesses like breakbone fever (dengue) are often mosquito-borne, and there are no such insects out and about during winter in the Dakotas, which brings us back around to wonder what terrible illness the men were fighting. Of the men, Leighton was noted as the most ill. Irish planned a trip to Fort Pierre the next day, if they did not improve.

Between tending to the men (he found that "large doses of quinine [were] the best in this fever") and, one assumes, the recuperating horse, Irish prepared the maps and profiles for transport to the railroad officers. His final observation for January 19 punctuated his concern that the river ice again appeared ready to break up, a situation that would have significantly impacted the men's ability to work.

The survey work wasn't the only casualty of the rampant illness that had felled so many of the crew; Irish was left to do many of the various chores around camp as well, whether it be feeding and care of stock, maintenance of the wood supply for stoves, meal preparation, or whatever other innumerable tasks needed attention.

While the sick men (except Dunlap, who was a recent victim of the fever) were feeling improved the next morning, Irish (along with Powers and Vernon, who were "just able to walk about") headed to Fort Pierre on January 20. Barely recovered, the men trotted cross-country on horseback, arriving around noon. The goal was to send the maps and profiles eastward via courier, then return to camp with mail and medicines, both of which would help bolster the men.

They stayed in Fort Pierre for the night, taking time to get the horses shod and their sounding rods repaired. The weather was degrading, and rain and snow fell overnight. Despite the worsening weather, Irish noted, "We have such glorious sunsets. Never before did I see such gorgeous tints in the clouds, and evening after evening they are repeated." Anyone who has had the privilege of seeing sunsets along the Missouri River in the Dakotas knows this to be true. During winter, those glorious colors reflect upon snow and river ice, bouncing back and forth between the bluffs that confine the river—simply beautiful.

Rain fell overnight, transitioning to snow throughout the twenty-first, blown about by a cold northwest wind. The men left Fort Pierre, crossed the ice, and traveled downstream, arriving in camp at 4:30 p.m. with the iodine, quinine ("all . . . there was in [Fort] Pierre, 1/2 an ounce"), linseed oil, and a patent medicine called "Spr Free Munate of Iron gargling oil." According to an 1877 list of medicinal gargle treatments, linseed oil was part of a particular recipe that must be used warm, as it "acts by softening the parts of the throat, and hastening the suppuration [discharge of pus] by its heat."[84]

Recent sunsets had been gorgeous, but the weather was changing. So would the focus of their efforts in the weeks to come, as getting west of the Missouri River became problematic in multiple ways.

REED'S RANCH

In February 2021, I took a research trip to explore camp and work locations in winter conditions. The overall trip was fruitful to the point of being overwhelming. One of my favorite harvests was standing at the foundation stones of what may have been a building at Reed's Ranch.

Among the various campsites, the surveyors may have spent the most time, in total, at Reed's Ranch. It sat approximately where modern Canning lies now, on Medicine Creek, about midway between the Missouri River, to the south, and modern Blunt, to the north.

I am reticent to approach strangers with questions, even when I desperately want to talk to them. The other person usually in the truck with me (my husband, Ray), however, is the opposite. He'll walk up and start talking to just about anyone, anytime, anywhere. Sometimes that is a good thing.

As we prowled around Canning, using both Irish's elaborate drawing of the Reed's Ranch location and a modern topographical map, we identified the likely spot. The bridge we wanted to cross, however, was marked private and barricaded, a rather perplexing thing since it was on a public township road. We turned instead onto a long dirt driveway that led to a couple of houses. In the driveway of one house stood a man, out feeding cats. Ray rolled down the window and greeted the man, who walked up to the truck, greeted us, introduced himself as Bernie, and asked how he could help. We explained what we were looking for, showing him the maps. He thought a moment, pulled out his phone, called someone, and relayed our purposes. After hanging up, he said, "Let's go talk to Don." Bernie climbed into the back seat of our truck and pointed us down the road and up a hill.

There, we went into a large garage and met Don. A quiet man, he listened as we explained our quest. We saw the spark of curiosity as he took the maps. He sat down behind his desk. As the rest of us chatted and his wife came out to greet us, Don examined the maps. I was watching out of the corner of my eye as he turned them, changing their orientation. He nodded, tilting his head one way, then the other. The rest of us continued chatting, but I could see that Don knew what he was looking at.

In a quiet spot in the conversation, Don spoke, his words giving me goosebumps and tingling my spine. "There are foundation stones right where this rectangle is," he said while pointing to the rectangle on Irish's drawing. The rectangle was labeled "Reed's Ranch," amidst the larger valley. The map also included the hills in their proper orientations, Medicine Creek, and the old military road and telegraph. He could look out his front window and see where that military road passed, along with its line of shadowing telegraph poles. "Right there," he said while pointing across the valley. "It crested the hill right there." I was standing where Irish had stood, looking across the valley Irish looked across.

Don, Bernie, Ray, and I climbed into Don's pickup truck and went cross-country over Don's property. We went around some buildings, then up to the top of the hill, the truck flexing a little this way and that as we hit ruts or irregularities in the ground along a short ridge. To our west was the Medicine Creek valley. To our east were more hills and, according to Irish's map, one of the best springs in Dakota Territory.

When the truck came to a stop, we got out and began searching for the foundation stones. I can't remember which of us found them first, but there they were. I've stood at other camp locations, seen the crew's view from other spots, but finding Reed's Ranch when I hadn't been expecting to was one of the high points of the entire research process.

The rocks in the right foreground may belong to the foundation of Reed's home or another of his buildings. This location matches the map drawn by Irish. S6-21

A view west-northwest across the valley of Medicine Creek from the crest of the hill where Reed's Ranch sat. The tracks that run through the modern valley can be seen just beyond the tree line. A foundation that may have been Reed's home is several hundred feet to the left, out of frame. S6-22

Don also showed us some tepee stones, still circular and in the size of a tepee base close to a century and half after last use, unmolested in all that time. He mentioned multiple effigies on his property that matched effigies drawn by Irish. The veil between the present and distant past sometimes thins, and my standing above Medicine Creek, where the crew sheltered so many nights at Reed's Ranch, was one such moment.

The tepee stones on the property that was once Reed's Ranch. The oval highlights the stone locations, mixed within the grasses. S6-23

Section Seven

EXPLORING WEST OF THE MISSOURI RIVER

JANUARY 22–MARCH 7, 1880

The depths of winter brought out not only the worst in the weather, but the worst in the humans too. The owner of their rented cabin—their warm, cozy, and personalized respite—demanded they vacate it, and they had little time to get out. Then some of the crew tried to mutiny; some were let go, some retained with a warning. As things were sorted out, a focus of the work became finding possible options for the tracks to cross the Missouri, and each had to be explored in turn. The terrain near the Missouri was wild and broken and complicated, and the location remote. There were weeks with no word from home, and Irish's family back in Iowa anxiously reported the same. Despite the recent mutiny attempt, Irish had to leave the men in charge of themselves as he and a few others departed for a scouting trip across the Great Sioux Reservation, being careful not to stray too far from the stage road the Lakota had granted permission for White people to trod. The trip was fruitful, but the weather made sure it was not an easy one.

Exploring the Mouth of the Cheyenne: January 22–February 25, 1880

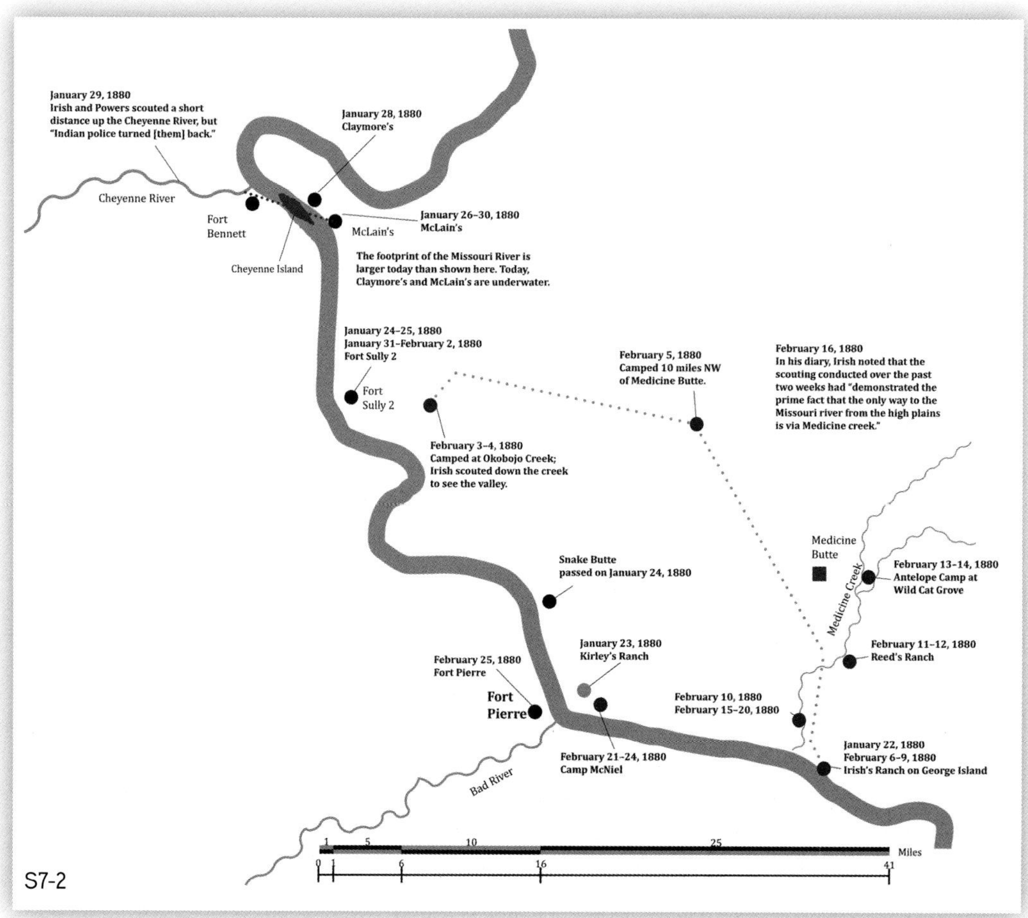

Irish, Powers, and Vernon returned from Fort Pierre with the medicine on Thursday, January 22, and the administered elixirs began to do their work. Irish reported, "The sick are better except Lewis and McNiel." Lewis was, in fact, not doing well—"poor fellow suffers much and calls for whiskey all the time."

While the men recovered, Irish prepared to leave on a scouting trip to the mouth of the Cheyenne River, where it empties into the Missouri River. On a cold and stormy January 23, it appears those who were well enough left camp and traveled as far as the ranch of Joseph Kirley, approximately where Pierre's old downtown is today. Irish had seen "many round bowl-shaped depressions" along the river bottoms, which he believed to be "the remains of . . . Ree houses." He linked past and future by writing, "Here is to be a future city and it once was a city. The Ree occupied it and for miles below here as far as old Fort Sully [Fort Sully 1]. The remains of their houses are to be seen all about here above [the] high water mark."

Today, the Cheyenne empties into the Missouri River northwest of Pierre as part of the Oahe Dam backup. In early 1880, this major tributary joined the larger river just to the west of Cheyenne Island, now mostly beneath the waters of Lake Oahe (same general location, different topography).

The crew departed the next morning, January 24, paying a bill to Kirley (which Irish also spelled as Kerley, Kerleigh, and Curley) totaling $4.75 (approximately $120 in 2019 dollars). About five miles north of Pierre, they crossed Snake Butte, the site of a turtle effigy. (The site is on private land, but the current owners encourage visitors, maintaining a path and interpretive sign. The reader is encouraged to learn more about this location.)

JOSEPH KIRLEY

One of the first White people to settle on the east bank of the Missouri, opposite Fort Pierre, Kirley and his wife arrived in early 1878. He established a road ranch and ferry, briefly partnering with another early settler. His ranch featured a "long log house with an extra room, which was used as a bunkhouse by stage drivers and wayfarers who stopped for the night."[85]

According to Kirley's daughter, Laura Kirley McAllister, a railroad surveyor "advised him to sell his land and business and move to Fort George," where the railroad planned to cross the river. Because the land had not yet been legally surveyed, it was not available for purchase, but "squatters right" held that the first to hold the land had first right to purchase the land.

Kirley eventually sold his squatter's right in what became Pierre, in exchange for a different parcel of land, $1,500, and "the newest model of a double barreled breech loading gun" (now held in the collections of the South Dakota State Historical Society), though his daughter claimed he was unaware that he had sold to the railroad company.[86]

Joseph Kirley and the gun that was a portion of the compensation for selling his land to the Chicago & North Western. S7-3

The winter weather played nice while the men traveled another twenty-five miles or so across the plateau above the broken Missouri bluffs. It may have been a calm day, for Irish mentioned none of the usual "violent gales" that were so common, and this land is high and unprotected from the winds, a rare and welcome situation; or perhaps he simply didn't mention them.

A wide view of the modern Missouri River valley, north of Pierre, looking to the southwest. This is the type of view the men would have beheld as they traveled between Pierre and Fort Sully. S7-4

The views were expansive. If any of the men had not yet seen the Missouri from the high bluffs, they had the opportunity now, and it would have been an awe-inspiring vista. The river itself is encased within a wide and jagged valley (and was even before the damming of the waters), with mound upon mound of craggy breaks below the rim, before resuming a flatter plateau off to the west. To the men responsible for determining a route down, across, and back up, it may also have simply looked like a headache—a beautiful, inspirational, and magnificent one, but a headache nonetheless. Or perhaps it looked more like a solid mathematical, geographical, and professional challenge.

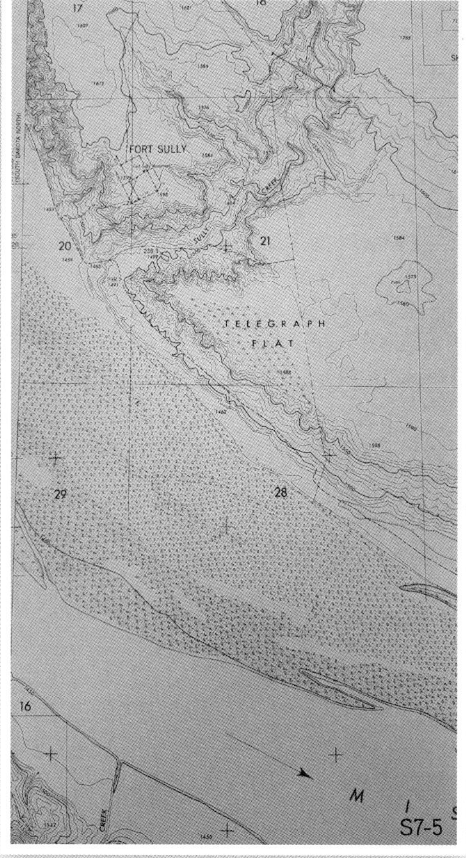

When they finally reached Fort Sully (Fort Sully 2, actually, but we will just call it Fort Sully), they obtained permission from Colonel Wood to camp "near the lines of the fort." Sunday,

January 25, was spent at the fort, which Irish declared "a fine location," except for the inconvenience of having to obtain their water from the Missouri River. The men set up camp "just west of the trader's store" (map on next page) while Irish became acquainted with some of the important men about the post.

Water duty at Fort Sully was a difficult task, as the river was 160 feet below the post. In his book *Fort Sully: Guns at Sunset*, Harold H. Schuler writes,

> The mile-and-a-half road was a steep climb for an 8-mule team army wagon carrying 495 gallons of water. The men had to make ten trips a day to provide the post's daily need of 5,000 gallons of water. Soldiers loaded the water wagon with buckets, a task made more difficult in winter when the men had to chop holes in the ice.[87]

Five thousand gallons of water—daily!

Officer's quarters at Fort Sully, circa 1880. S7-6

Sketch of Fort Sully from east. S7-7

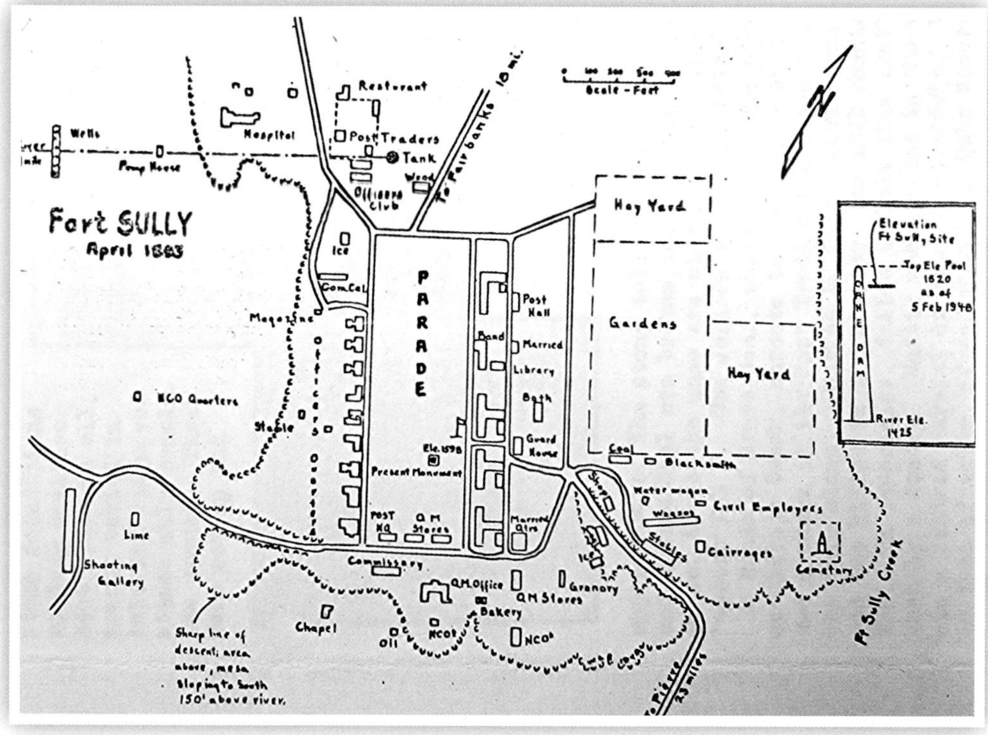

The post trader's store is seen just left of top-center on this 1883 map. Irish and crew set up "just west" of there (note the orientation of north). S7-8

On January 25, Irish's daughter Ruth wrote a newsy letter from Iowa. She enjoyed word play, writing clever letters that her sister Lizzie called "silly." In this letter, Ruth let her father know that a man they knew had "shot himself four times this morning and as a result of said shooting lies cold & dead at the present time."

The next morning, Irish and most of the men continued the journey of fifteen or so miles toward the mouth of the Cheyenne, enduring a "cold raw" day with a rising barometer reading. At least one (perhaps more fortunate) man was left behind at Fort Sully to "care for the camp."

After crossing the main river to visit Fort Bennett, near the mouth of the Cheyenne River, the men (Irish, Powers, and DeBarr) recrossed the Missouri to stay on the land of a man named McLain and his neighbor Basil Clement/Claymore, the two ranches within the "Little Bend" opposite the Cheyenne. (Due to the construction of the Oahe Dam—begun in 1948 and opened in 1962—much of this land now lies beneath the waters of the Missouri River.)

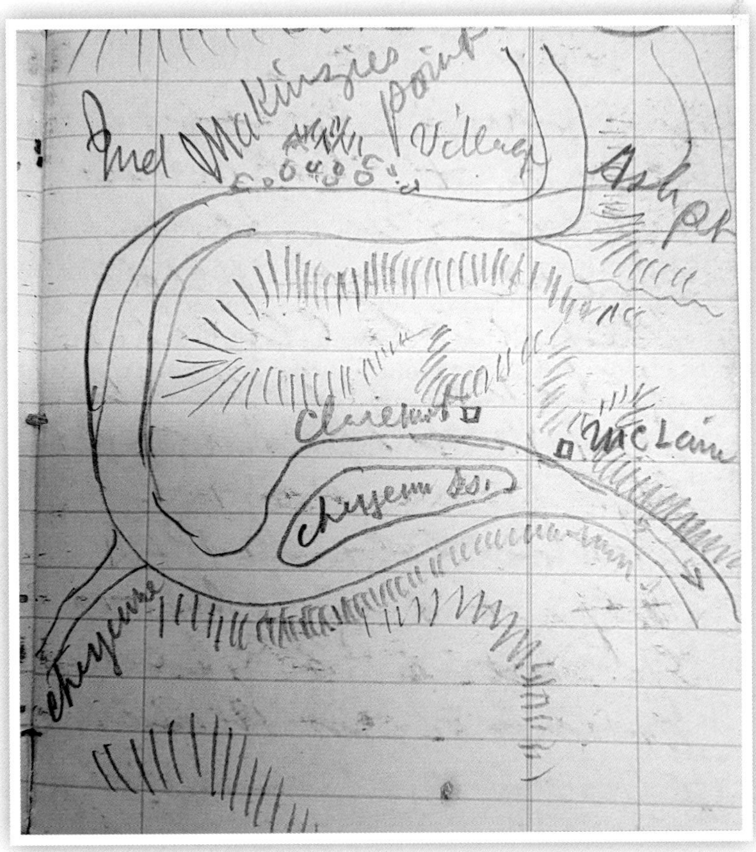

Irish's drawing of the area encompassing the mouth of the Cheyenne, Cheyenne Island, and the spit of land where Clement/Claymore and McLain had their ranches. S7-9

BASIL CLEMENT/CLAYMORE

Clement/Claymore was an early woodyard operator, having already been in the area for forty years by the time Irish stayed overnight while scouting a river crossing. His French name was Clement, but when heard by non-French speakers, it mutated into Claymore, so he was thus known by both names.

Due to having arrived in the vicinity of Fort Pierre as an employee of the American Fur Company around 1840, he played some role in many of the foundational events in the area. He married a local Lakota woman, and together they had many children. He was considered a member of the tribe, which led to a rather interesting example of bureaucracy in 1908 and 1909, when the Indian agent at the Cheyenne Agency tried to get official approval from Washington, DC, for this White man to receive annuities at the agency; it was eventually approved after a series of increasingly exasperated responses from the agent to increasingly ridiculous requests from Washington.

According to interviews done in the final decades of his life, Clement remembered speaking with "Indians" (not specifying further) who had spoken to Lewis and Clark in 1804, and "well remembered" artist George Catlin's visit in the 1840s. Clement himself served as a trapper, interpreter, guide, negotiator, and cattleman, the last of which made a considerable income and legacy for his large family. Basil died in November 1910.[88]

The pleasant weather that shone upon the area while the sick recuperated disappeared as health was regained and work resumed. While Irish and the men prowled around the sandbars where the Cheyenne River emptied into the Missouri, the temperatures fluctuated around zero. They measured the width and depth of the river both at the mouth of the Cheyenne and at its namesake island. These readings were to determine whether this was a reasonable location for the Dakota Central to cross the Missouri River.

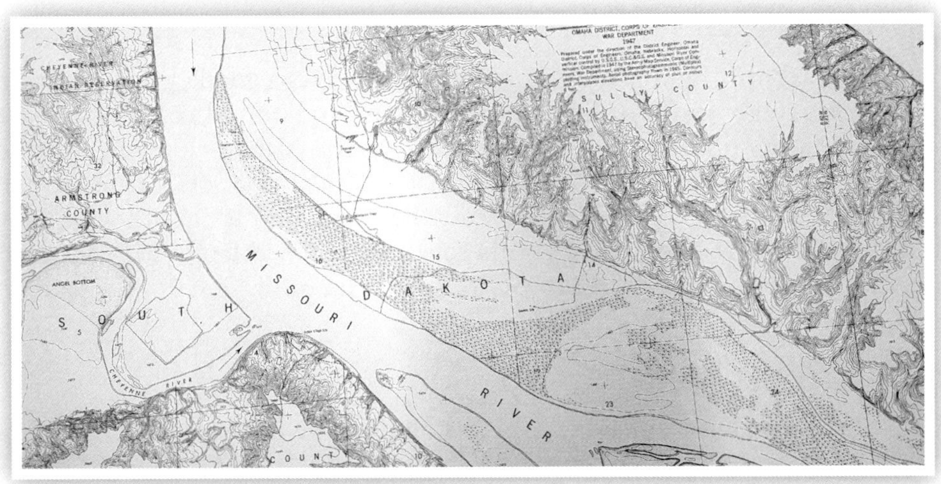

A 1947 map of the area where the Cheyenne empties into the Missouri, prior to the damming of the river. S7-10

While at Fort Sully on January 26, Irish wrote to his wife. He lamented not having received a letter from home "for over a week," but he'd chosen to believe that all was well there. He wrote,

> For my part I have a hard and busy time. Seven of the men were taken down sick of fever, and I had to doctor and care for them for over a week, and the work [is] pressing me hard all the time. Well they began to get better, and I left them in care of the well ones and came here on my way to the mouth of Big Cheyenne river. This trip is the last which I have to make this side of the river, and [I] shall come home before going further west. I have had a hard time this winter. It has been like taking care of so many spoiled and sick children. I am very well now, having got over my bad cold and the neuralgia which attended it . . . The misery of it was excruciating.

January 28 was cold enough to produce sundogs (–11 degrees at 6 a.m., 11 degrees above at 3 p.m.), but in a bit of serendipity, the wind was nearly calm. Irish and McLain explored the area, "seeing the full extent of the Little Bend," and Irish declared, "There is a chance to get down with a heavy grade." The location became a solid candidate to get the Dakota Central across the Missouri.

Note: This is a good place to remind the reader of the three major crossing options of the Missouri River, from south to north: (1) at Fort George, somewhat opposite the mouth of Medicine Creek; (2) the general Fort Pierre area, near the mouth of Bad River; and (3) the mouth of the Cheyenne River, via Okobojo Creek and using Cheyenne Island as a mid-river step. There is a map of these locations in section 8, which covers the resolution of this matter.

After determining that this crossing location was a good option, Irish and Powers tried to go up the Cheyenne River, but "Indian police turned [them] back," letting them know that the west side of the Missouri belonged to the Lakota and that White men belonged on the other side. (Traditionally, the Lakota had "police" who fulfilled the role the name implies. As they began to interact with the US government, this role began to overlap, with the Lakota supplying police to escort various White parties as well).

TENSIONS ALONG THE RIVER

It was January 29, 1880, when Irish and Powers were told to go back to the east side of the Missouri River. Several weeks later, rumors flew when a locomotive and caboose passed through Marshall, Minnesota, on a mission that was mysterious to observers. Station Agent T. A. Woodruff told the editor of the *Lyon County News* that the miniature train was taking railroad official A. G. Ryther to the Missouri River, where "a party of railroad surveyors [were] being held by Indians." Ryther, who Blunt had recently brought to meet with Irish, planned to negotiate the surveyors' release.[89]

The above could comprise a misinterpretation of the situation around Irish's crew, who were, in fact, never taken hostage. Woodruff may have been referring to an entirely different crew of surveyors, perhaps those surveying west of Watertown or toward a connection with the Northern Pacific. (Why else would the miniature train have been in Marshall instead of Brookings?) Or he could have been referring to officers heading along the Winona & St. Peter on an entirely different endeavor, with people having made up their own news and hoodwinking the editor into believing it as fact.

There were, in fact, surveyors for other lines killed in the line of duty. Fortunately, that never happened for our crew of engineers for the Dakota Central. News still wafted around, and in late March, the *New Ulm Weekly Review* reprinted a piece from the *Gary Inter-State* noting that the Chicago & North Western's survey crew had been twice turned back by the Lakota, with threats that a third attempt would be fatal.[90]

The men indeed turned back to the Missouri and continued their work there, taking measurements and river soundings in the vicinity of Cheyenne Island on Friday, January 30. However, a small mishap complicated the work, Irish recording, "I lost the ice chisel through the ice, and we broke the handle of the sounding rod."

To top it all off, it was a stormy and blustery day, with temperatures drifting around zero and snow swirling amidst the northwest gale. That afternoon they retreated to their lodgings and worked on the calculations to determine grade options. They finished the day with a shooting match, though their wisdom in choosing a location, as relayed in the diary, is absolutely in question: "Shot at candles in McLain's log house, had lots of fun."

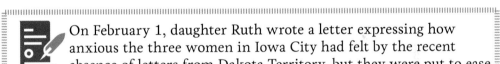

In addition to the shooting match, Irish told his wife he had spent the past week in territory belonging to the Sans Arcs, Blackfeet, Minneconjou, and Oglala while "making examinations and surveys" near the mouth of the Cheyenne River.

While updating his wife about the health of his crew members, Irish placed blame for recent illness on the fluctuating temperatures, penning, "The weather which was so very warm and unhealthy has now got cold." While he wrote that it was "very warm" through much of mid-January, with chinook winds and significant melting, no actual temperature readings were recorded.

He also told his wife that he'd finished the work near the Cheyenne River a full month sooner than estimated, thus hoping the Chicago & North Western officers would allow him a visit home. He was so hopeful, in fact, that he begged her to meet him in Sioux City, along the Missouri River in western Iowa, to extend their visit time during the potential furlough. To finish, he warned that the letter would be sent via a herdsman to Fort Bennett—"You may never get it."

The crew packed up to leave McLain's on January 31, leaving $4.00 behind to cover their board. They went as far as Fort Sully, taking "heights & distances as [they] went" and investigating signs of past habitation. A Lakota told them it had been at least eighty years since the Ree lived in the vicinity of the large village near the river bottoms, between Fort Bennett and the Little Bend.

On February 1, daughter Ruth wrote a letter expressing how anxious the three women in Iowa City had felt by the recent absence of letters from Dakota Territory, but they were put to ease by the receipt of the first correspondence in two weeks. Though the relief must have been great, it would not be complete, as they knew the news was old. Ruth then went on to share plenty of local gossip, adding that the house plants were "in a flourishing condition," as was the family bird, George, who was just then "out and perambulating amongst the plants." The plants and George were frequent mentions in letters back and forth between these family members, almost holding their own positions as members of the household.

The afternoon of Sunday, February 1, was stormy, Irish writing, "There is every sign of a blizzard on hand, or else fair weather"—rather interesting options, but his first instinct was correct. A storm blew up, continuing into the next day, ending at 2 p.m. after dropping snow and "hail" (probably sleet). While the storm did its business, Irish wrote letters to General Manager Hughitt and Chief Engineer Johnson, which were sent along with the next mail out of Fort Sully. Irish also made note that a previous explorer, during an 1877 scouting trip, had crossed the Cheyenne River "69 times in 77 miles" and "the river proper 50 times in 63 miles," making one wonder whether the remaining nineteen were across minor tributaries or slough areas. Regardless, that observation also meant that the Cheyenne may have presented too expensive a challenge for the railroad to follow on its path to the Black Hills.

On February 2, Irish wrote from Fort Sully to his daughter Lizzie. He'd received her letter written on January 20 "by an accident," as it had been sent to Fort Sully, where he just happened to be. It had been three or four weeks since he'd last received a letter from home, indicating that some had gone missing. Lizzie mentioned that her mother was ill, and Irish was alarmed. He begged her, "Now don't be afraid to tell if mother or any one else is sick; it is better for me to know it at once than to be startled in this way." (One does wonder, however, considering the time it took for news to travel, how knowing "right away" would be much different than a delayed telling on their part.)

He then told her about his work, and how he'd been taking readings and measurements at the spot where the Cheyenne River emptied into the Missouri. He was among the Lakota, but he reassured her, "They did not trouble us much but made many threats [as to] what they would do if we went further." While he did not say so, this may have been referring to the same recent threat of a fatal outcome mentioned in the newspaper.

The men left Fort Sully on February 3 under flurries, though by 11:30 a.m. the snow was falling thick. They reached Okobojo Creek, two miles south of Okobojo Buttes, where they decided to camp, seeking protection from the weather. Despite the conditions, Irish "went down the creek on horseback to see the valley," while the others got the tents set up. (Today, thanks to the Oahe Dam, the mouth of Okobojo Creek looks more like a backwater of the Missouri itself, before its course along the bluffs is truly visible.)

The next day, the fourth, under "raw and cold" conditions due to a northwest wind, the men further explored the Okobojo Creek valley, taking yet more measurements and determining whether this valley was a feasible option for descending the bluffs down to the Missouri. Finishing their work, they returned to camp and, pelted by continuing snow, prepared to leave in the morning.

Things did not go peacefully, however: "Joe DeBarr let the team get away in the darkness of nightfall. Billy the pony gave the alarm. We went out and found the team going down the creek towards the river." Remember that when Irish obtained Billy, he'd noted the horse's cleverness. Whether Billy gave that alarm while tattling on his fellow horses or was begging the escapees to wait for him will be left to speculation. Either way, the other horses had made a run for it, down the creek valley in steep bluffs on the banks of the Missouri River. "We had a hot chase," wrote Irish, but where they headed, they were fairly easy to round back up—a mistake on the horses' part if they'd been seeking freedom.

An abbreviated amount of sleep was scavenged, and the crew was up and on the road again by 9 a.m. on February 5. As with the previous segment of travel, they took measurements and readings along the way, this line being "out of the creek to the high lands on the east." The Okobojo Creek valley was another location that Irish considered a possibility for a descent down the bluffs.

Up on the high plain, back from the bluffs, the land is wide and flat, truly a "high plain," without much—if any—undulation in the surface of the land. But as the men traveled, Irish grumbled about a common winter complaint on the plains. "Had a fine plane to travel over," he wrote, "but [there were] many crusted snow banks, which made it hard for the horses . . . which hinders us much. We got only 17 miles." The snow had an annoying habit of forming a crust over the tops of the grasses, leaving air pockets below. Due to breaking through the snow crust over and over, they gave up hope of getting back to Reed's Ranch, instead making camp ten miles to the northwest of Big Medicine Hill.

While the day had been decent enough, the evening turned stormy, Irish writing, "Oh how threatening are its clouds, the wind blew a fearful gale at sunset." Rather than setting up the tent in the traditional manner, they laid it "on its side, pegged it down, put [their] beds under it, and turned in at 6pm." The horses were tied to the wagon. There was no telling how far they'd have been able to get away had they made an escape up on this high plateau, but fortunately they stayed put, hunkered with the men against the wind.

The storm did not let up with the sunrise on February 6. The morning dawned with precipitation from the northwest that made Irish exclaim, "Gracious, what a blizzard." He went on to write, "It had snowed all night and it had drifted over us and among us, but we had such good bedding that we did not know that we were buried." Yes, read that again—they were cocooned by snowdrifts, but woke up perfectly cozy. Irish drew a depiction of their situation, one of the author's favorite renderings of his.

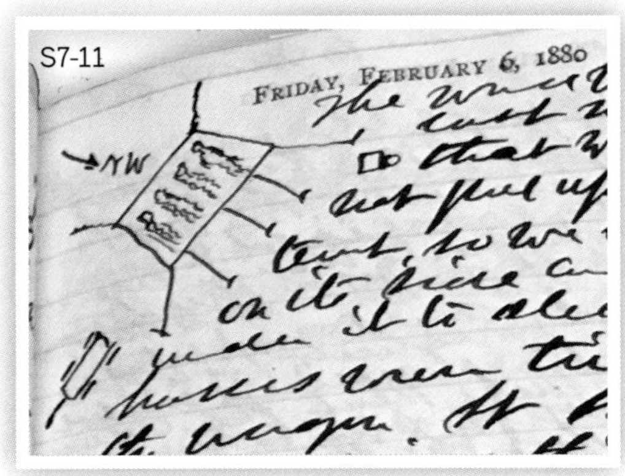

Irish's drawing of the men sleeping under the side-pegged tent, when they woke up buried in snow. The wagon is also drawn.

Despite pleasantly sleeping like sled dogs, "the storm was too severe to think of fire or breakfast even." Their next step was to pack up and set out toward the military telegraph line, then continue on to Reed's Ranch, traveling at times with a visibility of under ten feet. They reached Reed's at 2 p.m., refreshed themselves with a meal, then continued on, reaching the comfort of Irish's Ranch at 6 p.m., "out of provisions and horse feed."

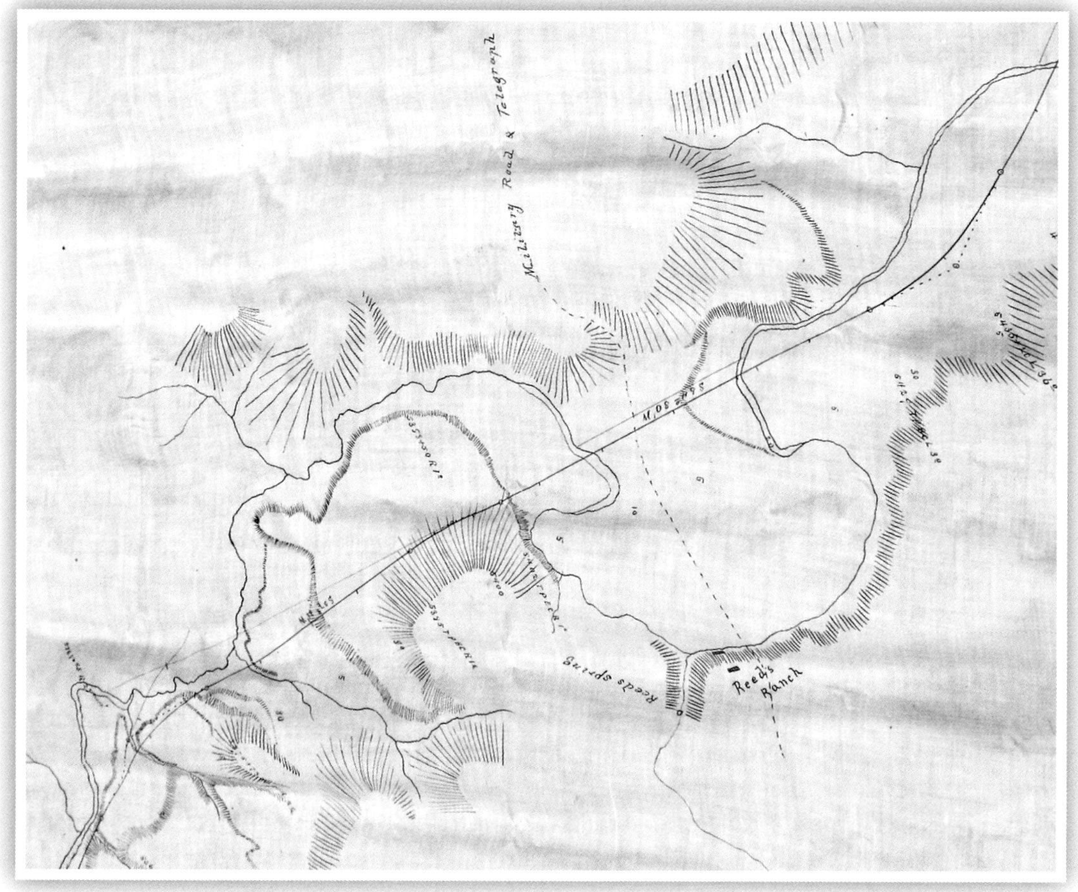

Irish's beautiful map, including the location of Reed's Ranch, shows the route of the military road and telegraph line, which he followed from their campsite between Fort Sully and the ranch itself. S7-12

Saturday, February 7, was spent doing chores and errands, and likely resting from the physical exertion of several days of travel and fighting snow, wind, and cold. Lewis was sent to Fort Thompson with letters, along with money to purchase medicines ($7.65) and pay off the promised amount for Billy the horse ($40). (It was also Laura Ingalls's thirteenth birthday, which the Ingalls family observed while living in the Engineers House, or Surveyors House, back at Silver Lake Camp.)

Irish was also relieved at the improved conditions of the sick men who had been left behind, attributing their recoveries to the use of quinine; they were again ready for work. Irish was also likely feeling grateful to be back in the comfortable log structure after having slept out in the open during the recent snowstorm.

Not all was well, however. Big Mike, owner of the ranch that the crew had moved to for the winter, returned and "made many threats," wanting the men out. "What can ail the brute?" wondered Irish in his diary. This was a significant and awful development. They'd done considerable work to improve the place for their needs, and just spent several days exposed to the elements. The shelter was a welcoming sight just the day before, and now they were told to leave. Anger, shock, concern, injustice, outrage—all of these must have raced through the men's minds as they realized their sudden change in situation.

Based on the next diary entry, Big Mike was agitated because the Indian agent at Fort Thompson, Captain William E. Dougherty, had threatened to "burn him out," and Big Mike suspected that Irish was an agent of Dougherty, occupying the location to squeeze him out. Big Mike believed that after the crew vacated the ranch, Dougherty's agents and the Lakota would set fire to the property. The story is told in such choppy language (likely the result of anger and frustration, running from the brain to the pen faster than he could write) that it is hard to nail down the details. In any event, Irish "made arrangements to move up river to Rousseau's place just above the mouth of Medicine Creek." On February 9, just two days after being notified they had to vacate the place, the crew members were reluctantly—maybe angrily—on the move, along with their "store tent and contents" and a significant portion of the rest of camp.

The kerfuffle with Big Mike was not the only bitter disappointment Irish had to contend with; he discovered several of his men had "enlisted for a mutiny." Perhaps the prospect of being tossed out of the comfortable cabin, forced to house in canvas tents for the duration, was too much for some of them. Or perhaps it was the cumulative stress of working in horrible weather.

Whatever the cause of the insurrection, Irish fired DeBarr, immediately sending him out of camp. "Will work it out of the others," he bristled, naming Dunlap, Carse, Selby, and Fatsinger—all men who had been important members of the team—as being the mutineers. In fact, Dunlap had, along with Old Joe, been one to stick close to Irish and seemed very well liked by the man. The sense of personal betrayal must have been sharp, on top of the disruption to the work at hand.

"We call them the Royal Family" was his final, growling note about the matter, with no further details, but this group of men will come up again. Perhaps the discomfort of tromping across the high plains during blizzards was but one of many reasons behind the discovered mutiny, but Irish was quiet as to their actual complaints, or what they had planned to do via this mutiny.

The final tasks of moving camp were completed on February 10, amidst a high southeast wind and falling barometer. The new, less cozy camp was set up in the "low bottoms 1 mile above [the] mouth of Medicine Creek." Irish declared, "Everything is good except the Royal Family," but again, he spilled no beans about what the situation was.

Irish and Perry Powers left camp early the next morning, the eleventh, with the intention of exploring the upper portions of Medicine Creek. After the excitement with Big Mike, the other men had their guns and "plenty of ammunition" at the ready. The day was warm, though a strong wind from the southeast threatened to blow the pair off their feet. By early afternoon, with the barometer falling, the wind shifted around to the northwest, and it "became very cold." The water that had been flowing along the hillsides from melting snow quickly froze. The two men trudged into Reed's Ranch at 7 p.m.

The night was not a quiet one. "A howling storm" raged "all night," and the next morning, February 12, Irish, uncharacteristically, declared it too severe to venture out. Perhaps he was trying to temper the work a bit in the wake of the recent mutiny. Restlessness may have set in, however, as Irish and Powers wandered around the grounds and took measurements of a spring on the property. The spring was 60 feet below the ranch's house, the notch the water flowed through was 3.25 inches deep and 11 inches wide, and the temperature of the water was 52 degrees, the same as they had measured it a few months prior. Irish declared it "the finest spring in Dakota," and he was not the only one to feel that way; he observed that "many wild duck stay at Reed's spring all winter." (The spring is shown on Irish's map of Reed's Ranch, on page 200.)

On February 12, Ruth wrote to her father, responding to his complaint that no letters from home had reached him for nearly a month. "I can't understand why you do not get our letters," she lamented, "for we never fail to write two per week and almost always three." The frustration appeared mutual, for after reassuring him, she added, "We haven't heard from you this week and are looking anxiously each mail for a letter."

The thirteenth brought "a sharp frosty morning but no wind." Irish and Powers explored up the creek, setting up a camp at what he called Wild Cat Grove, then continuing on foot to the top of Big Medicine Hill (also known as Medicine Knoll), which he measured to be 550 feet above the creek. At one time, it had been "a great Indian resort." Of specific interest was the assembly of small stones in the shape of a large rattlesnake, with "two large red stones" for the eyes and "two small black ones" forming the nostrils.

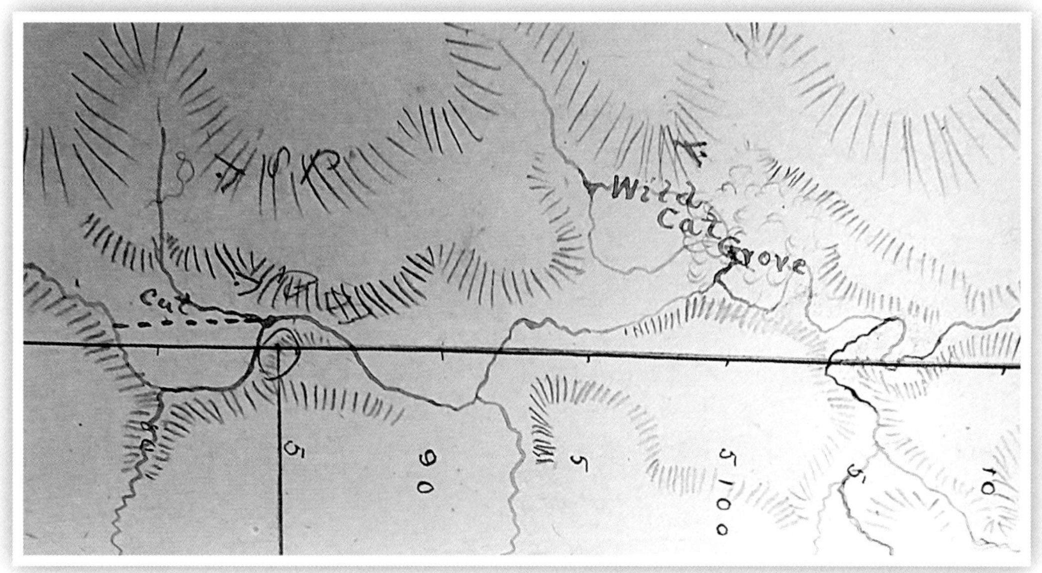

A map of the area around Wild Cat Grove, where Irish and Powers camped, oriented with west at the top. This is just a few miles south of the Lone Tree landmark along Medicine Creek. The illustration includes a proposed cut through a hill that would be needed to accomplish the grade. S7-13

The night was cold, and the 14th was both a "stormy windy day" and also "a fine day," the latter comment possibly referring to his sense of accomplishment in their work rather than the weather.

The two men continued their explorations, following the creek upstream, then returned along the "west side over the high prairie" above the valley of Medicine Creek. Along the way, Irish made note of significant, though fading, evidence of vast buffalo herds: "Old buffalo trails in great numbers run SE to NW, and many bones show how numerous they have been." The men "shot and ate several prairie dogs on the trip," noting that the buffalo were long gone, with only jackrabbits, antelope, and prairie dogs remaining.

Irish and Powers were up early the next morning, February 15, at the camp at Wild Cat Grove (recently renamed Antelope Camp after an animal Powers killed there), and they made it to Reed's Ranch for lunch. After a visit, they departed at 4 p.m., cutting straight across country rather than following the creek valley, and they reached the relocated camp at Rousseau's at 7 p.m. Along the way they saw, "on the high hill south of Reed's," some stone figures similar to those on Big Medicine Hill.

Big Medicine Hill (also called Medicine Knoll) from the north. S7-14

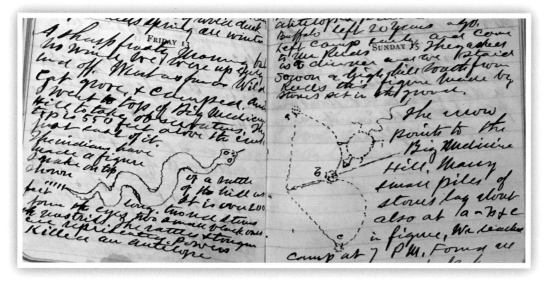

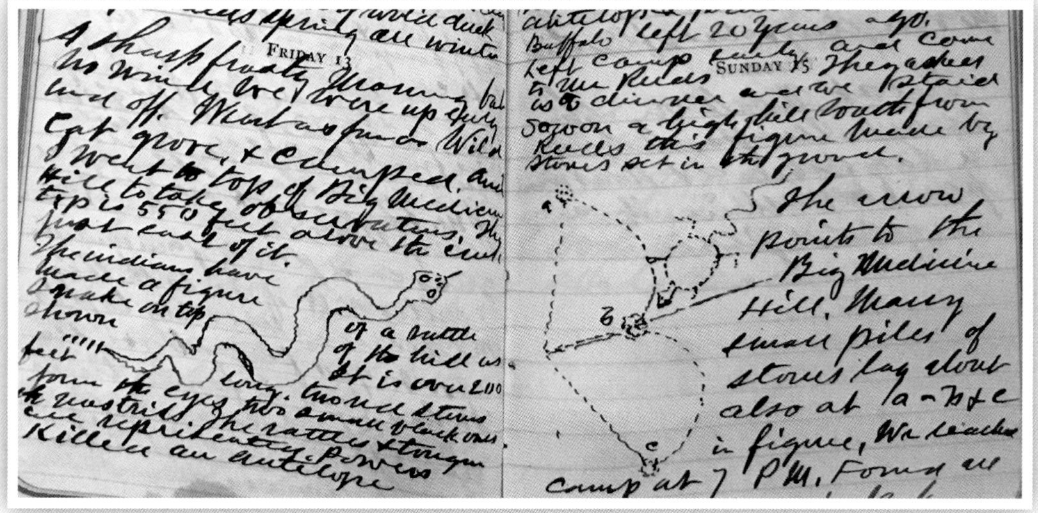

Irish made drawings of the rattlesnake figure atop Medicine Knoll and the turtle effigy he found south of Reed's Ranch. S7-15

Monday, February 16, began five days of work on maps to illustrate the recent scouting trip along Medicine Creek. An important observation resulted from the explorations: "These scouts demonstrated the prime fact that the only way to the Missouri River from the high plains is via Medicine Creek."

Irish had a log cabin to work in at Rousseau's, but it was "a very cold place." Fatsinger, the draught man (maker of detailed maps)—whom Irish had hauled off to Fort Thompson a while back for treatment and who was also one of the mutineers—returned and was set to work helping Irish with the maps. (Irish indicated that Fatsinger had been taken to Fort Hale, perhaps for better treatment.)

While Irish worked on maps, others were busy creating wooden stakes; 850 were created on the February 18 alone, and the work continued throughout the week. These stakes would mark the route, each indicating the grade level to be achieved, angles to be taken for curves, and other important information that the surveyors needed to relay to those who would turn the measurements into graded roadbed and, in turn, tracks. They were, in a way, the batons handed off in the railroad relay.

Just downriver, Big Mike's ranch, vacated just days before, was dismantled. Irish wrote, "Big Mike tore down his buildings as soon as I moved out of them and hauled them out on the bottoms above us. Dougherty came with police and burned all the houses on [Fort] George Island and destroyed the property + took all the cord wood."

CAPTAIN DOUGHERTY AND BIG MIKE

The Standing Rock Sioux Agency's 1879 annual report, written by Agent Dougherty, summed up the problem: steam navigation on the Missouri River meant that White men were cutting down trees along the river and selling the wood to fuel the boats, an act "clearly in violation of the law," but one that "cannot well be obviated." Much of the cargo carried by the boats supported the various posts up and down the Missouri, so the boats had to ply the waters, as the "closing of the wood-yards would cause the stoppage of this as well as private freight." Astutely, he noted, "The necessity of the wood still exists, but not the necessity of white men." Instead, he proposed that the Lakota chop the wood (which they legally owned) and reap the rewards of selling it to the steamboats "at the same price as the white man does." The White people, he said, could find another job.[91] This same complaint was mentioned by other agents, as well.

Exploitation of Native-owned resources by White people was a legal problem for the Indian agents. In his annual report for 1881, Lower Brule Agency's W. H. Parkhurst provided a background to the problem: the great diversity of the trees, which once "so thickly studded" the river bottoms, had "been ruthlessly stripped." He blamed military woodchoppers, Lakotas, and White people alike, adding, "Upon my arrival here there were but 12 cords of wood for agency use during the long and cold winter of 1880–'81." He especially wanted to make the commissioner aware of "the wonton and reckless manner in which the timber lands set apart for Indian use had been and are now mercilessly plundered of valuable standing timber and wood." To shed some light on what may have taken place at Big Mike's Woodyard, Agent Parkhurst added, "All cases that have come to my knowledge of wood chopping upon this or the 'general reservation' have been acted upon promptly, and the affenders [archaic variant of *offenders*] warned from Indian soil."[92]

A series of correspondence between Agent W. E. Dougherty at Crow Creek Agency–Fort Thompson and the commissioner of Indian affairs was preserved. The earliest one is very faded, but it appears that Dougherty described the situation upon Fort George Island, where a number of persons who had been "ordered off the Reservation" the previous year had returned to the location and resumed "cutting the timber" and selling it to the passing steamboats.[93] In his next letter, Dougherty reported that he "and nine (9) Indian police" had gone to Fort George Island and removed those who were guilty of "tresspass [*sic*] and depravation" of the Lakota land.[94]

An August 14, 1880, letter from Dougherty to the commissioner also recounted the incident:

> Sir, I have the honor to inform you that all the wood on Fort George Island was seized by the Government in February last and the trespassers expelled. Since that time some of the boats have purchased a portion of this wood from some person at Fort George who claims to own it. The sale was an illegal one.

Dougherty requested that the commissioner "refuse payment for any wood" that originated on the island or from additional woodyards on and near the reservation. "If your boats need wood at these points," he offered, "I will be pleased to have you take it, sending me a wood card for the amount taken, which you may replace at the landing here."[95]

A March 30, 1880, response letter from the commissioner acknowledged the wood seized from Fort George Island, then asked Dougherty to "ascertain at what rate per cord [he could] have the service performed [having the wood chopped and sold by the rightful owners], and report the same to [the commissioner's] office before further action [was] taken."[96]

On Friday, February 20, Irish was nearly done with the maps—one for Blunt, and a copy for Johnson. The strong wind, "a NW gale," blew sand around to such an extent that "no one could face it."

Saturday morning was "clear and fine" as the crew "pulled up camp and started for Pierre." The day was warm with no wind, and the trip was wonderfully uneventful. A new camp was set up at a point on the east bank, opposite Bad River, just "below" (south of) Kirley's ranch. The new campsite was within a "dense grove of Box Elder trees at [the] mouth of [a] small stream." They named it Camp McNiel, in honor of the group's cook. (Today this campsite is part of Griffin Park, in the city of Pierre, a block west of where Kirley's cabin once stood.)

On Sunday, February 22, the maps were mailed off to Blunt and Johnson, along with a "descriptive letter" to Hughitt. That task done—marking a good milestone for the project—Irish was otherwise silent about the day, excepting a list of expenses (such as $7.50 for hay) and a note saying the weather was so warm that the snow was gone and the ice was "thawing rapidly."

Monday, February 23, saw the beginning of work on the lines to determine a possible river crossing at or near Pierre. Soundings were taken on the east shore, opposite the mouth of the Bad River, with notes that the river ice was melting. That bad ice was a concern; Irish planned to take soundings for three possible routes across the river, a task that needed to be accomplished before the ice gave out.

Late on February 23, Irish sat down in camp at Fort Pierre and wrote home. After saying he'd recently received three letters from each of them, for a total of nine, he apologized that his work had kept him so busy that he'd "neglected writing." There was an upcoming trip of 120 miles to the "Forks of the Cheyenne River" (see tangent below), in the western part of Dakota Territory. Once that trip was complete, he expected Hughitt, Blunt, and Johnson to come out for a meeting, at which they'd discuss "plans for the future campaigns" and, he hoped, a furlough. The latter was becoming a regular refrain.

He reassured his family he was "very well"—"Never felt better than I do now"—though the "very bad attack of influenza" had hung on for "weeks and weeks." He wasn't the only one feeling improved. "My sick ones are all better, in fact well, and at work," he wrote. "We to day are sounding the Mo. River at Pierre. Lewis and Linkhart, do well indeed. I should be lost without them. Lewis is a very big eater, he eats like a hog."

He ended his correspondence by asking that they credit him "for writing this letter in the midst of hurry and confusion," citing that the work was "all sines, tangents, curves, grades, depths, heights, lengths, bearings and distances all the time night and day." After signing off, he added an excited postscript, almost two months after the event: "I have bought a love of a pony. I call him Billy paid $40 for him."

NAMES FOR THE CHEYENNE AND BELLE FOURCHE RIVERS

We'll establish a naming standard to ease confusion going forward. Looking at historic maps, the Belle Fourche River was frequently labeled as the "North Fork of the Cheyenne River," and the confluence of the Belle Fourche and Cheyenne Rivers was called "the Forks of the Cheyenne," or just "the Forks." Those are the names Irish most frequently used, and for simplicity we will as well, except where the Belle Fourche was specifically mentioned. He also used "Big Cheyenne" to refer to the main Cheyenne River, which is sometimes labeled "South Fork Cheyenne River" on some historic maps—today it is simply the "Cheyenne River."

Readings for the second line across the Missouri River and to the mouth of the Bad River were accomplished on February 24, at the "upper end of the bottoms." While taking level readings, Carse and Selby broke through the ice at the edge of a sandbar. They "were badly scared." Luckily the water was not too deep there, but it being February, the water must have been dangerously cold, and they were not in a position to quickly get to warmth.

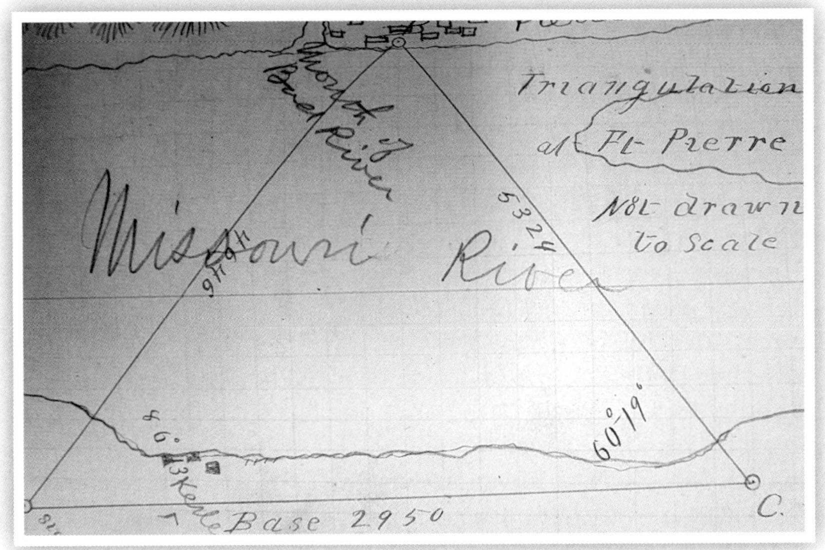

Irish's notebook entry for the measurements at the mouth of the Bad River. S7-16

The next day, February 25, the crew prepared to travel to Fort Pierre, on the western bank of the Missouri. Leighton and his team of horses, Irish and his pony Billy, and Powers and his horse Texas made the crossing, "using great caution, as the late warm weather [had] greatly weakened the ice." That is likely an understatement, but the warm spell was about over. The day had been "bad, and the barometer low." It was going to get worse, and soon. It was not a good time to take a long road trip.

Over the Fort Pierre to Deadwood Trail: February 26–March 7, 1880

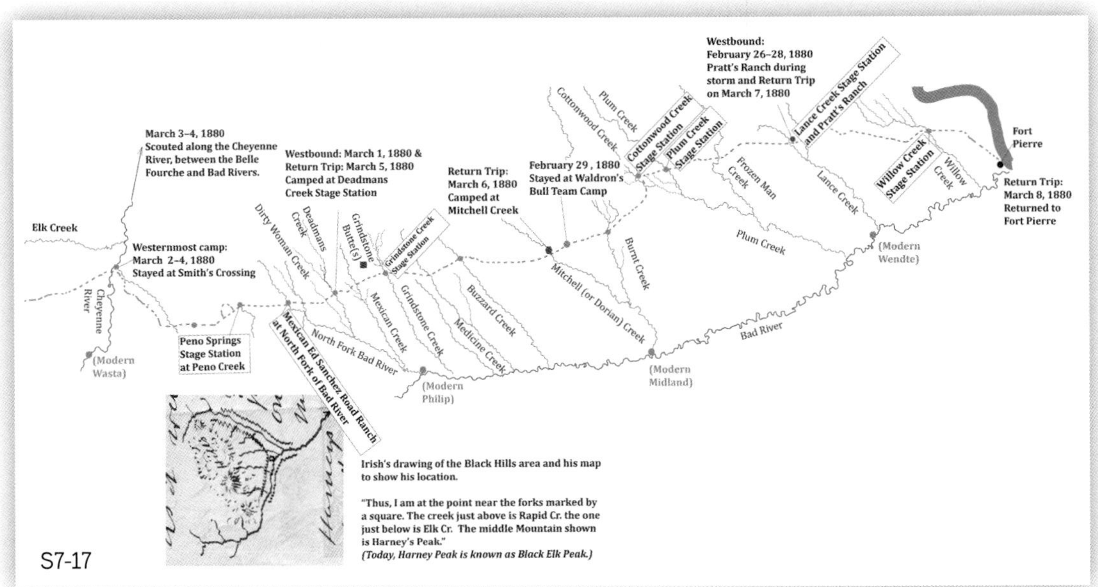

S7-17

After an overnight stay at Fort Pierre (where Ryther delivered a letter from Johnson), Irish, Leighton, and Powers were up early on the February 26, with "5 guns, 5 pistols, and all other things ready." They were joined by Sherwood (owner of Sherwood's Hotel) and his team of horses, with an odometer attached to a wagon wheel to make distance measurement easier.

The men were making final preparations for a scouting trip west to the Forks of the Cheyenne and the head of the Bad River, which would bring them nearly to the Black Hills. West of the Missouri River was Lakota land, except the one wagon road between Fort Pierre and Deadwood, regularly traveled by freight haulers and stagecoaches.

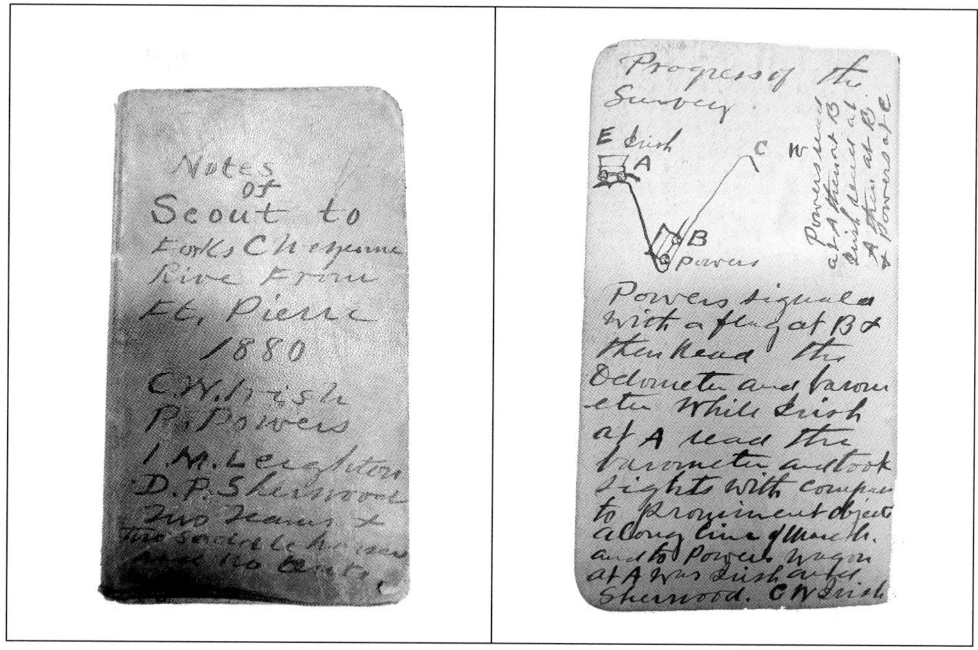

Irish recorded notes about the trip in this notebook—from weather, to topographical observations, to calculations. Among the pages was a description of how he and Powers used the barometer to measure elevations. S7-18, S7-19

They did not yet have permission to survey a route for the tracks, but this exploratory trip—using stage ranches along the approved road, which featured wide, sweeping vistas—would give them a sense of the terrain and opportunities to ask questions of people familiar with the locales. This information gathering would help later when they officially asked the Native people for permission to explore specific locations on behalf of the railroad company. But the survey party was already under surveillance. In fact, Irish's surveyor's notebook for this journey noted, "Several Indians on horseback maneuvered, suspicious about us." And with good reason, as Irish's party was apparently not the first to scout the land: "We so far have been closely watched by several mounted Indians. Today we found, on the ridge, marks of a survey made not long before. I suspect it is the work of the C. M. & St. P. engineers."

Stage ranches along the wagon road were located approximately every twelve to fifteen miles. There were meal stations at Lance Creek, Medicine Creek, and the Cheyenne River. The remaining ranches were way stations, where animals could be fed and watered, or swapped for fresh.

The group—Irish, Leighton, Powers, and Sherwood—headed northward along the Missouri River, passed the river bottoms at Old Fort Pierre, turned west to ascend "the long slope to [the] tops of [the] bluff on the Ft. Pierre and Deadwood" stage road, then trotted an additional ten and a half miles west to Willow Creek.

The Willow Creek stage station was somewhere in this valley. Willow Creek can be seen meandering within its deep, narrow channel, on the left side of this photo taken in late February 2021. S7-20

After a midday meal at Willow Creek Stage Stop, they continued an additional sixteen miles to Lance Creek Holes / Pratt's Ranch. The weather was "threatening," and the temperatures dropped until 7 p.m., when snow began. "It's a comfortless storm," Irish complained. "We were lucky to reach this ranch." The country they had passed over was "exceedingly broken," which would make for a challenging landscape to prepare for a roadbed.

The Fort Pierre to Deadwood Trail passed across the center of this image, from left to right, and the Lance Creek Holes / Pratt's Ranch stop was nestled against the hills on the right side, shown by an arrow. S7-21

The storm raged all night and all the next day, February 27, and the men were "crowded into a small cabin which [was] very cold and comfortless." The snow was still flying thick on the second night.

That small cabin was a stage stop along the road to Deadwood. The men remained there two full days while snow and winds continued to pummel the ranch. The temperature rose to a relatively balmy 26 degrees before abruptly falling to –10. After sundown on February 28, men "began to come in from the west." Irish added that some of them were "badly frozen," four having gone forty-eight hours "without fire or food."

This photo from the 1910s shows Borden's Ranch, built on land that previously hosted Lance Creek Stage Station / Pratt's Ranch, near Lance Creek Holes. While three decades farther along than what Irish saw, it gives an indication of what a stage ranch may have looked like.

It was a leap year, and on February 29 Irish and his men left Pratt's Ranch around midmorning, traveling throughout "a stormy cold raw day." Along the way, they passed many camps where travelers had waited out the storm, seeing the bodies of cattle that had not survived. They managed to travel twenty-eight miles, setting up their tents at Waldron's Bull Team Camp. Some of Waldron's bulls were among the casualties of the storm, smothered by the snow.

The general location of Waldron's Bull Team Camp, where the scouting group spent a night in tents on their trip to scout the Forks of the Cheyenne. The wide plateau gives a sense of the high plain over which the men were traveling. S7-23

Waldron's Bull Team Camp was a location where animals could be rested and possibly swapped for fresh ones (bull teams were a common method for pulling heavy freight). Before they left Waldron's on March 1, Irish and his companions "shared coffee and provisions with Waldron and his men." As the crew pushed westward, the day warmed, and the recent snow melted around them. It was a high plateau, with sudden creek gullies and the rare landmark, such as Grindstone Butte(s) (locals disagree about how many buttes make up the landmark). The road gently rose as they crossed the saddle between the southernmost two of the three buttes, then continued southwest toward the expanding horizon. After crossing Mexican Creek, they arrived at Deadman's Creek Stage Station.

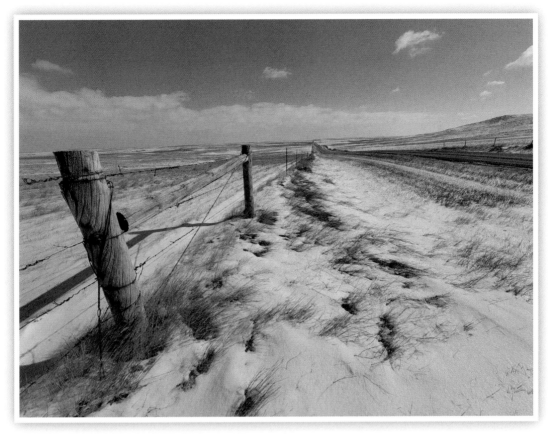

Looking toward the eastern approach to Grindstone Butte(s). The southernmost of the buttes is on the right. The stage road went generally on a diagonal through this photo, upper-left to mid-right. S7-24

The southernmost two hills that make up Grindstone Butte(s). The main stage road passed between them. Photo taken from the southeast, looking northwest. S7-25

The hospitality at the Deadman's Creek ranch was decidedly lacking in comparison to that received at Waldron's. "[The operators] would not let us have any wood," Irish complained, "so we made a fire of bull chips and cooked supper."

The general location of the Deadman's Creek stage station. This shows how narrow and steep some of these creek gullies (center of photo) were as they snaked across the high plain toward Bad River. S7-26

According to Irish's diary, the creek obtained its English name due to the death of four White men, killed by Lakotas. "There is much fear from that source now," wrote Irish, knowing that his party was on Lakota land, traveling the road, rather than heading cross-country, because the stage operators had negotiated safe passage for travelers upon this specific, narrow ribbon of land, and *only* that land.

Ruth wrote her father on March 1, scolding him for not writing and telling him of the nightmares shared in the household as they imagined various misfortunes that may have befallen him before a letter arrived. The most recent letter had told them about the purchase of Billy, and they were delighted both at the animal and of knowing that Irish was still among the living. So, too, were the houseplants, which were "flourishing splendidly." Ruth teased that her mother "[gave] more attention to them than she did her children when they were little." George the bird had been singing "at the top of his voice," and was a mischievous thing, getting "many a little scolding for slyly nipping off" the leaves of the beloved houseplants.

There was another matter that was consuming Mrs. Irish's attention, as related by Ruth:

> Mother I expect will have an open war with [neighbor] Mrs. Goetz this spring because of the latter's chickens, which are just turning things upside down in our yard since the death of Mink. They even roost in our outhouse. What is to be done? I say let them alone, as [the Goetzes] utterly defy us to help ourselves, and say they do not intend to check them up until they make their garden.

While Irish was approximately six hundred miles away, the goings-on at home were as important to him as if he were there—maybe more so.

THE IRISH-GOETZ HOME IN IOWA CITY

Let's fast-forward about a century or so—after a quick diversion backwards in time. In light of this minor tension between the Irishes and their neighbors the Goetzes, it seems appropriate to include this example of "all's well that ends well."

In 1849, Captain Frederick Macy Irish and his family, which included fifteen-year old son Charles, moved into a new house atop a hill in the southeastern portion of Iowa City. Dubbed Rose Hill, the abode went on to shelter subsequent generations of the Irish family until 1963. The structure then sat empty for several years, suffering the indignations of vandalism, stripped of anything valuable, and left to rot. But rot it refused to do.

According to an article about the house, "Captain Irish had built it to last. To build so massively and on such a large scale in this wilderness town of 1500 was quite in character for him, apparently, for he was a creative and adventurous soul, a huge man physically, with a big booming voice."

The house was solid, as was the connection felt by Carl and Janet Goetz, who purchased and lovingly restored Rose Hill in the late 1960s. Area residents assisted, helping to locate and return some original fixtures and reconstructing others. One piece returned to the house was an old whaling harpoon once treasured by Captain Irish, presented to the young Goetz couple by Charles Preston, whose mother, Ruth, was Captain Irish's granddaughter and the youngest daughter of Charles Wood Irish.[97]

On the morning of March 2, the party left the less-than-hospitable ranch on Deadman's Creek and continued their push west, coming upon a ranch that had been burned during the summer of 1879, just months before. They were also far enough west now that, upon climbing "Pino Hill" (Peno Hill on modern maps—northeast of modern Wasta, South Dakota), they got their first glimpse of the Black Hills. Irish sketched the region in a letter home:

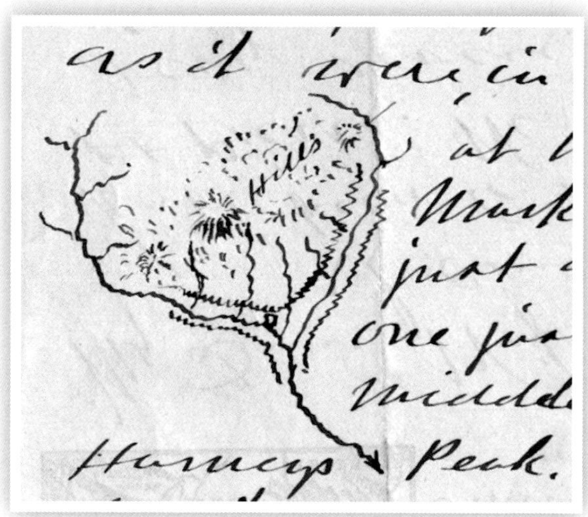

Irish's description of his map: "We are in full sight of the Black Hills. Harney's Peak [now Black Elk Peak] towers above all to the clouds; Bear Butte, Custer's Peak, and a dozen others rise up above the black ridge of the hills, which stretches itself along in a line from SE to NW for 150 miles, being about 80 miles broad. This river by its forks clasps the 'Hills' as it were. Thus, I am at the point near the forks marked by a square. The creek just above is Rapid Cr.; the one just below is Elk Cr. The middle Mountain shown is Harney's Peak. Look up the maps and see if you can find where I am." S7-27

Continuing west, the party arrived at Smith's Ranch, on the south fork of the Cheyenne River, south of Elk Creek. Here, too, White men had been killed within the year. These reminders likely kept the party alert. Due to the storm, it had taken them several extra days to reach this point, and Irish was anxious to get on with the work and back to the rest of the men.

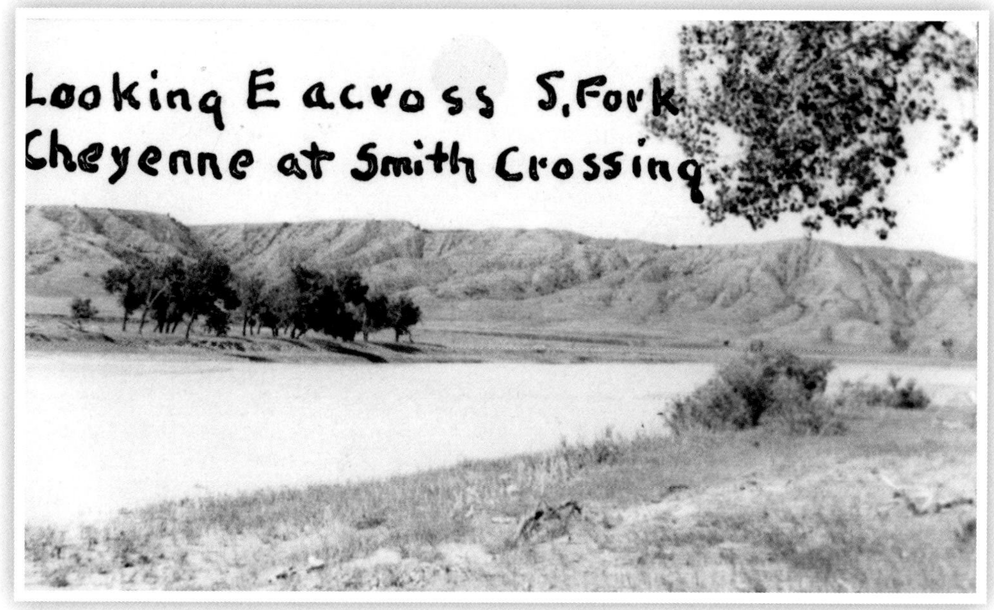

Historic photo of Smith's Crossing circa the 1950s. S7-28

A view to the northeast from the former location of Smith's Crossing Stage Ranch, showing bluffs to the east and north of the crossing location. S7-29

On March 3, Irish took Powers, ranch owner Smith, and a hunter named Reed (not the owner of Reed's Ranch) to examine the south branch of the Cheyenne. They crossed the river, followed it north to the mouth of Elk Creek, crossed the river again, then traveled south along the east bank before returning to Smith's Ranch.

Some of the rough terrain Irish described. This photo was taken southwest of the forks, on the west side of the Cheyenne, looking eastward. The Cheyenne is along the bluffs on the far side.

Another view of the terrain on the east side of the Cheyenne. This photo was taken from the west. The river itself is down in the valley between the meadow in the foreground and the cedar breaks on the far side. S7-31

It was "very far from pleasant to do this work," wrote Irish. The landscape was "very rugged," the "weather cold," and the snow deep—exhausting work all around. The area is, indeed, extraordinarily rugged. From a surveyor's viewpoint, it must have been nothing short of a daunting challenge. Suddenly those "bothersome hills" west of the James River may have felt like nothing more than mere ripples in the landscape.

The Cheyenne River winds through a wide valley flanked by high and rough bluffs. This modern photo is from a section several miles south of Smith's Ranch, but it provides a good impression of the landscape the men scouted on March 3, 1880. The Cheyenne's twisting, turning path is clearly shown. S7-32

While recuperating from the day's scouting, Irish took the opportunity to write to his wife, noting his location as "Smith's Ranch, Big Cheyenne River" (Cheyenne River). Before reminding her he would soon meet with the railroad officials—and hopefully be granted a longed-for furlough—he recounted for her the nearly week-long trek from Fort Pierre, beset by the storm, adding more depth than the diary afforded:

> I came here last night; have been 6 days getting here from Ft. Pierre. We were delayed by a very severe snow storm of 3 days duration, but were snug and comfortable while many others suffered severely. I saw several who had badly frozen feet and hands. A woman with her little child, 2 years old, travelled on in the storm; she had only 2 thin blankets, but such was her courage that she reached her husband at Twin Springs, 20 miles from here, without accident. Many a hardy man froze himself for want of courage, and hundreds of tough Texas oxen froze to death, while this poor woman, animated by the hope of meeting her husband and making a house in this wilderness of hills and mountains, kept on and found the storm happily without harm.

Such is the stuff of Western mythology—that a young mother and child would survive walking through a blizzard with "only 2 thin blankets," yet "her courage" caused the pair to survive where oxen and bulls would perish.

Another modern view of the Cheyenne Valley, showing the size of the surrounding hills. S7-33

The next day, March 4, featured a similar expedition of seventeen miles. "It's a wild place," observed Irish. "We saw tracks of Indians on horseback, fresh in the snow." There had been no interactions, however. The Lakota caused no problems, but a White man did. Following their evening meal, "a desperado by the name of McManns came to the house and stuck Mr. Sherwood over the head with a pistol, hurting him badly." Irish added, "I am very tired and worn out." For such a "Wild West" occurrence, he sure seems to have related the event casually.

The return trip to the Missouri River began on Friday, March 5, with improved weather, and they made it back to Deadman's Creek, where they spent the night. On the second day of travel, they made observations and notes along the route, passing Grindstone Butte(s) (which Irish noted the Lakota called Drum Butte) and getting as far east as Mitchell Creek (or Dorian Creek), just shy of Waldron's Bull Team Camp. There, they set up camp as another storm blew up. (By the early 1880s, there was a general store at Mitchell Creek Stage Station, but it is unknown whether it was there yet during this survey).

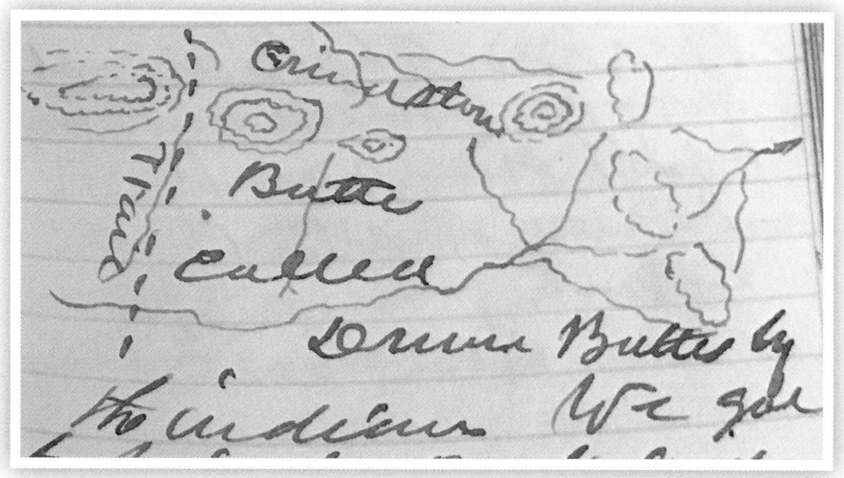

Irish's drawing of the topography around Grindstone Butt(e) and the Fort Pierre to Deadwood Trail, the road shown going around the buttes in three routes. S7-34

The night was "terrible": Leighton and Sherwood slept in the wagon bed, where Irish thought they were "like to have froze themselves." Irish and Powers were on the ground, without a tent, yet claimed to have been "warm enough," despite the thermometer reading a shuddering −36 degrees.

March 7 was "much better," Irish adding, "We got on finely, checking our work all the way." They arrived back at Lance Creek Holes / Pratt's Ranch, where they spent the night. By the end of the next day, they'd made their way back to the camp, "chilled and frozen almost through," Irish adding, "The snow now lies heavy on all the country."

This semi-clandestine scout had given Irish a glimpse of the terrain that would complicate the route west, but the landscape wasn't to be the only obstacle. In the meanwhile, simply finding a place to cross the Missouri, much less get beyond it, would occupy much of the crew's focus.

Upon reaching Fort Pierre, Irish took the opportunity to again write home. Just as the family had reassured him they'd written many more letters than he'd received, he, too, had written and sent six letters home between the dates they'd mentioned. Irish theorized, "Some scoundrel is stealing my letters." To put their minds at ease, he asked them not to fear, assuring, "I have a host of friends here, who would at once let you know if anything is the matter."

After instructions for paying a few bills in a specific manner, he turned his attention to the war Mrs. Irish was fighting with Mrs. Goetz over the wayward chickens:

> Now I must say to all as Christ did to all mankind. Be at peace with all men, or rather women. Don't you let old Mrs. Goetz poison any of you. She'd do it sure if a chance offers, but don't any of you say so. Get some one to fix up the fence and then get rat poison and kill the infernal things. I mean the rat exterminator. I have only to finish up my maps and figures and then shall come home but not to stay long. I am to have work here as long as I want it, and may be, when the line is done . . . Asst. Eng. I write this in a hurry to let you know that I am well and safe.

His career aspirations may have been helping to balance the hardships.

THE FORT PIERRE TO DEADWOOD TRAIL

In February 2021, I attempted to follow the route Irish, Leighton, Powers, and Sherwood took to the Forks, but without the awful weather. It was a success on both counts. With the help of Deb Schiefelbein at the Verendrye Museum, I was able to find the stage ranch locations and various stream crossings.

Back in 2008, a group of passionate people organized a ride to commemorate the centennial of the closing of the stage road. In cooperation with landowners, the trek followed the historic road as closely as possible, many participants using horse-drawn wagons. Through their pre-trip research (with the help of the South Dakota State Historical Society's archives), a map had been created, identifying the location of historic stops, as well as where the modern trekkers would stop for their nights.

On the first day of the winter 2021 research trip, with that map in hand, we followed the stage road as best we could, taking some "roads" that were really nothing more than ranch tracks across fields. We met several ranchers, some who pointed us toward specific locations. One escorted us through the gate leading onto their private land so they could point across a wide valley in the middle of grazing land, where a post showed where the road had crested a hill. Others shared stories about the history of their properties. Photos were taken, maps were marked, and hosts were effusively thanked.

What surprised me was that many of these "creeks," which had seemed formidable while reading the diaries, became little more than what would be created if a child took a stick and dragged it through the dirt—no secondary valley, just a deep channel with steep sides, following paths that looked more like what a panic-stricken snake would create while fleeing a predator. The imagination can create a landscape that doesn't exist, and I wanted to be accurate, which is one of the reasons I insisted on seeing each location myself.

For a stagecoach, getting across these twisting, turning, deep, and steep creek beds would have been an entirely different challenge. During research, I found mention that the Willow Creek crossing was notoriously difficult. We couldn't get close enough to the crossing to know exactly why, but I believed the account. Historically, the banks would be cut back to create a gentler slope on either side of the creek so the stagecoach could more easily traverse the dip. Sometimes stones or logs were laid to stabilize the banks, creating makeshift ramps down and up.

We zigzagged through township after township, observing the terrain and taking photos, documenting this creek crossing and that. As we turned down one road that turned out to be a long driveway, we met the property owners, Marianne and Lloyd Frein, who were on their way to town (at least forty-five minutes away). Turns out they were good friends with M. R. Hansen, who had been helping me identify remote locations, and they brightened at the mention of his name (more about M. R. later). They pointed us farther down their driveway to where a grave marker sits, and to where the Mexican Creek stage crossing had been, granting us access and sharing stories and good wishes for our research, with an invitation to come back in the summer. Again, good people, kind people.

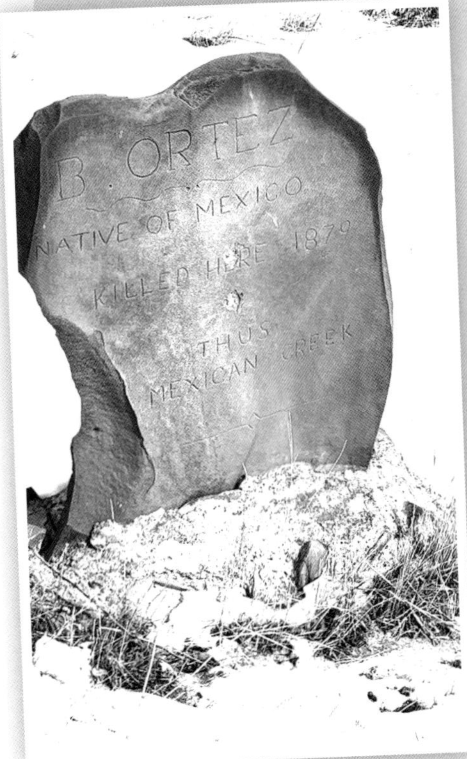

Inscription: "B. Ortez / Native of Mexico / Killed Here 1879 / Thus Mexican Creek." The current marker was placed in 1923, after the original one had become worn. S7-35

We pulled over at one of the stage stop locations and pulled out sandwiches for lunch. It felt like a long enough trip by modern vehicle on modern roads at modern speeds; what would it have been like to take the stage road in wagons—in February, days after a blizzard had deposited significant snow? We were grateful for the heated truck with a gentle ride and big windows. Irish, Leighton, Powers, and Sherwood had the view, but they didn't have the comfortable, protected environment of the truck. We were pleased to say that we had *not* suffered much on our version of the trek.

The most westward stop on Irish's exploratory trip had been Smith's Crossing, where the stage road crossed the Cheyenne. Irish and his party stayed at Smith's Ranch, on the west side of the Cheyenne, just beyond the crossing. The area around Smith's ranch was interesting, but getting close to Smith's Crossing was more emotionally satisfying.

We couldn't get all the way to the river, but we got as close as possible on modern roads without special permissions (I am always careful not to trespass). It was sunset. It was beautiful. One of my favorite photos of the entire trip was captured there (below). Again, the divide between March 1880, when Irish was there, crossing this spot to scout opportunities to get the tracks into Deadwood, and February 2021, when I stood there, felt thin. Very thin. He, too, had seen the sun set behind those same bluffs, and it likely looks very much the same, despite the passing of nearly a century and a half.

I stood there longer than I should have, just watching the sun go down, the colors that soaked the landscape changing from yellow to orange to pink to purple, each one stunningly beautiful and different than its predecessor. It was beautiful, but it was also frustrating. I was near the river, but I couldn't even *see* it.

A modern sunset close to the location where Smith's Ranch once stood. The Cheyenne River meanders beneath the far bluffs. You'll just have to imagine the colors—changing from yellow to orange to pink to purple. S7-36

Section Eight

RIVER CROSSINGS AND LOTS OF UPS AND DOWNS

MARCH 8–JULY 12, 1880

The officers arrived in Dakota Territory to review the surveyed routes to cross the Missouri River, personally inspecting things as they had at each prior step. The project was going well, and the officers were pleased with the work, even while giving Irish direction for changes. Irish was granted another furlough, after which he returned to Dakota Territory not only rejuvenated but in the company of Mrs. Irish. They experienced the adventure of a Missouri River steamboat trip, and she would spend the next several months near the work sites. The crew themselves were called back to the James River, where they were surprised to find a new town where just recently there had been only blowing grasses. While having Mrs. Irish nearby was of great help to her husband, there was more illness, missing crew members, another mutiny attempt, and a horse that accidentally killed itself. There was also the pressure of the approaching graders and tracklayers behind them. Meanwhile, a partial legal agreement had been reached with the Lakota, permitting some of what the Chicago & North Western had asked for, but not all—they did not yet grant permission for a survey west of the Missouri.

Exploring Another Route to the Missouri: March 8–27, 1880

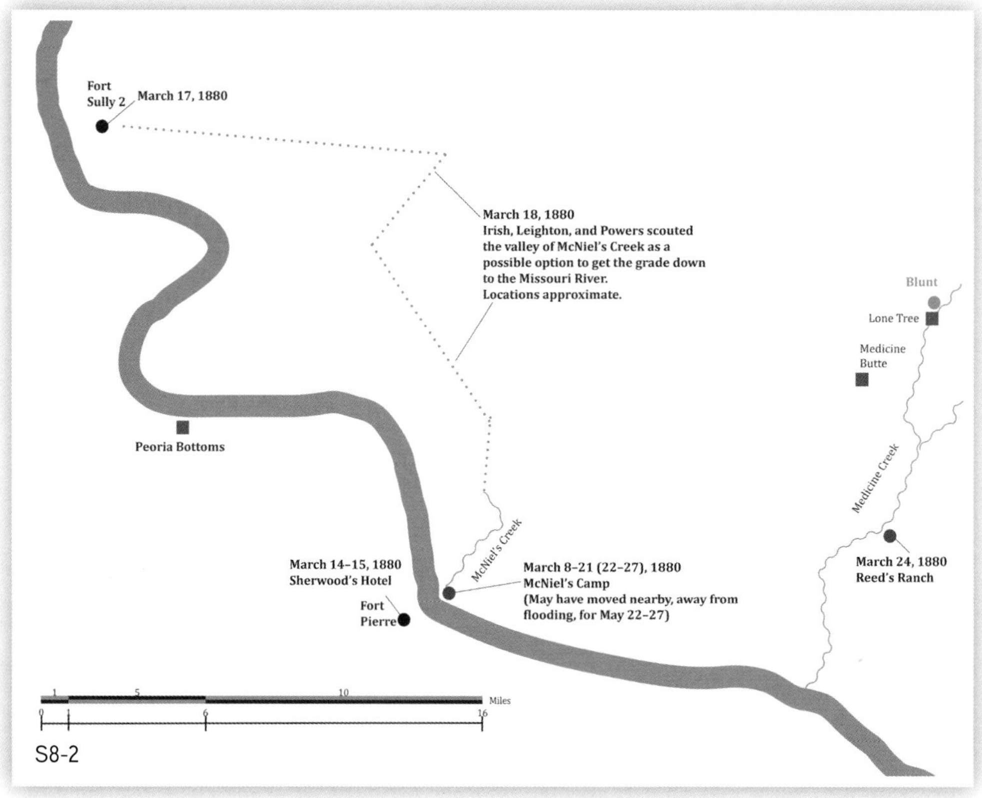

Back at camp, the weather remained "very cold and stormy." Snow fell, and the "wind [ran] around the circle each day." Irish set to work on maps and notes to document the scouting trip to the western reaches of the Cheyenne River. He was less pleased, however, by the work done by the men he'd left behind in camp.

The winter storms that affected Irish and his traveling party had also impacted the camp in Pierre, with temperatures ranging from –20 degrees to 3 above. It appeared the men had not ventured out, or at least not sufficiently to complete their work on a short line they'd identified. Considering the weather, this is understandable; however, Irish found it irritating.

While Irish remained in camp, documenting the Cheyenne River scout, he sent teams out to finish work on the short line. A portion of the party working on the Lone Tree line arrived back at camp the evening of March 11, having camped overnight at "Camp Blizzard" and presumably completed the needed survey work, but the men working on the levels did not return.

Meanwhile, Irish's work on the maps, profiles, notes, and the report about the Cheyenne River trip that he'd began on March 9 was completed by March 14, including profiles of "all the country between Bad and Cheyenne Rivers and from the Missouri to the forks of Cheyenne," Irish adding, "I find my work to tally well with former alternatives."

The fate of the level party began to worry Irish. They should have returned to camp on the eleventh with the rest of the men. On the thirteenth, he wrote, "The level party has not got in. I wonder what is the matter." The next day he added, "I can't imagine what has become of them, as they had only two day's work to do."

There were several possibilities that may have gone through his mind: Were any of the level party men part of the Royal Family (members of the group who had attempted mutiny on February 9)? Had they simply abandoned their work and returned east? Had they decided to try their hand in the gold camps of the Black Hills (a rather common "malady")? Had they met with foul play of some sort? Irish's recent trip west, crossing creeks named after various murders, likely drifted through his mind, not to mention the desperados who had shown up to batter stage ranch visitors. The weather was also worrisome; the light snow had stopped, but it was "still cold." (The party would reappear a few days later, but no explanation for their tardiness appears in the diary.)

On the night of March 14, Irish went to Sherwood's Hotel in Fort Pierre, staying overnight. He was crafting his report to Johnson, and he complained to his diary of being cold.

While Irish sat in his room at Sherwood's Hotel, in that "barn of a house," he wrote letters. One went to Chief Engineer Johnson. Others went to Iowa City. To his daughter Lizzie, he noted that it had been "dreadful cold" and snowy, but he was "warm, comfortable, and well." Lizzie had also sent him a diary for 1880 that failed to reach him, and he let her know he'd gone ahead and paid $3 for one available locally.

To his wife, he mentioned he'd seen in a newspaper that she'd gone to Toledo, Iowa, and he would send this letter to that locale. Due to a forty-eight-hour snowstorm, it was "fine sleighing" for the first time in twelve to fifteen years, and the people were worried about a spring flood. He was also still hoping his request for a furlough would be granted, saying, "I shall try to get home by April 1st (no fooling)."

He also provided some interesting insight into how those reports, maps, and other important papers were making their way to the officers of the railroad: "I have the same bad luck with letters to the company officers. So they have hired a man who now travels from Chicago here, gets my reports, and takes them back."

A third letter was written to daughter Ruth, repeating many of the things he had shared with his wife and Lizzie, adding, "You don't know how much lighter I feel when things are cheerful at home. I cannot enter into details now as I am writing against time for the mail. I have just finished 35 pages of reports +c for the company, so don't you think my arm is tired, and my eyes weak. My brain weary. I assure you they are."

The incoming mail from the Black Hills, likely carried by stage coach, had not made an appearance since March 9, the snow being about six inches deep. "Some fear the Indians," wrote Irish on the sixteenth. That day he also finished his report, made a copy, and got it off as a registered letter. "I am tired out entirely," he later wrote in his diary. "It's still winter. The ice in the river is solid as in Jan. and all the country buried in snow."

On March 17, "a fine day" that saw some thawing, Irish, Powers, and Leighton headed north to Fort Sully again, "an exploring trip," stopping at the stage ranch along the military road. It was St. Patrick's Day, and celebrations were taking place. Wryly, he noted, "I saw many black eyes."

THE MILITARY ROAD

Irish mentioned navigating his way to the military road, then following it to Reed's Ranch. On his lovely drawing of the Reed's Ranch area, the road is clearly marked (see page 124). The various forts across the region were connected by roads and waterways, facilitating the movement of men and supplies, work for which private civilians were frequently contracted.[98] "A good day's travel for a wagon with a heavy load was fifteen to twenty miles," in the best of circumstances and terrain.[99]

These roads saw heavy use from the 1860s to 1890s, and they remained in use by locals long after the military had moved on.[100] While steamboats were the fiscally preferred method of transportation for heavy or large shipments, trips via the roadways were usually shorter in distance and faster in time. For instance, there were 351 miles between Fort Sully 2 and Yankton by river, but via road it was only 262 miles.[101] Of course, roads had the advantage of not being as influenced by ice and drought.

The Missouri River was notoriously difficult and shallow, with sandbars and snags being two of the most common causes of demise for a riverboat. Wagons and stagecoaches could use roads most of the year, except on the muddiest or snowiest of days, and those conditions often improved quickly on their own.[102] Telegraph wires were strung along the road to facilitate necessary communications, so most travelers had some idea of what they were getting into.

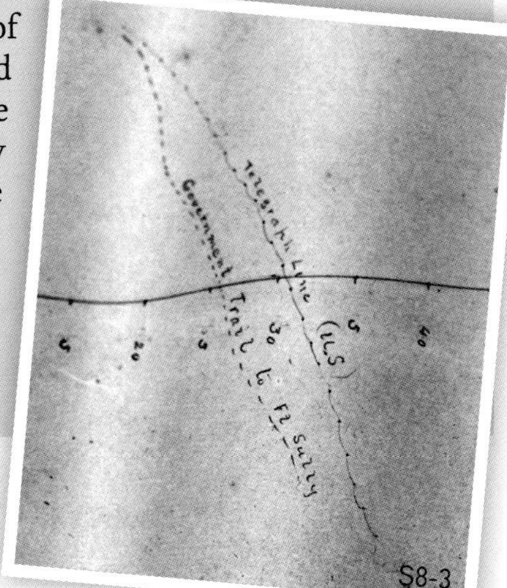

Irish drew the location of the military road and telegraph line as they crossed his survey down Medicine Creek.

On the morning of the March 18, the men set off for "the high plains eastward," where they scouted an alternative route to the Missouri, following McNiel's Creek, Irish noting, "Gracious how it thawed today." (As this creek descends down the bluff today, it passes the South Dakota State Historical Society and the Capitol complex, emptying into the Missouri River at Griffin Park.)

The "high plains" above the Missouri River, between Pierre and Fort Sully. Today the area is cultivated with rotating crops, but as the Dakota Central was being surveyed, the area would have been mostly prairie grass. The plain is flat and wide before descending into the rolling bluffs at the river. S8-4

The next day the crew reversed the trek, running a line back up McNiel's Creek, taking measurements and readings as they went. The air remained cold, yet thawing ground made the terrain "sloppy."

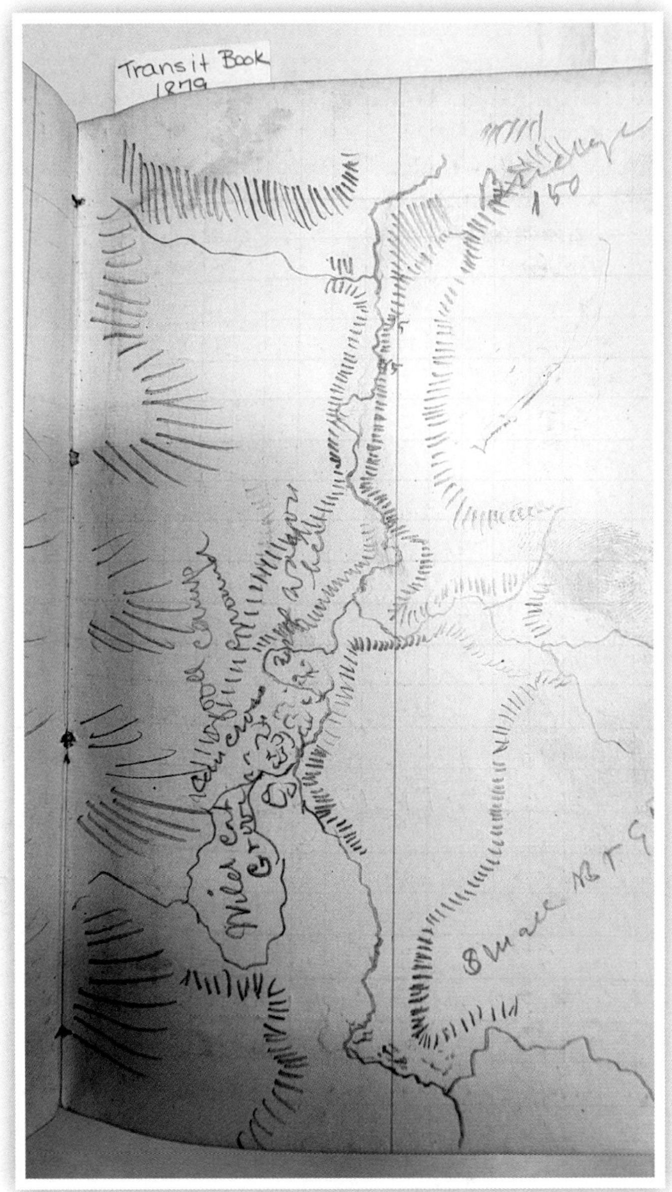

A page from a surveyor's notebook showing the area around McNiel's Creek as it descended the bluff, with topography and notes. S8-5

The diary never mentions washing clothes or other specific tasks, but the crew was working in the mud, which makes one think about those various "camp chores" Irish mentions now and then. Those chores certainly would have included washing mud and dirt out of their clothing, which must have been quite difficult. One also wonders whether the individual men were responsible for their own clothing, or whether—similar to the cook, who primarily handled a single task—one of the crew was charged with keeping the collective wardrobe in some sort of wearable shape.

After running five and a half miles up the creek, Irish returned to camp, then sent Powers and Selby out with the rod and level, respectively. This is the first recent mention that Irish made of someone taking levels. (Remember that his leveling crew had gone missing for days, and the diary remained silent as to their return, or which men had been absent.)

The melting continued, and Irish opened his diary entry for March 20 with, "Sloppy, very sloppy. Have to keep watch over the creek that it does not overflow camp." Amidst the mud, Irish continued work on maps, and the level party completed their work along McNiel's Creek.

Irish took the opportunity to send the new maps and profiles back to Johnson on March 21, sending them along with the camp cook, McNiel. The cook was so homesick, Irish gave him his blessing to return home.

The location where the creek Irish named after McNiel empties into the Missouri River, and where the men had set up Camp McNiel, before possibly moving it due to excessive muddiness. This location is in modern Griffin Park, in the city of Pierre, South Dakota. S8-6

As McNiel departed, Irish observed, "My camp is a mud hole." In fact, he declared that camp be moved. But the diary does not indicate whether the move actually happened or, if it did, exactly when. (An entry for March 23, two days forward, can be read two ways. When Blunt and Ryther arrived in camp, Irish lamented, "Sorry that we are in such a mudhole, but our new ground is still wet." Was the new ground also wet? Or was the new ground too wet for the crew to move camp? Oh, the vagaries of language!)

March 22 marked the one-year anniversary of the survey party's first work westward from Tracy, in weather that was "still stormy and wintry, but in the PM it thawed some." One year on, they were again working in thawing conditions. Fortunately, despite irritating mud, the river ice remained solid, and Irish surveyed the bluffs in the vicinity of Peoria Bottoms, enjoying the "fine spring weather" despite the mud.

Looking across the modern Missouri River, to Peoria Bottoms. S8-7

On March 24, Irish took Blunt and Ryther out to see various line options in person, traveling to Fort George Island, then on to Reed's Ranch. It had been "a fine day" weather-wise, though Irish suffered a "dreadful head ache."

The location that was Fort George Island is now beneath the waters of the Missouri River. However, this is the approximate location of the north end of the island. Across the river is the site of Fort George. This is one of the crossing options that Irish showed Blunt on March 24, 1880. S8-8

The next day's tour took the men across Medicine Knoll / Big Medicine Hill, Lone Tree Creek, and McNiel's Creek before they returned to camp, Irish suffering through his headache the entire time. He observed that the barometer was "very low," and he anticipated a storm. The wind increased in strength over the next day, Irish eventually declaring it a "high gale," though the storm itself merely produced some sprinkles.

Now having taken Blunt and Ryther to see each of the viable options for crossing the Missouri River, Irish spent the next day, March 26, reviewing the maps and profiles with Blunt; the men "had a good visit."

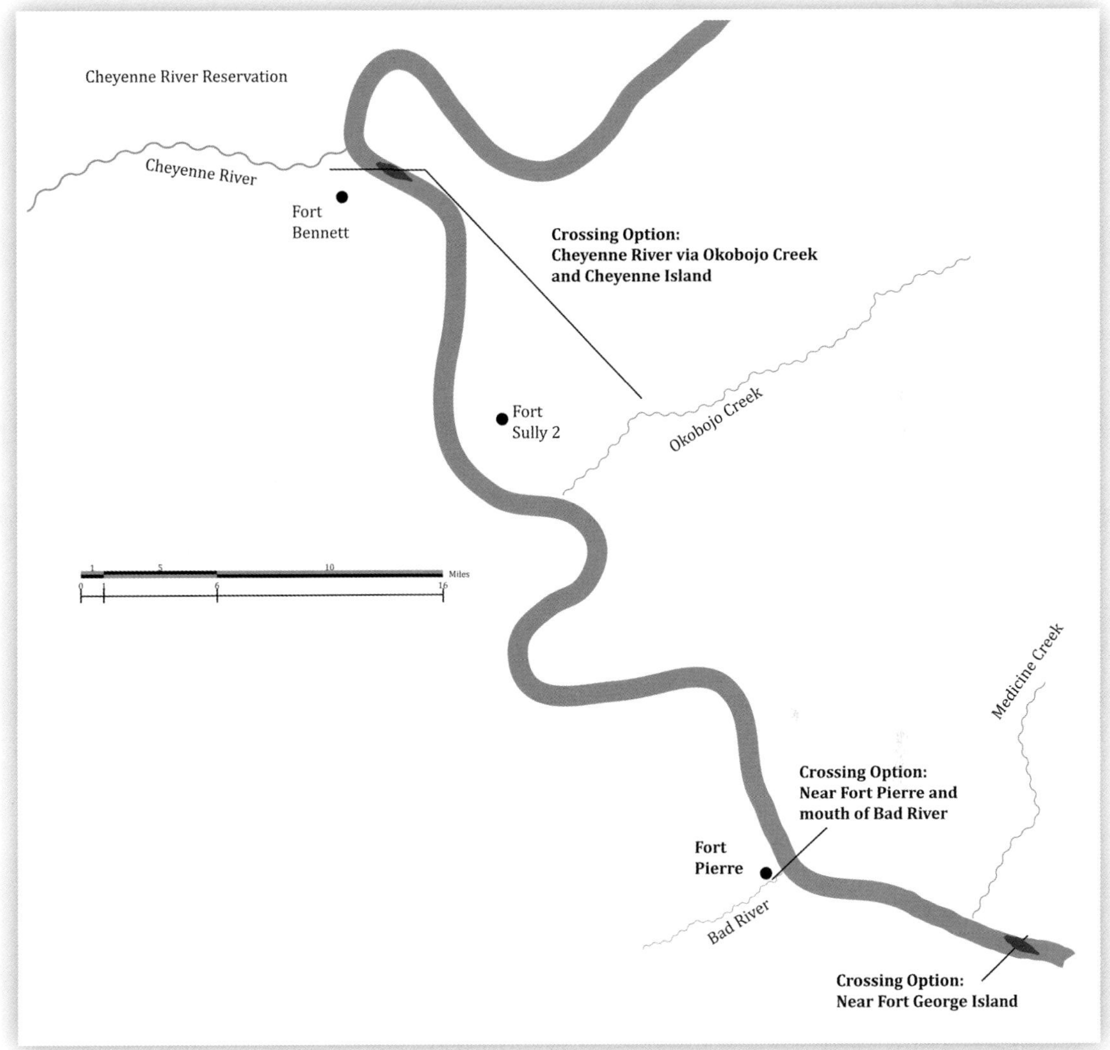

The three river crossing options that Blunt reviewed. S8-9

Irish made a terse note that he'd "sent No. 2 of Royal Family home"—after Blunt departed. The remaining members of the Royal Family—participants in the February mutiny—were Dunlap (who'd been close to Irish), Carse (who'd been shot in the right leg), Selby (who'd fallen through the ice on the Missouri), and Fatsinger (he of the "youthful indiscretions"). None of these men are mentioned again within the diary, nor are they noted in the jottings about payments made, addresses kept, and other topics Irish covered in the back of various notebooks. As such, it is not possible to reason out which one of the remaining members of the Royal Family were let go on March 26. But it is evident that the discontent among some of the workers had not entirely resolved with the dismissal of the first set of mutineers.

In Fort Pierre on March 27, waiting to depart for his long-awaited furlough, Irish wrote another letter, sending it ahead with Blunt so the Irish women would receive it in a day or two. He still hoped his wife would join him in Sioux City, writing, “I will telegraph from Yankton when you shall start to meet me, don’t disappoint me now. The girls can meet us at Cedar Rapids for a reunion there . . . You cannot imagine how I have been crowded the last two months.” He also told them to ignore some of the sensational articles in the newspapers meant to scare the settlers: “Well I am very well, no indian troubles. The papers enlarge too much.”

(Remember that last note about ignoring sensational articles in the newspapers regarding Indian troubles; there will be a fascinating admission about that, via a letter home, toward the end of the year.)

A Furlough Home: March 28–April 15, 1880

Irish spent Sunday, March 28, readying things for his long-awaited furlough. Letters had begun to show his impatience in some ways; for instance, Irish seemed to refer to his work as *the time between furloughs*. And again, he was ready to see his family. At 4 p.m., he boarded the Yankton-bound stage, passing “Chapelle Creek at 9 p.m. and the Soldier Holes at midnight.” It was “a cold, uncomfortable night.” They reached Fort Thompson at sunrise, where they disembarked, stopping to eat breakfast at Coon’s Ranch.

During their long day of travel, the winds were high, and upon their reaching Felicia’s Ranch at dark, Irish noted that “a great fire raged all day on the prairies.” The next morning, March 30, the driver was reluctant to continue due to the ferocity of the spreading blaze. Irish and another passenger (J. C. Beveridge of Crow Creek Agency) managed to persuade the driver on, and the journey continued. They ate breakfast at Yankton Agency, and the stage rolled into Yankton itself at 2 p.m. (Exactly where this fire burned remains a mystery, as no mention could be found in area newspapers aside from general mention of prairie fires without specific locations, probably because they were simply so common.)

Travel on the thirtieth may have been full of interesting conversation for Irish. Two of his fellow passengers were the previously mentioned J. C. Beveridge of Crow Creek Agency and H. H. Arthur of Washington, DC. One can speculate that at least a portion of the discussions revolved around the upcoming need to negotiate survey access to lands west of the Missouri.

Rain and snow fell overnight, likely putting an end to the prairie fires, though Irish makes no mention. The wind remained, and it was "fine overhead but muddy under foot." He settled in at Merchant's Hotel to recover from the long journey to Yankton, and to await Mrs. Irish's greatly anticipated arrival.

April began with a high wind and an early departure. After paying $3.50 for the hotel stay, Irish ate dinner in Sioux City, Iowa, then departed at 2:30 p.m., continuing to Missouri Valley Junction. There, he was elated to meet up with his daughters, though he "was so disappointed not to meet Mrs. Irish." (He did not include why she had not joined them.)

Irish and his daughters traveled south by train to Council Bluffs, and the next morning they crossed over the Missouri to explore Omaha before boarding a train for Cedar Rapids. After a short break, they boarded another train and arrived home in Iowa City at 10:30 a.m. on Saturday, April 3. Irish was "very tired" but noted that "the girls enjoyed the trip." In stark contrast to the cold weather he'd been dealing with in Dakota Territory, the temperature at home was 82 degrees.

Irish rested all day Sunday, April 4. The weather had turned cold, a high northwest wind had risen, and frost had settled upon the ground. By Wednesday he was already preparing to return to Chicago. First, however, he and Abbie celebrated their twenty-fifth wedding anniversary, on Thursday, April 8. Ruth and Lizzie gave them gifts, and Irish later wrote, "The presents warm us handsomely. We had a small party in evening. A fine day."

Friday was warm, reaching 72 degrees, though there was a "high gale" wind from the west-northwest. Despite the wind, Irish was likely grateful to be departing Iowa City in comfortable weather. By 2 p.m. he was on a train for Cedar Rapids, and from there, onward to Chicago at 7:15 a.m. McNiel, the cook who had returned home due to homesickness, met Irish at the depot, and the two went to McNiel's home, where Irish would lodge. After settling in, Irish went to the Chicago & North Western offices and met with Johnson, then returned to McNiel's home, where he remained the next day while a storm lashed the city.

NEGOTIATIONS BETWEEN THE LAKOTA AND THE DAKOTA CENTRAL

As the officers looked at the progress of their project to get the tracks to Deadwood, things were going well. However, there was a major item that needed to be accomplished before the survey portion could continue: The land west of the Missouri River belonged to the Lakota, and the next order of business was to obtain permission to survey across the Great Sioux Reservation, eventually construct a railroad along the chosen route, and obtain space for stations and other railroad infrastructure as needed.

On April 8, the secretary of the interior received a telegram from the agent at Lower Brule Agency that the Lakota there were "willing to sign road agreement but want to do it at Washington." The agent continued, "Can I so promise? They have not been represented there and claim promises have been made them of that privilege." The answer, telegrammed the next day, flatly said, "I think it best that you should settle the road agreement there. A delegation of three Lower Brule Indians will be authorized to visit Washington."[103]

In April and May of 1880, various councils were held between the Lakota and the Dakota Central, trying to come to an agreement whereby the company would obtain right-of-way through the Great Sioux Reservation, along a route that would be determined by survey. In exchange, the Lakota asked for ten thousand head of cattle. The Dakota Central rejected the proposal and therefore remained without permission to survey west of the river.[104]

Both the Chicago & North Western Railway Company and rival Chicago, Milwaukee & St. Paul Railway Company were negotiating for access rights, and the two were trying to coordinate similar terms.

Transcript: "4h That C. W. Irish the engineer of this Co may with suitable engineering assistance be permitted to make a preliminary survey sufficient to determine the question whether a practicable route for a railroad can be located between the point above mentioned for the crossing of the Missouri River and the Black Hills . . ." S8-10

On Monday, April 12, Irish again returned to the offices of the Chicago & North Western, followed by time spent "making purchases," needed items for the survey work in Dakota Territory. He was aboard a train back to Iowa City at 9:15 p.m., arrived home the next morning at 10:30 a.m., and immediately began preparing to leave for Fort Pierre. Wednesday was likewise spent preparing for the trip, but his diary entry for the day was more exuberant than most: "Mrs. Irish goes with me. We start tomorrow. This is a fine day."

A Riverboat Trip Up the Missouri River: April 16–27, 1880

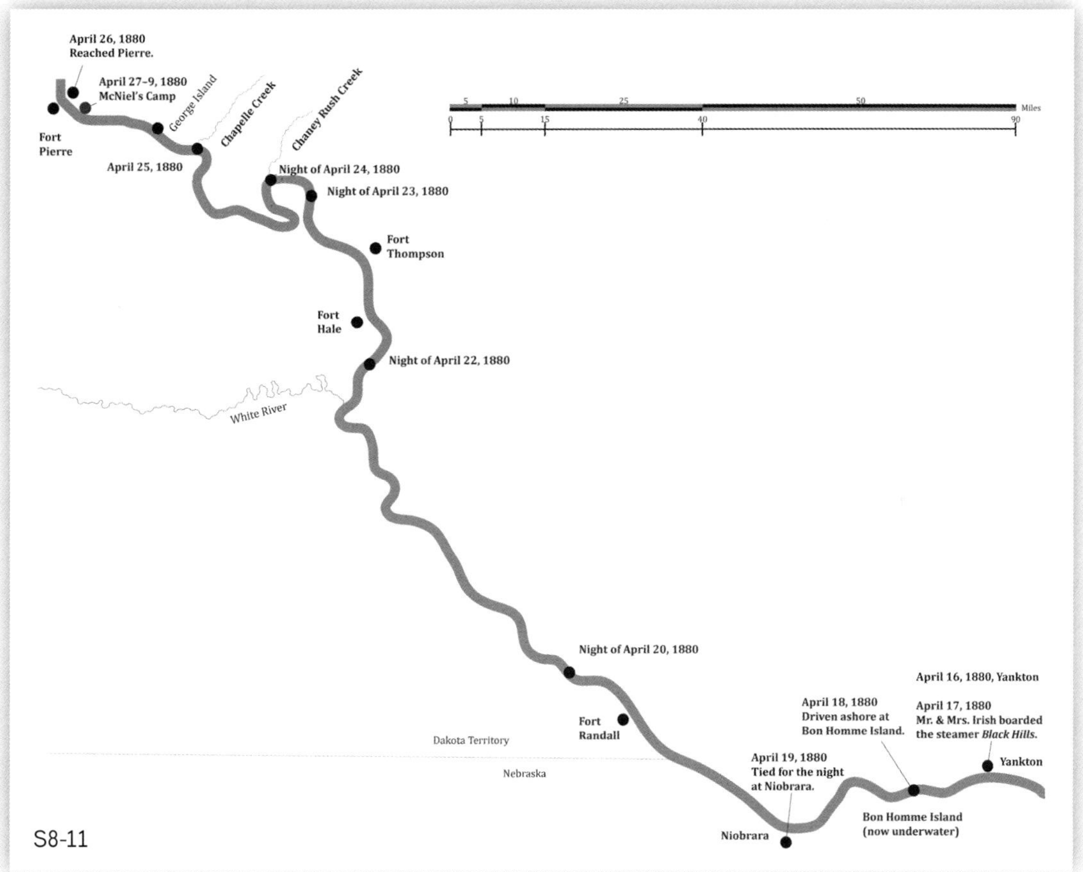

April 26, 1880
Reached Pierre.
April 27–9, 1880
McNiel's Camp
Fort Pierre
George Island
Chapelle Creek
Chaney Rush Creek
April 25, 1880
Night of April 24, 1880
Night of April 23, 1880
Fort Thompson
Fort Hale
Night of April 22, 1880
White River
Night of April 20, 1880
Fort Randall
Dakota Territory
Nebraska
April 16, 1880, Yankton
April 18, 1880
Driven ashore at
Bon Homme Island.
April 17, 1880
Mr. & Mrs. Irish boarded
the steamer *Black Hills*.
April 19, 1880
Tied for the night
at Niobrara.
Yankton
Bon Homme Island
(now underwater)
Niobrara
Miles

S8-11

In Cedar Rapids on April 16, the pair met up with friend and crew member Joe Mudra and new recruit Jack McCaddon (possibly a replacement for the recently fired mutineer). The four travelers arrived in Yankton in time for dinner the next day, with time enough for the Irishes to visit with friends before turning in for the night. The temperature stayed in the mid-fifties.

At 5 p.m. on Saturday, April 17, the group boarded the steamer *Black Hills* to begin the slow plod northward upon the Missouri River. After spending the night moored in place, the steamer started again at daylight, traveling until a storm blew up at 9 a.m., driving the boat ashore at Bon Homme Island. It began to snow, and the boat remained in place until the next morning.

THE *BLACK HILLS*

Mr. & Mrs. Irish were aboard the *Black Hills* from Yankton to Pierre. The steamer was a stern-wheeler (with a single paddle wheel at the stern, or back) packet (carrying both passengers and freight), with a wood hull and measuring 135 feet long and 27.5 feet wide. At the time of this trip, it had been on the water for two seasons, having launched in Pennsylvania in 1877 and floated down rivers to reach the Missouri. On March 28, 1884, while wintering at Bismarck, in northern Dakota Territory, the steamer was destroyed by ice.

April 19 was cold, with intermittent, strong winds that at one point required the steamer to "turn clean around once to get on." The boat eventually reached Niobrara, Nebraska, where it spent the night.

As the boat plied the river on the twentieth, Irish made note of the terrain, writing, "The river has been walled in from Yankton to Randall by high bluffs of a shaley stone which are from time to time about 60 feet high. From Randall the bluffs recede + become hills 300 to 400 [feet] high sloping to river."

Over the course of April 21 and 22, the boat and its occupants made their way from "a point 8 miles above [Fort] Randall" to "8 miles below Ft. Hale." Both days were warm, though the barometer was falling. The boat was helped along by a strong southeast wind on the twenty-second, but the river was "low for the season" and "troublesome to navigate."

Progress was made with "much difficulty" on April 23 due to sandbars and weather. However slow, the lumbering boat was making progress, having "ran around the first half of the big bend." That evening was stormy, and the steamer moored "at the north end of the point of Big Bend where Chain la Roche Creek" (Chaney Rush Creek) emptied into the Missouri. The storm, with strong winds, continued throughout the next day, though it didn't deter an antelope that was spotted swimming across the river.

The boat fought the continuing storm again all day on April 25, making it only as far as Chapelle Creek, about thirty-five river miles upstream, where it tied up. Irish again lamented, "The river is unusually low for the season, thus the tedious trip we are making."

On Monday, April 26, the steamer made it to Fort George Island, where it took on wood. It was yet again a stormy day, with wind and snow. Finally, at 7 p.m., the steamer pulled up at Fort Pierre, and the Irishes checked in at Sherwood's Hotel.

Upon settling into their room in Fort Pierre for the evening, Irish sat down to write his daughters to assure them of the safe arrival, including, "We had a good trip and good time on our way up, although it storms so much and so very hard." There were times, he said, the snow flew so thick while the boat was tied up that they could not see the shore. After detailing the slow advance up the river, he mentioned, "The steamers do not run at night in low water." Despite the frustrations, they had "found many new friends" aboard, and he added, "The whole town of Ft. Pierre comes along past the hotel to look at Mother";

apparently, the presence of a woman was "very scarce and indeed a curiosity in these regions." When he finished writing, Mrs. Irish added a note across the side of the page: "Did the plants in the yard freeze? How are the house plants?"

After a night of rest on land, Mr. Irish crossed the Missouri, back to the east side (it appears Mrs. Irish remained in Fort Pierre), stopped at Kirley's Ranch, then headed to the Box Elder Grove Camp, one mile south of the ranch, at the mouth of another small stream. He found the crew "all well."

Finishing Up between the James River and Medicine Creek: April 28–July 12, 1880

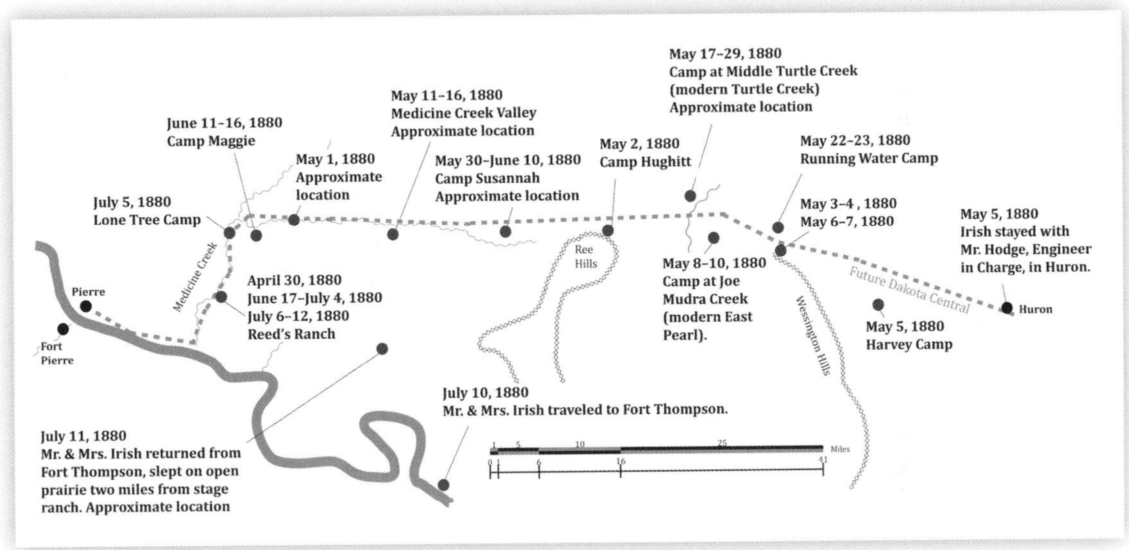

For much of the time spent reworking the final route from the James to the long tangent at the top of Medicine Creek, the crew worked out of both main, base camps as well as smaller work camps. The above represents the larger movements and campsites, but men were often scattered and sleeping away from camp as needed. S8-12

Immediately upon arrival at camp, Irish had the men prepare to move camp back to the James River—again. The spring construction season was beginning, contracts for grading the roadbed had been let, and his men were to "prepare the line for grading." While camp was being packed up, Mrs. Irish and another woman visited. His wife's presence seemed to inflate Irish's mood, and it was a fine day for finishing the camp takedown, Irish recording, "Not so bad today. It's beautiful weather. Grass is growing and many flowers are in blossom."

On Friday, April 30, camp was on the move. They departed Camp Kirley, traveling as far as Reed's Ranch. "Mrs. Irish was very tired, as was I," he wrote.

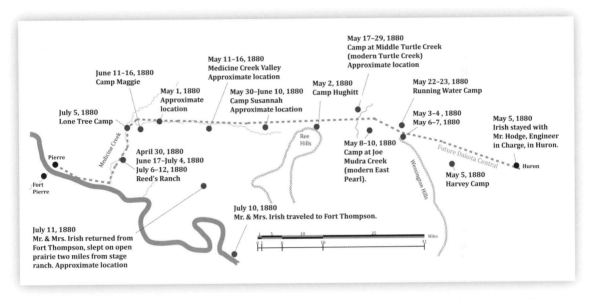

The temperature had soared to 95 degrees, which likely made travel more uncomfortable than in more temperate conditions.

The next day was hot too, though the temperature topped out at a cooler 88 degrees. The company traveled from Reed's Ranch to "a point 5 miles west of the upper water hole of Medicine Creek." They were traveling with a sick horse, and another became ill during the day, Irish adding that "the fall fires burned out the grass roots" and there was "no feed."

May 2 was another hot day, "92 in the shade." After reaching Camp Hughitt, in the Ree Hills (south of modern Ree Heights), the travelers "slept on the ground without tents." Fortunately it was cooler at night, though with a strong wind. The party was tired, and two horses were still ill.

The Ree Hills as seen from the north. S8-13

Sick or not, nearly all the horses ran off in the night—again—and it took over three hours to round them up. Irish did not indicate which direction they'd fled. In any case, once the horses were gathered up, the party pushed eastward to the Wessington Hills, camping near timber on the north side of a gulch, Irish writing, "Had a big hunt after water, found it."

The next morning, May 4, a third horse was declared ill, and Irish was relieved they were in an area with fresh grass for the animals to eat. Resting themselves and the animals, they remained in camp for the day, "making preparations for work."

The Wessington Hills as seen from the eventual track placement to the north. S8-14

The morning of May 5, the men headed toward the "line to the James," and Irish sent Harvey, McCaddon, and Chambers ahead to set up the main camp. Upon reaching the vicinity of the James, Irish was surprised to have "found a town of 6 houses called Huron." He discovered that while Huron had "just started," there was already "1 printing house" (newspaper) in operation. He visited with W. D. Hodge, the engineer in charge of operations (who had also been in charge at Silver Lake Camp during the Fall of 1879). Hodge came with Irish to the base camp set up by Harvey, then went farther west to where the rest of the men had remained, to begin the work. An additional horse was "played out," though whether due to illness or exhaustion is not clear.

When the men returned east to rework the lines between the James River and Medicine Creek, Mrs. Irish stayed behind at Reed's. On May 8, from a campsite seventy-eight miles from Reed's, Irish wrote her, "I have had you in my thoughts ever so much since we parted. Could I only know that you are comfortable and happy. Then I'd be happy also. I am very well. Have done but little work yet. Have had such very hot weather, but today cool. We have good water to drink that helps." He'd been waiting on a tent to arrive, and he assured her, once it did, "I shall send for you and any company you wish, to come and visit us."

He also provided a glimpse into the personality of his horse Billy, who he described as both tame and smart. Billy also seemed to have a sense of humor: "This morning I put the saddle on him and bridle and then turned him loose. He at once started off and walked quite a distance, then stopped and looked about to see if I came after him. He thought I'd chase him." There was "plenty of good grass" for the horses, and the flocks of returning birds made the plains "not so lonesome as in the winter." In general, work conditions were "so much better than last year."

After further instructions for his wife to pass along to their daughters, he added a postscript: "Tell Mr. and Mrs. Reed that the Iron Horse is within 113 miles of them." This was an exciting update for the residents along the Missouri.

May 7, a Friday, was rainy, with "sharp thunder" to their west. The men prepared for most of the party to head to Joe Mudra Creek, while Leighton was sent to the base camp set up by Harvey. By evening, Powers and Mudra were "quite sick."

It didn't help that the weather was wet and stormy, or that "the wind blew incessantly" from the northwest, bringing heavy rain overnight. Irish was anxious to begin the work of preparing for the graders, but the weather kept the men in camp for several more days, culminating in "a heavy hail storm," again with thunder—which meant lightning. Survey equipment included lots of metal rods; it would not have been prudent to be out in the field while lightning flashed anywhere nearby. The crew passed the time doing extra chores, and they "got [their] guns in order." Irish reviewed recent reports, maps, and profiles. Late in the day, the weather finally cleared.

Work finally began on Monday, May 10, but it wasn't necessarily to record measurements on stakes and plant them in the ground, as "preparing the line for grading" may suggest. Instead, they "ran a line 11 miles long and found splendid country and surface." It would appear that Irish was scouting an alternate route, with the graders not far to his east.

As we've seen, it did happen on occasion that after reviewing and scrutinizing the documents that Irish sent east—maps, reports, and profiles—the railroad officials would dash off a telegram and put an officer on a train headed west. Frequently when Irish noted he'd returned to camp to find Blunt there, this was the situation. After the meetings Irish had on his recent Chicago trip, it appears there was some discussion about the route west from the James River.

"We [Irish and Blunt] got off early to test the idea of running the Medicine creek tangent back to the main channel of Turtle river," recorded Irish on May 11. (This would take them north of the Wessington and Ree Hills, and in the area of the eventually built tracks.) The team camped on the eastern segment of the Medicine Creek valley. The wind had been strong from the southeast all day, and while they saw a handful of antelope, they did not harvest any. That evening, Irish fell ill (one wonders whether spring allergies were at play among the men).

The next morning, May 12, he felt indisposed all day, but he was out working in the heat and wind, covering forty miles of ground over the course of his scouting. Timing worked out nicely, as "it began to rain as soon as [they] got in. Such wind." A "severe gale" blew all night, and Irish "feared the camp would blow away."

He spent the thirteenth resting, still ill; Powers went out with the others, in Irish's place, to consider options for the long tangent. The severe gale of the night "increased in violence" throughout the day, and the temperature climbed to 86 degrees. That was to be the last temperature reading for some time, as the thermometer broke.

Irish felt better on the fourteenth, so he went out with the others to check the potential line Powers had set out the day before. Measurements were being taken "when a severe storm set in and drove [them] off." They were taking refuge in camp when Blunt arrived. Irish made a profile drawing of the new option, while the "wind blew so severe as to tear the cook tent open."

Blunt departed the next morning, May 15, and Irish ran yet another new line, offset about 1.5 miles from the one Powers had identified. Meanwhile, Irish sent the crew out to resume the work on Powers's line until it intersected with the existing long tangent. The storms that had pelted the men continued to inconvenience them in their work, as did illness; Irish was still "not very well," and two more men (Duncan and McCaddon), were also "troubled."

After a day of relative relaxation on the sixteenth (the men preparing for travel, Irish writing letters), the camp was moved on May 17 to about midway along Turtle Creek. Once in the new location, and despite the continuing threat of storms, they spent the seventeenth finishing the surveys for each of the possible lines to get to the long tangent that led to the Medicine Creek descent. Duncan's affliction, according to Irish, was "acute rheumatism," provoked by the stormy weather.

That evening, "the wind came with great violence and completely wrecked the cook tent." Irish recorded, "[Our tent was] torn all to pieces. We took the small tent and went to Running Water and made a camp." Once the tent was moved, they set out and ran nine miles of lines, probably as an option to reach the long tangent.

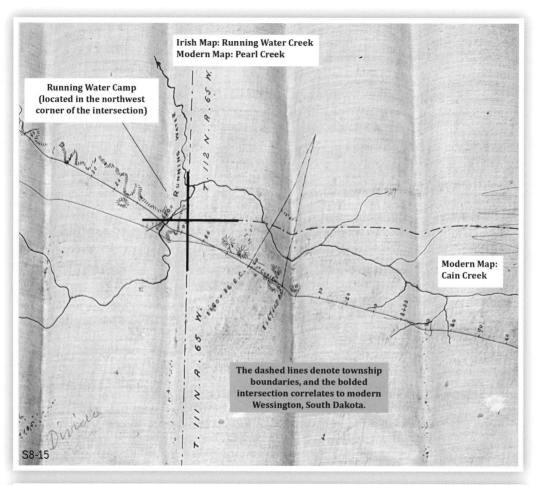

Irish Map: Running Water Creek
Modern Map: Pearl Creek

Running Water Camp (located in the northwest corner of the intersection)

Modern Map: Cain Creek

The dashed lines denote township boundaries, and the bolded intersection correlates to modern Wessington, South Dakota.

S8-15

The modern location of Running Water Camp is a dry hill and marsh in the northwest corner of US Highway 14 / Cook Street West and 374th Avenue in Wessington, South Dakota. S8-16

The next day, May 19, Irish worked on the tangent that would successfully connect to Powers's line. He was frustrated in the work, however, because needed supplies of stakes and profile paper had failed to arrive. He sent Fawcett west to look for them.

Harvey's job may have been to write the markings on the stakes, or to simply pound them into the ground in the proper locations. Regardless, he had "nothing to do" because there were no stakes. Finally, at 7 p.m. on May 20, Duncan (not Fawcett), showed up with eight hundred large stakes and "10 bundles of lath" (thin strips of wood), presumably to cut into more stakes.

"Work in earnest now," wrote Irish. "We have our line perfected and now go west. We are about out of grub. What a situation." On May 21, the route to, across, and beyond the James River was declared complete. Next they would head west to figure out how to get through the Wessington Hills.

On Saturday, May 22, the crew broke down their "little camp at Running Water" and started west in yet another gale of a wind. As was often the case when they moved toward a new camp, they were also "hard at work" on the surveying tasks. The group arrived at Turtle Creek Camp at 7 p.m.

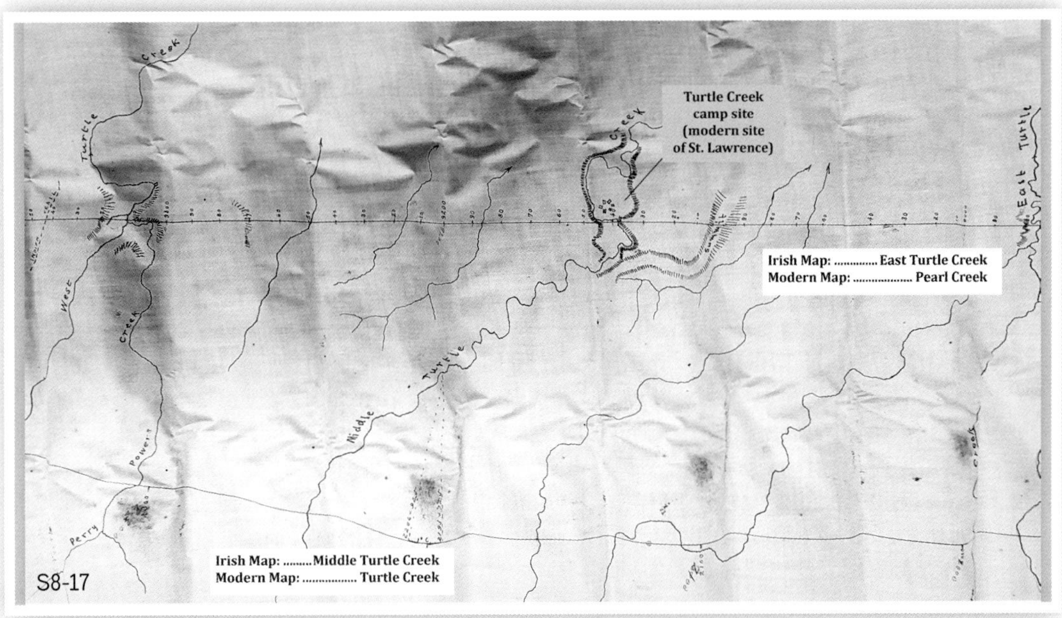

A messenger woke Irish at 5:30 a.m. on the twenty-third with instructions to meet Nichols at 6:30 a.m. seven miles to the east, "on important business." Nichols was the engineer in charge of construction, and he would soon be named superintendent of the Dakota Central. Roused out of sleep and likely in a state of mixed perplexity and annoyance, Irish saddled up Billy, then headed out in the heavy rainfall. The two men met up, then "travelled 30 miles and back without breakfast," which "took all day." Upon returning to camp at 5 p.m., Irish confided to his diary that he was "mighty tired out."

One of the more unusual incidents of the entire project was announced the next morning, Monday, May 24, at Turtle Creek Camp: "At daylight this AM [I] was awakened by Vernon saying that the horse Charlie had killed himself. He got a hind foot in his lariat and in his struggles broke his neck." This was a big event for the camp, impacting both operations and emotions.

The crew went out—somber and on foot—to level the tie line (the line that would link two previous lines together). A 3 p.m. rainstorm drove them back to camp yet again. Fawcett, who had been sent west on May 19, returned to camp.

From the camp on Turtle Creek, Irish wrote to his wife, either lamenting or boasting of having "ridden over 100 miles in the saddle yesterday and today," adding that he was "very well but quite tired out." He told her about Charlie, admitting that he'd at first thought it was Billy that had met his demise. Relieved that Billy was safe, he still grieved for the dead horse, writing, "Poor old fellow. He was a good horse. We all liked him, he was so kind and gentle. The boys intend to bury him tomorrow and put up a post with his name on."

He updated her on progress: "I have got 25 miles ready for the graders, and they will have 500 teams at work soon, this side [west] the James. The track comes right along." He cautioned her not to participate in any of the "loud squabbles . . . nor say anything that would lead the company officers to think that [Irish's crew] would be against them," adding, "It would hurt me much." Again, Irish was thinking about future jobs with the Chicago & North Western and wanted to ensure his reputation remained untainted.

Irish further warned Abbie not to put her flannels away too early, as it had cooled down. He also beamed with pride that the bread she made and shared with the crew had made Duncan the cook "quite jealous." Even better, the new tent had arrived, and she could now join him in camp. He planned to move the camp forty miles west, then either send for her or come himself to escort her back. His hope was that she would already be in camp by June 6, when Hughitt was scheduled to arrive. This camp would be named Camp Susannah, after Mrs. Susannah Abigail "Abbie" Yarborough Irish.

A short train crossing the James River near Huron in 1880. S8-18

The work continued the next day, May 25, despite having "to take to the wagons twice for shelter" due to heavy rainfall, which continued all day, interspersed with deluges. It was enough that Irish became concerned for their safety, working so near the creek, which he feared would bound from its banks and menace them all.

Fortunately the stream kept to its course, and the men "made a fine run with the chain" on the twenty-sixth, taking measurements. In the afternoon of this cold, windy day, Blunt appeared, and Irish brought him into camp. The evening—"very cold"; "We had to make fires"—was likely taken up with discussions pertaining to recent route updates and next steps.

The team split into smaller parties for work on May 27, one party going ahead to do transit work while Irish, McCaddon, and others checked levels. The day was warm, windy, and productive.

Blunt left the morning of the twenty-eighth, and camp was pulled up and moved. Two loads of "camp" were "sent ahead to Medicine creek," where main headquarters would be set up, while others plodded more slowly westward, doing levels along the way with Irish and McCaddon. It was another fine, productive day, but the night was a different matter. Irish was "sick all night, as was Cowan, McCaddon, Duncan, and Leighton." To further aggravate their situation, the morning of the twenty-ninth was "fiercely hot," followed by a midday rain that flooded the tents. Irish ended his daily entry with "We did no work today. Sickness and storm."

The levels team pulled up their temporary camp and worked throughout the next day, May 30. It rained all day, and as a result they "had a hard time of it." Cowan and Irish reached farthest west, the others making it only to Camp Hughitt. The rain continued its monotonous attack throughout the night.

Work resumed the next day. "I feel blue," lamented Irish. "We lose so much time from rain and used up horses. 3 are crippled and one dead." Vernon and his horse were left at Turtle Creek to await a new horse to replace Charlie. Once the horse arrived, Vernon rejoined the crew.

On June 1, Irish was up early "with the only team available," and he backtracked to check more levels. Vernon's new horse was not a willing partner in the work, however, spending considerable time "balking," and it "took all day to get him 12 miles." A quick campsite was set up north of Camp Hughitt, and two more miles of levels were run before daylight ran out.

A rare "calm night" led into Wednesday, June 2. The men ran three more miles of levels, "then started for camp." The early stoppage may have been because the men finished their work, or it could have been another horse issue. Ben, the horse owned by Leighton, was "crippled by a snag in his foot." As if the hobbled horse wasn't enough of a concern, the crew was running out of supplies. Cowan had been sent to bring back provisions from Fort Pierre, but the provisions were not available.

However, Cowan did not return entirely empty-handed—he had escorted Mrs. Irish to the camp from her lodgings in Fort Pierre. Abbie, upon taking up "quarters in her tent," was "well pleased with it." Irish also "gave the teams a rest," as they were "quite tired out." It is not clear whether the teams he spoke of were of the human or animal variety, but regardless, all were allowed a rare day of rest.

PREPARING FOR THE TRACKS

A June 3 letter to the secretary of the interior outlined terms sought by the Dakota Central: the right to construct a railyard and associated facilities around Fort Pierre, a wagon road to connect said railyard to an existing road (the Fort Pierre to Deadwood Trail), and permission to survey a route from the Missouri River to the Black Hills.[105]

The letter reiterated that the Dakota Central's tracks would soon reach the Missouri River, and while the exact location was unconfirmed, it was believed to be "at the mouth of Medicine Creek,"[106] which is the valley they had received permission to build in per the letter of November 6, 1879.

Because it was "necessary to examine the country west of the river," the company requested permission for "a corps of engineers under an escort of Indian police to start from Fort Pierre on June 15." This would make use of the information gathered during the exploratory trip Irish and others had taken in March, to scout the favorability of the terrain to the west. To facilitate the expedition, the Dakota Central's general solicitor, Mr. Cooks, proposed to "pay the wages of the police and for their rations at the generous prices and also to pay 40 cents a day to each one as hire for his pony."[107]

Exploring to the west was not the only task to be accomplished. The company also sought an agreement to purchase from the Lakota "ground for a freight depot and for residences of its employees not to exceed one section" on the west side of the Missouri. In exchange for all their requests, the company promised "to make reasonable and just compensation."[108] June 15, the date of the proposed examination, came and went with no agreement reached.

Page one of the June 3, 1880, letter requesting permission to survey west of the Missouri, the right to construct a wagon road to connect with the existing freight road, and land near the Bad River for railroad infrastructure.[109] Transcript: "Washington June 3 1880 / To the Hon. the Secretary of the Interior / The Dakota Central Railway Company respectfully represents / That it proposes to extend its Railroad to the Missouri river during the present season with the design to extend said Railroad westward to the Black Hills at some future time when it shall have acquired the right to do so, that the central point where its road shall strike the river has not been definitely settled but it is believed to be at the mouth of Medicine creek. It will be necessary to examine the country west of the river with references to the feasibility of extending the road westward . . ."

S8-19

Letter wrapper text, Dakota Central Railway Company, June 3, 1880. Transcript: "Proposes to extend its road thru Sioux Res. to Black Hills, asks leave to make examination of country by Corps Engineers. Agrees to pay wages of Indian Police & for their rations, and for the lands required for depot &c + $5.00 per acre. Asks authority to build wagon road from river to intersect wagon road from Ft. Pierre." S8-20

Four miles of line were run on Friday, June 4. That doesn't sound like much, but Irish wrote that they "had to travel 15 miles to begin work." In addition to the distance, the wind was strong and interfered enough that they were unable to run levels. That day, Engineer Hodge, along with his wife and their daughter Lillian, arrived in camp for an extended visit. With Mrs. Irish already on-site, the feeling in camp was becoming increasingly homelike, versus the all-male situation of the months before.

Irish was pleased to see that the Hodges "seem[ed] to feel at home." He was less pleased by how the relentless winds of recent days were testing the tents, but they seemed to be holding up alright.

On Saturday, the wind blew at a "35 mile gale all day," which was "hard to stand against." Irish added, "The level party could do nothing at all, my transit was very unsteady." Sunday was spent in place, the men getting camp back in order and Irish working on letters to the officers in Chicago.

Monday, June 7, was pleasantly without wind until near sunset, and the crew accomplished significant work. By the end of the day, Irish confided that he was, again, "quite tired out." The barometer was falling, and he worried more storms were on their way.

Indeed, rain began to fall in the night, and it persisted throughout the next day, increasing in intensity, and it was joined by a hailstorm. While Irish worked on profiles and grades, he sent the other men in camp ahead to set up the next location, which they would name Camp Maggie, after Mrs. Hodge. The company's report courier left camp with Irish's documents at 3 a.m. the next morning, and with that task accomplished, June 9 was spent doing more work on the line, and more team members were sent ahead to Camp Maggie.

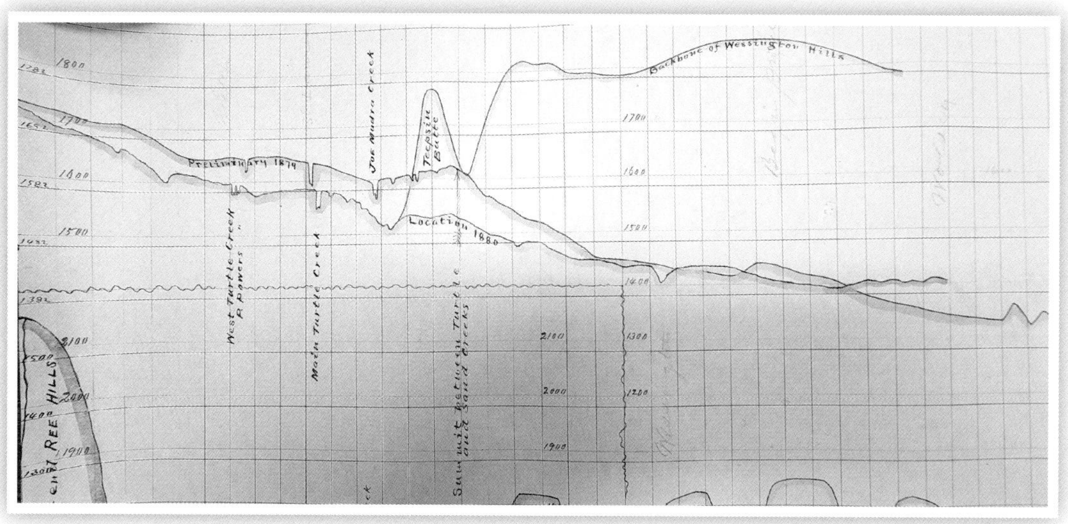

This profile map drawn by Irish shows the elevations of the preliminary 1879 line compared to the chosen line of 1880, along with the general elevations of the "backbone of Wessington Hills," Teepee Butte, the summit of the Wessington Hills, and the dips for West Turtle Creek, Main Turtle Creek, and Joe Mudra Creek. S8-21

On Saturday, June 12, Irish and Leighton headed for Pierre, arriving at 5 p.m. It is unclear whether the men hauled supplies with them from camp or acquired them there, but either way, as darkness fell, they ferried the items across the river to the western shore at Fort Pierre. The men then spent the night sleeping on the riverbank, protecting their goods.

After presumably leaving Leighton to watch over the goods at Fort Pierre (or having them stored away in a secured warehouse), Irish returned to camp, arriving at 6 p.m., to again find Blunt, and having missed a visit by Mr. and Mrs. Reed. "I am very tired," he wrote, closing out his entry for the day.

THE LAKOTA AND DAKOTA CENTRAL COME TO A PARTIAL AGREEMENT

On June 12, an agreement was reached between the Dakota Central and the Lakota, based upon the requests made on June 3. The Lakota granted to the Dakota Central "one section of land on the west bank of the Missouri river" for the construction of a depot and other necessary buildings to support the railroad, and the "right to construct and operate a wagon road to intersect with the one already established from [Fort] Pierre to the Black Hills." In exchange, the Dakota Central would pay $3,200 for the section of land (equivalent to $80,480 in 2019) and "$5.00 per acre for the wagon road" (equivalent to $125.75 in 2019), which was to be abandoned once the railroad replaced it. (The agreement was "approved by the Department [of Indian Affairs] and ratified by the Company on August 3, 1880.")[110]

What was missing from this agreement, of course, was any right to conduct a survey between the Missouri River and the Black Hills. Efforts to obtain this permission continued, and Irish would soon play a significant role in this endeavor.

The next day, June 14, Irish left camp to travel north to Fort Sully, arriving at 5 p.m. "We found the country well soaked," wrote Irish, and we can assume that Blunt was included in that "we." Irish dispatched a courier to Captain Schwan at Cheyenne Agency–Fort Bennett, on the other side of the Missouri, asking him to "not make up Indian escort" until Irish could reach him.

The next morning, the men left Fort Sully to return south, stopping in Pierre, where they picked up the mail. The day was "very hot and sultry," and they didn't reach camp until sunset. "Mr. Blunt wants to start in the morning eastward," wrote Irish, but it appears he did not leave camp until noon the next day, June 16.

On June 16, in camp along Medicine Creek, twelve miles northeast of Reed's, Mrs. Irish sat down to write to Ruth and Lizzie. As she hadn't been keeping a journal, she worried she might accidentally "leave out the most spicey episodes." And some of the stories were indeed different from the type her husband shared.

One day, she'd dashed off a letter to send along with a teamster who was going to Pierre to get provisions. He was supposed to return right away, "but he got drunk and didn't arrive until Friday" morning, just as the crew was preparing to move camp. Those who had been left in camp while the teamster was on a bender "had a slim living for some three days." With so many people in camp, they "were reduced to hard tack + canned tomatoes + one ham." When the ham was boiled, the water was saved to season gathered greens and wild peas.

According to this letter, Mrs. Irish had assumed some cooking responsibilities in camp. Some of the crew gathered lamb's-quarters (a plant that tastes like spinach or chard), which she then stewed in the ham broth. Berries were harvested, and when the wayward teamster finally arrived with the provisions, Mrs. Irish and Mrs. Hodge, using flour and bacon, were able to provide the camp with biscuits, coffee, and fried meat. "I never saw such pleased fellows," she effused. "They thanked us before they eat + after too."

Tired out, she went into her tent to rest, kicking off her shoes and loosening her dress. Just as she got all comfortable and began to nap, Mrs. Hodge alerted her to a group who had come out from Pierre to visit with her: Mr. and Mrs. Reed and their child, Mrs. Reed's sister and a friend, and Judge Waldron. She scrambled to find seating for everyone in the small tent. "I tell you it's sociable," she wrote. "I amused them for a time then went to the kitchen. I was mad enough at the cook to shoot him." Apparently, he was still puttering around, working on the breakfast dishes, not having yet begun lunch. She swept him aside and "got most of the dinner for 37 people" accomplished, while Mrs. Reed set the table, cut bread, and divided the pies.

As the guests were leaving, Blunt and another man came into camp. Again Mrs. Irish and Mrs. Hodge, wanting to be good hosts, cooked "all day long" to feed the new arrivals and washed all the dishes. "The cook is a beast," Mrs. Irish emphatically declared to her daughters. Observing the drama between the women and the camp cook, Blunt commented to Mrs. Irish that the women were "doing too much." She said she wanted to treat the men to a feast but would "abandon the kitchen" afterward. The men certainly appreciated her efforts. "Joe is by my door playing waltzes on the mouth organ, it is real nice," she wrote. She appreciated the gestures of the crew, but had no kind words for the cook, calling him "a contrary old sailor."

Meanwhile, Irish sent a portion of the crew on to Reed's Ranch, taking part of the camp with them, and once Blunt departed, they "got levels checked and ran on down creek." The men were "correcting the mistake made in numbers."

On June 17, the rest of camp was prepared for the move, and work continued in running the line down Medicine Creek. Powers accompanied Irish, as did Mrs. Irish, on horseback. A heavy rain descended, along with a high wind, and the camp was a muddy affair.

In an addendum to the letter she was writing back home, Mrs. Irish noted that it was raining as camp was moved to Reed's. The teams with the wagons had to go around the bluffs. She and Powers, however, came down the creek valley on horseback, with Irish on foot. Her characterizations are worth including in full: "The rain began to pour, the lightning flash + thunder peal. The water ran in the trail like branches + Billy would walk in it like a little fool boy + every little while he would whirl his hind end to the storm. It was too funny, altogether it was ridiculous."

With the crew again assembled in one location, the men set up the full camp and hung wet things out to dry. "The ground [was] soppy" as the men gathered wood and hauled water. Fortunately, the weather was hot and windy, which, despite being a "full blast" that "tried [their] tents severely," was most helpful in reducing the "soppy" part.

On June 18, Irish scribbled off a quick note to Ruth and Lizzie on the back of Mrs. Irish's letter: "The work of grading had to be pushed hard along, and I had to work night and day to do it. I am about over the rush of work, but am about to begin work west of the Mo. River, which will take up much of my time. So don't think ill of me, but overlook and pardon me for apparent neglect."

The nineteenth was "very hot + sultry." The wind continued, and so did the transit and level work "just above the scout camp." Irish wasn't scouting a route, but for the marker stakes they'd set on prior trips. He later wrote, "I rode Billy up + down the creek looking up points. The cattle have destroyed many. We got on slowly."

June 20 was "hot, very hot," and the entire group "laid about the camp and did all [they] could to keep cool." The group had company, as "a camp of soldiers came from Yankton and camped on the creek."

The next day, Leighton and Duncan headed to Pierre on an errand. The morning was hot and sultry, followed by a rain with a "sharp + severe" lightning storm throughout a 90-degree afternoon. The rest of the team worked their way down Medicine Creek, despite the weather, particularly the dangers posed by standing in a lightning storm with metal rods in their hands.

The heat continued on June 22, with "hot, very hot" appearing for the second time in three consecutive diary entries. It was 96 degrees at 10 a.m., and readings were underway for "the first 4 degree curve" of the route when Irish was summoned to Reed's Ranch. Reed was injured, having fallen from his horse, and he was experiencing back spasms and was having difficulty breathing. Irish was silent on a specific diagnosis or how he treated Reed.

The next day, Irish reported that Reed was "some better," as was Mrs. Irish, who had been ill for the past four days. Working through the rainy day, the "men all got very wet."

June 24 brought a hot morning and a stormy afternoon, with significant rain and "very sharp" lightning. While the weather raged, Irish updated the profile maps to be consistent with recent work. Reed came out of his house at some point, but he found "himself very weak." Again, the diary does not hint at a diagnosis, but one suspects Irish was concerned about internal injuries.

On Friday, June 25, Hodge and a party were sent down Medicine Creek to run lines on the Winnebago Reservation, an area overseen by the officials at Fort Thompson. They "had no success out of it," however.

Several Lakota men had joined the team, including two named Pole and Drum. Newcomer Drum was declared "a fool" soon after arriving, though Irish gave no clues as to what the man had done to earn his annoyance.

Despite considerable rainfall on June 26, the camp at Reed's Ranch was "in good shape," and Irish was content as he worked on more profiles and reports. Drum left on the twenty-seventh, and Irish's diary seemed to take a deep, relieved breath.

The twenty-eighth was spent working on a change in the line upstream of Reed's Ranch, and the next day, the men worked on section lines, while Irish kept up with profiles and maps. Medicine Creek, while in a relatively wide and gentle valley, was managing to give the men a run for their labors.

On June 30, Irish hosted contractors Wells and "Ford" (possibly meaning Hiram Forbes), who brought "dispatches and letters" from Hughitt and Blunt. They stayed overnight, then departed for Pierre on July 1. In their wake arrived a new crew member named H. H. Tubbs, who brought with him a second new man and a new team of horses. Irish was feeling ill, so he stayed in camp to continue work on the profiles and maps, sending the men out to locate section lines down the creek.

CONTRACTORS MAKING PROGRESS

The June 30 *Fort Pierre Weekly Signal* noted that twenty-five miles of grade had been laid west of the James, and the worker camps were again on their move westward, rapidly catching up to the surveyors, plowing and turning to dust the ground so recently measured by Irish's crew. Back in Volga, freight and passenger receipts had totaled over $11,000 (equivalent to $276,650 in 2019) during the month of May alone.[111]

Of course, it wasn't just the activity behind the surveyors that was filling column space. Newspapers in the Black Hills were excitedly sharing updates as well, in the same way local papers east of the Missouri had done the previous year. The rails were on their way from the east, bringing with them future opportunities.

The first few days of July were plenty hot, reaching the low nineties, with cooling rains each afternoon. Irish (with help from Hodge) kept at work on profiles and maps. By July 3, Tubbs and McCaddon had taken over the work on the profiles, allowing Irish to focus on the maps.

Holidays were often treated like any other day, but on July 4, the men celebrated with a shooting match. Then Mr. and Mrs. Irish, Mr. and Mrs. Hodge, and two young women who were visiting camp that day climbed "the Big Hill" near Reed's to enjoy the afternoon.

The rare day spent lounging had been pleasant enough, but the crew got back to work on the fifth, leaving camp at 6 a.m. to get to Lone Tree. There, they spent the day working on a large curve on the proposed route, getting the measurements and markings just right before camping nearby for the night.

They were up and at it again early the next day, after a "sultry and quiet" night. The men took readings along the creek, though they were interrupted by another storm of lightning and hard rain. They finished their work at 4 p.m. and retreated to camp, but their rest would be interrupted.

It appears that some sort of incident took place that evening. The next day, July 7, Irish paid and discharged both Lewis and Linkhart. Neither of these men were part of the "Royal Family," though both had previously suffered illnesses during their work. Irish tended to remain quiet (frustratingly for this author) on the reasons for most discharges, these included. Whatever the reason, Irish, though "quite sick," continued working on the maps during another hot, rainy, and lightning-filled day, down two more men.

On July 8, another "hot, very hot" day, Irish continued work on the maps, still "very sick," and he "went to bed sick" in the afternoon, though he managed to get letters sent off by messenger. "Still sick; had a hard night of it," was his first entry for the ninth as well.

The rest must have helped, as his health had improved enough by the morning of July 10 that he borrowed Reed's ambulance (an enclosed delivery wagon) and, with Mrs. Irish, Leighton, and Leighton's team, traveled to Fort Thompson, a journey that began at 7 a.m. and stretched thirteen hours. Upon arrival, they "had some trouble to get quarters [lodging] but at last succeeded."

"Hot, oh! very hot. +98 no comfort anywhere" was the grievance that shimmered like a mirage on the page on July 11. On this day, he "wrote a long letter to Hughitt detailing the Indian situation, which [was] bad indeed." This entry coincided with the start of an interesting phase of Irish's role for the Chicago & North Western. The landscape would not be the only thing he was observing, measuring, and negotiating; he would soon be working as a diplomat on behalf of his employer, though not by assignment.

PRESS REPORTS

The Irish surveying party of the Northwestern railroad are in camp at Medicine creek, fifteen miles below Fort Pierre, awaiting orders. S8-22

As we've seen, the crew had been plenty busy, so they probably weren't idly waiting for some word to be given. They were, though, waiting for news as to whether they would get permission to pursue work on the western side of the Missouri.

After leaving Fort Thompson, the Irishes and Leighton traveled twelve miles before camping on the open prairie, just two miles shy of the next stage ranch. A heavy wind and rainstorm blew up overnight, and the couple were forced to take shelter in the ambulance instead of their tent. The diary was mum on how Leighton sheltered from the storm.

The next day, the trio kept moving, stopping for dinner at the main fork of Chapelle Creek, where they held a shooting match. It would be within character for Mrs. Irish to participate in this competition along with the men, but that's supposition. The party arrived back at camp at 2 p.m., where Irish again found "several of the men sick"—a frustrating way to start an important period in Irish's career.

MYSTERIOUS CAMPING LOCATIONS

As I previously explained, it was not easy to find specific locations for the various camps along this route, due to vague location descriptions and topographical features that have changed names over the years.

Another factor is that Irish's crew frequently named some of those nearby topographical features—such as creeks and buttes—after themselves, among themselves, and those names have had little, if any, bearing on official or modern nomenclature. Blunt's Butte, near Manchester, South Dakota, is a rare exception. More common are examples like Joe Mudra Creek and Camp Susannah, the latter named in honor of Mrs. Irish. Another was called Fox Camp, likely where they'd spotted a fox. Likewise, the newest (in the narrative) campsite was named Camp Maggie, after visitor Mrs. Hodge, and it was clearly noted on a map of the Medicine Creek work. Fortunately, using mentions of distances within the diary or letters, we can extrapolate and guesstimate other locations with relative accuracy.

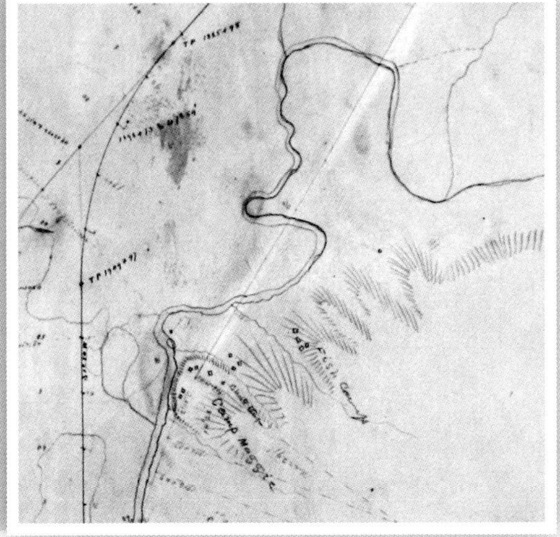

The bend southward along Medicine Creek just south of modern Blunt. Irish's drawing shows the locations of Camp Maggie and Fish Camp. S8-23

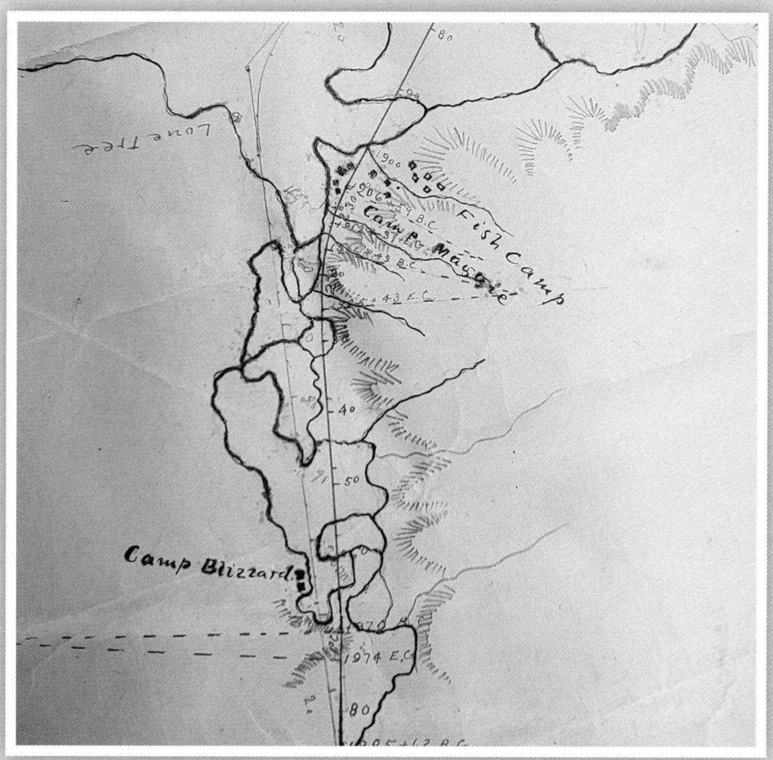

A map showing clearer detail for Fish Camp, Camp Maggie, and Camp Blizzard, in relation to the Lone Tree landmark just south of modern Blunt, South Dakota. S8-24

Section Nine

CRITICAL NEGOTIATIONS AND WORK WEST OF THE MISSOURI

JULY 13–SEPTEMBER 25, 1880

Without permission to survey west of the Missouri River, the project would stall. The day-to-day work on completing the survey east of the Missouri had to continue, but Irish himself prioritized participating in negotiations with the Lakota. His mood was boosted by the arrival of his daughters for an extended visit, bringing all four family members together in camp. Irish's efforts paid off, culminating in a successful grand council in mid-August. By the end of August, the crew was established in a new camp, at the mouth of the Bad River, on the west side of the Missouri. Hardest for Irish, he bid his wife and daughters goodbye as they returned home and left him to his work. As the men began their tasks up the Bad River, they also encountered the clay that vexes people to this day; called gumbo, it slowed the work in frustrating new ways. Worst of all, however, was the accidental shooting of a beloved crew member.

Negotiation Duties: July 13–August 18, 1880

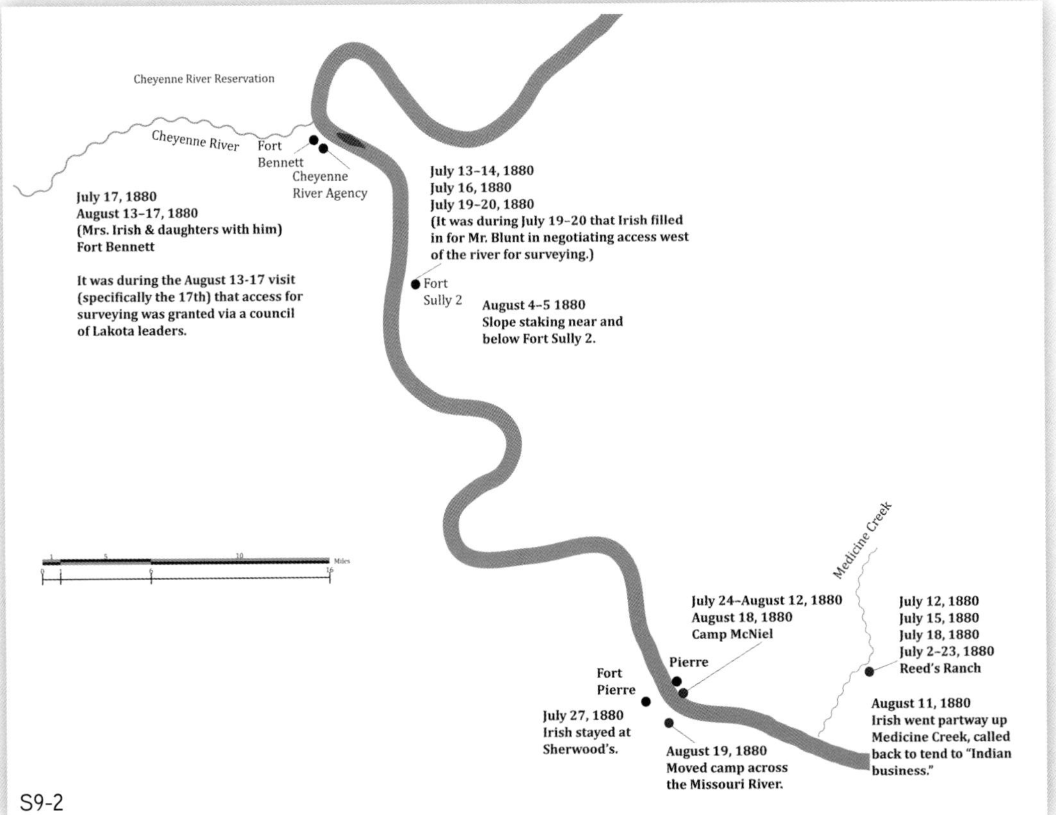

Cheyenne River Reservation

Cheyenne River

Fort Bennett

Cheyenne River Agency

July 17, 1880
August 13-17, 1880
(Mrs. Irish & daughters with him)
Fort Bennett

It was during the August 13-17 visit (specifically the 17th) that access for surveying was granted via a council of Lakota leaders.

July 13-14, 1880
July 16, 1880
July 19-20, 1880
(It was during July 19-20 that Irish filled in for Mr. Blunt in negotiating access west of the river for surveying.)

Fort Sully 2

August 4-5 1880
Slope staking near and below Fort Sully 2.

Medicine Creek

July 24–August 12, 1880
August 18, 1880
Camp McNiel

Pierre

Fort Pierre

July 12, 1880
July 15, 1880
July 18, 1880
July 2-23, 1880
Reed's Ranch

July 27, 1880
Irish stayed at Sherwood's.

August 19, 1880
Moved camp across the Missouri River.

August 11, 1880
Irish went partway up Medicine Creek, called back to tend to "Indian business."

S9-2

After a single overnight at camp, Irish and Leighton were off to Fort Sully, where Irish embarked upon the sensitive work of obtaining permission to survey a route through Lakota land. The day was again hot, with yet another torrential rainstorm in the afternoon, leaving the men drenched as they rode. Upon their 4 p.m. arrival at Fort Sully, Irish met with both Colonel William Wood, the post commander, and Major C. P. Bartlett, speaking to them about "the Indian affairs."

Major Bartlett is seated on the steps, second from the left. S9-3

After a night at Fort Sully, Irish and Leighton set off early on July 14 to visit Cheyenne Agency, with N. H. Young from Fort Sully joining them. At the agency, they discussed the proposed survey with Lakota representatives and the agent. "All advise me to wait for an understanding," Irish later wrote. He, Leighton, and Young arrived back at Fort Sully at 4 p.m., perhaps disappointed and frustrated that the survey could not yet be started.

A little after 8 a.m. the next day, Irish and Leighton left Fort Sully and headed back to camp, the day hot with a high wind, dust blowing in a swirling rush around them. Irish likely spent much of the ride contemplating "the situation" with the Lakota, eager for their permission to allow the survey to begin west of the Missouri River. He knew that this critical and touchy situation would determine whether his job would continue, and those of his crew members. The men arrived at camp at 3 p.m., finding it in good order and all inhabitants well. At 4 p.m., Blunt and Ryther also arrived in camp.

The very next day, July 16, Irish returned north with Leighton (and presumably Blunt and Ryther, though they are not mentioned), arriving at Fort Sully at 2 p.m. There, he spoke with General William Tecumseh Sherman, and "a salute was fired." Irish's documentation provides no other details about his conversations with the inhabitants of Fort Sully, nor with this powerful visitor.

GENERAL WILLIAM T. SHERMAN

General Sherman—famous for his role in the Civil War, serving as the commanding general of the US Army from 1869 to 1883—was known for his "hard war" tactics (destroying anything that might be useful to the enemy), and the same was true as he oversaw the US Army's role in the so-called Indian Wars of the latter half of the nineteenth century.

A major emphasis for him was ensuring the Plains would be safe for European immigrants to inhabit, and he believed railroad expansion was critical to maximizing the US Army's influence on the frontier. Thus, he focused on protecting the railroad's operations from hostile Native parties.[112]

Perhaps it was in this capacity that Sherman was at Fort Sully on July 16, 1880, ahead of the negotiations between the Chicago & North Western and members of the various Lakota tribes. Or it may have been a coincidence, as during the summer of 1880, Sherman, his daughter, and some aides were inspecting various military forts throughout Dakota Territory.[113]

The evening of the sixteenth, settled in at Fort Sully, Irish wrote to his daughters with instructions for a journey to join him and their mother in Dakota Territory. Upon reaching Yankton, they were to stay at Jencks' Hotel. Its proprietors, friends of Irish, would deliver them to the steamer *Black Hills*, which had a regular schedule between Yankton and Fort Pierre. Once they reached Pierre, they were to go to Sherwood's Hotel and ask Sherwood to send a messenger to camp "near to Willson's Ranch, 7 miles below Pierre."

He was worried about them falling overboard, writing, "Now I want you to be very careful on board the boat, and do not go near to the sides without great caution and keeping continuously on your guard." He then reassured them that he and their mother were well and informed them that he was at Fort Sully "with Mr. Blunt to try and make a treaty with the Indians."

On July 17, Irish left Fort Sully and headed northwest, across the river, reaching Fort Bennett, relatively adjacent to Cheyenne River Agency. The river crossing was difficult due to high water, and dinner was significantly delayed. When the men arrived at Fort Bennett, they conferred with Captain Schwan and Lieutenants L. R. Brown and Meyers, and found "the Indians angered much." On top of the usual frustrations about annuities and broken agreements, the prospect of a railroad through their increasingly shrinking lands had the Lakota alarmed. The men stayed overnight in Lieutenant Meyers's quarters.

The next morning, they obtained breakfast from the trading store of W. E. Caton before starting for camp. Of the weather, Irish wrote, "The day was hot and dusty except where a storm half mile wide crossed the road," which could suggest they saw a tornado or similar.

Whatever the weather event, the storm that was the impending negotiations with the Lakota was the true focus of Irish's attentions. The men arrived back at camp "quite late," but they were up early yet again the next morning to return to Fort Sully, this time in the company of Mrs. Irish.

Here begins one of the most interesting circumstances revealed within Irish's diaries from his time as surveyor: "Mr. Blunt, who is commissioned to do this Indian work, is afraid to go anymore," Irish candidly elaborated, "so [he] stays in camp to run lines for a passtime while I do his work." This is significant; the railroad officer tasked with the negotiations was staying behind, but the hired surveyor would be performing the officer's critical role. Perhaps Irish was the more appropriate representative, due to his personality, knowledge of the landscape, or both. Whatever the reason for the switch, Irish now held a great responsibility on his shoulders.

Mr. and Mrs. Irish, along with Leighton, stayed at the Fort Sully home of a Mr. and Mrs. Hoover on the night of July 19. The next morning, Irish and Leighton rode on the front seat of the spring wagon, and Mrs. Irish and Mrs. Hoover rode on the back seat. Irish shot at a wolf from the wagon seat, the gun's report startling the horses so badly that the women were tossed from their seats, "hurting them badly." The women must have reassured the men that they were alright, for the party continued to Fort Bennett.

After conducting their business at Fort Bennett, they again crossed the river and returned to the Hoover home for another overnight. Irish later wrote, "The wounded are now better but Mrs. Irish is very sore. Mrs. Hoover [is] not so bad off but feels poorly."

The next morning, July 21, they (presumably just Mr. and Mrs. Irish and Leighton) departed for Pierre, then on to camp at Reed's, where Irish recorded that the day had been "dreadful hot" and that he was "quite worn out." Blunt, who had remained in camp while Irish ricocheted between there, Fort Sully, Fort Bennett, and Cheyenne Agency the previous several days, left the next morning, July 22. Irish was still feeling "completely worn out," so he set Hodge and Tubbs to work on the maps and profiles "of the line made by Blunt while [Irish] was at Cheyenne Agency." In addition to his fatigue, it is possible he was irritated with Blunt for having put him in the position of negotiating on behalf of the Chicago & North Western; either way, Irish handed off the labor of drawing up Blunt's line work too.

While Irish was looking to the west and dealing with the diplomatic crisis that loomed there, he was also responsible for ensuring the surveyed route was properly marked and ready for the graders, who were rapidly working their way from the east.

While we know that newspapers were not always reliable when it came to reporting the locations of graders and tracklayers, it was reported at about this time that the graders were twenty-five miles east of Pierre and the tracklayers fifty miles west of Huron (putting them approximately at the Ree Hills), "progressing at the rate of fifteen miles per week."[114] This rate, using very generalized math, placed the tracklayers two and a half weeks from the descent down Medicine Creek.

It is worth stepping back and taking another look at Irish's movements over the last two weeks or so, using approximate straight-line distances between each step, to get a general idea of how far he was traveling. Leaving camp at Reed's, he rode to Fort Thompson and back (an 80-mile round trip), then to Fort Sully (33 miles one way), to the Cheyenne Agency–Fort Bennett area (11), back to Fort Sully (11), back to Reed's (33), back to Fort Sully (33), on to Fort Bennett specifically (12) followed by Cheyenne Agency (2), back to Reed's (40), back to Fort Sully (33), on to Cheyenne Agency–Fort Bennett (23), back to Pierre (33), and then to camp (15). Totaled, those trips represent roughly 360 miles (give or take a dozen or so for route deviation). It is no wonder he was feeling "completely worn out."

Why did Irish keep going back and forth, versus utilizing the military telegraph at one of the various forts? Or was that off-limits to civilians, even railroad officials? Could he have stationed himself midway and sent runners? Perhaps the discussions were confidential, too sensitive to trust to others. Regardless, this time spent doing Blunt's work took him away from his own responsibilities.

On July 23, Irish assigned men to make stakes, but "timber [was] very scarce." It was also "deathly hot, so some men were sick," Irish among them, writing, "We did but little in camp. It's so very hot and dry that the grass is dead and water very scarce."

On July 24, an achingly hot 101-degree day, Irish and Hodge remained at Willson Creek Camp while a portion of it was pulled up and moved to two miles south of Pierre. The next day was even hotter: "Oh! How hot! 106 in the shade, no air stirring." Still, the rest of camp was picked up and moved to the new location, nearer the river. The heat took its toll: "I am very sick now and had to go to bed." Irish's final observation for the day was that the river, winding through an area prone to erosion, was "very dirty."

On July 26, Irish sent Hodge and a number of men to set slope stakes along Willson Creek. It was another "100° in the shade" type of day. Despite the heat, Irish reported feeling better, so he headed out and "began the topographical survey at E. Pierre." In other words, he was looking at that narrow stretch of land between the base of the undulating bluffs and the bank of the Missouri River, weighing options to get the tracks from the mouth of Medicine Creek northward toward Pierre. We don't know at this point which of the northern options for crossing the river had been selected, but we can deduce that the Fort George option had been eliminated, as it was south of where Medicine Creek emptied into the Missouri.

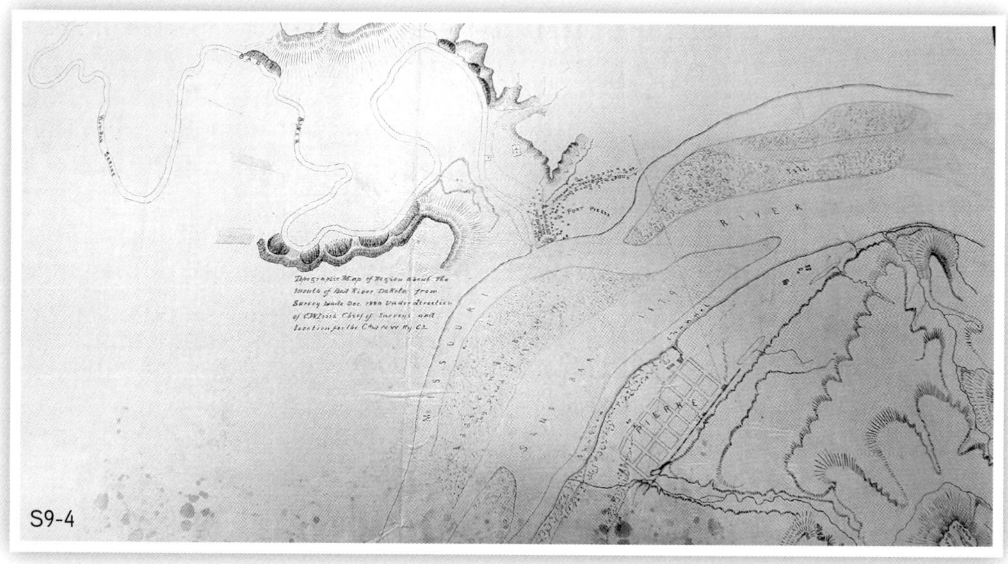

S9-4

It took Irish until the next day to finalize that topographical survey of the Pierre area. Upon completion, he, his wife, and Mr. and Mrs. Hodge went into Fort Pierre, stayed overnight at Sherwood's Hotel, and enjoyed the extravagance of a restaurant meal.

The next day, July 28, they crossed the river on Cowan's Ferry (probably not named for crew member Cowan) for $1.00 and had lunch in Pierre for an additional dollar. They continued on to camp, where Irish learned that some of the animals had run off—"a mule got 17 miles away." To top it all off, the "flies [were] very bad."

On the twenty-ninth, Engineer Hodge "pulled down his tent, packed up his family, and started for Huron with two teams." While Hodge headed east toward Huron, some men worked to make the needed stakes, and others went to work setting those stakes in place along the route, northward along the

Missouri, toward Pierre. While they were at work, Irish noted the riverboat *Fontenelle* passing by on its way north.

July 30 was a cool day, with a strong wind from the northwest—"delightful weather." The men continued working on slope staking and prepared the camp "for a reception to the girls [Ruth and Lizzie], whom [they expected] every hour on the steamer *Meade*." (This despite the letter Irish had sent telling them to board the *Black Hills*.) Irish's diction could suggest he was fairly excited, awaiting the arrival of his daughters.

Disappointment reigned, however, as they did not arrive. "Still on the watch for the girls," he later wrote. At the time, transportation was at the mercy of many factors; weather, drought, sandbars, and snags were among the big issues for the steamboats. The weather had been hot and dry, and the crops in the area were perishing.

The wait for the girls' arrival continued, as did work on the stakes. Irish had Perry Powers in charge of a number of men, churning out the needed legion of stakes. In turn, Tubbs (either on his own or with his own group of men) was out along the line, getting those hot-off-the-press stakes into the ground in the appropriate spots.

Sandbars and snags were constant dangers on the Missouri River in Irish's time, and they remain so today. S9-5

The waiting and staking made the time tick by from July 30 through August 1, and still Lizzie and Ruth had not arrived. Their parents got even more anxious when a southeast "gale" rushed straight up the river. Unable to stand the wait any longer, Irish headed to Pierre, where he, one supposes, stood on the landing dock, hand held above his eyes to block the sun, squinting downstream against that gale, watching for the steamboat bearing his beloved daughters.

It did no good—neither the steamer nor the daughters appeared. Dejected, Irish returned to camp. At 1 p.m., he and the others were surprised and joyously delighted by the arrival of Ruth and Lizzie in camp. As Irish was returning south to camp, the steamer had slipped upriver. Unable to get to the landing due to low water, the *Meade* had deployed its yawl (essentially a rowboat), unseen by the anxious father. The belated reunion now had an entertaining backstory to bring it to life in the future.

THE DANGERS OF STEAMBOATING

Irish had been worried his daughters would find themselves tossed overboard. That was not likely, as they were sensible women; however, the dangers of this mode of transportation were real. Steamboats were an important cog in the economies of the frontier, and they were also very dangerous. They were mostly made of wood coated with highly flammable linseed oil, and the vessels became perilously dry over their relatively short lifespan; many were lost to fire. If they didn't catch fire by sparks from the steam engine, exploding boilers, or the carelessness of those onboard, they also commonly succumbed to river snags.

Christopher Alan Gordon, in his book *Fire, Pestilence, and Death: St. Louis, 1849*, explains the danger beautifully:

> Many passengers eventually came to realize that boarding a steamboat and arriving safely at their point of destination was a roll of the dice. Any kind of calamity could strike as you chugged down the Big Muddy [the Missouri] or the Mighty Mississippi. Snags, whole sunken trees embedded upside down in a river's muddy bottom, were one of the most frequent boat killers on the Missouri River. Jagged roots or a broken trunk pointed up, waiting to catch an unsuspecting boat. Upon hitting the snag, the boat's wooden bottom would splinter, quickly sending it—and its passengers and cargo—to the bottom.[115]

In fact, that is how the *Meade* met its fate. The *Meade* had a relatively long lifespan for a Missouri River steamer, having launched in 1875. It had been moored at Yankton the March 1881 morning that the raging Missouri waters, full of ice, catastrophically ended the careers of many other boats. Instead of being crushed, the *Meade* broke loose of her moorings and floated downriver, surviving for several more years. Then, on September 4, 1888, while passing through Pelican Bend, near St. Louis, it hit a snag and sank.

See appendix V to learn about each of the five steamboats Irish mentioned in his diaries, and their eventual fates.

August 2 was a "cool and pleasant" day, though by 2 p.m. it was "very hot" and "the flies were bad." The day was productive nonetheless, with Powers and his crew enduring more hours making stakes, Tubbs sticking said stakes into the ground, and Irish getting letters dispatched to the officers back east.

The next day was "hot, hot, hot [with] no wind to speak of." Irish went to Pierre and back, picking up provisions and mail, in the company of daughter

Lizzie. While in town, Lizzie stopped by the offices of the *Fort Pierre Weekly Signal*, a visit memorialized by the next day's edition.[116] While cultured, Irish's daughters were also rustic, not averse to physical activity. On August 4, Ruth and Lizzie went to a nearby prairie dog town with crew member Morse, and Lizzie herself shot a prairie dog, presumably for use in the camp meal. The weather was still quite hot, and Tubbs and his party were setting stakes in the vicinity of the abandoned Old Fort Sully (now referred to as Fort Sully 1), on the southeast end of modern Pierre.

August 5 was "hot as blazes," and despite the throbbing heat, Tubbs and his crew forged ahead with staking, having gotten past the original Fort Sully. "Flies are bad," complained Irish as he sent off letters to Blunt and other officers of the Chicago & North Western.

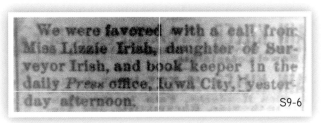

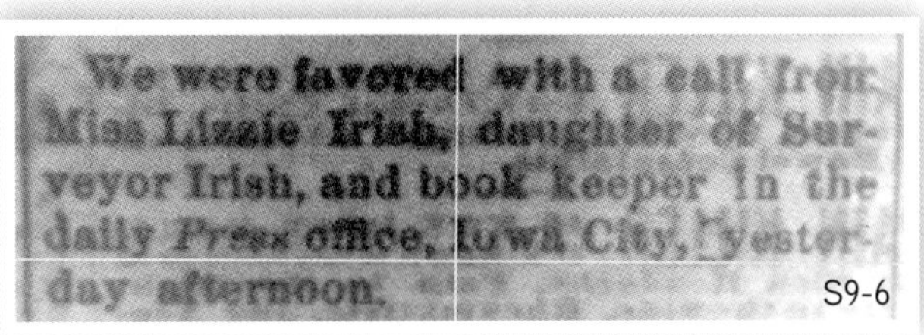
We were favored with a call from Miss Lizzie Irish, daughter of Surveyor Irish, and book keeper in the daily *Press* office, Iowa City, yesterday afternoon.

S9-6

There was evidence of a wildfire in the air on August 6, which was "very smoky but not so thick as last year." In addition to the hot weather, "the wind [was] veering about all the points of the compass each day." Conditions were on the *less than pleasant* end of the hospitable scale, but the nights were lovely, and Irish recorded they had seen "many meteors." That same note about meteors was added to the diary for the next four nights, too. This was likely the annual shower of the Perseids, which appear to hail from the constellation Perseus.[117]

It was time to move camp to the west side of the Missouri River, so it would be in place for the permission Irish was sure he would receive, and preparations began on Saturday, August 7. There were myriad items that needed to be checked, accounted for, and even repaired before such an undertaking could proceed, and this move was no exception. The wagons, it was discovered, needed repair: "The hot dry air has loosened all the tires of the wagons."

On August 8, Mr. and Mrs. Reed came to camp for a visit, and Mrs. Irish and her daughters went home with them for a visit of a few days. In their absence, Irish was feeling "almost sick"; whether from heat, stress, or actual illness is not explained. Caton, who ran the trading post at Fort Bennett, brought news to camp in the morning, after which Irish sent Perry Powers ahead to where Harvey was working to set up the new camp across the river. What was the news that Caton brought? Irish does not say. But the next week would be an important one.

The night of August 8 was cool and comfortable, and the ninth a "fine day." Irish spent it doing chores, during which he "overhauled [his] clothing, letters + papers." He also sent some of the men "to run in a change of line."

The night of August 10 brought a short burst of excitement when Irish discovered a horse thief in camp and gave chase. "Fired 8 shots at him," he later wrote, "[but] he got away in the river. He got my saddle + bridle and was going to take Jacket's Pony." Jacket was a Lakota police officer assigned to assist the surveyors.

HORSE THIEVERY

Horse theft was a common hustle and a serious problem. The newspapers assisted in the recovery of stolen horses by publishing descriptions of them, such as "one bay horse, star in forehead, black mane and tail. Lame in left hind foot; weight 900 pounds."[118] That horse had been stolen from the Norton Camp along the Dakota Central grade, and information could be sent there or to a Mr. A. S. Mitchell via Oakwood. It was a serious enough issue that an organization, the Horse Thief Protective Association, was founded to prevent it.[119]

Beginning in late June 1880, an uptick in reported horse thefts was noticed in the papers. Captain Waldron, in Fort Pierre, had a "valuable pony" taken from his yard. The article then reported that the "thief or thieves rode the animal to Willow Creek, where it either escaped or was turned loose, and returned home last night."[120] (How they knew how far the horse had gotten before returning home was not explained.) A week later, two more of Waldron's ponies were stolen.[121] The editor suggested that a hanging may need to take place to set an example for other thieves.

Horses were not the only items tempting the less honest types roaming around Fort Pierre. The safe of local merchant Harris was nearly cracked open "while he with his family were in attendance at the dance at the school house."[122] The criminals were scared off by neighbors, but people were on edge. A week or so later, the homes of Mrs. Chamberlain, L. Parent, Zach Sutley, and several others were plundered. Mrs. Chamberlain was deprived of about $10; Parent lost jewelry and $5; and, most brazenly, $45 held within the vest pocket of the sleeping Sutley was taken as he used the vest as a pillow beneath his head. The residents, reported the paper, had made a concerted effort to arm themselves against this band of miscreants, should they strike the area again.[123]

Correspondence.

For The Signal.

On the night of the 9th a festive horse thief came into the camp of Mr. Irish on the east side of the river, about two miles below here. His intention was, no doubt, to steal interpreter Tacket's fast horse. In this he was foiled by Van Norman, the night watch, who detected him in the act of putting Mr. Irish's fine California saddle upon the fleet beast. Van fired three shots at the fellow driving him into the thick brush just below the camp. Mr. Irish and the balance of the party were at once upon the ground and so corralled the fellow that his only escape was by the river. By this channel he tried to elude the pursuit, but was detected and fired upon. It is the belief of the party that the thief was killed and is now food for the fishes.

Mr. Irish and his men wish to give notice that they want a frightful ex-

The article stated the event as happening on the ninth, but Irish's diary has it on the tenth. S9-7

The episode that most unsettled Irish's camp landed in the newspaper, with the *Fort Pierre Weekly Signal* sharing, "A festive horse thief came into the camp of Mr. Irish on the east side of the river, about two miles below here."[124]

Additionally, Irish was anxious to hear from Hughitt again. "Lawler is daily expected to make an adverse treaty." (This referred to John Lawler, agent for the competing Chicago & Milwaukee Railway, which was also working to obtain access rights to reservation land, an agreement that could give an edge to that line, over the Chicago & North Western, and that would set the framework for future agreements for both railroad companies.)

The next day, August 11, Irish followed Medicine Creek upstream to Reed's Ranch, where his family was staying, but then decided that he "had better go back to camp on the Indian business." Powers, who had been sent to the new camp Harvey was setting up, met Irish at Reed's Ranch, which may be where he heard whatever he heard that made him return to camp with Powers. What news had he been given? Again, Irish was silent on the details. His wife and daughters also returned to camp, a comfort for him on this "dreadful hot day."

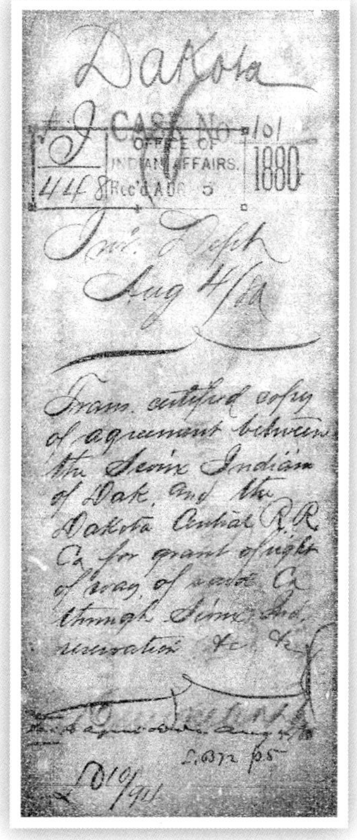

Letter wrapper dated August 4, 1880. Transcript: "Transmission: Certified copy of agreement between the Sioux Indians of Dak. and the Dakota Central R.R. Co for grant of right of way of said Co. through Sioux Ind. reservation +c." This letter presumably contained the prewritten agreement that the officers of the Chicago & North Western wanted the Lakota to accept through the negotiations soon to be held. S9-8

August 12 brought the long-awaited telegram from Hughitt; the officer would be arriving on August 13. The rest of the crew, who had been working on the line change along Medicine Creek, also returned to camp.

Irish made a quick trip to Pierre and reported upon his return that the "river [was] cutting away the warehouses." There had been recent heavy rains, and the *Fort Pierre Weekly Signal* reported, "The bank of the river is cutting badly. Jim Doud has had to move a part of his warehouse to keep it from going into the river." Not only that, but the dance hall's roof had caved in, and roads were in impassible condition.[125]

After experiencing "a beautiful aurora borealis" overnight, Irish, with his wife and daughters, headed for Fort Bennett on the thirteenth. Upon arrival, Irish and Canton went at once to meet with Leonard Love, the Indian agent in charge at Cheyenne Agency. Irish was able to convince Agent Love to "send off for Indian chiefs" so that conversations could take place.

At 2 p.m. the next day, August 14, Hughitt, Blunt, and a man named Bullard arrived at Cheyenne Agency. It had begun raining at 10 a.m., and it continued all day, throughout the night, and all through the fifteenth—"which ruins our chances for a council," lamented Irish. "We did the best to get over a dark rainy day."

The situation did not improve. "Rain! Rain!" penned Irish. "It is so heavy that the streams are all swollen, and the Indians cannot get to the agency. As it is, many have come in and are putting up the teepees on the slope north of the agency." Finally, around 2 p.m. on the sixteenth, the rain hinted toward clearing, raising hopes for receding streams. The rain resumed, however, and kept it up until about 10 a.m. on the seventeenth, when it finally cleared.

With the parting of the clouds came, finally, the conversations that Irish was anxious for. "The Head Chiefs are now here and held a council," he wrote, and a more general council took place at 2 p.m. There was "no result," and Irish was "tired out." The council continued, and an agreement was reached at midnight. The only glimpse we get of the talks is that they were successful: "We are to go on with the surveys."

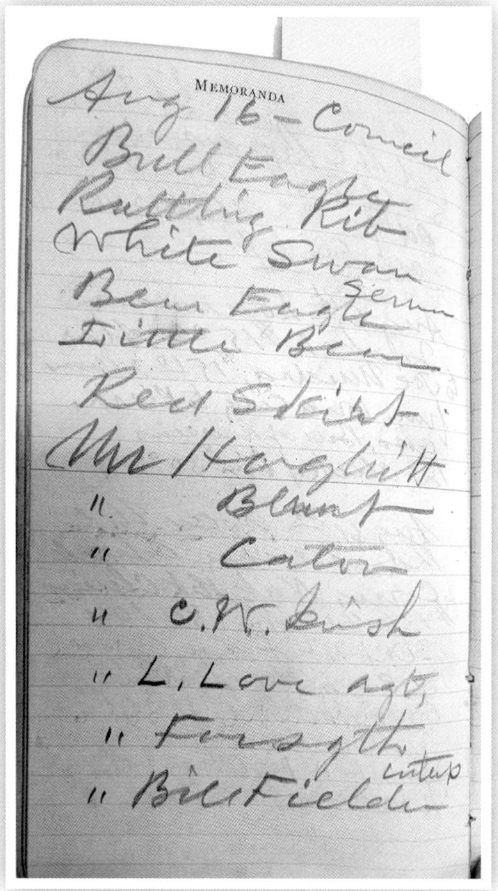
MEMORANDA
Aug 16 – Council
Bull Eagle
Rattling Rib
White Swan
Bear Eagle
Little Bear
Red Shirt
Mr Hughitt
" Blunt
" Cator
" C.W. Irish
" L. Love agt,
" Forsyth
" Bill Fielder

Irish's listing of participants in the August 16, 1880, council to reach an agreement allowing the Chicago & North Western to survey a route west of the Missouri River. S9-9

It is unfortunate that Irish's diary allotted so few lines each day, for the council likely discussed, offered, rejected, and renegotiated some fascinating matters, and Irish could have elaborated. Regardless, he was now able to resume the survey. He was also, diplomatically, silent on what role Hughitt, Blunt, and Bullard played in the negotiations. Remember that a few weeks prior, Blunt had left Irish to begin the initial conversations, and one wonders what had taken place between the officers and this talented surveyor in the intervening time. It does appear that, with Hughitt present, Blunt took part in these councils rather than remaining back at the surveyor camp.

One result of the negotiations was that an "Indian police" corps (sometimes called a "guard" by Irish) was assembled from men trusted by the negotiators to accompany the survey team, making sure they stuck to their word about where they would wander, and to protect Irish and his men from any who may have disagreed with the arrangement. Irish remained at the agency until noon, waiting for the police corps to assemble. It took until 8 p.m. to reach the camp two miles south of Pierre. The time to begin work on the west side of the Missouri had arrived.

THE AGREEMENT AS REPORTED BY A LOCAL INDIAN AGENT AND THE REGIONAL PRESS

This tangent will be on the longer end, but it's important for context. Around midnight between August 17 and 18, 1880, an agreement was reached at Cheyenne Agency–Fort Bennett, allowing Irish and his men to survey a route for the Dakota Central to cross the Great Sioux Reservation and approach Deadwood, in the northern Black Hills. The chosen route would include the confluence of the Belle Fourche and Cheyenne Rivers.

In October 1876, less than four months after the events at the Little Bighorn, Colonel Nelson Miles negotiated an agreement with Lakota leader Sitting Bull. In the book *Yellowstone Command*, author Jerome A. Greene details the event:

> It appears that the surrender Miles negotiated was somewhat tainted with promises that he had neither the authority to make nor the power to deliver. Indian accounts substantially confirm that throughout Miles's discussions with them, the colonel, sensing their growing destitution, allowed that provision would be made either for establishing an agency at the confluence of the Cheyenne and Belle Fourche rivers, near the Black Hills, or for moving the existing Cheyenne River Agency to that location, traditionally cherished by the Indians.[126]

The inclusion of that location in the railroad's plans must have made the negotiations for the survey access all the more difficult. Disappointingly—aside from Irish's diary entries—little immediate information was found about that August council, whether in surviving letters from the various Indian agencies, newspaper editions (a few articles follow), letters from Irish, or annual reports from the Indian agents.

What we do have about the August negotiations, however, are late-1880 and early-1881 letters and legal documents that outlined the intended route of the Dakota Central. These documents, a few of which are quoted below, likely comprise the official outcome and next steps of the August councils.

In his annual report to the commissioner of Indian affairs and secretary of the interior for the year 1880, Agent Love of Cheyenne River Agency wrote,

> In regard to the proposed extension of the Chicago and Northwestern Railroad through the Sioux Reservation, I have had a number of consultations with the . . . Indians. I have expressed to them in general terms my opinion that a railroad would prove of incalculable benefit to them and their children if their rights were

> carefully guarded, and that they might fully rely on such protection of their true interests by the department having them in charge.[127]

The following year's report (dated August 20, 1881) from Cheyenne River Agency noted,

> During the summer and fall of 1880 the Indians were wrought up to no little excitement by the appearance of the railroad officials, who were endeavoring to secure the right of way through the Sioux reservation. This state of feeling continued until about the 1st of January 1881, when a treaty was completed for a right of way for two railroads through the Sioux reservation.[128]

Crow Creek's acting Indian agent, Dougherty, wrote the following in his 1880 annual report:

> The two greatest railroads in the northwest [the Chicago & North Western and the Chicago, Milwaukee & St. Paul] pass along its boundaries and are now bringing in thousands of settlers who will soon have the reservation inclosed by farms and stock ranches. It is evident, therefore, that it will not be long until a demand will be made for the cession of this land, or a part of it, and perhaps for the removal of the Indians. Already steps have been taken in pursuance of that object.[129]

(The agent, rather caught in the middle, was correct in observing that it would not be long; a significant portion of Native lands were "reallocated" by the future Dawes Act of 1887.)

This agreement was big news, yet the *Fort Pierre Weekly Signal* published only a short piece completely devoid of details, as shown in the image here:

A more detailed account appeared a week later, reprinted from the *Yankton Daily Press and Dakotaian*:

> General Manager Hughitt, of the Chicago & Northwestern road[,] accompanied [by] Mr. Bullard, of Omaha and Mr. Blunt, chief engineer, are just returning from the Cheyenne agency, where they had a conference with the Indians, and obtained the right to make a preliminary survey across the reservation. This is substantially what the Milwaukee and St. Paul company has obtained through Lawler. It is stated that neither company has yet obtained the right of way in fact: that this will not be done until it is positively determined what course they wish to pursue after crossing the Missouri. The Northwestern surveyors have crossed the river, and will push the

The Northwestern surveyors, under charge of Mr. Irish started out last Monday morning from here to survey a route to the Hills. A big council was held at Cheyenne agency which granted them the right to run the survey.

S9-10

> preliminary survey toward the Black Hills with all reasonable dispatch. Meantime tracklaying from Huron to the Missouri river is proceeding with remarkable speed. On Wednesday the force laid over two miles of track, and the average has been over a mile and a half a day on the whole work. The track is now in operation for the construction trains for sixty-two miles beyond Huron, leaving only about fifty miles to the Missouri, which space is now all under construction, and will be completed doubtless and in operation to Fort Pierre by October.[130]

Since we know how much work Irish put into making these negotiations a success, it is interesting that he was not in any way credited along with the railroad officers.

A week later, an article appeared reminding readers of a similar negotiation a year prior:

> It will be remembered that the last winter when Spotted Tail, Red Cloud, and other Sioux chiefs were here, B. C. Cook, attorney for the Northwestern railway, made an unsuccessful attempt to negotiate with the Indians for the right of way across their reservation from Fort Pierre to the Black Hills. The chiefs demanded 10,000 head of cattle which after a good deal of talk, was rejected by the road, with no intention however, of abandoning the enterprise. They at lengths succeeded in securing the right of way desired for a money consideration, and it has been approved by the interior department rather reluctantly. There has been an intense rivalry between the Milwaukee & St. Paul road and the Chicago & Northwestern to secure a line through to the Black Hills, and so persistent have they been that now both have secured the concession from the Indians, and there will now be, no doubt, the fastest exhibition of track-laying in the race to the Hills ever witnessed in this country.[131]

Crossing the Missouri and Up the Bad: August 19–September 25, 1880

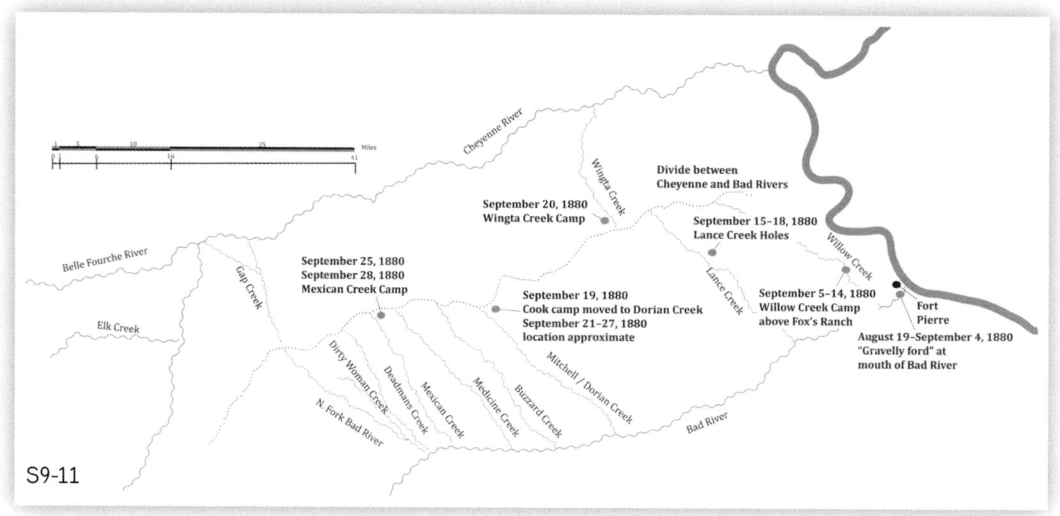

S9-11

The relief Irish must have felt at the conclusion of the council was slightly counteracted by the discovery that sickness again afflicted the men, with Chambers, Mudra, and Chase all suffering fever.

The next day, August 19, Irish began final preparations to move the full camp to the west, crossing the river at Pierre; some of the bits and pieces were moved, and stacked on a lot belonging to a man named Dan Chamberlain. The remaining camp equipage was moved the following day. One tent was set up on Chamberlain's lot, housing some of the men. However, Irish took his family and the sickest of his men, Chase, to stay at Sherwood's Hotel.

On the twenty-first, Hodge, who had been visiting, returned east while the men worked to establish the new camp on a "gravelly ford" along the Bad River, which Irish described as "a fine, level piece of ground on the west side of Bad River in a great bend of the river with a high hill to the southwest." It was about the longest description of a camp location Irish had written down in quite some time.

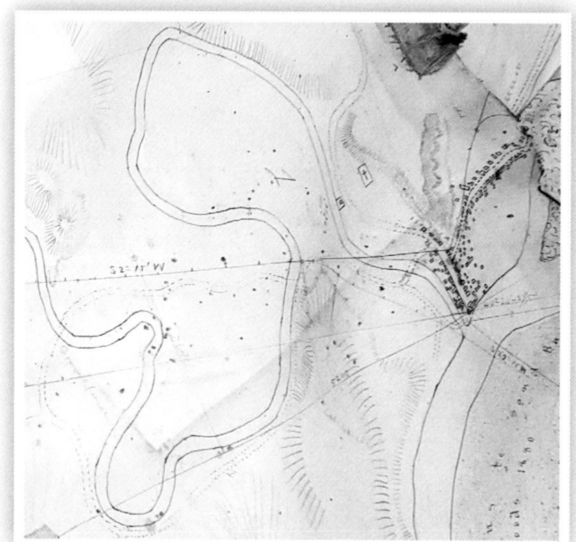

The section of the Bad River that meanders toward the Missouri, near Fort Pierre. The new camp location was within that "great bend of the river" and along a "gravelly ford"; those descriptions appear in light pencil on the left side of the image. S9-12

The *Fort Pierre Weekly Signal* also reported the move, saying the camp was "above the gravel crossing, where [Irish and crew] will remain a week or two."[132] While the surveyor's camp had moved west of the river, the supply camp for the graders and tracklayers had moved over Medicine Creek and would soon be at Pierre.[133] This may be as physically close as the graders and tracklayers had gotten to the survey activities, except when the surveyors were specifically reworking a stretch of the route.

The modern mouth of the Bad River, part of a city park in Fort Pierre. The men set up their camp within half a mile off the lower-right side of this image. S9-13

August 22 was another hot and windy day. Most of the sick men were improving, though Chase still suffered. Another man, Bingham, had become drunk and left camp; whether of his own volition or under Irish's direction is not clear. Ryther also departed. A few final tasks were completed to get the camp in order. Then, on August 23, the men "got at work on the lines W. of the river."

The next day, Irish had the crew work "on the island to clear lines and then took them over the river to check up lines and connect with the late surveys." Although work had begun on the west side of the river, there was still work to do to connect with the line to the east. While the men were focused on surveying, the women were making plum butter, "some for camp use and some to take home."

The next several diary entries were filled in after-the-fact, the one for August 25 being written by his daughter Ruth. She reported that she and others had gone to Pierre and "hunted Bingly, brought him home." If "Bingly" was Bingham—the man who had gotten drunk—his skills must have been needed, as Irish seemed to have a zero-tolerance policy for drunkenness while in camp. Another man, Scott, had arrived via the Deadwood stage and was settling into camp.

A significant rain fell overnight between the twenty-fifth and twenty-sixth, and "all things [were] afloat" in camp, and they "could not work today." Worse than that, "a scoundrel fixed a shot through the camp at 9" at night, and the crew "sent 15 or 20 after him." It is unclear whether the "15 or 20" were crewmen chasing on foot or bullets fired into the darkness—likely the latter—but whatever the "15 to 20" were, they were not successful at catching the scoundrel.

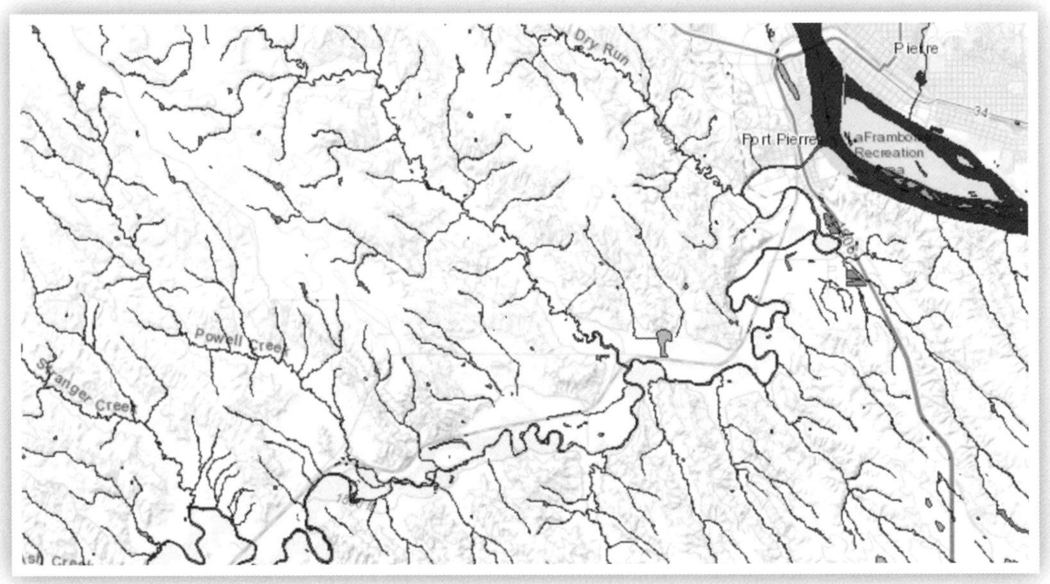

It is dry west of Fort Pierre, but not entirely without water. This modern map shows where creeks form between the many hills west of the Missouri River. S9-14

Work on August 27 was difficult. Rain caused the creeks and rivers to rise, and the ground transformed into a muddy, slippery goo sometimes called gumbo, despite it being hot and windy. The next day, running a line up the Bad River, beyond the camp, was the same kind of muddy mess, though the day was cool. To bypass walking in the mud, Irish obtained a boat to help with the work. Another vessel, the steamboat *Red Cloud*, passed the group, heading south on the Missouri.

The barometer was low on the twenty-ninth, but the temperature was quite high. This was also the last full day in camp for Mrs. Irish, Ruth, and Lizzie. Irish had seen the steamboat *Western* go upriver the day before, and he'd noted that it would whisk his family away on its return trip. The Irishes ferried across to the Pierre side of the river at 7 p.m., Irish noting, "Just as we left [Fort] Pierre, a man was shot and killed."

The family spent the night in Pierre, during "a most terrific storm." At 4:30 a.m. on August 30, the captain of the *Western* steered the boat into the current of the Missouri, and the female Irishes were on their way home after "a tearful parting," though Irish felt it was "best for them to be off." (The

Western would not survive much longer. The flood of March 1881, which opened this book, destroyed the *Western*, along with the *Fontenelle*, which Irish had seen plying the river in late July.)

The Fort Pierre paper also made note of their departure.[134] The reason that Irish felt it prudent for them to return home—possibly because the work was becoming more demanding again, or maybe due to ongoing concern about the dangers on the west side of the Missouri—was not recorded in the diary. In any event, Irish returned to camp with gossip: "The man killed last night was Black Dick, Lou Bently killed him."

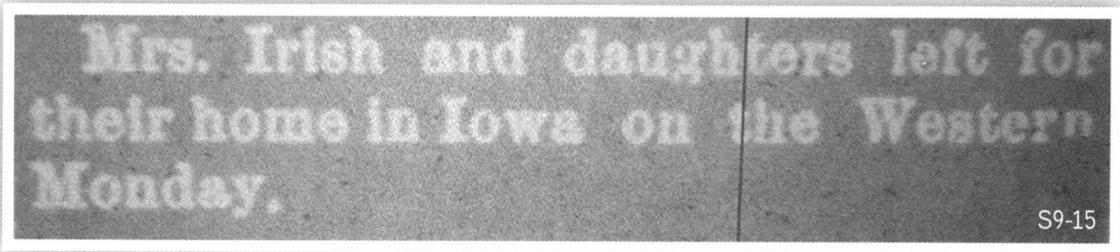
Mrs. Irish and daughters left for their home in Iowa on the Western Monday.

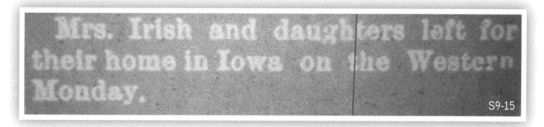

S9-15

LIZZIE AND RUTH RECOUNT THEIR TRIP TO DAKOTA

Upon their return to Iowa City, Lizzie and Ruth submitted an overview of their trip to the local newspaper, the *Iowa City Daily Press*, which was run by their uncle. (Lizzie wrote for them both, so any singular first-person pronouns refer to her.)

After receiving a letter from their parents begging them to "come at once," they were, two hours later, on a "coal train bound for Cedar Rapids." They then traveled west to Sioux City, situated on the Missouri River, where they boarded the steamer *General Meade* on Thursday night. The boat had been scheduled to leave that evening, but its heavy load of freight did not get aboard until the next morning. Meanwhile, "the river had fallen so much as to leave [the steamer] stranded upon a bar of mud." The fluctuating waters of the Missouri were a constant bane to river travel. Lizzie wrote, "The Missouri mud is similar to putty, so the longer we remained there the tighter we were stuck. They put on a full steam and puffed hard all day Friday, but Friday eve. found us safely anchored on the same bar of mud."

After having spent the previous evening loading the boat full of cargo, the crew spent the next night reversing the process. With the help of a ferryboat, the cargo was removed from the *Meade* to reduce weight and hopefully let it float free of the sandbar.

The Irish daughters watched the work unfold, describing it in their account: "The moon being full, the river presented a very pretty picture, with its boat loads of freight, and busy men." That wasn't the only entertainment, however. The ferryboat hosted "an excursion," and was "illuminated beautifully with Chinese lanterns, and the young people on board of it kept time with flying feet to the music of the band." Lizzie and Ruth went to bed about 2 a.m., only to be called back at 3 a.m. for "ice cream and cake."

While the young people partied, the men "worked faithfully all night, and by early dawn" the *Meade* was pulled off the bar by the ferryboat, "to the great joy of all." The *Meade* moved upriver to a deeper spot, "reloaded its freight, and then made a good start up stream."

The steamboats *General Meade, Peck, Milwaukee, Terry,* and *Thompson.* Irish's daughters traveled from Yankton to Pierre aboard the *Meade.* One can see why the father begged his daughters to stay away from the edges, so as not to be tossed into the river. S9-16

The Missouri did not release her prey easily, however: "We had gone but a few miles when we found ourselves stuck upon a sandbar." This time the delay was short, and they were soon again on their way. At noon on Monday, the *Meade* pulled up to the dock in Yankton. After a short stop, taking on six additional passengers and allowing a short visit in town, the boat pulled out and headed north.

There were scheduled stops at Yankton Agency, Lower Brule Agency, Fort Randall, and Fort Hale. Next were two more unscheduled stops upon sandbars, one Friday night and another on Saturday. Then, around 10 a.m. on Sunday, August 1, Lizzie and Ruth saw something exciting:

> We caught sight of father's camp, about fourteen miles distance. The sight interested all our friends as well as ourselves. We took our glasses and ascended to the hurricane deck so as to obtain a better view. When we came opposite the camp we could see them hurrying to and fro, waving handkerchiefs and table-clothes. [Irish had missed this fanfare because he was in Pierre, squinting downriver.] We returned the salute by waving, and the Captain had the boat whistles blown with great vim; thus we landed at Fort Pierre amidst great rejoicing. I had heard descriptions of the people and place, still could not help feeling some surprise when I caught sight of women dressed in the latest styles, wearing men's hats and carrying revolvers and fans at their belts. The men wore buck-skin pants with fringe and beads on the side seams, cartridge belts around their waists, with knives and Colt's revolvers attached thereto, moccasins upon their feet, their hair falling upon their shoulders and crowned by large sombreros. Taken all together the town presented quite a fantastic scene."

While in Fort Pierre, they observed some of the freight teams preparing to head west to Deadwood, their "trains composed of from three to five very large wagons loaded with freight to which were attached five to seven spans of mules or seven to nine yokes of oxen waiting patiently for their drivers to give the word with bullwhack in hand, curses in their mouths, and trusty arms at their sides."

In a slightly different description of events, compared to what Irish noted in his diary, Lizzie wrote that when they arrived in camp around 4 p.m., they "found that [their] parents had gone up the river to the ferry, but had not succeeded in getting over the river. One of the boys jumped upon a pony and was after [Mr. and Mrs. Irish] in a second. Inside of an hour he returned with them."

Their account also spoke of the negotiations between the Lakota peoples and the railroad officials, though the details they included seemed geared more toward entertaining the readers of the *Iowa City Daily Press* than mirroring even the sparse details their father provided in his diaries. The letter did accurately note that "at the close of the council the President of the C. N. W. R. R. gave father permission to employ an interpreter and thirty Indians as scouts to accompany the surveying party to the Black Hills." Also, being well acquainted with the landscape to the west, the scouts were "sent ahead to select camping places where good water, wild game and fish abounded."

As a final story of adventure, Lizzie noted that she and Ruth had been invited to tag along when a local ranch family were dispatched to drive a herd of beef cattle to Fort Sully. Partway to the fort, the "cattle became unruly," and the rancher had to leave the wagon to help his men wrangle. His family members were reluctant to drive the team of horses attached to the wagon, feeling the animals were too wild and unpredictable in their less experienced hands. Lizzie volunteered to do the job: "I mounted the high seat in the spring wagon, took the reins and raw-hide whip into my hands, and to the surprise of everyone in the party showed them that an 'Iowa girl' was not afraid to drive their wild broncho animals." It wasn't just the family who were impressed; the Lakota who were helping drive the animals were also "interested in the way [she] managed those wild horses." She added, "I was as much of an attraction as though I were a captain of a Pony Express. With my assistance we reached Fort Sully in time for supper. I was not only tired but hungry."[135]

Stories of death and danger had Irish worried. He'd recently heard about the burial of another murdered man, and that an accused murderer named Arkansas (unrelated to the Black Dick / Lou Bently episode) had been fired at on the streets. "It's very lawless here," he wrote. This may be another reason he felt it best that his family return to the eastern reaches of Iowa. It was widely believed the man named Arkansas was behind a group of marauders impacting many of the residents of Fort Pierre. (Irish will mention this Arkansas character again in the months to come.)

BLACK DICK AND LOU BENTLY

The first accounts published in newspapers were nearly as matter-of-fact as Irish's notation, then grew with each subsequent newspaper edition. To summarize the situation, Black Dick and Lou Bently were two good friends who ran afoul of each other over a woman, one "of ill repute," as the phrase went at the time. Black Dick became angered upon seeing Bently in her company, and while his temper stewed, he marinated the emotions in alcohol. Once properly soused, he went in search of Bently.

Black Dick was considered an expert marksman with his pistol, but on this day he was so inebriated that his shots harmed no one. Bently was more in control of his actions, and two of his three shots hit their mark. Bently himself was reportedly anxious to turn himself in to have the matter resolved and over. Witnesses fully supported Bently's action as self-defense, and the papers surmised that the case would be quickly dismissed. Mr. Caton, of Cheyenne Agency, heard the case. Bail was set at $250, and promptly paid. But Caton wavered on whether bail should be granted for so serious a crime as murder. After consideration, bail was granted.[136]

With his wife and daughters on their way home, Irish got back to work. The mud, which was "horrid deep," continued to play a starring role in the diary entries. Despite the high water and soggy ground, Irish and Scott scouted up Willow Creek on August 31, returning to camp for the night. The other men in camp were making stakes—it seemed that someone was *always* making stakes.

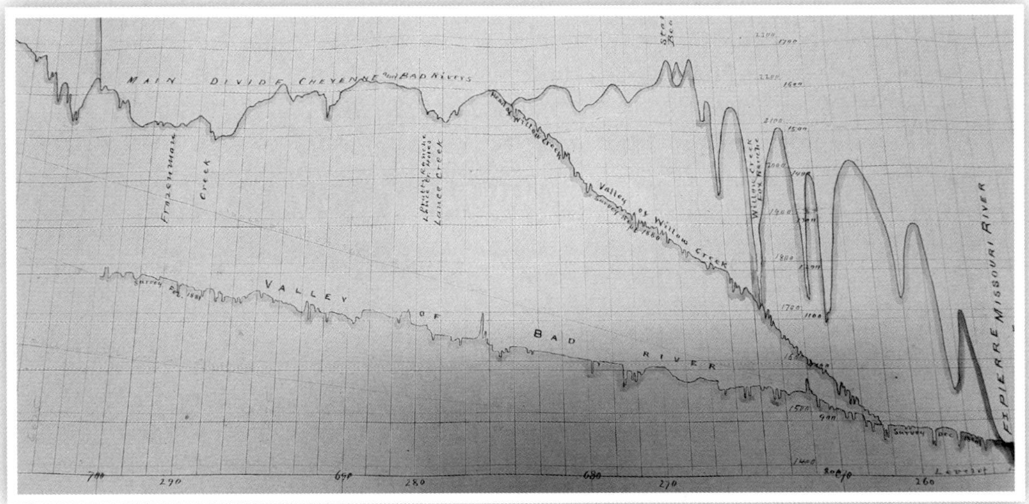

This elevation profile map shows the preliminary route the men were exploring up Willow Creek, to reach the ridge between the Bad and Cheyenne Rivers. These first months of work along the Bad River would focus on using the ridge between the two rivers. The work beginning in November would focus on following the Bad River valley. S9-17

The general vicinity of where Willow Creek empties into the Bad River. S9-18

September dawned cool, and the mud was drying fast, though the waters of the Bad River were "higher than ever." Ryther, who seems to have replaced Blunt in communicating directly with Irish, appeared in camp. Irish "set the boys reloading shells and at camp work." Irish's demeanor appears to have been more unsettled now that he and those under his watch were on the western bank of the river, compared to the last few months spent on the eastern side.

The afternoon of that first day of the month, a passing team and driver attempted to cross the Bad River near camp, got caught in the muddy clay, and needed to be rescued by the surveyors, an event that broke up the tedium of camp chores.

While the cool weather was hastening the drying of the mud, it was not yet dry enough for "easy travel." On September 2, the men "ran 8 miles of bluff line," though the work was difficult due to the mud. "It is all a team can do to get along," wrote Irish. "This Bad River clay is the worst of its kind." Along the route, they passed Old Fort Pierre, the already long-abandoned fur trade location.

MUD . . . CLAY MUD

I am amazed at the amount of work the men carried out while dealing with this mud. If you've ever tried to hike in Badlands National Park while the ground is wet, you can appreciate what Irish's crew were contending with. With your first step, your shoe will sink down about a quarter inch. With the second step, both shoes will now have a good weight of clay stuck to them. When a third step is tried, you will slide in some unpredictable direction and flail to keep your balance. You will try bringing the other foot forward, only to find that moving either foot is not as much under your control as it is subject to the auspices of that soppy, gloppy, gooey mess—which has a considerable weight—stuck to your shoes. That the men kept at their work in that mess is a lesson in great tenacity—or just plain stubbornness.

Despite the mud, Irish seemed pleased with the work progress. On September 3, one team was sent "to run onto Willow creek," while a second party was investigating a good route up and over the bluff about halfway between Willow and Lance Creeks, going up what today is called Ash Creek.

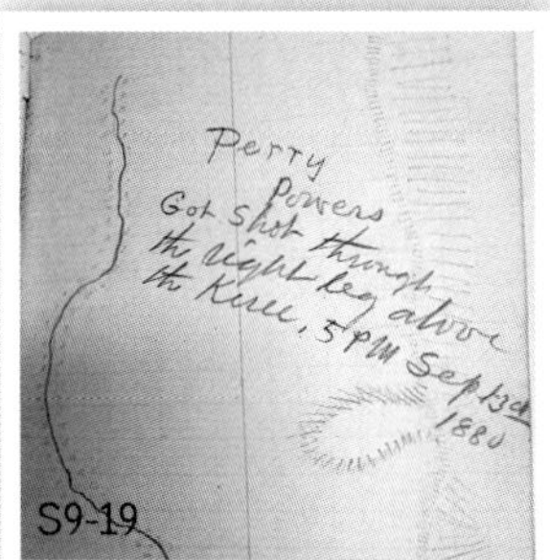

S9-19

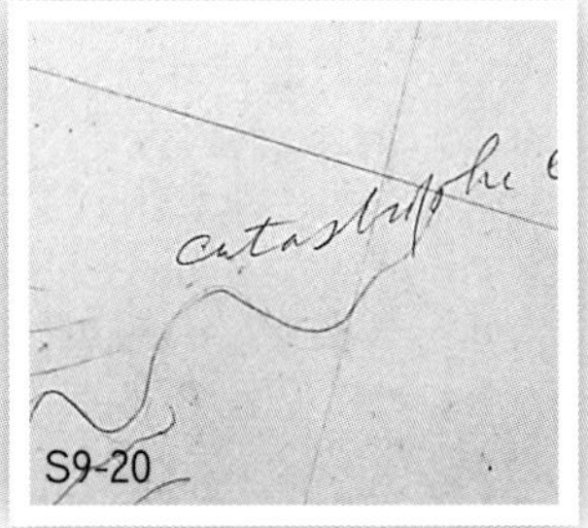

S9-20

The work was successful until, on September 3, upon their turning to head back to camp, "5 or 6 of them fired at a jack rabbit." This may have been bad for the jackrabbit, but it turned out far worse for one of the team members. In his diary, Irish unemotionally recorded that a "pistol went off accidentally and shot Powers in the left leg above the knee." Other notations would show that the incident was a blow to Irish, unsettling enough that he made note of it on the corresponding map in his surveyor's notebook and marked the location with the word "Catastrophe" on another map. This was a most unwelcome diversion and an emotional shock to the entire crew.

THE ACCIDENTAL SHOOTING OF PERRY POWERS

Powers was well-liked, and this injury became news across the region. The first two mentions are shared below.

On September 8, under the headline "Accidentally Shot," the *Fort Pierre Weekly Signal* shared the following:

> Perry Powers formerly of Sparta Wis., but now with Irish's surveying party was accidentally shot in the leg last Thursday evening while returning to camp, about two miles above this place, from surveying. There was a number of the surveyors in the wagon jogging along when a large jack rabbit started up in front of their horses, and all of them attempted to get a shot at it. Powers was sitting in the front seat with the driver Leighton who was trying to get a shot at the rabbit with his revolver, but when he got his revolver cocked, one of the men on the back seat shot and scared the horses into a run, and Leighton [was trying] to stop them when his revolver was discharged, with the above result. P. was brought to town and taken to the Grand Central, and the next day when the

> *Benton* came up he was to be sent to Sully to be taken care of, but the Captain, who is what we would call a first-class "stinker," refused to take him up unless he should be put in a state room or down on deck, neither of which would do in his condition. No cause was given by the captain for not taking him. Early Saturday morning the doctor at Cheyenne was sent for and arrived in the afternoon. He pronounced it a bad but not necessarily fatal wound. This is hard luck for the unfortunate young man, who will loose [archaic variant of *lose*] his whole summer's work.[137]

The next day, the *Yankton Daily Press and Dakotaian* relayed similar details, adding a few others that also appear in a letter Irish would send home (keep reading); the article ended with, "Powers was a great favorite among his associates, and the accident produced a feeling of profound sorrow.—Special Correspondent."[138] Irish himself was likely that "special correspondent"—based on the snippet's wording and that of similar articles tied to him—making the sentiment about Powers especially poignant.

The next day, September 4, was hot as well as "very muddy and trying," and Irish missed having Powers on hand for the day's work. After a 6 p.m. meal in camp, Irish rode the short distance north to Fort Pierre to visit with Powers and check on his condition. Somewhere around 9:30 p.m., while Irish was in town, "5 shots were fired through [the] camp by some scoundrels."

On September 5, a portion of the camp was sent ahead to get re-established along Willow Creek, "with instructions to put it up about 4 miles above Fox's ranch." L. C. Fox's Willow Creek Ranch, or just Fox's Ranch, advertised "groceries, canned goods, tobacco, cigars, cider, and everything needed by freighters," as well as "meals at all hours of day and night"—and it was located on Lakota land.[139]

According to the diary, Irish was pleased to learn that Powers was "getting on well" despite the severity of his injury. (Whether Irish went himself, sent a runner, or a runner came to him is not indicated.) What may have been less welcome—though there is not enough information to judge one way or another—was that Arkansas, the perpetrator who had killed a man in Pierre, was about their camp that day. The visit must have gone without incident, most certainly not resulting in another murder.

September 6 saw the remainder of camp moved up Willow Creek, farther from the ruffians of Fort Pierre. Due to the bluffs and the mud, it was "a hard pull and it took [them] until about 9PM to get in." The landscape was not the only complicating factor. Several of the men were afflicted with dysentery, and others were hinting that they, too, would soon be under its sway.

After finalizing the camp setup, Irish traveled to the head of Willow Creek with two of the Lakota scouts, White Bull and Whirlwind. His conclusion was that this line would not be favorable as a route. Willow Creek's deep and narrow valley—more a channel, really—would not provide the gentle slope needed for a railroad grade. Upon returning to camp, he discovered more men had fallen ill, for a total of seven. "It beats all," he sighed. On the other hand, Powers was healing well.

September 8 was a less pleasant day. It was only 46 degrees in the morning, with a wind that was "raw and cold." Most of Irish's crew was out of commission, and the work was additionally hindered by brush and mud. Returning to camp, he found headmen Little Bear and White Swan. The men had a conversation, but about what, there is no information. One could surmise, based on upcoming events, that different bands of Lakota were concerned about which of the police were—or were not—participating in the survey project.

Lance Creek is typical of the tributaries to the Bad River, with winding, steep, narrow paths.

On Thursday, September 9, Irish went farther up Willow Creek, "almost to the Big Bend in it," which was just south of their camp. Additional Indian police arrived, setting up camp nearby. Irish sent White Bull along with Hodgkiss and Corn (also Lakotas) out to hunt. Another of the Lakota, Jacket, was down with dysentery, like the others.

That evening saw the arrival of Agent Love, Lieutenant Hoffman, and interpreter Fielder as well as Lakota headmen Little Bear and White Swan, who had visited the day before. Irish recorded no further clues about the talks, though we can surmise the topics centered around the railroad survey, possibly the hunting of game, and perhaps internal tribal politics and/or many other concerns.

Little Bear and White Swan insisted that Irish hire two of their men and send away two of the currently employed Lakotas. "I expect that to keep the peace I will have to do this," Irish acknowledged. The situation was, of course, hot. The air was too, reaching nearly 100 degrees, contributing to discomfort all around.

After the agents left on the morning of September 10, Irish reported a solid day's work, as they followed the creek up to the top of the bluff and out onto "a high ridge." Overnight, however, "a severe gale of wind came up from NW. It blew down a store tent, both cook tents, and pulled the others over. Mrs Tobacco Sack's teepee fell too." The cover, top box, and bows from Leighton's wagon were carried a quarter mile down the creek, wrecking them. Four of Irish's men remained ill, and "the Indians [were] all sick too." The camp was in a shambles, and all able hands were tasked with picking up the mess. (Other locations saw similar destruction; for example, the wind blew down the new photographer's gallery in Fort Pierre, "and did various other damages."[140])

On September 11, from the camp on Willow Creek, twenty miles west of Pierre, Irish wrote to his family that he was "still in the land of the living." It was a very long letter, one of the longest surviving letters written during this job. It began on "that very muddy + wet Monday morning" that the Irish women left. "It rained all that day and I staid at the hotel," wrote Irish. "The boys let all my stuff get wet." He listed the provisions that were ruined, including 200 pounds of flour.

Worse was the loss of several maps and papers, which had taken hours to produce: "You cannot imagine how grieved I felt when I got to camp very sick and to find that they, to whom I had shown so much favor, would so entirely neglect me and my interests while my back was turned." Apparently, two young men, one of them a Mr. Sanborn (not the railroad superintendent), had been entrusted to watch over the maps and papers. Irish suspected that the two resented their having been denied the adventure of a trip across the river and back, and that they took it out on his possessions. "Be that as it may," wrote Irish, "I met with much loss from that rain, all of which might have been avoided by shutting up the tents." Irish shared his hurt and anger, at both this personal betrayal as well as the damage done to the physical items; perhaps it also reminded him of the mutiny by earlier crew members.

There were also stories right out of the Wild West, with outlaws being shot and buried in the mud, others threatened and on guard. There were complaints about a new crew member who Irish deemed a "stubborn fellow and as lazy as he can be," and Irish was forced to do much of the man's work as well as his own.

But the bigger story was how Powers came to be shot in the leg, which we touched on earlier. "It came about thus," began Irish in a letter home. In full, the story reads as follows:

> The party had done its day's work and was returning to camp. They had two teams. Powers was riding on the front seat with Posey [a Lakota police officer] as driver. The rear wagon scared up two jack rabbits, and at once they pulled out their pistols. Powers leaned over to the left and looked backward; so did Posey, who had a pistol cocked in his hand, [and] the fools behind began to fire. Sanborn, just behind Powers, fired; so did Morse. The horses

> started up, and the idiot Posey, with a cocked pistol in his hand, began to pull in on the reins when off went the pistol. It's a great wonder that he did not kill someone or himself with it. Sanborn and the others kept on firing until Bob Chambers [threatened to] knock some of them down, [then] they began to come to their senses. Scott came to me on horse back to tell me of it. I sent [Scott] back and had Powers brought to town at once, and I then set at work and probed and dressed the wound, taking out some small splinters of bone. Then my troubles began afresh. What a disappointment you cannot know it was to me. I did not like to depend upon my judgment, so [I] sent to Ft. Bennett for Dr. McChesney. He came and examined the wound and said I had done all that could be done for it. Since then [Powers] has had no other treatment. Poor Posey, they said he looked as if he was dying as they came along. At last he asked others to stop, said he was so very sick, raised up and fell out of the wagon as if he were dead. He had fainted. He feels very bad about the affair and says he will pay all the bills.

It is interesting that Irish indicated in this letter that it was the Indian police officer Posey who was to blame for the errant bullet, as he'd named Leighton as the shooter in his initial diary entry. This letter included enough details about how the incident happened and how badly Posey felt about it that one might consider this account the correct version.

The version published less than a week after the incident had also named Leighton instead of Posey. Perhaps Leighton had initially covered for Posey, but it seems the truth came out eventually. It is also possible that the story relayed to the papers cast Leighton as the shooter so as not to cause unnecessary nervousness among the White population, knowing Leighton would be forgiven by the readers, but Posey would not.

The wind continued to blow all the next day, September 12, so severely that the men did not work until late afternoon, when Irish, Scott, and Tubbs took to their horses and scouted the area to determine which direction to head next. The temperature dropped to 22 degrees in the early hours of September 13, and ice formed. The men who were healthy enough to work, including Irish, rose early and ran a line nine and a half miles up Willow Creek, reaching the head. Upon their return to camp, Irish "was gratified to find all the sick ones better." The temperature was also better; it was a comfortable 65 degrees at 8 p.m.

Typical of the wide but broken valley terrain to the north of Bad River. S9-22

The valley along Lance Creek. S9-23

DEBATING HOW FAR TO FOLLOW THE BAD RIVER

In these initial surveys, Irish was looking for a route that would take the line a few miles up the Bad River, then northward to connect to the ridge above the Cheyenne River valley, then on to Deadwood via the Belle Fourche. The trip he and others made in March out to the Forks of the Cheyenne had provided a view of the landscape along that divide, and the map below is a handy reference for the two options.

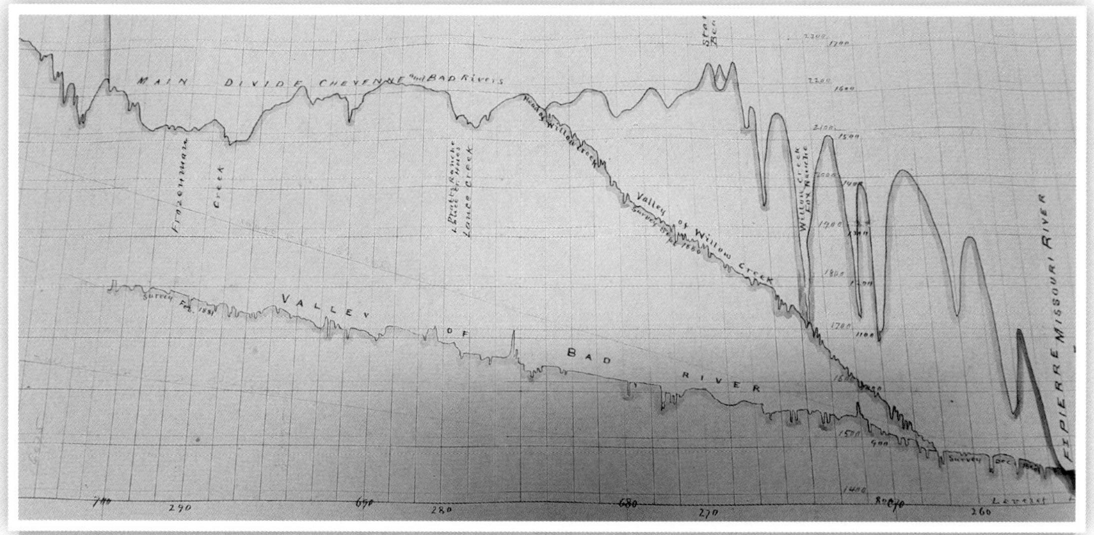

One of the high-level profile maps that showed the two options Irish was investigating: (1) branching off the Bad River early and crossing over to the ridge dividing the valleys of the Bad and Cheyenne Rivers (September 1880), or (2) going well up the Bad River before crossing over (December 1880). S9-24

On September 14, Irish went west along *a* ridge—we don't know exactly which; it could have been a random ridge above the Bad, a random ridge above the Cheyenne, or the divide between the two major watersheds. Whichever ridge he followed, it was "rough country," which would be true for either route option. It was clear that establishing a route west from the river was going to involve terrain much more erratic than what they'd encountered in the area between the western edge of the Big Sioux divide (just beyond De Smet) and the Missouri River.

While his own crew members had recovered from their illnesses, the Indian police had fallen desperately ill: "The Indians are nearly all sick, 11 out of 12 . . . and 4 of my men are also sick of a virulent dysentery. It's a very painful disease. I find Squibbs Tinct[ure] of opium the only remedy I have."

And Irish was not immune, falling ill himself "with the prevailing camp disease" overnight, though he felt better by morning; seven of the sick Indians had also improved. The camp was moved "to the heads of Lance Creek holes, called by the Indians Horseheads."

On a "very hot" September 16, Irish took Leighton's team, McCaddon, and Corn to explore to the west. They reached the top of Arrow Creek, "a branch of the Cheyenne," seeing thirteen antelope and two deer along the way, and returned to camp that evening. On the seventeenth, they resumed work on the line the main party was working on, progressing eleven and a half miles.

Mentions of rattlesnakes became common in the diary once camp was set up on the west side of the Missouri. Some entries simply described their size—large, or long—while others reported the men dispatching the reptiles for having intruded upon the camp. On September 17, two rattlesnakes were killed, one of which "came near to biting Billy, my horse." Staying alert for rattlesnakes took extra energy, on top of regular work along the line during the heat, and the men got back to camp "after dark, tired almost to death."

The day's heat faded, and the air turned cool, warning of a storm. The rain, with thunder, began overnight, and while the men did get out to do work on September 18, they turned around after only four and a half miles, Irish later writing, "The rain of last night wet up the clay prairie so that a team cannot pull an empty wagon." Not one to waste time, Irish instead set about working on the maps for the recent scouting trip, also checking on his sick men. By the end of the day, Albright and Standing Elk were added to the list of those who had fallen ill, and Irish mentioned that Jacket, who had been the first to come down sick on the ninth, was still out of commission, nine days later.

The rain continued into September 19, though more peacefully and without thunder. No matter—it wasn't the thunder that made the clay into a slippery, clinging mess that prevented the men from going out to work the lines. It was the confounded rain.

Where Plum Creek (seen via trees in the center of the image) empties into the winding Bad River (on the right side of the photo). This is west of modern Wendte, South Dakota. This image shows the wide valley of the Bad River and the undulating landscape that surrounds it.

A strong wind came in from the northwest, and Irish must have hoped it would dry the mud enough for serious travel, as he sent the cook's portion of camp and related accoutrements off to be set up along with a new camp at Mitchell/Dorian Creek, and prepared to resume work on the line they'd been working.

Mitchell/Dorian Creek near the mouth where it empties into the Bad River. S9-26

A photo of Bad River just upstream of the mouth of Mitchell/Dorian Creek. This image shows the bank of the Bad River as well as the bluffs farther from the riverbed. S9-27

The next day, September 20, Irish and a portion of the crew "took the part of the camp the teams could haul" and "struck out into the wilderness." The work went well, and a temporary camp was set up on Wingta Creek (a tributary of the Cheyenne). They also crossed the ridge into the Cheyenne River drainage system, and apparently "the Indians [were] mad about it." Out this far were Irish and three Lakotas—Hodgkiss, Scarleg, and Corn. Irish was not specific enough for us to know whether it was specifically Hodgkiss, Scarleg, and Corn who were angry or the Lakota in general. Regardless, Irish looked over the landscape and declared it "wild."

A hard frost appeared overnight. The men awoke at 5 a.m. on the twenty-first, had a "hurried breakfast," and went off to do their work. "It is a hard broken country," Irish observed, and after crossing a ridge, saw more "high and broken" land, stretching all the way to the horizon. The wild land held wild horses, and three of them were captured by the Lakotas. "Scarleg is the lucky man," Irish cheered. Turning back toward the ridge to the Bad River, the men camped at the head of Mitchell/Dorian Creek, ending a "clear and calm day."

On September 22, the crew continued up the creek, joining with the crew that had been doing similar work up Lance Creek. "All in good order," Irish reported, "the sick are better, all of them." Irish worked on letters to Blunt and Ryther, and made plans to do another scout the next day.

The landscape just south of the Bad River, west of modern Van Metre, showing the transition of the landscape west of the Missouri River; this is about three-quarters of the way between the Missouri River and Mitchell/Dorian Creek. S9-28

A view of the "high and broken" Bad River valley, east of Mitchell/Dorian Creek. S9-29

Alas, the next day was "a bad stormy day." The level party had set out to do work, but they came back "broke down"—Irish was probably referring to their wagon(s) or other wooded equipment, as he sent a few men down the creek to retrieve timber so that whatever had broken down could be made right again, but the men were probably tired too. Otherwise, the day was spent in camp, waiting out the weather. September 24 was also stormy, another "bad day," another day working on maps and chores instead of scouting. There was also a change in the Lakota team, as "Red Skirt [took] the place of Crane +

Afraid of Nothing of Hodgkiss." This probably finalized the member swap that began with the camp visit by headmen Little Bear and White Swan.

On the twenty-fifth, Irish headed out at 6 a.m. on a scouting trip, taking Leighton, Scott, and Whirlwind with him. They traveled half a mile up Mitchell/Dorian Creek, then turned west. The various other creeks they encountered were their landmarks; they ate their noontime meal at Buzzard Creek, and they ended their twenty-mile scout, against strong northwest winds, on the banks of Mexican Creek, where they set up camp for the night.

A view of the wide Bad River valley, in the vicinity of Buzzard Creek. S9-30

The meandering tree line through the center of this winter photo marks the location of Mexican Creek, showing the surrounding terrain. The Fort Pierre to Deadwood Trail crossed at about the halfway mark across this photo, from left to right. S9-31

Those strong northwest winds were but a whisper of what lurked just a few weeks ahead. The rugged terrain that so frustrated the crew would provide at least some protection when those winds unleashed a pandemonium of frigid temperatures and blinding snow—a Dakota Territory blizzard.

SCRIBBLES

Sometimes Irish's scribbles turned out to be, well, perfectly decipherable words—once you knew the answer. I spent considerable time and involved multiple people in trying to identify a "Weekilinks" or "Welliance" Creek, only to suddenly realize, in a rush of embarrassment, that he had written "*Medicine* Creek." Once I realized what it was, the scribble only needed to be squinted at sideways to see it. Now it looks obvious—because I know the answer, of course.

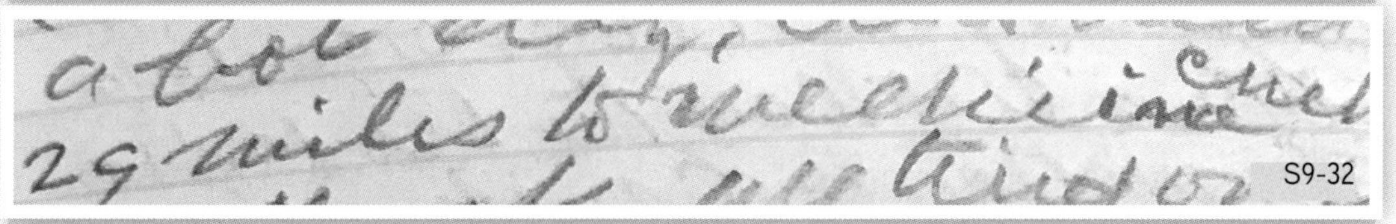

I encountered one such head-scratcher on my very first read and transcription of the diary, and it perpetuated from there, even after showing it to many peers and experts on riverboating, all perplexed by the scribble. Then, while reading a book about forts of the Upper Missouri River region, the answer popped up. Suddenly, the diary scribble became perfectly obvious. Rather embarrassing, actually. It wasn't a scribble at all—the problem was all mine. The story is as follows.

When daughters Ruth and Lizzie arrived in camp on August 1, Irish's diary noted, "The girls came at 1 P.M. and were brought to the camp by the steamer [indecipherable scribble]." During my initial read and transcription, and many subsequent readings, the word appeared to be *Yarel*. I searched all known lists of Missouri riverboats. I contacted the Dakota Territorial Museum in Yankton, as well as several other sources. People became intrigued, doing their own research and sharing the contact information of experts in Missouri riverboating. The result was always the same: they couldn't find anything resembling the scribbled word on Irish's diary page. (I always sent a copy of the actual page, in Irish's handwriting, not just my transcription.) After I received yet another "unable to identify a boat with a name even close to this" email, I was about to dismiss this quandary as too tangential and no longer worth pursuing.

At the time, I was reading a book about Upper Missouri River forts, learning about their structures, histories, and purposes, so I would have context for their existence as Irish visited them. On one page was an episode from the 1860s where a steamboat had been unable to make a landing due to low water. Instead, it loaded passengers and cargo onto its "yawl" and sent it to shore. Ah-ha! The day after this discovery, I received an email from one of the people I'd reached out to for help, Megan Hansen at the Dakota Territorial Museum. She'd also been reading, and came across this definition of *yawl*: "a rowboat which belongs to a steamboat, and is used as part of the steamboat's equipment."[141] Now it made perfect sense!

Yawl. All this time, I'd been thinking Irish had been referring to a big boat, a steamer whose name was obscured by bad handwriting. But it turned out that he was talking about the big boat's little boat—a shuttle boat. The diary page didn't say "the steamer *Yarel*"; it said "the steamer's yawl." Punctuation (and capitalization) is important, but Irish was not much of a practitioner—hence some of the punctuation I've added for ease of reading—and this particular absence of an apostrophe set a small army of people aflutter, searching for a nonexistent steamboat. The steamboat expert verified my conclusion, and with a whew and a chuckle, I marked this research item as completed.

Other scribbles were even more elusive. There was something he added to quinine. There are buttes out near the Cheyenne. But at least I know about Medicine Creek and some steamer's yawl. Still—that was a hell of a snag!

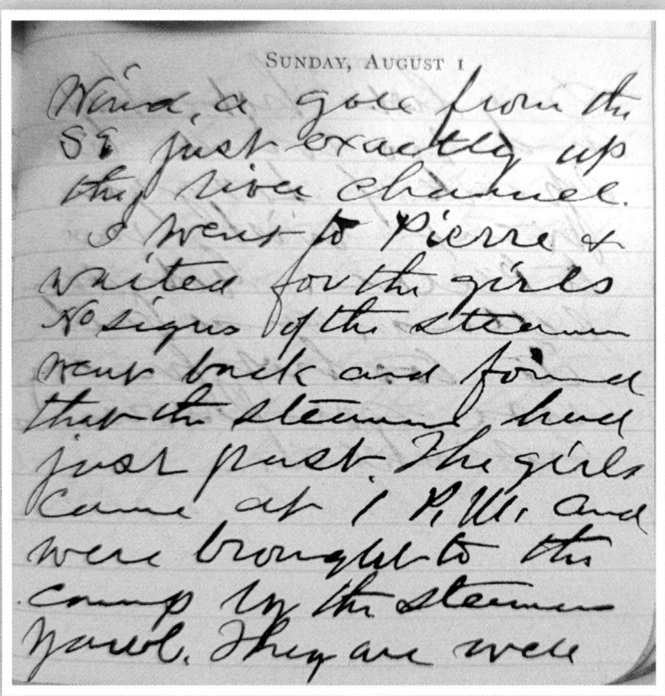
SUNDAY, AUGUST 1

Wind, a gale from the SE just exactly up the river channel. I went to Pierre & waited for the girls No signs of the steamer went back and found that the steamer had just past. The girls came at 1 P.M. and were brought to the camp by the steamer yawl. They are well

Now that we know what it says, the word *yawl* stands out neat, clean, and easy to read (first word of the last line). S9-33

Sunset along the Missouri River not far from Fort Sully 2. S9-34

Section Ten

THE FORKS OF THE CHEYENNE AND THE FIRST MONTHS OF THE HARD WINTER

SEPTEMBER 26–DECEMBER 21, 1880

The terrain was rough, and the weather was rougher—and that doesn't even factor in the "gumbo" mud. The men scouted well to the west, eventually reaching the Forks of the Cheyenne. With winter approaching, efforts were pushed to get as much exploring done as possible before conditions slowed the work even more than the gumbo. Then, one warm October day dissolved overnight into the first blizzard of what became known as the Hard Winter of 1880–81. Tents were re-engineered into tepees to better withstand the winds and hold in the little heat they could generate from a sod furnace. It was a difficult time, with low provisions, extreme cold, serious illness, and a most definite drop in morale. When the storm cleared, work resumed in earnest, and the crew needed to make up for lost time. A bright side for Irish appeared when he encountered Mrs. Irish walking across the ice of the Missouri River upon his return to Fort Pierre.

Approaching the Cheyenne: September 26–October 12, 1880

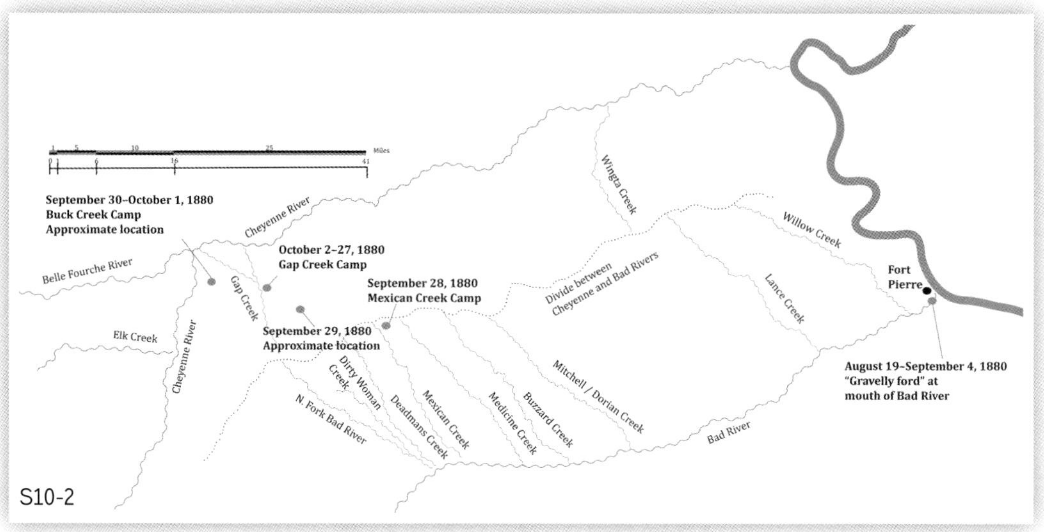

The men slept out in the open the evening of September 26, not having brought tents, and they awoke to find the ground covered in frost. Fortunately, the day warmed into the seventies, and the wind had rotated to come from the southwest. Again, creeks marked their progress as they headed back toward camp by following along the "south side of the divide between the Bad + Cheyenne rivers." Their noontime meal was again taken at Buzzard Creek, and they arrived in camp at 6 p.m. That night was cold, and "signs of storms" worried the men.

On the twenty-seventh, Jacket, evidently feeling better, was among a group of men who "killed 6 deer and 3 antelope" while Irish's party was scouting, so the food in camp that evening was hearty and filling. The diary provides lots of survey-centric notations, including that they covered thirteen and three-quarters miles of "tough work" before reaching camp at 7 p.m.

After enduring another cold night, camp was uprooted yet again the morning of September 28. This time, Irish sent Jacket and some others ahead with the bulk of camp things, with the responsibility of re-establishing the living quarters another twenty-five miles to the west. The main group's dinner was again eaten at Buzzard Creek, in a cold northwest wind. The men slept for the night at the "heads of Mexican creek," and Jacket and his crew were only two miles farther on; travel was no simple matter in this rough country.

That night, Irish dug out his equipment and took solid readings to establish, based on "magnetic" (compass) and star readings, a benchmark location for the survey work. It was cold again, and by the morning of September 29, there was plenty of ice. The men kept moving, crossing "the ridge at heads of Medicine creek."

This image shows Medicine Creek close to where it empties into the Bad River. A few of these trees may be old enough to have been young when the surveying crew was passing through. While over the past few days the men had camped at its head, they also scouted along this stretch, looking to see if they could follow its valley up toward the Cheyenne, then to the Belle Fourche, then into Deadwood. S10-3

There, along the ridge, the survey party overtook the party in charge of moving the camp. The surveyors reached the campsite at 7:30 p.m., but their tents were still somewhere to the east, trudging along in the gloppy gumbo with heavy wagons.

Ice formed again overnight, and Irish was up and out early on September 30 to scout along the Cheyenne, taking Bishop, Leighton, Jacket, Red Skirt, and Whirlwind with him. Irish was suffering from "severe neuralgia," possibly triggered by the cold night, though the day itself was hot. The party came upon a creek "with plenty of timber." Between them, Jacket and Red Skirt killed an antelope and two buck deer. After the hunt, however, Jacket again fell ill.

The men spent that evening near a small branch of Crow Creek, which they named Buck Creek, likely in honor of the animals dispatched by Jacket and Red Skirt. The scouting trek continued along the Cheyenne on October 1, reaching a point about two miles from the forks. It was a hot day, and the men "had a good time," despite being "in the saddle all day." They were back at the Buck Creek Camp by 8 p.m., "tired out" and hungry. The antelope and two deer shot the day before had not just lent themselves to a creek name, but were transformed into various "venison steak + ribs +c," which were ravenously devoured by the hungry men—except Jacket, who was "quite sick."

On October 2, as had happened once or twice, the men discovered upon waking that "the ponies had gone." Camp was hastily packed up, and they found "the lost ponies" during the journey back to the main camp.

The party was greeted back in camp around 2:30 p.m., at which point Irish orchestrated sending three "loads" of camp equipment "ahead to Gap Creek," where the next base camp would be established. He also "sent the Indians to Pierre + Cheyenne agency," though he did not indicate why. We know at least some of the Lakotas remained, as Jacket (still sick) and Red Skirt are mentioned in the diary as present in camp over the next few days.

The survey party of the railroad are now out to the Grindstone Buttes, and in no place is it more than eight miles from the stage route. They are striking for the Cheyenne river, and when they reach it they will follow up a high level plateau to the mouth of the Belle Fourche, where they will cross, and then up that stream to a point we know not where. This route has been looked over and found to be a good one.

S10-4

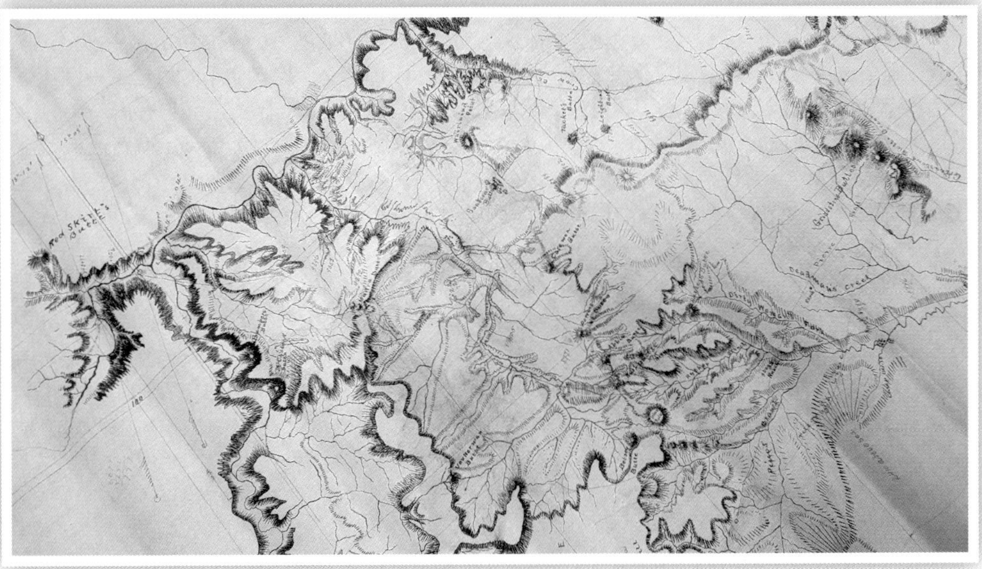

Irish's map of the western portion of the region. The Grindstone Butte(s) landmark is on the right, the Forks of the Cheyenne on the left. S10-5

A hard frost settled upon the landscape overnight into October 3, and the temperature at 6 a.m. was 22 degrees. Irish spent the "fine" day working on "payroll + bills + other business + letters." The teams he'd sent ahead to establish the new camp had not returned, however, which must have caused some level of concern.

Early the morning of October 4, the missing teams appeared. No explanation for the delay was recorded, though one suspects the usual mud and difficult terrain. With the focus back on the work at hand, the crew "ran over the heads of Crow Creek," then spent the night camping exposed, with no tents, on the west side of the creek. While the day had been hot, the night was very cold.

Irish took special interest in the geology of the area they were exploring on the fourth, remarking on "the number of hills capped with sand stone slabs," mentioning, "I found an exposure of soft sandstone and cut my name in it." The next day, October 5, they passed near the Posey Buttes (named for the Lakota police officer), then on into the valley of Gap Creek, an area of "heavy canyons." When Irish arrived at camp (the one he'd ordered established ahead), he was pleased to see there was plenty of timber. The water, however, was bad, and everyone in camp as well as three horses became sick. Jacket and Albright were particularly ill. Irish himself was "tired out," not riding back into camp until 8:30 p.m.—"Boys thought I was lost."

Most of the men had remained in camp on the fifth, doing various chores, including stake-making. As timber was handy, one imagines that Irish set the men to making as many stakes as they could, to prevent the earlier situation where they were unable to work due to the lack of stakes. As the saying goes, *Make hay [or stakes] while the sun shines.*

This photo was taken near Creighton, South Dakota, looking east across a wide valley that contains many smaller creek valleys, including the North Fork of the Bad River, on the east end. S10-6

Irish and Leighton explored six or seven miles down Gap Creek, taking in the options. They found "plenty of water + wood in the canyon," as well as nine deer—"All is now ready for business." He seemed perfectly pleased with this option for getting the tracks down to the Cheyenne and up the North Fork of the Cheyenne on that final leg into Deadwood.

The Lakotas in the crew were less pleased. "The Indians give me much trouble" was how Irish closed his diary entry for October 6, suggesting the Lakotas did not agree that this route option was optimal.

On October 7, Irish, Leighton, Whirlwind, and Red Skirt explored "up to the ridge S. side of Gap Cr. Thence towards the forks." The heat was "oppressive," and camp was made near a "branch of Gap Creek about 5 miles from the forks of the Cheyenne." The night was "not so cold as usual," though there was still a spotty frost in the morning.

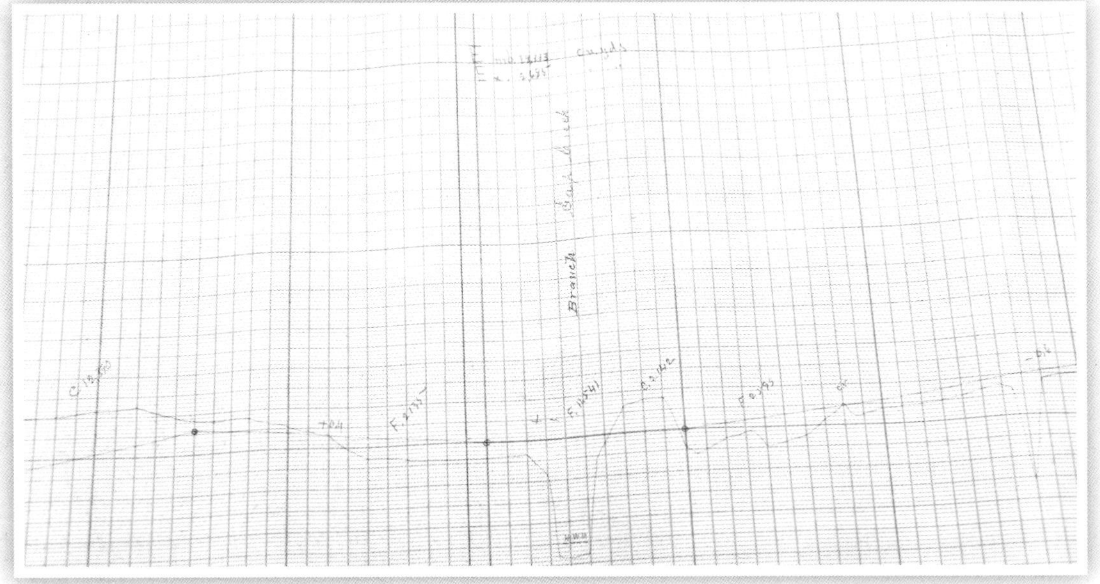

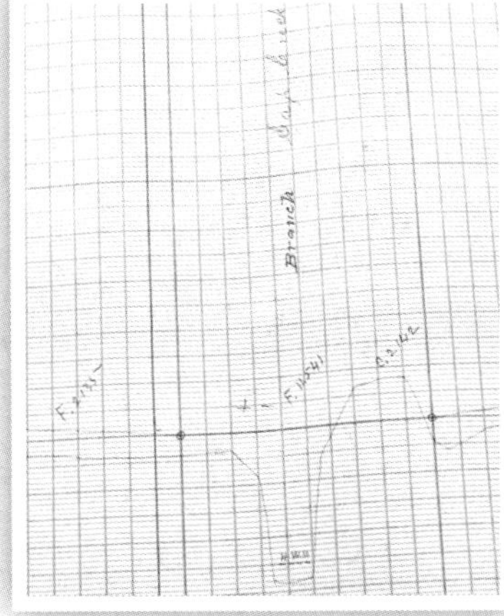

This profile map segment is an excellent example of one of the responsibilities of a surveyor. Irish had to determine the level of grade, then calculate the amount of ground that had to be removed ("c" = cut) or filled in ("f" = fill) in order for the track to meet grade. The total cubic yards of material are noted at each location. This also shows our mysterious Gap Creek, but without the context of surrounding geographic features that would allow us to correlate it to a modern map. We merely get to see its profile. S10-7, S10-8

On Friday, October 8, the party explored "over a very rough country down to the forks." At some point, on the east side of the bluffs, the party built a mound to mark the site, as there were no good trees to blaze. All but one member of the crew placed a rock onto the mound, with Red Skirt refusing to participate in the ceremony.

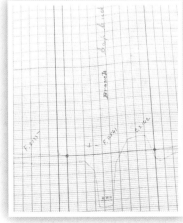

The "very rough country" near the Forks of the Cheyenne. This photo was taken on the east side of the Cheyenne, looking northwest, toward the Forks, which are within the valley visible at top-right. S10-9

On October 9, there were "strong signs of a storm." Nevertheless, the men traveled to the west, following the North Fork of the Cheyenne River, until they were about eight miles from its mouth, crossing the river once along the way. The afternoon had brought "renewed signs of storms," and overnight a "severe wind storm" swept down from the northwest. They camped for the night, without tents, on the bank of the Belle Fourche. Upon waking, Irish declared the morning "cold."

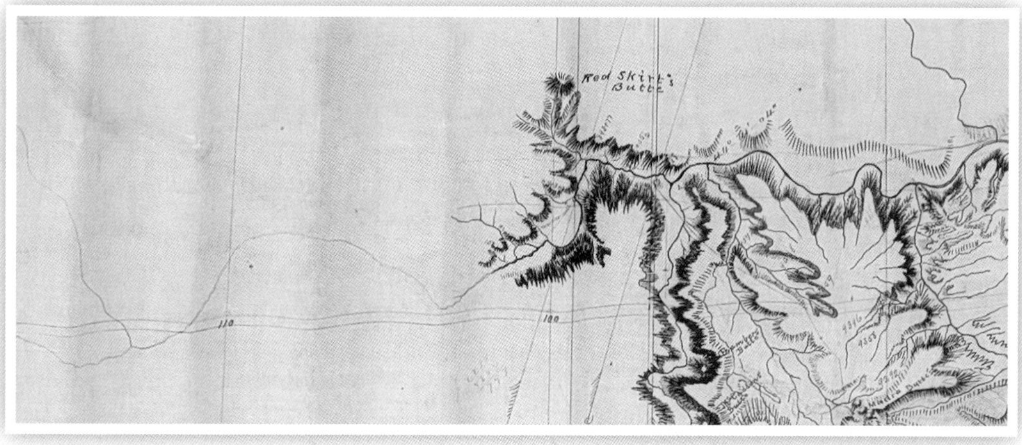

The Belle Fourche River (or the North Fork of the Cheyenne) wending westward as an undefined line beyond the area that Irish had been able to investigate. S10-10

Irish and Red Skirt spent Sunday, October 10, on horseback, exploring the area "above" camp (which could have meant to the north, or it could have meant upstream, which, where they were, would have meant to the south). They traveled about twenty miles out before turning around, reaching camp at about 8 p.m. Irish declared the day successful, despite the cold air and "severe gale."

Overnight between the tenth and eleventh was "very cold," and the wind continued to plague the temporary camp. On the eleventh, the men returned to the Forks of the Cheyenne, "over very high and almost impassable hills just above the forks." There they established another camp for the night, and the level party, which had been exploring a different line, joined them. The weather had been fine during the day, but that night the temperature dove to 12 degrees.

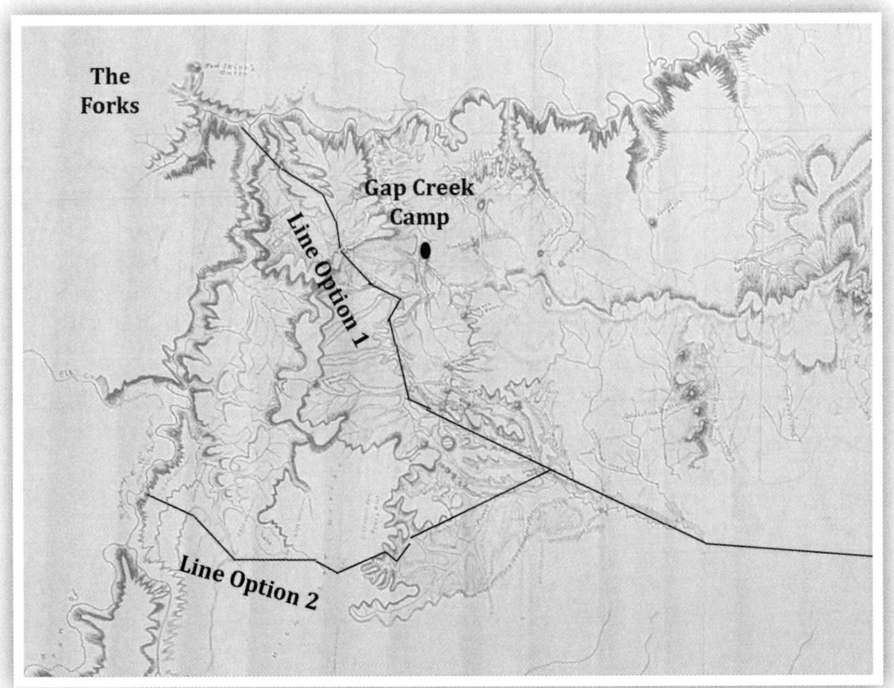

The two line options the men were investigating to get the tracks from the North Fork of the Bad River down to the Cheyenne. S10-11

"My canteen of coffee froze solid in the bed, at my head," Irish wrote of his waking on October 12. They were up and going by 8 a.m., starting their return to the main camp at Gap Creek. "The wind blew chilly . . . a gale from [the] SE," making the trek less than pleasant. Irish and Red Skirt rejoined the main camp around 4:30 in the afternoon, finding four men ill. Jacket was one of the sick, along with Chase and two others. "It's the villainous water," declared Irish in frustration.

The weather, too, continued to antagonize the crew. The barometer, which had "been very high," suddenly "got very low." The temperature was not low, however, reading 80 degrees at 2 p.m. Irish's instincts were good, and he sent Chamberlain and Sherwood back to Medicine Creek Camp to pick up supplies. They would be unable to return for several days.

The Start of the Hard Winter: October 13–28, 1880

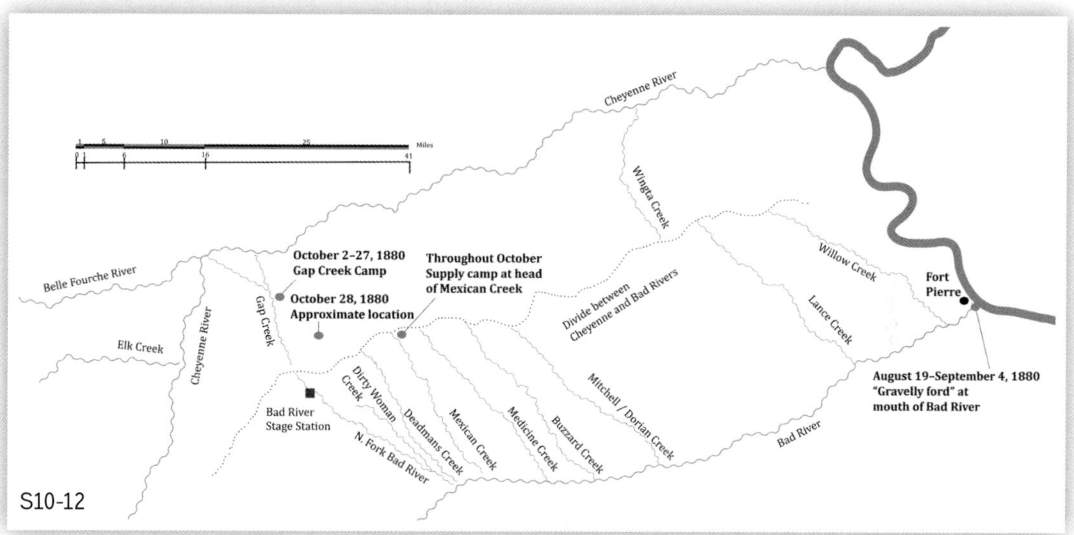

It was 80 degrees at 2 p.m. But overnight, into October 14, a "hard storm" blew up. It began with rain, then turned to snow around midnight, Irish recording, "It snowed all day and the wind [was] a perfect gale." In addition to the unwelcome snow, the camp was "comfortless," and the sick had gotten worse. Irish noted that the men were doing all they could "to keep warm in this gale."

The fifteenth was just as bad: "Stormy, stormy high wind. The snow fell 3 inches deep and still the wind blows. I feel quite under the weather, tried to get my tent warm with stove pipe + tin pan; it was not a success. We have one stove. I have set the boys to make a teepee to warm up in."

It might be useful here to reiterate the list of bedding that Irish had shared in a letter home in the first months of the survey; he and another were sharing sleeping quarters:

> We have two water proof blankets, 1 buffalo robe, and 4 wool blankets under us on a bed of hay. Then 4 wool blankets and a buffalo robe over us, and use my quilt for a bolster. Then I have another robe and my gray over coat, which I lay between me and the wall of the tent, so you see we cannot help but be warm. Then we have such a good tent! It is of cloth that weighs 12 ounces to the square yard. It's as thick as buckskin, and [I] have a large sheet iron stove to heat up with.

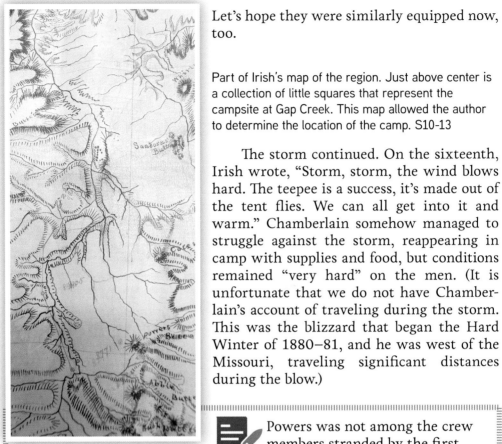

Let's hope they were similarly equipped now, too.

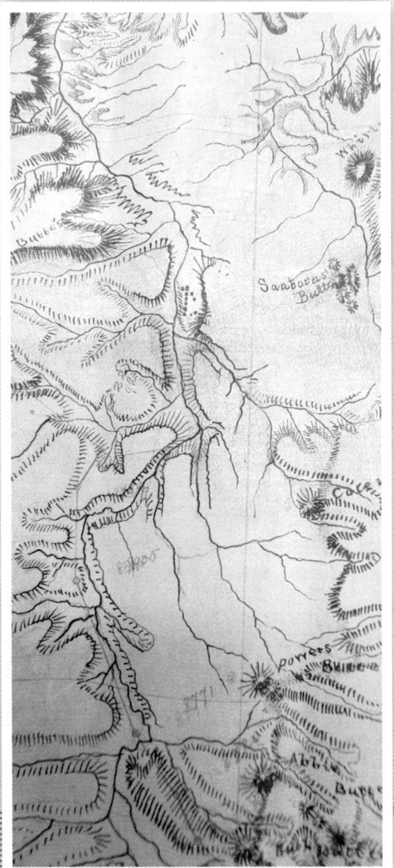

Part of Irish's map of the region. Just above center is a collection of little squares that represent the campsite at Gap Creek. This map allowed the author to determine the location of the camp. S10-13

The storm continued. On the sixteenth, Irish wrote, "Storm, storm, the wind blows hard. The teepee is a success, it's made out of the tent flies. We can all get into it and warm." Chamberlain somehow managed to struggle against the storm, reappearing in camp with supplies and food, but conditions remained "very hard" on the men. (It is unfortunate that we do not have Chamberlain's account of traveling during the storm. This was the blizzard that began the Hard Winter of 1880–81, and he was west of the Missouri, traveling significant distances during the blow.)

Powers was not among the crew members stranded by the first blizzard of the Hard Winter. On October 16, Reed wrote a letter to Mrs. Irish, including, "Perry Powers stopped here on his way home. It was too bad; he is such a nice young man." The sentiment refers to Powers's leg injury after being shot.

This letter must have been written about a month after Powers was escorted eastward, as the September 22 *Fort Pierre Weekly Signal* reported, "A. S. Shannon went to Winona in charge of Perry Powers last week, and will return via Mankato, and bring Mrs. Shannon and all the little Shannons back with him."[142]

While the storm raged around camp, Irish worked on maps and profiles for the recent scouting trips. And so it went on the seventeenth too. The ground had three inches of snow, with more falling. Because it had been so warm the days prior to the storm, much of the snow was melting as it fell, until the ground cooled enough to allow snow accumulation.

As the storm continued, Irish created a "sod furnace" in his tent. The men also "built a sod bank around the teepee" to help protect it from the winds. An additional teepee was constructed out of a tent fly for Jacket, who had been ailing for much of his time on the crew.

Monday, October 18, the fourth day of the storm, found the ground "hard frozen, [snow] 4 inches deep." A sod furnace and accompanying chimney were constructed in the store tent, and Irish declared it "a success." However, the men were "still far from comfortable," and Chase was getting worse. "Will have to send him off as he will die here," wrote Irish.

THE START OF THE HARD WINTER OF 1880–81

The *Black Hills Daily Pioneer* of October 18 published a long account of this initial "Polar Wave," its impact felt for hundreds of miles—from west of Dakota Territory to the Great Lakes to the east, and well to the south too. Railroad tracks were blocked by snow, bringing trains to a halt, and ships on Lake Michigan were wrecked. The ground had frozen across a wide swath of territory, even ruining potato and other root crops. "Telegraph lines are generally prostrate," wrote the *Pioneer*'s editor. "It was with much difficulty that Manager Emery could secure last night even the brief report which we published."[143]

The *Fort Pierre Weekly Signal* reported that the railroad company paid residents of Kingsbury and Beadle Counties thirty cents per hour to shovel snow from the tracks during the blockade following the October storm.[144] This would be the beginning of the railroad company's great outlay of money over the coming winter, with very little freight or passenger funds coming in across the same region.

(For deeper details about the Hard Winter, read *The Beautiful Snow: The Ingalls Family, the Railroads, and the Hard Winter of 1880–81.*)

The storm released its hold on October 19, which Irish declared a "better day." The sod furnaces warmed the tents to the point that hands were limber enough to work, and Irish again spent the day drawing the maps and profiles. "It goes slow, as my co-laborers take no interest in the work. I am not at all well, can hardly keep my feet."

Between the bitter cold and illness, things in camp were not going well. Irish sent a crewman named Blair and a Lakota named Meat to escort the ailing Chase to Fort Pierre. After possibly crossing paths with Blair, Meat, and Chase, Ryther appeared in camp at 8 p.m., bringing welcome supplies. Ryther may have started out in Pierre, alarmed and looking for his crew, or he may have been at the Medicine Creek base camp prior to the start of the storm; we don't know how far he traveled to get supplies to the men at Gap Creek Camp. Regardless, he was an incoming hero.

Wednesday, October 20, was another "cold blustery day." Irish, Ryther, Red Skirt, Leighton, and Chambers left the snowed-in Gap Creek Camp and made the difficult trek to the Forks of the Cheyenne. After showing Ryther the proposed route Irish had his eye on, the men returned to camp at 7 p.m.

The night was again "very cold." On top of that, upon waking on the twenty-first, the men discovered that the horses got away during the night—again. The horses were rounded up, and Irish returned to Gap Creek Camp, near the Forks. There, he found Jacket had worsened to "quite sick." Irish himself was not well, writing, "I am about to go to bed. I have fever and headache."

PIERRE READY TO WELCOME RAILROAD PATRONS

While Irish was retrieving provisions from the supply camp and getting them back to the men at Gap Creek Camp, the newly built tracks were within three short miles of Pierre. A large hotel was being constructed near the future depot site, ready to welcome passengers. However, the newspapers had already brought a hint of what was to come. The *Fort Pierre Weekly Signal* of Wednesday, October 20, reported, "The train . . . was delayed last week between Lake Benton and Huron. The mail due here Sunday morning was also delayed on account of snow."[145] The trains would soon arrive in Pierre. But it was not going to be the rush of business the Chicago & North Western had expected.

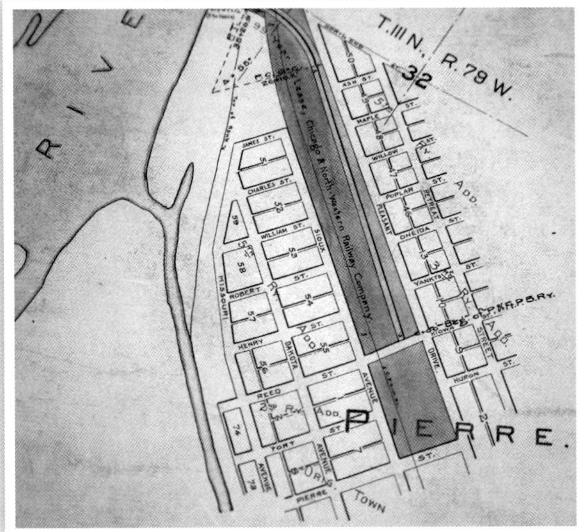

A map of the layout of Pierre; the grey area is the railroad property. S10-14

The next day, the twenty-second, Irish was "sick, sick" and could "hardly stand it." As leader, he had responsibilities to fulfill. Ryther was anxious to get on his way, so Irish "worked all day to get the map and profiles ready." The illness won, and Irish was unsuccessful at finishing the documents for Ryther, who left at 4 p.m. without them. Irish immediately went back to bed, feeling "used up." He remained in bed throughout the twenty-third, writing, "Quinine and Dover's Powders are the remedies."

ILLNESS, TREATMENT & RAMIFICATIONS

An 1877 encyclopedia of remedies includes a description of Dover's Powder: "Ipecacuanha, in powder, 1 drachm; powdered opium, 1 drachm; powdered saltpetre, 1 ounce. All well mixed. Dose, from 8 to 20 grains."[146] The main ingredient, ipecacuanha, is better known today as ipecac, as in ipecac syrup, once widely used to induce vomiting but now discouraged for over-the-counter use.

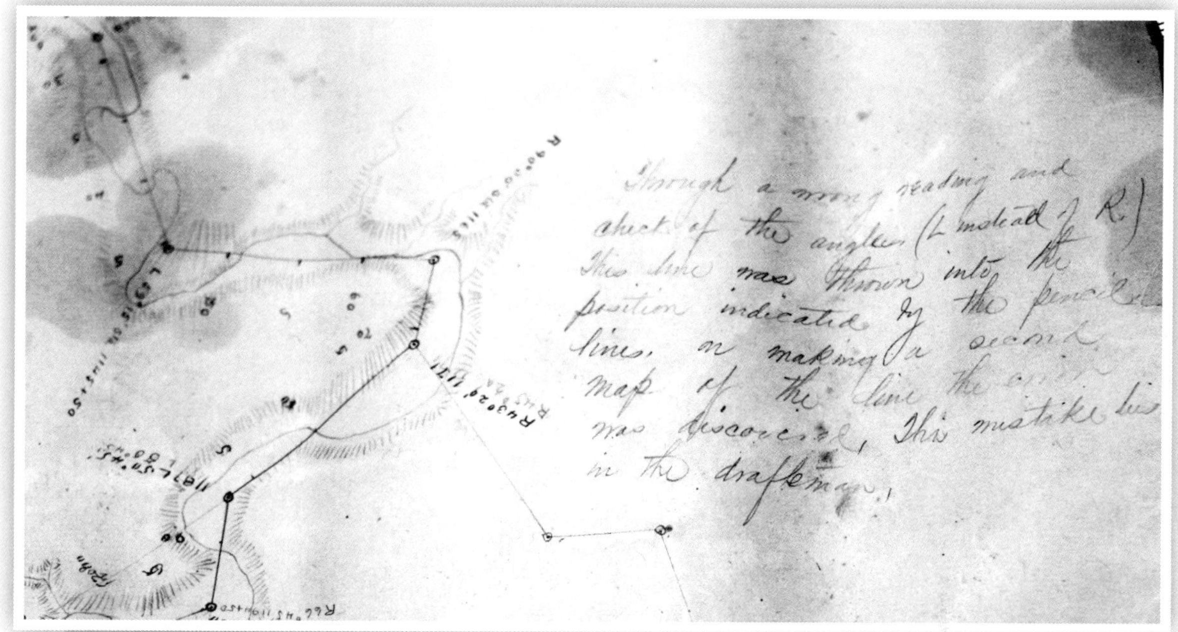

Working on the maps while sick may have had ramifications. This example may not be among the maps Irish worked on that day, but it does illustrate how much detail, concentration, and focus were required to create an accurate map. The note upon this map states, "Through a wrong reading and check of the angles (L instead of R.) this line was thrown into the position indicated by the pencil lines. On making a second map of the line, the error was discovered. This mistake lies in the draftsman!" S10-15

While Irish felt he was improving under the regimen of quinine and powders, Chase was sent home, as the water available had "hurt him so." Jacket was also failing, "very sick and [getting] worse," having "not been well since [leaving] Pierre."

Irish felt well enough upon waking on October 24 that he set about writing letters and reports for Hughitt and "a long letter home." As previously stated, Jacket was getting worse, and Irish tried a mixture of "laudanum + chloroform, which eased [his suffering] some."

It did not ease Irish's concern, however, and on October 25, he sent Whirlwind and Ree (probably also a Lakota) to Rosebud Agency to bring back Jacket's family. "Jacket is worse and I am better," was Irish's concerning note.

The barometer had fallen very low again, and sure enough, a "hard storm of snow and rain" hit the camp overnight into the twenty-sixth. The diary says that half an inch of rain fell first, followed by enough snow to cover the ground come morning, which we can take to mean that much—or all—of the snowfall from the storm that started on October 13 had melted by the twenty-fifth. He sent Scarleg and Corn off to Fort Pierre with the reports, letters, and other mail matter, then departed toward the head of Gap Creek for the next stage of work.

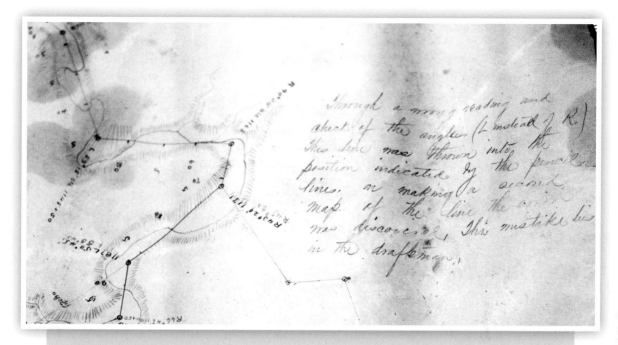

Early the next morning, October 27, the men were scouting along "the summit at the Gap and ran the Bluffs of the Bad River." The day was pleasantly warm, and they were able to check out seven miles of terrain. The group may have misjudged time, staying longer than anticipated, as by the time they turned to go back to camp, they were racing sunset, and "got lost in the dark and had quite a time." Joe Mudra got lost alone, not getting back until 9 p.m.

"I was quite out of sorts all night, being very tired, did not sleep easy," Irish wrote on October 28. The day did not allow for rest, however, as the men began to move camp to the "top of hills" near some buttes. Chamberlain had returned with mail, and a letter for Irish let him know that his wife was feeling poorly, leaving him feeling "very uneasy about her," and he was unable to sleep. The day had been warm, but the barometer was low again, "threatening storm." It seems that both Irish and the weather shared a disposition.

NEWS FROM THE CHEYENNE RIVER REGION

The October 27 *Fort Pierre Weekly Signal* included a brief piece noting, "Deer and antelope are said to abound numerously on the Cheyenne river, and up Bad River."[147] This news likely came from Ryther or Chamberlain, making use of the information obtained during their visits to Gap and Medicine Creek Camps to look in on the men following the winter's first blizzard. Meanwhile, the final bridge below Pierre was being constructed, and train cars had reached a spot just a few miles south of that final bridge. Residents were again anxious to welcome the trains, as lumber had become scarce in Pierre; orders were en route from Minneapolis and Winona. The *Signal*'s editor printed, hopefully, "We expect to see great improvements in Pierre in the next month if not too cold."[148]

Work Resumed: October 29–November 6, 1880

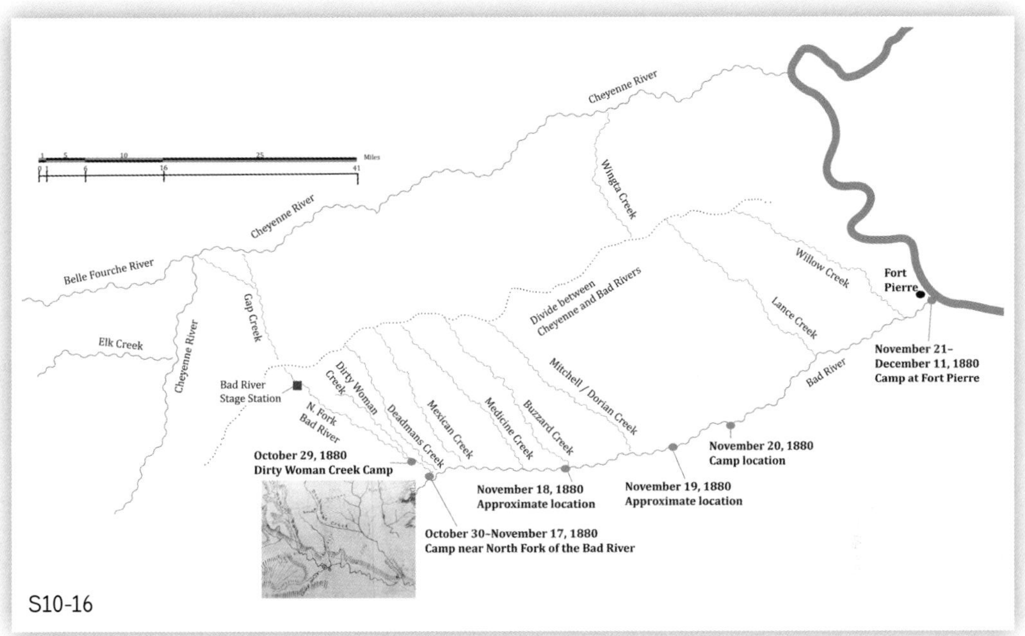

Regardless of the barometric changes, the men were up and out early on October 29. The route included scouting along the ridge to the head of the North Fork of the Bad River, where they ate their midday meal. After the break, they went cross-country to the mouth of Dirty Woman Creek, where they again set up camp.

"Jacket is very sick," Irish wrote, "I fear he will not last long." It is unclear whether they were hauling poor Jacket hither and yon, or whether Irish was hearing word from a base camp where Jacket was suffering.

That night brought another hard freeze, and the men had no tents. Their "blankets and robes were frozen stiff over [them]." For a few moments, simply think about the conditions these men were working under—it is simultaneously impressive and horrifying.

On October 30, the crew worked their way down the North Fork of the Bad River, where they decided on "a nice place" to camp. Irish "sent teams back for balance of camp," and they got the new location set up with tents "in good order." After nights of sleeping out in the open, the tents must have seemed quite luxurious indeed that evening. It was 12 degrees as the sun rose on the thirty-first, and they "worked all day to get camp ready." Jacket's stepfather, Mr. Elston, and family also arrived in camp. Jacket was no healthier, but Irish likely felt better having the man's loved ones there to tend to him.

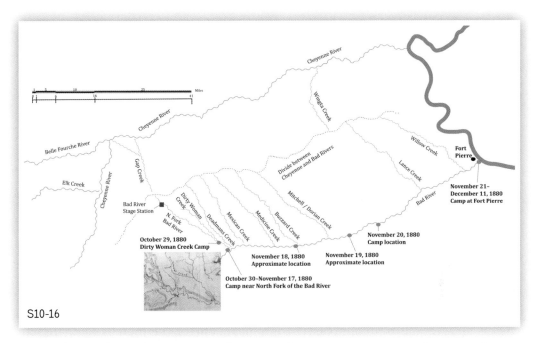

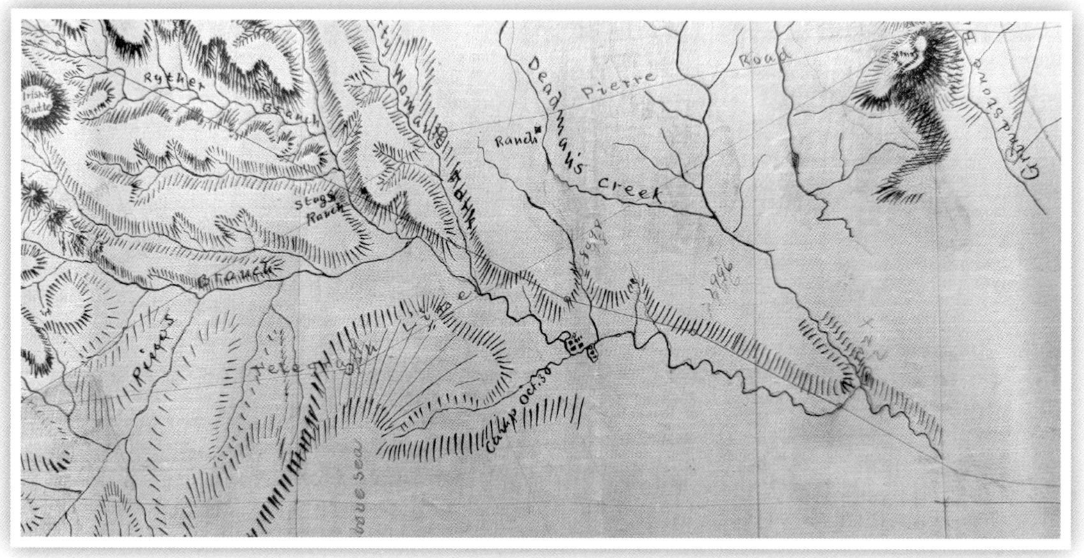

Irish's map detail showing the location of the October 30, 1880, campsite. S10-17

Another 12-degree night was endured, and as November dawned, Jacket needed most of Irish's attention. Before doing the medical watch, Irish "set all hands at work on camp chores," but it appears one of the men balked. "Barch [or Barsh—the handwriting is sloppy] left today[;] glad of it." He'd clearly left because he wanted to, but Irish was likely also glad to be rid of a man who didn't want to be there. While tending to Jacket, Irish wrote letters—some for work, some for family—and kept his eye on the barometer. It was again falling, sitting at 27.3 as the day ended.

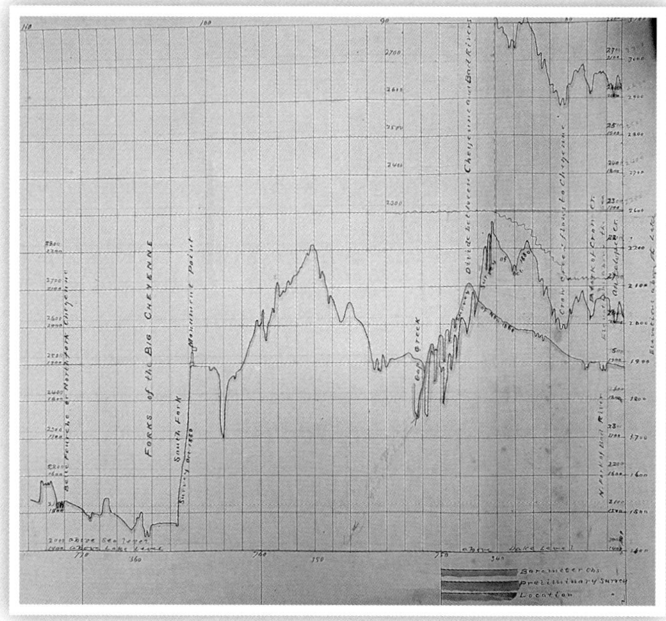

An elevation profile map that compares the October 1880 and November 1880 line routes explored to the east of the Forks of the Cheyenne (right half of the image). S10-18

With Jacket under the care of family, Irish got out of camp to work on November 2. Following another ridge, he worked until about 4:15 p.m., having completed six and a half hours of observations and readings—among the best progress made for several weeks since the first storm of the winter. It was a "fine" day, and warm. The geese and ducks were earnestly flying south, however, and Irish made note.

November 3 was another productive day, with nine and a half miles of lines recorded, "nearly to the forks of the river." A storm had "threatened" all day, and by 4:15 p.m., the rain had finally begun, getting the men "very wet on [their] way back to camp." The rain turned to snow overnight, and on the fourth, Irish noted, "All is winter now."

Irish told the men to remain in camp on the fourth, as it was a "cold, wintry day." And at last, after several weeks, Jacket was feeling better, providing a surge of relief for Irish. Along with that fact, however, was the notation that Tubbs was now sick. Ryther arrived in camp too. The tents were lashed by a northwest wind that began that evening, with "snow and sleet all night."

The next morning, November 5, Ryther and McCready left camp to catch the stage east to Pierre. When they got there, the stage only had one spot left; Ryther boarded the stage, and McCready returned to camp. Amidst camp activities, another trip was in the works, and Irish and others spent the day finishing up profiles and maps so the papers could be sent along.

Saturday, November 6, was yet another stormy day, rain and sleet falling all night. The weather was slowing the work; the level party took four days to complete a line that, Irish felt, would ordinarily have taken two. Fortunately, the day was warm, the temperature reading 58 degrees at 2 p.m. "Jacket is very low," Irish lamented, likely fearing a relapse for the man. He added, "I am tired out."

FIRST TRAIN INTO PIERRE

Back in Pierre, all was celebration. A flurry of squibs excitedly shared the big news, then jumped to the *next* big plan:

> Hurrah for Pierre! The railroad is here! The telegraph line was completed up to Pierre day before yesterday. The cars have commenced running into Pierre, carrying freight and passengers. The Northwestern Transportation company's coaches commenced running from Deadwood this way Monday. The coach bound for the Hills left here yesterday morning. A railroad from Bismarck to the Black Hills is being strongly agitated.[149]

Pierre was settling into the new situation, and so were the towns in the Black Hills, to the west. The excitement of getting a train to the Hills quickly took a bit of a hit when the *Central Herald* noted that a two-year contract had been agreed upon between the railroad and the stage company, an indication that the rails may, after all, be at least two years away.[150]

A Return to Pierre and Back to the Cheyenne: November 7–16, 1880

Irish worked throughout Sunday, November 7, on more maps and more notes. Once all was in order, he left camp and traveled to "the Bad River Station of the NW stage Co and stopped there for the stage to Pierre." At 3 a.m. he boarded the stage heading toward Fort Pierre, joining three others already onboard, all bundled up in their robes. When they approached Deadman's Creek, there was "an upset[,] fortunately without serious injuries." The stage reached Fort Pierre at 9:30 p.m. on the eighth—an eighteen-and-a-half-hour journey, including the upset, which reminds us how long—and dangerous, given the weather and other factors—travel could be. The day had been cold, and Irish's three meals cost him 75 cents. (His return was later reported in the November 10 *Fort Pierre Weekly Signal.*)

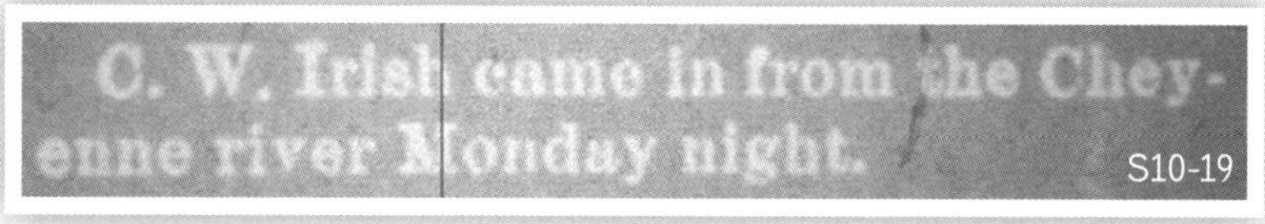
C. W. Irish came in from the Cheyenne river Monday night.

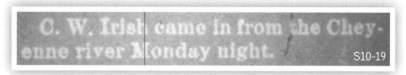

S10-19

THE FIRE FIEND.

Fort Pierre Almost in Flames—Loss About $4,000.

Monday night about 10 o'clock a fire was discovered in Mr. Marion's hay stack, situated right in the central part of the town, and containing about 100 tons of hay. The alarm was given at once, and in a very few moments a hundred men were on the ground rendering all the assistance in their power to prevent a general conflagration. There were two log stables adjoining the hay, both filled with horses, grain and machinery. All the horses except one were rescued, but it was impossible to save the grain and machinery, as the fire covered the stables in a very few moments after it was set.

At one time it was thought that the town was doomed, and our citizens were preparing to move their property to a place of safety. Had there been any wind nothing could have prevented the whole town from utter destruction.

Tho principal losers are as follows: Marion $2,000; Waldron $500; La Plant $1,500. Geo. Harris stable and contents, with the exception of horses.

Messrs. Ryther and Tracy were injured quite severely in their attempt to tear down a fence near the scene of the fire, the former getting an ugly wound on the head, and the latter spraining his ankle.

The cause of the fire is not known, but supposed to have been set for the purpose of pillage. $500 reward is offered for the cowardly miscreant who applied the match.

S10-20

That same evening, November 8, Fort Pierre experienced a fire. It burned "90 tons of hay + 1 horse," and Ryther suffered a serious head cut while helping to fight the flames. Fires in frontier towns were often fully or nearly cataclysmic; they were either quickly put out, leaving anxious and relieved people in their wake, or they swept away large swaths of the hastily assembled wooden buildings. In this instance, the residents of Fort Pierre may have felt relief at losing *only* ninety tons of hay and a horse. But with the Hard Winter beginning its long slog toward spring, those 90 tons of hay were a serious—but not yet fully understood—loss.

The next morning, Irish crossed the river and met Hughitt, Blunt, and Johnson in Pierre—which Irish described as "growing finely." The four men spent the "wintry" day examining the maps and profiles and making plans. Irish mysteriously spent the tenth on "special business," likely tied to the meeting with the officers the day before. He also "settled bills and bought supplies needed, and had a pleasant visit with Mr. Ryther."

Early on November 11, Irish was back on the stage, headed west. Creeks and stage stations again served as his landmarks, the stage crossing Lance Creek and Medicine Creek before arriving, finally, at North Fork Bad River Station at 11 p.m. He summarized his day with, "Cold, tired, and hungry."

It did not improve. "Got off on foot in a snow blizzard for camp," began his entry for the twelfth. "Had a 2 hour walk in the storm but made it all right. I am suffering from neuralgia." In pain, he walked into camp and went straight to bed.

Snow continued throughout the thirteenth, but Irish and his horse, Billy, went twenty-five miles out and back along the Bad River. He was not impressed, declaring, "Bad River is bad for any purpose." The pair returned to camp around 8:30 p.m., "quite tired out"—Irish for sure, but probably Billy too.

"Storm stormy all the time," penned Irish on the fourteenth. He spent the day getting "everything ready for a trip and survey down the [Bad] river." He also wrote several letters and sent them off with a courier. He then settled in and hoped for an improved weather situation. Perhaps it worked.

On November 15, the precipitation continued, but it was only rain. Irish didn't seem to trust it, however, writing, "I am uneasy and troubled about the weather." The wagons were loaded and ready to haul, but unable to move. Then the rain turned to snow. Instead of heading out on the trip, Irish and some of the men "ran 6 miles of line."

The night was "clear and cold," but by morning it was again snowing, with a strong northwest wind. The men attempted to work, but they "had to abandon [the] survey, it [was snowing] so hard." A Mr. Peterson, with his buckboard, arrived in camp "out of health." Irish liked him, however. It appears that Peterson was there to help move camp to a less remote location.

Hopefully the man was prepared for camp conditions, as it was a "very cold night," and things did not warm up throughout the seventeenth. Preparations were finished to begin the scout east along the Bad River, downstream to the Missouri. The camp also prepared to move back to the gravel bar near the mouth of the Bad, where they had begun their work west of the Missouri River. "It's awful cold," closed that day's entry.

HUGHITT AND ROUTE INSIGHTS

An article appeared in the November 12 edition of the *Black Hills News* that provided significant insight into the business analysis for the route into the Black Hills. This initial article was vague as to the identity of a *mystery gentleman* who generously shared information about the Chicago & North Western's plans. A little over a month later, the December 15 edition indignantly groused that their carefully veiled interview with Hughitt had been republished by the *St. Paul Pioneer Press* without attribution. Thus we know it was Hughitt himself providing these insights.[151] While the November 12 article slyly called their informant "the gentleman," we'll simply call him Hughitt for expediency.

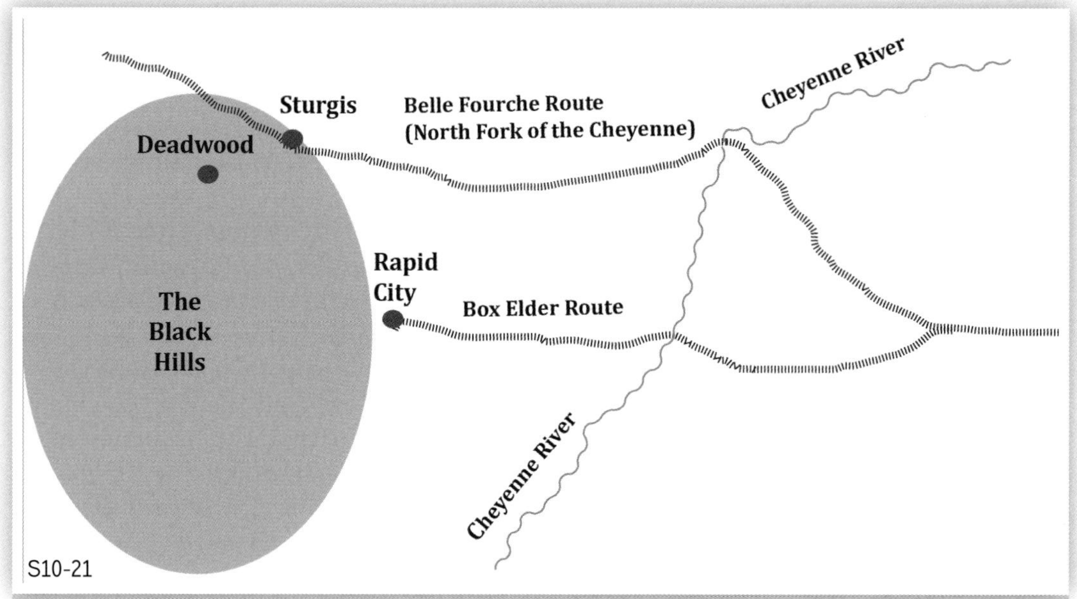

A visual overview of the options Hughitt described.

Hughitt disappointed the editor by confirming it would probably be two years yet before a railroad reached the Hills. As to the route, he predicted it would be the Sturgis area, not Rapid City, that would be the "future foothills metropolis." In his opinion, a railroad "could be constructed . . . at a much less expense" near Sturgis versus Rapid City. The reason, he explained, was the crossing location of the Cheyenne had ramifications beyond a bridge across the river. To target Rapid City, the logical crossing of the Cheyenne would be near the mouth of Rapid Creek, a location that would "require a very steep grade."[152] A steep grade was an expensive grade, not just for construction but for ongoing operations.

After explaining the difficulties of the Rapid Creek valley, Hughitt then admitted there was, in fact, a workable alternative. The relatively easy grade of Box Elder Creek's valley could be reached where the bluffs along the Cheyenne were "not so high." In fact, the valley of Box Elder Creek would allow tracks to be "constructed at a comparatively small cost with very little grading" to reach Rapid City. But Rapid City was not the goal. Hughitt explained, "The principal object of a road into the Hills will of course be to catch the trade of Deadwood, Lead, and Central [City]."[153] While they *could* run a relatively easy and inexpensive line into Rapid City, they did not *want* to go to Rapid City.

Hughitt further posited it was unlikely that any existing towns would be specifically targeted, as they knew that "an entirely new town" could be built where most advantageous to support the new rail line.[154]

Despite Hughitt's caution that his proposed line might skirt the Black Hills, rather than go into them to physically meet Deadwood, the editor added his own optimism to close the article, stating, "We believe, however, a road will reach us first from the Missouri river, and in that event it will probably come in at some point further north."[155]

Back Down the Bad River to Fort Pierre: November 18–December 21, 1880

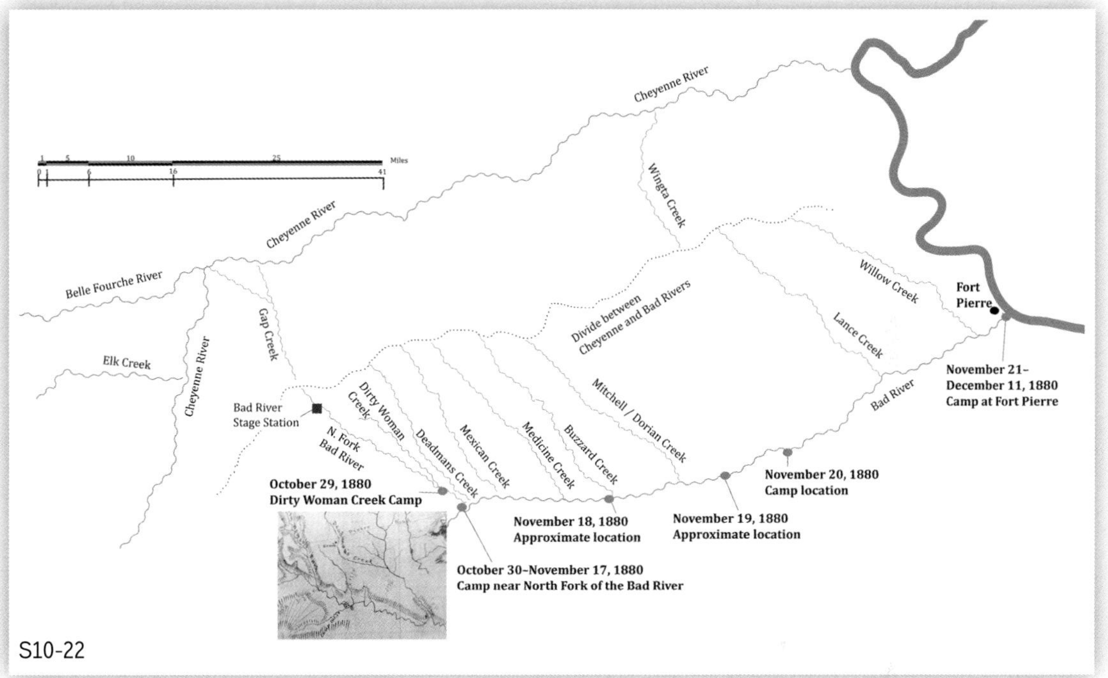

S10-22

The thermometer read –6 degrees—"a stinger." By 11 a.m. the men were again on the move, Leighton and McCready sticking with Irish, who wrote, "Day very cold and stormy." They made nearly twenty miles over "very rough ground," then set up a quick camp on the riverbank. It was "a severe night," though they had chosen a campsite nestled within a timbered valley where "there was plenty of wood" to keep fires going. The barometer was high—which meant storms were less likely, but the cold would persist.

Saturday, November 20, was "severely cold" and besieged with a strong northwest wind. The terrain was more favorable for travel, and the crew were fortunate to find another wooded campsite, on the south side of the Bad. The barometer continued to rise, the wind continued to blow, and Irish wryly mused, "It seems as if winter has come to us."

The men continued to follow the Bad downstream on the twenty-first, forced to cross the water (or ice) multiple times—"The buckboard team had a hard time, it's so hard to get along the river." They reached their destination camp at Fort Pierre around 4 p.m., glad to be done for the day as well as back to the best shelter they'd had since early September, almost two months prior. Irish set about work on a report that Ryther would transport back to Blunt in

Winona. The profiles and maps covered about twenty-five miles of the Bad River area.

The reunion with more comfortable lodging wasn't the only improvement to Irish's situation. The next morning, November 22, he "met Mrs. Irish in company with Mr. Ryther on the ice, coming over." Irish put off his work for a few hours while she settled in. It is unclear whether the return of his wife was a planned meeting or an unexpected but wonderful surprise; regardless, she'd made the journey from Iowa in the rough weather, and it seemed the couple would endure the coming winter together—though they did not know it would be a historic one.

On November 23, Mrs. Irish was set up in the more comfortable chambers of Sherwood's Grand Central Hotel in Fort Pierre. The day was cold and windy, and the river was frozen solid. In his diary, Irish noted, "Three steamers are frozen fast in the channel between here and Yankton. Winter has come early much before it was expected." And it was going to get worse—much worse.

The weather continued to comprise "real winter." The Lakota police came back to camp on the twenty-fourth, "some of them badly frozen. They were united in saying that they [could not] stand the trip." In another case of vague diary entries causing curiosity for later researchers, he noted that he left "3 boxes in care of Ryther at the Big Warehouse." Were these boxes of things for Ryther to haul eastward for the officers? Were they provisions and supplies that Irish had accumulated in Fort Pierre and stored in the warehouse, with instructions that Ryther had permission to retrieve and haul out to the survey camps as needed? While the more direct, clear entries provide interesting insights into the work of running a frontier survey group, these vague, oddball entries are almost more informative, making one consider various possibilities and question the validity of prevalent theories, resulting in even more insights into day-to-day operations.

There had been several nights with temperatures between −18 and −22 degrees, Irish reflecting, "I am astonished that the winter sets in so early and so severe." He must have spent considerable time deciding whether to keep the full crew on board, trying to force the work. On November 25, he made plans to discharge some of the crew, including the Lakota police. He must have recognized that it would not be practical to continue the work as earnestly as prior.

The diary entry for November 26 was possibly the shortest of the two years: "Paid off the Indians and got them ready to go home. It's now milder weather." The twenty-seventh was another day of decent weather, and one wonders whether Irish second-guessed his decision to release some of the crew.

The fair weather continued November 28, and Blunt arrived. Also joining the group was Nichols, recently (November 15) promoted to superintendent of the Dakota Central. Irish recorded that Blunt and Nichols left later in the day; the diary was silent on the topic of the conversations they'd had, but they likely discussed the recent, deeper explorations along the Bad River—though the crew would go on to work lines across the Missouri, instead, in the coming days.

The second-to-the-last day of November was likewise "quite a fine day." However, the barometer was again dropping, and McCaddon and Peterson had fallen sick. It seemed there was always something amiss with the men, the weather, or both.

November closed out with "a fine day," and the remaining men got "things in readiness for trip." By December 1, the two sick men (McCaddon and Peterson) were "quite out of sorts." The measuring chains were straightened, and the maps made ready. After six weeks of rain and snowstorms, December began with an all-day *sandstorm*.

On December 2, they "ran [a line] across the river," confirming the "intersect with the old line," making sure the line from the track terminus at Pierre would easily link with the route going up the Bad River. The temperatures were cold, ranging from –2 degrees at 6 a.m. to 2 degrees at 2 p.m. The night was "terribly cold," further complicated by a "high wind from NW." Still, the men were out connecting the new track terminus across the Missouri, via measurements, with the mouth of the Bad River. "It snows all the time," Irish wrote once again.

While in Fort Pierre on December 3, Irish wrote a letter home to his daughters, reporting the good with the bad:

> Mother has as nice a nest as a squirrel or mouse could make and I think she will be comfortable. I now go to camp and on up Bad River. It snows here now and is mid winter. Jack McCaddon is not able to stand the weather, he has a very weak back and poor constitution. I don't think he will live long.

December 4 was "very stormy," forcing the men to abandon their work only halfway through the day. Irish rode out to the mouth of Willow Creek, then returned to camp. Stoves had been ordered to help warm the men; they were expected but had not yet arrived, likely due to railroad blockades to the east.

Sunday, December 5, was "very cold and stormy," and Irish stayed "in house all day." This comment raises the possibility that their camp was not entirely comprised of tents. Perhaps by "house" he simply meant "home," which for now was the camp. Or maybe he was at the hotel in Pierre with Mrs. Irish. One hopes there was a solid-walled structure, as the temperature dropped to –26 degrees overnight, rising to a grand –10 degrees by 2 p.m. on the sixth—"A clear day at last, but oh! how cold." Again, the crew were out doing work, following creeks, checking cross-river measurements.

On the seventh, Irish's diary has one of the fairly uncommon entries full of measurements—degrees, minutes, angles of deflection, and the like. This particular set of measurements involved a point "near camp," so perhaps the men were able to return to the tents and stoves to get warm now and then.

On December 7, Irish wrote his daughters from Pierre. Sherwood's Hotel, he told them, was now on "the north edge of Murderer's Flat." The Irishes were not terribly happy living at the hotel, as it was too loud and rambunctious, the inhabitants having "as many eruptions as Mt. Vesuvius." Those eruptions caused, within the Irishes, "jars which like nervous earthquakes tremble[d] through one's systems, when hours of ease [were] excepted and sought for."

"Well, where am I?" he mused, as he lost his train of thought. "Oh! yes, Billy has got the Epizoo, bad, so have all the horses here that I know of. Also many folks, especially little children." ("The epizoo" is a colloquial term for an *epizootic disease*, meaning it affects many animals of one kind simultaneously. And there is some evidence supporting that equine influenza, at least, can spread to humans.[156]) He also shared that their friend Reed was now "one of the new county commissioners."

He expressed fatherly worries too:

> Well, Ruth, I want you to take all the recreation you can. I am so glad that you turn to books for a pastime, but don't put in all [Irish's underline] your time that way. Get good warm meals of digestible food + take good care of yourself on account of the calling you follow. Lizzie, you should be very careful about that skating and not go near the ice until you can skate. Seriously, I don't like to hear that you do so. One can so easily overdo at it, and then the other dangers. Well, I can not be always with you, so you must care for yourself.

The same day, he sent "by express 6 deer heads + hooves" as well as a porcupine skin. There were instructions about who should receive each of the sundry items within the package, along with the caution, "Look out when you handle the sack, or you will get the quills of the porcupine in your hands."

The men were out again on the eighth, and while they had accomplished a good amount of work, Irish observed that they seemed "very glum." In the same entry, he mentioned the crew had "so many new men," so the low morale could have been partially due to a disparity between the newbies' expectations and the reality of working in such hideous conditions; the more seasoned crew members would have been more accustomed to the cold and snow. Fortunately a stove arrived in camp, likely one of the more welcome additions in quite some time. And while the weather was cold, Irish framed it as "much better . . . –2 at 6am." One wonders how the new recruits were truly adjusting.

December 9, too, was spent determining measurements for crossing the river, creating a fourth line option. Once they determined the point where that line would meet the west bank of the river, they ran a "guide line . . . up to 6 miles above town, 1 mile above Willow creek." Irish ran an errand to Fort Pierre, and while there he took some benchmark readings to use on future maps.

"Weather warmer," Irish penned with cautious optimism on the tenth. The men had a "fine day" of work, getting to a "high point below Lance creek." The weather had been so nice that Irish was afraid to hope for a repeat. "I am very tired and sore," he concluded, the result of several days of steady work in the steady cold.

LAKOTA DELEGATION GOES TO WASHINGTON

On November 12, permission was granted for a delegation of Brule Sioux to visit Washington, DC, to celebrate the agreement, and the headmen from Cheyenne River Agency were invited as well.[157]

The delegation got their trip to Washington, but it did not go smoothly. To the east of New Ulm, Minnesota, at about 2:30 a.m. on December 9, a passenger train carrying 330 passengers, including the Lakota delegation, derailed near Courtland. Articles about the incident varied in detail and perspective, and some left out the Lakota passengers altogether. The *New Ulm Weekly Review*'s version identified the five Cheyenne River Agency headmen as "Little No-Heart, Rattling Rib, Blue Coat, White Swan, and Four Bear, under the charge of U.S. Indian Agent Leonard Love." While repairs to the train and tracks were made, the delegation returned to New Ulm, where they were the object of much attention. One of them "had never seen a train of cars until he reached Fort Pierre, and after the accident near Courtland he expressed his disgust of the white man's mode of traveling, in strong terms."[158]

Both Rattling Rib and White Swan had participated in the August council with the officers of the Chicago & North Western, and White Swan had visited one of Irish's camps to swap out some team members.

Lance Creek, near the location where it empties into the Bad River. S10-23

Irish had developed plans detailing various options for scouting and exploration. To accomplish one of these options, he sent a party out to explore one of the lines. "They did but little," he recorded, probably with a sigh. The weather had turned warm enough that the snow was melting, and the mud had returned. Again, *mud* is too kind a word. This was that clingy, gloppy gumbo that is a scourge upon the region when wet, making the men's work a miserable trudge.

At least the warm weather made for a comfortable night, and the next day, December 12, was also workably warm. Camp was mobilized and moved to the mouth of Lance Creek, and it would remain a main camp as the men worked up and down the river, camping at satellite locations as needed. The barometer had dropped throughout the day, reaching 28.10 by 7 p.m. Once at the new camp, Irish wrote several letters—some home, some to the officers of the railroad.

While some men worked to get camp fully established, Irish scouted upstream along the Bad River "to take a look at the topography." It was again "a fine day, warm and very pleasant." McCaddon remained ill, as was a man named Raymond, possibly a new crew member. Mrs. Irish, who had recently been ill, was "now better," up and about at Sherwood's Hotel in Fort Pierre.

On December 14, another "very pleasant" day, the men worked yet another river crossing option, Irish later writing, "We got in the 6° curve + ran to 5th crossing, where I found I had to change line; went back + shortened curve and ran on." Entries like this help to highlight how frustrating and fascinating the engineering was to determine the straightest path possible in a land full of hills, valleys, "rough country," and all manner of other challenges, especially given the physical constraints on how tight a curve could be for a railcar and its wheels.

Irish's skill set was well suited to the task, and progress was made in determining workable options. Two different curves were calculated and examined on the fifteenth, and while the temperatures were "fine," cloud cover had moved in. Somehow he also learned that Mrs. Reed and her mother, Mrs. Broadine, had visited the recuperating Mrs. Irish.

MAKING THE AUGUST COUNCIL AGREEMENTS OFFICIAL

Meanwhile, the work accomplished at the council in late August was being solidified via legal documents. Because this was an important step in the process, this longer tangent outlines the parameters of the agreements on both sides, setting the framework for Irish's work going forward. Various letters were written over a period of two weeks in December 1880, but they are shared together here for context.

The August councils granted permission for the survey. While Irish had done some preliminary explorations in March 1880, his reports from those explorations were likely

S10-24

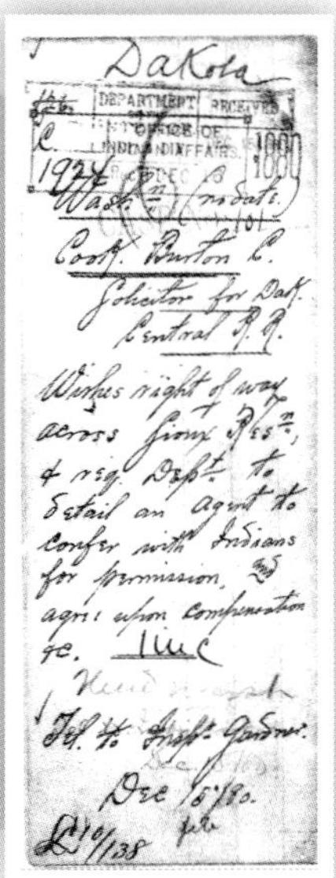

Dakota
DEPARTMENT OF INDIAN AFFAIRS RECEIVED DEC 1880
1924
Wash.
Coolf. Burton C.
Solicitor for Dak. Central R.R.
Wishes right of way across Sioux Res.n, & req. Dept. to detail an agent to confer with Indians for permission and agree upon compensation &c.
Fd. to Asst. Gardner.
Dec 15/80.
L 10/138

insufficient to determine an anticipated route in anything but general terms during the councils. Therefore, whether the August agreement involved a right-of-way for the eventual tracks based on this newly allowed survey is unknown, but a specific route was known by December. A telegram dated December 15, 1880, to Robert Gardner, inspector in the Indian services, read,

> Dakota Central has applied [to the Department of Interior] for right of way, two hundred feet wide, depot stations +c from West Pierre up Bad River to north fork, up north fork to head Gap creek, down Gap creek to Cheyenne River up Cheyenne River Valley to mouth north fork Cheyenne, up said fork to western boundary said Reservation. If Indians are willing to grant right of way, the Dakota Central will compensate them on same terms as Chicago, Milwaukee and Saint Paul. It is desirable that this be accomplished both for Indians as well as the general intent. Return to Standing Rock and endeavor to obtain assent of Indians as in case of the other railroad, from there proceed to the other Sioux Agencies formerly visited by you. The Cheyenne River and Lower Brule delegations will discuss the matter here.[159]

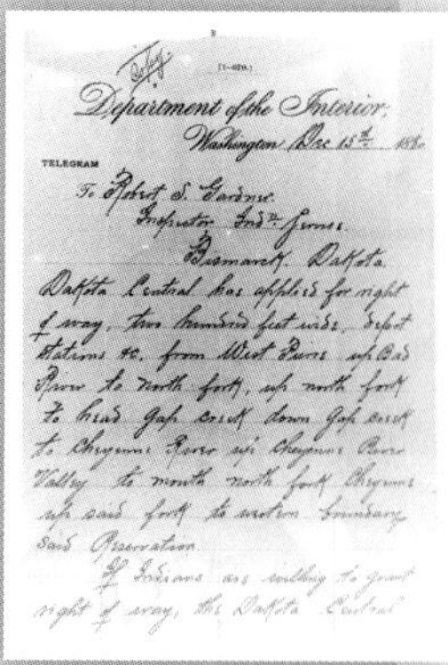
Department of the Interior,
Washington Dec 15th 1880
TELEGRAM
To Robert S. Gardner
Inspector Ind. Service
Bismarck, Dakota
Dakota Central has applied for right of way, two hundred feet wide, depot stations &c. from West Pierre up Bad River to north fork, up north fork to head Gap creek down Gap creek to Cheyenne River up Cheyenne River Valley to mouth north fork Cheyenne up said fork to western boundary said Reservation.
If Indians are willing to grant right of way, the Dakota Central

The wrapper for the telegram sent on December 15, 1880. S10-25

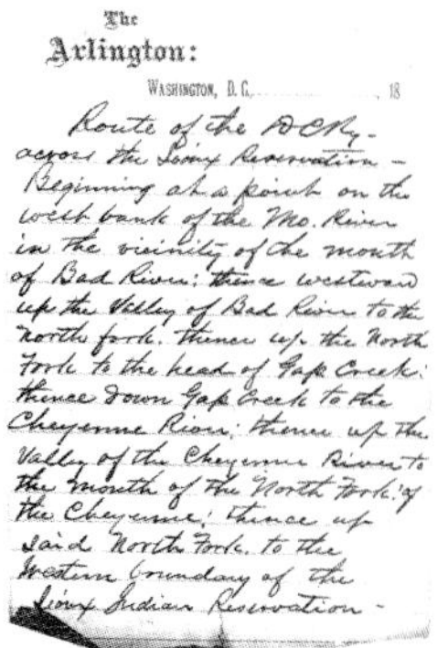
The Arlington:
WASHINGTON, D.C. 18
Route of the D.C.Ry. across the Sioux Reservation — Beginning at a point on the west bank of the Mo. River in the vicinity of the mouth of Bad River; thence westward up the Valley of Bad River to the north fork. thence up the North Fork to the head of Gap Creek; thence down Gap Creek to the Cheyenne River; thence up the Valley of the Cheyenne River to the mouth of the North Fork of the Cheyenne; thence up said North Fork to the western boundary of the Sioux Indian Reservation —

The December 15 telegram that outlined the route the Dakota Central intended to take from the Missouri River to the western edge of the Sioux Reservation, along the North Fork of the Cheyenne. S10-26

On December 23, 1880, a new document was established that detailed the agreement for the Dakota Central right-of-way through the Great Sioux Reservation, based upon the route Irish had identified as being the best to the northern Black Hills. The names and seals of individual members of the various tribes were listed, along with the names of the interpreters, witnesses, and agents. Written in flourishing legalese, it broke down into these elements granted to the Dakota Central:

- the free and undisturbed right to locate, construct, operate, and maintain its line of railway, commencing at a point on the west bank of the Missouri River at or near the mouth of Bad River, running in a westerly direction on the line surveyed and located by the said Dakota Central Railway, from West Pierre up Bad River to North Fork [of the Bad River], up North Fork [of the Bad River] to Lead Gap Creek, down Gap Creek to Cheyenne River, up Cheyenne River Valley to North Fork Cheyenne, up said fork to western boundary of said Sioux Indian Reservation in Dakota Territory.

- to occupy and hold . . . a strip of land not exceeding two hundred feet in width, extending the entire length of said line of railway, over and across the Great Sioux Indian Reservation in said Territory of Dakota.

For these considerations, the railroad, prior to the start of construction, would . . .

- [pay] the sum of one hundred and ten dollars per mile not exceeding two hundred feet in width, for lands located on the line as surveyed by the Dakota Central Railway Company.
- upon the commencement or beginning of work of constructing said railway [pay] a sum of money equal to one-half of the full amount to be paid for the sole use and benefit of said Indians.

Once construction reached 100 miles west of the Missouri, the railroad would . . .

- [pay] the remaining one-half and residue of the amount of money herein stipulated for the construction and operation of said railway.

Further, the Dakota Central had the right to . . .

- occupy and hold [station locations] along the line of said railway exclusively for railway purposes, not exceeding one hundred and sixty acres of land at any one point, [for the price of $4.00 per acre, paid according to the requirements of the secretary of the interior.]
- open and use for the purpose of constructing and operating said railway, a wagon road upon the line of said railway as located by the engineers [and connecting to the Black Hills] or with any wagon road intersecting or near the line of said railway over and across the Great Sioux Indian Reservation.

The Indians would . . .

- protect the railroad and its employees for the peaceful location, construction, and operation of the railway over and across the Sioux Reservation.

The agreement was then signed and approved by the "chiefs, headmen, and heads of a majority of families of the various Sioux Indians" located at several agencies. The dates each agency submitted their signed documents varied. The final version, signed a week later in Washington, had slightly different language, though the basics remained unchanged.

The Standing Rock Sioux signed on December 23, 1880; those at Lower Brule, Crow Creek, and Cheyenne River Agencies, on December 31, 1880; those at Rosebud Agency, on January 12, 1881; and Pine Ridge Agency, on January 18. Albert Keep, Marvin Hughitt, and Special Agent George Bliss affixed the corporate seal of the Chicago & North Western on July 1, 1881.[160]

The documents were progressing toward being legally binding, and Irish was doing his work. Full legal processes can be as slow-moving as survey work in the winter. This was no ordinary winter, and the legal machinery would prove even slower.

Back along the Bad River, the cloud cover of the fifteenth continued on the sixteenth, and lack of wind made the 26-degree air manageable. In fact, "the last vestige of the late snows [had] gone." Irish did not mention mud, despite the melting, and the men "ran ahead to a creek [they] called Peterson Creek," named for the man who brought the buckboard (yet another example of how maddeningly difficult it is to follow, exactly, their path.), at which point snow began to fall at such a rate "as to drive [them] off." The barometer read 28.10, seven inches of snow had fallen by 7 a.m., and it continued until 2 p.m.

The snow stopped on the morning of December 17, and the men managed to get over two miles of line run. Jacket and his wife also left camp, but no mention was made of Jacket's health status.

The snow had stopped, but it remained overcast, and on the eighteenth clouds appeared "threatening." The men got out on the line, though "snow [made] it very laborious walking," as they had to slice through brush as they went. The feared storm did not blow up, and there were signs of clearing as night descended. Fresh snow also has a way of softening the landscape, covering what lies beneath it, which could be a dormant bush to scratch the skin, a hole to twist an ankle or break a leg, or simply a deep pocket of snow to be dug out of. That conditions were slippery goes without saying. "Laborious" was the kindest of descriptions that could be used.

On December 19, Irish complained they'd "not seen the sun since the 15th," and "it [had] been mostly cloudy since the 10th"—grey mornings, grey days, and grey nights take a toll. In addition, Peterson was still laid up with a sore leg, which had afflicted him since soon after his arrival. Irish worked on maps and profiles of the recent lines, lines mapped to the "end of run," and the profiles "to end of levels."

The clouds parted enough on December 20 that Irish took time to celebrate, writing, "We saw the sun." This simple entry helps to illuminate how welcome the sun's appearance was. The air may not have been warm, but the sky was no longer grey—now a brilliant blue, which can do much to brighten the mood, even with cold air. It didn't last long, but a short time under a blue sky was appreciated.

By afternoon the weather again looked threatening, and though cold, it remained pleasant. On the twenty-first, they backed up a bit to try another variation on a line, then, when pleased with that location, ran another four and a quarter miles forward from that point. Leighton, Hutchinson, and Peterson fell sick, and snow began to fall.

It was a "two steps forward, one step back" type of effort. That stubborn trudging would continue, but not for long.

THE SAGA OF GAP CREEK

I really (*really!*) wanted to find the location of Gap Creek Camp. The crew spent the mid-October blizzard of 1880 there—the historic first blizzard of the Hard Winter of 1880–81—so I felt it was an important site to find. For me, having written a whole book about the Hard Winter, it was the most important campsite left unidentified. The problem was that many locations Irish mentioned as landmarks in any direction from Gap Creek were named *by the crew, for the crew*, and thus were on no maps other than Irish's.

As the surveyors moved upstream along Bad River, the tributary creek names correlated nicely to both modern and historic maps, but one varied: Dorian Creek, which some histories identify as also being called Mitchell Creek. Mitchell Creek is on modern maps, perfectly in place among the tally of other creek names the crew crossed over one after another. The Bad River tributaries were, in fact, the easiest to map of any landscape they traveled.

The same wasn't true for the eastern tributaries of the Cheyenne, nor did it remain true once the men traveled away from the Bad River, headed up the North Fork of the Bad, and into the area of land that drained into the Cheyenne near its confluence with the Belle Fourche (or North Fork of the Cheyenne).

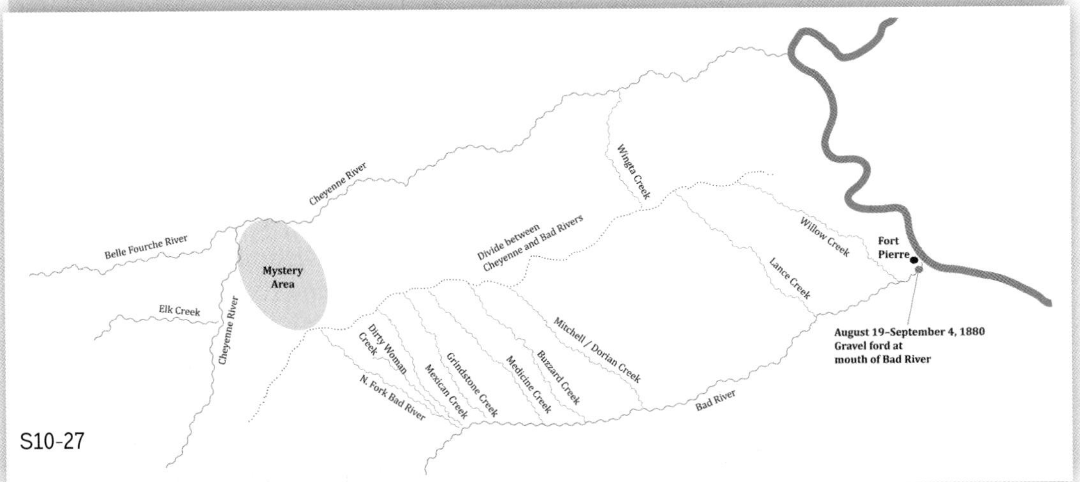

S10-27

Within that swath of land, northwest of modern Philip, South Dakota, lie landmarks that Irish did a fairly good job of describing, but with names that simply do not correlate to modern maps.

Because the pandemic delayed my access to Irish's maps, I tried to figure it out without his visual aids. I reached out to county historical societies, state historians, state hydrologists, state geologists . . . They did their best, referencing privately held databases. These sources were very useful in identifying some things, but none mentioned the elusive Gap Creek or the tributaries mentioned by Irish. I reached out to the National Archives, which houses the Chicago & North Western's route map that was filed with the US House of

Representatives. They were short-handed, and I could not go to Washington, DC.

The search included some absurdly comical incidents, several trips, and conversations with landowners. Then one magical day, the long-sought map was rolled out onto a table in the University of Iowa Libraries Special Collections and Archives department. I stood there for several moments, stunned, staring at it in silence. I may have even become a little teary. But even with (most of the) answers laying in front of me, I ended up letting out a laughing gasp—this incredibly detailed map was almost like a wink from beyond, with Irish telling me, "Ha, gotcha!"

See appendix III for a deeper dive into the humorous quest to locate Gap Creek. It was quite the adventure all on its own.

Section Eleven

WINTER CHANGES EVERYTHING

DECEMBER 22, 1880—SPRING 1881

The weather had turned brutal—with perilously cold temperatures and continuing blizzards—yet Irish and his crew kept at their work, bundled in buffalo coats and gloves, persevering against the inhospitable conditions. Due to the vast amounts of snow falling to the east, the railroads had become blocked, and the trains that had just recently arrived at the bank of the Missouri could not get through. A series of fires in Fort Pierre left Mrs. Irish in constant fear for her life. While she feared being incinerated, her husband was at risk of freezing to death. Finally, the blizzards and cold overwhelmed the work, and it was reluctantly halted altogether. Irish retreated to the new town of Pierre, where he and Mrs. Irish settled in, trapped until either the trains could run or the river became navigable. Before the river had a chance to host transportation, however, it went on a cataclysmic rampage.

Continued Work along the Bad River: December 22–31, 1880

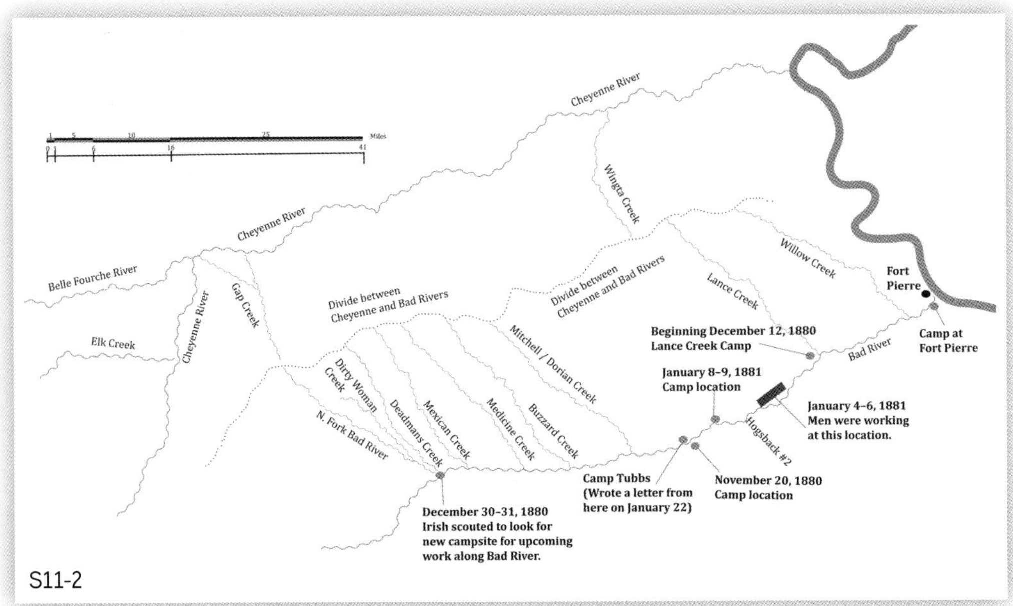

S11-2

The morning of December 22 was –9 degrees with a northwest wind. The men put in "a hard day's work" analyzing notes from the recent scouts. The sun again teasingly peeked out from the clouds, and Irish took the opportunity to make a reading. Through his efforts, he determined that his watch was slow by four minutes and thirty-two seconds.

The twenty-third was sunny and warm enough to be comfortable for the men, but fortunately not warm enough to thaw the ground and make mud. "We jump into estimates + maps deeply + get well; it's very hard work," wrote Irish. Peterson was also still lame.

On Christmas Eve 1880, the men "hurried [their] work on maps and profiles," and Irish resolved to work on the related reports once he was in Fort Pierre. It was a busy day. He and a crew member named Henry Brown took a team, "drove 15 miles up Bad River, and got back to camp at 4 PM, left for Fort Pierre at 5 PM, arrived 11 PM."

That late arrival from a camp relatively close by was due to becoming a bit . . . disoriented. "We had quite a time coming down last night," he confessed the next day, Christmas Day. "Got off the track and lost an hour of time. It was dark and stormy."

That same day, he finished his report, but there was a great deal of math yet to do. He may have been calculating distances; curves; the number, heights, and lengths of bridges needed; cuts and fills; or any number of other minute details that would make up the finished railroad. "The final figures take time," he wrote. "Ryther helps me much." The day was stormy, but the barometer read high. It was also a holiday, and "folks [were] all merry."

Irish spent the twenty-sixth in Fort Pierre, "work[ing] hard all day on the final figures." After finishing around noon, he declared himself "relieved." The calculations were for the initial twenty-mile run up the Bad River, including nearly twenty miles of line, 12,356 yards of truss bridge, and 71.5 feet of trestle.

SURVEYOR NOTEBOOKS

Throughout the surveying, Irish recorded the minutiae of the work in various leather-bound notebooks such as those pictured here. On the left side of each two-page spread was noted the location number along the line. On the right side were his drawings of the landscape (as shown below), along with any important notes, such as "creek banks steeper on this side." Understanding what he did with these notations is well beyond the scope of this book. But it is worth taking a moment to consider the engineering and mathematics that the men were undertaking.

S11-3

The columns upon columns of numbers, as shown in the sample here, were ingredients in calculations needed to determine every facet of the route. Where Irish mentioned there were many calculations to be done, this is the type of thing he was working with.

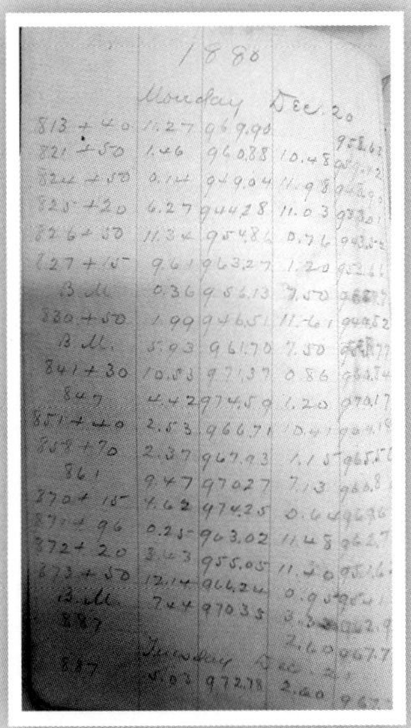

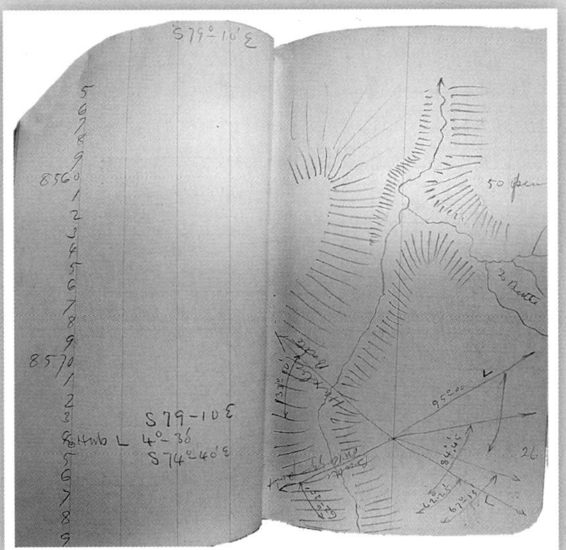

S11-4, S11-5

On December 26, Ruth sat down to compose a lengthy letter to her parents, sharing stories about their Christmas in Iowa. Lizzie had been away at a wedding, and upon returning, she decided to bring some cheer to the household. Ruth wrote,

> This being the time of year for Santa Clause to make his annual calls and donations, I will proceed to relate how I was treated by the generous "Old Fellow" . . . She [Lizzie impersonating Santa] called early and inquired at the door if there was an antiquated female in this house who answered to this description: namely in stature short, color dark but radiant as the [indistinct noun—possibly *poppy* or *pot fry* (seasoned cast iron pan?)], eyes dark as the hidden deeds of the midnight peace disturber, hair dark and short, same which resembling a well-worked broom. Expression resembling a thundercloud in the distance, which at one moment threatened destruction to all creation, the next, light breaks through the dense cloud and lights up the vast territory of her countenance with such a golden light (caused by biliousness) that her face resembles the full moon, both in shape and brilliance. Fannie [a hired woman], immediately recognizing me in this novel form, answered the inquiry in the affirmative.

Ruth was not a conventional woman of her time. Her parents sometimes expressed concern about her future and had evidently written something that caused this soliloquy on her part:

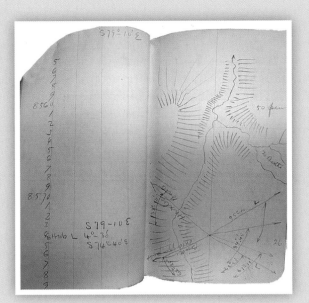

I do sincerely pray that you both will have a little confidence in me in regard to myself and my most mysterious future . . . I shall insist upon your ceasing to worry because you think me a fool on certain subjects. For I assure you I'm not and that I do not intend to marry anyone to reform them, because I have not time or inclination to do so, and then too I'm not quite so romantic. Now I've told you this several times [and] still you persist in worrying your selves + me too.

She then reassured her mother that "the plants and the bird [were] getting along nicely."

At 2:35 a.m. on December 27, Irish "was awakened from sound sleep by a cry of fire." The wind was high, and the temperature was –22 degrees—two factors that would complicate any firefighting effort. It was Harris's store. "In 25 minutes 4 houses log + frame were in ashes," and damages were estimated to fall between $7,000 and $10,000 (between $176,050 and $251,500 in 2019). The Irishes were staying at Sherwood's Grand Central Hotel, which was "in great danger for a time." Irish was concerned, so he "took [his] cash, papers + report + by help of Mrs. Irish tied them up in a blanket and threw them into the Bad River." They did the same with their clothes and other belongings, "but fortunately [they experienced] no loss." The excitement did, however, take at least a small toll. "This upset us for today," he conceded. The report that he'd worked so hard on was muddy, and the "trains [were] blocked by snow." It was his first mention of what would be a serious problem for the rest of the winter, as farther to the east, one of the winter's biggest storms had struck with significant force in the eastern part of Dakota Territory and in western Minnesota. Another casualty of the fire was Mrs. Irish's sense of security, a loss that would continue to plague her.

Despite the weather and Mrs. Irish's insecurity, Irish prepared to return to camp, the temperature reading –16 degrees at 6 a.m. on the twenty-eighth, with a high wind. He added, "I made haste and got off with Henry Brown at 11 AM. The gale was severe and snow was drifted badly. But we got on well and reached camp at 3 PM. Sharply cold. I was sick of colic when we got in camp."

On December 27, following the fire, Irish composed a letter to Ruth and Lizzie. He let them know that on Christmas Eve, he'd arrived at Sherwood's Hotel "at 11 PM, wrapped in robes and covered with frost," thus appearing the "veritable Santa Claus."

Unconstrained by the limited space of a diary page, he was able to share details of the fire more fully, telling them he was about to share with them "one of Fort Pierre's choicest excitements excepting a shooting match."

He had just finished writing a letter to Blunt and crawled into bed. Just as he drifted off to sleep he heard the cry, "Fire, fire!" The account continued as follows:

> I got out of bed in an instant. Mother as well struck a light. I ran to the front of the hotel and saw that Geo. Harris' store and house was all ablaze. It looked threatening. Wind high and very cold. I ran back, Mother had dressed, and made up a good fire. We packed up, tied up and bunched up. I took the valuables and threw them over the back fence into Bad River. Then waited results. The fire went down gradually and we were safe. We moved back, went to bed, got some sleep, and today it all is quiet on Bad River. Geo. Harris' place, Rousseau's old quarters, and all else on that side of the street is a total wreck up to the Drug Store. . . . Mother had kept up bravely until . . . she broke down, took a good cry over it. Is now quiet also, and full of cider . . . Well, I am off for camp way up towards the head of classic Bad River. . . . Mother says she shall start back at once. I hope she will change her mind for, really, she is improving in health.

Here, Irish may have used the word *cider* as a euphemism; Mrs. Irish was not anti-drink, as was so common among the "proper women" of the era, and who could blame her for indulging after such an experience?

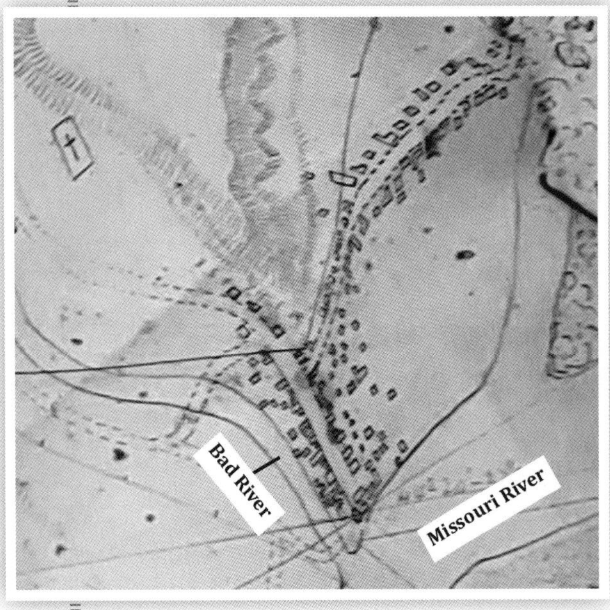

Irish had made a map of the area where the Bad River emptied into the Missouri River. This close-up of that map shows the structures along the main street of Fort Pierre, one of which was Sherwood's Grand Central Hotel. Irish noted that he'd bagged up his papers and tossed them over the back fence, into the Bad River. S11-6

After Irish left for the camp up the Bad River, Mrs. Irish wrote a letter of her own. Knowing her daughters would be worried about their father's safety in the cold, she told them, "I am anxious about him but he said I should not be for he had been out when it was worse. He was dressed very heavy + had lots of robes + blankets to wrap in, had a man with him too."

Still deeply unsettled by the fire, she nervously told her daughters, "I am in a terrible sweat, expect to get all my things burned any time." After all, her room was full of paper, fabric, and wood. The building itself was wood and tar paper, as were the surrounding buildings, some as close as three feet away. Not only that, but there was "hay + lumber all around."

She wanted to flee Dakota Territory and return home, but her husband wanted her to stay. Her solution was to demand that he build her a cave to protect her from the fire hazards. "Such a time as we did have Sunday night," she remembered. "I never saw buildings go so quickly, even the log ones that had dirt roofs."

With fire threatening their lodging, Irish had told her to run towards Waldron's Bull Team Camp, but she "could not get out, for the blaze leaped across to Sherwood's porch," igniting the hotel. With the first escape route blocked off, she then "planned to run up Bad river + out of the way."

Despite that plan, and for whatever reason, she remained at Sherwood's, which, due to a heavy layer of snow on its roof, was saved "to the delight of all."

She was an emotional wreck in the fire's aftermath, and while she had her "things all packed," she admitted that it hardly mattered, as she'd not be able to get them out of the hotel on her own. She worried, too, that with the bitter cold, "one would freeze" if forced to go out into the elements to escape a fire. By the end of the letter, she'd perhaps spent her immediate emotions, and wanted to calm any alarm she had caused for Ruth and Lizzie, adding, "Well, I must try + be light hearted."

Mrs. Irish's fear of fire would continue.

COMBATING FIRE BEFORE IT BEGINS

Fire was a constant threat in the hastily built frontier towns, where hay, dried lumber, and other flammables were jumbled together near stoves—easily taken advantage of by people with nefarious purposes. For example, one such person took a horseshoe, heated it to a glow, wrapped it in burlap, and tossed it up on a blacksmith shop's roof in an attempt to burn it down; fortunately he was unsuccessful.[161]

At the beginning of the new year, the citizens of Fort Pierre gathered for a "Fire Meeting" to discuss organized methods of combating the age-old foe, the editor of the *Fort Pierre Weekly Signal* writing, "Every business man should be present as the company is a benefit to all."[162]

December 29 was "severe," with the temperature reading –22 degrees along with a "high wind all day and snow flying badly." The next day, the men stubbornly crept up the Bad River valley, "the wind NW a gale. Snow flying thick." Irish and Elston (who may have stayed in place of his stepson, Jacket) "pushed on and passed the S Fork Bad River and camped for the night at upper forks." Irish lamented, "I am quite sick with a bad cold. This was a bad day.

Snow drifted." They'd made nearly seventy miles since leaving Fort Pierre the day before.

Pause to again think about the conditions these men and their horses were enduring—the frightful cold. It was quite the opposite of what Mrs. Irish was fearing—the frightful flame.

On December 28, Mrs. Irish again wrote to her daughters. First, she reassured them that their father was safe, a man having come to Fort Pierre to let her know Irish had safely reached camp. She then mused, "One can stand the cold here better than in Iowa if the wind does not blow," adding that the wind had stopped, and the temperature had dropped to −20 degrees.

She remained quite unsettled in the wake of the fire, telling her daughters, "I packed all I could of my things last night + slept with a goodly share of my clothes on so I could get out if I had to in double quick time. My surroundings are anything but desirable." She clarified, "I [had] gotten so I liked my room after I had [a] window put in on [the] south side + the other cleaned + decorated, but I can't overcome my fear with my surroundings of hay + other quick combustibles."

Her fear was so strong that she'd taken all of her "pretty things" down from the walls. "I dare not take dovers powders," she noted in her rattled state of mind, "for fear of not being unable to waken in danger." Of course, what she *meant* was that Dover's powder, a common opium-containing medicinal of the time, would knock her out such that she'd sleep right through any fire alarm. Her words, however, ricochet into all sorts of contradictions via her terror—on top of the double negative "not being unable to waken."

After getting to the bottom of the page, she had more to add, writing sideways on the edge of the sheet, "I am expecting to be cremated any time. People that [prematurely] mourned my death . . . may have a reality yet."

While Mrs. Irish was prepared to spring from the hotel room while wearing her entire wardrobe and carrying the rest of her belongings, Irish was in camp at Lance Creek, writing of his trip from Fort Pierre, "I drove in all the bad windy plains, for Henry had nothing over his face." He also thanked her for the winter clothes she had prepared that allowed him to manage the ordeal: "I had a slight attack of neuralgia of the bowels after we got here, it lasted until 10 PM. I am over it now and this morning feel as happy as you please."

He also sent her instructions, though whether to keep her healthy or to keep her calm may be up for debate:

> Now you keep warm, take some quinine of mornings, before breakfast mind you now . . . take good doses for three days, only one as above each day. Gargle your throat often, and take the

> Collinsonia 4 days at a time, then drop it for 3 days and take quinine as above. Keep warm. Keep quiet [Irish's underlines], don't go about much until this cold spree is over.

(Collinsonia is an herbal remedy often associated with relief of pain as well as respiratory and digestive issues.)

The year 1880 took its final bow after "a bad night" for Irish. Fortunately, he was feeling improved by morning, and after breakfast, he and Billy the horse "rode on up the river to look for a camping place. Found a nice one. Snow 12 inches deep on levels and drift 2 to 3 ft deep." He returned to the main camp at 2:30 p.m. and declared it "a fine day, no wind, clear, much warmer."

On New Year's Eve, from camp at Lance Creek, Irish wrote to his wife:

> I am well, and hope that you will not for a moment think that I suffered coming up. Why, we had ourselves so nicely bundled that had we to sit out all night in a storm, we should have been warm. It was a hard storm, though. Today was nice. I have been up 27 miles above here to find a new camp ground. I found a perfect heaven of a place. It's above the herder's camps, and the game is thick. Now we will start Indian stories afloat to keep hunters and cattle men out of our way, so if you hear Indian stories, it is from this source.

This is the admission hinted at earlier, in Irish's March 27, 1880, letter written from Fort Pierre. To keep locals from pestering them in their work, Irish planted "Indian stories" to keep people afraid and away. This is one of the few times Irish did something less than admirable in the course of his work, leveraging fear to create a false "reality." Unfortunately, false stories such as these could make their way into newspapers, creating a false sense of danger among White people, resulting in true danger to the Native peoples.

He then told her he planned to return to Fort Pierre, writing,

> I shall come down as soon as I get the west 20 miles run, which will be, I think, about the end of next week if no blizzard comes. So don't run off. You should have seen Billy when I got on his back this AM; he was as proud as a peacock. He and I are great companions. He scared up a herd of 7 deer—lord, how they ran off. Billy wanted to follow the rascals; he has been used to hunting them.

Mrs. Irish also wrote a letter on New Year's Eve, this one home to Ruth and Lizzie, including, "I must say that I am tired of waiting for a train. It will be a week tomorrow since we had any." She expressed her desire for the railroads to bypass Minnesota, for the blockades that would define the coming winter had already been a serious problem, and most of them were, in fact, in Minnesota. This refrain would appear many times in newspapers across Dakota Territory.

The weather, she declared, was dreadful: "The cold first of this [year] was the severest of the winter so far; one of the stages coming from the Hills has not been heard from since Monday. The Agent stops here + he is dreadfully worried. . . . The drive between stations is 30 miles." She also lamented having to entertain at the hotel. It was more convenient than living at home in terms of having to clean, but the kitchen was well below her standards. "It is so dirty," she complained, and there was evidently a pig lying on the kitchen floor. "Everything tastes + smells of dirty hog."

In Iowa City, a letter was being written for the parents as well. Ruth let them know that George the bird had stopped singing. He was alive and well, but apparently brooding: "I'm sure George would sing for joy at hearing your voices again until his little throat would burst. I honestly believe the reason he doesn't sing is just because he misses you and so is exceedingly lonely."

New Year and Worse Weather: January 1–February 23, 1881

Trains were not running, and the mail was also waylaid, so the book Irish intended to serve as his 1881 diary had not yet arrived. He found some blank pages in the back of the previous one, within the "memos and accounts" section. There he scribbled that 1881 began with the men working on maps "all day, hard, but [they] did not get it done." Chinook winds blew, warming the day to a welcome 27 degrees.

January 2 also began warm, and he hoped to make up for lost time, but it got colder as the day went on, Irish writing, "Had a hard time. Peterson cannot do the work." Despite the bitter cold, the men defiantly tried to work, and five loads of camp gear were sent ahead to the next campsite, indicating they had no intention of giving up.

By January 4, a mix of rain and sleet was falling while the men worked a couple dozen miles to the west of Fort Pierre, along a ridge they called the "Hogs Back." In fact, there were two, as on January 5, they were working on a second "Hogs Back." They "had a hard time" and "did not get [it] done," and the rain continued all morning before turning to snow. "It spit snow all day," he complained. Additionally, the thawing and freezing had caused a crust to form on the snow. Such crust makes travel difficult; rather than simply giving way when stepped on, the crust breaks, creating sharp, jagged edges that can cut skin.

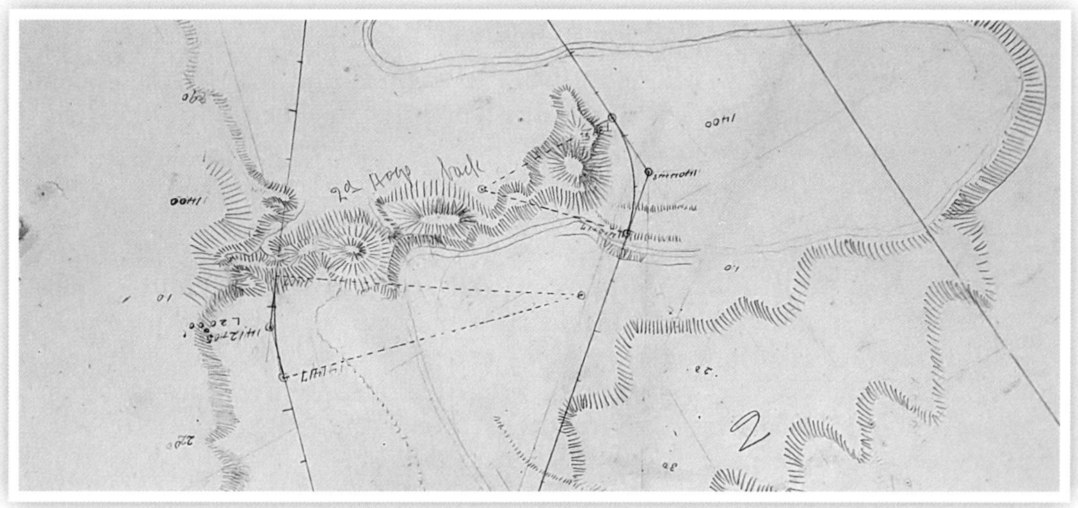

The second of the two locations labelled "Hogs Back"; Irish did not draw the first one on the final map. Two route options are shown: one that would require a cut (left side) and one that would have skirted around the formation. The cut option was eventually selected. S11-7

RAILROAD BLOCKADES SETTLE IN

According to the *Fort Pierre Weekly Signal*, the winter was already taking a toll on the new railroad, keeping most of the trains well away from the shiny new town of Pierre and the enterprising new merchants waiting for the newly completed rails to deliver customers out to where the tracks met the Missouri. Despite the operational delays, the railroad company had recently made an agreement with the Lakotas on the west side of the river, purchasing "640 acres of land." An article intimated that the weather was too bad for the survey work to proceed.[163]

The Dakota Central R. R., is hav-ing a devil [illegible] a time with the snow.

[illegible]y. It is hardly probable that the company intend pushing the road toward the Hills, unless they are compelled to do so by their great r[illegible]al.

S11-8, S11-9

Thursday, January 6, saw more work on that second Hogs Back, under "very cold and getting colder" conditions. On only a few occasions did Irish continue to take weather readings, but this day was one of those. He took readings at 6, 8, 9, and 9:30 p.m., and they were, respectively, –12, –26, –30, and –32 degrees.

At the 5:30 a.m. reading on January 7, the sky was clear, and the thermometer read "–38/–40" degrees. In addition to the dangerously cold temperatures, Irish had four sick men: Chamberlain, Leighton, Mudra, and Griffin (a recent addition). Rather than trying to work, the men stayed in camp. While the sick ones rested, Irish worked on maps, with Tubbs assisting on the profiles. The day was "intensely cold," though the 2:30 p.m. reading was 21 degrees, a significant warm-up since that morning.

In an undated letter that was likely sent not long after Irish learned that George the bird had stopped singing, Irish wrote to his daughters, "'It's true blue winter here. But I have Mother nicely fixed up and will soon have my camp also well fixed."" He then turned his attention to the bird. "Keep George warm with plenty of green stuff to eat and plenty of water, and hang up another bird for company in the room if he likes it."

By "nicely fixed up," it's unclear whether he meant Mrs. Irish was still housed at Sherwood's Hotel—anticipating being cremated in a flash fire—or whether he had made arrangements for her to move to a different location. The answer would come a little further on, via another letter.

Irish was worried about the cold. In fact, he confided, in a note of resignation in his diary on January 8, that perhaps it would be best to "move camp, as [it was] too cold to work the line." It was –16 degrees when they began the move at 10 a.m. They were able to travel thirteen miles, a decent distance considering there was snow, mud, and a high wind blowing. They found a spot with timber and set up camp there.

The timber may have provided wood for fires and some protection from the wind, but the air didn't care about such conveniences. It was "an awful, cold night," and Irish was awoken by his cold feet at 2 a.m. on January 9 and had to warm them. While up, he looked at the thermometer, which read –36 degrees. Another crew member, Royston, was also suffering from cold feet. When 5 a.m. came, it was -43 degrees with calm air, and the men got up to begin the move again, wanting to reach the main camp and keep their bodies in motion. They came into the main camp at 10 a.m. and "found Sherwood all right." Three tents were set up, and the 2-degree reading at 2 p.m. meant there had been "a rise in temp of 45 degrees." That relative warmth did not last, for it was yet another "awful cold night."

The men spent January 10 getting the camp in order to keep their blood flowing, while the atmosphere threatened an impending storm. A storm did not seem to develop, but a wind must have blown up, as Irish noted that by night it was snowing hard, yet there were no clouds. In fact, he noted, "The moon shines brightly." It is likely that a strong wind was picking up already-fallen snow and swirling it around, imitating a storm. Irish set himself to work on the topographic maps of the recent work.

The intrepid men again tried to work on the eleventh. It was –10 degrees at the morning reading. After a mere two miles, they gave up the effort, having "suffered much" by the cold and the "sharp wind." The barometer was dropping, reading 27.80 at sundown—a worrying sign.

There was no raging storm on the morning of January 12, however, so the men headed out at sunrise, another attempt at work. "It was sharply cold," followed soon by a northwest wind that blew up and "caused us much suffering." They kept working, "in snow 7" to 12" deep," until 2 p.m., when the "wind was so high," causing the snow to fly about so much that the work was again stopped. The men returned to camp, dejected. "It was a very cold day," wrote Irish, as if it needed repeating.

The conditions were inhospitable enough that the twelfth was yet another "cold stormy day" spent in camp, the only mentioned accomplishment being that of taking "sights of latitude"—and, one can assume, hoping for better conditions.

The hinted-at storm finally brewed up on January 13, striking overnight. It did not last long, however, and the wind had stopped by the morning thermometer reading, which taunted the men at –22 degrees. Irish decided to stay in camp rather than push out into the cold, despite the lack of wind. By 9 p.m. it was –31 degrees.

January 14 began with a –26-degree reading and developed into a "cold, stormy day." The thermometer read zero at some point—a kind relief, relatively speaking. The men busied themselves around camp again, and Irish "completed the map to end of line," possibly meaning the Hogs Back lines they had experimented with earlier. A team and wagon came into camp from Fort Pierre in the evening.

On January 15, the men awoke to a bright –23-degree morning and headed out to work. They discovered that the transit was broken, but they continued taking readings until 2:30 p.m., using the transit as best they could. They had to stop at 2:30 due to snow and wind that had again blown up to besiege them.

DIPHTHERIA DEATHS

While the men tenaciously fought the weather, two children, beloved of friends, were lost to diphtheria back in Fort Pierre; a ten-year-old granddaughter of Sherwood (Maud Norwood) and four-year-old Minnie Chamberlain were both lost to the disease days apart, both funerals presided over by

Reverend W. B. Williams.[164] One wonders whether Mrs. Irish attended one or both of these heartbreaking observances, especially since little Maud's was held at the hotel owned by her grandparents.

The conditions were beginning to impact the crew. Peterson, Leighton, and Chambers all headed east towards Fort Pierre. Joe Mudra was feeling better, and it appears he stayed with Irish. Of the weather, Irish wrote, "How stormy it is, wind not high but very cold. Range from +10 to −25, −38, +c for the past 12 days." One imagines that Irish may have spent more time considering the merits of pushing the work forward at this point.

Unfortunately, the final diary entry was recorded on January 15, 1881, closing the window that allowed us to tag along with the men. That may be disappointing, but there are still some bits and pieces that allow us to wrap up the story a bit.

A letter written to Mrs. Irish on January 22 from Camp Tubbs, approximately thirty miles west of Fort Pierre, helps fill in details after the diary entries stop:

> I am working on towards the setting sun. I have a bad cold, nothing serious. Joe is better, Elston can't speak above a whisper, and Tenney is not at all well. But we all got out at work today and got within 3 miles of the end of [the] 2d 20 miles. Joe was so weak that I gave him a small bottle of his favorite remedy [another euphemism for alcohol?] and told him that you sent it to him. You cannot imagine what a change it has wrought in him already. I have one more day on the line and two or three on the maps, then I come down. I have the teams [running regular morning] trips between Pierre and our camps; I send this down tomorrow + it should reach you on Tuesday at farthest.
>
> Tell me all the news you can, write if only a short letter. I feel sure that you are comfortable, and how I do hope [you are] happy and well. You do not know how blue I felt that morning when I came away and that room [was] not fixed. But the report you gave of work begun cheered me up. We had a very hard storm, a real blizzard of snow to drive in the second day, but no one suffered at all except Raymond. He was somewhat scared. I shall have Shorty (Mr Sinclair) come to see you each trip and get the letters.

A segment of the preliminary survey map of the Bad River, showing both the location of Camp Tubbs (left of center) and the campsite for November 20, 1880 (lower right). S11-10

Irish intended to keep the survey work going, despite the worsening winter. It is also likely that none of the women let Irish know that his wife expected death by conflagration as she awaited his return to Fort Pierre. Whether Mrs. Irish remained there by choice is irrelevant; it was impossible to leave.

On January 23, Irish wrote home from Camp Tubbs, letting his daughters know about a new arrangement he had made to protect their mother from news that might upset her, as he was concerned about her level of anxiety. "Mother is about the same," he told them. "She got a bad set back at the Sherwood Hotel and laid abed sick for a week. When I left her, she was cheery and looked much better. I moved her over to the Stebbins House in Pierre, got her a good room, clean bed, and good victuals [food], so [I] think she will get on."

The arrangements for this move were evidently unknown to Mrs. Irish, however:

> I pay $10 per week for her, but she must never know it . . . Be careful not to tell too much of family troubles in letters to Mother. Send all your letters to Matto PO Pierre Dak. When you write anything for me only, [send it] direct to Fort Pierre, and it will come to me direct. I am in great haste, as the team is waiting. 25° below zero this AM. −43 the coldest, on morning 9th Jan.

Thus, family letters would land on the east side of the river, and anything the daughters wished only their father to know were sent to the west side. (Pierre was temporarily named Matto by a post office official.[165] The railroad officials were unhappy and must have used their sway, as the name disappeared very quickly, Pierre being on the official plat drawing. *Matto* was a derivation of the Lakota word for *bear*.[166])

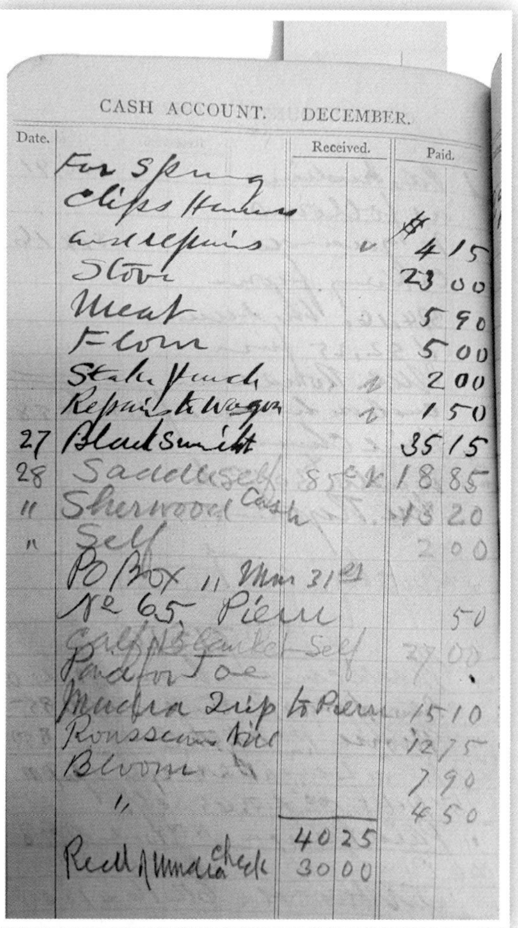

CASH ACCOUNT. DECEMBER.

Date.		Received.	Paid.
	For Spring Clips Hinges and repairs		$4 15
	Stove		23 00
	Meat		5 90
	Flour		5 00
	Stake Punch		2 00
	Repair to Wagon		1 50
27	Blacksmith		35 15
28	Saddle Self		18 85
"	Sherwood Cash		13 20
"	Self		2 00
	PO Box " Mar 31st No 65 Pierre		50
	[illegible]		[illegible]
	Paid for [illegible]		
	Madra Trip to Pierre		15 10
	Rousseau Bill		12 75
	Bloom		7 90
	"		4 50
		40 25	
	Recd Amanda check	30 00	

A page from the expense journal that included PO Box #65 in Pierre, where mail intended for Mrs. Irish could be sent. S11-11

Ruth wrote a letter on January 29 that was likely on its way before she received the one mentioned above from her father. In it, she was glad to let her parents know that George, the family bird, had resumed singing. Despite that good news, the daughters were experiencing their own anxieties, worried about their parents, out on the isolated frontier.

"We have had extremely cold weather this winter," she wrote, "and we have worried so much about both of you, especially during the past two weeks." No letters had reached the daughters during those two weeks, and due to the "heavy fall of snow" they knew was afflicting Dakota Territory, they feared their father "would be snowed in and run short of provisions" and that their mother "would get burned out, &c." She continued, "But I sincerely trust that neither of these calamities overtook either of you. We received a letter from Mother on Thursday which had been on the road fifteen days." It must have been excruciating for all four of them to not have regular reassurances about the safety of the others.

The Bad River follows its twisting path against the base of the far bluffs. The 1881 survey came to an end within this stretch. S11-12

Survey work on the Dakota Central came to an end in February 1881, just to the west of modern Van Metre, South Dakota, in a bend of the Bad River. The men were just short of thirty miles west of Fort Pierre, Dakota Territory. Irish sent a telegram home—the date is not clear—to tell his daughters that the survey party had moved to Pierre and that they were well.

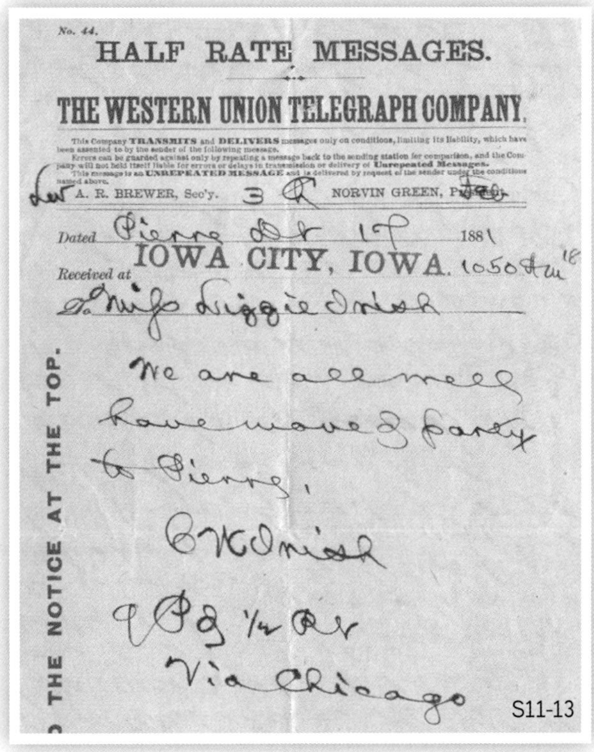

No. 44.

HALF RATE MESSAGES.

THE WESTERN UNION TELEGRAPH COMPANY.

This Company TRANSMITS and DELIVERS messages only on conditions, limiting its liability, which have been assented to by the sender of the following message.
Errors can be guarded against only by repeating a message back to the sending station for comparison, and the Company will not hold itself liable for errors or delays in transmission or delivery of Unrepeated Messages.
This message is an UNREPEATED MESSAGE and is delivered by request of the sender under the conditions named above.

A. R. BREWER, Sec'y. 3 NORVIN GREEN, President.

Dated Pierre 1881

Received at IOWA CITY, IOWA.

To Miss Lizzie Irish

We are all well
have moved party
to Pierre.

C W Irish

Via Chicago

THE NOTICE AT THE TOP.

S11-13

MIDWINTER CONDITIONS

The railroad snow blockades in Minnesota were well established by February, and the little communities on either side of the Missouri were settling in, waiting for spring. Snow was "something less than ten feet deep on the prairies," and the stages were unable to run. It was "fearful cold" and windy. The mail was being brought in by sled, and men were shoveling out the tracks up and down the line, only to have the wind sift it right back in before trains could even try to break through.[167]

It wasn't all hopeless, however. Due to the approximately two months that trains were able to operate on the western end of the Dakota Central, there were warehouses full of goods in Pierre. A local hotel and restaurant—whose operator was curiously named Snow—advertised plenty of oysters for sale. Another business, Sparks & Allen's, also had eggs for sale. A masquerade ball was held at the end of February, luring three soldiers down from Fort Sully, a considerable distance in good conditions, and a life-risking venture in the unpredictable weather.[168] For now, the residents of Pierre and Fort Pierre were weathering their isolation without too much trouble.

Work Comes to a Stop: February 24–March 26, 1881

On February 24, Irish wrote a long letter to his daughters to bring them up to date on the hair-raising incidents that had brought his survey job for the Dakota Central to an end for the winter, and how he and Mrs. Irish were awaiting spring—like so many other tens of thousands of people impacted by the great railroad blockades.

In his February 24 letter home from Pierre, Irish provided considerable interesting details about what he and his crew encountered in their final days of survey work, so a large chunk of the letter is included below:

> The storms and blockade of this winter have played many pranks with business and plans of all the people of this great territory. Indeed, most serious has it been to some. Now I am one of the victims, for all my plans have been upset, and here I am with mother, living in the depot while I get my office work done and the snow gets ready to melt. It would take a book to contain the incidents of our experience here. We are very well and have some fun as the winter days and storms roll along, but I will first tell you of my experience on Bad River. We got on slowly, for the winter was very cold and blustery from the outset, and at last had reached 40 miles from the mouth. The snow kept on getting deeper and deeper, and at last, on the 4th of Feb., came a storm

such as I never saw the like before. The snow fell for 62 hours to the depth of 2 1/2 feet, making, with what was on the ground before it, 3 feet 4 inches deep.

I tell you, I was in a fix; I was about 15 miles from camp with a team and one man. We started back, had to leave the buckboard, all our bedding, and other things to the mercy of the elements and of the wolves, and on horseback we made our way into camp late at night, starved and nearly frozen.

Then I had to go on horse back to Pierre for help to get the camp away, so that I was travelling 5 days in the storm.

Well, we got back in good order, except Elston, Jacket's stepfather, who shot himself through the hand. Well, I put the men and all the camp things into the log dance house on the left hand side of the road as you go out of Pierre [possibly Fort Pierre] towards our old camp.

I built a stable against the side of it and have the horses in there safe and sound. My goodness, the snow which is piled up about here! I am sure from all that I can see and learn that when all this snow and ice thaws out, there will be a great flood below as well as here. It is a season which no one here, however old, has seen the like of. Then again, the snow is so much deeper down from the east that it is impossible to get a train along for 300 miles . . . It is now 37 days since we have had a mail or any other communication except by telegraph, and it will be weeks yet before we can get out of here. We, that is mother and I, keep well. We live in the depot building with Mr. Williams the agent. . . .

We have a good time and [are] well indeed. It's so quiet and nice here. Old Joe [Mudra] boards here and works for his board. Tubbs is the Boss over at the Dann house, and we all are waiting for the snow to get out of the way. Mother and I attended the masquerade ball on the night of 22nd, had a good time, will let her describe it. It was too funny. Of course, I have no news, can only say that the men who own cattle here expect to lose about all their cattle from sheer starvation. The snow is so deep that no grass is to be seen. Feed of all kinds is scarce and [its cost] high, and there are small towns in both Minnesota and Dakota which have long since burned their last gallon of oil and can see ahead to the time when they will be eating the last of the provisions.

At Watertown, Dakota, they have no wood and are at work cutting up the RR bridges for fuel. There is plenty to eat at this point. Wolves are hungry and go about in droves, and many a luckless antelope and deer gets run into a deep snow bank and is torn limb from limb before he has quite drawn his last breath.

Today (the 24th) it is warm and thawing rapidly, while from a point 35 miles east of here or down the RR for 15 miles, a hard storm is raging. Mother says she is too lazy to write. She lies on a lounge near by while I write. I am awful busy on payrolls, vouchers, bills, maps, and profiles. Hope to get them all off my hands soon and that by that time it will be so that we can start home. Reed will move to town soon. We look for a flood and will get out on a big hill to escape it.

Back in Iowa City, Ruth was wondering whether it was of any use to write back; would her letters ever reach her parents with the blockades in place?

Conditions were snowy in Iowa too. Despite the blockades and her doubts about the mail, Ruth wrote and sent a letter in early March:

I just feel as if it were hardly any use to write, for the continued storms will keep the roads blockaded from snow until next Aug., hence prevent the letter from reaching you. I do really hope that you both have succeeded in keeping well and comfortable, but I have my doubts and fears in the matter.

The snow has been to the top of our north fence now for six weeks, of course the deepest places are caused by drifting, yet we have not had less than two feet on the level since New Year's. The farmers cannot get into the towns for their necessary comforts or to bring in the much needed butter, eggs, and wood. Yet we continue to live in the hope that things will not be always thus.

By early March, the residents of both Pierre and Fort Pierre were getting restless and worried. The Missouri was notoriously unpredictable, and fears of a flood were growing. Some residents were "building ware houses up on the high ground where the water [could not] reach them."[169] The snow and cold had been treacherous, and the freighters were taking heavy losses. The March 5 *Fort Pierre Weekly Signal* reported that the cold and snow were killing many work animals: "La Plant lost about forty head of oxen. Frank Alderich lost nearly all of his [oxen or mule] train, and many other freighters have lost heavily."[170]

Word had it that the Cheyenne River was running "very high," but the surplus water had yet to reach the Fort Pierre area."[171] It was only a matter of time—and when it burst loose, it would be cataclysmic.

Work on maps, profiles, reports, and letters continued, and by March 10, Irish felt he was approaching the final documentation of the physical work.

While taking a break on March 10, Irish wrote to Ruth and Lizzie:

We are surrounded by vast fields of snow. It is over 2 1/2 feet deep all about us, and although we have had several days of thaw, still the earth in every direction that the eye can reach to is a blank white. This has had effect upon the eyes, and I hear of many cases of snow blindness. My own eyes are very weak on that account. . . .

No man however old . . . remembers such a winter and such a snow fall. The Missouri river here has ice three feet thick over it. The water has been raising so as now to be 8 feet above low water mark. Yet the ice does not break up. We all expect a frightful flood when the vast snow field comes down, and every one in the two towns is ready to move to the bluffs. Cattle are dying off in large numbers, and I expect that fully 3/4 of all the cattle in this country will die of starvation. . . .

We have had only one train here since the 12th of Dec. and for 28 days only one stage got here from Deadwood. They now make the trip in 6 to sometimes 4 days. It takes them only 32 hours in good roads and weather, and this is our only way out from here now. . . .

We have plenty to eat as yet but there is no butter nor bacon in town. We can stand it until the snow permits a train or the ice a boat. We shall leave here the first opportunity. Now write and direct via Yankton as that is the only way to reach us by letter. When you telegraph, do so by half rate message. . . .

We are having the first real March storm now; it has blown great gales and rained and sleeted all day.

UPDATE ON THE RAILROAD BLOCKADES

While the Irishes wrote letters back and forth, the *Fort Pierre Weekly Signal* reported that Sherwood's Hotel was provisioned "to last . . . until the blockade is over." He'd made his own butter over the winter, and also had "plenty of meat and vegetables." Sherwood's business was doing well enough that plans were afoot to "raise the roof of his house [hotel] one and one-half stories, and extend the dining room to a length of fifty feet, by turning the office into a dining room and building a new office on to the east side of the hotel."[172]

There was optimism, too, as residents knew the blockades would eventually come to an end. Shovelers were working to clear the tracks west of Sleepy

Eye, Minnesota,[173] bringing renewed hope to the readers. Of course, the shovelers had been working west of Sleepy Eye all winter, and there were storms on the horizon yet, too.

The Missouri experienced a five-foot rise by March 19, and water was reported to be "nearly up to the doors,"[174] though it was still behaving in a relatively manageable fashion. Only one more edition of the *Fort Pierre Weekly Signal* would go to press before calamity struck.

Based on previous letters, it can be said that Mr. and Mrs. Irish, while adventurous, valued peace and quiet. But frontier living came with aggravations, and not just from the weather. "The society of Pierre was as bad as ever was Fort Pierre," groused Irish to his daughters in a March 21 letter. He was becoming anxious to leave the entire region, adding, "I have my work about done and hope that we may soon be out of this." The next day, March 22, 1881, marked the two-year anniversary of the start of work in Tracy.

But the trip home was something for the future, and for now, they were essentially trapped in Pierre until the heavy snowpack melted enough for travel. So, he took the opportunity to update Ruth and Lizzie on the circumstances he and their mother were experiencing, including his hope that things would soon improve:

> Here we are, up stairs in the ticket office, late at night. Snow all about us. Snow so deep that [neither] man nor animals are able to make their way through it except where by force of circumstances a way must be made. The road from here to Deadwood is daily getting better. That trip is shortened up from 17 days to 4 or 6 as the case may be. From here to Yankton, the trip is made in from 14 to 20 days. So you see that we are hemmed in.

He appears to have been in a reflective mood, shifting to a more philosophical tone:

> Seriously we are in the wane, we have gone over the rugged side and are now about to slide down the swift and more regular descent of human life. We are both well. I am much the strongest of the two. Mother is not as well as usual, but I think that a sight of the first boat or train will help her much.

He illustrated his metaphor at a corner of the page.

S11-14

In a recent letter, Ruth had detailed a storm that struck Iowa City. Irish had made note of the storm's date, and in this March 21 letter, he reminded her of his own experience in that same storm, which he had detailed for his daughters in correspondence dated February 24. In that letter, he had told them how Elston was shot through the hand. Elston's situation had improved by March 21, but the same was not true for others:

> Gracious, how the cattle are dying off. Mr. Reed will lose about all he has, as will many others. The poor things get into small bands, and one after one they lie down and die. Starved to death . . . The river is now at a stand still. But it's almost a flood over at Fort Pierre. I have loaned the [surveyor's] tents to people there to live in.

Reinforcing the isolation there on the banks of the Missouri River, he let her know that none of the things she mentioned having sent had reached them, and not to bother sending any more, as he expected that he and Mrs. Irish would likely make it back home before the items would arrive in Pierre. He added,

> You know that we have had but one train since 10th Dec. and that for a month after that, there was no communication except by telegraph or when a man would undertake to walk out to the "outside world" . . . They are now talking up an Indian scare. It's all folly, so if you see it in dispatches, don't get scared. A bundle of newspapers came the last mail, but one, and although more than a month old, [it] was a treat, I tell you . . . The snow is from 30 to 60 feet deep on the RR down in Minnesota and bad enough all along. It may be a month before we can get a train, but [we] shall take the first boat. The ice has not yet broken up.

That last sentence would prove portentous—as in just days, all hell would break loose.

Such Scolding, Swearing & Yelling: March 27–April/May 1881

The original Dakota Central / Chicago & North Western depot in Pierre (right side). This is where Irish and his wife were living after the surveying stopped in early 1881. At one point the water was three feet deep on the first floor. It also reached the second floor of Sherwood's Grand Central Hotel in Fort Pierre, where Mrs. Irish had previously lived. S11-15

The newspapers of the region—and even the nation—were filled with column after column of large, bold, excited headlines depicting the devastation along the Missouri River that began when an ice dam broke in the early hours of March 27, 1881. No detail, no description of the scenes, no terrifying experience was too small to put to print, and the articles kept coming for several weeks as news was shared and reshared, updated and embellished.

On April 8, still confined in Pierre, Irish wrote another long letter home to Ruth and Lizzie. They had likely already heard about the calamity that scoured the banks of the Missouri River for hundreds of miles, causing death, destruction, shock, and horror. Mr. and Mrs. Irish had probably sent an earlier telegram to their daughters, alleviating their anxiety over their parents' fate.

A telegram is, by necessity, the briefest of communications. This letter from their father would be the opposite, providing a fascinating and personal look at the chaos that took place that day as well as the conditions leading up to it. It was from this letter that the preface of this book was crafted. Because of its value in this narrative, a large percentage of that letter appears below:

The snow has been very deep here this winter. The various falls aggregate about 89 inches (7 feet 5 inches) deep, but from time to time it has thawed, so as to leave the snow now 3 1/2 feet deep all over the plains, and this white matte reaches as far as I can learn, from northern Iowa westward to the Rocky Mountains and northward to the 46th parallel of latitude and eastward to the [Great] Lakes. My goodness, what a flood it will send down in June along the Iowa rivers and the Mississippi.

Well, we have had a flood here of no small proportions. It began about March 24. The river raised slowly to bank full on March 26. On the morning of the 27th, the ice broke, and soon after beginning to run, it gorged 7 miles below here, and the river rapidly rose . . .

It was about 6AM, and many of them [the people in Fort Pierre] had to leave their beds and, without their clothes, fly to the top of that clay hill where we ran our line the day you were with us. Lots of the folks on this side stood on the bank and laughed to see the Fort Pierre folks run. When all at once the muddy waters took a sudden surge of four feet upward, which drowned out the folks in about half a dozen houses on the low banks on this side. They were mostly hard cases and came out to dry land dragging the beds and their children, some of the women swearing, others crying, and the children squalling. In a few minutes the water took another lift of about 2 feet, which sent it into the town. Then there was hurrying to and fro.

Teams were in demand, and on came the black and muddy waters. It was a funny sight. Men came wading out waist deep with all sorts of bundles on their backs. One fellow came jogging along in great excitement with a pie on his plate, tied up in a rag—this was all his burden. Others had trunks on their shoulders. Teams came rushing through the hurrying throng. High loaded, off would go a feather bed or pillows, or maybe a young one. Then such scolding, swearing, and yelling. About 3/4 of the people got drunk at once, which greatly added to the bedlamite condition of things. About 2 PM the water was so deep that teams could no longer travel. Then boats were in demand, and the boatmen demanded [$]5.00 per trip.

Before sundown about all the inhabitants were perched on the bluffs in tents, wagons, huts, and one fellow sat upon the top of a solitary mound with only a sheetiron camp stove, a camp stool, and a pistol for a shelter. The affair all the afternoon looked serious and still more so as the shades of evening drew upon us. For the water came higher, and higher. The men got drunker, and drunker. Shouts and yells, mingled with rapid pistol shots. The threatening demeanor of a gang of outcast scoundrels who were consorts of Arkansas [murderer], who was killed last fall, together with the deepening shades of approaching night, conspired to fill the heart of anyone with terror.

We had staid in the 2d story of the depot building and looked down upon all this through the day, but still, up came the water, and we could see in the dim light a hive of rugged ice pushing up over the banks above us. It came on as if by stealth to take us unawares in the darkness and overwhelm us. I took the little tent which we used last summer and put it up on the bluff in as good a place as I could find, took over bedding provisions, and arranged to take Mother and Mrs. Williams over. Which I did about 9 PM, for the water steadily increased and now stood 3 feet deep on our lower story floors.

A Mr. Cessna, who had a board shantie, let the women in there about 2 AM Monday [the] 28th. The water had got so high and for a short time rose so fast, 10 inches in 10 minutes, that the ice lifted over the banks and came through the town at first here, and then a cake of 8 or 10 tons weight came along, but they rapidly multiplied in numbers when one went into a small house, crushing it like as if it was an egg shell. When another struck the Nicholas House Hotel it sounded like a bomb shell. Then one struck a telegraph pole and cut it off. We nearly lost our telegraph instrument by this. One large cake struck the passenger car standing on the track near us and made a terrific noise. The [Black] porter of the sleeping car, who was in the Pullman at the time, came to the door and called loudly for help. None came.

People down town who had the temerity to stay in 2 story houses began to ring bells, fire guns, and call for help. The [porter] not getting a boat began to sing camp meeting hymns. As the water was rising so fast, the ice would soon cut the town to pieces, so Williams [presumedly Mr.] and I went ashore. We had not been there long when we heard a crash and roar, splashes, crunchings, and groanings on the river which defy description. It caused the earth to tremble under our feet like an earthquake. We knew the gorge had broke. It soon settled down to a steady roar, and the water at once began to fall. We went back and got a sound sleep to find the water standing 3 inches deep on the floors. It ran down that day, Monday [the] 28th, and left the town covered by ponds of ice and all sorts of things, houses turned over, broken up, and every thing looking as if an earthquake or tornado had come that way.

Well, this day 3/4 of the town was drunk, and the Arkansas band of thieves took possession. They broke open houses, plundered hotels, spread out over the overflowed district, and took possession of any and every article of value which they could find. They drove off citizens who were picking up their own property, and this they did with arms in their hands. I went to the sheriff and soon found he was in league with them. The citizens soon found that they had no protection from law, banded together, and with arms in their hands proceeded to arrest the scoundrels.

They had to fire 5 shots to scare them. I was at work ditching to get the water off. I saw a man coming by me in a hurry, believed he was the fellow (Texas, he is called) who lived 6 days on Bad River in the storms a year ago without anything to eat. He is no thief but gets on a glorious drunk when he has money enough. Well, Texas had just come up to me and shook hands when bang went a sharps rifle just in front of us, and I saw the ball throw up the dirt between 40 feet of the fellow who was hurrying along . He and Texas both turned at once, facing the rifleman, and held up their hands. He commanded them to come to him, which they did, Texas saying, "Well, I'm comin' but don't like the way you call me." They told Texas to go his way, [as] they did not want him, and then took the other fellow along. One of the gang refused to go, [but] when a rope was around his neck quicker than you could think, he turned white as a ghost and said he'd go. They took them to the bank of the river and put them into their own boats and turned them loose on the river. They went over to Ft. Pierre, where they came from.

Well, the telegraph soon told us that another flood was coming. It came and went and did us no harm. I got most of the water off the town plat, and people moved into houses and cleaned up. Fort Pierre is no more a town, only 3 houses are left standing in it. The ice is piled up all over the town plat from 8 to 20 feet deep. The great warehouses which stood upon the bank at the steamboat landing are crushed and gone; one of them lies in the mouth of Bad River. Judge Waldron's house is uninjured. I am so glad. They are such kind people.

It's hard to describe the wreck. The steam ferry boat was pushed up on the shore 200 yards from the river and left lying on top of ten feet deep of ice. They are trying to get her down.

All the people of Ft. Pierre are now camped in tents and wagons on the clay hills just above the old town. One thing shows how muddier the rush of water and ice was when it came upon them. There was a large train of 4 mule teams hitched up and starting out for Deadwood. The ice came so fast that they had to pull out the bolts and let the doubletrees [mechanisms for hitching teams] go, and run the mules at a gallop to save them. The train was destroyed, wagons and all, included 18,000 pounds of flour.

> Well, now it's the provision question; starvation stares many a fellow in the face. All the prodigals are in want, and there are no husks to feed upon. It's too bad that industrious people have to perish themselves to feed the horde of scoundrels who in better times do nothing but drink and gamble and steal.

And so our story is nearly over, with Mr. and Mrs. Irish awaiting their exit from Fort Pierre and return home to Iowa and their daughters. The trains were still weeks away from getting through, and many of the steamboats that worked the Missouri River had been damaged or destroyed when the raging waters reached Yankton.

Over the course of this terrible winter, newspaper accounts had reported Pierre and Fort Pierre as having plenty of food, mostly due to warehouses stocked full before the trains stopped, and those stocks were supplemented by occasional resupply trips up from Yankton. Unfortunately, the flood wiped away a good percentage of what was left of that food, leaving these towns, too, waiting in earnest for the return of the trains.

It would be six weeks after the flood before the first train swept into Pierre, on May 8, 1881.[175] It would be even longer before a train rolled up the Bad River or crossed the Missouri to reach the area.

The snow blockades were significant, as captured in photographs published via the Elmer & Tenney "Snow Blockade Series of 1881." The series of sixty-six photos showed the depth of compacted snow within railroad cuts in southern Minnesota. S11-16 (top), S11-17 (bottom)

EPILOGUE

The end of the Hard Winter seems to have also paused the Chicago & North Western's plans for reaching Deadwood. The time was not right to cross the Great Sioux Reservation. In fact, it would be another quarter century before Irish's survey work west of the Missouri would be dusted off and reworked. A lot would change in the intervening years (1881–1906), and while the survey along the Bad River was employed, the route changed significantly from that which Irish had envisioned when it reached the area near modern Philip. For his part, Irish continued in the employ of the Chicago & North Western for a couple more years. His career aspirations took a turn, however, and he spent the final decades of his life in the Nevada gold fields. The diaries and letters shared here are but a tiny fraction of the material he left behind, after a life well lived—a life full of curiosity, exploration, and productivity.

A Project Interrupted

After following Irish and his men for two years of work, in all conditions, through successes and dangers, it may be a disappointing shock that their work west of the Missouri sat dormant for a quarter century. After all that intense focus between 1879 and 1880—and the stubborn push to continue through the brutal early months of the Hard Winter—how could the railroad officials just shelve the project for so long?

The Chicago & North Western's Intentions

We saw the December 1880 *Black Hills Daily Pioneer* interview recounting Marvin Hughitt's plans pertaining to route options and timing.[176] Yet those ambitions seem to be washed away with the spring snowmelt. Let's look at another article that paper published—in their November 23, 1880, edition—that outlined some of Hughitt's inclinations, providing further insight into the larger regional goals of the Chicago & North Western.

The article related how Hughitt intended progress to continue as rapidly as ever, with the caveat that winter could, of course, slow the work. Once spring weather arrived, however, he anticipated work would resume west of the Missouri, culminating in functional tracks. The article writer stated that

Hughitt "evidently comprehends the present value of the Hills trade and realizes that a prosperous future is in store for the entire northwest." The mineral-rich land of the Black Hills was valuable, but there were other riches being eyed. The article continued,

> [Hughitt] intimates that the Black Hills are merely a side-issue with his company as compared to the vast territory to the northwest which they propose to penetrate at the earliest possible moment, and to be the first to place the wonderland of America, Yellowstone park [established in 1872], within easy reach of the most distant city. The tenor of his conversation created an impression that the direct line of the road will not touch the Hills, but striking the Cheyenne near the forks, continue up the Belle Fourche valley to the big bend, thence northwest through Montana.[177]

The company had bigger plans than the Black Hills. But there were realities at play, and those realities put plans on hold. Work-around options were implemented, and those work-arounds became the established day-to-day operations. It isn't that inertia set in so much as that economic energies were redirected.

The Disincentives to Building the Tracks in 1881

For context, let's back up a bit. In 1881, much of what today is the western half of South Dakota was the Great Sioux Reservation, which was established by the Fort Laramie Treaty of 1851. Subsequent treaties, agreements, and acts carved more and more land away from the Lakota, as noted earlier. There were a handful of White people living on or near the reservation, mostly White men with Lakota wives living in community with the Lakota, but the land belonged to the Lakota.

The Chicago & North Western was confident they'd soon be laying tracks across that land, as found in era publications. For instance, the *Railroad Gazette* of January 21, 1881, reported that the Chicago & North Western was "putting in a winter bridge over the Missouri at Pierre, Dak., for the purpose of carrying across material for the extension to the Black Hills, on which work will be resumed in the spring."[178]

However, things did not work out that way. While Irish had *surveyed* (with permission from the Lakota) a route through the Great Sioux Reservation in late 1880 and the first months of 1881, the actual *construction and operation* of a railroad through the same land was a different proposition. The railroad would need stops every handful of miles to replenish water and fuel (both scarce), and these sites would be vulnerable at this turbulent time.

The company had not yet obtained full legal permission to cross the Great Sioux Reservation. While the Chicago & North Western officers and Lakota leaders had signed an agreement to allow the crossing, it remained unratified by the US Congress. Once Irish and his crew left Gap Creek Camp a few weeks after the blizzard in October 1880, they did not return that far west. The portion of the survey stretching from modern Philip to the Forks of the Cheyenne and on to Deadwood would never come to fruition.

Why? Risk and expense were both high, and without settlers along the route to help prop up the economics of a railroad infrastructure, motivation waned to build the physical rail line through the contested land. And so, the survey remained in a preliminary state for years as time and focus moved on.

A few years later, the General Allotment Act of 1887, more commonly known as the Dawes Act, changed the communal structure of the reservation lands, giving each Native household a certain amount of land. (It's much more complicated than that, but we'll simplify it here). After the land was assigned to Native households, the remaining acreage was considered "surplus" and made available for sale to settlers. This also turned the Great Sioux Reservation into several smaller reservations. On February 14, 1890, the lands south of the Cheyenne River and north of the new Pine Ridge and Rosebud Reservations (including the land Irish had surveyed between the North Fork of the Bad River and the Forks of the Cheyenne) were declared open to settlement and the building of tracks. But several factors still slowed settlement.

The climate and ecosystem of the area was more favorable to ranching than farming, and the 160-acre parcels of land made available were known to be insufficient, so White settlement was slow until the 1910s, when the Enlarged Homestead Act doubled the offerings to 320 acres each.

Also suppressing White settlement in this region were the general relations between Lakota and White people through the 1880s and early 1890s. Tensions were at their height following the 1876 event at Little Bighorn and the rise of the Ghost Dance, culminating with the 1890 tragedy at Wounded Knee.

Then came the Panic of 1893, often considered the worst economic calamity of the nineteenth century, if not all American history up to that point in time.[179] Like the Panic of 1873, two decades before, it put the brakes on railroad development.

And so, the residents of Fort Pierre and Pierre adjusted. Many of Fort Pierre's residents and merchants moved eastward to Pierre for the convenience of direct access to the tracks. For instance, the *Fort Pierre Weekly Signal* announced in their November 24, 1880, edition that they themselves had up and moved their business across the river to Pierre.[180] (Unfortunately, that new space for the *Fort Pierre Weekly Signal*, an important source of information about the construction of the Dakota Central and happenings during the Hard Winter, was swept away by the great flood. Its March 26 issue was the last until May 14.)

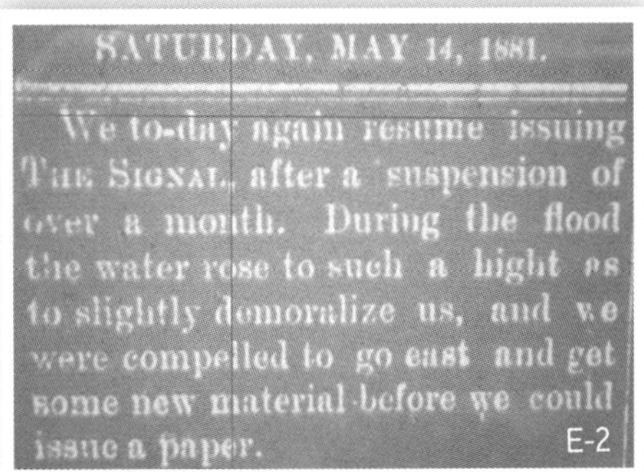
SATURDAY, MAY 14, 1881.

We to-day again resume issuing The Signal, after a suspension of over a month. During the flood the water rose to such a hight as to slightly demoralize us, and we were compelled to go east and get some new material before we could issue a paper.

E-2

Without official permission to proceed across the Great Sioux Reservation, the Chicago & North Western stepped back and reevaluated how to best invest in the area and support the infrastructure and markets established over the past two years. An additional 331 miles of track were laid in Dakota Territory during the fiscal year that ended May 31, 1882, the year immediately following the end of Irish's work.[181] These tracks greatly expanded the Chicago & North Western's network in the eastern half of the state, filling in north–south routes and making connections between burgeoning market centers. The eastern portion of what is today South Dakota became a web of towns connected by tracks—not just those of the Chicago & North Western but of other railway companies too.

Eventually, the Chicago & North Western found its long-sought route to Deadwood. Turning north from Chadron, Nebraska, a branch of the Fremont, Elkhorn & Missouri Valley Railroad reached Rapid City in July 1886 and the city of Belle Fourche in 1890, a decade after that railroad's officers originally set their sights on the northern Black Hills.[182]

The Tracks from Fort Pierre Eventually Reached Rapid City, Not Deadwood

By the time construction commenced west of the Missouri River in 1906, a quarter century after Irish's work, Deadwood had long waned in vibrancy; the loose gold had played out, leaving the harder-to-reach underground minerals for the big mines, such as the Homestake Mine, between Lead and Deadwood. Rapid City had become the more desirable destination.

Still, it may have felt a bit like a lost opportunity, at least at the time. Railroad historian H. Roger Grant wrote, "While persistent efforts made by the North Western and its principal rival in South Dakota, the Milwaukee Road, resulted in the opening of the Indian lands between the Cheyenne and White rivers in 1890, this was a hollow victory; the Great Dakota Boom had largely ended." Circumstances just hadn't been right. Grant further explained, "The North Western could have surely won an easement for its nearly 170 miles of track through Sioux country just as the Elkhorn Route had done in scattered areas of northwestern Nebraska about the same time, but Hughitt concluded that traffic to and from the Hills would not justify the cost."[183]

Therefore, when the time came to execute a final survey, the route followed Irish's work much of the way up the Bad River, but then diverted toward Rapid City and the more favorable Box Elder valley. The difficult terrain that had vexed Irish near the Forks of the Cheyenne became a nonissue when that area was bypassed for the one that crossed the Cheyenne thirty miles to the south (near modern Interstate 90), where a wide and gentle turn allowed the tracks to easily run up Box Elder Creek's valley into Rapid City. Lastly, a 1907 bridge across the Missouri River between Pierre and Fort Pierre completed the coveted link between Chicago and the Black Hills that Irish had begun planning in secret in January 1879.

Glimpses of the 1906 Construction Project

There were settlers in the region before 1906, but they were fewer in number than those that would wash in with the arrival of the railroad. But even that wave would not match the intensity of the one that had followed Irish's crew west along their line of stakes across the prairie grasses east of the Missouri. The land west of the river wasn't lush with prairie grass; it was dry pasture grass, drawing a different type of settler. Still, plenty came in to try their luck.

An interesting story pertaining to the town of Philip can be found in a county history book. Even before the coming of the railroad, there had been a post office at Philip, but it was not yet an official town. According to local lore, when the town itself was platted in 1906 by the railroad's Western Town Lot Company, resident Frank Slocum recommended an area just to the west, up on a bench and thus protected from flooding. The railroad's engineers resisted, "because they had planned a branch of the new railroad to extend up the east side of North Fork as far as Mexican creek, to cross the divide there and head north and northwest to the Cheyenne River and on to Belle Fourche."[184]

Aside from the head-scratcher as to why the railroad's own representatives would reject the higher ground in favor of an oft-flooded patch of ground for their infrastructure and the town lots, this tidbit shows that the plan of utilizing Irish's route up to the Forks was not yet entirely forgotten. Those plans did not come to fruition, and thus in the research for this book, considerable time had to be spent hunting for specifics within the entire Gap Creek region, as it was impossible to follow any ghostly remnants of an abandoned grade.

The bench land Frank Slocum had recommended as a better alternative for the town of Philip, which sits in a lower part of the valley and closer to the riverbed. E-3

The Bad River valley allowed a wide, relatively flat roadbed along much of its route. E-4

This and the next image show the modern tracks following the Cheyenne River (the structure in the top image is the bridge that crosses the Cheyenne), staying within the valley westward beyond Irish's plan. Once leaving the Bad River valley, the roadbed found a wide, gentle valley to follow until it could cross the Cheyenne, follow it to Box Elder Creek, then follow that creek up to Rapid City. E-5

A modern train traveling the Bad River Valley, to the west of Fort Pierre. E-6

Marvin Hughitt

The Dakota Central was just one of many projects undertaken by the Chicago & North Western in this era, and Hughitt went on to have a long career with the company. Railroad historian H. Roger Grant summed up Hughitt's career by writing, "After [President Albert] Keep's departure in 1887, Hughitt guided the railroad for more than a generation. During this long tenure he symbolized the stability and profitability of the property." Hughitt served as president until 1910 and remained on the board until his death in 1928. Grant recounted a Chicago journalist describing Hughitt thusly: "Tall, straight of figure, broad of shoulder, firm of face and alert of step, Mr. Hughitt is the very personification of success and power. He is the North-Western Railway."[185]

Further supporting Hughitt's hands-on involvement (such as coming out to campsites to see route options for himself on occasion), Grant confirmed that Hughitt "wanted to 'know the facts' about his company's operations and the region it served or planned to reach. Hughitt had a good command of finances as well, and he consistently showed a sense of commitment to the public." Hughitt was "optimistic about the future of the North Western and its territory," noted Grant, but he "resisted needless expansion, although he considered a possible extension to the Pacific coast." He was a steady man with "an antispecultive bent, something that set him apart from more colorful contemporary railroad leaders. 'Hughitt liked to stick to his knitting,' remarked an associate. He did, and the North Western prospered."[186]

Irish Working in Minnesota After the Great Flood

Mr. and Mrs. Irish left Pierre sometime between Irish's letter of April 8, detailing the great flood, and a letter written by Ruth on May 20, to her father and sister.

Irish resumed surveying tasks for the Chicago & North Western soon after leaving Pierre, but that work was not in Dakota Territory, completing the survey his crew had begun toward the Forks of the Cheyenne, as would be expected. Instead, he was in Minnesota, identifying a route for a branch line to connect the towns of New Ulm and Redwood Falls, and the warmer conditions there mirrored those he'd experienced in Dakota Territory.

On July 24, 1881, from a camp at Swan Lake, near New Ulm, Irish told his family,

> Last Friday two tornadoes passed us not more than 15 or 20 miles on each side. The day was exceeding hot, 105 in the shade. We saw and watched the two clouds. They were approaching each other, one from the SW, the other from the NE. They met and united about over our heads at 1/2 past 3 PM. The north one passed over a small town called Montevideo and one or two smaller villages, tearing down and scattering the houses and killing several people. The south one passed over New Ulm. . . . The storm unroofed nearly every house in it, threw down many, and killed in the town and vicinity 30 people and wounded twice as many more. We have had but one bad storm that broke the ridge pole of one of our tents.

Powers and Tubbs were with him, and Irish entertained Ruth by telling her of the men's camp activities. Local young women liked to visit camp to flirt with the men, an activity Irish suspected was intended for little more than making their local beaus jealous. Then, those local beaus came and hung around the camp, looking as mad as they could. Powers had become particularly enamored of a young woman who was "engaged to marry a young farmer."

When the young farmer appeared in camp to retrieve his betrothed, she and Powers were singing

New Ulm Review.

NEW ULM, MINN

Wednesday, July 20th, 1881

DEATH AND [DE]STRUCTION.

NEW ULM DEVASTATED.

A Large Portion of the City a Shapeless Mass of Ruins.

Six Killed and Fifty-Three Wounded. The Towns of West Newton, Cairo and Wellington add 13 Killed and Many Wounded.

The Damage to Property in New Ulm alone Will Reach $250,000.

E-7

New Ulm Weekly Review, New Ulm, Minnesota, July 20, 1881

songs about crossing proverbial rivers. She did not budge despite the appearance of her fiancé. Irish used elusive wording to describe what he thought the outcome would be, saying, "I expect that there will be a jewel here soon [Irish's underline]." Irish even made a sketch of the scene (below).

E-8

The account of youthful flirting wasn't the best story Irish shared in that same July 24 letter, however. Consider the following:

> Well, this lake is full of water newts. The first that we knew of it, they came out of the water in the night and crawled into the tents. Powers sleeps next to us, Tubbs next. Well, I was sound asleep, as were the rest, when all at once I heard Powers scream like a woman in afright for all the world. Scream after scream. We got a light, and then he had caught a slimy, cold, wiggling [or wriggling] newt under the collar of his shirt just as it was going down his back. My goodness! What a scare! Well, we got over that, lay down again, and soon, one got under Tubbs's shirt, on his belly. He jumped up and yelled. . . . The other tents were visited by them by this time, and I tell you the commotion was great.
>
> Last night they killed 25 in one tent. I have not as yet had a visit, but if I do, you know it will not scare me. They look exactly like the one which we made a pet of. I tell you, but Tubbs's face was a study when he caught that one. I do not think he could have looked worse if the cholera had taken him suddenly. His red hair

> stood up and he was a picture of fright. Don't you wish you were here to enjoy such fun.

Powers had obviously recovered enough from the early September gunshot wound to the leg to be back on the job and flirting with the locals, something that must have been a joy to Irish, who'd obviously brought the man back onto the team.

Unfortunately, Powers's story may not have such a happy ending. A newspaper article had indicated his hometown as Sparta, Wisconsin. In Sparta's Woodlawn Cemetery stands the tombstone of a Perry Powers, born in 1858 and deceased in 1893. A little math shows a death at the terribly young age of thirty-five, and a mere twelve years after the end of the Dakota Central survey work.[187] It turns out the name Perry Powers was relatively common at the time, but assuming the grave belongs to *our* Perry Powers, he would have been about twenty-one years of age when he began work with Irish on the Dakota Central job.

Irish continued surveying, but he transitioned away from his railroad work for the Chicago & North Western and was soon in Nevada, where he focused on mining projects (more about that in appendix VII). The Chicago & North Western moved on to other projects as well, with Marvin Hughitt continuing to command the mighty company until the final few years before his death, in 1928, at the age of ninety.

And that brings us back around to the survey work that resulted in the route from Tracy to Deadwood.

Irish died in September 1904, less than two years before his work up the Bad River was put to use. It is certain that Hughitt was involved, for he remained chair of the Chicago & North Western's board until 1925. In the bigger picture, that twenty-five-year gap is a minor blip in the story.

Yes, Irish's crew battled storms and mosquitos, winds and blizzards, blazing hot and bitter cold, comradery and mutiny, suffering and joy, and the many other adventures, good and bad, that unfolded within the brief diary entries and more informative letters home that he left behind. It has been an honor to share the significant role they played in establishing a transportation route that remains heavily used today.

As the author of his printed eulogy put it, Irish inherited "the spirit to go forth and do the world's work regardless of the vicissitudes which beset the way, and in many of his engineering trips across our great untamed Western plains and through the mountain fastnesses[,] the way was as pathless for him, the pioneer, as had been the ocean to his forefathers."[188] What a life he had, indeed, charted.

ACKNOWLEDGMENTS

A project of this huge scope requires a group of people every bit as expansive. I am deeply grateful to everyone who played a role, and I apologize right now if I do not mention you below. If you helped me put this together in any way, I am grateful!

The staff at the South Dakota State Archives at the South Dakota State Historical Society, for digging out old maps, fort documents, and historic photographs, as well as contributing their own curiosities that led to further discoveries. Halley Hair, Matthew Rietzel, and Virginia Hanson were especially supportive.

Vice President and COO Greg Keil and Senior Survey Technician Jim Staberg of Barr Engineering, for patiently answering questions about surveying both old-school and modern.

Emily Berry, Christopher Pellowski, and Bill Roggenthen from the Museum of Geology at South Dakota School of Mines and Technology and Galen Hoogestraat of the United States Geological Survey (USGS), for helping to chase down landmarks and creeks in an area of erosion and variable naming practices.

Lesley Martin of the Chicago History Museum and Sandley Howell of the Chicago Public Library, for helping to chase down modern addresses of historic buildings after streets were renamed and houses were renumbered.

Linda Gross of the Hagley Museum and Library, for answering questions about patent- and frontier-medicine practices.

Katherine Lamie of the Archaeological Research Center at the South Dakota State Historical Society, Sunny Hannum of the Fort Pierre Development Corporation, and archaeologist Sara Pfannkuche, for helping me understand the Dirt Lodges site and village locations within the region between the James and Missouri Rivers.

Doug Hansen of the Hansen Wheel & Wagon Shop, for describing the multiple types of vehicles mentioned in the diaries and letters.

Deb Schiefelbein of the Verendrye Museum in Fort Pierre and Darby Nutter, who was trail master of the 2008 Fort Pierre to Deadwood Trail Ride, for their research to identify the historic locations of stage ranches along the trail.

MaryAnn and Lloyd Frein, for welcoming us onto their land and pointing out the stage road crossing, as well as the grave marker of B. Ortez.

Meggan Hansen of the Mead Cultural Education Center, the Yankton County Historical Society, and the Dakota Territorial Museum, and steamboat researcher Craig Ernster, for helping to track down information about each of the steamboats mentioned in the diaries and letters, and for helping to figure out the scribbles within the diaries.

Jakob Etrheim of the Murray County Historical Society, for information about Neil Currie.

Michael Johnson of the Fairfield County Heritage Association / Sherman House Museum in Lancaster, Ohio, for providing information about William T. Sherman's presence at Fort Sully 2 in July 1880.

Executive Director Alexandra McKendree and Collections Manager Becky Dewing of the Johnson County Historical Society in Iowa City, Iowa, and County Recorder Kim Painter of Johnson County, Iowa, for tracking down old records to see if we could determine birth and death records in an era when neither were required. Becky also answered questions about the Irish-Goetz House, also known as Rose Hill.

Ryan Mattke and Dana Peterson of the John R. Borchert Map Library at the University of Minnesota and Jennifer Andries of the Lyon County Historical Society, for helping to chase down the location of Rush Lake Camp.

Stetson Kastengren, for explaining the Dawes Act and its ramifications, as well as how to interpret maps that use different perspectives.

Don Korkow, for his tour of the property that was once Reed's Ranch. That day was one of the major highlights of the research portion of this project.

Hang Nguyen of the State Historical Society of Iowa in Iowa City, for walking me through the Charles Wood Irish Papers in that organization's collection.

Jenna Silver, Rich Dana, Mac Gill, and Giselle Simón of the Special Collections and Archives department at University of Iowa Libraries in Iowa City, for being partners in this project since 2017. I am eternally grateful for their roles in protecting Irish's papers and for their passion in making them available for research.

M. R. Hansen of Philip, South Dakota, for guiding me toward the landmarks I wanted to see and the people I needed to meet, such as his brother David K. Hansen, Linda Eisenbraun, and local ranchers who welcomed me onto their lands. M. R. has supported my research for several years now, keeping his eyes and ears open and sending packages full of information. He is a gem of a person and the true soul of the West River region of South Dakota.

Craig Pfannkuche and the volunteers of the Chicago & North Western Historical Society in Chicago, for their unending patience, enthusiasm, and support. One of the very best things to come out of the research related to the C&NW is my friendship with Craig.

Steve Devore for navigating a drone over the Gap Creek campsite location so that I could see it, and capturing video and photographs of the same.

My beta readers, for reviewing the very early manuscript. On a recommendation from my editor, I'd "thrown it all in there!" and hoped that the early readers would tell me that this or that could be cut, but instead they said, "WOW, IT'S ALL GREAT! KEEP IT ALL, AND ADD MORE ABOUT [ANY

NUMBER OF THINGS]!" Thank you, Jim Hicks, Tim Lundahl, Bob Sandeen, Laura Whitaker, and Ray Wilson, for the comments and insights, and for all the stuff you said had to stay and what had to be added. Sadly, I trimmed about thirty thousand words, but hopefully you'll like it even better now and not miss what was cut.

Sincere, deep gratitude to experts-in-their-fields William Anderson, Nancy Tystad Koupal, Rick Mills, John Berg, Giselle Simón, and Bob Sandeen for reading the completed manuscript and providing their professional endorsements. More importantly, I am grateful for the friendships we have developed. It has been a delight to get to know each of you as individuals, and I now think of you first and foremost as friends.

My daughter, Laura, for supporting my deep dive into one of the few eras of history that she, for some inconceivable reason, is not interested in. She's always ready with a positive word. My niece, Jamie, for always being an enthusiastic cheerleader.

Ray, for patiently driving up and down dusty roads, squinting at tiny maps, and helping transfer Irish's maps onto modern USGS topographical maps so that I could stand in the exact spots where Irish and his men worked. It was Ray's map skills that determined the location of the elusive and remote Gap Creek campsite.

My eternal gratefulness and thanks go to "Team Snow": Angela Wiechmann, my developmental editor—your insights, support, and shepherding gave me the confidence to dive into this project. Kris Kobe, my copy editor—you have a gift, and you are a gift; working with you is a joy from beginning to end, making me laugh and making the hard parts easy. Patrick Donnelly, who did the tedious task of proofreading and making sure that all those endnotes were in the proper style. Kendra Millis, who had the task of creating a functional index from the details, when the lead character appears on nearly every page. James (Jay) Monroe, the incredibly talented designer who took bits and pieces and crafted this beautiful finished product. Lily Coyle, Laurie Herrmann, and the team at Beaver's Pond Press—thank you for your support, wisdom, and experience. My life has significantly changed since you welcomed my projects.

APPENDIXES

I: People
II: Surveying before GPS
III: Where Exactly Was the Gap Creek Camp?
IV: Township, Range & Section Delineations
V: Steamboats Mentioned in the Diaries
VI: Forts and Agencies
VII: Biography of Irish Family

APPENDIX I: PEOPLE

This list was assembled from diary and letter mentions, notations in payment books and ledgers, and newspaper articles. Crew roles appear as they did in the sources, but certain roles/tasks were likely shared or rotated.

Crew Members

- **Adams:** Died of illness.
- **Albright, L. B.:** Included in a list of ill men in September and October 1880.
- **Barch (or Barsch):** Scout; lead chain. Left team on October 31, 1880; Irish was "glad of it."
- **Bingham:** Got drunk and left camp, then was brought back.
- **Bishop:** Scout.
- **BJ:** Joined the crew on Monday, December 22, 1879, when they were headquartered at Reed's Ranch.
- **Blair:** Along with Meat (Lakota), sent back to Pierre from Gap Creek Camp on October 19, 1880, escorting the ailing Chase.
- **Caldwell:** Courier; scout; brought letters, pistols, and powder. Escorted Adams to seek medical care.
- **Carse, C. J.:** Initial crew member. Rod; levels. Present at Blunt's Butte time-capsule event. Accidentally shot himself through right leg with

small pocket pistol. Camp Carse was named after him. Part of the February 1880 mutiny; deemed part of the "Royal Family," but kept on the crew. Broke through the ice on the Missouri River.

- **Chambers, Bob:** Set up a main camp. Listed among the sick in late August 1880. Was with the group when Perry Powers was shot. Among those at the Gap Creek Camp for the October 1880 blizzard.
- **Chase:** Listed among the sick men in late August 1880. Still sick in mid-October; Irish worried he would die if he remained with the group, so he was sent home. Among those at the Gap Creek Camp for the October 1880 blizzard.
- **Christianson, L.:** Present at the Blunt's Butte time-capsule event.
- **Cole, W. C.:** Cook. Present at the Blunt's Butte time-capsule event. Discharged on July 19, 1879.
- **Collins, I. D.:** Present at the Blunt's Butte time-capsule event. Discharged on July 19, 1879, for getting drunk.
- **Cornell:** Scouted for water.
- **DeBarr, Joe:** Initial crew member, 1st aux. Courier (maps); sent for provisions; fuel and wood duty; scout (with Irish, mouth of the Cheyenne River). Present at Blunt's Butte time capsule event. Listed among the ill in mid-December 1879 and mid-January 1880. Part of the February 1880 mutiny; discharged that day.
- **Duncan:** Courier; sent on errands. The cook who was "quite jealous" of Mrs. Irish's bread, which the men raved about. Listed among ill men in mid-May 1880. Brought 800 large stakes and 10 bundles of lath to camp on May 20, 1880.
- **Dunlap, D. C.:** Member of initial crew. Assistant, leveler, transit, hunter, courier (notes), scout (with Irish). Was close with Irish, "like brothers." Present at the Blunt's Butte time-capsule event. Face was blistered during firefight at Rush Lake Camp. Married around May 1879; tried to get his wife set up near camps. Listed among ill men in mid-June and November 1879 and January 1880. Helped Irish haze the new recruits in late November 1879. Part of the February 1880 mutiny; deemed part of the "Royal Family," but kept on the crew.
- **Fatsinger:** Draughtman (draftsman); scout. Exhibited "youthful indiscretions." Listed among ill men in mid-December 1879; eventually taken to Fort Thompson for medical care. Part of the February 1880 mutiny; deemed part of the "Royal Family," but kept on the crew.
- **Fawcet:** Sent on errands; general camp tasks.
- **Griffin:** Listed among sick men in early January 1881.
- **Harvey:** Stake work; setting up camps.

- **Henderson:** Teamster; hunter.
- **Hodge, W. D.:** Oversaw Silver Lake Camp and a camp near Huron. Joined Irish's crew on occasion (bringing his family)—running lines, maps and profiles, slope staking. Camp Maggie was named after his wife.
- **Hughitt, A. J. "Amos":** Present at the Blunt's Butte time-capsule event. First cousin of Marvin Hughitt Sr.
- **Hughitt, O. N. "Orin":** Son of Amos. Nephew of Marvin Hughitt Sr. Present at the Blunt's Butte time-capsule event.
- **Hutchinson, Charley J.:** Levels; hunter. Present at the Blunt's Butte time-capsule event. Listed among ill men in mid-August 1879 and late December 1880.
- **Irish, Charles Wood:** Lead surveyor, present from beginning to end. Present at the Blunt's Butte time-capsule event. Among those at the Gap Creek Camp for the October 1880 blizzard.
- **Latio, H. M.:** Present at the Blunt's Butte time-capsule event.
- **Leighton, I. M.:** Initial crew member. Scout (with Irish, March 1880, Forks of the Cheyenne); errands (had a wagon and team of horses). Overpowered by heat August 1879. Helped move camp late August 1879. Present at the Blunt's Butte time-capsule event. Listed among sick men in mid-January, late May, and late December 1880 and in early January 1881. Among those at the Gap Creek Camp for the October 1880 blizzard. Initially listed as the man behind the accidental shooting of Perry Powers.
- **Lewis:** Rear chain; courier. Described as having hair that stood up. Recruited for the winter work on Fort George Island—"the best of the lot . . . has such good sense"; "got on very well"; "eats like a hog." Listed as ill in mid-January 1880. Noted as doing well in the work in late February 1880. Irish said he'd be "lost without" both Lewis and Linkhart. Discharged with pay on July 7, 1880.
- **Linkhart:** Initial crew member. Head chain. Listed among sick men in mid-January 1880. Suffered terrible homesickness. Noted as doing well in the work in late February 1880. Irish said he'd be "lost without" both Lewis and Linkhart. Discharged with pay on July 7, 1880.
- **McCaddon, Jack:** Leveler; scout (with Irish); helped create profile maps. Sent to set up a new camp. Listed among sick men in late May and late November 1880.
- **McCready, Dave:** Was among crew in far western region when the October 1880 blizzard struck.

- **McNiel:** Cook. Listed among sick men in mid-December 1879 and January 1880. Camp McNiel and McNiel's Creek were named after him. So homesick that Irish sent him home in March 1880. Hosted Irish at his home at 148 West Madison Street when Irish was in Chicago in April 1880 (today that address is 679 West Madison Street).
- **Meyers, "C. H.":** (Initials according to Irish's diary; other entries merely say "Meyers.") Courier; errands. Went with Irish to the Dirt Lodges.
- **Meyers, "F. S.":** (Initials according to the newspaper article.) Present at the Blunt's Butte time-capsule event.
- **Miller, E. S.:** Hunter. Present at the Blunt's Butte time-capsule event.
- **Morse:** Escorted Ruth and Lizzie to a prairie dog town. Present during the accidental shooting of Perry Powers. Left the crew on October 31, 1880.
- **Mudra, Joe ("Mudree"):** Hunter. Present at the Blunt's Butte time-capsule event. Took personal interest in feather collecting for Mrs. Irish. Overpowered by heat in August 1879. Joe Mudra Creek was named after him. Listed among sick men in early May and mid-August 1880 and early January 1881.
- **Nettiburgh, J. S.:** Scout (with Irish). Present at the Blunt's Butte time-capsule event. Camp Nettiburgh and Nettiburgh's Grove (near the camp) were named after him.
- **Olson:** Hunter. Overpowered by heat in August 1879.
- **Parke:** Levels.
- **Pearsall:** General camp tasks.
- **Peterson:** Brought team and buckboard. Listed among sick men in early December 1880. Peterson Creek was named after him. Suffered from sore legs, being out in the cold in late 1880 through early 1881. Left the crew on January 16, 1881.
- **Powers, Perry:** Scout (with Irish, March 1880, Forks of the Cheyenne); rod; transit; stake making; fishing; hunting; identifying line options. Trusted by Irish; put in charge in Irish's absence. Powers Camp was named after him. Listed among sick men in mid-January 1880 and early May 1880. With Irish when turned back by Indian police along the Cheyenne River in late January 1880. Present at the Blunt's Butte time-capsule event. Accidentally shot on September 3, 1880. Was with Irish and Tubbs on a survey in Minnesota in July 1881.
- **Quinn:** Courier.
- **Raymond:** Listed among ill men in mid-December 1880.

- **Scott:** Scout (with Irish). Arrived via stagecoach. Notified Irish about Perry Powers's accidental shooting.
- **Segur, I. E.:** Scout (with Irish). Present at the Blunt's Butte time-capsule event.
- **Selby:** Levels. Fell through ice at a sandbar on the Missouri River. Part of the February 1880 mutiny; deemed part of the "Royal Family," but kept on the crew.
- **Shanklin, W. N.:** Created the canals and trenches to drain Camp Irish, along the Big Sioux. Present at the Blunt's Butte time-capsule event. Discharged on July 19, 1879.
- **Styers, G.:** Present at the Blunt's Butte time-capsule event.
- **Thompson, A. B.:** Leveler; slope staking. His wife set up a shanty near a camp.
- **Thorn, G. W.:** Courier (frequently got lost); provisions; hunter; scout; fuel and wood duty; moving camp. Thorn's Grove was named after him. Present at the Blunt's Butte time-capsule event.
- **Tubbs, H. H.:** Levels; scouting; slope staking; helped with profiles and maps. Camp Tubbs was named after him. Listed among sick men in early November 1880. Joined Irish and Powers on a survey in Minnesota in July 1881.
- **Vernon:** Teamster; errands. Listed among sick men in mid-January 1880. Delivered the news that Charlie the horse had killed himself.

Lakota Police and Guards

- **Afraid of Nothing:** Replaced Hodgkiss on September 24, 1880.
- **Corn:** Scouted; hunted; courier trusted with reports and letters.
- **Crane:** Replaced by Red Skirt on September 24, 1880.
- **Drum:** Declared a fool by Irish; left on June 27, 1880.
- **Elston, Mr.:** Jacket's stepfather. Came to tend to the very ill Jacket; stayed behind when Jacket returned home. Listed among sick men in mid-January 1881. Accidentally shot himself through the hand during the final weeks of work along Bad River.
- **Hodgkiss:** Hunter; scout (with Irish). Replaced by Afraid of Nothing on September 24, 1880.
- **Jacket:** Hunted; helped move camp; scout (with Irish). Among those at the Gap Creek Camp for the October 1880 blizzard. Frequently very ill; family eventually came to tend him; family took him home, but father-in-law stayed.

- **Meat:** Along with Blair, sent back to Pierre from Gap Creek Camp on October 19, 1880, escorting the ailing Chase.
- **One Eye:** Teamster; brought provisions. Discharged for letting horses get away.
- **Pole:** Team and harnesses.
- **Posey:** Wagon driver. The Posey Buttes were named after him. Named, in private, as the accidental shooter of Perry Powers; horrified by episode.
- **Red Skirt:** Scout (with Irish); hunted. Participated in the August 1880 council. Replaced Crane on September 24, 1880. Refused to participate in the commemorative mound marking at the Forks. Among those at the Gap Creek Camp for the October 1880 blizzard.
- **Ree:** Sent with Whirlwind to Rosebud Agency to get Jacket's family.
- **Scarleg:** Scout (with Irish); courier (reports and letters).
- **Standing Elk:** Among men listed as sick in mid-September 1880.
- **Tobacco Sack, Mrs.:** A woman in camp with her husband.
- **Whirlwind:** Scout (with Irish). Sent with Ree to Rosebud Agency to get Jacket's family.
- **White Bull:** Scout (with Irish); hunted.

Lakota Camp Visitors

Headmen **Little Bear** and **White Swan** participated in the August 1880 councils. Both men appeared in camp on September 8, 1880, and they came back the next day with Agent Leonard Love. They insisted that Irish hire two of their men and send away two of the Lakotas already hired.

APPENDIX II: SURVEYING BEFORE GPS

- **Chains:** Survey crews measured distance using metal chains of standardized lengths, with intermittent markers to denote shorter increments. A-2

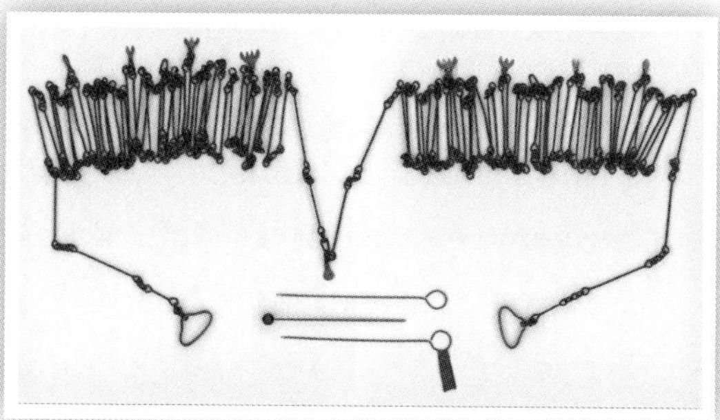

- **Creek and River Valleys:** These were preferred locations for track placement because nature had already done the work to erode wide, flat valleys through rougher terrain.
- **Curves:** Where not straight, the tracks of a railroad are made up of curves that gently change direction at an angle the cars can maneuver.
- **Elevations:** Surveyors determined the elevation above sea level of relevant points on the landscape.
- **Grades/Grading:** Grading is the creation of a level base, or foundation, for construction; railroad grading requires specified slopes.
- **Levels/Leveling:** Leveling involves determining the elevation difference between two points, then the amount of material to be "cut" (removed) or filled to make a navigable grade (road base) between the two spots.
- **Lines:** The overall path or route being investigated. Survey crews frequently ran multiple lines in an area to determine which was most efficient, referring to them as Line A, Line B, etc.
- **Maps:** A "bird's-eye view" of the area traveled. Some maps were detailed topographical representations, while others featured lines, curves, and markings for distances, with associated calculations.
- **Offset:** A line run mostly parallel to another line, a particular distance away.
- **Profile Maps:** Drawn on grid paper, these represented the profile of a route, showing the grade and incline or decline along the route—a specialized line graph.
- **Scout:** A preliminary investigation of an area to get a general idea of whether the area could warrant more detailed work to define a through route.

- **Soundings:** The method of measuring the distance to the bottom of a river, creek, or lake from the water or ice surface.
- **Stakes:** Stakes were used to mark the routes, tops of cuts, and bases of slopes, as well as for many other purposes. Once a preliminary route was selected for further work, surveyors would mark its stakes with specific directions for the graders.
- **Tangent:** A straight line (of track) between two points.
- **Tie Line:** A line of track that links two lines together.
- **Transit:** A piece of equipment similar to a small spotting scope, used to measure angles.
- **Water Tables:** Measurements of how far one has to dig/drill into the ground to find water.

Curves, Tangents & Water Tables

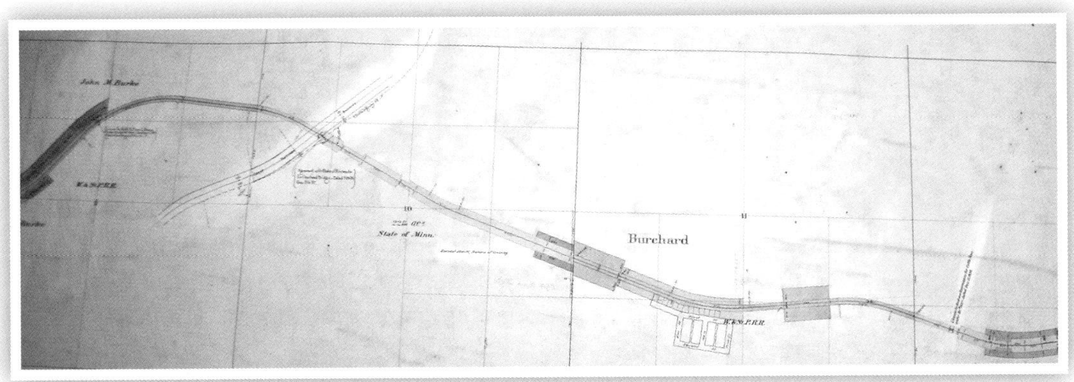

The final route to, over, and beyond the Redwood River, which the tracks cross in section 10 on the map. The number and degree of curves illustrates the adjustments needed to navigate the terrain. A-3

A modern satellite image of the same stretch of the route, showing the river crossing in section 10. A-4

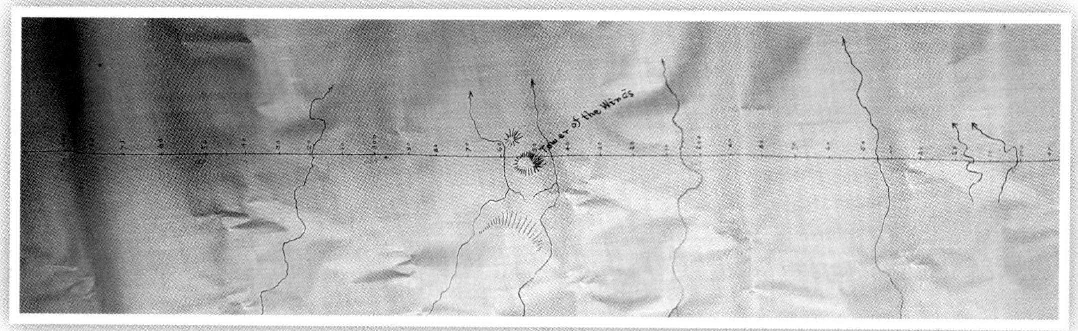

An example of one of the long tangents of the route. One ran west of Lake Benton, approaching the Big Sioux River. Another ran from the northern end of the Ree Hills to the start of the descent down Medicine Creek. This illustration is of that second tangent, east of modern Blunt, South Dakota. A-5

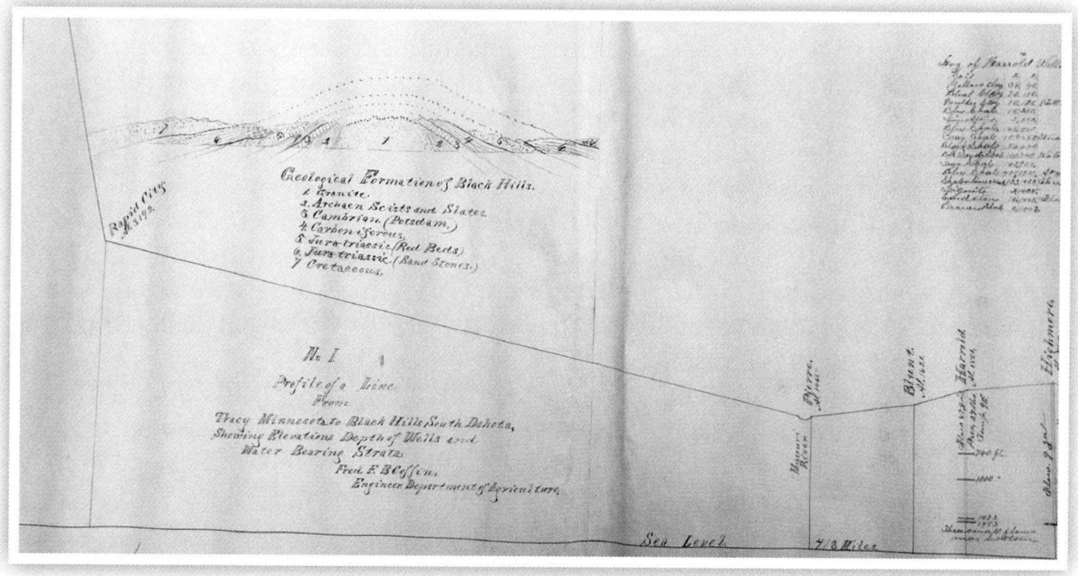

Another of Irish's tasks was to take water table readings, to determine the availability of water for locomotives. This profile shows the depth below ground where water was found. A-6

APPENDIX III: WHERE EXACTLY WAS GAP CREEK CAMP?

In the main text of this book, I introduce the quest to identify Gap Creek, which was not labeled on any modern nor historic maps that could be found. I became increasingly obsessed with finding not only Gap Creek but also Gap Creek Camp, and thus the route Irish planned to follow to get the tracks to Deadwood.

Partly, I was intrigued by the incredibly difficult terrain, curious as to exactly what route he found to get the tracks through the region and down to the Forks of the Cheyenne. I had a secondary interest, however: having already written a book about the Hard Winter of 1880–81, I became fixated on finding the location of the campsite where the men endured that October 1880 blizzard.

The region that held the elusive Gap Creek was Lakota land, not well mapped nor explored. Further, Irish named landmarks such as creeks, ridges, buttes, and bluffs after family and crew members, notations that were relevant only to him and the crew. Most modern and historic maps tend to have no labels attached to creeks in the area (or often no creeks drawn at all), making identifying the surveyor's path in the area between modern Philip and the Forks of the Cheyenne an investigative puzzle.

The COVID-19 pandemic shut down research locations. Further complicating my efforts, maps drawn by Irish were crumbling, so they were removed from access until they could be tended to by the preservation department. Instead, I turned to other sources.

I reached out to dozens of people familiar with the landscape of this region, but enough time had passed that Irish's descriptions were not ringing bells for modern geologists, hydrologists, or ranchers whose families had been on the land for generations.

M. R. Hansen Trip Number One

In the meanwhile, one of the people I'd reached out to sent the name and email address of a retired man who "knew that region inside and out." In research, each bread crumb leads to another—and this bread crumb led to the entire bakery.

M. R. Hansen (a resident of Philip) turned out to be a true soul of the West River region of South Dakota. He not only has deep family roots in the area going back to the first White settlers, but he knew just about everyone. Once upon a time, he taught old-style surveying at the South Dakota School of Mines and Technology. He knew all of the landowners within the region I needed access to. I felt incredibly fortunate to have found such a treasure chest in the shape of a human.

On my first trip to meet him, he excitedly handed over history books of the region, pointing out extended relatives and their connections to various pieces of local lore. It was mind-spinning and fascinating. His energy is every bit as expansive as the landscape.

He enlisted several of his friends, too. We met up with them at a popular gathering spot in Philip, and all were enthusiastic in presenting ideas for where the mysterious Gap Creek could be. More importantly, they had recommendations for which present landowners would be great to contact—along with phone numbers.

The author and M. R. Hansen, on land that his family homesteaded when the region was opened to White settlement. Just over the ridge behind us, one can view the region Irish and his men surveyed to determine the route to the Forks of the Cheyenne. A-7

We were also given advice on which properties we could drive along even before getting official permission. We stopped and talked to countless people who'd driven out to see what we were doing, and upon learning, they gave up whatever information they had as well. Again—good people, kind people.

That first trip to meet M. R. in person, after long correspondence, was in mid-February 2021. I was determined to visit the various scouting and campsite locations during the same seasons that the surveyors saw them. So I needed to see the area between the Missouri and Cheyenne / Belle Fourche Rivers in winter. I wanted to see the terrain in this least hospitable of seasons, behold the sky, feel and smell the air—get a true sense of the place, as best as I could, nearly a century and a half later.

The landscape is beautifully overwhelming near the Cheyenne River, southeast of where the Belle Fourche joins in on the way to the Missouri. It is wide. It is high. It is rough, rough country. Irish described it that way, and it remains so today, even with our modern roads and bridges.

Sitting in our truck, we got as close to the Forks of the Cheyenne as we could without official permission to cross over the invisible line between "It's okay for you to be here" and "Do not trespass." We were on the bluffs, well above the rivers, unable to see down the jagged bluffs to where they joined. We could see dozens of miles eastward across the wide valley that, somewhere, held the secret of Gap Creek and the elusive campsite.

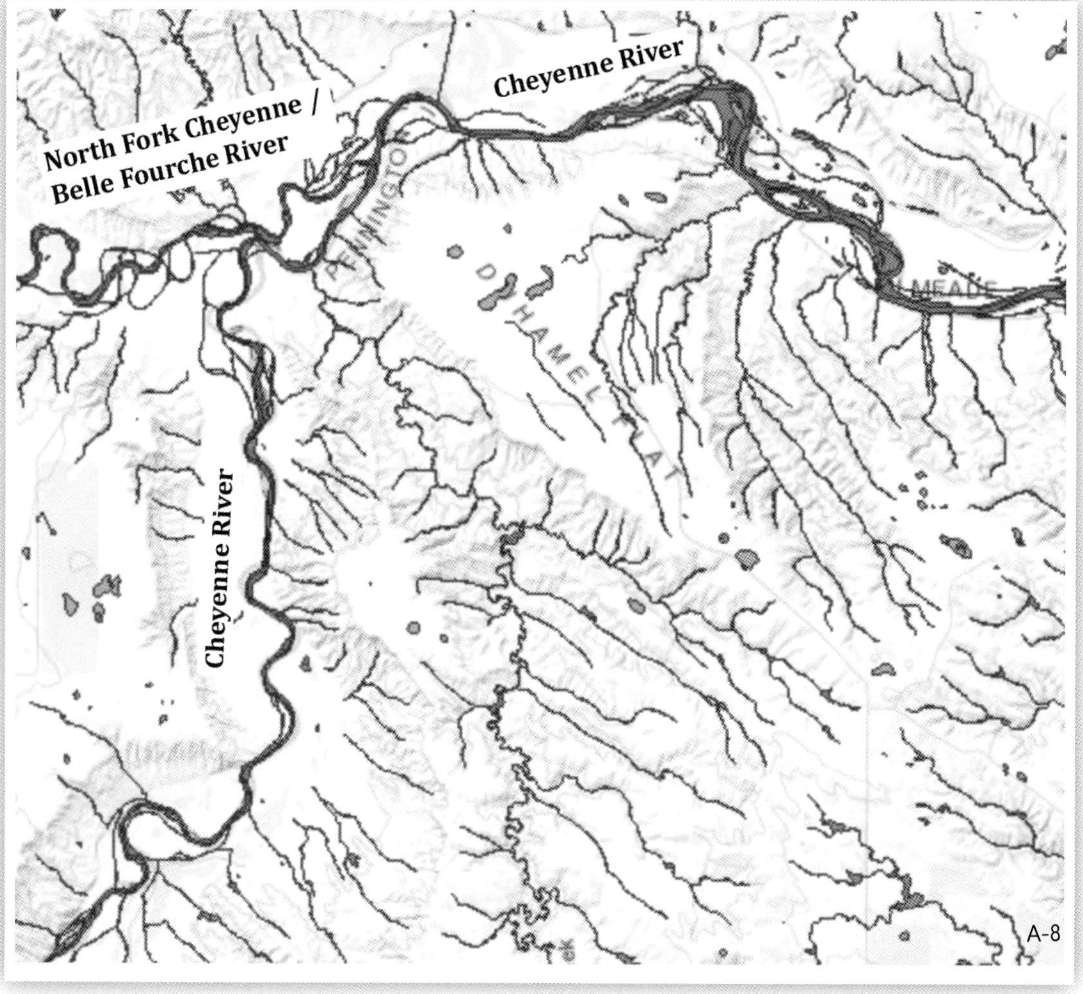

Much of the valley itself looks hospitable enough for a railbed, at least until one gets closer to the Cheyenne. But Irish's mysterious descent down to the Cheyenne remained locked behind "no trespassing" cattle gates. Time had run out on this particular trip, so we made a mental note to visit in the summer, after making phone calls and arrangements.

View north down the valley towards the Gap Creek campsite and, near the top of the photo, the Cheyenne River. This drone photo shows the broken land, yet Irish found a suitable route for the tracks. A-9

Maps in Pierre

After significant roaming around; scanning maps (both modern and historic) with magnifying glasses; talking with many ranchers, hydrologists, geologists, and a surveying instructor; and taking advantage of modern satellite and terrain maps, a couple of theories developed.

I was tantalizingly misdirected for a while when I opened a county history book that showed modern Deep Creek labeled as Opening Creek, thinking, "Hmm . . . *opening* could be a synonym for *gap*." I spent significant time analyzing the landscape along Deep Creek, trying to match its terrain to Irish's tributary names and distance measurements.

Soon after the COVID-19 restrictions were lifted, I packed up a bunch of masks and some paperwork and headed to Pierre. The staff at the South Dakota State Archives were fabulous, and they became curious as well. One staffer in particular, Virginia, went out of her way to dig deep into the archives and records, knowing that landmark names had changed over the years. Many maps were looked through, some getting us teasingly close, only to reveal nothing.

On the next page are but a sample of the maps we perused; they show various levels of detail, but none provided the answers I was looking for. It became increasingly humorous how forgotten that wedge of land seemed in these otherwise relatively detailed maps.

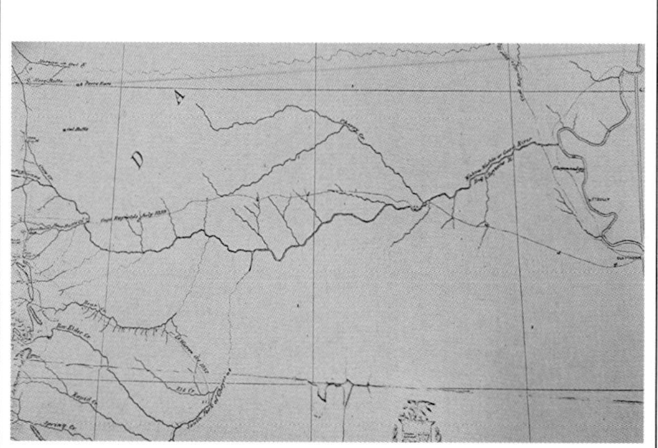

This early map was very generalized and undetailed. A-10

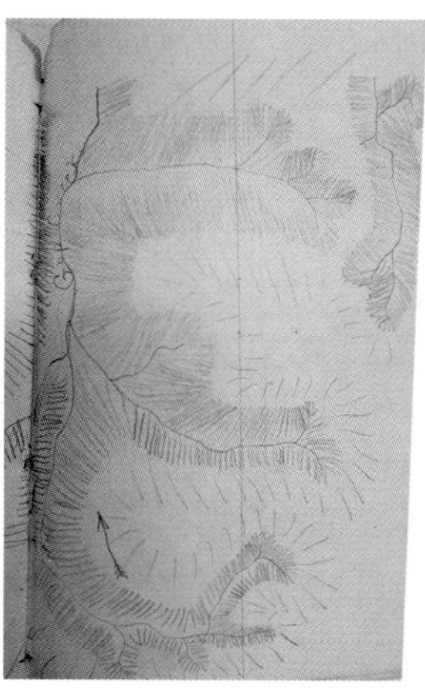

One of Irish's notebook drawings, labeling Gap Creek but without wider context. It shows the creek running north–south, which could indicate modern Deep Creek. A-11

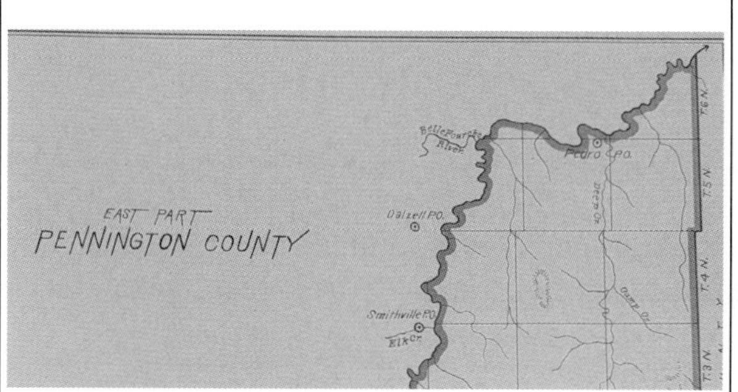

The creek seems to appear on this map, but it is not labeled. The length of the drawn creek also doesn't match Irish's distance descriptions. A-12

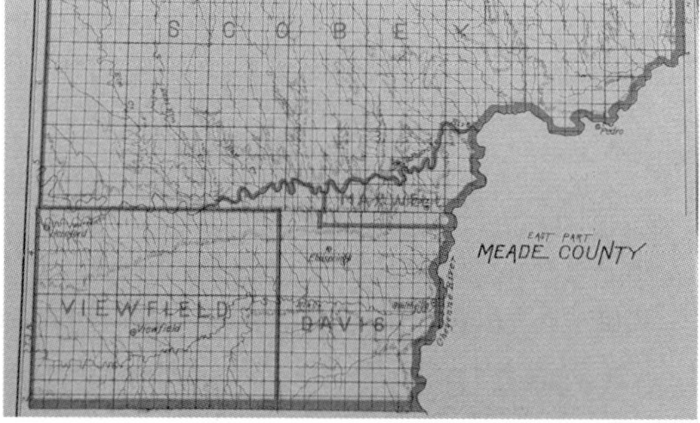

This particular atlas did not contain a page for "East Part Meade County." This experience was typical of the sleuthing using maps of this area. A-13

Halfway through this weeklong researchfest in the South Dakota State Archives, a binder of maps was delivered by the increasingly invested Virginia. Flipping page after page, I was confronted with white space, or an unlabeled wiggly line, but nothing that could help me identify Gap Creek; the maps above are perfect examples of my frustrations.

Fortunately, I am detail-oriented and stubbornly optimistic, and I was afraid I would miss out if I gave up and failed to turn even one page. I was no longer entirely paying attention, though, having developed that stare one gets when having mentally checked out. I flipped a page . . . and then, suddenly, something caught my attention. There, in the back of a simple spiral-bound compilation of map photocopies . . .

I stopped. I stared. I felt a chill. I felt . . . odd. I tilted my face closer to the page. I squinted. I took a deep breath, then looked again.

The map showed a line labeled "Chicago & North Western R. R.," running diagonally from the valley of the Bad River up to the Forks of the Cheyenne. I knew that line had never been built. But . . . here it was, a map illustrating Irish's proposed route to Deadwood—the route that followed Gap Creek down to the Cheyenne, which would then lead them to the valley of the Belle Fourche and thus to Deadwood.

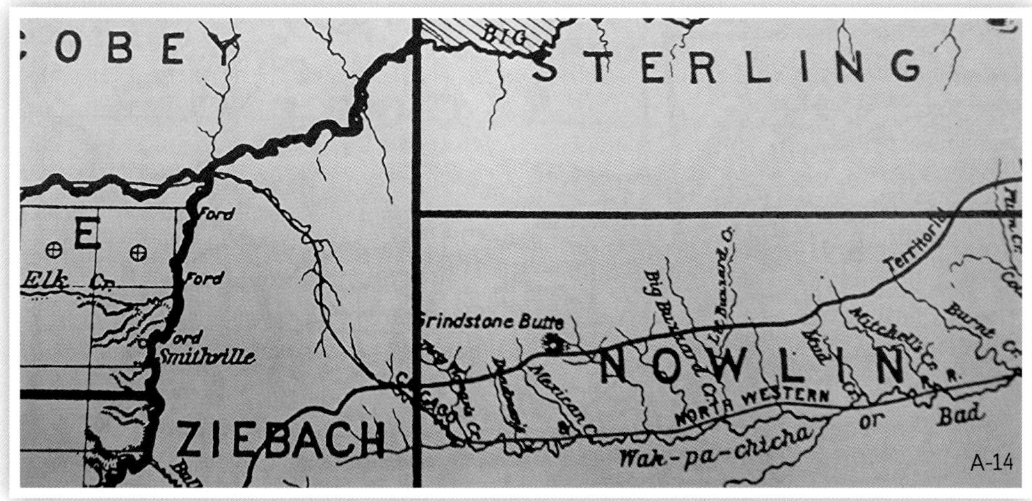

I dug out the pages that described the route as agreed upon between the railroad company and the Lakota; the description matched the map perfectly. I could now compare other historic maps to this map and, using the rest of Irish's clues, narrow the general location where Irish and his men spent that first blizzard of the Hard Winter of 1880–81.

Researchers know the thrill of the find, and the especially thrilling effect of finding something hard wrought. This simple map was one of those moments. It also earned A. F. Dinsmore, the principal draftsman who generated the map in 1889, a special thank-you in this book.

With that said, this map was just a starting point. I then reached out to the National Archives, referencing the House of Representatives bill under which the map had been filed, hoping the record still existed. The online options skipped most of the 48th Congress, which caused concern that the records had somehow been lost. A few days later, an email arrived indicating that the maps did exist, but that due to short staffing, I would have to submit my request at another time. Eventually it became clear that if I wanted to see that map, I would have to go to Washington, DC, which simply wasn't feasible at the time. Instead, I turned back to thinking about Irish's maps at the University of Iowa.

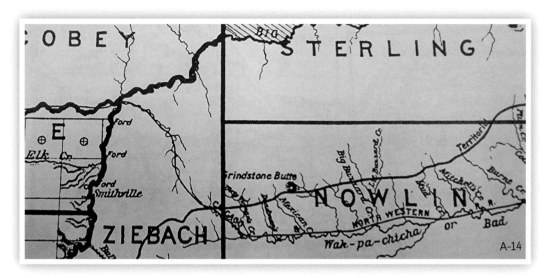

Maps at the University of Iowa–Iowa City

Oh, the most glorious of days! It started frustratingly enough. I had only skimmed the website for parking information; there was a giant lot right next to the library, so I made a cursory mental note and got in the car. I arrived only to discover that not only that lot but all other lots were usable by permit only, with no visitor parking, and street parking was limited to two hours. I eventually found a public ramp and walked the several blocks back to the university library. I got to the Special Collections room just before it opened, then, in stuffing my items into a locker, promptly gashed my arm. Things were starting off bumpy, but they would improve. More than once, I was covered in goose bumps as I again held the original materials I had already been working with for over five years.

Day two was smoother. I knew where to park, and I knew the shortcut through buildings to get to the library more directly. Giselle Simón, the map conservator, met me in the Special Collections room, a cart full of long rolls beside her. The next several hours were the stuff that researchers live for.

My goal was not only to find a detailed map of that large Gap Creek region, but to also see the maps along the route which Rich Dana and I had looked at via our video conference the summer before. I hoped to rephotograph the maps that had been blurry in the video and reexamine the locations of the mystery camps. (You may remember that the videoconference software defaulted to recording the "focus" of the meeting, the person speaking, and I was making plenty of noises when I saw those maps initially. Ugh, that still irritates me!)

Giselle and I looked at each map in the collection related to Irish's time on this project, except one that was so fragile that I deemed it not worth risking a look (a region that was duplicated on other maps and would not have held any new answers). As mentioned earlier, there were maps covered in desiccated mold, some with possible live mold, some that were torn or threatened to tear, and others that looked brand-new. Some were on thin paper, some on thick, some on a coated linen. Some were little more than lines and numbers without context, while others were beautifully detailed. Some were multicolored—an aspect that sadly does not reproduce as well in gray scale, but lovely nonetheless.

Several were stunning. One of the most stunning was so in two ways: First, it was visually beautiful, full of details. Second, it stunned me into disorientation for a few moments—it held the answers.

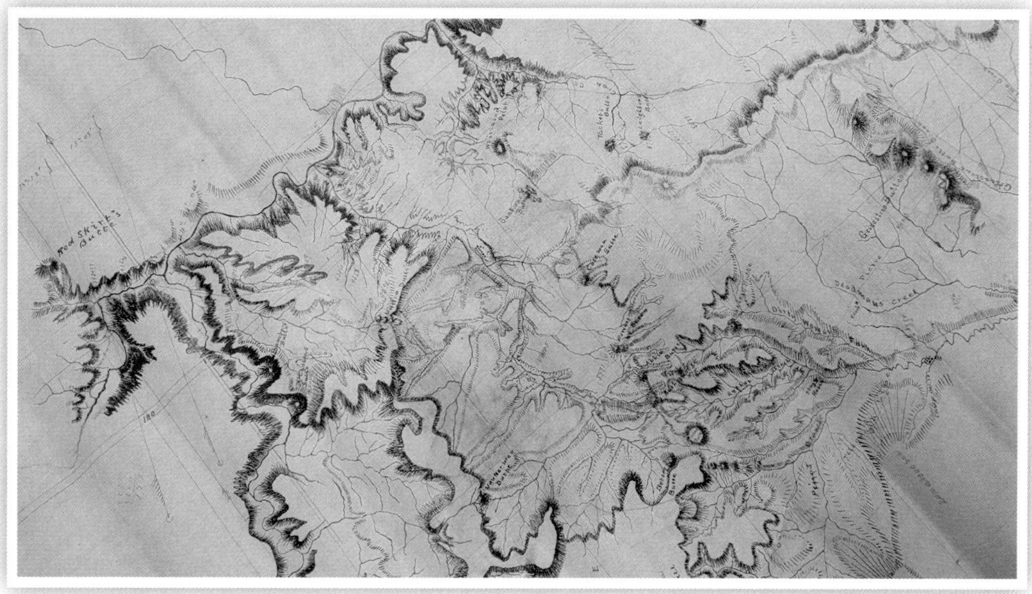

The beautifully executed map on linen that held the answers to the mysterious region between the North Fork of the Bad River and the Forks of the Cheyenne. A-15

Running through the map were red lines showing the main proposed route, as well as alternate lines the crew had identified. The map was also covered in topographical features, all labeled. The ridges and buttes were labeled. The tiny little tributaries that were not the focus of the work were labeled. Most of the larger creeks mentioned in the diaries were labeled. Locations not mentioned in the diaries or letters were labeled. So many labels! But nowhere on this map does the name Gap Creek appear.

I chuckled as I momentarily groused at Irish for having purposefully neglected that label just to tease me. Then, almost as if he'd winked at me, I saw it—he hadn't labeled the camp, but he did draw it.

An example of the small details and many landmark labels on the map. A-16

Bending close to the surface of the map, I saw an assembly of little squares protected on the side of a ridge. The squares were Irish's way of denoting a camp location. Gap Creek Camp, where the men had endured the first blizzard of the Hard Winter, stared back at me. Jackpot! Bingo! Hallelujah! Happy dance! Giselle even had me pose with the map, knowing how momentous this moment was for the wrap-up of my research for this book.

The remaining mysteries were solved, with one minor exception: the camp at Rush Lake, near the Redwood River, would remain a mystery. But it had otherwise been a marvelously fruitful day!

M. R. Hansen Trip Number Two

The unfortunate part of the timing of my two back-to-back trips in early autumn 2022 was that my trip to western South Dakota came a few weeks *before* that fruitful trip to Iowa City. Therefore, I was still working from conjecture and guesses—informed guesses, but guesses nonetheless. Still, it was a productive trip.

Thanks to the map that showed the proposed route, we had a general idea of the location. But the specific valley or ridge that was followed remained to be determined. On the first day of the trip, we met up with M. R.'s brother David, who looked over the maps, listened to the clues, recommended contacts to talk to. The second day, M. R. gave a delightful tour of old family homesteads in the area.

The third day began at the venerable tourist stop Wall Drug, along Interstate 90, on the western end of Badlands National Park—where I got to meet the current, fourth-generation owner of the store, thanks to M. R. knowing, it seems, everyone. Another fun piece of trivia is that M. R.'s father was responsible for painting the original (and ubiquitous) Wall Drug billboards that graced so many roadsides in the middle part of the century.

There, I had the honor of speaking with Linda Eisenbraun, owner of the land where the proposed route would have descended the bluffs to reach the Cheyenne River. After looking at the maps and reading some of Irish's descriptions, she felt that modern Deep Creek was a solid candidate for Gap Creek. She even made a profile drawing of why it was named Deep Creek . . . a drawing that matched one Irish had made. Another bingo! She was likewise confident, however, that they would have followed that creek all the way north to the Cheyenne River, instead of following the creek that meandered through her property. That left us debating back and forth a bit about the discrepancy between her very logical reasoning and the map Irish had drawn.

That map had been filed for congressional approval, and it showed the route following Deep Creek for only part of its run before veering off to the west. With Linda's information freshly in my mind, now full of possibilities, we left the town of Wall and headed north to explore the wide area between Wall and the Forks of the Cheyenne a second time, now with more confidence.

We drove through the plain, following ridges, looking down valleys, speculating. We jumped out of the truck, squinted into the sun, walked along fence lines. Maps were held steady against the wind as we speculated and debated more, then jumped back into the truck and moved to the next location. At each location, we walked up and down the road, peering into smaller valleys as far as we could see from the road. We paid particular attention to one site that was a major candidate for the Gap Creek campsite (this was before I'd had the opportunity to study Irish's pen-on-linen map).

We followed a long, gradual ridge eastward and crossed it on the east side after turning south, taking lots of photographs and talking through many possibilities. In hindsight, we had identified the correct ridge. These in-person reconnaissance treks were paying off, even without the map that confirmed our conjectures. Plus, they were simply fun.

One ridge made a beautiful curve while retaining a suitable width for a rail bed. A-17

The same photograph with a line drawn to show Irish's proposed route along the ridge. A-18

The eastern edge of the area, where the ridges began, showing ridge after ridge leading toward the Cheyenne. A-19

The gentle ridges in the midsection of the plateau, suitable to carry the tracks down toward the Cheyenne River. A-20

Getting closer to determining the route Irish identified for taking the tracks from the head of the North Fork of the Bad River down to the Cheyenne had been intellectually fulfilling, but something was still missing for me as the researcher. Whether my determination was authentic curiosity or inching closer and closer to obsession, I really wanted to find the location of the campsite along Gap Creek where the men spent the October 1880 blizzard. And by "find," I mean *see*.

Captured! The Gap Creek Campsite and the Route to the Cheyenne

During the late morning of Sunday, June 11, 2023, I was part of a group of four people standing on a remote dirt road in western South Dakota, not far from the confluence of the Belle Fourche and Cheyenne Rivers. I was both excited and cautious, trying not to get my hopes up too much about this long-pursued goal of actually *seeing* the Gap Creek camp location.

My friend Steve was nervous, standing there with the brand-new drone he was tasked to operate without the benefit of time to learn how to operate it. The drone used for other outings had sat idle for a while and, inexplicably, was inoperable when he pulled it out to pack it up for the trip. After ascertaining that time was too short to order a replacement part, he purchased a new drone, put it in the car, headed to western South Dakota, and hoped for the best. He now found himself squinting against the sun at the drone's display console, a mix of confidence and perplexity on his face, hoping he wouldn't deliver disappointment instead of footage.

The other two attendees, Ray and Tim, weren't nervous. They were along for the fun of it, and to help Steve keep the drone pointed in the right direction, based on what they knew about my research and the maps they held in their hands.

My priority for flight targets was the Gap Creek campsite, where Irish and a portion of his men hunkered down in canvas tents while the first blizzard of the Hard Winter lashed around them. We stopped the car just outside of a gate that demarked public road from private ranch access, the nearest we could get to the long-sought valley.

The time had come, and the four of us piled out of the car with anticipation and excitement. It only took a few minutes to unpack the drone and get it set up on the road, ready for duty. The drone whirred to life, lifted into the sky, and zipped off to the north. Honestly, it felt a little like sending a child off to kindergarten. We watched until the little drone became a spot, then simply disappeared against the white clouds. Then we could only wait, half holding our breath, hoping all would go well.

The only indications that the drone was still on its mission were reassurances from Steve, who was steadfastly staring at the display console. Since this was a new drone, Steve wasn't always sure what it was doing, and he'd sometimes make "oh" or "oops" sounds, while the rest of us interrupted our conversation to look at Steve for indications that all was well or that disaster had struck.

Suddenly the console sprang to life, beeps and buzzes indicating that battery drain required the drone to return to its starting point. According to the display, it had not yet reached its destination. The campsite was too far from the road, beyond the range of the drone.

With no small feeling of dejection, we awaited its return while brainstorming solutions. Was there a setting that could be changed to reduce battery drain? As it turned out, *yes*! And since we had several fully charged batteries, a second attempt was made.

They say three is lucky, but for us, standing on that sun-soaked ridge, a gentle, drone-friendly breeze blowing across the grasses, the second try was the charm.

On its second flight, the drone flew straight to its destination, revealing with incredible resolution and colors the beauty that was the Gap Creek campsite. Watching the video feels like peacefully hang gliding over the site in awe.

Looking south, this drone photo shows the waterway that Irish called Gap Creek. According to Irish's map, the campsite was on the west (right-hand) side of the creek, on the flat in the area that shows recent erosion. A-21

After several years of reading and rereading diary entries, holding magnifying glasses to maps, working with many manners of experts, and trying to reconcile Irish's ink-and-linen map with modern topographical maps, my efforts had *finally* yielded visuals of the location. Celebratory SweeTarts, courtesy of Tim, were consumed in commemoration.

After the success of the Gap Creek expedition, we moved on, with more confidence, to recording the ridges and route that Irish had identified for getting the tracks from the head of the North Fork of the Bad River down to the Cheyenne.

On an earlier trip, we'd identified a ridge we believed Irish planned to use to get the final few miles down to the Cheyenne. We sent the drone down that ridge, though we had a bit of trouble pointing it in the proper direction. The sun was bright, the wind was a bit stronger along this ridge, the display was difficult to read—and remember, this was the first time Steve was flying this new drone. We hoped for the best, not entirely sure what it would capture.

Later that evening, watching the footage, we were not only surprised but *thrilled* to discover that the drone had gone a bit wayward, but in so doing, it showed that the ridge we had originally identified was not in the least conducive to tracks, while the ridge immediately to the south was smooth and unbroken nearly all the way down. The drone hadn't gone where we wanted it to go, but it had captured exactly what we wanted to find.

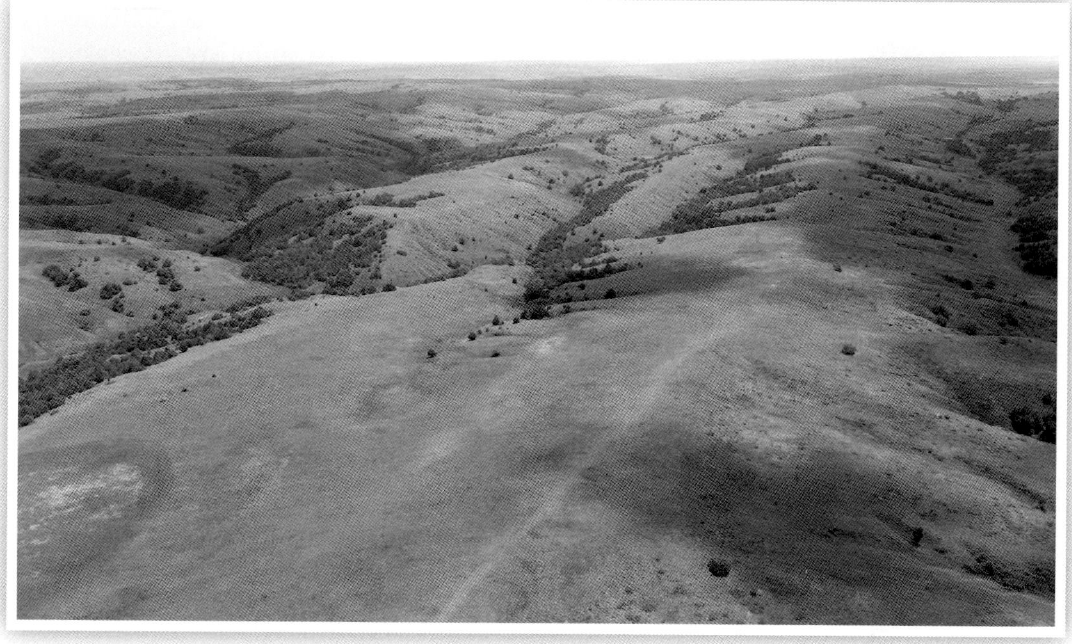

After crossing the ridge from the head of the North Fork of the Bad River, Irish proposed taking the tracks along one ridge, using a bridge to span a short gap onto another ridge, then follow that ridge (above) all the way down to the Cheyenne. A-22

The day was so successful as to be almost overwhelming, but watching the captured footage felt exciting no matter how many times I replayed it. This was another of those days that a researcher lives for.

APPENDIX IV: TOWNSHIP, RANGE & SECTION DELINEATIONS

It is helpful to understand the township-range-section (called the Public Land Survey System, or PLSS) layout of the region. The images here illustrate the concept, using the irregularly shaped Redwood County in Minnesota as an example.

A *range* represented a six-mile-wide swath of land, east-to-west, with the numbers increasing as one moved westward. Each range was then subdivided into six-mile-long squares of land called *townships*, with numbers increasing from south to north. Townships were named as White people settled them, as shown below.

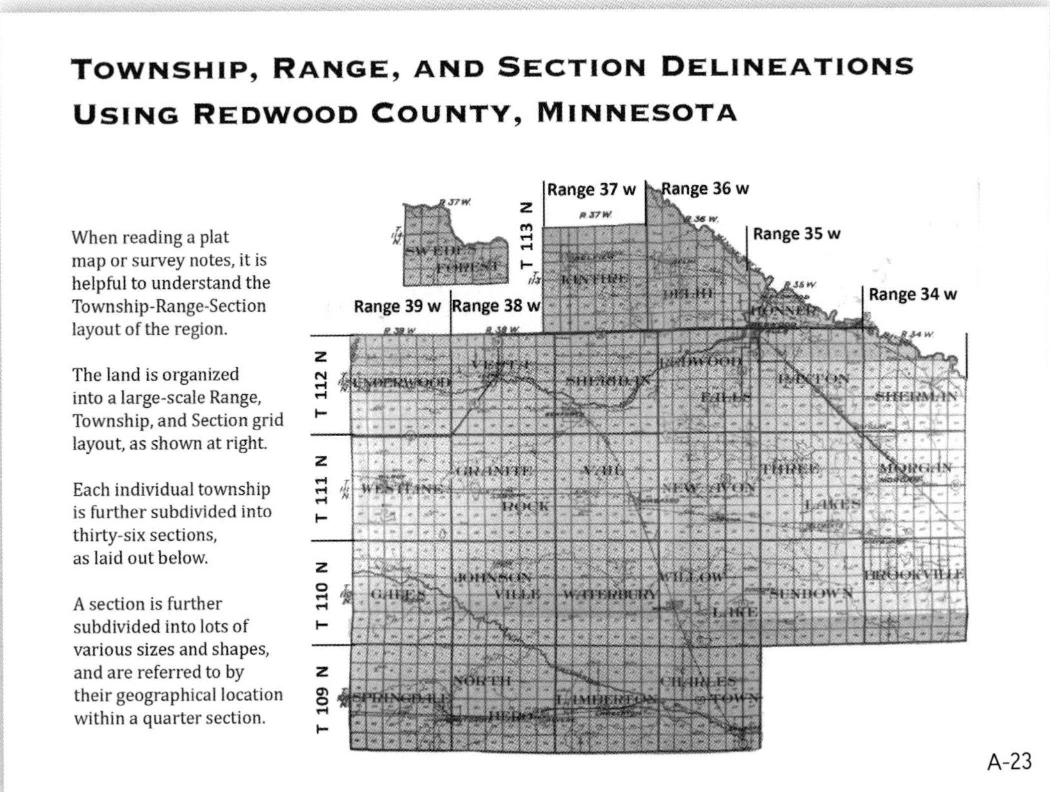

Township, Range, and Section Delineations
Using Redwood County, Minnesota
When reading a plat map or survey notes, it is helpful to understand the Township-Range-Section layout of the region.
The land is organized into a large-scale Range, Township, and Section grid layout, as shown at right.
Each individual township is further subdivided into thirty-six sections, as laid out below.
A section is further subdivided into lots of various sizes and shapes, and are referred to by their geographical location within a quarter section.
Range 39 w
Range 38 w
Range 37 w
Range 36 w
Range 35 w
Range 34 w
T 113 N
T 112 N
T 111 N
T 110 N
T 109 N
A-23

Each township was further subdivided into thirty-six one-mile-square *sections*, as laid out on the next page.

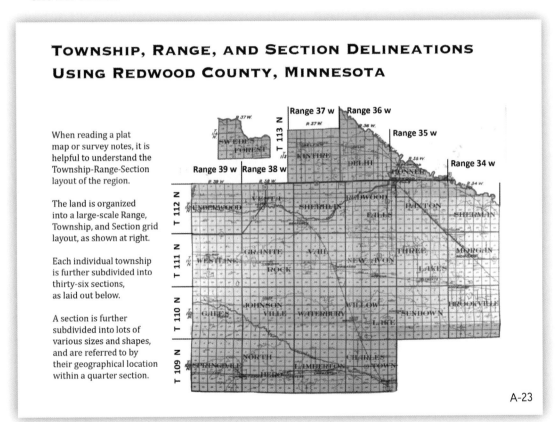

Township Section Grid

This diagram is of a single township. Each number represents an individual section within that township.

[----------------------6 miles----------------------]

6	5	4	3	2	1
7	8	9	10	11	12
18	17	16	15	14	13
19	20	21	22	23	24
30	29	28	27	26	25
31	32	33	34	35	36

[----------------------6 miles----------------------]

[1 mile] [1 mile]

A-24

The *sections* could then be further subdivided into various shapes and sizes and referred to by their geographical location within the section—for instance, "the northwest quarter of the northeast quarter of Section 18."

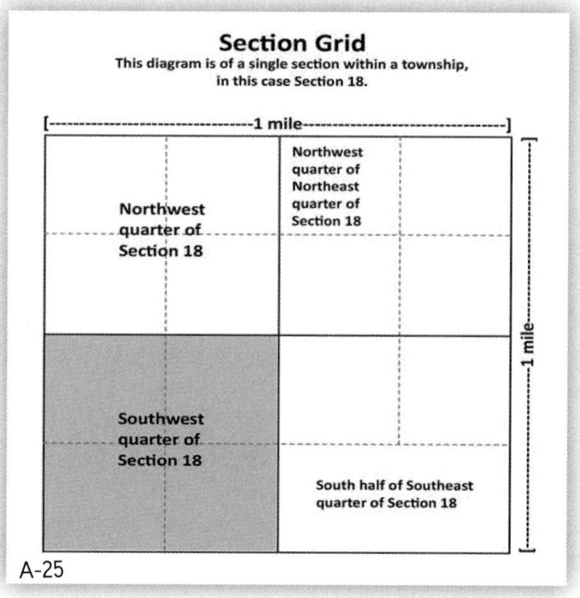

A-25

APPENDIX V: STEAMBOATS MENTIONED IN THE DIARIES

According to author Michael Gillespie in his book *Wild River, Wooden Boats*, "the untamed Missouri was as close to a living thing as a river could get. And it seemed very disinclined to become a highway of commerce."[189] Yet that is exactly how it was used. Full of snags and sandbars, frozen about five months of the year, and either too high or too low much of the remaining months, it was a frustrating pathway to travel.

In *Forts of the Upper Missouri*, author Robert G. Athearn detailed how army bureaucracy compounded the natural opposition of the river. River transportation was, in theory, inexpensive. So the army purchased the fur post at Fort Pierre, planning to ship goods upriver to that point before they were sent over land. Experienced river pilots noted that existing boats were too heavy for the river, so the army had lighter, lower-draft boats built for the purpose. Several other boats were enlisted to haul goods from St. Louis to Fort Pierre. As Athearn writes, "The 'Big Muddy' answered the challenge so successfully that not a single vessel reached its objective with a full cargo."[190] That was in 1855. In 1863, General Sully was trying to lead troops around the region against various Native tribes. It was not a success, partly due to their unfamiliarity with the landscape, but also due to the river. "The enigmatic Missouri had frustrated his efforts so effectively," writes Athearn, "that the navigational season almost passed before he could get his force in the field."[191] So it would go, season after season.

Several methods of plying the waters were employed, but steamboats were the largest, most impressive, and most problematic. Their large paddlewheels—fixed on the sides of the boat (sidewheelers) or on the back (sternwheelers)—provided propulsion, but they were frequently damaged by driftwood and snags; the individual paddles (called buckets) would break, but they were replaced as necessary with spare parts carried on all steamers.

Of travel on the finicky river, early missionary Father Pierre-Jean De Smet wrote, "I fear the sea I will admit, but all the storms and unpleasant things I have experienced in four different voyages did not inspire so much terror in me as the navigation of the somber, treacherous and muddy Missouri."[192] (Father De Smet traveled widely among the Native peoples of the Midwest and Northwest during the mid-nineteenth century. The town of De Smet, South Dakota, was named for him.)

Steamboats were insatiably hungry for wood (estimated to burn about a cord an hour), which fueled the boilers that created the steam. Along the river, private "woodyards" were operated by individuals who harvested whatever wood they could find to sell to the boats. As a boat moved along the river, it would stop at any number of these woodyards to replenish supplies. An April 1880 logbook for the steamer *Benton* listed the woodyards stopped at, which included eleven between the upper end of the Big Bend and Pierre: upper end

Big Bend, Medicine Creek, Joe Creek, Cedar Island, Dorion-Loisel Island, Chapelle Creek, Fort George, Medicine Creek, Farm Island, Bad River, and Pierre. Seven more were listed between Pierre and Cheyenne Agency: Lost Island, Oahe Mission, Chantier Creek, Okobojo Creek, Fort Sully, Fort Bennett, and Cheyenne River.[193]

Boats frequently ran aground on sandbars, but the worst hazard in the river were the snags—old trees that had fallen into the river and lay mostly below the surface, their limbs waiting to puncture the hulls of the passing boats. Some sank in just minutes. One researcher noted that 204 of the 289 confirmed sinkings in the Missouri River were due to striking snags or rocks.[194]

Terrors on the boat itself involved fire and explosions. The boats were made of wood and coated with paint based in linseed oil, and with fires heating the boilers—not to mention stoves for cooking or heat, lanterns, etc.—even a minor mishap could set off a conflagration.

For White people, use of the Missouri River evolved from exploration to fur trade highway to army fort resupply channel. In the late 1870s, gold seekers looking to get to the Black Hills or Montana were also making heavy use of river transportation, and the population around Fort Pierre began to grow. Below are summary details of each of the boats mentioned by Irish:

- ***Black Hills*:** (Mr. & Mrs. Irish rode this boat from Yankton to Pierre.) Sternwheel packet boat. Launched in 1877 at California, Pennsylvania. After wintering at Bismarck, it was destroyed on March 28, 1884, cut down by ice.
- ***Fontenelle*:** (Irish saw it on the river.) Sternwheel packet boat. Launched in 1870 at Brownsville, Pennsylvania (some records say 1868). Destroyed March 1881 in Yankton, Dakota Territory, cut down by ice.
- ***Meade*, or *General Meade*:** (Ruth and Lizzie took this boat to Pierre.) Sternwheel packet boat. Launched in 1875 at Pittsburgh, Pennsylvania. Broke loose from its mooring during the March 1881 Yankton flood and was carried downriver, but was recovered. Destroyed September 4, 1888, by a snag at Pelican Bend.
- ***Red Cloud*:** (Irish saw it on the river.) Sternwheel. Destroyed July 11, 1882, after hitting a snag in Montana Territory.
- ***Western*:** Took Mrs. Irish, Ruth, and Lizzie back to Yankton. Sternwheel packet boat. Launched in 1872 at Pittsburgh, Pennsylvania. Destroyed March 1881 near Yankton, Dakota Territory, in an ice crush.

APPENDIX VI: FORTS AND AGENCIES

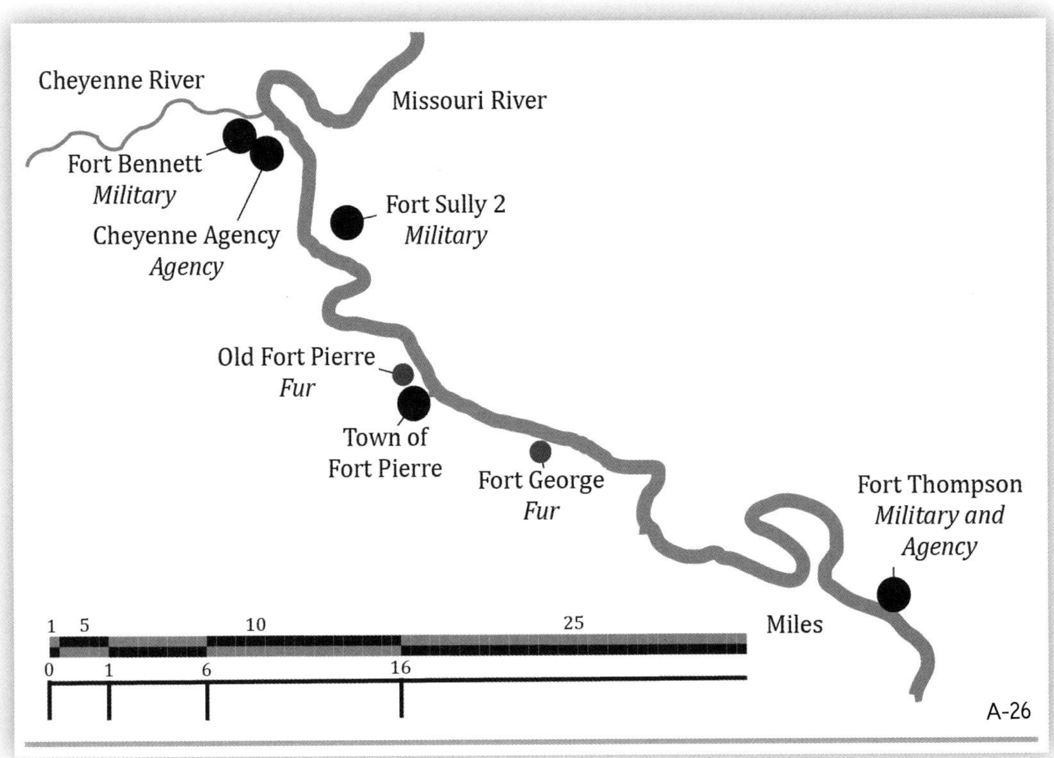

The history of the forts along the Missouri between the Cheyenne River, to the north, and the "Big Bend," to the south, is its own fascinating tale. It can also be confusing and convoluted. Some forts began as trading posts for the old fur companies. Some were military forts. Some were fur posts that became military posts. Some were military forts that became Indian agencies. Many had more than one location, due to being unfavorably sited the first time, and sometimes the second time, too. With all those differences and changes, tracking them requires deep attention to detail and an archaeologist's patience for finding tiny bits of data to piece things together, which at times are intimately interwoven.

One could easily dive too deeply into this aspect of history (you are encouraged to do so—it is very interesting). However, to keep to the scope of Irish's survey duties, a basic history of the forts mentioned within his diaries and letters is included, covering the years 1879–1881, just enough to provide some context for the diary and letter mentions (and okay, maybe a little bit of history thrown in).

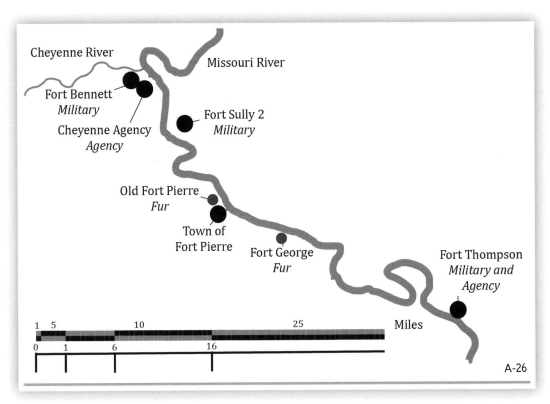

Basic History

The military's official role was to keep the peace between the White settlers and the Native peoples, the latter being pushed ever westward of the ever-moving "frontier."

The Yankton Treaty, signed in 1858, was one of many with the Lakota, and it set in motion the expansion of White settlers into Dakota Territory. The military's role soon expanded to protecting Native land from White encroachment. The two purposes would occupy various governmental agencies for the next several decades.

In 1868, the Treaty of Fort Laramie officially and legally noted that the land upon which Fort Pierre sat belonged to the Lakota. At the same time, it legally opened southeastern Dakota Territory to White settlement (except those areas already designated as reservations). Then an 1877 act of Congress opened the Black Hills to White settlement.

Fort Pierre (Fur Post, Then Military Post, Then Town)

The story of Fort Pierre—originally Fort Pierre Chouteau, named after merchant Pierre Chouteau Jr., whose family's wealth came from the fur trade—is a great example of how interwoven the histories of the Missouri River forts can be.

There had been some assembly of White residents in the vicinity of modern Fort Pierre since 1817 (as Fort LaFramboise), but Fort Pierre began life as an American Fur Company trading post in the early 1830s, located a few miles north of modern Fort Pierre (the town). Years later it was moved three miles to the north, then sold to the United States in 1855 to serve as a military post. It was not well placed for that purpose, so the army dismantled most of the structures in 1857 and moved them downstream to help construct buildings at Fort Randall, which had been established the year before.

In 1858, a second Fort Pierre was established two miles to the north of the previous Fort Pierre; it, too, would be abandoned, this time in 1863, and its items were moved over to Farm Island (near modern Pierre, on the east side of the Missouri River) to be near the first Fort Sully during the punitive expedition in Minnesota led by Colonel Sibley after the Dakota War of 1862. Gold had also been discovered in Montana in 1862, and the main access to the gold fields was via the Missouri River, drawing thousands through the tiny settlement on Farm Island. This iteration, too, was then deemed unfavorable, this time for being so vulnerable on a low island, so Fort Sully moved a couple dozen miles upriver to become Fort Sully 2.

In 1876, a larger (though still relatively small) wave of settlers began to establish themselves near the mouth of the Bad River, borrowing the old fort's name to establish the town of Fort Pierre. By 1877, there was a main street that ran perpendicular to the Missouri River, hosting "a group of business buildings . . . Sherwood's Hotel among them."[195] An 1877 act of Congress opened the Black Hills to White people following the discovery of gold there. The intervening years had seen various attempts to keep White people out, but the 1877 act made their presence legal. However, getting to the Hills required trespassing on Lakota land. The allowance of a wagon road from Fort Pierre to Deadwood meant a relatively safe route to the gold fields, across the Great Sioux Reservation. Situated on the eastern end of that road, the thriving business community of Fort Pierre catered to the needs of these transients.

By 1879, Fort Pierre was a community of about two hundred, and one of few communities allowed west of the Missouri. It was also the eastern terminus for the Fort Pierre to Deadwood Trail, a stage and freight road.

Fort George (Fur Post)

There were two, both long gone by 1879. It was the second location—Fort George 2, about fifteen miles downstream from modern Fort Pierre—that was mentioned in Irish's diaries. This fort was for the Union Fur Company, a competitor of the American Fur Company (Fort Pierre). The operators of Fort George were notorious for liberally dispensing alcohol among the Lakota.

Irish and his men scouted a few miles up Fort George Creek, investigating a route across and westward away from the Missouri. The team's winter encampment on Fort George Island, used in late 1879 and early 1880, was on the east side of the Missouri, across from Fort George 2.

Fort Thompson (Military Post & Indian Agency)

Originally created as the Upper Missouri Agency in 1861, this is where bands of Minnesota Dakota were sent following the Dakota War of 1862. In 1871, the military post of Fort Thompson became Crow Creek Indian Agency, and it was operating as such during the time Irish visited. Built in 1864, it was abandoned just a few years later. In 1870, it was deemed a "sub-post" of Fort Sully 2, and the military post was dismantled in 1878; the agency remained, though the location was still referred to as Fort Thompson.

Fort Sully (Military Post)

There were two Fort Sully locations, the first operating from 1863 to 1866 on Farm Island, near the modern city of Pierre. That location was unfavorable, and in 1866 it was moved about twenty-five miles upriver. It is this northern location, Fort Sully 2, that is referenced throughout this work, except where "old Fort Sully" is mentioned, which means Fort Sully 1.

Fort Sully's population was tasked with keeping White people out of the Great Sioux Reservation, protecting the lives of employees at the nearby Indian agencies, keeping the Lakota within reservation boundaries, and upholding the rights of Lakota and White people alike.

Life at Fort Sully was mostly quiet, though the post did participate in some of the larger campaigns against the Plains tribes. It also provided escorts for surveyors working to find a route for the Northern Pacific in the years prior to the Panic of 1873, and when construction work resumed on multiple lines in 1879.

The August 6, 1879, *Yankton Daily Press and Dakotaian* contained a description of Fort Sully from a "Special Correspondent." In part it read,

> We rode through a hilly and broken country for ten miles and then traveled over a level country for about eight or more miles, and we could see the prairie for a distance of about fifty miles . . . Reached Fort Sully at 2 o'clock p.m. and took quarters at the Frandy hotel, kept by a discharged soldier. Ft. Sully is built on an elevated plateau and is surrounded on the south and west by the Missouri river, and on the east and north at a distance of 1800 yards by high bluffs. As a military post to protect itself against an attack, Ft. Sully is the best situated fort on the Missouri river. The buildings are in the shape of a quadrangle, the officer's quarters to the west, the hospital, bakery and laundry to the south, the soldiers quarters to the east, and the offices, post library and Odd Fellow's hall to the north. There is a magnificent square inside of the buildings, covered with grass, in the centre of which is an immense cistern containing 100,000 gallons of water. Surrounding the buildings inside there is a gravel sidewalk planted with trees and outside of the sidewalk a road, also made of gravel. The road and sidewalk are free of weeds, and the place looks so clean that one would think himself transported inside of a public square in the city of Philadelphia or Washington.[196]

Fort Sully 2 was abandoned in 1894, and it is now partially submerged beneath the waters of the Missouri, in Lake Oahe, due to the Oahe Dam. The modern Fort Sully Game Refuge is upon land that hosted the fort and was the focus of much of Irish's attention in the summer of 1880.

Fort Sully 2 in the 1880s. A-27

Fort Bennett & Cheyenne River Agency

Cheyenne River Agency was established in 1869 (part of the Fort Laramie Treaty of 1868). The following year, a military post was built next door to protect it, as the next closest military post was seven miles away (Fort Sully). "The post at Cheyenne River Agency," as it was initially referred to, was renamed Fort Bennett in 1878 in honor of Captain Andrew S. Bennett, who had fallen in battle. As the settlements grew side by side—separated by nothing more than "a picket fence"[197]—Cheyenne Agency came to be described as "the town adjoining Fort Bennett."[198]

The two entities—Fort Bennett and Cheyenne Agency—worked in physical and administrative conjunction. The *Yankton Daily Press and Dakotaian* related some nicknames for men at both locations that give a sense of the comradery between them: "Captain Schwan, Indian agent, is called by the Indians 'The-man-that-never-laughs'; Lt. Brown, commander of the scouts, assistant agent, is called by the Cheyennes 'Pretty Boy.'"[199] (Irish interacted with both Captain Schwan, acting agent until May 27, 1880, and Leonard Love, who assumed the post at that time; Agent Love was in charge during the

August 1880 negotiations that allowed the surveying to continue west of the Missouri.)

The same "Special Correspondent" who described Fort Sully in glowing terms was equally *unimpressed* with Fort Bennett, saying,

> The fort does not present a beautiful appearance. The officers' headquarters, numbering seven, face the Missouri and back of them, at a distance of fifty feet, is a long building, which looks like a large barn occupied by the companies. At the back of the fort is a chain of bluffs, which if occupied by the Indians, would give them a splendid chance to pick off the troops one by one with their rifles. There are at present five companies at the fort. Mr. James C. Robb is post trader at Fort Bennett, and is doing an immense business. His store is larger than any in Yankton.[200]

As to the state of Cheyenne Agency, the correspondent said the buildings were "distributed on the place without any symmetry, but [were] new and commodious"[201]; those buildings included a trading post, "the prosperous Hammond Cattle ranch,"[202] and B. P. Hoover's milk ranch, which also operated as "an ice cream saloon."[203]

The local Lakota had taken a deep interest in cattle, with each family averaging "25–50 head." Cattle ranching quickly outpaced agriculture as the vocation of the Cheyenne Agency, as would be true for settlers, too.

Following the Dawes / General Allotment Act, Fort Bennett was abandoned on November 18, 1891, and Cheyenne Agency was moved fifty-six miles up the Missouri, across from Forest City.

Fort Bennett (1878–1891) in the late 1880s. The old Cheyenne River Agency No. 1 (1870–90) is visible in the center background. A-28

APPENDIX VII: BIOGRAPHIES OF THE IRISH FAMILY

Charles Wood Irish (1834–1904)

Upon Irish's passing, obituaries and articles sprung up in newspapers not only from across Iowa and Dakota Territory but from Minnesota, California, Nebraska, Washington (state), Connecticut, Wisconsin, New York, Missouri, Kansas, Massachusetts, Colorado, and doubtless many others. His impact stretched coast to coast. Many noted his passing with sorrow and included some level of extract from the in memoriam bulletin shared below (unfortunately, often with errors sprinkled in).

One newspaper edition published on September 28, 1904—it is unclear where, though likely somewhere in Iowa, possibly Iowa City—noted that in the days before Irish's passing, he had sent several telegrams, "all of startling, but preparatory import, warning" daughter Lizzie "of his dangerous illness." He knew the end was near, and "for 36 hours prior to his end, he was unconscious, and there was no hope for his recovery."[204] The article continued,

> He was 80 miles from a railroad, when stricken down with his old ailment—traemic poisoning [see note below]—and it was only the indefatigable efforts of the loving workmen to whom he had accorded countless favors, that made possible even the crude attention that he could promptly receive. The gently ministering hand of but one woman was present, the wife of a member of the camp lending all possible eassistance [*sic*] in the easing of his last hours.

("Traemic" may refer to *hyponatremia*, or low concentration of sodium in the blood, which can cause many issues within the body; there is also *hypernatremia*, an abnormally high sodium concentration, though rehydration usually resolves that.)

The article finished with, "In Mr. Irish's death, the profession loses one of the ablest men in this country. The Hawkeye state loses a citizen who has given it magnificent service, and [Iowa City] loses a truly noble-natured, upright, honorable and beloved citizen."

He was living in Gold Creek, Nevada, and making plans for a visit home to Iowa City when he became ill and died. His remains were escorted home by his brother John, and the funeral was held on October 3, 1904, at All Souls' Church in Iowa City. The solemn event was well attended, and "the assemblage which accompanied the body to Oakland Cemetery was a long one, befitting a man who spent fifty years as one of the most prominent citizens" of Iowa City. A significant biography was published in memoriam; it is included in the subsequent pages in full:

IN MEMORIAM

GENERAL CHARLES WOOD IRISH

The death of General Charles Wood Irish, September 27, 1904, at Gold Creek, Nev., marks the loss of a worker—a man of high purpose and strength of character. He was suddenly stricken down while engaged in his life's work, that of engineering. From earliest manhood he had engaged in this profession and as lasting monuments to his technical skill the United States has, especially through the great West, many excellent railroads that are the result of his labor and ability as an engineer.

A NETWORK OF RAILS

As a pioneer of Iowa his earliest work was done in this state, beginning with the old Clinton and Lyons road, which was one of the first attempts at railroading in Iowa, and was never completed. Soon after it fell through, General Irish was employed by John I. Blair of New Jersey, the famous railway builder, in locating the Chicago & Northwestern from Clinton to Council Bluffs. He also located in this state several branches to the main east and west lines as the C. G. W. and the B., C. R. N., the C. & N. W. from Mankato, Minn., to the Black Hills, Dakota, the C. B. & Q. of Illinois, and a branch of the C. & N. W. in Wisconsin, are the results of his labor in the north. Because of illness he had to refuse a call to help locate the Northern Pacific. In the Southwest he helped to locate the Atchison, Topeka & Santa Fe and was the builder of the Royal Gorge bridge across the canon [*sic*] for the Arizona and Colorado road. During his residence at Iowa City he was for a number of years the city engineer and helped in many ways towards the development of the city and county.

IN GOVERNMENT SERVICE

In 1886 he removed to the state of Nevada having been appointed by President Cleveland surveyor general of that state. He remained in this capacity until 1893, when he was called, again by President Cleveland, to be chief of the Irrigation Bureau, with headquarters at Washington, D. C. For this office his previous experience particularly well suited him.

Later he opened an engineering office at Reno, Nev., whence he was called to Gold Creek, where he was General Manager of the Coleman Placer Gold Mines of Hope Gulch. Here it was after years of skilled and faithful service, he received the final summons. He has also been deputy mineral surveyor of the State of Nevada for the past eight years. His motto was work, and few and brief were his vacations.

AS A SCIENTIST

When not engaged in the engineering field he was studying and investigating in the realms of science. He was an astronomer of no small fame, and were his writings on this subject collected they would make a valuable little volume.

His own private observatory was well equipped with instruments and the result of his observations were sought by noted students in this subject, and were published not only by the bulletins issued by the Smithsonian Institution, but also in those issued by the Astronomical Observatory of the Academy of Sciences, Paris, where they were accorded first rank with those made by astronomers of the famous world observatories.

He was the promoter of and one of the charter members of the Iowa State Engineering society, also a member of the National Engineering Association. General Irish was a warm friend of the Iowa State University, and in its museum are to be found a large and valuable collection of specimens generously donated by him, especially the minerals and flora of the United States. He has also contributed generously to the museum of Rochester, N. Y. Prof. Ward, its founder, was one of his warmest personal friends.

A HELPFUL FRIEND

General Irish was in the 50's a resident of Tama County, Ia. This region of our state was then on the frontier and was full of possibilities for a young man of his tastes and ability. Here he was county surveyor. He made the preliminary survey, and with J. H. Hollen first discovered the feasibility of Tama's water power. He laid off and plotted Oak Hill cemetery. He surveyed and plotted Bodfish and Brown's addition to Iuka and the J. H. Hollen addition to Tama City. He lived in Toledo and for some time on a farm west of Toledo, and was for a brief while a teacher. His library and his electrical and scientific instruments were a boon to the pioneer residents, for General Irish made all welcome who came to his home seeking intellectual help. He was a close observer of men and things; had an excellent memory and a mind stored with a fund of rare experience. Being a charming conversationalist and genial in nature his company was sought by young and old. Of the young he was very fond and never lost an opportunity to help and encourage them. To this end he assisted the young people of Iowa City interested in science to organize an Agassiz association. To this he gave much time, taking the club into the field for observation and then meeting for a time in his own study with them, giving talks and helping them with miscroscopical [*sic*] work. Thus were his moments employed; were we to count the length of his life in achievements we should find he had really lived a much longer time than his three score years and ten.

HIS INHERITED TASTES

He was of Quaker parentage and was born in New York City, February 11, 1834, and came with his parents to Johnson County, Ia., in 1839. He was the eldest son of Captain Frederick Macey Irish, one of the leading pioneers of this state. His mother was Elizabeth Ann Robinson of Mamaronneck [*sic*], Westchester County, New York, a descendant of the notable Rev. John Robinson who led the Pilgrims to Leyden and invoked God's blessing upon the Mayflower and her freight of lives that July morning nearly 200 years ago. General Irish's father, Captain Frederick Macey Irish, was of a sea-faring family whose ancestors for generations had followed the sea. Their home was the Island of Nantucket. Shortly after the close of the Revolutionary war, a colony left the island and settled at Hudson, N. Y. With this colony came General Charles Irish's grandfather, Jonathan Irish and family, also the Worths, Folgers, Coffins and Maceys; all of kin, for the Maceys, who first settled the island under the circumstances practically told by Whittier in the "Exciles," early became confident with the Irishes and these in turn with the other families mentioned.

All were brave Quaker sailors and Hudson became a whaling port, but Jonathan Irish and his wife Ruth, sought to rear their sons to a less dangerous calling, so they plunged into the wilderness of central New York, where amid the forest they built them a home. Here they reared a family of 12—but futile was the forest refuge against that long hereditary passion for the sea. Several of the sons, amongst them Frederick, felt the sea spell strong upon them and returned to Nantucket to realize the dreams of their youth by going on the same pathless waves of their fore-fathers.

General Charles W. Irish inherited much of this brave spirit of his ancestors—the spirit to go forth and do the world's work regardless of the vicissitudes which beset the way, and in many of his engineering trips across our great untamed Western plains and through the mountain fastnesses the way was as pathless for him, the pioneer, as had been the ocean to his forefathers.

A LOVER OF NATURE

His was a rugged constitution which helped him to endure cheerfully for so many years the hardships of camp life; hardships made doubly hard by the severe winter storms of the North or the debilitating heat of the plains of the South and West. Often far from the centers of civilization and entirely without communication with the outside world for months at a time, he was sustained and cheered in his isolation by his great love of Nature and his cheerful, studious habits. In this isolated life he was often compelled to subsist entirely upon wild fruits or game, and was a fine marksman but not a sportsman. He never wantonly destroyed the life of any creature. On the contrary he, if possible, gained its confidence and studied its habits, often succeeding in so taming the wild animals that they would come to his camp and even eat from his hands. With the wild Indians also he never had trouble though he was in the heart of the Apachee country when Geronimo and his band were at large, and on the plains of Dakota when the Sioux led by Sitting Bull, were on the war-path; yet though General Irish was in daily contact with them he by kindness and never deceiving gained and held their confidence, teaching them and in turn learning their language and customs. This love of Nature, good judgment, and sound moral worth, particularly fitted him for so broad and active a life, while his kindness of heart made him a helpful friend to those in trouble. General Irish was quick to respond to the calls of the sick and suffering and skillful in relieving their pain. In this capacity alone he has endeared himself to hundreds to whom in the absence of medical aid he has gladly ministered, riding many miles, often at night, to set broken bones, dress wounds or nurse the sick. His heart was full of that tender feeling which to the last glorified his life and works. He was truly one of Nature's noblemen. While not united with any church he was raised under Quaker principles and was a man of broad and liberal religious faith and the trust he felt in God is well expressed in these lines of Whittier:

I know not where His islands lift

Their fronded palms in air;

I only know I cannot drift

Beyond his love and care.

FAMILY TIES

General Irish was married at Solon, Ia., April 8, 1855, to Miss Susannah Abigail Yarbrough, whose father, Zachariah Yarbrough of Lexington, N. C., was a grandson of Benjamin Merrill, one of the famous band of Regulators of North Carolina who captured and executed Governor Tryon in 1771.

Mrs. Irish and two daughters, Miss Elizabeth Irish of the University Business College of Iowa City, and Mrs. Dr. Charles H. Preston of Davenport, are left to deeply mourn the loss of so truly a good husband and father. There are also three grandchildren, the Misses Abbie and Ella Preston of Davenport and their brother, Charles Irish Preston. Gen. Irish also leaves three brothers, Hon. Gilbert Robinson Irish of Iowa City, Prof. Thomas Irish of Dubuque, Colonel John P. Irish of Oakland, Cal., and one sister, Miss Ruth Elizabeth Irish of Iowa City.

General Irish's whole life was lived in accordance with this sentiment ef [*sic*] Epictetus:

"God has delivered yourself to your care, and says: I had no one fitter to trust than you. Preserve this person for me as he is by nature; modest, beautiful, noble, tranquil."

[End of published biography.]

Susannah Abigail "Abbie" Irish (1837–1925)

Abbie was born in North Carolina but moved with her family, at age nine, to Iowa City. In her teens, she moved to live with her married older sister, five miles to the north. There, she became intrigued with her teacher, Mr. Charles Wood Irish, and the two married a year later.

As she wrote for a biographical sketch in a Johnson County Iowa history,

> Mr. Irish and I together braved many dangers on the Dakota plains; experienced severe winters, with deep snows and famine—followed by floods and a reign of terror due to the attempt of desperadoes filled with bad whisky to gain control of the settlement and its meager supply of food stuffs. We knew personally many of the

> foremost Indian chieftains of the Dakotas, for Mr. Irish had to meet them in council and obtain the right of way across their territory before he could proceed with the building of the railroad. We often entertained them in camp. When Crow Dog was seeking the life of Spotted Tail, the old chieftain, Spotted Tail, first sought protection in Mr. Irish's camp.[205]

(Spotted Tail was a controversial leader, some calling him "the white man's chief," and it was frequently reported in newspapers that he was going to be deposed in favor of others less likely to cooperate with the encroaching White people.)

She had seen a great change in technologies over her lifetime, which she mused on in the same sketch:

> I am now in my seventy-fourth year and as I watch the automobiles and electric [cable] cars flash past my window and read of the trips made in actual flying machines, I can but wonder if I am dreaming or am lost in some wonderful Arabian Nights tale, so different does this world of 1911 appear from that upon which my eyes first gazed in 1837. . . .
>
> When I had left the South, in my childhood, travel was mainly by team over rude roads or by water if one chanced to be going to points reached by the navigable rivers, and as I before stated, I practically walked most of the way to Iowa; but my return—how different. In a comfortable, yes luxurious palace car, I was speeded along, covering in thirty-six hours the distance that we, as emigrants, forty-nine years before, had wearily accomplished in six weeks. The patient team of oxen of that day are now retired and steam and electricity are doing their work. Will the next fifty years produce as great changes in transportation as the past fifty have I often ask myself. The flying machine is now here—will it be practical? What a boon the telephone would have been to the isolated frontiers-man and his family fifty years ago.[206]

As found in the diaries and letters, she was unafraid to participate in camp life or take on camp workers she felt were not living up to the task. She rode on horseback up and down the bluffs with the men. She moved casually between frontier lodgings, whether canvas tents or hotel accommodations. Letters and diary entries do indicate some nervousness, especially when the Hard Winter of 1880–81 set in and trapped her and her husband in Pierre, Dakota Territory, for several months. Over the years, those concerns shifted from fear toward confidence: "Mr. Irish and I had become by this time good travelers, birds of passage as it were, winging our flight from one point to another across the United States, feeling at home wherever our camp chanced to be pitched, be it in the wilderness or in the center of civilization."[207]

Caption on back: "Elizabeth Irish and her mother Mrs. Chas. W. Irish, Reno, Nevada. Mother had on her back an Indian baby basket." A-29

Lizzie Irish (left), Mrs. Susannah Abigail "Abbie" Irish (top center), and Ruth Ann Irish Preston (right), with Ruth's twin daughters, Abigail (left) and Ella (right), 1890, Reno, Nevada. Photo taken by Charles Wood Irish. A-30

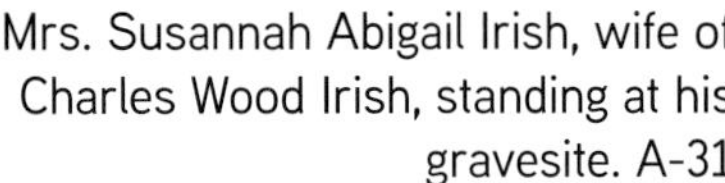

Mrs. Susannah Abigail Irish, wife of Charles Wood Irish, standing at his gravesite. A-31

Hannah Elizabeth "Lizzie" Irish (1856–1952)

Lizzie was independent and possessed a strong personality in an era when this was not encouraged for women. She worked for her uncle as his business manager and bookkeeper, then held various positions with the United States Mint and Wells Fargo Bank while living in California. She also served as her father's "chief clerk, stenographer, and bookkeeper" while he worked in Nevada as surveyor general. She remained very close to both her father and his brother, her uncle John P. Irish, but eventually settled back into life in Iowa City. She opened a business school and operated it until 1940, retiring at the age of eighty-four. She died at ninety-six.[208]

A 1913 biographical sketch of Lizzie in a Johnson County, Iowa, history noted, "The story of such a busy life, is truly an inspiration to the young who are longing to meet and conquer the problems of the world."[209]

Lizzie Irish. A-32

Irish's brother, John P. Irish. A-33

Ruth Ann Irish Preston (1859–1949)

Ruth showed herself through letters to also be independent, though less so than her sister. Ruth worked as a teacher until she married at age twenty-eight. While the more traditional of the sisters, she remained active outside the home and was also a writer and artist. She and her husband, Charles Preston, had twin daughters, Abigail and Ella, as well as a son, whom they also named Charles. The last descendent of Charles Wood Irish died with the passing of Ruth's son in 1977.[210]

There is also a grave marker in the Irish plot at the Oakland Cemetery in Iowa City for a son, Frankie, who died (possibly on the day of his birth) in 1882. Abbie would have been about 45 years old at the time of his birth. This was an era before required registrations of births and deaths, and the Johnson County records do not show a birth nor death for this child in 1882, so details are lacking.

Final Notes About the Irish Family

The summary of the Charles Wood Irish Papers collection noted that Abbie and her daughters, Lizzie and Ruth, "all lived past the Biblical three-score-years-and-ten, and the daughters recorded the difficulties they encountered as their mother grew older." The collections summary implores a researcher with a background in women's history to delve into the massive collection of letters, journals, and other items that document the lives of these three women.[211] I share this here to raise awareness so that someone will take on the worthy task.

In 1849, Frederick Irish (father of C. W.) built a home at 1415 East Davenport Street in Iowa City, naming it Rose Hill; it was placed on the National Register of Historic Places in 1992. Weaving through the letters between Irish and his family back in Iowa City were mentions of their neighbors, the Goetz couple, who caused the Irish family trouble—whether it be their dangerous dogs menacing the Irish women or their feral chickens taking up roost within the Irishes' outhouse. The fascinating twist is that today, Rose Hill is officially known as the Irish-Goetz House.[212]

The Irishes were a family with personality and flair. Not only did they dress up their dog, but they took a photo. This photo is undated, and it was mixed in with a variety of photos, mostly from Nevada. A note on the back identified the dog as "Herb." A-34

Among the family photographs was this one, "Father's pet squirrel, Gold Creek, Nev. 1902." (The "squirrel" is actually a chipmunk.) A-35

ILLUSTRATIONS CREDITS

Author's Note and Introduction

AI-1 Cover materials: (1) The photo of Irish is from the Charles Wood Irish Papers, University of Iowa Libraries, Iowa City, Iowa. (2) The image of Rice's sectional map of Dakota Territory, produced by G. Jay Rice and Fred Sturnegk and published by St. Paul Lithog. & Eng. Co. in 1872, is from the Library of Congress, Geography and Map Division (https://www.loc.gov/item/2012593215/). (3) Landscape photo by author.

AI-2 Map by author.

AI-3 Charles Wood Irish, portrait, ca. 1870. From Isaac Wetherby Collection. Special Collections, State Historical Society of Iowa, Iowa City.

AI-4 Susannah Abigail Yarborough Irish, portrait, ca. 1870. From Isaac Wetherby Collection, Special Collections, State Historical Society of Iowa, Iowa City.

AI-5 Photograph taken by author. Charles Wood Irish Papers, University of Iowa Libraries, Iowa City, Iowa. Series 3: Diaries. Box 5, diaries 1879, 1880, and 1881.

AI-6 Maps by author.

AI-7 South Dakota State Historical Society.

AI-8 South Dakota State Historical Society.

AI-9 South Dakota State Historical Society.

AI-10 South Dakota State Historical Society.

AI-11 Map by author.

AI-12 Map by author.

AI-13 Map by author.

Section One

S1-1 Photograph by author.

S1-2 Charles Wood Irish Papers, University of Iowa Libraries, Iowa City, Iowa.

S1-3 Map by author.

S1-4 https://www.findagrave.com/memorial/152537906/john-ellsworth-blunt.

S1-5 Charles Wood Irish Papers, University of Iowa Libraries, Iowa City, Iowa.

S1-6 Photograph by author.

S1-7 Photograph by author.

S1-8 Map by author.

S1-9 Map by MapBox.com.

S1-10 Map by author.

S1-11 "National Wetlands Inventory," US Fish and Wildlife Service, US Department of the Interior, November 21, 2001, https://www.fws.gov/program/national-wetlands-inventory/wetlands-mapper.

S1-12 Joseph N. Nicollet's 1839 Manuscript Maps of the Missouri River and Upper Mississippi Basin. Compiled by W. Raymond Wood. Scientific Papers, Vol. XXIV, Illinois State Museum, 1993. South Dakota State Historical Society Collections.

S1-13 Photograph by author.

S1-14 "Byron E. Pay," Find a Grave, https://www.findagrave.com/memorial/8128333/byron-e-pay. Some information about Byron E. Pay found at https://www.minnesotamedalofhonormemorial.org/wp-content/uploads/2017/12/Pay-Byron-Edward-Original-Bio.pdf.
S1-15 *New Ulm Weekly Review*, New Ulm, Minnesota, February 19, 1879.
S1-16 Map by author.
S1-17 Photograph by author.
S1-18 Map by author.
S1-19 Chicago & North Western Historical Society.
S1-20 Chicago & North Western Historical Society.
S1-21 Photograph by author.

Section Two

S2-1 Photograph by author.
S2-2 Map by author.
S2-3 Charles Wood Irish Papers, University of Iowa Libraries, Iowa City, Iowa.
S2-4 South Dakota State Historical Society.
S2-5 Charles Wood Irish Papers, University of Iowa Libraries, Iowa City, Iowa.
S2-6 Charles Wood Irish Papers, University of Iowa Libraries, Iowa City, Iowa.
S2-7 Chicago & North Western Historical Society.
S2-8 Plat Book of Lincoln County, Minnesota, compiled from county records and actual surveys, Northwest Publishing Co., 1898.
S2-9 Charles Wood Irish Papers, University of Iowa Libraries, Iowa City, Iowa.
S2-10 Photograph by author.
S2-11 Photograph by author.
S2-12 Photograph by author.
S2-13 Chicago & North Western Historical Society.
S2-14 Photograph by author.
S2-15 Charles Wood Irish Papers, University of Iowa Libraries, Iowa City, Iowa.
S2-16 Google Maps.
S2-17 Lyon County, Minnesota, Township Grid, State of Minnesota Plat Book—1916, John R. Borchert Map Library, University of Minnesota Libraries, accessed February 2, 2019, http://geo.lib.umn.edu/plat_books/stateofmn1916/counties/lyon.htm.
S2-18 An Inventory of Minnesota Lakes, Bulletin No. 25, Division of Waters, Soils, and Minerals. Minnesota Conservation Department, page 261. 1968.
S2-19 Map by author.
S2-20 Photograph by author, Chicago & North Western Historical Society.

Section Three

S3-1 Photograph by author.
S3-2 Map by author.
S3-3 Map by author.
S3-4 Map by author.
S3-5 Photograph by author, Charles Wood Irish Papers, University of Iowa Libraries, Iowa City, Iowa.
S3-6 Charles Wood Irish Papers, University of Iowa Libraries, Iowa City, Iowa.
S3-7 Lyon County, MN, Township Grid, State of Minnesota Plat Book—1916, John R. Borchert Map Library, University of Minnesota Libraries, accessed February 2, 2019, http://geo.lib.umn.edu/plat_books/stateofmn1916/counties/lyon.htm.
S3-8 Map by author.
S3-9 Map by author.
S3-10 Charles Wood Irish Papers, University of Iowa Libraries, Iowa City, Iowa.

S3-11 Map by author.
S3-12 "National Wetlands Inventory," US Fish and Wildlife Service, US Department of the Interior, November 21, 2001, https://www.fws.gov/program/national-wetlands-inventory/wetlands-mapper.
S3-13 Photograph by author.
S3-14 (1) Map by author. (2) The map of Brookings County, South Dakota, originally published by E. Frank Peterson and E.P. Noll & Co. in 1897, is from the Library of Congress (https://www.loc.gov/item/2012592516/).
S3-15 Drone photograph by Steve Devore.
S3-16 *Brookings County Press*, Fountain, Dakota Territory, June 12, 1879.
S3-17 Map by author.
S3-18 (1) 1909 Outline Map of Kingsbury County South Dakota, Manchester Township, Geo. A. Ogle & Co. (2) Map by author. (3) Photograph by author. (4) Charles Wood Irish Papers, University of Iowa Libraries, Iowa City, Iowa.

Section Four

S4-1 Photograph by author.
S4-2 Map by author.
S4-3 Map by author.
S4-4 Photograph by author.
S4-5 Map by author.
S4-6 Charles Wood Irish Papers, University of Iowa Libraries, Iowa City, Iowa.
S4-7 Charles Wood Irish Papers, University of Iowa Libraries, Iowa City, Iowa.
S4-8 Map by author.
S4-9 "National Wetlands Inventory," US Fish and Wildlife Service, US Department of the Interior, November 21, 2001, https://www.fws.gov/program/national-wetlands-inventory/wetlands-mapper.
S4-10 Map by author.
S4-11 Map by author.
S4-12 Charles Wood Irish Papers, University of Iowa Libraries, Iowa City, Iowa.
S4-13 Charles Wood Irish Papers, University of Iowa Libraries, Iowa City, Iowa.
S4-14 Photograph by author.
S4-15 Map by author.
S4-16 Photograph by author.
S4-17 Photograph by author.
S4-18 Charles Wood Irish Papers, University of Iowa Libraries, Iowa City, Iowa.

Section Five

S5-1 Photograph by author.
S5-2 Map by author.
S5-3 Photograph by author.
S5-4 Charles Wood Irish Papers, University of Iowa Libraries, Iowa City, Iowa.
S5-5 Charles Wood Irish Papers, University of Iowa Libraries, Iowa City, Iowa.
S5-6 South Dakota State Historical Society Archives, G4055-64-1947, Sheet No. 64, Missouri River, Drawer 33, Folder 3.
S5-7 Charles Wood Irish Papers, University of Iowa Libraries, Iowa City, Iowa.
S5-8 Photograph by author.
S5-9 Map by author.
S5-10 Photograph by author.
S5-11 Charles Wood Irish Papers, University of Iowa Libraries, Iowa City, Iowa.
S5-12 Map by author.
S5-13 Map by author.
S5-14 Map by author.

S5-15 *Brookings County Press*, Fountain, Dakota Territory, November 13, 1879.
S5-16 Winona County Historical Society.
S5-17 Map by author.
S5-18 Collection of Marcy Schramm.
S5-19 Photograph by author, Laura Ingalls Wilder Memorial Society, De Smet, South Dakota.
S5-20 Charles Wood Irish Papers, University of Iowa Libraries, Iowa City, Iowa.
S5-21 South Dakota State Historical Society. Special Case #101: Dakota Central Railroad Right of Ways on Sioux Reservation, 1879–1881 (MF5042).
S5-22 South Dakota State Historical Society. Special Case #101: Dakota Central Railroad Right of Ways on Sioux Reservation, 1879–1881 (MF5042).
S5-23 Video screen capture by author, Charles Wood Irish Papers, University of Iowa Libraries, Iowa City, Iowa.
S5-24 Video screen capture by author.
S5-25 Charles Wood Irish Papers, University of Iowa Libraries, Iowa City, Iowa.
S5-26 Charles Wood Irish Papers, University of Iowa Libraries, Iowa City, Iowa.

Section Six

S6-1 Photograph by author.
S6-2 Map by author.
S6-3 *Yankton Daily Press and Dakotaian*, Yankton, Dakota Territory, August 9, 1880. Chronicling America: Historic American Newspapers, Library of Congress, https://chroniclingamerica.loc.gov/lccn/sn91099608/1880-08-09/ed-1/seq-1/.
S6-4 *Brookings County Press*, Brookings, Dakota Territory, December 11, 1879, reprinted from the *Yankton Press*, Yankton, Dakota Territory, November 18, 1879.
S6-5 Charles Wood Irish Papers, University of Iowa Libraries, Iowa City, Iowa.
S6-6 South Dakota State Historical Society Archives, G4055-64-1947, Sheet No. 64, Missouri River, Drawer 33, Folder 3.
S6-7 *Yankton Daily Press and Dakotaian*, Yankton, Dakota Territory, December 11, 1879. Chronicling America: Historic American Newspapers, Library of Congress, https://chroniclingamerica.loc.gov/lccn/sn84022144/1879-12-11/ed-1/seq-4/.
S6-8 Charles Wood Irish Papers, University of Iowa Libraries, Iowa City, Iowa.
S6-9 Map by author.
S6-10 Charles Wood Irish Papers, University of Iowa Libraries, Iowa City, Iowa.
S6-11 Photograph by author.
S6-12 Charles Wood Irish Papers, University of Iowa Libraries, Iowa City, Iowa.
S6-13 Charles Wood Irish Papers, University of Iowa Libraries, Iowa City, Iowa.
S6-14 Charles Wood Irish Papers, University of Iowa Libraries, Iowa City, Iowa.
S6-15 Charles Wood Irish Papers, University of Iowa Libraries, Iowa City, Iowa.
S6-16 Charles Wood Irish Papers, University of Iowa Libraries, Iowa City, Iowa.
S6-17 Charles Wood Irish Papers, University of Iowa Libraries, Iowa City, Iowa.
S6-18 Photograph by author.
S6-19 Photograph by author.
S6-20 South Dakota State Historical Society.
S6-21 Photograph by author.
S6-22 Photograph by author.
S6-23 Photograph by author.

Section Seven

S7-1 Photograph by author.
S7-2 Map by author.
S7-3 South Dakota State Historical Society.
S7-4 Photograph by author.

S7-5 South Dakota State Historical Society Archives, G4055-74-1947, Sheet No. 74, Missouri River, Drawer 33, Folder 3.
S7-6 South Dakota State Historical Society P97 Mixed Subject File, Fort Sully folder. Donor: Lawrence Riggs, Pierre, South Dakota, May 1984.
S7-7 South Dakota State Historical Society P97 Mixed Subject File, Fort Sully Folder.
S7-8 South Dakota State Historical Society.
S7-9 Charles Wood Irish Papers, University of Iowa Libraries, Iowa City, Iowa.
S7-10 South Dakota State Historical Society Archives, G4055-87-1947, Sheet No. 87, Missouri River, Drawer 33, Folder 3.
S7-11 Charles Wood Irish Papers, University of Iowa Libraries, Iowa City, Iowa.
S7-12 Charles Wood Irish Papers, University of Iowa Libraries, Iowa City, Iowa.
S7-13 Charles Wood Irish Papers, University of Iowa Libraries, Iowa City, Iowa.
S7-14 Photograph by author.
S7-15 Charles Wood Irish Papers, University of Iowa Libraries, Iowa City, Iowa.
S7-16 Charles Wood Irish Papers, University of Iowa Libraries, Iowa City, Iowa.
S7-17 Map by author; inset image from the Charles Wood Irish Papers, University of Iowa Libraries, Iowa City, Iowa.
S7-18 Charles Wood Irish Papers, University of Iowa Libraries, Iowa City, Iowa.
S7-19 Charles Wood Irish Papers, University of Iowa Libraries, Iowa City, Iowa.
S7-20 Photograph by author.
S7-21 Photograph by author.
S7-22 South Dakota State Historical Society, H2018-060, 50520 folder "Old Stanley County."
S7-23 Photograph by author.
S7-24 Photograph by author.
S7-25 Photograph by author.
S7-26 Photograph by author.
S7-27 Charles Wood Irish Papers, University of Iowa Libraries, Iowa City, Iowa.
S7-28 South Dakota State Historical Society.
S7-29 Photograph by author.
S7-30 Photograph by author.
S7-31 Photograph by author.
S7-32 Photograph by author.
S7-33 Photograph by author.
S7-34 Charles Wood Irish Papers, University of Iowa Libraries, Iowa City, Iowa.
S7-35 Photograph by author.
S7-36 Photograph by author.

Section Eight

S8-1 Photograph by author.
S8-2 Map by author.
S8-3 Charles Wood Irish Papers, University of Iowa Libraries, Iowa City, Iowa.
S8-4 Photograph by author.
S8-5 Charles Wood Irish Papers, University of Iowa Libraries, Iowa City, Iowa.
S8-6 Photograph by author.
S8-7 Photograph by author.
S8-8 Photograph by author.
S8-9 Map by author.
S8-10 South Dakota State Historical Society, Pierre, South Dakota. Special Case #101: Dakota Central Railroad Right of Ways on Sioux Reservation, 1879–1881 (MF5042).
S8-11 Map by author.
S8-12 Map by author.

S8-13 Photograph by author.
S8-14 Photograph by author.
S8-15 Charles Wood Irish Papers, University of Iowa Libraries, Iowa City, Iowa.
S8-16 Photograph by author.
S8-17 Charles Wood Irish Papers, University of Iowa Libraries, Iowa City, Iowa.
S8-18 South Dakota State Historical Society.
S8-19 South Dakota State Historical Society, Pierre, South Dakota. Special Case #101: Dakota Central Railroad Right of Ways on Sioux Reservation, 1879–1881 (MF5042).
S8-20 South Dakota State Historical Society, Pierre, South Dakota. Special Case #101: Dakota Central Railroad Right of Ways on Sioux Reservation, 1879–1881 (MF5042).
S8-21 Charles Wood Irish Papers, University of Iowa Libraries, Iowa City, Iowa.
S8-22 *Yankton Daily Press and Dakotaian*, Yankton, Dakota Territory, July 21, 1880. Chronicling America: Historic American Newspapers, Library of Congress. https://chroniclingamerica.loc.gov/lccn/sn91099608/1880-07-21/ed-1/seq-1/.
S8-23 Charles Wood Irish Papers, University of Iowa Libraries, Iowa City, Iowa.
S8-24 Charles Wood Irish Papers, University of Iowa Libraries, Iowa City, Iowa.

Section Nine

S9-1 Photograph by author.
S9-2 Map by author.
S9-3 South Dakota State Historical Society Fort Sully folder, Misc. Subject File, P97.
S9-4 Charles Wood Irish Papers, University of Iowa Libraries, Iowa City, Iowa.
S9-5 Photograph by author.
S9-6 *Fort Pierre Weekly Signal*, Fort Pierre, Dakota Territory, August 4, 1880.
S9-7 *Fort Pierre Weekly Signal*, Fort Pierre, Dakota Territory, August 11, 1880.
S9-8 South Dakota State Historical Society, Pierre, South Dakota. Special Case #101: Dakota Central Railroad Right of Ways on Sioux Reservation, 1879-1881 (MF5042).
S9-9 Charles Wood Irish Papers, University of Iowa Libraries, Iowa City, Iowa.
S9-10 *Fort Pierre Weekly Signal*, Fort Pierre, Dakota Territory, August 25, 1880.
S9-11 Map by author.
S9-12 Charles Wood Irish Papers, University of Iowa Libraries, Iowa City, Iowa.
S9-13 Photograph by author.
S9-14 "National Wetlands Inventory," US Fish and Wildlife Service, US Department of the Interior, November 21, 2001, https://www.fws.gov/program/national-wetlands-inventory/wetlands-mapper.
S9-15 *Fort Pierre Weekly Signal*, Fort Pierre, Dakota Territory, September 1, 1880.
S9-16 South Dakota State Historical Society.
S9-17 Charles Wood Irish Papers, University of Iowa Libraries, Iowa City, Iowa.
S9-18 Photograph by author.
S9-19 Charles Wood Irish Papers, University of Iowa Libraries, Iowa City, Iowa.
S9-20 Charles Wood Irish Papers, University of Iowa Libraries, Iowa City, Iowa.
S9-21 Photograph by author.
S9-22 Photograph by author.
S9-23 Photograph by author.
S9-24 Charles Wood Irish Papers, University of Iowa Libraries, Iowa City, Iowa.
S9-25 Photograph by author.
S9-26 Photograph by author.
S9-27 Photograph by author.
S9-28 Photograph by author.
S9-29 Photograph by author.

S9-30 Photograph by author.
S9-31 Photograph by author.
S9-32 Charles Wood Irish Papers, University of Iowa Libraries, Iowa City, Iowa.
S9-33 Charles Wood Irish Papers, University of Iowa Libraries, Iowa City, Iowa.
S9-34 Photograph by author.

Section Ten

S10-1 Photograph by author.
S10-2 Map by author.
S10-3 Photograph by author.
S10-4 *Yankton Daily Press and Dakotaian*, Yankton, Dakota Territory, October 6, 1880.
S10-5 Charles Wood Irish Papers, University of Iowa Libraries, Iowa City, Iowa.
S10-6 Photograph by author.
S10-7 Charles Wood Irish Papers, University of Iowa Libraries, Iowa City, Iowa.
S10-8 Charles Wood Irish Papers, University of Iowa Libraries, Iowa City, Iowa.
S10-9 Photograph by author.
S10-10 Charles Wood Irish Papers, University of Iowa Libraries, Iowa City, Iowa.
S10-11 Charles Wood Irish Papers, University of Iowa Libraries, Iowa City, Iowa.
S10-12 Map by author.
S10-13 Charles Wood Irish Papers, University of Iowa Libraries, Iowa City, Iowa.
S10-14 Chicago & North Western Historical Society.
S10-15 Charles Wood Irish Papers, University of Iowa Libraries, Iowa City, Iowa.
S10-16 Map by author.
S10-17 Charles Wood Irish Papers, University of Iowa Libraries, Iowa City, Iowa.
S10-18 Charles Wood Irish Papers, University of Iowa Libraries, Iowa City, Iowa.
S10-19 *Fort Pierre Weekly Signal*, Fort Pierre, Dakota Territory, November 10, 1880.
S10-20 *Fort Pierre Weekly Signal*, Fort Pierre, Dakota Territory, November 10, 1880.
S10-21 Map by author.
S10-22 Map by author.
S10-23 Photograph by author.
S10-24 South Dakota State Historical Society, Pierre, South Dakota. Special Case #101: Dakota Central Railroad Right of Ways on Sioux Reservation, 1879–1881 (MF5042).
S10-25 South Dakota State Historical Society, Pierre, South Dakota. Special Case #101: Dakota Central Railroad Right of Ways on Sioux Reservation, 1879–1881 (MF5042).
S10-26 South Dakota State Historical Society, Pierre, South Dakota. Special Case #101: Dakota Central Railroad Right of Ways on Sioux Reservation, 1879–1881 (MF5042).
S10-27 Map by author.

Section Eleven

S11-1 Photograph by author.
S11-2 Map by author.
S11-3 Charles Wood Irish Papers, University of Iowa Libraries, Iowa City, Iowa.
S11-4 Charles Wood Irish Papers, University of Iowa Libraries, Iowa City, Iowa.
S11-5 Charles Wood Irish Papers, University of Iowa Libraries, Iowa City, Iowa.
S11-6 Charles Wood Irish Papers, University of Iowa Libraries, Iowa City, Iowa.
S11-7 Charles Wood Irish Papers, University of Iowa Libraries, Iowa City, Iowa.
S11-8 *Fort Pierre Weekly Signal*, Fort Pierre, Dakota Territory, January 8, 1881.
S11-9 *Fort Pierre Weekly Signal*, Fort Pierre, Dakota Territory, January 8, 1881.
S11-10 Charles Wood Irish Papers, University of Iowa Libraries, Iowa City, Iowa.
S11-11 Charles Wood Irish Papers, University of Iowa Libraries, Iowa City, Iowa.

S11-12 Photograph by author.
S11-13 Charles Wood Irish Papers, University of Iowa Libraries, Iowa City, Iowa.
S11-14 Charles Wood Irish Papers, University of Iowa Libraries, Iowa City, Iowa.
S11-15 South Dakota State Historical Society Box 5644, H2009-101, R. C. Lathay Collection.
S11-16 Winona County Historical Society.
S11-17 Chicago & North Western Historical Society.

Epilogue

E-1 Photograph by author.
E-2 *Fort Pierre Weekly Signal*, Pierre, Dakota Territory, May 14, 1881.
E-3 Photograph by author.
E-4 Photograph by author.
E-5 Photograph by author.
E-6 Photograph by author.
E-7 *New Ulm Weekly Review*, New Ulm, Minnesota, July 20, 1881.
E-8 Charles Wood Irish Papers, University of Iowa Libraries, Iowa City, Iowa.

Appendixes

A-1 Photograph by author.
A-2 *Gunter's Chain and a Manuscript Manual for Its Use*. [England?: manufacturer not identified, between 1800 and 1900?, 1800] Map. https://www.loc.gov/item/2020587048/.
A-3 Chicago & North Western Historical Society.
A-4 OpenStreetMap, https://www.openstreetmap.org/copyright.
A-5 Charles Wood Irish Papers, University of Iowa Libraries, Iowa City, Iowa.
A-6 Charles Wood Irish Papers, University of Iowa Libraries, Iowa City, Iowa.
A-7 Photograph by author.
A-8 "National Wetlands Inventory," US Fish and Wildlife Service, US Department of the Interior, November 21, 2001, https://www.fws.gov/program/national-wetlands-inventory/wetlands-mapper.
A-9 Drone photograph by Steve Devore.
A-10 South Dakota State Historical Society, Pierre, South Dakota, Map Collection.
A-11 Charles Wood Irish Papers, University of Iowa Libraries, Iowa City, Iowa.
A-12 South Dakota State Historical Society, Pierre, South Dakota, Map Collection.
A-13 South Dakota State Historical Society, Pierre, South Dakota, Map Collection.
A-14 South Dakota State Historical Society, Pierre, South Dakota, Department of the Interior, General Land Office, Hon. Lewis A. Groff Commissioner, A. F. Dinsmore, Principal Draughtsman, 1889.
A-15 Charles Wood Irish Papers, University of Iowa Libraries, Iowa City, Iowa.
A-16 Charles Wood Irish Papers, University of Iowa Libraries, Iowa City, Iowa.
A-17 Photograph by author.
A-18 Photograph by author.
A-19 Photograph by author.
A-20 Photograph by author.
A-21 Drone Photograph by Steve Devore.
A-22 Drone photograph by Steve Devore.
A-23 Redwood County, Minnesota, Township Grid, *State of Minnesota Plat Book—1916*, John R. Borchert Map Library, University of Minnesota Libraries, accessed February 2, 2019, http://geo.lib.umn.edu/plat_books/stateofmn1916/counties/redwood.htm.
A-24 Map by author.
A-25 Map by author.

A-26 Map by author.

A-27 South Dakota State Historical Society Archives, Pierre, South Dakota, Fort Sully folder, Misc. Subject File, P97.

A-28 South Dakota State Historical Society Archives, Pierre, South Dakota. Fort Bennett folder, Misc. Subject File, P93.

A-29 Charles Wood Irish Papers, University of Iowa Libraries, Iowa City, Iowa.

A-30 Photographed by C. W. Irish. "Elizabeth Irish, Abigail Preston, Mrs. S. A. Irish, Ella Preston, Mrs. Ruth Irish Preston. Reno, Nevada, August 1890." From Irish-Preston Papers, Ms 105, Box 20b, Folder 2, Special Collections, State Historical Society of Iowa, Iowa City, Iowa.

A-31 Charles Wood Irish Papers, University of Iowa Libraries, Iowa City, Iowa.

A-32 Charles Wood Irish Papers, University of Iowa Libraries, Iowa City, Iowa.

A-33 Charles Wood Irish Papers, University of Iowa Libraries, Iowa City, Iowa.

A-34 Charles Wood Irish Papers, University of Iowa Libraries, Iowa City, Iowa.

A-35 Charles Wood Irish Papers, University of Iowa Libraries, Iowa City, Iowa.

ENDNOTES

Note: All diary entries and personal letters throughout the work are cited as "Charles Wood Irish Papers, University of Iowa Libraries, Iowa City, Iowa."

1. Charles Wood Irish Papers, University of Iowa Libraries, Iowa City, Iowa.
2. Dr. Barb Mayes Boustead, meteorologist, National Weather Service, email correspondence with author, October 14, 2019.
3. "Inflation Calculator: 1881 Dollars in 2019," Official Inflation Data, Alioth Finance, https://www.officialdata.org/us/inflation/1881.
4. James D. McLaird, *Wild Bill Hickok & Calamity Jane* (Pierre, South Dakota: South Dakota State Historical Society Press, 2008), 132.
5. *History of Winona County, 1883, Together with Biographical Matter, Statistics, etc. Gathered from Matter Furnished by Interviews with Old Settlers, County, Township and Other Records, and Extracts from Files of Papers, Pamphlets, and Such Other Sources as Have Been Available* (Chicago: H. H. Hill and Company, Publishers, 1883), 525–6.
6. "John Ellsworth Blunt," Find a Grave, accessed June 8, 2023, https://www.findagrave.com/memorial/152537906/john-ellsworth-blunt.
7. "Great Oasis WMA," Minnesota Department of Natural Resources, accessed September 19, 2020, https://www.dnr.state.mn.us/wmas/detail_report.html?id=WMA0020600.
8. Pipestone National Monument, National Park Service, accessed September 19, 2020, https://www.nps.gov/articles/the-power-of-the-pipe.htm.
9. The town of Flandreau (pronounced FLAN-droo), currently spelled with the *e*, was named for US Indian Agent Charles E. Flandrau, and that is how the town's name was spelled throughout the Hard Winter. Since the town officially calls itself Flandreau, I spelled it that way when outside of quotes from the era.
10. "Byron Edward Pay," Minnesota Medal of Honor Memorial, accessed September 20, 2020, https://www.minnesotamedalofhonormemorial.org/wp-content/uploads/2017/12/Pay-Byron-Edward-Original-Bio.pdf.
11. *Moody County Enterprise*, Flandreau, Dakota Territory, February 6, 1879.
12. "Slaughter Slough, Waterfall Production Area," (pamphlet, Windom, Minnesota: US Fish & Wildlife Services), accessed August 8, 2023. https://murraycountymn.com/wp-content/uploads/2015/06/SlaughterSlough.pdf.
13. Maxine Kayser Luehmann, *The Sun and the Moon: A History of Murray County* (Slayton, Minnesota: Murray County Board of Commissioners, 1982 [reprint 2002]), 308.

14. "History of Currie," (Currie, Minnesota: End-O-Line Railroad Museum), video.
15. William Stennett, *Yesterday and Today: A History of the Chicago and North Western Railway System* (Chicago: Winship Co., 1910), 49.
16. Carl Smith, *Chicago's Great Fire: The Destruction and Resurrection of an Iconic American City* (New York: Atlantic Monthly Press, 2020), 331–7.
17. *Brookings County Press*, Fountain, Dakota Territory, March 27, 1879.
18. *Brookings County Press*, Fountain, Dakota Territory, April 3, 1879, reprinted from the *Marshfield Tribune*, Marshfield, Minnesota.
19. *Brookings County Press*, Fountain, Dakota Territory, April 10, 1879.
20. *Brookings County Press*, Fountain, Dakota Territory, April 17, 1879.
21. *Brookings County Press*, Fountain, Dakota Territory, April 17, 1879.
22. *Brookings County Press*, Fountain, Dakota Territory, May 1, 1879.
23. "Why do meteors glow in vibrant colors?" Accuweather.com, accessed February 4, 2021, https://www.accuweather.com.
24. *Brookings County Press*, Fountain, Dakota Territory, May 15, 1879.
25. *Brookings County Press*, Fountain, Dakota Territory, May 15, 1879, reprinted from *Marshfield Tribune*, Marshfield, Minnesota.
26. *Currie Pioneer*, Currie, Minnesota, May 22, 1879.
27. *Lyon County News*, Marshall, Minnesota, June 25, 1879.
28. *Brookings County Press*, Fountain, Dakota Territory, May 22, 1879.
29. *Brookings County Press*, Fountain, Dakota Territory, June 5, 1879.
30. *Brookings County Press*, Fountain, Dakota Territory, June 5, 1879.
31. *Brookings County Press*, Fountain, Dakota Territory, June 19, 1879.
32. "From Oakwood," *Brookings County Press*, Fountain, Dakota Territory, July 10, 1879.
33. Lathrop, "Early History of Lake Henry Neighborhood and Church," De Smet, South Dakota, archives of the Laura Ingalls Wilder Memorial Society, accessed February 9, 2022.
34. *Brookings County Press*, Fountain, Dakota Territory, June 12, 1879.
35. *Brookings County Press*, Fountain, Dakota Territory, June 12, 1879.
36. Andro Linklater, *Measuring America: How the United States Was Shaped by the Greatest Land Sale in History* (New York: Penguin Random House, 2002), 167.
37. "Clear the Track!" *Brookings County Press*, Fountain, Dakota Territory, June 19, 1879.
38. "The Road," *Brookings County Press*, Fountain, Dakota Territory, June 19, 1879, reprinted from the *Marshfield Tribune*, Marshfield, Minnesota.
39. *South Dakota Place Names, Part I State, County and Town Names, Compiled by Workers of the Writers' Program of the Work Projects Administration in the State of South Dakota* (Vermillion, South Dakota: University of South Dakota, 1940), 49.
40. *Manchester Times*, Manchester, Dakota Territory, May 21, 1887.
41. Thomas W. Haberman, "The Randall Phase Component at the Dirt Lodge Village Site, Spink County, South Dakota: Late Woodland/Early Plains Village Transitions on the Northeastern Plains," *Plains Anthropologist* 38, no. 145: 75–116.
42. A. J. Edgerton, *Compilation of the Railroad Laws of Minnesota* (Saint Paul, Minnesota: William S. Combs, 1872), 262.
43. *New Ulm Weekly Review*, New Ulm, Minnesota, August 27, 1879.
44. *Brookings County Press*, Fountain, Dakota Territory, July 3, 1879.
45. *Brookings County Press*, Fountain, Dakota Territory, July 24, 1879, reprinted by *Yankton Daily Press and Dakotaian*, Yankton, Dakota Territory, July 31, 1879.
46. "From Lake Village," *Brookings County Press*, Fountain, Dakota Territory, July 10, 1879.

47. *Brookings County Press*, Fountain, Dakota Territory, July 3, 1879.
48. While there are newspaper accounts that mention the new townsite being named Hughitt, the prior local name of Lake Benton is what became permanent.
49. John Charles Fremont, *Memoirs of My Life: Including in the Narrative Five Journeys of Western Exploration* (Chicago: Belford, Clarke, 1887), 45–46.
50. *Brookings County Press*, Fountain, Dakota Territory, July 17, 1879.
51. "From Lake Village," *Brookings County Press*, Fountain, Dakota Territory, July 17, 1879.
52. *Brookings County Press*, Fountain, Dakota Territory, July 24, 1879, reprinted from *Watertown News*, Watertown, Dakota Territory.
53. "Oakland Cemetery, Iowa City, Johnson County, Iowa," Interment.net, accessed August 16, 2022, http://www.interment.net/data/us/ia/johnson/oakland-cemetery/records-hi-hy.htm.
54. "Chicago, Winona & Dakota Railroad," *Brookings County Press*, Fountain, Dakota Territory, August 14, 1879, reprinted from *Winona Republican*, Winona, Minnesota.
55. *Brookings County Press*, Fountain, Dakota Territory, August 21, 1879.
56. William B. Dick, *Encyclopedia of Practical Receipts and Processes, Fourth Edition* (New York: Dick & Fitzgerald, 1877 and 1884), 434–5.
57. *Brookings County Press*, Fountain, Dakota Territory, September 11, 1879.
58. *Brookings County Press*, Fountain, Dakota Territory, October 2, 1879.
59. *Brookings County Press*, Fountain, Dakota Territory, September 11, 1879.
60. *Brookings County Press*, Fountain, Dakota Territory, September 18, 1879.
61. *Brookings County Press*, Fountain, Dakota Territory, September 18, 1879.
62. *Brookings County Press*, Fountain, Dakota Territory, September 18, 1879.
63. Laura Ingalls Wilder, *Pioneer Girl: The Annotated Autobiography*, ed. Pamela Smith Hill (Pierre, South Dakota: South Dakota State Historical Society Press, 2014), 164–5.
64. *Brookings County Press*, Fountain, Dakota Territory, October 2, 1879, reprinted from the *Pioneer Press*, Saint Paul, Minnesota.
65. "Freight Business," *Brookings County Press*, Fountain, Dakota Territory, October 2, 1879.
66. *Brookings County Press*, Fountain, Dakota Territory, October 9, 1879.
67. *Brookings County Press*, Fountain, Dakota Territory, October 9, 1879.
68. *Brookings County Press*, Fountain, Dakota Territory, October 2, 1879.
69. *Brookings County Press*, Brookings, Dakota Territory, November 13, 1879.
70. *Brookings County Press*, Brookings, Dakota Territory, October 22, 1879.
71. *Brookings County Press*, Brookings, Dakota Territory, October 22, 1879.
72. *Brookings County Press*, Brookings, Dakota Territory, October 22, 1879.
73. *Brookings County Press*, Brookings, Dakota Territory, October 22, 1879.
74. "The First Train," *Brookings County Press*, Brookings, Dakota Territory, October 22, 1879.
75. Laura Ingalls Wilder, *Pioneer Girl: The Annotated Autobiography*, ed. Pamela Smith Hill (Pierre, South Dakota: South Dakota State Historical Society Press, 2014), 162.
76. *Brookings County Press*, Brookings, Dakota Territory, October 29, 1879.
77. *Brookings County Press*, Brookings, Dakota Territory, November 5, 1879.
78. "Special Case #101: Dakota Central Railroad Right of Ways on Sioux Reservation, 1879–1881 (MF5042)" (South Dakota State Historical Society, Pierre, South Dakota), accessed July 12, 2021.
79. "From Volga," *Brookings County Press*, Brookings, Dakota Territory, December 18, 1879.
80. Harold H. Schuler, *Fort Sully: Guns at Sunset* (Vermillion, South Dakota:

The University of South Dakota Press, 1992), 89.

81. "BIA: Letters Received, 1824–1880, Cheyenne River Agency, 1879–1880, Reel 5 (131), MF4, 1432, Correspondence from Caton to Hayt (manuscript collection, South Dakota State Historical Society, Pierre, South Dakota), accessed July 15, 2021.
82. "BIA: Letters Received, 1824–1880, Cheyenne River Agency, 1879–1880, Reel 5 (131), MF4, 1432, Correspondence from Caton to Hayt (manuscript collection, South Dakota State Historical Society, Pierre, South Dakota), accessed July 15, 2021.
83. *Brookings County Press*, Brookings, Dakota Territory, January 8, 1880.
84. William B. Dick, *Dick's Encyclopedia of Practical Receipts and Processes, Fourth Edition* (New York: Dick & Fitzgerald Publishers, 1877), 455–6, item 5072.
85. Harold H. Schuler, *A Bridge Apart: History of Early Pierre and Fort Pierre* (Pierre, South Dakota: State Publishing, 1987), 70.
86. Harold H. Schuler, *A Bridge Apart: History of Early Pierre and Fort Pierre* (Pierre, South Dakota: State Publishing, 1987), 71–72.
87. Harold H. Schuler, *Fort Sully: Guns at Sunset* (Vermillion, South Dakota: The University of South Dakota Press, 1992), 64.
88. "Clement/Claymore, Basil (see also Claymore)" (biographical files, South Dakota State Historical Society, Pierre, South Dakota), accessed July 16, 2021.
89. "Scalps," *Lyon County News*, Marshall, Minnesota, February 25, 1880.
90. *New Ulm Weekly Review*, New Ulm, Minnesota, March 24, 1880.
91. *Annual Reports, Commissioner of Indian Affairs to the Secretary of the Interior for the Year 1879* (Washington, DC: Government Printing Office, 1879), 47.
92. *Annual Reports, Commissioner of Indian Affairs to the Secretary of the Interior for the Year 1881* (Washington, DC: Government Printing Office, 1881), 39.
93. "RG75, Crow Creek/Lower Brule Correspondence, Copies Letters Sent to Commissioner, MF 6622, 2004-5" (correspondence, South Dakota State Historical Society, Pierre, South Dakota), accessed July 15, 2021.
94. "RG75, Crow Creek/Lower Brule Correspondence, Copies Letters Sent to Commissioner, MF 6622, 2004-5" (correspondence, South Dakota State Historical Society, Pierre, South Dakota), March 20, 1880, accessed July 15, 2021.
95. "RG75, Crow Creek/Lower Brule Correspondence, Copies Letters Sent to Commissioner, MF 6622, 2004-5" (correspondence, South Dakota State Historical Society, Pierre, South Dakota), August 14, 1880, accessed July 15, 2021.
96. "RG75, Crow Creek/Lower Brule Correspondence, Copies Letters Sent to Commissioner, MF 6622, 2004-5" (correspondence, South Dakota State Historical Society, Pierre, South Dakota), March 30, 1880, accessed July 15, 2021.
97. "Headline of Article," *Iowa City Press Citizen*, Iowa City, Iowa, May 4, 1971.
98. Gary S. Freedom, "Moving Men and Supplies: Military Transportation on the Northern Great Plains, 1866–1891," *South Dakota History Journal* 14, no. 2 (June 1984): 115.
99. Gary S. Freedom, "Moving Men and Supplies: Military Transportation on the Northern Great Plains, 1866–1891," *South Dakota History Journal* 14, no. 2 (June 1984): 116.
100. Gary S. Freedom, "Moving Men and Supplies: Military Transportation on the Northern Great Plains, 1866–1891," *South Dakota History Journal* 14, no. 2 (June 1984): 116–117.
101. Gary S. Freedom, "Moving Men and Supplies: Military Transportation on the Northern Great Plains, 1866–1891," *South Dakota History Journal* 14, no. 2 (June 1984): 119.
102. Gary S. Freedom, "Moving Men and Supplies: Military Transportation on the Northern Great Plains,

1866–1891," *South Dakota History Journal* 14, no. 2 (June 1984): 124.

103. "Special Case #101: Dakota Central Railroad Right of Ways on Sioux Reservation, 1879–1881 (MF5042)" (South Dakota State Historical Society, Pierre, South Dakota), accessed July 15, 2021.
104. "Special Case #101: Dakota Central Railroad Right of Ways on Sioux Reservation, 1879–1881 (MF5042)" (South Dakota State Historical Society, Pierre, South Dakota), accessed July 15, 2021.
105. "Special Case #101: Dakota Central Railroad Right of Ways on Sioux Reservation, 1879–1881 (MF5042)" (South Dakota State Historical Society, Pierre, South Dakota), accessed July 15, 2021.
106. "Special Case #101: Dakota Central Railroad Right of Ways on Sioux Reservation, 1879–1881 (MF5042)" (South Dakota State Historical Society, Pierre, South Dakota), accessed July 15, 2021.
107. "Special Case #101: Dakota Central Railroad Right of Ways on Sioux Reservation, 1879–1881 (MF5042)" (South Dakota State Historical Society, Pierre, South Dakota), accessed July 15, 2021.
108. "Special Case #101: Dakota Central Railroad Right of Ways on Sioux Reservation, 1879–1881 (MF5042)" (South Dakota State Historical Society, Pierre, South Dakota), accessed July 15, 2021.
109. "Special Case #101: Dakota Central Railroad Right of Ways on Sioux Reservation, 1879–1881 (MF5042)" (South Dakota State Historical Society, Pierre, South Dakota), accessed July 15, 2021.
110. "Special Case #101: Dakota Central Railroad Right of Ways on Sioux Reservation, 1879–1881 (MF5042)" (South Dakota State Historical Society, Pierre, South Dakota), accessed July 15, 2021.
111. *Fort Pierre Weekly Signal*, Fort Pierre, Dakota Territory, June 30, 1880.
112. Robert G. Athearn, *William Tecumseh Sherman and the Settlement of the West* (Norman, Oklahoma: University of Oklahoma Press, 1956), 24.
113. Michael Johnson, Fairfield County Heritage Association, Lancaster, Ohio, email correspondence with author, February 10, 2023.
114. *Fort Pierre Weekly Signal*, Fort Pierre, Dakota Territory, July 28, 1880.
115. Christopher Alan Gordon, *Fire, Pestilence, and Death: St. Louis, 1849* (Saint Louis, Missouri: Missouri Historical Society Press, 2018), 96–98.
116. *Fort Pierre Weekly Signal*, Fort Pierre, Dakota Territory, August 4, 1880.
117. H. Corder, "The August Meteors, 1883," *The Observatory* 6: 338–9.
118. "Strayed or Stolen," *Brookings County Press*, Fountain, Dakota Territory, June 12, 1879.
119. *Brookings County Press*, Fountain, Dakota Territory, June 26, 1879.
120. *Fort Pierre Weekly Signal*, Fort Pierre, Dakota Territory, June 30, 1880.
121. *Fort Pierre Weekly Signal*, Fort Pierre, Dakota Territory, July 7, 1880.
122. *Fort Pierre Weekly Signal*, Fort Pierre, Dakota Territory, July 7, 1880.
123. *Fort Pierre Weekly Signal*, Fort Pierre, Dakota Territory, July 28, 1880.
124. *Fort Pierre Weekly Signal*, Fort Pierre, Dakota Territory, August 11, 1880.
125. *Fort Pierre Weekly Signal*, Fort Pierre, Dakota Territory, August 18, 1880.
126. Jerome A. Greene, *Yellowstone Command: Colonel Nelson A. Miles and the Great Sioux War, 1876–1877* (Lincoln, Nebraska: University of Nebraska Press, 1991), 111.
127. *Annual Reports, Commissioner of Indian Affairs to the Secretary of the Interior for the Year 1880* (Washington, DC: Government Printing Office, 1880), 19.
128. *Annual Reports, Commissioner of Indian Affairs to the Secretary of the Interior for the Year 1881* (Washington, DC: Government Printing Office, 1881), 24.
129. *Annual Reports, Commissioner of Indian Affairs to the Secretary of the Interior*

for the Year 1880 (Washington, DC: Government Printing Office, 1880), 21.

130. *Yankton Daily Press and Dakotaian*, Yankton, Dakota Territory, August 23, 1880, reprinted by *Fort Pierre Weekly Signal*, Fort Pierre, Dakota Territory, September 1, 1880.
131. "A Railroad Race," *Fort Pierre Weekly Signal*, Fort Pierre, Dakota Territory, September 8, 1880, reprinted from *Chicago Times*, Chicago, Illinois.
132. *Fort Pierre Weekly Signal*, Fort Pierre, Dakota Territory, August 25, 1880.
133. *Fort Pierre Weekly Signal*, Fort Pierre, Dakota Territory, August 25, 1880.
134. *Fort Pierre Weekly Signal*, Fort Pierre, Dakota Territory, September 1, 1880.
135. Irish-Preston Family Papers, State Historical Society of Iowa, Iowa City, Iowa, accessed November 29, 2021.
136. "Another Man Killed," *Fort Pierre Weekly Signal*, Fort Pierre, Dakota Territory, September 1, 1880; "Fatal Affray at Fort Pierre," *Yankton Press and Daily Dakotaian*, Yankton, Dakota Territory, September 1, 1880; "A Shooter Shot," *Black Hills Daily Pioneer*, Deadwood, Dakota Territory, September 2, 1880; "One by One," *Yankton Press and Daily Dakotaian*, Yankton, Dakota Territory, September 6, 1880; "Up River Notes," *Yankton Press and Daily Dakotaian*, Yankton, Dakota Territory, September 9, 1880.
137. "Accidentally Shot," *Fort Pierre Weekly Signal*, Fort Pierre, Dakota Territory, September 8, 1880.
138. "Up River Notes," *Yankton Daily Press and Dakotaian*, Yankton, Dakota Territory, September 9, 1880.
139. Advertisement, *Fort Pierre Weekly Signal*, Fort Pierre, Dakota Territory, July 7, 1880.
140. *Fort Pierre Weekly Signal*, Fort Pierre, Dakota Territory, September 15, 1880.
141. "yawl," Steamboats.org, accessed June 30, 2021, https://www.steamboats.org/history-education/glossary/yawl.
142. *Fort Pierre Weekly Signal*, Fort Pierre, Dakota Territory, September 22, 1880.
143. *Black Hills Daily Pioneer*, Deadwood, Dakota Territory, October 18, 1880.
144. *Fort Pierre Weekly Signal*, Fort Pierre, Dakota Territory, November 10, 1880.
145. *Fort Pierre Weekly Signal*, Fort Pierre, Dakota Territory, October 20, 1880.
146. William B. Dick, *Dick's Encyclopedia of Practical Receipts and Processes, Fourth Edition* (New York: Dick & Fitzgerald Publishers, 1877), 462, item 5176.
147. *Fort Pierre Weekly Signal*, Fort Pierre, Dakota Territory, October 27, 1880.
148. *Fort Pierre Weekly Signal*, Fort Pierre, Dakota Territory, October 27, 1880.
149. *Fort Pierre Weekly Signal*, Fort Pierre, Dakota Territory, November 3, 1880.
150. *Fort Pierre Weekly Signal*, Fort Pierre, Dakota Territory, November 3, 1880, reprinted from *Central Herald*, Central City, Dakota Territory.
151. *Black Hills Daily Pioneer*, Deadwood, Dakota Territory, December 15, 1880.
152. "Railroad Prospects," *Black Hills News*, Deadwood, Dakota Territory, November 12, 1880.
153. "Railroad Prospects," *Black Hills News*, Deadwood, Dakota Territory, November 12, 1880.
154. "Railroad Prospects," *Black Hills News*, Deadwood, Dakota Territory, November 12, 1880.
155. "Railroad Prospects," *Black Hills News*, Deadwood, Dakota Territory, November 12, 1880.
156. Mick McCluskey, "Can You Get the Flu from Your Horse?" *Equus Magazine*, July 25, 2019.
157. "Special Case #101: Dakota Central Railroad Right of Ways on Sioux Reservation, 1879–1881 (MF5042)" (South Dakota State Historical Society, Pierre, South Dakota), accessed July 12, 2021.
158. *New Ulm Weekly Review*, New Ulm, Minnesota, December 15, 1880.
159. "Special Case #101: Dakota Central Railroad Right of Ways on Sioux Reservation, 1879–1881 (MF5042)" (South Dakota State Historical Society,

Pierre, South Dakota), accessed July 12, 2021.

160. Vine Deloria, Jr. and Raymond J. DeMallie, *Documents of American Indian Diplomacy: Treaties, Agreements, and Conventions, 1775–1979, Volume One* (Norman, Oklahoma: University of Oklahoma Press, 1999), 536–544.

161. *Fort Pierre Weekly Signal*, Fort Pierre, Dakota Territory, October 6, 1880.

162. "Fire Meeting," *Fort Pierre Weekly Signal*, Fort Pierre, Dakota Territory, January 8, 1881.

163. *Fort Pierre Weekly Signal*, Fort Pierre, Dakota Territory, January 8, 1881.

164. "Died," *Fort Pierre Weekly Signal*, Fort Pierre, Dakota Territory, January 22, 1881.

165. *Black Hills Daily Pioneer*, Deadwood, Dakota Territory, October 18, 1880, reprinted from *Yankton Daily Press and Dakotaian*, Yankton, Dakota Territory.

166. Harold H. Schuler, *A Bridge Apart: History of Early Pierre and Fort Pierre* (Pierre, South Dakota: State Publishing, 1987), 72.

167. *Fort Pierre Weekly Signal*, Fort Pierre, Dakota Territory, February 12, 1881.

168. *Fort Pierre Weekly Signal*, Fort Pierre, Dakota Territory, February 19, 1881.

169. *Fort Pierre Weekly Signal*, Fort Pierre, Dakota Territory, March 5, 1881.

170. *Fort Pierre Weekly Signal*, Fort Pierre, Dakota Territory, March 5, 1881.

171. *Fort Pierre Weekly Signal*, Fort Pierre, Dakota Territory, March 5, 1881.

172. *Fort Pierre Weekly Signal*, Fort Pierre, Dakota Territory, March 19, 1881.

173. *Fort Pierre Weekly Signal*, Fort Pierre, Dakota Territory, March 19, 1881.

174. *Fort Pierre Weekly Signal*, Fort Pierre, Dakota Territory, March 19, 1881.

175. Harold H. Schuler, *A Bridge Apart: History of Early Pierre and Fort Pierre* (Pierre, South Dakota: State Publishing, 1987), 54.

176. *Black Hills Daily Pioneer*, Deadwood, Dakota Territory, December 15, 1880.

177. "Coming Railroads," *Black Hills Daily Pioneer*, Deadwood, Dakota Territory, November 23, 1880.

178. *Railroad Gazette* 13 (January 21, 1881): 42.

179. Gary Richardson and Tim Sablik, "Banking Panics of the Gilded Age," Federal Reserve History, accessed September 23, 2021, https://www.federalreservehistory.org/essays/banking-panics-of-the-gilded-age; "Panic of 1893," Encyclopedia.com, accessed September 23, 2021, https://www.encyclopedia.com/history/united-states-and-canada/us-history/panic-1893.

180. *Fort Pierre Weekly Signal*, Fort Pierre, Dakota Territory, November 24, 1880.

181. William H. Stennett, *Yesterday and To-day: A History* (Chicago: Rand, McNally, 1905), 66.

182. William H. Stennett, *Yesterday and To-day: A History* (Chicago: Rand, McNally, 1905), 31–32.

183. H. Roger Grant, *The Northwestern: A History of the Chicago & North Western Railway Company* (DeKalb, Illinois: Northern Illinois University Press, 1996), 59–60; Duane Robinson, *Encyclopedia of South Dakota, First Edition* (Pierre, South Dakota: self-published, 1925), 601.

184. Elsie Hey Baye, ed. *Haakon Horizons* (Phillip, South Dakota: State Publishing, 1982), 280.

185. H. Roger Grant, *The Northwestern: A History of the Chicago & North Western Railway Company* (DeKalb, Illinois: Northern Illinois University Press, 1996), 43.

186. H. Roger Grant, *The Northwestern: A History of the Chicago & North Western Railway Company* (DeKalb, Illinois: Northern Illinois University Press, 1996), 44.

187. "Perry Powers," Find a Grave, accessed June 23, 2022, https://www.findagrave.com/memorial/140742342/perry-powers.

188. Charles Wood Irish Papers, University of Iowa Libraries, Iowa City, Iowa.

189. Michael Gillespie, *Wild River, Wooden Boats: True Stories of Steamboating and the Missouri River* (Stoddard, Wisconsin: Heritage Press, 2000), 5.
190. Robert Athearn, *Forts of the Upper Missouri* (Lincoln, Nebraska: University of Nebraska Press, 1967), 37.
191. Robert Athearn, *Forts of the Upper Missouri* (Lincoln, Nebraska: University of Nebraska Press, 1967), 127.
192. Hiram Martin Chittenden and Alfred Talbot Richardson, *Life and Travels of Father DeSmet among the North American Indians, Volume 1* (New York: Francis P. Harper, 1905), 154.
193. "Steamboats, Log of Steamboat Benton," South Dakota State Historical Society Archives, Pierre, South Dakota, April 1880, accessed July 15, 2021.
194. Michael Gillespie, *Wild River, Wooden Boats: True Stories of Steamboating and the Missouri River* (Stoddard, Wisconsin: Heritage Press, 2000), 85.
195. Harold H. Schuler, *A Bridge Apart: History of Early Pierre and Fort Pierre* (Pierre, South Dakota: State Publishing, 1987), 70.
196. "Up River Sketches," *Yankton Daily Press and Dakotaian*, Yankton, Dakota Territory, August 6, 1879.
197. "Up River Sketches," *Yankton Daily Press and Dakotaian*, Yankton, Dakota Territory, August 6, 1879.
198. "Recovered Post: Cheyenne River Sioux History," Cheyenne River Sioux Tribe, February 18, 2019, accessed July 15, 2021, https://crst.home.blog/2019/02/18/recovered-post-cheyenne-river-sioux-history/.
199. "Up River Sketches," *Yankton Daily Press and Dakotaian*, Yankton, Dakota Territory, August 6, 1879.
200. "Up River Sketches," *Yankton Daily Press and Dakotaian*, Yankton, Dakota Territory, August 6, 1879.
201. "Up River Sketches," *Yankton Daily Press and Dakotaian*, Yankton, Dakota Territory, August 6, 1879.
202. "Up River Sketches," *Yankton Daily Press and Dakotaian*, Yankton, Dakota Territory, November 15, 1878.
203. "Up River Sketches," *Yankton Daily Press and Dakotaian*, Yankton, Dakota Territory, August 6, 1879.
204. Charles Wood Irish Papers, University of Iowa Libraries, Iowa City, Iowa.
205. Clarence Ray Aurner, *Leading Events in Johnson County Iowa History, Volume Two* (Cedar Rapids, Iowa: Western Historical Press, 1913), 436.
206. Clarence Ray Aurner, *Leading Events in Johnson County Iowa History, Volume Two* (Cedar Rapids, Iowa: Western Historical Press, 1913), 436.
207. Clarence Ray Aurner, *Leading Events in Johnson County Iowa History, Volume Two* (Cedar Rapids, Iowa: Western Historical Press, 1913), 436.
208. Joyce Giaquinta and Billie Peterson, "Manuscript Collections: The Irish-Preston Papers, 1832–1972," *The Annals of Iowa* 44 (1978), 475–9.
209. Clarence Ray Aurner, *Leading Events in Johnson County Iowa History, Volume Two* (Cedar Rapids, Iowa: Western Historical Press, 1913), 425.
210. Joyce Giaquinta and Billie Peterson, "Manuscript Collections: The Irish-Preston Papers, 1832–1972," *The Annals of Iowa* 44 (1978), 475–9.
211. Joyce Giaquinta and Billie Peterson, "Manuscript Collections: The Irish-Preston Papers, 1832–1972," *The Annals of Iowa* 44 (1978), 475–9.
212. "Rose Hill," US National Register of Historic Places, accessed June 1, 2020, https://npgallery.nps.gov/NRHP/GetAsset/NRHP/92000425_text.

INDEX

Adams, 121–122, 125, 129, 171, 180
Afraid of Nothing, 290
Albright, 287, 299
Alderich, Frank, 346
American Creek, 155
American Fur Company, 192
American Meteorological Society, 61
Antelope Camp, 201
archive work, 144–148
Arrow Creek, 286
Arthur, H. H., 232
Ash Creek, 280
Atchison, Topeka & Santa Fe Railway, 11
August council agreement, 320–322
aurora borealis, 267

Bad River
- camp near, 272
- exploration of, 129, 141, 207, 278*fig*, 285, 313, 317
- fire and, 332–333
- height of, 279
- map of, 272*fig*, 286*fig*, 302*fig*, 332*fig*, 341*fig*
- measurements at mouth of, 205, 206*fig*
- photograph of, 273*fig*, 279*fig*, 287*fig*–288*fig*, 299*fig*, 343*fig*
- report on, 316
- terrain/landscape near, 285*fig*, 289*fig*–290*fig*

Badlands National Park, 279
Bancroft, 129
Bandy, 128, 138
Bandy Town, 128, 130, 134
Barch (Barsh), 310
Bartlett (Bart) Low, 10–11, 18, 24
Bartlett, C. P., 258
Bear Butte, 214*fig*
Bear Lake, 10, 24
Bell, W. H., 11
Belle Fourche River, 205, 301, 301*fig*
Ben (horse), 246
Bender family (Bloody Benders), 132
Bently, Lou, 275, 278
Benton, 281
Beveridge, J. C., 232
Bidwell, Mr., 47
"big cut west of Tracy," 35
Big Medicine Hill, 197, 200, 202*fig*, 230
Big Mike, 155*fig*, 156–157, 199–200, 203
Big Mike's Woodyard, 123, 127, 156, 203
Big Sioux camp, 75–76, 79, 84
Big Sioux River, 12, 49, 56–58, 68–69, 82, 82*fig*, 101–102
Big Slough, 104
Billy (pony), 175, 196, 198, 205–206, 212, 239, 243–244, 251, 287, 313, 318, 335
Bingham, 273
Bingly, 273
Bishop, 297
BJ, 170
Black Dick, 275, 278
Black Elk Peak, 214*fig*
Black Hills, 2, 6, 213, 214*fig*, 358
Black Hills, 235–236, 259
Black Hills Daily Pioneer, 305, 357
Black Hills News, 313
Black Rush Lake, 50–51
Blackfeet, 195
Blair, 305
Blake, Mr., 169
Bliss, George, 322
blockades, 337, 347–348, 355*fig*
"Bloody Benders," 132

Blunt, John Ellsworth
  butte named for, 88
  cake for, 68
  in camp, 47, 62–63, 66, 92, 102–103, 111, 229, 240, 245, 249–250, 259
  Cheyenne Agency and, 267
  correspondence with, 19–20, 67, 132, 252, 265, 289, 332
  at Fort Sully, 260
  home of, 135, 140
  with Irish, 230–231, 241, 312
  Irish's taking on work of, 261
  at Medary Creek, 59
  meetings with, 7–8, 133, 136, 205
  Mrs. Irish and, 250
  negotiations and, 260, 268
  photograph of, 7*fig*
  river crossing options and, 231*fig*
  Ryther and, 194
  sun burn of, 107
  surveying agreement and, 270
  in Tracy, 136–137
  in Winona, 25, 30
Blunt's Butte, 87–89, 101, 254
Bon Homme Island, 235
boosterism, 60
Borden's Ranch, 209*fig*
Box Elder Creek, 314, 360
Box Elder Creek Camp, 237
breakbone fever, 121, 179–180
Broadine, Mrs., 320
Brookings
  competition with Watertown, 97, 128
  location of, 57
Brookings County, 45, 48
Brookings County Press
  camp visit and, 79, 82*fig*, 83
  construction workers and, 66
  on harvest, 64, 84
  on "Indian troubles," 60
  Native Americans and, 99
  on progress of town, 137
  on settlers, 129–130
  town locations and, 121, 128
  updates in, 36, 47–48, 73–74, 86, 98, 106, 134–135, 167, 176–177
  on Volga, 140
  on weather, 101–102
Brown, Henry, 328, 331
Brown, L. R., 260
Bruce (town), 132
Bryan, G., 42
Buck Creek, 297
Buck Creek Camp, 297
Buffalo Camp, 100
buffalo herds, 201
Buffalo Ridge, 13
Bullard, Mr., 267–268, 270
Burke, 136
Buzzard Creek, 290, 296
By the Shores of Silver Lake (Wilder), 129

Caldwell, 109, 115, 117, 125
Camp Blizzard, 166, 166*fig*, 224, 255*fig*
Camp Carse, 134
Camp Greenhorn, 161–163, 165
Camp Hughitt, 120, 120*fig*, 129, 238, 246
Camp Irish, 79, 80*fig*, 82*fig*
Camp Kirley, 237
Camp Maggie, 248, 254
Camp McNiel, 204, 229*fig*, 254*fig*–255*fig*
Camp Nettiburgh, 109, 109*fig*, 111
Camp Susannah, 244, 254
Camp Tubbs, 340–342, 341*fig*
Canton, 267
Carse, C. J., 88, 106, 155–156, 199, 205, 231
catarrh, 178
Catlin, George, 192
Caton, W. E., 175, 175*fig*, 260, 265, 278
Central Herald, 311
Cessna, Mr., 352
Chamberlain, Dan, 266, 272, 303–304, 308, 338
Chamberlain, Minnie, 339–340
Chamberlain, Mrs., 266
Chambers, Bob, 239, 272, 284, 305, 340
Chapelle Butte, 123
Chapelle Creek, 123, 165, 254
Charlie (horse), 243–244, 246

Chase, 272–273, 302, 305, 307
Cheyenne Agency, 192, 249, 258, 267, 269
Cheyenne Island, 187, 191*fig*, 192, 194
Cheyenne River, 191*fig*, 192–193, 193*fig*, 195–196, 205, 215*fig*–216*fig*, 224–225
Cheyenne River Agency, 175, 269–270, 319, 322
Chicago
  description of, 28
  Irish and wife in, 136
Chicago, Milwaukee & St. Paul, 99, 234, 270
Chicago & Dakota, 69
Chicago & Milwaukee Railway, 267
Chicago & North Western
  expansion of, 1
  goals for, 357–358
  Lakota people and, 194, 234, 259, 267*fig*
  offices of, 27–28, 27*fig*, 31
  Panic of 1873 and, 2
  parallel surveys and, 96, 98
  possible route for, 117
  presidents of, 26
  rail passes on, 95
  surveying agreement and, 268*fig*, 269–271
Chicago & North Western Historical Society, 50, 52
Chicago Times, 87
Chickamauga, 15
Christianson, L., 88
Christmas Eve/Christmas Day, 170–171, 178, 328, 330–331
Civil War, 15
Clement/Claymore, Basil, 191, 191*fig*, 192
Clermont (may be Clement), 175
Cole, W. C. (cook), 41–42, 88, 106
Collins, I. D., 88, 106
Collinsonia, 335
Commercial Hotel, 24, 34, 138
Cook, B. C., 271
Cooks, Mr., 246
Coon's Ranch, 232
Corn, 282, 286, 288, 307
Cornell, 109–110
Cowan, 245–246
Cowan's Ferry, 262
Crane, 289
Crater, George W., 79
Crow Creek, 155, 297, 299
Crow Creek Agency, 203, 232, 270, 322
Currie (town), 8, 11, 18–20, 22, 24–25
Currie, Neil, 22–25, 34
Currie Pioneer, 65
Custer's Peak, 214*fig*
cut-and-fill tasks, 10

Dakota Central Railway
  charter for, 96–97
  connecting with Northern Pacific, 116
  incorporation of, 65
  Lakota people and, 233–234, 246–247, 249
  name change point and, 69
  permission sought by, 246–247
  right of way for, 320–322
  scouting trip and, 6
  Sioux people and, 267*fig*
Dakota people, 58
Dakota Territorial Legislature, 16
Dakota Territory
  crossing into, 48–49
  first locomotive to, 137
  impact in, 64–65
Dakota War (1862), 22
Dana, Rich, 144–148, 146*fig*
Dann house, 345
Dawes Act (1887), 270, 359
De Smet, 76*fig*, 79, 86, 101, 138, 140
De Smet's Surveyors House, 167
Deadman's Creek, 312
Deadman's Creek Stage Station, 210, 212, 212*fig*, 213, 218
Deadwood, 69–70, 77, 98, 115, 360
DeBarr, Joe, 38, 75, 88, 130, 133, 167, 179, 191, 196, 199
dengue fever, 121, 180
Dewey's Camp, 155
diphtheria, 153, 155, 339–340
Dirt Lodges, 96
Dirty Woman Creek, 309

diseases/illnesses
- breakbone fever, 121, 179–180
- catarrh, 178
- dengue fever, 121, 180
- diphtheria, 153, 155, 339–340
- dysentery, 286
- influenza, 176, 205
- malaria, 121
- mumps, 83
- neuralgia, 297, 313
- quinsy, 178
- syphilis, 173
- *see also* medicines and treatments

Dorian Creek, 324
Doud, Jim, 267
Dougherty, William E., 199, 203–204, 270
Dover's Powder, 306, 334
Drum, 252
Duncan, 241, 243, 245, 251
Dunlap, D. C.
- cake for, 68
- in camp, 43
- correspondence with, 122
- fire and, 41–42
- health of, 86–87, 158, 180
- hunting and, 163
- with Irish, 37, 49, 88, 100
- mutiny and, 199, 231
- new men and, 156
- surveying by, 124–125
- wife of, 70, 77, 93

dysentery, 286

Egberg, Halverson, 56
Elk Creek, 214*fig*, 215
Elkhorn Route, 360
Elmer & Tenney, 355*fig*
Elston, 309, 333, 340, 345, 349
Emery, Manager, 305
Engineers House (Surveyors House in De Smet), 140
Enlarged Homestead Act, 359
expense journals, 159*fig*, 342*fig*

Fannie (hired woman), 168
Fatsinger, 167, 171–174, 199, 202, 231
Fawcett, 242, 244
feathers, 22, 31, 38–39, 42–43, 46, 58, 60, 85
Felicia's Ranch, 232
Felt, Mr., 174
Fielder, 282
Fire, Pestilence, and Death: St. Louis, 1849 (Gordon), 264
fires
- in Flandreau, 16–17
- in Fort Pierre, 312, 331
- Mrs. Irish and, 332–334
- near Oakwood, 131–132
- on prairie, 232
- preventing, 333
- in Rush Lake camp, 41–42, 49, 69
- Wilder's description of, 131–132

Fish Camp, 254*fig*–255*fig*
Flandreau, 16–17
flood of March 1881, xxi*fig*, xxii–xxiv, 350*fig*, 351–354
Fontenelle, 263, 275
Fool Soldiers, 23
Forbes, Docia, 74
Forbes, Hiram, 74, 86, 102, 134, 252
Ford, 252
Fort Bennett, 191, 249, 260, 269
Fort George, 230*fig*
Fort George Creek, 178
Fort George Island
- camp on, 160, 166
- Dougherty and, 203–204
- Irish on, 163, 230
- map of, 123*fig*, 158*fig*
- survey crew on, 141, 171
- travel to, 153–154
- weather on, 165
- Woodyard on, 123, 127, 203, 236

Fort Hale, 171, 173, 202, 276
Fort Laramie Treaty (1851), 358
Fort Pierre
- fire in, 312, 331
- flood of March 1881 and, xxii–xxiv, 351–354

Irish in, 158, 177, 180, 205, 318, 328–329
Irishes in, 236
map of, 332*fig*
Fort Pierre to Deadwood Trail, 209*fig*, 218*fig*, 219–221, 246, 290*fig*
Fort Pierre Weekly Signal, 252, 265–267, 270, 273, 280–281, 304–306, 308, 333, 337, 346–348, 359
Fort Randall, 276
Fort Sully, 186, 188–189, 189*fig*–190*fig*, 193, 195–196, 226, 249, 258–259, 277
Fort Sully: Guns at Sunset (Schuler), 189
Fort Thompson, 152, 155, 155*fig*, 156, 173–174, 176, 198, 202–203, 252
Fouber Holes Stage Ranch, 174
Fouber Water Holes, 175
Fox, L. C., 281
Fox Camp, 254
Fox's Ranch, 281
frame houses, 78
Frein, Marianne and Lloyd, 220
Frémont, John C., 103, 134

Gap Creek, 298–300, 300*fig*, 304*fig*
Gap Creek Camp, 305–306, 308, 324–325, 358
Gardner, Robert, 321
Gary Inter-State, 194
General Allotment Act (1887), 359
General Meade, 263–264, 275–276, 276*fig*
George (bird), 168, 195, 212, 336, 338, 342
Ghost Dance, 359
Giles, 8, 11, 19, 23–24
Gilmore (butcher), 174
Goetz, Carl and Janet, 213
Goetz couple, 21, 213, 219
Goodwin, 106, 133, 135
Gordon, Christopher Alan, 264
Grant, H. Roger, 360, 362
grasshopper scourge, 21
Great Chicago Fire, 136
Great Dakota Boom, 360
Great Oasis State Wildlife Management Area, 10
Great Sioux Reservation, 233–234, 269–271, 321–322, 358–359
Green Horn Camp, 161
Greene, Jerome A., 269
Griffin, 338
Grindstone Butte(s), 210, 211*fig*, 218, 218*fig*, 298*fig*

Hansen, M. R., 220
Hansen, Megan, 291–292
Hard Winter (1880–81), 21, 35, 84, 132, 304–305, 312, 324, 357
Harney's Peak, 214*fig*
Harris, Geo. (merchant), 266, 332
Harvey, 239–240, 243, 265, 267
Hawes, Mr., 60–61
hay stoves, 21–22
Hayt, Commissioner of Indian Affairs, 141, 142*fig*–143*fig*, 175, 175*fig*
Hickcox, Mr., 10
Higgins, Dr., 106
high plains, 227*fig*
Hodge, Lillian, 248
Hodge, Mrs., 248, 250, 253–254, 262
Hodge, W. D., 138, 239, 248, 253, 261–262, 272
Hodgkiss, 282, 288, 290
Hoffman, Lieutenant, 282
Hogs Back, 336, 337*fig*, 338–339
Hole in the Mountain, 47, 47*fig*, 66
holidays, 46
homesickness, 11, 49, 85, 117
Homestake Mine, 360
Hoover, Mr. and Mrs., 260
horse theft, 266
Horse Thief Protective Association, 266
Huffman, Louisa (sister-in-law), 28, 48, 69, 87, 114–115, 135*fig*
Huff's House Hotel, 135
Hughitt, A. J., 88
Hughitt, Marvin
August council agreement and, 322
Brookings County Press on, 81
as C&NW president, 26
in camp, 92, 102–103
career of, 362, 365

correspondence with, 19, 141, 195, 252–253, 267, 307
cost evaluation and, 360
Deadwood and, 69–70
goals of, 357–358
interview with, 313
with Irish, 77, 312
meetings with, 25, 59, 141, 205
negotiations and, 268
portrait of, 26*fig*
rail passes and, 75
raise from, 62
on route options, 313–315
second surveyor hired by, 73
surveying agreement and, 270
in Tracy, 136
Hughitt, O. N., 88
Huron (town), 239
Hutchinson, C. J. (Charley), 88, 95, 115, 323
Hutchinson Lake, 93, 100, 107

illnesses. *see* diseases/illnesses; medicines and treatments
Indian Lakes, 40–41, 41*fig*, 43, 45
"Indian police" corps, 268–269, 282, 286, 316
"Indian stories," 335
influenza, 176, 205
Ingalls, Caroline, 139
Ingalls, Charles, 45*fig*, 66, 67*fig*, 68, 74, 101–103, 107, 139
Ingalls, Laura, 18, 66, 198
iodine, 180
Iowa City Press, 275–277
Iowa State Press, 84
ipecacuanha, 306
Irish, Charles Wood
death of, 365
description of, 48
handwriting of, 122
health of, 34, 48, 58, 61–62, 65–66, 71, 73, 76, 121, 126, 128–129, 176–178, 245, 252–253, 297, 306, 333
later career of, 363, 365
portrait of, iv*fig*
wages for, 62
see also individual camps and survey locations
Irish, Frederick Macy, 213
Irish, John P., 84, 95, 153
Irish, Lizzie (daughter)
attempts to wake, 168
in camp, 263–265, 267
correspondence with, 17, 19, 31, 38, 46, 59–60, 62, 71–72, 77, 82–83, 138, 154, 156, 165, 196, 225, 236–237, 249–251, 259–260, 283, 317–318, 330–336, 338, 341–342, 344–354
departure of, 274–275
Irish's furlough and, 233
as notary public, 74
Reeds and, 265
telegram for, 343
trip to Dakota and, 275–277
Irish, Ruth (daughter)
in camp, 263–265, 267
correspondence with, 18, 29–30, 56, 61, 111, 123, 138, 154, 156–157, 163–165, 168, 177, 191, 195, 200, 212–213, 225, 236–237, 249–251, 259–260, 283, 317–318, 330–336, 338, 341–354, 363
departure of, 274–275
diary entries written by, 273
furlough for, 232–234
health of, 71–72, 74, 76, 83, 205
Irish's furlough and, 233
Reeds and, 265
telegram for, 343
trip to Dakota and, 275–277
Irish, Susannah Abigail (née Yarborough)
in camp, 237, 246, 267, 316
in Chicago, 136
correspondence with, 20, 37, 41–42, 48–49, 58, 62, 67–70, 77, 85, 95–98, 152–153, 177–178, 193, 216–217, 225, 232, 239–240, 244, 249–251, 283, 304, 332–336, 340, 343
departure of, 274–275
dishes and, 160
fire and, 331–333, 341
flood of March 1881 and, 352
at Fort Sully, 260–261
health of, 252, 320, 341–342, 348

with Irish, 234–235, 251, 253–254, 262, 344
Irish's furlough and, 233
Irish's reflections on, 157
July 4 and, 253
portrait of, iv*fig*
Reeds and, 265
sister's health and, 87
in Tracy, 137–138
Irish's Ranch, 159, 163–164, 168, 174–176, 178, 198
iron camphor, 153–154
iron tonic, 48

Jacket, 266, 282, 287, 296–299, 304, 306–307, 309–311, 323
James River, 60, 68, 73, 80, 86, 94, 94*fig*, 245*fig*
Jencks' Hotel, 153, 155, 259
Joe Mudra Creek, 116, 116*fig*, 240, 248*fig*, 254
Johnson, Chief Engineer
butte named for, 179
correspondence with, 19, 195, 207
gloves from, 178
meetings with, 28, 59, 136, 205, 233, 312
Johnson's Butte, 179
Jones, S. G., 18
Jones's Ranch, 123

Keep, Albert, 25–26, 26*fig*, 28, 136, 322, 362
Kirley, Joseph, 186–187, 187*fig*, 204, 237

La Plant, 346
Lake Benton
camp on, 43, 59, 68, 74
first locomotive to, 134
grading work and, 121
Ingalls and, 102–103
map of, 45*fig*, 67*fig*
photograph of, 12*fig*
scouting trip near, 11–12, 18
surveying work near, 45–53, 60, 65–68, 70–71
travel to, 24, 40
Lake Campeska [Kampeska], 97
Lake Cavour, 93
Lake Oahe, 187
Lake Oakwood, 15
Lake Poinsett, 134
Lake Preston, 75, 76*fig*, 82, 84–85, 102–105
Lake Sarah, 23
Lake Shetek, 22
Lake Shetek State Park, 23
Lake Tetonkaha, 15
Lake Whitewood, 57, 82
Lake Yankton, 23, 37, 40*fig*, 60, 64
Lakota people
agreement with, 269, 358
Big Mike and, 199
in crew, 300
evidence of, 217
hunting and, 108
Irish and, 169, 196, 252, 288
land belonging to, 152, 194, 207, 212
men captured by, 289
negotiations with, 233–234, 258–259, 267*fig*, 277
purchase agreement with, 246–247, 249, 337
scouts from, 281
tensions with, 260, 359
timber and, 127, 203
Washington delegation and, 319
see also individual people
Lance Creek, 282*fig*, 285*fig*, 289, 312, 319*fig*, 320, 334–335
Lance Creek Holes, 208, 209*fig*, 218
Latio, H. M., 88
Lawler, John, 267, 270
LeCompt, Louison, 155*fig*, 158
Leighton, I. M.
in camp, 240
departure of, 340
health of, 112, 179–180, 245, 323, 338
horse of, 246
with Irish, 88, 158, 177, 206–208, 218–220, 226, 249, 253–254, 258–260, 315
Medicine Creek Camp and, 125
in Pierre, 251

Powers's shooting and, 280, 284
scouting trip and, 290, 297, 299–300, 305
Soldier Water Holes and, 176
wagon wreckage and, 283
Lewis, 156, 160, 179, 186, 198, 205, 253
Lewis and Clark, 192
Lindermans, 63
Linkhart, 160, 178–179, 205, 253
linseed oil, 180–181
Little Bear, 282, 290
Little Bighorn, 359
Lone Tree Creek, 230, 253
Lone Tree line, 224
Long Winter, The (Wilder), 35
Love, Leonard, 267, 269–270, 282, 319
Lower Brule Agency, 203, 233–234, 276, 322
Lowville Township, 10
Lyon County News, 194

malaria, 121
Manchester, C. H., 87–88
Manchester Times, 87–88
Marshfield, 24, 38, 65
Marshfield Tribune, 36, 65, 86
McAllister, Laura Kirley, 187
McCaddon, Jack, 235, 239, 241, 245, 253, 286, 317, 320
McChesney, Dr., 284
McCormick, 167
McCready, 311, 315
McKinley, William, 16
McLain, 191, 191*fig*, 193–195
McManns, 217
McNiel, 164, 167, 179, 186, 229, 233
McNiel's Creek, 227, 228*fig*, 229, 229*fig*, 230
Meade, 263–264, 275–276, 276*fig*
meal stations, 208
Meat, 305
Medary, 11–12, 15
Medary Creek, 56, 59, 74
Medicine Butte, 125
Medicine Creek, 116, 124–125, 124*fig*, 126–129, 126*fig*–127*fig*, 142*fig*–143*fig*, 144, 202, 297*fig*, 312
Medicine Creek Camp, 303, 308
Medicine Knoll, 125*fig*, 200, 202*fig*, 230
medicines and treatments
iodine, 180
ipecacuanha, 306
opium, 286, 306
quinine, 122, 129, 153–154, 158–159, 176, 180, 198, 306
Spr Free Munate of Iron gargling oil, 180
Squibbs Tincture, 286
see also diseases/illnesses
Merchandise Mart building, 28
Merchant's Hotel, 233
meteor, 60–61, 101, 105, 265
Mexican Creek, 290, 290*fig*
Mexican Creek stage crossing, 220
Meyers (unspecified), 101
Meyers, C. H., 96, 98, 125
Meyers, F. S., 88
Meyers, Lieutenant, 260
Miles, Nelson, 269
military roads, 226
Miller, E. S., 88
Millet, Mr., 175
Milltown, 155, 155*fig*
Milwaukee, 276*fig*
Milwaukee & St. Paul, 270–271
Mink (dog), 76, 136, 165, 213
Minneconjou, 195
Missouri River
Bad River and, 332*fig*
crossings of, 127–128, 193–194
difficulty of shipping on, 226
flood of March 1881 and, xxii–xxiii
photograph of, 230*fig*, 263*fig*, 293*fig*
reaching, 123–124
Missouri Valley Junction, 233
Mitchell, A. S., 266
Mitchell Creek, 218
Mitchell/Dorian Creek, 287, 288*fig*, 289–290, 324
moon dogs, 18
Morse, A. W., 42, 45, 45*fig*, 56, 71, 76, 265, 283–284
Mosquito Camp, 107

mosquitos, 76*fig*, 89, 92, 100, 101*fig*, 102, 104–107, 120
mound building, 86
mud, 228–229, 274, 278–280, 282, 320
Mudra, Joe (Old Joe)
in Cedar Rapids, 235
Dunlap compared to, 199
feather collection and, 39, 42
furlough for, 135–136
getting lost, 308
health of, 112, 240, 272, 338, 340
mention of in letters, 36, 38, 46, 49, 96, 345
mule deer supplied by, 115–116
Mudree [Mudra], Joe, 88
mumps, 83
muriatic acid, 176
Muser Waterfowl Production Area, 101
mutiny, 199, 225, 231–232

Native Americans, 98–99. *see also* Lakota people; Sioux people; *individual people and agencies*
Nero (dog), 46, 72
Nero, Mr., 154–155
Nettiburgh, J. S., 86, 88, 92, 108–110, 115, 122–123
Nettiburgh's Grove, 109, 111
neuralgia, 297, 313
New Ulm Weekly Review, 98, 194, 319, 363*fig*
Nicholas House Hotel, 352
Nichols, Tracy Minn, 78, 243, 316
Nicollet, Joseph N., 14*fig*
Nielson's Camp, 78
Northern Pacific, 2, 69, 98, 116
Northwestern Fur Company, 15–16
Norton Camp, 266
Norwood, Maud, 339
notebooks, 329, 329*fig*–330*fig*

Oahe Dam, 187, 191, 196
Oakwood, 15–16, 18, 75, 77–78, 106–107, 131–132, 138
Oakwood Farm, 16
Oakwood House Hotel, 16, 132
Oglala, 195
Okobojo Buttes, 196
Okobojo Creek, 196–197
Old Joe. *see* Mudra, Joe (Old Joe)
Olson, 112
opium, 286, 306
Ordway, Territorial Governor, 132
Ortez, B., 220*fig*

pandemic, work during, 144–148
Panic of 1873, 1–2, 98
Panic of 1893, 359
parallel survey, 96–98
Parent, L., 266
Parkhurst, W. H., 203
pasqueflowers, 46
Pay, Byron E., 15–16, 15*fig*, 75, 78, 78*fig*, 79–80, 88, 131–132
Peck, 276*fig*
Peoria Bottoms, 229
Perrine, Mr., 66
Perry's Ranch, 128
Perseids, 265
Peterson, Mr., 313, 317, 323, 328, 336, 340
Peterson Creek, 323
Pfannkuche, Craig, 52–53
Philip (town), 361
Pierre (man), 72–73
Pierre (town)
arrival of tracks in, 306, 308, 311
flood of March 1881 and, xxii–xxiv, xxii*fig*, 350*fig*
map of, 306*fig*
Pierre, Captain, 276
Pine Ridge Agency, 322
Pine Ridge Reservation, 359
Pino Hill, 213
Pipestone, 8, 10
plants, 46
Plum Creek, 287*fig*
Pole, 252
Posey Buttes, 299
post traders, 175, 190*fig*
poverty, 21
Powers, Perry
camp setup and, 265, 267

on exploring trip, 226, 229
food and, 65, 171
health of, 179–180, 240
with Irish, 88, 186, 191, 194, 200–201, 201*fig*, 206–207, 207*fig*, 208, 215, 218–220, 240–241, 251
local woman and, 363–364
Mrs. Irish and, 251
return of, 170
shooting of, 280–281, 283–284, 304
supervisory work of, 263
tombstone for, 365
Powers Camp, 108–109
Prairie Coteau, 12–13, 13*fig*–14*fig*
Prairie Pothole Region, 103
Pratt's Ranch, 208, 209*fig*, 210, 218
Preston, Dr. Charles, 123, 213
Preston, Ruth, 213

quinine, 122, 129, 153–154, 158–159, 176, 180, 198, 306
quinsy, 178

rail passes, 95
Railroad Gazette, 358
Rapid City, 314
Rapid Creek, 214*fig*
rattlesnakes, 286–287
Rattling Rib, 319
Raymond, 320
Red Cloud, 271
Red Cloud (steamboat), 274
Red Skirt, 289–290, 297–298, 300, 302, 305
Redwood Coteaus, 37–45, 40*fig*, 60
Redwood County Gazette, 102
Redwood River, 24, 37, 39, 41, 43, 44*fig*, 60, 63, 65, 69, 71
Ree, 195, 307
Ree Hills, 238, 238*fig*
Ree houses, 186
Reed, J., 124, 215, 249–250, 252, 265, 304, 318, 320, 349
Reed, Mrs., 249–250, 265, 320
Reed's Ranch
author's visit to, 181–183
importance of, 124
map of, 124*fig*, 198*fig*, 200
military roads and, 226
Mrs. Irish at, 239
photographs of, 182*fig*–183*fig*
Robb, J. C., 175
Rock Lake, 50–51, 51*fig*
Rose Hill, 213
Rosebud Agency, 307, 322
Rosebud Reservation, 359
Rousseau, 199, 201–202
Royal Family, 199, 225, 231–232, 253
Royston, 338
Running Water Camp, 242*fig*, 243
Rush Lake, 37–38, 41, 49
Rush Lake camp, 41–42, 49–53, 51*fig*, 60, 63, 65–66, 69
Ryther, A. G.
arrival of, 111
assistance from, 329
in camp, 229, 259, 279, 305, 311
correspondence and, 207, 289, 308, 315–316
departure of, 273, 306
injury to, 312
with Irish, 230–231
Native Americans and, 194

Sanborn, Mr., 283–284
Sanborn, Superintendent, 47
Sand Creek, 114, 114*fig*
Sans Arcs, 195
Sarah Gregory Stage Ranch, 155
Scarleg, 288–289, 307
Schiefelbein, Deb, 219
Schuler, Harold H., 189
Schurz, Carl, 141, 143*fig*
Schwan, Captain, 249, 260
Scott, 273, 278, 284, 290
Segur, I. E., 86, 88
Selby, 199, 205, 229, 231
Shampo, Mr., 169
Shanklin, W. N., 81, 88, 106
Shannon, A. S., 304
Sherman, William Tecumseh, 259

Sherwood, 207–208, 217–220, 259, 303, 338–340, 347
Sherwood's Grand Central Hotel, 177, 225, 236, 259, 262, 272, 316, 318, 331, 332*fig*, 333, 347, 350*fig*
shooting match, 113
Silver Lake, 86
Silver Lake Camp, 138–139, 198, 239
Simón, Giselle, 148
Sinclair, Shorty, 340
Sioux people, 267*fig*, 269–271
Sioux River, 81
Sitting Bull, 269
Slaughter Slough, 22–23, 23*fig*
Sleepy Eye, Minnesota, 347–348
Slocum, Frank, 361, 361*fig*
slope stakes, 66
Smith, 215
Smith's Crossing, 214*fig*, 220–221
Smith's Crossing Stage Ranch, 215*fig*
Smith's Ranch, 214–215, 216*fig*, 221
smoke, effects of, 112, 114, 114*fig*, 115
Snake Butte, 187
Snow, 344
"Snow Blockades Series of 1881" (Elmer & Tenney), 355*fig*
Snyder, John, 42, 45, 45*fig*, 69, 71
sod furnaces, 304–305
Soldier Water Holes, 171–172, 172*fig*, 173–174, 176
Sparks & Allen's, 344
Spotted Tail, 271
Spr Free Munate of Iron gargling oil, 180
squatter's right, 187
Squibbs Tincture, 286
squibs, 73–74
St. Paul Pioneer Press, 313
stage ranches, 208
Standing Elk, 287
Standing Rock Sioux, 322
Standing Rock Sioux Agency, 203
steamboats, 203, 235–236, 264. *see also individual steamboats*
Stebbins House, 341–342
Stennett, William H., 26
Stowe, W. R., 59, 73–74, 86
Sturgis, 314
Styers, G., 88
Surveyors House (Engineer's House), 167
sutlers, 175
Sutley, Zach, 266
syphilis, 173

Teepee Butte, 248*fig*
telegraph poles
  military roads and, 226
  setting of, 137
Tenney, 340
tents, 36*fig*
tepee stones, 183
Terra Coteau, 128, 130
Terry, 276*fig*
Terry, Thomas, 23–24
Texas (horse), 206
Texas (man), 353
thief, encounter with, 265–266
Thompson, 276*fig*
Thompson, A. B., 46, 70
Thorn, G. W.
  absence of, 38–39, 64, 130
  correspondence/dispatches and, 71, 76, 106
  with Irish, 73, 75, 88, 109–111, 122–123
  Medicine Creek Camp and, 125
  scouting trip and, 115
  supplies and, 60, 101
Thorn's Grove, 110
timber, 16. *see also* Big Mike's Woodyard; Fort George Island
time capsules, 87–88
Tobacco Sack, Mrs., 283
tornadoes, 363
town locations, 121, 128
Tracy, Minnesota, 2, 6, 19, 24–25
Tubbs, H. H., 252–253, 261, 263–265, 284, 311, 338, 345, 363–365
Turtle Creek, 241, 246
Turtle Creek Camp, 243–244
turtle effigy, 187, 202*fig*
Twin Lakes, 82

University of Iowa Libraries Special Collections and Archives department, 63
Upper Missouri River Basin, 14*fig*

Verendrye Museum, 219
Vernon, 167, 176, 180, 186, 243, 246
Volga, 128, 130, 132, 134–135, 140, 176, 252

Waldron, Captain, 266
Waldron, Judge, 250, 353
Waldron's Bull Team Camp, 210, 210*fig*, 333
water
  at Fort Sully, 189
  illness from, 302
  lack of, 115–116, 131
Waterman, Mr., 130
Watertown, 68, 97–98, 132–135
Watertown News, 107
way stations, 208
weaponry, 99
Wells (contractor), 66–67, 74, 252
Wells & Company, 45*fig*, 66, 167
Wells Street Depot, 27–28
Welsh, Mrs., 138
Wessington Hills, 108–117, 110*fig*, 112*fig*, 149*fig*, 162*fig*, 239*fig*, 248*fig*
West Turtle Creek, 248*fig*
Western, 274–275
Western Town Lot Company, 361
Wetherby, Isaac Augustus, iv*fig*
Whackers, Bill, 175
Whirlwind, 281, 290, 297, 300, 307
White Bull, 281
White Swan, 282, 290, 319
Wild Cat Grove, 200–201, 201*fig*
Wilder, Laura Ingalls, 35, 129, 131–132, 139
Williams, Mr., 345, 352
Williams, Mrs., 352
Williams, W. B., 340
Willow Creek, 220, 278–279, 278*fig*–279*fig*, 281–282, 284
Willow Creek Ranch, 281
Willow Creek Stage Stop, 208, 208*fig*
Willson, P. A., 152
Willson Creek, 262
Willson Creek Camp, 261
Wingta Creek, 288
Winnebago Reservation, 252
Winona, 7–8, 25, 30–31, 35, 115, 135–136, 140, 304
Winona & St. Peter, 1–2, 6, 8, 96–98, 115, 194
Winona Republican, 98
Wood, Colonel William, 188, 258
"wooding up" locations, 127
Woodruff, T. A., 194
Wounded Knee, 359
Wright, John and Julia, 22

Yankton Agency, 232, 276
Yankton Daily Press and Dakotaian, 99, 154*fig*, 159*fig*, 270, 281
yawls, 291–292
Yellowstone Command (Greene), 269
Young, N. H., 258–259